STRATEGIC MA

MW01174804

Concepts, Skills and Practices

R.M. SRIVASTAVA

Former Professor, Head and Dean
Faculty of Management Studies
Banaras Hindu University
and
Director, Northern Coalfields Ltd. (Coal India Affiliate)

SHUBHRA VERMA

Management Consultant
Mumbai

PHI Learning Private Limited

New Delhi-110001
2012

₹ 375.00

STRATEGIC MANAGEMENT: Concepts, Skills and Practices
R.M. Srivastava and Shubhra Verma

ISBN-978-81-203-4512-6

Published by Asoke K. Ghosh, PHI Learning Private Limited, M-97, Connaught Circus, New Delhi-110001 and Printed by Baba Barkha Nath Printers, Bahadurgarh, Haryana-124507.

Dedication

This work is dedicated to our beloved parents and grandparents
who have been a perennial source of exuberance,
inspiration and effervescent spirit.

Contents

Section IV   Strategy Implementation and Strategic Audit

Section V Real Life Indian Cases in Strategic Management

List of Illustrative Capsules

Preface

Constant and continuous tectonic and tumultuous changes in national and international economic environment during the last three decades in the context of liberalisation of economic systems at a path breaking pace, revolution of information technologies and realignment of economic forces, have changed cataclysmically the dynamics of business landscape, both in terms of customers' choice set and complexion of competition. In addition, the momentous changes in global trading regulations and the emergence of new institutions, markets and innovative instruments leading to globalisation of business, growth of economic power houses and new centres of activity across the globe, increased economic interdependencies, free flow of capital and knowledge and evolution of much more efficient, internationally linked market, offer raft of opportunities to corporate enterprises to expand and diversify their operations all over the world. However, with growing globalisation, problems of corporate enterprises have magnified; thanks to the enormous economic, competitive and political risks, resulting in volatility in global market place and violent exchange rate fluctuations on the one hand, and differences in cultural, financial, marketing and personal environment alongwith diverse governance practices, on the other.

Sustained survival and success of corporate enterprises in a complex, competitive and discontinuous environment hinge primarily on their resilience and dynamism to continually anticipate the environmental changes, and in tandem revisit their vision and business models, redefine their core business faster than the changes in circumstances, and transform their process, structure, human and financial resources proactively. Their goal is a strategy that is forever morphing, forever conforming itself to emerging opportunities and incipient trends and build organisational skills and infrastructure which can constantly make its future and catapult it to the global marquee.

Corporate enterprises in India and abroad in their relentless endeavour to cope with mindboggling changes and concomitant challenges and capitalise on the burgeoning opportunities across the globe and stay ahead of their rivals, have of late, exhibited remarkable dynamism and vibrance in their strategic thinking and action, adopting with unswerving speed new concepts, frameworks, skills, paradigms, new architecture as also world class practices. They are realigning their business and operating models in terms of distribution reach, competitive and value added product offerings and differential customer services through competence-enhancing disruptions so as to strengthen their competitive position in the market.

In this scenario it is exciting to capture the dynamically changing policies, strategies, business models, frameworks and practices of corporate enterprises in India and abroad, and convey them to the learners and future entrepreneurs in a structured and stimulating manner, and hence, the present work.

Keeping in view the syllabi of different university departments and business schools and professional courses, the work has been organised into five major sections.

Section I on 'Introduction' contains 4 chapters, which are intended to provide background materials necessary to comprehend the concept of strategic management and its various dimensions.

Thus, **Chapter 1** 'New Paradigms of Managing Challenges for Indian Corporate Enterprises' attempts to throw light on emerging paradigms, templates and techniques that can aid Indian corporates to combat impending global challenges and achieve enduring competitive superiority.

Chapter 2 'Concept and Components of Strategic Management' provides understanding of evolution of strategic management concept, the redeeming characteristics of strategic management concept, components of strategic management, tasks of corporate managers and pre-requisites to effective strategic management.

Chapter 3 'Strategic Management Process—A Synoptic View' explains the model of strategic management, discerning the various activities involved in formulation of strategy and its execution and control. This chapter also provides an insight into interrelationship between management policy and strategic management.

Chapter 4 'Corporate Governance in Corporate Enterprises' introduces the notion of corporate governance, and deals with the fundamentals of corporate governance. A bird's eye view of recent catastrophic corporate scandals also finds place in this chapter. An extensive discussion of nature and objectives of effective corporate governance for corporate enterprises in India forms an integral part of this chapter.

Section II on 'Scanning Business Environment: Processes and Techniques' comprising 4 chapters discusses the process involved in scanning external as well as internal business environment and the various tools which are used for the purpose.

Thus, **Chapter 5** 'Scanning Macro Environment' delves into the basic features of external business environment, process of scanning the external environment, and the forces influencing such scanning and techniques of external environmental scanning.

Chapter 6 'Scanning Competitive Environment' discusses how competence of an enterprise can be analysed to discern its competitive strengths and weaknesses, and explore synergistic advantages. 'Core competence' perspective also finds prominent place in this chapter.

Chapter 7 'Scanning Internal Business Environment' seeks to provide a vivid view of various forces that bear upon the competitive position of an enterprise.

Chapter 8 'Value Creation and Competitive Advantage' deals with the concept of value chain analysis and its constituents, and undertakes value chain analysis and establishes linkages. Besides, this chapter intends to focus on insights into value system and its role in gaining competitive advantage. New paradigms of value creation have also been discussed.

Section III on 'Dynamics of Strategy Making' contains 7 chapters that are exclusively devoted to the focus on how decisions are made in regard to the choice of objectives and strategies for achieving sustained competitive advantage in dynamically changing environment.

Thus, **Chapter 9** 'Formulating Corporate Objectives' intends to impart conceptual understanding of corporate vision, mission, objectives and goals and provide insights into the mechanisms of setting and balancing corporate objectives in an enterprise.

Chapter 10 'Developing Competitive Strategy for a Firm' deals with the foundations of competitive strategy and a company's quest for competitive advantage which is framed around five generic competitive strategies. Discussion on the approach to making competitive strategy also forms a part of this chapter.

Chapter 11 'Crafting Corporate Strategy' is concerned with dilating upon three critical issues which an enterprise as a whole faces in a fiercely competitive environment, viz., the firm's overall orientation towards growth, stability or retrenchment, the industries or markets in which the firm competes through its products and business units and the manner in which management coordinates activities, transfers resources and cultivates capabilities among product lines and business units.

Chapter 12 'Devising Strategy for a Diversified Company' addresses how a company can use diversification to create or compound competitive advantage for its business units and examine the strategic options of an already diversified company to improve its overall performance. In this process, the analytical spotlight is on the techniques and procedures for assessing the strategic attractiveness of a diversified company's business portfolio.

Chapter 13 'Making Strategy for Mergers and Acquisitions' is directed to dilate upon various drivers for mergers and acquisitions and discuss in detail how mergers and acquisitions should be managed to create added value for corporate shareholders.

Chapter 14 'Designing Strategy for Entering Overseas Markets' seeks to explore a company's strategic options for expanding beyond its domestic turf and competing in the markets of either a few or a great many countries.

Chapter 15 'Strategy and Corporate Social Responsibility' attempts to provide an incisive understanding of the concept of social responsibility and its various dimensions and also to provide seering insights into process of incorporating social responsibility in making strategic decisions.

Section IV 'Strategy Implementation and Strategic Audit' comprises of 5 chapters which deal with the modern approach of implementing strategy and dilates upon various parameters of strategy execution.

Chapter 16 'Strategy Implementation—A Synoptic View' discusses the major ingredients of strategy execution and focuses on how critical resources of an organisation should be allocated to support strategy.

Chapter 17 'Organising for Competitive Advantage' seeks to discuss relationship between strategy and structure and to focus on how organisational structure should be designed to gain sustained competitive advantage.

Chapter 18 'Cultural Dynamics and Strategy Execution' is devoted to address major aspects of organisational culture and their relevance in organisational effectiveness. This is followed by a discussion on methodology for establishing and maintaining effective organisational culture.

Chapter 19 'Strategy Execution Through Leadership' is directed to examine the role of leadership in strategy execution and provide perspicacious view of new paradigms of leading an organisation in competitive scenario.

Chapter 20 'Strategic Audit and Recycling' begins with providing conceptual understanding of strategic audit and its thrust areas, followed by discussion of various methods of conducting strategic audit. Recycling of strategy also finds a place at the end of the chapter.

Section V 'Case Studies in Strategic Management' includes 13 real-life Indian cases which provide an invaluable opportunity to the readers to apply their theoretical knowledge to real-life business problems by analysing the strategic issues of specific organisations in much greater depth. This, in itself, develops their conceptual and analytical skills in sizing up company's strengths and weaknesses and in conducting strategic analysis in a variety of industries and competitive situations.

'A guide to case analysis' has been included at the beginning of this section to provide the learners knowledge about the case method, and offer suggestions of approaching case analysis.

The work is structured around the decision-making process with a view to exposing in an enlightening manner the practising managers, potential managers and researchers, the contemporary concepts, frameworks, skills, practices and techniques pertaining to strategy making and execution with suitable examples. The work is intended to hit the bull's eye with respect to content, and represent the best thinking of both academics and practitioners:

- The overall approach followed in this book is integrative and the one in which all functions of business are synthesised within the framework of corporate strategy.

- The focus of the present work is squarely on what every student needs to know about making and executing business strategies in today's competitive environment.

- Concepts, skills and models have been explained with the help of Illustrative Capsules and end-of-the-book case studies pertaining to Indian organisations.

- Learning objectives at the beginning of every section and its chapters would enable readers to identify key points and ideas contained therein.

- Conclusion at the end of each chapter provide summatic view of the key ideas embodied in the chapter.

- Conceptual questions at the chapter end allow learners to test their understanding of the text.

- Key terms crucial to understanding various dimensions of strategic management have been highlighted throughout the book.
- A list of selected references and internet resources at the end of each chapter would help learners to easily locate references providing additional information about specific topics.
- Inclusion of 13 carefully structured and integrated real-life cases based on Indian business organisations along with a guide to case analysis would deepen understanding of the learners about various concepts, approaches, frameworks and techniques in strategic management and develop their analytical skills to conduct strategic analysis perspicaciously.

The book is intended to satisfy the needs of students pursuing professional programmes, viz., MBA, MIBA, Chartered Accountants, Cost and Works Accountants, Company Secretaries, M.Com. and various other sectoral programmes being conducted currently by Indian Universities, Institutes of Management, ICAI, ICWA and Corporate Undertakings where strategic management and business policy form core and compulsory course. This work will also be useful for practising managers who need to develop strategy for a particular business. The middle level executives will find this work helpful in honing their integrative skills and prepare themselves for discharging responsibilities at the higher level of management.

R.M. Srivastava
Shubhra Verma

Acknowledgements

We express our profound sense of gratitude to all those who aided us during the preparation of this work. We owe enormous debts of gratitude to those management prodigies whose wondrous works inspired us to complete the present book. We are highly appreciative of the senior managers of various corporate organisations for providing practice materials for the book and for sharing their brilliant insights with us.

Special thanks are due to Shri Neeraj Nigam, General Manager, Reserve Bank of India, Mumbai for his professional support. We are also grateful to Dr. Divya Nigam for her sagacious and sapient advice that helped us improve the quality of our work.

We would also acknowledge our families, especially Mrs. Sneh Prabha and Ms. Ishita Nigam for their continued academic and moral support, inspiration and stimulus without which this work would not have seen the light of the day.

Last but not the least, we deeply feel obliged to the Almighty for his unswerving blessings that provided stupendous energy to us to complete this work.

We value constructive recommendations and thoughts from management scholars and practising managers about the coverage and contents of the book.

R.M. Srivastava
Shubhra Verma

List of Acronyms

ACB	Audit Committee of the Board
AHCL	Amrutanjan Health Care Ltd.
AI	Air India
ALL	Ashok Leyland Ltd.
BBy	Best Bay
BCG	Boston Consultancy Group
BEP	Break-Even Point
BFL	Bharat Forge Ltd.
BHEL	Bharat Heavy Electricals Ltd.
BOS	Blue Ocean Strategy
BPCL	Bharat Petroleum Company Ltd.
BSC	Balanced Score Card
BSM	Business Service Management
CEO	Chief Executive Officer
CIAL	Cochin International Airport Ltd.
CII	Confederation of Indian Industry
COO	Chief Operating Officer
CRE	Corporate Real Estate
CSCO	CISCO system
CSR	Corporate Social Responsibility
CT	Computed Tomography

CVBU	Commercial Vehicle Business Unit
CVP	Customer Value Proposition
DART	Dialogue, Access, Risk Management and Transparency
DICV	Diamler India Commercial Vehicle
EDPs	Executive Development Programmes
EPS	Earning Per Share
ERCs	Engineering Research Centres
FDA	Food and Drug Administration
FEMA	Foreign Exchange Management Act
FERA	Foreign Exchange Regulation Act
FICCI	Federation of Indian Chambers of Commerce & Industry
FMCG	Fast Moving Consumer Goods
GCPL	Godrej Consumers Products Ltd.
GDP	Gross Domestic Product
GE	General Electric
GM	General Motors
GNP	Gross National Product
HDFC	Housing Development Finance Corporation
HPC	Hindustan Petroleum Company
HUL	Hindustan Unilever Ltd.
IFAS	Integral Factor Analysis Summary
ILI	Infosys Leadership System
IOC	Indian Oil Corporation
IRR	Internal Rate of Return
ISO	International Organization for Standardization
IT	Information Technology
ITC	Indian Tobacco Company
IVRS	Interactive Voice Response Service
JV	Joint Venture
L&F	Li & Fung
L&T	Larsen & Toubro
LCC	Low Cost Carriers
M&A	Mergers & Acquisitions
M&M	Mahindra & Mahindra

MNC	Multinational Corporation
MOU	Memorandum of Understanding
MPB	Management Plan Budget
MSIL	Maruti Suzuki India Ltd.
NPA	Non-Performing Asset
NTPC	National Thermal Power Corporation
OECD	Organization for Economic Cooperation and Development
ONGC	Oil and Natural Gas Corporation
P&G	Procter & Gamble
PBDIT	Profit before Depreciation Interest and Tax
PSBU	Passenger Car Business Unit
PSU	Public Sector Undertaking
R&D	Research & Development
R&R	Rehabilitation & Resettlement
RBI	Reserve Bank of India
RIL	Reliance Industries Ltd.
ROI	Return on Investment
S&C	Scenario & Contingency Planning
SBI	State Bank of India
SBU	Strategic Business Unit
SCP	Structure Conduct Performance
SEBI	Securities Exchange Board of India
SWOT	Strengths, Weaknesses, Opportunities and Threats
TBL	Triple Bottom Line Perspective
TCS	Tata Consultancy Services
TDABC	Tim-Driven Activity-Based Costing
TQM	Total Quality Management
TSE	Toronto Stock Exchange
UTI	Unit Trust of India

SECTION I

Introduction

1

New Paradigms of Managing Challenges to Indian Corporate Enterprises

LEARNING OBJECTIVES

The present Chapter aims at:
- Familiarising readers with competitive challenges to Indian corporates.
- Discussing new paradigms of coping with these challenges, and the emerging managerial practices in India.

INTRODUCTION

Indian economy and India Inc. have had chequered performance and unsustained growth during the post liberalisation period. Indian economy was in a somnolent state since 1996 with almost all the critical sectors in the vertex of crises despite cataclysmic macro economic reformatory measures undertaken by the Government of India in 1991 to salvage the country from precarious economic crisis, improve underlying strengths of the country, foster developmental objectives of growth and self reliance and to infuse competitiveness in Indian business. The overall economic growth of the country during the first decade of liberalisation @ 5.75% was a shade lower than an annual average growth of 5.8% during the decade of pre-liberalisation. Industry sector grew @ 5.8% during the post-liberalisation period, as contrasted with 7.7% over the pre-liberalisation decade. Service sector, which contributed a hefty 50% growth rate in 1999–2000, recorded a growth rate of about 5% in the subsequent years. Large number of companies is reported to be switching over to trading from manufacturing for margin sake. Public sector undertakings (PSUs) registered dismal performance and became a net drain on the society as a whole, incurring a whopping net loss of ₹10,904 crore in the year 2000. Agriculture sector, which averaged about 4% annual growth between 1981–1990, clocked just 2.3% growth a year between 1991–2000.

3

Some of the Indian companies, in their frenetic efforts to defend their turf against the onslaughts of multinational companies (MNCs) embarked on a host of strategic moves such as restructuring of business portfolio, selling business units, scouting funds abroad to lower cost of capital and scale up faster, and building up relationships with international design and engineering firms to blunt the technological edge of the foreign entrants. Many Indian corporates including PSUs focused on the cost-reduction strategy to improve their competitiveness. Some companies tried to gain competitive advantage by changing the rules of the game. They did this by taking advantage of the anomalies in the import duty structure to generate monopoly profits through business integration. Despite these measures, most of them failed the acid test. They were not able to grow their business in a manner that was profitable, sustainable and capital efficient.

Indian financial institutions and markets with gargantuan amount of Non-Performing Assets (NPAs) (of the order of ₹1.9 lakh crore), with persistently declining profitability, and with poor customer service were in grave mess. Repeated scams on large scale in these institutions and UTI fiasco shattered and shook the public confidence in them.

Thus, Indian economy in general and industries, in particular, were tottering and a pall of gloom was spreading everywhere leading to a downward ranking of India in terms of global competitiveness from 48 to 57 out of 75 countries. Indian corporates almost faltered to counterpoise the global threats.

However, since 2003 Indian economy accelerated mainly due to the global economic boom, clocking over average growth rate of 9% during 2003–07, industry sector chugging over 12%, and service sector over 11%. Exports doubled from 53 billion in 2002–03 to over $103 billion in 2006–07, Foreign Direct Investment (FDI) surged from one billion in 1991 to over 49 billion in 2006–07 and Foreign Institutional Investments (FIIs) soared to $49 billion. Foreign exchange reserves burgeoned to over $248 billion.

Resurgent domestic economy and emergence of global opportunities infused enormous confidence among Indian business leaders to take risk and become big. They were in delirious hurry to expand globally and so pursued an inorganic route to seamlessly access new overseas markets, achieve cutting edge technology, develop new product mixes, acquire global brands, improve operating margins, gain scale, enhance market share and thereby pole-vault into the rarefied global leagues. This is borne out of the increasing offshore deals clinched at a scorching pace during the period 2004–07, rising from Mergers and Acquisitions (M&A) deals of 40 in 2004 for $2 billion to 661 deals for 51 billion in 2007. What was most interesting to observe was that irresistible appetite for becoming global was not only among big Indian Corporates like Tatas, Birlas, Ambanis, Mahindras, Oil and National Gas Corporation (ONGC), Wipro and so on but also among medium-sized companies who scouted aggressively the world over for the best buys. Firms like Dishman Pharmaceuticals and Chemicals, GHCL, Suzlon Energy, Essel Packaging, Amtek auto, Sundaram Fasteners, and Havel even acquired foreign firms which were comparatively bigger in size.

Economic growth at blistering pace was halted in 2007 due to a sub-prime crisis in the US and its ripple effect all over the world in terms of slump in global economies, global financial meltdown and global liquidity and tended to decline to 5.3% in 2009. India's exports plummeted by 33% on global demand dip in 2008–09. Capital inflows in the country too dwindled significantly inasmuch as total net foreign investment inflow amounted to just $19.6 billion in 2008–09 compared with $63.8 billion in 2007–08. Another disconcerting feature of the emerging economic scenario is reflected in the slackening of industrial growth in 2007 with rates touching the negative lows in March 2009. IT sector suffered the most due to drop in demand of software services from the US and UK. Indian corporates across the sectors, which till recently were basking in the glory of international conquests and burgeoning domestic demand are now bearing the brunt of a sudden downswing in their earnings due to rise in price of industrial raw materials and high cost of capital which have already crimped domestic demand. Big corporates like Tatas, Birlas, Vijya Mallyas, Suzlon Energy and others are experiencing enormous problems in digesting the mega deals stitched in the boom years. Stock prices came crashing down, making yesterday's buyouts suddenly look obscenely dear, prices of many of the products of the acquired companies slipped, the debt resorted to burn these buyouts threatened to burn holes in the balance sheet. Thus, as large Indian companies scramble to refinance and repay the debt taken to buy overseas companies, the archetype of the ambitious Indian overseas acquirer seems gloriously undone. Many of these deals were premised on plentiful liquidity, the India story continuing to shine and the world continuing to boom. The reality, of course, is now different, with world economic growth being a contraction of 1.3% and slowdown in global demand. Questions are thus being raised about the corporates' appropriateness to scenario planning and valuation of deals. Even for strategically appropriate deals, valuations need to be aligned to the most conservative scenarios. In their mad rush to impenetrate international markets, some big corporate leaders offered higher value to acquire overseas firms which subsequently backfired in terms of deterioration of financial health of the combined entity, owing to highly leveraged buyouts at peak valuations and softening of the demand of the products of the acquired firms, bout of mergers and acquisitions in boom times.

The economy bounced back in 2009–10 when Gross Domestic Product (GDP) shot up to 8.7% and industrial growth rate zoomed to 17% in the last quarter of 2010. However, Indian economic growth rate decelerated to 7.6 per cent during 2010–October 2011 and industrial growth rate slimped to almost 5.1 per cent in October, compared with a robust expansion of 11.3% in the same month of 2010.

Indian companies, which were being patted on their back for their acquisitive itch a few years ago, are now hogging the limelight for the selling spree they have embarked upon—of assets and shareholding. Right from India's biggest conglomerates like Tatas and the Birlas, to mid-sized sector leaders like pharmaceutical major Wockhardt and real estate major Unitech promoters like Tulsi Tanti of Suzlon Energy, India Inc. is preparing for its own end-of-season gargantuan scale.[1]

However, there are companies—both big like Bharti Airtel, Larsen & Toubro, Hero Honda, and Mahindra & Mahindra and small like Sun Pharma, AIA Engineering, Everest Kanto and Simplex Infrastructures who have been notching smart growth even as their rivals flounder. This is the testament to the conviction that focused vision and strong values accompanied by robust strategic planning and smart execution and continuous monitoring to adopt most suitable business model can help a firm in riding any challenge and achieving smooth and sustainable performance.

Blame for unstable growth and unsustained performance of the economy in general and India Inc in particular cannot be placed squarely on global recession and economic slowdown because Indian economy is not a globalised one and its participation in World Trade is negligible (0.7%). In fact, the continuing sluggishness of Indian economy and so also corporate sector is a problem of our own making collective failures in identifying the ongoing challenges and taking suitable strategic measures to combat these challenges to improve our performance on endurable basis.

COMPETITIVE CHALLENGES BEFORE INDIAN CORPORATES

Sheeny and sizzling performance of Indian corporates until recently have now become glum and gloomy, and Indian entrepreneurs—both big and small—barring few like Mahindra & Mahindra, Bharti Airtel, Bharat Forge, Larsen & Toubro and Tata Motors—are struggling hard to maintain their performance and save themselves from extinction. This is despite the munificent natural, physical and intellectual resources available to them. Reasons for wavering performance of corporate India may be traced in constraints and constrictions in their strategic thinking and action to cope with litany of challenges stemming out of fast changing environmental forces, as is evidenced from the following discussions.

Challenge of Coping with Change

The greatest challenge which Indian companies have been facing since liberalisation and globalisation of the economy, is their inability to take full advantage of opportunities offered by the new globalised economy and minimise risks associated with the process of globalisation. Nevertheless there has been perceptible change in business models and paradigms of managing business and people, the speed and thoroughness with which the change was needed are woefully lacking because of absence of forceful and specific interventions on the one hand and feudalistic and ethnocentric mindset of corporates in India on the other. They have yet to fully realise that in ferociously competitive and dynamically changing environment where only certainty is uncertainty and discontinuity, smugness is the kiss of death. Companies to survive and succeed in such an environment on sustainable basis have to be resilient and continually anticipate the environmental changes and reinvent business models and redefine their core businesses faster than the change in circumstances. Indian organisations need to appreciate that to be successful on enduring basis, being better or bigger is not good enough; one has to be always different. It is wrong to assume that good companies are invincible. Tom Peter and Robert Waterman generated a list of successful companies in their pathbreaking 1980's work *In Search of Excellence*. In the late 1990s, James Collins and Jerry Porrass did list a similar number of companies in their book on *Built To Last*. But merely a few years after these books were written, many of the great companies enumerated in these books lost their sheen because they developed complacency, and did not change their strategies, process, structure and people in consonance with environmental changes. Air India of the 1970s was one of the best in the world. Once it was nationalised, it became complacent and started to collapse. General Motors, that ruled the car industry for more than half a century with broad range of vehicles, reflecting the company's promise to offer a car for every purse and purpose, has now crashed into bankruptcy, primarily because it did not bother changing its business model in tandem with changing customers' demands. Apple toppling Microsoft is a case in point (Illustrative Capsule 1.1).

ILLUSTRATIVE CAPSULE 1.1

APPLE TOPPLING MICROSOFT

On May 25, 2010 *Wall Street* valued Apple, the maker of iPods and iPhones at $222.12 billion and Microsoft at $219.18 billion. Thus, the former shot past Microsoft, the computer software giant, to become the world's most valuable technology company. This changing of the guard caps was the most stunning turnarounds in business history for Apple, which had been given up for dead only a decade earlier and its co-founder and visionary chief executive, late Steven P. Jobs. The rapidly rising value attached to Apple by investors also heralds an important cultural shift: customer tastes have overtaken the needs of business as the leading force shaping technology.

Microsoft, with its windows and office software franchises, dominated the relationship most people had with their computer for almost two decades. But the click clack of the keyboard has ceded ground to the swipe of a finger across a smart phone's touchscreen.

Apple is in the right place at the right time. Although it still sells computers, twice as much revenue is coming from handheld devices and music. Overall, the technology industry sold about 172 million smartphones in 2009, compared with 306 million smartphones PCs, but smartphone sales grew at a pace five times faster.

Microsoft depends more on maintaining the status quo, while Apple is in a constant battle to one-up itself and create something new. Apple is a bet on technology.

Source: Business Standard, May 28, 2010

The vast majority of companies, which succeeded by accident, tended to take more credit for themselves leading to arrogance, as noted in the case of General Motors. Wal-Mart and Microsoft created a culture of arrogance and have gone down in their performance. Most Indian companies made huge investments in developing their core competencies but did not update and hone them afterwards, create new skills, depreciate the old ones and match the rivals. As a result, many of them have lost their market share and are confronting with problem of survival.

Challenge of Growth

The biggest challenge to Indian companies lies in their ability to grow in the midst of competition. The changing landscape has made it more and more difficult for organisations by narrowing their competitive capabilities. The days of product, technology and advertising are behind us.[2] There are increasing choices for the consumer today.

In Indian manufacturing, the most worrying evidence is that of the lack of visibility into strategic information. In fact, and somewhat alarmingly, the more strategic the information, the less the visibility. This makes it difficult to take the right decisions in strategy making and execution.

The markets are getting saturated with high penetration levels that challenge organisations to explore bottom of the pyramid opportunities and expand their horizons into rural geographies and international markets. This calls for recognising that ideas have a limited shelf life and creating a culture where ideas will flower and keep flowing continuously.

Challenge of Innovation

Innovation as a powerful source of differentiation, growth and competitive advantage is an integral to the competitive battle in which organisations are constantly trying to get ahead of one another. Most innovative companies have realised that innovation is not about developing new products and services but more fundamentally about discovering new ways to create value. Innovation is more than invention. The translation of an invention into a commercial application is an equally important dimension of innovation. Thus, novelty and utility are two major dimensions of innovation. Further, innovation is not limited to R&D and product design, but extends across the entire value chain—it is equally important in organisational design, the supply chain, manufacturing, financial innovation and, in branding. Incremental innovation in all aspects of the organisation is the lubricant of ongoing competitive success.

To meet competitive pressures, global firms are increasing R&D expenditure. The top firms such as Microsoft, IBM, Xerox, Motorola and Phillips have spent around 4% of their annual turnover on R&D. In contrast, our country has accorded low priority to innovation, spending a mere 0.8% of GDP on R&D. Fortune 100 companies alone spend more. In contrast, a large number of Indian companies are spending meager sum on R&D. For example, Reliance provides for one-fourth of 1% towards R&D efforts. Companies like Tata Motors, Mahindra & Mahindra, Infosys Technologies, Tata Consultancy Services (TCS), Wipro Technologies, and Maruti Suzuki India have catapulted on to the global marquee simply because of their focus on technological innovation to do things differently. Such examples, however, are rare. Hardly there are few organizations in India who prepare road maps for identifying opportunities and technological breakthroughs. It is a matter of serious concern when the analysis shows that Indian industry's efforts to innovate is less than what they were ten years ago.

Indian firms do not lack innovative abilities. But the ability to harness this innovative capacity and convert it into global and systematic way currently eludes us. Ranbaxy's fiasco—one time pharmaceutical leader in India—is a testament to the neglect of innovation by the company. Unable to make patent breakthroughs, Ranbaxy reached a stage where it was forced to sell itself to the Japanese major Dauchi Sarkyo for $4.6 billion. This deal exposes the fact that across industries Indians are still incapable of being thought leaders. They lack firms with the wherewithal to make pathbreaking discoveries. Several firms across industries could be potential takeover targets since their growth formula depends on incremental volumes and cost arbitrage unlike global leaders who are innovative thinkers and have proprietary research in their portfolios. Particularly vulnerable are firms in the IT, Textile and Pharma sectors. A very large percentage of second-rung IT firms are nothing but glorified code of developers.

According to a survey conducted by *Business Today* and *Monitor Group*, more than 90% of 75 senior executives surveyed across sectors, believe that innovation is very important to achieve their organisational goals but more than 73% of the executives are not satisfied with the current level of innovation in their organisations. They felt that their organisations having many competing priorities were overly focused on short-term results and faced resource constraints that make innovation difficult.[3] Indian companies have yet to realise that innovation is a necessity rather than a choice and have to fight to overcome the various barriers.

Indian manufacturers lack the technology support for looking at the lifecycle data of the products. Without this data, innovation on the product portfolio is difficult. Indian firms are far behind multinationals in India when it comes to adopting leading technologies, despite the (perceived or real) a low cost of technology in India compared to the developed countries. This low rate of technology adoption poses a real risk to Indian manufacturers' future, limiting their participation in global value chains where these technologies are required. Unlike the US, ideas not only take longer to find financial backers in India, but also, once a start up succeeds in taking its initial idea forward, its owner finds its very difficult to sell out. The reason is that such promoters are unable to form a realistic value of their businesses, and so workable deals with buyers become difficult. This price discovery becomes more daunting in the absence of a developed market for start ups.

Challenge of Focus

One of the biggest problems with Indian corporates is that they never have had focused business. They have engaged themselves in related and not related activities regardless of their core competencies with the result that they could not maximise value of the firm. They get afflicted with the MOU, or the Master of the Universe Syndrome. Two giant corporate groups, viz., Tata and Birla, have had conglomerate business group with a portfolio of several related and unrelated activities. Tata group embraced businesses like textiles, tea, watch, telecom, software, engineering goods, automobiles, and so on. Likewise, Birla's business scope encompassed copper, fertilisers, textiles, cement, telecom, software and branded garments.

According to a research study, highly focused companies, deriving more than two-thirds revenue from one business, had median annual earning rate that was 8% in excess of their industry average. In contrast, moderately diversified group (having atleast 2/3rd revenue from two segments) had notched up 13% a year in excess of the average. Highly diversified companies (having less than 2/3rd revenue from two segments) earned only 4% higher than the industry average.

Challenge of Productivity

Low productivity of Indian corporate is a drag on their global competitiveness. Value added per worker in India is reported to be about $62.00 as compared to $44,000 in the case of the US, $47,000 in Japan and $38,200 in Germany. Productivity of Indian labour compared to China is almost five times lower. Reasons for this can be ascribed to the use of substandard and obsolete product and communication technologies, under-utilisation of capacities, relatively less proficiency of workers, peevish labour-management relations and high labour turnover. Existence of non-performing culture and ineffective leadership has contributed significantly to low productivity. Poor infrastructure in the country is reported to have adversely affected productivity to the extent of 5%. For example, most businesses in India such as IT, banks, telecom networks and manufacturing processes who require uninterrupted power supply are suffering huge losses in between ₹25,000 and ₹1 lakh per hour.

Challenge of Quality

Another blockage to competitiveness of Indian organisations is appallingly poor quality of standards. On global benchmarks of the Total Quality Management (TQM) practices, the world competitiveness report has ranked India as number 38 in a sample of 41 countries. While multinationals are setting quality standards at 99.9995%, their Indian corporate counterparts are struggling for quality standards at 95%.

Growing competitive pressures in domestic and global markets has compelled Indian companies to stop treating quality as a cost and start looking at it as an investment.

The challenge lies in error-proofing on products and services as also in improving the quality of input materials and processes to achieve global levels of quality. This calls for increasing investments in R&D as well as testing systems.

It all boils down to whether TQM, ISO and Six Sigma are feel-good words used only in promotional materials or whether they are real, living and passionately practiced systems in the organization.

Recent seizure by the USFDA of the entire stock of drugs manufactured by Sun Pharma's US subsidiary Caraco Pharmaceutical Laboratories on the charge of repeated manufacturing standard violations bears eloquent testimony to the low quality standards of Indian organisations. Similar action was earlier taken against Ranbaxy when it was banned from importing over 30 generic drugs into the US because of manufacturing violations at its two domestic plants. Companies like Lupin and Cipla are also under the FDA scanner over quality issues.

Challenge of Cost

One of the factors affecting a company's ability to expand and compete globally on enduring basis is cost of product/service. On the cost front, Indian organisations have been relatively less competitive. High cost of product is not only because of low productivity but also due to small scale of operations, large amount of wastages and high inventory turnover. International scale of operations in many industrial sectors is generally five to ten times bigger when compared to India, giving large global operations a distinct cost advantage. Absence of cost consciousness, indifferent attitude towards innovation and automation, existence of unhealthy work culture among organisational people and their diminutive loyalty towards their work life and strong and militant trade unions have been bane for cost ineffectiveness of the enterprises. Another challenge comes from our lack of a global mindset in sourcing. Barring few organisations, Indian enterprises have to learn to operate in the global sourcing arena, locating world class sources and coping with multi-cultural negotiations. The surest way to move towards world class is for ruthlessly benchmarking every element of our cost and relentlessly squeezing out non-value added costs.

Challenge of Talent

In highly competitive environment, where knowledge is the sole differentiating factor that separates a good organisation from an average one, talent (value-based competency) has become the world's most sought after quality because it contributes significantly to product innovation and development, deep understanding of market and customer needs, originality of service and creation of global infrastructure. Since organisations across the globe are vying with each other to attract the best and the brightest, competition for talented people is becoming fiercer than competition for customers. Battles of the future will be battles for talent among companies and countries, which fret about balance of brains as well as the balance of power.

One of the major stumbling blocks to high competitiveness of Indian companies is inflexible and incapable labour force. Given the feverish pace of business growth, the demand for talent has already outstripped supply. A talent famine is now staring us in the face.

According to Mc Kinsey report, the quest for workers is creating a talent crunch that, some believe, might dull India's competitive edge in outsourcing. This is an irony that while there are 40 million unemployeds, corporate India is busy trying to cope with an unprecedented demand for committed people having right technical and leadership skills. This problem is going to assume alarming proportions in the near future. Projections show that by 2010, the IT/ITES sectors will need a work force of 2.3 million to maintain its current market share. However, there will be a potential shortfall of nearly 3.6 million qualified employees.[4] India Inc. is, thus, faced with the daunting task of attracting the talented people, in addition to retaining and growing its people.

The problem will not only be in the availability of IT or technical talent but also in the availability of good managers who understand the needs of the global economy and execute accordingly. Further, quality of management talent will also be an issue. Indian organisations will need managers with skillsets considerably different from those in the past. They will need a new kind of managers who can think strategically and operate effectively in a global market place in order to compete with global rivals.

Another serious problem which India Inc. is grappling with in recent years, is not only losing fair bit of top talents but plenty of the "Universal Leavers", who form any company's top performers. In the current economic downturn, organisations that have shed chunks of the workforce are left with insecure employees who tend to jump ship if they can to avoid a pink slip. Losing employees to the competitors is at the top of mind for many organisations including SRF Ltd.

Challenge of Managing Customers

The plethora of choices coupled with cost competition has triggered a move from a supply-led to a demand-led economy. This is compounded by two major forces—consolidation among customers and the emergence of modern retail at a scale never known before. The result is shift in balance of power from the supplier to the customer characterised by a customer resurgence bordering on toughness. A related challenge is our mindset of selling on "price" and inability to sell "value". The undue focus on price versus value is at the heart of several businesses being unable to unlock their value potential adequately.

The other challenge relates to our ability to develop and maintain productive partnerships with customers. This calls for changes in our approach to customer dealings from a selling focus to one of customer business development.

Challenge of Managing People

The biggest and most important challenge that corporate India is facing and which has been responsible for unsustainable corporate commendable performance and low global competitiveness relates to people. Barring quite a few excellent companies like HCL Infosystems, Microsoft India, Proctor and Gamble, Infosys Technologies, Dr. Reddy's Laboratories, Jonhson & Johnson, HLL, Godrej Consumers, Sapient, Ashok Leyland, Mind tree Consulting and Accenture, Indian organisations have not paid much attention to people and their aspirations. In India, people have never been considered as a source of value and competitive advantage. They are treated as a cost to be controlled and not the asset to be developed. In fact, organisations in India have been pursuing blinkered approach to manage human resources, even though the latter contributes almost two-thirds of the wealth of nations, according to World Bank study[5]. Barring a few, most organisations have yet to realise that knowledge people cannot be managed by theory X nor theory Y nor any other specific theory of managing people. It needs to go beyond this and should involve cohering the employees' goals with those of the organisation and the vice-versa.

Challenge of Land Acquisition

An emerging but pernicious problem plaguing Indian Inc. ambition of polevaulting into the top business league pertains to acquisition of land. Industrial investors—Indian and foreign—with plentitude of funds in hands, are struggling to get their projects off the ground, literally. Every big industrial house in the country is confronting problems with land acquisition. The high decibel case of the Tata Group's *Nano* project near Kolkata is just one, though the most instructive, example. Investments worth over ₹2.5 lakh crore are on hold because of rehabilitation and resettlement (R&R) roadblock. This roadblock can deepen the impact of the current slowdown of the economy and the corporates' global competitiveness. The current problem over land acquisition in the country seems a bit out of place, especially, when one considers the fact that India has abundant arable land (49% of total, compared to 18% in the US and 15% in China) and some of the biggest industrial projects in independent India have been built on vast tracks of land acquired from farmers.

The major stumbling to land acquisition in India is the existence of archaic law— Land Acquisition Act, 1894, though there have been amendments to it. Until recently, the country did not have a law on R&R issues. Past acquisitions were done without a framework or guideline. The R&R track record of the governments inspires little confidence which leads to obdurate resistance to land acquisition by local communities.

Challenge of Execution

Key to success of an organisation in highly uncertain and discontinuous environment is how fast it can execute its strategy and how well it can adapt to cope with the changes. Today, half-life of strategy is shrinking. Strategies are getting outdated faster than before. Their underpinnings are being shaken and they die much more quickly than in the past.

Every organisation seeking to be a part of those admired, or in the top 100 companies in the country, aims for execution excellence. However, in the real world, around 90% organisations either stagnate or decay due to poor execution.[6] Inept and delayed execution of project cause enormous losses. For example, inordinate delay in taking decisions on proposals of the erstwhile Air India and Indian Airlines to expand fleets and in executing plans presented by respective managements, resulted in loss of their market dominance. Likewise, Haldia Petrochemicals in West Bengal is a classic case of delay in execution, costing the government and investors thousands of crores (the project cost jumped from ₹2,000 crore at the time of conception of the project to over ₹10,000 crore when it got implemented) and resulting in huge losses. Another example is the National Highway plan conceived by the Government of India at a cost of ₹11,000 crore, a decade ago. It has ended up costing over ₹30,000 crore to the national exchequer, largely due to delays in execution. Similar has been the case of the Bangalore International Airport. However, Bharat Sanchar Nigam Limited (BSNL) could counteract the competitive threat from new private telephony players by reinventing its strategy and focussing on execution.

Private sector corporate enterprises in India have been found more smart in executing their plans as compared to their public sector counterparts basically because of nihilistic attitude and action flippant of the senior executives in the public sector. The primary cause for delayed execution is that planning is separated from doing. Executing strategy requires ownership at all levels. It is wrong to assume that execution is a lower-level responsibility.

Challenge of Mindset

A challenge to sustainable performance in globalised and integrated economy is developing a global mindset of the corporate managers. Ever since the Indian economy opened up, a good number of companies—both big and small—globalised their operations and achieved commendable performance; but most of them could not sustain it. One of the factors responsible is their failure to realise the difference between global mindset and global experience. Thinking global and becoming global is different from going global. Global mindset has nothing to do with geographies of how many countries an organisation's manager has worked in; global mindset is about being global in attitudes, thinking and action. A manager with a global mindset, though working locally, sets skill and efficiency bar extremely high, is eager to leverage resources seamlessly, build unique capabilities to transcend the barriers of language and culture to create value. Such managers develop a global pool of managerial talent and have strong governance practices.

Ethnocentric mindsets and action flippant Indian corporate managers especially in public sector have been frigid onlookers to dramatic developments occurring across the country turf, and bothered little to prognosticate the impact of these developments on their product-market complexion and dovetail their business plans and operations. This tendency has been responsible for the utter failure of most of the organisations. In fact, the greatest threat to Indian corporates is not from transnationals but from Indian corporate sector's practice of endowing senior managers with tremendous authority and holding them responsible for little.

NEW PARADIGMS TO MEET COMPETITIVE CHALLENGES

The centre of a modern society, economy and community is neither technology, nor information and productivity, but the managed institution which is the society's way of getting things done.[7] In fact, management is the specific approach, the specific function to make institutions capable of producing results. It has gained paramount importance during the last three decades which witnessed complete revolution in world economy, leading to emergence of global village where organisations are striving hard to match the competitors of their new global rivals so as to achieve competitive edge on sustaining basis.

However, management being social discipline dealing with behaviour of people and human institutions which are susceptible to continuous change, has to respond quickly to pathbreaking environmental developments. As such, what worked yesterday in closed and controlled economic system is not going to work today and tomorrow in market-driven and discontinuous economic system where organisations and technology are changing so fast and the productivity of capital and labour, sophistication of human intelligence and human ingenuity to process information have emerged as the key variables to survival and success, most of the recipes that have been employed to manage the business do not work. It is, therefore, necessary to keep pace with continuously evolving technology and to be receptive to new ideas, concepts, skills, fundamentals and to change the mindset (Illustrative Capsule 1.2).

Illustrative Capsule 1.2

NEW STRATEGIC PARADIGMS OF RELIANCE INDUSTRIES LTD. (RIL)

In Mid-October, 2007, at the annual general meeting (AGM) of RIL, Chairman Mukesh Ambani talked about five fundamental strategic shifts that were under way at the Petrochemicals and refining Goliath. Ambani declared that RIL would now pursue acquisitions for global size and scale. The second big departure from the past is Ambani's willingness to accept partnerships—primarily joint ventures—as a way of life. The other changes involve relying on agriculture and rural sectors for growth, focusing on research and innovation, and getting a global footprint in a bid to be recognised as a true Indian multinational.

A couple of these shifts were noticeable within a fortnight. The head of RIL's global oil business let on at an investment summit that acquisitions of oil and gas assets, worth up to $1.5 billion were on the anvil. Around the same time, RIL signed an initial agreement with the state-run gas transporter GAIL (India) Ltd. to jointly set up petrochemicals units in foreign markets.

Source: *Chairman's speech*, 2007

Strategizing Business Plan

Nevertheless, the DOT-Com boom of the 1990s changed the rules of business and new concepts, tools and techniques were adopted to achieve superior business performance and it has been proved beyond doubt that companies that outperformed their industry peers had a strong grasp of the business basics and excelled at the four primary management practices: strategy, execution, culture and structure.[8]

Strategising business plan does not mean simply three-year or five-year rolling resource budgets and some sort of market share projection. Such plan coordinates the deployment of resources, but does not deliver what senior managers want: a path to substantially higher performance. Strategising business plan signifies focused strategy making. Focused strategy making implies strategic thinking which is nothing but capturing what manager learns from all sources and synthesising that learning into vision of that business should pursue. Strategic thinking is about positioning an organisation for sustainable competitive advantage. This calls for addressing three major issues, viz., What are we now? Where do we want to go? and How do we get there? The foundation of strategic thinking is based on the Strengths, Weaknesses, Opportunities and Threats (SWOT) analysis and its outcome is an integrated perspective of the enterprise. Such kind of thinking cannot always be developed on schedule and immaculately conceived.

In view of the uncertainty and discontinuity of changes in the environment, organisations need to be agile and flexible, both in terms of their thinking and their organisational processes. There must be constant alertness, awareness of what is going on around the organisation—constant mental sensitivity and agility, and constant questioning. At the same time, that too would remain completely useless unless it has the ability to redeploy resources fast. In the early 90's Nokia won over Ericsson and Motorola because of its strategic agility. But then, over the years, some of these capabilities began to deteriorate so much so that it became difficult to change.

The secret of continuous success of top companies of the world is that they have a strong vision and clear focus. These companies have kept one eye on their growth and the other on the ever-changing business environment, and kept evolving. This has ensured that they can respond to challenges of new technologies, trends and changing customer needs.

Strategic agility demands specific leadership skills. Leadership unity or the collective commitments are needed at the top to make bold decisions. Strategy making should begin with drawing up strategic vision and intent of the organisation.

In sum, the greatest challenge before Indian corporates today is how effectively to meet international competition and take full advantage of opportunities the new globalised economy offers, and minimise risks associated with the process of globalisation. This calls for adoption by Indian corporates new theories, concepts, principles, skills and practices, a new mindset in diverse fields of the organisation, society, and the nation to cope with the perilous but promising challenges.

Drawing up Strategic Vision and Intent of the Organisation

So as to achieve competitive edge over its rivals on an enduring basis an organisation has to draw up futuristic vision, articulating the fundamental line of future business and its thrust areas. Conceptualising the future or seeing what others cannot see is the hallmark of a successful organisation. In doing so, the corporate management should have global perspective to see the world that is literally at its feet. AT&T spells out its vision as 'to become the world's best at bringing people together giving them easy access to each other and to the information and services, they want and need anytime anywhere'. Tata Motors aspires for creating a global empire encompassing the entire gamut of motorised vehicles.

The vision so set should be ambitious and customer oriented. Companies should have ambitions beyond their resources and capabilities and then create an obsession with winning at all levels of the organisation and then sustain that obsession for a long period, say 10–20 years, in quest for global leadership. This long-term obsession is termed as 'strategic intent'. Strategic intent does more than paint a vision for the future. It signals the desire to win. With such a mindset, disparities between resources and goals become challenges rather than constraints and 'winning' becomes a corporate obsession capable of sustaining a sense of urgency for a long period of time. It turns the organisation's focus on key competitive targets, and provides clear goals about which competencies to develop, what kind of resources to harness and what segments to concentrate on.

Strategic intent envisions a desired leadership position and establishes the criterion an organisation will use to chart its progress. Canon, for instance, sought to beat "Xerox". Honda strove to become a second Ford—an automotive pioneer. These are expressions of strategic intent. The strategic intent of Infosys is precision, measurement, de-skilling, de-risking processes, systems and routines. This has helped it to become one of the most formidable programming services. Also, an active management process is imperative to achieve the ambition. Active management process encompasses focussing the organisation's attention on the essence of winning, motivating people by communicating the value of target, leaving room for individual and team contributions, sustaining enthusiasm by providing new operational definitions as circumstances change, and using intent constantly to guide resource allocations.

Strategic intent should be so spelt out as to capture the essence of winning. Coca-Cola's strategic intent has been to put the coke within "arm's reach" of every consumer in the world.

Strategic intent should be stable overtime. In its endeavour to achieve global leadership the organisation's attention span should be lengthened so that strategic intent provides consistently to short-term action, while providing scope for reinterpretation as new opportunities emerge. For instance, strategic intent of Komatsu, a Japanese Company, to encircle the US Caterpillar encompassed a succession of medium-term programmes so as to exploit specific weakness in Caterpillar or build particular competitive advantages. When Caterpillar threatened Komatsu, it responded by first improving its quality, then driving down its costs, then cultivating export markets, and then finally undertaking new product development.

Strategic intent should set a target that deserves performal effort and commitment. A company with strategic intent "to unseat the best or remain the best" can secure the commitment of its employees.

Achieving strategic intent demands enormous creativity and innovation with respect to means. For instance, Fujitsy employed strategic alliance to Europe to beat IBM. Besides, the culture of entrepreneurship needs to be developed in the organisation. An *intrepreneur* is an entrepreneur within an organisation. Also, organisations need high risk takers who can think creatively of ways and means of converting an idea into a profitable reality.

Further, companies and their managers should not only be dreamers; they must also have knack to translate dreams into reality. They have to passionately own vision and drive to completion. Top management has to act as the custodian of vision and should be committed to realise it.

Customerising Strategic Intent

With a view to enhancing a firm's share in business opportunities and creating customers at profit, its strategic intent should be customer oriented, so that the strategy, process, structure, information systems, reward systems and people are aligned to the customers' delight.

It is important to touch the customer's nerve and create empathy so as to attract them. Companies have to learn to please customers in new ways. In Toyota, the management keeps constantly watching its customers and not the competitors, and addresses the needs and expectations of their customers. It is to be recognised that cost, quality and incremental innovation are leading toward parity across industries. Companies must understand what customers wish to experience in doing business with them. They have to put themselves in their customers' shoes and then look at their companies to see how they must change to please the customers. McDonald, for example, required getting 'adult' managers to put themselves in the shoes of little children.

Companies have to manufacture what the customers want and not sell them what they choose to make. They have to recognise the sordid fact that markets are not a homogeneous mass but a heterogeneous aggregation of individuals with differing requirements in terms of price, product, delivery, expected performance and service. The customers have indeed become variety seeking and hence a product and its brand need to be constantly updated.

Flexible manufacturing systems capable of responding speedily and cost-effectively to the customers' requirements are critical to success. Companies should strive to meet the unique demands of their product and market segments without compromising their economies of scale. In all these efforts, information will be the glue that will bind all the links in the value chain and enable swift and accurate response.

What is important to note is that the firms should not shift their focus from consumers to competitors. The philosophy of Sapient is to help clients who need to keep in touch with their end customers.

Customisation of Product Offerings by *Dainik Bhaskar*—a leading Hindi language newspaper—is a case in point (Illustrative Capsule 1.3).

ILLUSTRATIVE CAPSULE 1.3
CUSTOMISATION OF PRODUCT OFFERINGS BY *DAINIK BHASKAR*

Until the early 2000s, *Dainik Bhaskar* was a Hindi language newspaper circulated in Madhya Pradesh, Jaipur in Rajasthan, Chandigarh in Punjab and Haryana. Having established itself in these regions, *Dainik Bhaskar* decided to expand its business and for that, wanted to break the geographic as well as the language barriers.

The first step in choosing to change its geographical track was to choose the market. After careful consideration, it decided to choose Ahmedabad having the potential of a metro with a proven consumption pattern.

After this, it set out to understand the needs of potential customers. For this, it contacted over 1,450 researchers to survey 1.2 million homes and conducted 54 focus groups in Ahmedabad and six neighbouring districts. In the survey, people were asked what they wanted from a newspaper and what the current newspaper lacked.

The feedback received from the focus groups helped *Dainik Bhaskar* to shape the content of the newspaper to the needs of customers and also give it new insights into the Gujarati market.

In the second stage, it revisited the 1.2 million people, surveyed with a pre-paid subscription offer to *Divya Bhaskar*. Conversion rates were high as people saw their feedback being incorporated in the design of the paper. It also helped rope in vendors who saw a large reader base already demanding this paper.

The large numbers of pre-paid subscribers were also helpful in roping in advertisers faster, leading to much higher revenues. The result was heartening. *Divya Bhaskar's* launch edition sold 4,52,000 copies, taking it straight to the number one position.

Dainik Bhaskar employed consumer research for two-way communication, effectively doubling the impact of each interaction. This approach partook the form of 'crowdsourcing', where a company finds a way to get the input of a large number of consumers to help configure an offering. In addition to extracting the relevant information for the creation of a new market appropriate product, the experience that consumers received during the course of the two visits was enough of a differentiator to cement a relationship that resulted in high conversion to subscriptions.

Divya Bhaskar has continued to leverage its knowledge of the Gujarati market to launch other editions in Gujarat to fill market gaps and niches. *DB Gold* became Surat's first afternoon paper catering to the needs of industrialists, traders and the business community.

Leveraging the learning from Gujarat, *Dainik Bhaskar* has launched *DNA* in Mumbai—another new language in a new geography. *DNA* is at present number 2 in terms of circulation in that city.

At present, *Divya Bhaskar* has a circulation of 11.5 lakh in Gujarat with nine editions.

Focussing on Innovation

So as to stay ahead of their global competitors on an enduring basis, Indian organisations have to strengthen innovation and new product development efforts, and imbibe innovation as an integral part of corporate strategy. There is a strong need to foster culture of innovation across the organisation. Business leaders must lead the innovation agenda. They must define innovation broadly and build space for individuals to innovate. They must set 'stretch' targets to encourage employees to look beyond the core business. It is wrong to presume that the top management is responsible for innovation in the organisation. As innovation is a response to fundamental changes in the industry in terms of technological shifts, customers shifts, changes in demographics and in distribution channels, etc. it is the people at the bottom of the organisational pyramid, who are in close and constant touch with the customers and competitors. They can be better innovators than the CEO, who is far removed from the customer and the market place. Indian firms need to create a role for individuals or teams to operationalise the innovation agenda, build innovation, capabilities and support business units' innovative efforts. Quite a number of Indian companies such as LG India, Wipro and ICICI have energised an innovative culture and employees' drive change. Also to promote innovative culture, organisations need to measure and reward employees for innovation related activities. Procter and Gamble (P&G), for example, has made innovation central to its strategy and has integrated innovation into its personal goal setting and reward system. Organisations must create a collaborative, risk-free environment, empowering people to experiment with new ideas. Various global innovation leaders such as 3M and Google allow their employees to spend some of their office time on projects that specifically interest them.

For affecting innovation on a rapid scale, companies will need to invest more and more in research and development and acquire business know-how. Indian companies will need to innovate new products and services or invent completely new product categories. Companies that move into completely new product categories and business segments and create new demand will be able to seize growth and profit opportunities. For coming out with breakthrough products, they must look at non-customers rather than customers. Tata Motor's ₹1 lakh priced *Nano* car is targeted at the non-consumers of automobiles in India today, viz., the two-wheeler population.

It will also be useful for Indian companies to identify partners equipped with robust research capabilities and forge alliances with them. Nokia, for example, collaborates with local universities, institutes and companies to facilitate the exchange of ideas and to achieve collaboration among mobile, wireless, software and electronics manufacturing communities. This local cluster of innovation has led to various innovative products in Nokia.

In India, most partnerships are used for transactional purposes such as information gathering for addressing short-term needs. Hardly 50% of innovation leaders such as Infosys, TCS and Samsung Electronics (India) use partners for market-forming alliances. Indian firms need to assess their own strategic direction and the role of partnering in their competitive positioning.

In order to speed up innovation from idea generation to commercialisation, an organisation needs innovation processes to reach its innovation goals. These structures improve the interfaces between functions for optimal resource allocation, teaming and rapid decision making.

Finally, Indian companies must cultivate a global mindset if they are to realise their dream of becoming globally-dominant players. With such a mindset, companies understand the differences across cultures and across countries and engage in business model innovation locally to satisfy the unique needs of customers in a particular country.

Bharti Airtel's innovative initiatives to provide mobile solution to rural folk have paid rich dividends in terms of phenomenal increase in penetration in rural hinterlands and hogging leadership in the telecom industry (Illustrative Capsule 1.4).

ILLUSTRATIVE CAPSULE 1.4

BHARTI AIRTEL'S INNOVATIVE INITIATIVES TO PROVIDE MOBILE SOLUTION IN RURAL HINTERLANDS

Bharti Airtel—India's largest mobile telephony player—felt in 2004 that with the entry of additional operators across the country's telecom circles, competition for urban consumers would intensify while rural India in view of growing prosperity offers burgeoning opportunity. However, this opportunity carries with it a set of challenges, especially in distribution, service, product knowledge, and affordability. Still, Airtel has successfully cracked the code by dint of innovative interventions. It embraced communication paradigm to hit the rural market.

While Airtel had no problem in putting up telecom towers in rural areas, it found that handset makers had a scant distribution presence there. So, Airtel entered into strategic partnership with Nokia to bundle a handset with a connection. It helped that both Airtel and Nokia had the same, popular brand ambassador, Shah Rukh Khan. The management believed that rural consumers were extremely brand aware, and they would pay a bit more and get a top brand rather than a cheaper brand.

The management also noted that rural consumers could ill afford to pay the steep validity charge—the money they had to pay to stay connected on the network. This needed to be changed. Airtel began playing around with its recharge schemes, prodded no doubt by changes in government tariff policy. Recharge rates came down, eventually, culminating in 'lifetime validity' connections for as little as ₹99 and micro-recharges where consumers could top up as much as they needed in multiples of ₹10.

To increase reach and distribution Airtel created a two-tiered structure with Rural Super-stockists (approximately 2,000) and Rural Distributors under them. The Rural Distributors were young entrepreneurs (about 30,000) who were allotted territories around a few mobile towers and were responsible for consumer acquisition. Airtel also entered into alliances with Indian Farmers Fertiliser Cooperative Ltd. (IFFCO), which helped it sell connections through 35,000 agricultural societies.

Airtel also forged alliances with various micro-finance institutions which built an enabling system allowing 7,00,000 rural retail outlets to sell recharges through a mobile device.

For service purposes, Airtel created 25,000 Airtel Service Centres (ASCs), across rural India. It also provided training to local people in a village to handle service requirements, in addition to selling new connections and recharge. This gave the retailer higher credibility leading to increased walk-ins, while Airtel provided a face to customer service interactions. Moreover, a dedicated helpline or call centre in each circle provided real time back-up support to these ASCs.

Over a period of time, Airtel continued to innovate to drive more value from its rural initiative. It introduced value-added services like fixed duration music radio, job alerts and for consumers buying connection through the IFFCO joint venture—information about produce, prices and tips on crop management, among other things.

Airtel has also introduced SMS-based self-service systems in nine vernacular languages. It is now piloting call centres dedicated to rural customers in Tier III and IV Forms with Interactive Voice Response Service (IVRS) options in 16 local languages. The massive-up demand for value-added services in rural India surprised the management. The rural consumers are quite aware of what is available and what they want.

The impact of Airtel's rural innovative initiative has been phenomenal. Not only has penetration in rural India increased manifold, given that two out of three net subscriber additions in India today come from its villages, but also, the drive has also placed Airtel in a strong position.

Re-inventing Business Model

In an intensifying competitive environment continued success of a company rides on resilience. Strategic resilience is about continuously anticipating and adjusting to deep, secular trends that can permanently impair the earning power of a core business. It is about having the capacity to change before the case for change becomes desperately obvious. The quest for resilience cannot start with an inventory of best practices. Today's best practices are manifestly inadequate. Instead, it must begin with an aspiration, minus trauma. The goal is a strategy that is forever morphying, forever conforming itself to emerging opportunities and incipient trends. The goal is an organisation that is constantly making its future rather than defending its past.[9]

Indian companies have the tendency to look for best practices and then try and replicate the model. These companies, according to Professor Prahalad, should look at next practices and not best practices because best practices lead to agreement on mediocrity. If all the companies benchmark each other, they will gravitate towards mediocrity in a hurry. What we really need to do is to ask what the next practices are, so that we become the benchmark companies, and the benchmark institutions around the world.[10]

To sustain competitive superiority in the turbulent environment, organisations should focus on dynamically reinventing business models and strategies as circumstances change. Reinventing new business model encompasses the entire value chain. It is about bringing about new product, putting in a whole new process, thinking around it and marketing it. It is about working on practical utilitarian features that enhance customer experience. In 2003, Apple—an MNC—introduced the iPod with iTunes store, revolutionising portable entertainment, creating a new market, and transforming the company. In just three years, the iPod/iTunes combination became a $10 billion product, accounting for almost 50% of Apple's revenue. Apple's market value capitalisation catapulted from around $1 billion in early 2003 to over $150 billion by late 2007. A key to this wondrous success was adoption of a new business model. Apple was the first to invent a business model which could make downloading digital music easy and convenient by combining hardware, software and service.

Stories of business model innovation from well-established companies like Apple, however, are rare. According to a recent American Management Association study, no more than 10% of innovation investment at global companies is focused on developing new business models.[11] GE has decided to focus on designing lower-cost technologies that will appeal to customers in emerging markets. This is intended to boost GE's chances of success in emerging markets.[12] In India, cases of inventing business model such as Tata's *Nano* car and Bharti Airtel's least-cost business model are far and few. Airtel has a big portion of its innovation portfolio in breakthrough projects.

An interesting trend emerging in recent few years in India's business landscape and catching the attention of Multinational Companies (MNCs) across the globe is innovative managerial practices, known as 'Indovation' which are highly flexible and economical to manage business complexities and respond to fast changing dynamic market conditions. A detailed account of these practices is contained in the last section of this chapter.

Moser Baer—the world's second largest product of blank optical disks—has created value for Indian consumers by offering a quality product at a very low price by adopting new business model (Illustrative Capsule 1.5).

ILLUSTRATIVE CAPSULE 1.5

MOSER BAER'S MODEL OF CREATING VALUE

The home video market in India has been highly fragmented and no single company had been able to capture a significant share until 2007 as none had the distribution capability or a large content base in multiple languages. Also rampant piracy was eating into the market share of brands. The legal players used to price home VCD/DVDs at a large premium and lay emphasis on the quality difference compared to pirated videos.

With so many small players competing and using essentially the same strategy, there was tremendous pressure to use innovation for breaking out of the pack.

Delhi-based Moser Baer—the world's second largest producer of blank optical disks—decided to challenge the dominant orthodoxies and adopted innovative strategy of moving up the value chain beyond its present business and created an entertainment model to this industry. Moser Baer looks at four aspects, viz., reapplying its manufacturing and technology capabilities, building the distribution capability of a fast moving consumer goods (FMCGs), acquiring and exploiting content, and building a sustainable brand with a clear value proposition.

The technology adopted by Moser Baer enabled it to break the mould in the home video space. Before Moser Baer entered the market, there were two price products for each VCD/DVD—the legitimate content came in disks priced at ₹300–500 each, while the pirated stuff was available at ₹30–40 per disk. Moser Baer solved this price or quality puzzle to produce high-quality VCDs/DVDs at prices up to 80% less than those charged by the established players. Consumers always want a quality product, but Indian consumers want a quality product at a very low price. For Moser Baer, low prices mean high volumes and a strong business case.

Moser Baer's strategy completely changed the industry from a high margin to a high volume one. The company could effectively challenge the pirates and change the very basis of competition.

Sensing that the application of superior technology is not enough to sustain competitive edge, as the same will be copied by the competitors in course of time, Moser Baer focused on innovation in distribution, content and brand.

In order to create a distribution network having a wide reach at a very low cost, Moser Baer aggressively hired talent from the best FMCG companies and borrowed tactics that were new to home entertainment. Harish Dayal, CEO, of Moser Baer's Entertainment Division says: "If the price of our DVD is comparable to that of a chocolate, it must be sold in a shop that sells chocolates". This included activating new channels like cycle carts in cities. Each cart is expected to carry 35 best sellers.

Moser Baer also felt that control over content was necessary to defend its new business model. After launching its home entertainment business, it acquired the rights to 10,000 titles (or over half at the total content created in India) in Hindi and 14 regional languages. It also entered into tie-up with regular content producers like UTV to release their productions on home videos after a certain period of theatrical release. Moser Baer is now moving into new content generation, with plans to produce content specifically for DVDs in direct-to-home educational and devotional categories.

All this helped Moser Baer to create a brand with a clear consumer benefit—a high quality product widely available at delightful prices.

When prices of blank DVDs fell sharply in late 2008, pirates were able to bundle more movies into a single disk at a low cost. For Moser Baer, more content per disk would have meant higher cost. So, it started innovating to reach new audiences. It created an extended offering with collections (like the "Shah Rukh Khan 6 Pack" of six movies of the Bollywood Superstar) priced at a premium and aimed at high-end customers. It also created a brand 'Super DVD' priced at ₹27–30 with three movies to cater to the rural markets and take the pirates head on.

In just a few years, Moser Baer created a disruptive change in the home entertainment business. The average cost of movie VCD/DVD has come down from ₹125/250 to ₹25/50, respectively. Moser Baer's home entertainment business now accounts for 10% of group revenues of ₹2,344 crore, and it has become a household brand.

Moser Baer's future strategy is to extend the distribution reach so as to reach the million retail outlets that are in mofussil India.

Focussing on Core Activities

So as to sustain superior competitive advantage over their rivals, organisations should focus their energy on a few essential things such as quality, product development capability, management development and global expansion. There is nothing wrong with diversification per se, but creating skills is important.

The concept of focus is a lot more complex than being in a few businesses. 3M is very focused, with 60,000 products, as is Cargill, whose products range from seeds to mini steel mills. So, focus is not limiting the number of businesses, but creating multiple businesses which are built on and exploit core competencies.[13] Core competencies connote managerial capability to consolidate corporate wide technologies and production skills into competence that enables organisations to bring out innovative products of world class standards at competitive price to cater to the ever-changing needs of customers.

The core competence perspective is about creating new businesses and enlarging the scope of the corporate portfolio, while underlying the necessity of developing and exploiting core skills in all the areas. This again does not mean restricting oneself to the existing competencies, but creating new ones as well. The idea is to be focused on core competencies and be diversified in businesses.

Without focused attention on a few key things at any one time, improvement efforts are likely to be diluted and the company ends up as a perpetual laggard in every critical performance area.[14] Wal-Mart started its retail businesses with a single focus: "To bring the lowest possible prices to its customers." Today, it is not only the world's largest retailer, but also the world's largest company.

It is true that companies which concentrate their resources on their core businesses fare better than that of their counterparts. However, they must branch out into new businesses to compensate for the declining prospect of creating value in the older ones. The thrust should be on building a portfolio with an appropriate balance of current performance and growth potential and an intense management focus to meet the market's expectations through dynamically reshaping assets.

Focussing on Leveraging of Resources

In resource starved competitive world where organisations are struggling ceaselessly to procure resources to meet their strategic investment requirements, the 'concept of fit', or the relationship between the organisation and its competitive environment, focussing on allocation of resources among competing investment opportunities should pave way to the 'concept of stretch' where the thrust is on 'how to close the capability gap between the resources and the organisation's ambitions'. Concept of stretch with focus on getting more value from existing resources is the most potent approach to garnering greater resource productivity inasmuch as it seeks to get the most of the resources one has to get a much bigger bang for the buck. It is based on the philosophy that a company with limited resources should focus on moving more with less, go far to undefended niches rather than confront its competitors in defended market, and invest in core competencies where management feels it has the potential to become world leader.

While the concept of fit implies allocation of resources across business and geographies, the concept of stretch signifies leveraging what a company already has rather than simply allocating it.[15] This is a more creative response to scarcity. In the continuous search for less resources-intensive ways to achieve ambitious objectives, leveraging resources provides a very different approach which is essentially energising. Management can leverage its resources by concentrating them more effectively on key strategic goals, by accumulating them more efficaciously, by complementing one kind of resource with another to create higher order value, by conserving resources wherever possible and by recovering them from the market place in the shortest possible time.

Focussing on Co-option and Collaboration

An important route to achieve competitive superiority on a continuing basis is co-option and collaboration. Co-option enables an organisation to conserve and maximise the use of resources. Enticing a potential competitor into a fight against a common enemy, working collectively to establish a new standard or develop a new technology, and building a coalition around a particular issue is to co-opt the resources of other companies and thereby extend one's own influence. The process of co-option begins with a question: "How can I convince other companies that they have a stake in my success?" The logic is often, "My enemy's enemy is my friend". Philip, for example, has a knack for playing with Matsushita against each other, enrolling one as a partner to block the other. Being slightly Machiavellian is no disadvantage when it comes to co-opting resources.[16]

Collaborative approach, which signifies formation of strategic alliances between two or more organisations belonging to the same country or different parts of the world or different ends of supply chain with a specific objective of minimising business risk and maximising corporate value through product innovation and development market penetration, market development or through diversification, has come to be recognised as a powerful source of competitive advantage because of its humungous potentiality to enable the partners to achieve excellence in their operations and become global players by rationalising their existing operations, melding complementary skills, creating innovative ideas and their exploitation, selecting integrated suppliers and appropriate sharing and allocating risk. Through partnering arrangements, companies can gain access to new technologies, new distribution channels, impenetrate global markets and capitalise on new market opportunities at relatively less cost and risk but with greater speed.

This is why corporate organisations around the globe have been pursuing collaborative approach during the last three decades. Indian corporates have, of late, begun jumping on to the brand wagon of alliances, mergers and acquisitions to access seamlessly new overseas markers, acquire global brands, improve operating margins and efficiencies, gain hefty scale, enhance market share and thereby pole-vault into the rarefied global league. Collaborative competition by Mahindra & Mahindra (M&M) is a case in point (Illustrative Capsule 1.6).

ILLUSTRATIVE CAPSULE 1.6

COLLABORATIVE COMPETITION BY MAHINDRA & MAHINDRA

Mahindra & Mahindra (M&M) acquired Punjab Tractors in 2007 by paying ₹1,370 crore. Punjab Tractors—one of the most efficient tractor companies in India—was not doing well in recent few years and its market share shrunk from 18.6% in 1999–2000 to 8.1% in 2006–07 and profit after tax fell more than half from ₹133 crore to ₹65 crore during the seven-year period and return on average net worth had slumped from 39.8% to 9.9%. However, three years later, Punjab Tractors did better than what was hoped.

Punjab Tractors run as an independent business unit called the Swaraj division (*Swaraj* is the brand of its tractors); so its profits and loss numbers are not in the public domain. But there are some indications that the Swaraj division's turnover reached about ₹1,900 crore and profit in excess of ₹400 crore in 2009–10.

Punjab Tractors sourced engines from Swaraj Engines which it owned 51% along with the Kirloskars. The engines were well known for their ruggedness. What was lacking was fuel efficiency. Up to 70% of the operational cost of a tractor can be fuel. The efficiency of the engines has since been improved 4% to 5% which can save a farmer up to ₹8 per hour of usage.

Mahindra & Mahindra (M&M) has left its research department more or less independent. It shares just a handful of services with the M&M team like computer aided engineering. To put it in perspective, M&M has merged the research teams of its automatic and Mahindra tractor divisions.

Also, the Swaraj Vendors have not been replaced enbloc with M&M vendors. "A lot of the Swaraj Vendors are local producers in and around Chandigarh; those we have decided to leave untouched. Some of the critical components that come from outside have been aligned with M&M", says Pawan Goenka, President M&M (Automotive & Farm Sector).

"The marketing teams of M&M and Swaraj have been kept separate, and both are encouraged to slug it out in the market place. Territories too have not been demarcated between the two brands, though Swaraj has stronger brand equity in the North. Both the brands are free to compete wherever they want. If we make boundaries, the value of each brand is lessened", says Goenka. "Mahindra is number one in all states except two or three. Swaraj is not number one in any state but is number two in few states and number three in others. I have coined a team called collaborative competition for the two". M&M wants to set up a tractor factor in the South; it is likely that it will not roll out Swaraj Tractors as well. And this will help Swaraj spread into the Southern markets. Of course, Mahindra is the chosen brand for overseas markets and not Swaraj. Adds Goenka: "Swaraj is an Indian brand and its focus will be India".

Despite the tremendous potentiality of collaborative approach, a significant portion of alliances, mergers and acquisitions (70%) have failed to add value due to a plethora of factors both on planning and execution. As such, it is advisable to manage prudently strategic alliances and mergers and acquisitions.

Focussing on Excellent Execution

In a changing and challenging world, brilliant strategy, blockbuster business product or breakthrough technology can put an organisation on the competitive map, but only excellent execution can keep it there. How the corporate investment translates into results is determined by strategy, and more importantly execution. Around 90% organisations either stagnate or decay due to poor execution. Excellence in execution is what enables the organisation to grow better than competition, achieve higher customer satisfaction, improve efficiency of operations and become consistently successful.

Execution excellence is achieved when execution quality is excellent and the execution happens on time. Today, very often, the difference between a company and its competitor is the ability to execute. If a company's competitors are executing better than it, they are beating in here and now.

Following are the pre-requisites to excellent execution:

(i) Articulate the corporate objectives and goals of the organisation;

(ii) Build a strong foundation by putting in place the right infrastructure, people and resources;

(iii) Align the entire organisation to the corporate objectives and goals;

(iv) Continuous free flow of information across organisation boundaries;

(v) Create invigorating environment for people to execute;

(vi) Measure success and progress by breaking strategy into smaller goals and into smaller tasks. Clear metrics for each business unit, team and individual, along with an accountability system to track progress are inevitable;

(vii) Detailed planning and follow up on each activity;

(viii) Establish a sense of urgency. No compromise of delay should be accepted on the agreed goals;

(ix) Remain focused and continue to execute the strategy irrespective of the changing circumstances;

(x) Invest in the future by continuously training and developing a new lot of people to excel in execution.

Focussing on Integrated Organisation

In increasingly jerky and competitive environment, where consumers are fastly moving in the direction of increased expectations of value addition, response time sensitivity, reliability, cost consciousness and information sensitivity, organisations can have competitive edge over their rivals if they satisfy heterogeneous demands of the customers with competitive advantages in terms of price, product, delivery, expected performance and service without compromising on the economies of scale. For this, it is imperative to build interdependent, vertical and horizontal clusters for procuring, converting, distributing and servicing goods. Thus, route of collaborative manufacturing has to be chosen.

The most powerful vehicle for developing such clusters is to create an integrated and virtual organisation, distinct from the one created by law. A virtual organisation is the seamless work of all entities engaged in the procurement, conversion, distribution and servicing to configurate and reconfigurate value chains. This entity can serve as a potent means of focussing on core competencies of the organisation, leveraging those of its vendors and lowering their costs, and becoming more responsive to finicky customers. As such, it will be pertinent for the organisation to confine itself to core process and outsource the rest from specialised units so as to add real value and capture maximum profits. In fact, advantages of outsourcing can be derived from a well-knit virtual organisation.

Not long ago, manufacturing was considered to be the single-most important activity that a company performed so much so that car makers like Ford and General Motors chose to self-make all the components that went into their vehicles. The underlying belief was simple: if you do not make it, you can't control the price, the quality, or the supply of those components. However, with emergence of highly specialised units engaged in the manufacturing of component parts and growing consolidation in vendor base, organisations are increasingly realising that trying to do everything in the company is not only expensive, but also unprofitable.

It is not just manufacture-intensive industries that are debating the issues. For instance, Sara Lee which sells confectionery and household goods like Kiwi Shoe Polish and Brylcream, announced two years ago that it would divert all its manufacturing operations, and would focus solely on marketing and brand building.

In the near future, many big car makers—Ford, Diamler-Chrysler, and Toyota—and even pharmaceutical companies, will increasingly want to take the Sara Lee route. Besieged by competition and diversity of global consumer preferences, companies are discovering that there is more value-addition in product development, brand management and marketing than in manufacturing. Thus, from mass production, the shift will be to mass customisation.

Organising Business with New Approaches

Corporate managers must recognise that there is no one right way of organising business. For the first time after World War I it was realised that there should be formal organisation structure to manage large business. Further, Fayol's functional structure was not the one right organisation for massive undertakings. Highly centralised management could not work on that scale. Need was felt to develop a structure that could push down decision-making into the organisation. Hence, Pierre S. Du Port (1870–1950) and Alfred S'olan (1875–1955) evolved decentralised structure which came to be recognised as the managerial mantra, the one right way.

In recent few years, 'team' form of organisation has become a potent method of organising business. Thus, there can never be one right organisation for all the time to come. In fact, organisation is not an absolute entity. It is a tool for making a product by working together. As such, a given organisational structure fits certain tasks in certain conditions and at certain times.

There has been a good deal of discussion on decimation of hierarchy. It will be irrational to talk of hierarchy less structure because any institution to function effectively must have a final authority, which is the best to take the final decision, and who can then expect to be obeyed. As a matter of fact, hierarchy, of course, lean, thin and flat, is the only hope in a crisis.

What the management must keep in mind while designing a suitable model of organisation are the following cardinal principles:

(i) There has got to be transparency at all levels and in all spheres of activities in the true sense of the term. Organisational people must know and understand the organisational structure they are in, their role and responsibilities, and their inter-relationships.

(ii) There should be an organisation where everybody feels responsible for creating new mindsets, the right incentives and fora where young people can be heard. This is significant, for global competition brings a sense of purpose to people at the lower levels who are closest to technology and customers. Listening to them will be crucial. Management has to be egalitarian rather than elitist.

(iii) There must be someone in the organisation who could take commands in times of crisis.

(iv) An organisation must have only one master.

(v) It should have the fewest number of layers, that is as flat and lean as possible.

(vi) It should be flexible so as to be alacer and responsive to the environmental changes.

Pursuing People's Approach to Manage People

In the process of reconstructing business architecture to cope with seismic changes and to achieve competitive edge, organisations must remember that it is not technology, not the net, but intellectual capital which will be the key differential factor in the current century. Companies will have to focus on product innovation and development, deep understanding of market and customer needs, originality of service and global infrastructure network. Knowledge provides all these abilities. The only source of knowledge is people. Human beings are the drivers of the knowledge juggernaut. For, it is their knowledge that integrates the diverse functional departments and operations of the company into a single pool for achieving customer satisfaction. People are both the source and conduit of knowledge. It is people who lie at the heart of the core functions of the organisation as well as of the management initiatives. There is, therefore, a growing realisation that the employee is the most valuable asset of an organisation.

In view of digitalisation, deregulation and globalisation where organisations are shifting from being product-based to knowledge-based competitiveness of an enterprise is now being decided not by its ability to source raw materials, cheap capital or good workers, but by its ability to build, enhance, share and leverage knowledge and to know how to do things better than its competitors.

In a market-driven competitive economy, the focus is on the work that adds value to the organisation, that is highly specialised and not easily duplicable by competitors. The work of tomorrow demands a high degree of talents-value based competencies. This is why talent has come to be recognised as a potent source of competitive advantage. Organisations should, therefore, focus on attracting talents across diverse geographical regions of the country and the world and create talent pool through structured plan.

In order to attract talents and retain them, organisations should make the work environment more open and invigorating for their employees, providing them the opportunity to work across business units and geographies. Organisations will have to create small entrepreneurial islands where an organisation can house its best talent to pursue experiments, innovate, develop cutting edge products, dream up now and then, better ways of running a business and create value in an unrestrained manner, a positive value addition to the organisation. From employees, they will want to become employees-partners in business. Young talented managers should be fully empowered to come up with business plans of their own ideas and provide funds to execute the potential ideas. This is what organisations like Accenture and Johnson & Johnson are providing to their employees. In HCL, employees are allowed to take risk and they are not crucified, if they fail.

Organisations must device long-term plan for development of talent pool. They should adopt the strategy of developing its own talented people. They have to take a far-sighted view of engaging and developing talent beyond the scope of their immediate job requirements. They need to provide people with structured learning interventions, regular information, dialogue and feedback around career prospects so that people may grow with the organisation. At HCL Infosytsem, emphasis is on talent creation. It looks for people with emotional quotient. HCL's Human Resource (HR) department has launched a dizzying array of initiatives that help employees to constantly reinvent themselves and strive for higher growth. It constantly stokes a culture of innovation and entrepreneurship.

Organisations must also remember that talented and knowledge people need to be managed differently. For over 50 years, organisations have realised that money alone cannot motivate employees to perform much more. Of course, dissatisfaction with money demotivates. What motivates knowledge workers is what motivates volunteers. Volunteers get more satisfaction from their work than their paid employees precisely because they are not paid. They need, above all, challenges.

Organisations should imbibe organisational values of excellence including integrity, fairness and growth in the people, policies and processes of companies. They have to ensure fair and unbiased employee treatment in all respects. There is also a need to weave transparency into the organisations' processes. Best companies have in place management process that links employee performance goals with those of the organisations. They devise performance centric incentives and bonuses. At IGate, an IT company, meritorious employees across all levels are granted stock options so as to make them owners of the organisation. Now, the time has come for organisations to adopt a 360° feedback so that the employees get opportunity to evaluate the managers' performance in respect of strategic decisions. Thus, employees should also be involved in decision-making process.

Strategic relationships between employer and employees need to be developed and strengthened. An employer has to deal with his employees like their preferred customers. In fact, employees have to be managed in marketing way. In marketing, one does not begin with the question 'what do we want'? One begins with the questions like 'what does the other party want?' 'What is its value?' 'What are its goals?' 'What does it consider results?' and so on.

This is neither theory X nor theory Y nor any other specific theory of managing people. It goes beyond this and involves cohering the employees' goals with those of the organisation and vice-versa. The managers must treat their employees not as a cost to be controlled but as an asset to be developed. Employees need to be supported and nurtured so that they contribute their best to the organisation. Top managers will have to own the responsibility of converting the contractual employees of an economic entity into committed members of a purposeful organisation. They have to create an organisation where everyone feels responsible for creating new mindsets, the right incentives, and where young people can be heard and bloom and blossom. This is significant, for global competition brings a sense of purpose to people at the lower levels, who are closest to technology and customers. Listening to them will be crucial. Talented people will have to be given free hand. They will expect enormous latitude in the way they work and the manner in which they take their work forward. Organisations will have to live with flexi-time, working from home (depending on the job's role), round-the-clock accessibility to the work place, in-house health clubs, and full-fledged day care centres and so on.

As such, employees have to be managed as associates, and partners in the true sense. The definition of a partnership is that all partners are equal and partners cannot be ordered but are to be persuaded. To stay a step ahead of the aspirations of their people, companies have to do more than provide a stimulating work environment. Senior managers must focus on nurturing talent and possess the ability to manage a talented hand of renegades. While conventional training programmes may continue, organisations will need to keep talented employees enthused by continuously upgrading their knowledge and skills-set by way of cross-divisional transfers, working with vendors, collaborating with competitors in the knowledge arena and the like.

Corporate Governance

Corporate managers must remember that organisations utilise the resources of the society and some of their activities deplete raw material resources and/or cause pollution and as such they cannot operate in isolation, with wealth creation as their only objective. They have to be socially responsive and give greater emphasis to ethical conduct, honesty and integrity, complying with society's moral fabric and values while working to achieve their economic objectives. This requires self-regulation and fair corporate governance. A detailed discussion on corporate governance is provided in Chapter 4.

Creating Performing Culture

An organisation aspiring to achieve sustainable competitive advantage over its rivals must establish a performance culture which focuses on wondrous and excellent performance. This culture produces a work climate and organisational *esprit de corps* that thrive on meeting performance targets and being part of winning effort. Performing culture enhances the strategic direction of the organisation and allows for individual expression and creativity. Entrepreneurship is encouraged and rewarded in this culture.

Transparency, freedom of expression, total involvement of organisational people in the functioning of the organisation, and fairness to all are the hallmarks of an effective culture. The behaviour of an organisation's leader is to be consistent with his spoken values. Top management does seriously and sincerely care about the well-being of all stakeholders and try to satisfy all the legitimate demands simultaneously.

Developing performance oriented culture and reinforcing it is a complex task involving a network of policies, practices, words, symbols, styles and values pulled together to produce extraordinary results with ordinary people. The drivers of the system are a strong belief in the merit of the individual, strong company assurance to job security, and promotion from within managerial practices that encourage employees to exhibit their individual creativity and pride in doing their jobs. Godrej has a performance-oriented culture. It has instituted a lot of business processes and initiatives to succeed as a performance-oriented and people-oriented organisation. There is a 360° evaluation for all its senior people including the chairman. There is a very strong bottom-up feedback mechanism for the management and a strong leadership development tool for young leaders.

New Leadership Paradigm

Excellent strategic thinking and action and adoption of new rules of game to cope with competitive challenges are contingent upon leadership of the organisation. Generally the term 'leadership' is used to refer to the style and behaviour of leaders for providing direction, influencing people, obtaining their commitment and mobilising their talent and energies to achieve organisational goals. Leadership is the glue that holds an organisation and propels it toward greater achievement; it can also be a toxic element that destroys once powerful companies. The scandals at Enron, Tyco, World Com and Satyam gave the world a glimpse of the havoc leadership can cause. Equally, we have seen how leaders with great personal integrity and credibility such as Ratan Tata of Tata Sons, Narayan Murthy of Infosys, Sunil Mittal of Airtel, Deepak Parekh of HDFC, and Anand Mahindra of M&M have turned super achievers without even seeking to be stand-out leaders. Thus, leadership matters for better or worse.

The nature of leadership has changed dramatically over the years. In this new business environment, leadership is no longer a title; it is a set of behaviours. A fancy title is not only an opportunity, it is also an obligation to engage in certain behaviours.

In the changed business milieu, corporate leaders have to practice transformational style of leadership for influencing the behaviour of the people. Transformational leaders inspire organisational success by profoundly affecting a followers' beliefs in what an organisation should be as well as the followers' values. Unlike transactional leaders who guide and motivate their followers in the direction of established objectives by classifying roles and task requirements, and intervene only if standards are not met; transformational leaders inspire their people by way of vision creation, articulation, empowerment, trust, knowledge and performance. They have unflinching commitment to the fulfillment of their destinies.

In an escalating competitive environment, the traditional role of a leader has to be changed from commander to coach, manager to mentor, director to delegator and from one who demands respect to one who commands respect.

INNOVATIVE MANAGERIAL PRACTICES IN INDIA

During the last few years Indian business entrepreneurs—both large and small—have adopted innovative and non-conventional managerial practices spanning from manufacturing to marketing communications to meet competitive challenges from MNCs effectively both on cost and quality scores while catering to the varied needs of mass poor customers who live in the country side. These maverick entrepreneurs have spotted opportunities in developing high volume products tailored to the demands and incomes of Indian consumers. Thus, the business mantra propounded by C.K. Prahalad in his book *The Fortune at the Bottom of the Pyramid* has entered the lexicon of modern India.

Until recently, the flow of management and strategy models was one way and Indian entrepreneurs absorbed them from foreign corporations and institutions. As India Inc. raced to globalise and global companies sought to exploit the country's low cost talent pool, managerial concepts like Kaizen, TQM, Six Sigma and so on of the industrialised economy gained currency.

However, the scenario has now changed. Having being satisfied with the inadequacy of the above concepts in view of their being punctilious in nature, insisting on strict manufacturing practices which are time consuming and costly in operations to manage the complexities of doing business in India both in terms of the regulatory environment and scarce resources on the one hand, and to cope with fast changing dynamics of Indian market on the other, Indian business entrepreneurs have, of late, thought of evolving a fast and flexible but inexpensive approach to respond quickly to dynamic and competitive market conditions.

Mahindra & Mahindra (M&M), for instance, rescheduled the launch of the *Xylo* Utility Vehicle to accommodate the installation of a dual air-conditioner once it discovered that this would have been a critical element of customer demand.

Failure of Logan—a car jointly produced by a 51.49% joint venture between M&M and Renault in 2007 to capture market in India because of higher pricing was mainly owing to the delay in taking decision by the French company to reduce the wheel base to below 4 metres to take advantage of the lower excise duty. In contrast, Tata Motors was able to display the kind of rapid and adaptable approach and reduce the length of the Indigo to benefit from the duty differential.

Likewise, the speed with which automobile companies in India have been able to respond to the credit crunch after the Lehman Brothers bankruptcy is another key take away for global conglomerates. While the credit market in Mumbai completely dried up between October 2008 and March 2009 and spreads were out of whack, companies like M&M and Bajaj Auto moved really fast to manage inventories and reduce stocks and align working capital management so much so that M&M actually had enough cash to buy Satyam some months later.

Indian businessmen have the knack of making things differently so as to get the maximum out of the minimum. For instance, Tata Motors and M&M source second hand assembly lines from the west and re-configure them in India for their car projects. This innovative approach has helped them to pare costs by as much as 30%.

Indian companies have also adopted a unique approach to lean manufacturing and maintenance management. Bharat Forge's maintenance management is a case in point. Developed over 15 to 18 years in Bharat Forge's Indian factories, it is an extremely mechanised process that focuses on minimising downtime or the time scheduled for machine maintenance. Obviously, lower downtime means higher plant profitability. The system that Bharat Forge developed in India and that was implemented by its best practices group in plants it acquired overseas entailed creating a robust information system that anticipates problems before they occur. As a result, Bharat Forge plants worldwide have an average downtime of less than 10%, the norm for efficient plants worldwide.

What is important to note is that Bharat Forge has not laid down any hard and fast rule. In fact, it has established a 'best practices group' comprising two to three people from each of its plants worldwide to focus on improving its all round performance, and implementing the maintenance management system is a part of that exercise.

Indian entrepreneurs by dint of their technological ingenuity and innovative mindset are developing products suited to the habits and needs of India's 1.2 billion people whose per capita income is $1,000 a year. Across the Delhi Auto Expo, Electrothem India was modeling its *Ride-to-School*, one of a wave of products designed and priced for low-income Indian consumers. The three-wheel transporter, adapted for school runs, is an auto-rickshaw that carries eight children and runs on a battery. It has a top speed of 45 km/h, with a battery life of four hours and costs ₹1,50,000.

The shimmering innovative managerial approach can also be seen in Tata Motor's much hyped *Nano*, a bare-bones sub compact car that the company sells for $2,500 to the so called bottom-of-the-pyramid consumers who had been priced out of the auto market.

Tata has taken the lead in other areas too. Of late, it has launched the *Swatch*, a low-cost water filter named with the Hindi word meaning 'clean'. The *Swatch* is targeted at poor rural households that have no electricity or running water.

Indian entrepreneurs have also stretched their innovative thinking to produce a battery-powered, ultra-low cost fridge, resistant to power cuts, an automatic teller cash machine for rural areas; and even a flour-mill powered by scooter.

Godrej Group has recently produced 'nano' refrigerators, named *Chotu Kool* (Little Cool) for rural folk at a cost of ₹3,250 which is almost 35% less than the cheapest category of refrigerators available in the market today.

Indian entrepreneurs endowed with frugalmind set think differently for mass and volume. Mittal's mobile phone services company is the leader in a market where tariffs as low as 30-paise a minute are the lowest in the world.

Many small entrepreneurs have a burning passion to change the way things are done and an innovative bent of mind to translate their ideas into products. Best of all, their products mostly fashioned out of locally available inputs or parts, are not patentable but yield a profit because these products sell readily without the aid of a power point spiel. For instance, an entrepreneur from Coimbatore has developed a machine costing ₹75,000 that can produce sanitary napkins from rags. Another entrepreneur from Bangalore has built battery-powered stick which alerts a blind person about an obstacle more than an inch high or a depression greater than a foot within a diametre of one metre from the tip.

An entrepreneur of Rajkot—a potter by profession—has produced *Mitti Cool*— a rural fridge that would not need electricity. The *Mitti Cool* fridge uses the same principle of cooling as the clay pots in which villagers store drinking water.

Marketing communication firms are also working innovative ways to allow country consumers develop an appetite for branded products and services. For instance, Ogilvy outreach—the rural marketing arm of O&M conducting the supplying exercise— engaged some 120 local youth with portable DVD players and screens strapped on their chests to move door to door in a remote town about 100 km off Hyderabad.

Indian companies have also adopted a novel approach, what is now called, 'partnering to manage overseas acquisitions, so as to maximise global competitiveness. This partnering approach entails keeping an acquisition structurally separate and maintaining its own identity and organisation. Instead of rushing to integrate acquired businesses, they allowed the acquired companies to continue operating independently within the framework of their values to serve as a beacon. Big business groups like Tata, A.V. Birla and M&M are using this partnering approach. While allowing each entity to retain its local identity, they created a structure to leverage global strengths. For instance, in case of Tata Chemicals, the HR Chief of each organisation reports to an overall head in India but also to the chief of each area. This flexibility has enabled the group to cherry-pick the best practices from within the organisation.

The partnering approach has proved a great success, as is evident from the financial performance of the Indian companies which acquired 204 companies abroad between 2008 and 2009, creating value for shareholders.[17]

These few amongst many examples of best managerial practices based on ingenuity of Indian entrepreneurs supported by technology are getting recognition across the business world because they are highly flexible and less expensive and yield advantages for businesses transcending labour costs. A new word '**Indovation**' (*Jugaad* in Hindi) has been coined to these evolving practices and is on its way to enter the lexicon of management consultants, mingling with Six Sigma, Tom, Kaizen and Toyota's logistics system.

Indovation (India+Innovation) or *Jugaad* (pronounced "joo-gaardh") is an Indian style of creating improvisation that is driven by scarce resources and concern for customers' immediate needs. The key theme is to skim prices down till they fit into the Indian hip pocket, while creating a product, often from scratch, that fits Indian needs like a glove. Indovations have already been applied in a wide sphere of business covering transport and telecommunication, solar power, medical equipment, toiletry, ultra-low cost fridge, automatic teller cash machine for rural areas, flour mill powered by scooter and many more.

Indovations evolving from the exigency of doing business in recession-slammed business landscape are catching the attention of MNCs who do not have money to burn on R&D. They have come to believe that problems involved in doing business in emerging markets like India to exploit burgeoning opportunities are complex and need different business models and a different approach. Already companies as varied as Best Bay (BBy), Cisco Systems (CSCO) and Oracle are employing *Jugaad* as they create products and services that are more economical both for supplier and consumer. Top executives at Cisco which opened its second global headquarter in Bangalore in 2007 are importing the Indian mindset as they weld teams of US engineers with Indian supervisors. Even the iPhone maker is a champion at repurposing existing ideas and technologies in simple ways which enable it to reduce R&D outlays and produce high-margin products. The appeal of small and low-cost, and India's fast growing economy has caught on Toyota, Honda, Renault and Ford who are aggressively pitching their small cars at the Indian market.

MNCs are increasingly looking at India as a means of drawing lessons on resource maximisation. For instance, Renault-Nissan's first greenfield plant in Chennai was completed in 21 months against an average time of 36 months for plants of comparable capacity. This experience has encouraged the alliance to examine the kind of "safe shortcuts" that can deliver a huge leap forward in terms of time and cost for future projects. Renualt-Nissan, a late-comer to India is trying to derive business learnings with its multiple alliance with Bajaj Auto to develop a low-cost car, and Ashok Leyland for light commercial vehicles. This "cross pollination" of ideas is being extended to the alliance's design studio in Mumbai where talent is being hired locally.

The latest trend emerging in business world today is the adoption of innovative management models developed in India by MNCs, thus making India a new innovation destination. The concept of **Reverse Innovation** is taking root in India. Over the last few decades, it was observed that innovation was taking place in the developed nations and then moving to the developing countries. Now, "Reverse Innovation"—an innovation that is likely to be first evolved and adopted in the developing world and then move to the developed world—is receiving attention of the US Companies because of the emergence of frugal mindset among consumers in developed markets and increasing demand for 'value for money' products. For instance, in November 2009, a dozen executives from companies including investment banks Rothschild and Goldman Sachs and tech research firm Gartner (IT) ringed a conference table in a brownstone on New York's Upper East Side to learn how US businesses could develop products more cheaply and quickly by borrowing strategies from India.

Another illustrous example is of Deere & Company—the world's top maker of tractors—who developed a no-frills tractor model in Pune for its India model and then launched it in the US market to compete with its rivals including M&M.

Likewise, a low-priced electrocardiograph designed, developed and manufactured in India by GE Healthcare is finding takers not just in India but in other emerging markets. The *Mac 400*, developed at one-third the cost of a comparable imported version, has buyers in kerbside medical assistance in the US At Suzlon, while some engineering work is done out of its Indian factories, most of the high-end innovation including mind energy management solutions are carried out of its labs in Germany and Netherlands. Even Tata Technologies, the equipment and design subsidiary of Tata Motors, has been engaged by the US based Genovation cars to design prototype of an electric car for the company.[18] A German company Siemans also adopted Indian business strategy for developing its high-quality engineering technology for low-cost emerging market.

General Electric in its strive to resurrect itself has, of late, decided to focus on introducing more new products at more points and practices to capture new opportunities. It has developed a full line of high-margin, low-cost healthcare devices, and now marketed successfully in the developed world.

With the increasing pace of globalisation leading to fierceness in competitive environment, India is emerging as the source of best practices in management and strategy. The big hurdle before the Indian will be the lack of scale to take advantage of reverse innovation and go global. As such, Indian companies should innovate through partnerships in the same way as Procter & Gamble which already has more than half its products having R&D elements from external sources, and Nokia has partnered Reuters for data such as market prices and weather reports.

Summary

Indian corporates have had unstable and unsustained performance during the post liberalisation period. After initial economic gloom and India Inc.'s dismal performance despite tremendous economic reforms, the economy recovered and started blooming; so also the corporate sector shined. Corporate leaders enthused with economic prosperity and emergence of global opportunities began to expand their business domestically and overseas at whirring speed and some of them pole-vaulted on to the global marquee. However, this pace of expansion could not be sustained in the recent few years due to sub-prime crisis in the US and unpreparedness of the corporate sector to meet this challenge.

The reasons for this wavering performance of corporate India may be traced essentially in constraints and constrictions in their strategic thinking and action to cope with litany of challenges stemming out of fast changing environmental forces. Among various challenges plaguing the corporate sector in India, important ones pertain to coping with change, growth, innovation, productivity, quality, cost, talent, management of customers and people, land acquisition, execution and mindset.

Indian corporates will, therefore, have to adopt new concepts, principles, skills, practices and new mind frame in diverse fields of the organisation, society and the nation. They have to strategise the plan which signifies focused strategy making. Organisations have to conceptualise the future and be ambitious beyond their resources and capabilities and then create sustainable business, winning at all levels of the organisation.

So as to stay ahead of their global competitors on sustained basis Indian organisations need to strengthen innovation and new product development efforts and imbibe innovation as an integral part of corporate strategy. They should focus on dynamically reinventing business models and strategies as circumstances change.

The time has come when Indian companies must focus only on that segment of their business where they have core capability and can outsource the rest. Adopting the concept of integrated organisation will be significantly useful in this respect.

There is also a strong need to shift focus from allocation to leveraging of resources so as to get more value from existing resources. In the continual search for less resource-intensive ways to achieve ambitious objectives, leveraging resources provides a very different approach which is essentially energising.

Co-option and collaboration could be another potent means to gain competitive edge in terms of product innovation and development, market development and penetration in global markets.

For translating the strategy into desired results, excellent execution in all segments of business is essential. In order to implement strategy, such kind of structure has to be created as ensures, among others, transparency, freedom to work, few number of layers, flexibility and responsiveness.

People's approach to managing needs is to be followed in the knowledge economy. Organisations will have to accord high tech focus development of the people's talents. Building the required skills and competencies among employees demand new paradigms of managing them.

Organisations will have to be socially responsive and lay greater emphasis on ethical conduct, honesty and integrity, complying with society's moral fabric and values while working for achieving their economic objectives.

Above all, an organisation aspiring to achieve sustainable competitive prowess over its rivals must establish a performance culture. This demands not only heroic leader at the top but leaders throughout the organisation at every level. Corporate managers have to play the role more of a leader than as a manager.

Key Terms

Cocreate value	Ethnocentric mindset	Reverse innovation
Collaboration	Global mindset	Strategic intent
Concept of fit	Indovation	Strategic vision
Concept of stretch	Innovation	Sub-prime crisis
Cooption	Integrated organisation	Talent
Core business	Jugaad	Value chain
Core competence	Keirtsu	Virtual organisation
Corporate governance	Leveraging of resources	
Customer value proposition	Resilient	

Discussion Questions

1. Why has Indian Inc.'s performance not been sustainable?
2. What are the major challenges that Indian companies are facing?
3. What steps and paradigms would you suggest to overcome the competitive challenges?
4. Why should Indian organisations focus on innovation?
5. "Reinventing business model enables organisations to remain strategically resilient". Comment upon this statement with the help of suitable examples.
6. What is people's approach to managing business? How far will this approach be helpful to organisations in combating competitive challenges?
7. What approach should Indian corporates follow in organising business?
8. Outline the latest innovative managerial practices in India's business milieu.

References

1. *Business Today*, June 14, 2009.
2. *Business Line*, April 17, 2006.
3. *Business Today*, April 20, 2008.
4. *Asian Banking Outlook*, 2006.
5. *Times of India*, January 29, 2006.
6. *Indian Management*, June 2006.
7. Drucker, Peter F., "Management's New Paradigms", *Forbes*, October 5, p.152, 1998.
8. Nohria, Nitin, Willian Joyce and Bruce Roberson, "What Really Works", *Harvard Business Review*, July, 2003.
9. Hamel, Gary and Liisa Vlikangas, "Does Your Strategy Work?" *Indian Management*, November, 2003.
10. Prahalad, C.K., "Companies Need Continuous Changes-Not Episodic Breakthroughs", *Indian Management*, May, 2008.
11. Johnson, Mark W., Clayton M. Christensen and Henning Kagermann, "Reinventing Your Business Model", *Harvard Business Review*, South Asia, December, 2008.
12. *Business Standard*, September 23, 2009.
13. Prahalad, C.K., *The Economic Times*, February, 23–29, 1996.
14. *Indian Management*, May, 2008.
15. Hamel, Gary and C.K. Prahalad, "Strategy, Stretch and Leverage", *Harvard Business Review*, March–April, 1993.
16. Hamel, Gary and C.K. Prahalad, "Strategy as Stretch and Leverage", op. cit.
17. *Business Standard*, June 13, 2010.
18. *Business Standard*, June 14, 2010.

Internet Resources

- *www.apple.com*
- *www.bharti.com*
- *www.bhaskar.com*
- *www.moserbaer.com*
- *www.business-standard.com*
- *www.businessweek.com*
- *www.hinduismtoday.com*

2

Concept and Components of Strategic Management

INTRODUCTION

The history of corporate world amply reveals that over the centuries some organisations experienced meteoric growth, achieving industry leadership, while others faltered, stagnated or failed. Some seemed to squeeze every opportunity, while others were found laggard in moving. Consider, for example, the sterling performance of Coca-Cola in relation to its initial public offering in 1919 which would have been worth over $2,00,000 in 2000, while a dollar invested in a portfolio of representative large US stocks over the same period would have been worth less than $4,200.[1] Moreover, companies while successful were started when Coca-Cola was founded, many more disappeared from the scene.

Failure of accomplished corporate giants like Enron, World.Com, General Motors, Lehman Brothers, Mortgan Standley, AIG and others in the face of wondrous performance of Toyota, Honda, Nike, Nokia, IBM, Hindustan Petroleum (HP) and CISCO forces one to find out what distinguishes success from failure. A review of the history of successful firms suggests a broad range of ways to achieve superior performance. Some firms have succeeded by innovating and others by eschewing innovation in favour of operational efficiency. Some successful firms have sought to grow as rapidly as possible, while others have pursued modest growth. Some dominate their market, while others prosper by concentrating on a small market segment.

Variations in the performance of organisations have been the outcome of the vast differences in the industries in which the organisation participates, the regulatory requirements confronting it and the human, financial and physical assets it can bring to bear. But the variation is perplexing for the management who must navigate the organisation's external environment in a way that makes most of the organisation's assets. Those who have good grasp of the business basics have been found more successful in exploiting business opportunities and achieving sustainable competitive edge than their rivals. Without exception, companies that outperformed their industry peers excelled at what is generally termed as primary management practices—strategy, execution, culture and structure. And they supplemented their great skill in those areas with a mastery of any two out of four secondary management practices—talent, innovation, leadership, and mergers and partnerships.[2]

Thus, despite the 'dotcom' (.com) boom of the 1990s which had changed the rules of business forever, and even entrepreneurs and venture capitalists which discarded traditional business models as antiquated and conventional business wisdom as old school, strategic management as an approach of managing business even in complex, competitive and uncertain environment has always remained highly relevant with varying focus on its different dimensions. As such, it would be pertinent to have deep insights into the concept of strategic management and its components.

Concept of Strategic Management—A Dynamic View

The concept of strategic management is subtle and dynamic inasmuch as the concept of strategy has changed over times depending on the context in which the organisations act.

'Strategy' is a term that can be traced back to the ancient Greeks who used it to mean a chief magistrate or a military commander-in-chief. Over the next two millennia, with all refinements, the concept of strategy continued to focus on military interpretations. In military sense, tactics involves the use of armed forces in the engagement, while strategy referred to the use of engagements for the object of the war.[3] The adaptation of strategic terminology to a business context, however, had to await the Second Industrial Revolution, which began in the second half of the nineteenth century but really took off only in the twentieth century.

The First Industrial Revolution (spanning the mid-1700s to the mid-1800s) had failed to induce much in the way of strategic behaviour. This is for the fact that the industrial revolution was largely driven by the development of international trade in a few commodities (especially cotton). Most of the companies being small lacked the power to influence market outcomes to any significant extent and hence required little or no strategy.

The Second Industrial Revolution, which began in the last half of the 19th century in the US, witnessed the emergence of strategy as a way to shape market forces and affect the competitive environment. In the US, the construction of key railroads after 1850 made it possible to build mass markets for the first time. Alongwith an improved access to capital and credit, mass markets encouraged large-scale investment to exploit economies of scale in production and economies of scope in distribution.

By the late 19th century, the large, vertically integrated companies that invested heavily in manufacturing and marketing began to emerge first in the USA and then in Europe. Overtime, these companies began to alert the competitive environment within their industries and even cross industry boundaries.[4]

The World War II supplied a vital stimulus to strategic thinking in business as well as military domains. The concept of long-range planning took birth amid a flurry of optimism and activity during the post-war period. A large number of American and West European Companies adopted this approach during 1949–65. However, the contents and dimensions of long-range planning have changed considerably and the methodology followed for this sort of the planning has improved over the years.

The earliest long-range planning consisted principally of forecasting trends in sales, profits and perhaps in capital requirements of the existing operations of the business on annual basis, using substantially the same procedures and techniques as entailed in the preparation of the annual operating budget. These annual forecasts were usually made for two years as operating executives often inclined to regard any planning beyond two years as a theoretical exercise. These forecasts when summed together and well-documented and ratified by the top management came to be accepted as basic long-range plan of the enterprise furnishing adequate basis for a simple definition of sales and profit objectives or for checking the reasonableness of objectives which the management might already have defined, formally or informally. On the basis of such forecasts, the management used to assess the impact of a product or marketing changes in their plans, their distribution system or their sales force.

Thus, in the 1950s long-range planning was primarily involved in goal-setting and did not provide the mechanism for implementing the plans. Long-range plans during this period were excessively bludgeoned with projections and business data.

In the 1960s, the concept of economic planning was incorporated in long-range planning and the management gave overriding emphasis on resource allocation while formulating long-range plans for the enterprise. This was for the fact that the management during this period encountered serious problem of financing expanding needs of several business units of the company. Economic and financial concepts and techniques including cash flow analysis, capital budgeting and portfolio analysis were frequently applied to study cost of capital, company valuations and profitability determinants.

The long-range plans based on the concept of economic planning were inward-looking, largely quantitative, devoid of any interaction with external environmental force. Large number of organisations having adopted long-range forecasting received severe setback because the management failed to consider the possibility of future developments in the economic and industrial fields as technology, competition, government policies and values of society were changing fast. The resulting disappointments highlighted the need for a dynamic concept of long-range planning guided by a clear-cut but flexible overall concept of strategy and hence the concept of strategic planning during the 1970s. Strategic planning came to be identified as the process of determining the major objectives of an organisation and policies and strategies governing the operation, use and disposition of resources to achieve these objectives.[5] The thrust of strategic planning approach was on environmental scanning wherein choice of objectives and strategy are based on opportunities and threats arising out of changes in the environmental forces. The strategists tried to look at their companies' product offerings and those of their competitors from the viewpoint of an objective outsider. For instance, when a company experienced swift decline in sales in one of its major products following the introduction of a new, cheaper competitive product, the management decided to find out the reason. Through field interviewing of customers, they discovered that the sales slide was nearly over—something the competitors had not realised. Since sales of the product had dropped off to a few core markets where no cost-effective alternative was available, the management decided to put more support behind this product line, just as the competition was closing their plants. The management trained the sales force to service those distributors who continued to carry the line, and revised prices to pick up competitive distribution through master distributor arrangements.

In the subsequent years, management recognised that strategic planning should not only be limited to defining the company's basic purpose, articulating objectives and delineating the course of action to achieve these objectives but should also encompass all activities pertaining to the implementation of strategy, recycling and reformulating strategy. It is not so much planning that sets the organisation apart, but rather the thoroughness with which management links strategic planning to operational decision–making. This can be achieved through formulation of strategic plan, development of functional and action plans, creation of suitable organisational climate and structure, entrepreneurial drive among managers and technical personnel at all levels and involvement of wide niches of relatively junior people in many aspects of the corporate strategic plans.

The nineties witnessed turbulent changes in terms of global competition, emergence of the market forces for corporate planning and control, and the changes in the paradigms of corporate governance leading to greater involvement of shareholders and directors in strategy making exercises. A greater discipline in shaping corporate strategy was noticeable.

In view of the above, the concept of integrated planning came to receive greater attention from the top corporate management in the US who frequently used the term corporate planning instead of long-range planning. Since corporate planning shedded some of its baby fat and began to take on some of the responsibilities of a full-fledged management discipline, it came to be designated as strategic management with greater focus on action orientation.[6]

The sophisticated annual 5-year strategic plan was replaced with strategic thinking at all levels of the organisation through the year. Instead of a large centralised planning staff, internal and external planning consultants came to be available to help guide group strategy discussions. Although top management still initiated the strategic planning process, the resulting strategies might come from anywhere in the organisation. Planning was typically interactive across levels and was no longer top-down. People at all levels were now involved.

General Electric (GE), one of the pioneers of strategic planning, led the transition from strategic planning to strategic management during 1980s.[7] By the 1990s, most corporations around the world had also begun the conversion to strategic management.

In closed, controlled and stable environment, strategy was the management's principal game plan for strengthening the organisation's position, pleasing customers and achieving performance targets. However, in highly complex, uncertain, discontinuous and competitive business environment, that set in since the beginning of the 21st century, key to success of an organisation is how fast it can execute and how well it can adapt. This is why, in recent years, greater emphasis is being laid on execution of plan than on strategy making.

In recent years, there has been growing focus on the use of scenario and contingency planning (S&C) to manage uncertainty in an increasingly turbulent world. According to the survey conducted by Darrell Rigby and Barbara Bilodeau,[8] companies' use of S&C planning tools lagged behind the average for management tools' use overall. This changed abruptly after 9/11.

As the Figure 2.1 shows, in its first 8 years on the radar, S&C's use remained relatively flat, tracking well below the mean usage rate for all tools. But in 2002, its use leaped above the mean, nearly doubling to reach 70%. Its use has remained at or above the mean ever since, hitting 69% globally in the 2006 survey, 72% in North & Latin America, 74% in Europe and 64% in Asia-Pacific.

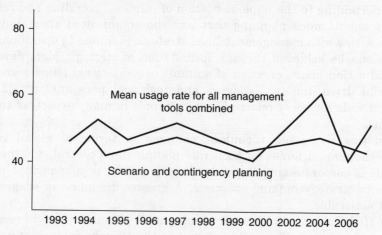

Figure 2.1 Use of S&C over the years.

More and more executives are finding the tools more valuable. This is probably due to improvement in the S&C tools, increased experience with them, and a broader appreciation for them, as global events have underscored their value. The survey further reveals that companies recognise the greater opportunity and risk that come with globalisation and the increasing need to anticipate crisis and develop robust contingency plans. The growing use of S&C tools suggests that companies are finding value as never before in planning for an uncertain future.

Strategic management, in brief, is thus an action-oriented corporate planning that positions an organisation within its external environment. Strategy is a game plan of top management for strengthening the position of an enterprise, delighting customers and achieving corporate objectives. It is concerned with achieving an overall integration of an organisation's internal divisions while simultaneously integrating the organisation with its external environment.[9] Strategic management does this in two basic ways. First, it considers formulation of the planning that leads to the achievement of organisational objectives and specific statements of action. Second, it involves implementation of the design and use of organisational subsystem and resources to operate.

Although strategy had considerable breadth in the past, it did not have much rigour. The ubiquitous SWOT model was used to assess a company's internal strengths and weaknesses and the opportunities and threats in its external environment. But the tools for doing so were pedestrian by all measures. Advances over the next few decades not only refined the tools but spawned a new industry around strategy. Corporate planning departments emerged and introduced formal systems and standards for strategic analysis.

While gaining depth, strategy has lost breadth and stature. It has become more about formulation than implementation, and more about getting the idea right at the outset than living with a strategy over time.[10]

Figure 2.2 portrays the historical development of concept of strategic management.

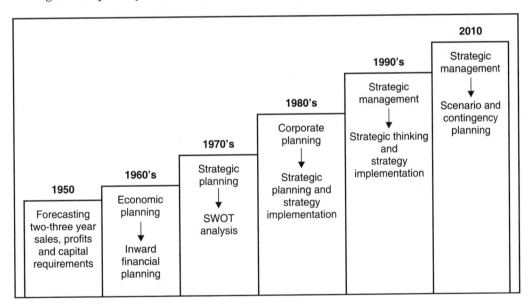

Figure 2.2 Historical development of strategic management concept.

In the wake of increased uncertainty of business climate and ferocity of competitiveness, a new management model, viz., **collaborative strategic management** is receiving serious attention of the top management. Collaborative strategic management signifies the process of coalescing the activities of key functional areas, viz., human resource (HR), corporate real estate (CRE) and information technology (IT) with one another and with the organisation's corporate objectives and strategies so as to optimalise the existing resources and achieve the ultimate objective of sustained competitive prowess.

IMMANENT FEATURES OF STRATEGIC MANAGEMENT

Strategic management as a modern approach to managing enterprises has certain basic characteristics which make it distinct from other approaches. A brief discussion of these characteristics would provide deep insight into the substantive nature of strategic management approach:

(i) Strategic management is an organised and systematised process of managing an enterprise. It is exclusively concerned with reasoning where we are going and how we intend to get there. The answer to the first question lies in the strategic planning and that to the latter in strategy execution. Strategic planning encompasses the activities of defining the company's basic characteristics (purpose), the qualitative and quantitative projection of its achievements (objectives and goals) and determining the most profitable way of deploying resources to exploit present and future opportunities and to counteract present and future threats. The implementation phase of strategic management covers all activities involving developing functional, organisational and action plans and monitoring, recycling and reformulating strategies.

(ii) Strategic management involves making decisions on how one should manage the business one is in, and intends to be in, so as to achieve the objectives desired by the organisation and reach the destination articulated by it. It guides the managerial action regarding construction of business portfolio in the changed environment and deployment of resources to do so. Strategic management seeks to lay down priorities for allocating corporate resources among different activities and decides which organisational unit shall get how much. Without a strategy, a manager has no thought to follow, no road map to manage by and no united action programme to produce the intended results.

(iii) Strategic management approach is based on structure of plans consisting of strategic plans, functional plans, operating plans and organisational plans. Strategic plans spell out a company's fundamental characteristics, the composition of its business mix, objectives and goals and a general programme of action providing guidance regarding deployment of resources, the various areas in which the company has to make thrusts, the strongholds it has to defend, the combination, and the timing and sequence of major initiatives and moves.

Within the parameters of an overall plan, detailed functional plans in critical business areas such as production, marketing, finance, personnel and research and development are developed. Each of these plans contains objectives and goals, policies and strategies of the concerned functional department.

In order to translate strategic and functional plans into action, operating plans are formulated. The principal focus of these plans is on establishing goals, action programmes and budgets for the ensuing year.

Another plan developed to implement corporate and other plans is organisational plan which is concerned with structuring the company's human resources in a way which creates a maximum performance potential.

This plan lists specific decisions pertaining to structuring of authority and responsibility relationships, work flows, information flows, personnel training and development, wage and incentive system.

(iv) Strategic management concept based on the systems approach is the overall planning of corporate enterprise concerned with configuring and directing the resource conversion process in such a way as to optimise the attainment of the objectives.[11] It is developed from the point of view of general management. It does not deal with each separate element of the business by itself; instead it permits the chief executive to see things as parts of a whole. In this system, the interests and purpose of the total enterprise take precedence over departmental claims in determining objectives, priorities and resource allocation.

The overall approach of strategic management provides a mechanism for the interrelated parts to be coordinated, thereby avoiding sub-optimisation of parts at the expense of the whole. Further, it supplies an integrated framework within each of the functional plans: divisional and departmental plans are interlinked and all are tied together into overall plans for the entire business.

(v) Strategic management is fundamentally concerned with the futurity of present decisions. It does not deal with future decisions. It assesses the impact of present decisions on the future product-market path of the company. The strategic management system is based on the belief that while the future is uncertain and the environment is complex, it is possible and necessary to cope with them through active intervention. It also believes that the future can be prognosticated and that change is not to be feared or frowned upon. It can be managed for the benefit of the enterprise.

(vi) Strategic management process is dynamic in character because it is exclusively concerned with improving competitive advantage of the firm on a sustainable basis and the firm's internal ambience changes over time. No firm—however successful—can afford to view current strategy as valid for all times to come. The quest for corporate resilience demands a strategy that is forever latching on to emerging opportunities. Thus, the impetus for a change in the firm's deployment and acquisition of its assets is frequently a change in the context in which it operates. As a matter of fact, strategic management is a continuous dynamic process that goes on throughout the corporate life. A firm has just to contend with three primary external forces—customers, competitors and the government. These forces decisively affect the firm's strategies.

(vii) An astute corporate manager is always amenable to changes in the internal as well as the external environment and brings about necessary adjustments in objectives, goals, strategies, policies, procedures and budgets with the intention of seizing potential opportunities and minimising impending threats. A one time plan not subjected to periodic review and modification inspite of changed conditions will be a fiasco because conditions change to such an extent that the plan is no longer relevant or helpful but only a hindrance. Strategic planning should, therefore, not be static. It has to be continuously adapted to changing conditions.

There are, however, practical limits to the frequency of change; an element of stabilisation is necessary to realise results. The benefits of quantity production, for example, are never made in unbroken succession. Major alternation in an industrial structure during its construction affects costs, schedules, plans, operations and personnel: a significant restriction on the frequency of adjustment in planning its human tolerance. People cannot show results in a state of perpetual analytical motion or manage successfully in response to continuously changing information. Periods of relative stability are required to comprehend the existing situation to formulate and carry out managerial actions and to consider the future.

The periodic review of short-range plans takes place only as often as required by the type of enterprise and improved profit performance overtime, usually quarterly. Long-range corporate plans are revised usually once a year but adjustments brought about by current events are accumulated and formal revisions are made in the interim, if necessary.

(viii) Corporate strategy is usually considered in terms of concept of fit signifying relationship between the company and its environment and allocation of resources among competing investment opportunities. In the changed environment, 'concept of fit' must be supplemented by 'concept of stretch' which demands focus on leveraging of resources in addition to their allocation.

Concept of leverage is based on the philosophy that a company with limited resources should focus on doing more with less, go for undefined niches rather than confront its competitors as well as defended market, investing on basic competencies which enable the organisation to bring forth its global leader. Leveraging implies allocating the existing resources in a more creative way so as to improve resource productivity.

Concept of stretch is based on the belief that copious resources cannot guarantee continued industrial leadership and conversely, modest resources cannot be deterrent to future leadership. General Motors, Phillips and IBM with burgeoning resources at their command were found on the defensive with Honda, Sony and Compaq. IBM challenged Xerox in the copier business but failed, while Canon, a company with 10% of the size of Xerox in the mid 70's, eventually displaced Xerox as the world's prolific copier manufacturer.

(ix) Strategic management process is cross-functional in nature which signifies synthesisation of organisational human resources and expertise from critical functions such as marketing, operations and finance in a comprehensive way. This enables management to resolve conflicts in recommendations of individual functions operating in isolation. A cross-functional approach allows no one, not marketing nor manufacturing nor finance, to control or dominate the process; each contributes simultaneously to create a better plan and result.

(x) The time span of the strategic planning is long-range. The basic task of long-range planning is to visualise the enterprise as it would be 5 to 10 years hence. Generally, long-range projection of economic environment, customer demand for products or new technology of interest to the company is made for 10 to 20 or more years in the future. Similarly, long-range objectives are set for 10 years in the future. However, operating plans developed to achieve these objectives and translate strategies into action are prepared for shorter periods of not more than 3 years.

No organisation should, however, be dogmatic about the time spectrum. The planning period should be suitable for the business. It should be long enough to take into account any normal cycle in the foreseeable future. Further, the time span also puts a responsibility on the management of building up sufficient infrastructure so as to ensure that what the system decides for a given period is feasible and manageable. The planning period reflects the philosophy of the management and is conditioned by a host of other factors including the size of the enterprise, technology and the environmental forces under which a given enterprise has to operate.

It is worth noting that long-range planning for a particular span of time does not imply that a corporate plan is prepared at intervals of that time period, nor does it suggest that the company should make no study of trends beyond the period. According to Devid Hussey,[12] a five-year plan is on that rolls. It may be revised and updated once a year and at every revision an additional year is added. So, there is always a five-year plan. The plans must be flexible and the company must be prepared to reconsider the whole of its strategy if events show it to be necessary. What it must never do is to formulate a five-year plan and then follow it blindly for the given time period. The trends beyond the planning cycle will have an effect on the company's strategies. For example, an enterprise engaged in quarrying must take into account the life span of the quarry while formulating corporate plan because it is likely to restrict the investment the enterprise is prepared to put into the quarry, or cause it to search for some other area of activity so that it can be well established by the time the present quarry is exhausted.

In India, most of the companies have corporate plans of more than five years. Only a few organisations have adopted a 10-year span for preparing their plan.[13]

(xi) Strategy is not only influenced by environmental developments and resource capability of an organisation but also by the values and expectations of those who are at the helm of affairs in and around the organisation. In some respects, strategy can be thought of as a reflection of the attitudes and beliefs of those who are most influential in the organisation. Whether a company intends to expand or is concerned with consolidation, and where the boundaries are drawn for a company's activities reflect much about the values and attitudes of managers engaged in strategy making and executing. At times, values of stakeholders including workforce, buyers, suppliers, shareholders and the local community bear upon the strategy development of an organisation.

COMPONENTS OF STRATEGIC MANAGEMENT SYSTEM

The essence of strategic management system is making strategy and executing it in such a way as to achieve the avowed corporate objectives. Hence, this system of management is composed of strategic planning and implementation planning. Monitoring of plans is also ingrained in strategic management approach as it ensures that planned performance corresponds to the actual results.

Strategic Planning

Strategic planning is an intelligence—design choice activity concerned with defining the basic character of the firm, the composition of its business mix, the qualitative and quantitative projection of the firm's achievements, and the crafting of strategies for the organisation as a whole as well as for different critical functions. This is done after making extensive and dispassionate appraisal of the environmental forces and matching the product market opportunities so discerned with corporate competencies.

Strategy is inherently action-oriented. It is practically impossible to plan all the bits and pieces of a company's business in advance and then go for long periods without change. Reacting and responding to happenings either inside the firm or outside of it is a normal part of the strategy making process. Highly dynamic and partly unpredictable character of competition, fast changing values and expectations of customers, unplanned increase or decrease in costs, mergers and acquisitions among major industry players, new regulation, tumbling of trade barriers and other innumerable events can render parts of strategy obsolete. There is always something new to react and some new strategic window opening up. This is why the task of crafting strategy is a never ending process. In fact, a company's actual strategy is a blend of its intended or planned strategy and its unplanned reactions to fresh developments.

It is pertinent to note that strategic planning, as it has been practiced, has really been a strategic programming—the articulation and elaboration of strategies or visions that already exists. But strategic thinking signifies capturing what the manager learns from all sources both the soft insights from his or her personal experiences and experiences of others throughout the organisation and the hard data from market research and the like and then synthesizing that learning into a vision of the direction that the business should pursue.[14]

Strategic planning in actual practice has always been about analysis—about breaking down a goal or a set of intended actions into steps, and formalising those steps so that they can be implemented almost automatically, and articulating the anticipated results of each step.

Strategic thinking, in contrast, is about synthesis. It involves intuition and creativity. The outcome of strategic thinking is an integrated perspective of the enterprise, a not-too-precisely articulated vision of direction, such as the vision of Ratan Tata, Chairman of Tata Sons.

Such strategies often cannot be developed on schedule and immaculately conceived. They must be free to appear at anytime and at any place in the organisation, typically through messy processes of informal learning that must necessarily be carried out by people at various levels who are deeply involved with the specific issues at hand.

Strategy making needs to function beyond the boxes to encourage the informal learning that produces new perspectives and new combinations. In fact, strategic planning in terms of strategic programming has not only ever amounted to strategic thinking but has, in fact, often impeded it.

Strategic thinking helps a firm to take positions in a world that is complex, confusing and uncertain. One cannot get rid of ambiguity and uncertainty which are the flip side of opportunity. If a firm wants certainty and clarity, it has to wait for others to take a position and see how they do. Then it will know what works, but it will be too late to profit from the knowledge.

Strategy is needed for any organisation as a whole, for each business the company is in and aspires to be in and for each functional part of the business, viz., marketing, production, finance, research and development and human resources.

Thus, strategic planning of an organisation, especially large and multinational one, exists at three levels, viz., corporate, business unit level and functional level.

Corporate Strategy

Strategy at the corporate level is termed as **corporate strategy**. It is the top management plan to direct and conduct the business of the corporate group. It encompasses an organisation wide business comprising of moves proposed to be made to establish business positions in different industries and the approaches to be used to manage the company's group of business successfully.

Corporate strategy sheds light on how one should manage the business one is in and intends to be in so as to achieve competitive edge over its rivals. Corporate level strategy represents the patterns of entrepreneurial actions and intents underlying an organisation's strategic interests in different business, divisions, product lines, techniques, customer groups and customer needs.

Corporate strategy thus consists of the following moves intended to be made to establish a company's niche in different industries and the approaches to be followed to manage the company's group of business:

Determination of business portfolio of the organisation: A business, like a flower, is born: it flourishes and withers. But the fact that a company's business blossoms and then fades does not mean that the company must die. A company to succeed must outline its individual business. Its continual growth is the objectives; the pace of replenishment has to be faster than the pace of decline. To sustain growth, there must be a continuous pipeline of new businesses that represent new sources of growth.

Thus, the first major issue to be addressed is to decide about the company's business portfolio so as to achieve the target levels of corporate performance. Thus, corporate management has to determine what industries to diversify into? When and how to start a new business? Which of the existing businesses to continue and which one to get out? and whether to enter the new business on its own or by acquiring another company, and so on.

A company aspiring to expand its business outside the national boundary has to address various strategic issues such as which countries to be entered into? What products/services to be offered? What would be the approach to handle foreign markets? What would be the mode of entry into different countries, and the like.

Initiating moves to improve the combined portfolio of the organisation: Once the decision regarding business mix of the company has been taken, corporate strategy must focus on ways to get better result of the business portfolio. The management has to decide on how to strengthen the long-term competitive positions and profitabilities of businesses the company is presently engaged in or proposes to embrace in future. The strategy should, therefore, specify the approach the organisation would employ in each of the different activities, viz., grow or build, hold or maintain, shrink and manage for decline.

The overall plan for managing a group of diversified business usually involves pursuing rapid growth strategies in the most promising business, keeping the other core activities healthy, initiating turnaround efforts in weak performing businesses with growth potential and divesting businesses which are no longer attractive or that do not fit into management's long-range plans.

Conceiving ways and means to synergise organisational efforts: So as to gain competitive advantage over its rivals for all the time to come, an organisation should explore the possibility of synergistic potentials in the organisational move to diversify its business. Related diversification offers abundant opportunities to utilise fully the existing skills and expertise, and infrastructural facilities in the new business, thereby resulting in reduction of overall cost and strengthening competitiveness of some of the businesses of the company and boosting its corporate value.

Establishing priorities for allocation of resources: This is a crucial strategic issue which has to be addressed very seriously as it supplies a much needed management rationale for evaluating competing requests for corporate resources particularly for the fact that the company's different businesses are generally not equally attractive and promising. The corporate management has to decide on the kind of fit between internal resource capability and mix of business activities which will yield a level of performance and results commensurate with corporate objectives. This is the crux of the corporate level strategy. If high level organisational performance is to be achieved, both the availability of internal resources and patterns of their deployment have to be tethered to the requirements of each line of business the company is in.

Thus, for sustainable competitive advantage and high profitability, business activities having high market potentials have to be allocated greater funds than those having lower market earning potentials. Consistently poor performing units need to be dropped to release the funds needed for funding promising projects.

Various other decision issues pertaining to these major questions are:

- Choice of domestic market, countries and regions for setting up new business or for expansion
- Products to be marketed and/or produced in a particular domestic market and a country

- Best form of entry in foreign markets
- Competitors in different domestic markets and foreign countries and their significance in these markets
- Level of the business risks existing in different global markets
- Major source of industry innovation
- Homes of the most demanding customers
- Extent of product adaptation required by local markets
- Sharing activities with other company businesses
- Possibility of using upstream capacity
- Possibility of using downstream capacity
- Proximity to other markets
- Scope of financial sourcing
- Scale of economies in production and marketing in different global markets
- Opportunities for product differentiation in different countries
- Possibility of disaggregating the production and marketing functions for an efficient blending of scale of economies and learning curve effects and the differentiation necessary to respond to market peculiarities.

It must be noted that corporate strategy is more value-oriented, conceptually based and less concrete than strategic decisions made at the unit, division and department level. The choice of the businesses and markets in which to compete, the dividend policies, the priorities for expansion, and the methods of long-term capital generation are examples of more corporate level strategic decisions.

In brief, corporate strategy is what makes the corporate whole and up to more than the sum of its business limit parts. Unfortunately, corporate strategies of most companies have dissipated instead of created shareholders value. Hence the need to realise the sordid fact that diversified companies do not compete; only their business units do. Unless a corporate strategy places primary attention on nurturing the success of each unit, the strategy will fail, no matter how eloquently constructed.

Business Strategy

Business strategy, also known as strategic business unit (SBU), is the managerial plan for directing and running a single business. Such a strategy defines the product-market posture of its individual business units. It is mirrored in the pattern, approaches and moves crafted by management to produce successful performance in one specific line of business. Business strategy deals specifically with issues such as (i) How the organisation intends to compete in that specific business? (ii) What will be the role/thrust of each key functional areas in contributing to the success of business in the market place? and (iii) How resources will be allocated within the business unit?

Corporate strategy and business strategy are one and the same in case a company markets one product or service line (a group of similar products or services) in one country. However, for companies engaged in several product or service lines, for each business or services, business strategy called the SBU is formulated. A strategic business unit for an MNC may also take the form of a regional or national affiliate that has a certain degree of autonomy. For example, Pepsi-Cola USA, Pepsi-Cola-Bottling Group, Pepsi-Cola International, Pepsi-Cola Bottling International, Pepsi Co. Wins and Spirits International, Pepsi Co. Foods International, Pizza Hut, Taco Bell, Pepsi Co. Food Service International, North American Van Line, Lee way Motor Freight, and Wilson Sporting Goods are the principal divisions and subsidiaries of Pepsi Incorporated. Some of these SBU groupings are based on product and service lines, while some other SBUs are geographically based.

Although large number of strategies have come into operations and have proved successful for organisations over the years, recent years have witnessed emergence of a handful of generic strategies which achieved astounding results in many industries and countries. These generic strategies enable firms to maximise gains from their competitive advantages and to build defensible positions to ward off threats from rival firms. Each strategy is evolved to suit a business unit of a firm. A firm looking for new business opportunities or seeking to get out of existing business should consider the suitability of each activity into each unit.

Like corporate strategy, business strategy has also two aspects, viz., external and internal. The external aspect of the business strategy is concerned with the way an organisation can entrepreneurially be effective in that particular business—What sort of competitive edge to strive for? Which customer needs and customer groups to emphasise? and Whether or not to differentiate the firm's product offerings from those of rivals? How to position the business in the market place *vis-à-vis* rivals and to appeal to customers? and What must be done to keep the firm's market approach abreast of the evolutionary aspects of industry trends, direction, social changes and economic conditions?

The internal aspects of business strategy focus on how the different components of business (manufacturing, marketing, finance, research and development) ought to be aligned and coordinated in order to be responsive to those market forces upon which competitive success depends. The line of business strategy provides guidance for organising and providing funds for the performance of sub-activities within the business, for doing so in ways which speak directly to what is needed for successful performance. Perhaps, the key internal concern is about the kind of distinctive competence to develop and how to develop it.

The thrust of business strategy is how to build and strengthen the company's long-term competitive position in the market place. This demands forming responses to changes underway, addressing specific strategic issues facing the company's business.

A powerful business strategy is the outcome of the strategist's ability to cohere a series of moves and approaches capable of producing sustainable competitive advantage. With a competitive advantage, a company has good prospects for showing above average performance and achieving success in the industry. Absence of competitive advantage lands a firm, however, in risk of being outcompeted by stronger rivals, and results in mediocre performance.

Three major forces that render a business strategy effective in yielding sustainable competitive advantage are:

(i) deciding where a company has the highest scope to win a competitive edge;

(ii) developing product service attributes that have strong buyer appeal and set the company above its rivals; and

(iii) neutralising the competitive moves of rival organisations.

An example of how effective business strategy was to Havels India is shown here as Illustrative Capsule 2.1.

ILLUSTRATIVE CAPSULE 2.1

STRATEGIC MOVES OF HAVELS INDIA

In the year 1958, Quimat Rai Gupta, a young school teacher of Punjab, reached Delhi to pursue his dream of starting his own business. He invested his entire savings of ₹10,000—a substantial amount then—to launch a small trading business in cables and wires at the Bhagirath place wholesale electrical goods market.

Over the next decade, the school teacher took the next step backward, into manufacturing. But he needed a brand. He acquired Havels for the princely sum of ₹10 lakh in 1971, thus moving up from being a trader in electrical equipment to a manufacturer of switch gear.

Indeed, this laid the foundation for the success story that is Havels India today. Quimat Rai was not satisfied with the existing state of affairs, and was always looking to do something new. This is why he moved on to manufacturing, even though the trading business had taken root.

Over the next couple of decades, Quimat Rai aggressively expanded his manufacturing base in Delhi. In the '70s and '80s, Havels started making change over switches, HBC fuses, and miniature circuit breakers (in a joint venture with Geyer, Germany). By 1990, revenues had hit ₹30 crore.

In 1992 his son Anil Gupta joined the family business armed with an economics degree from Delhi's Shri Ram College and an MBA from Wake Forest North Carolina.

Anil had global ambitions for the group. He felt that the firm had to adopt a two-pronged strategy. One, the firm's products should be world class in terms of quality rapid technology. Two, it should rapidly scale up its distribution network, both in India and abroad, to gain market share.

To achieve this, he gradually shut down the old manufacturing plants. All ten plants that Havels today has, are new and have the latest technologies. At the same time, he expanded the product portfolio to include industrial cables and wires, switches, fans, compact fluorescent lamps and lighting fixture. Havels India is among the top three in most of its products and is increasing market share with some aggressive brand building.

Anil and his core team are now planning to take the Havels brand global. The acquisition of Sylvania, the world's fourth-largest lighting and fixture brand, has given it a distribution network spanning 50 countries, mainly in Latin America and Europe and a diverse product portfolio.

Today, the school teacher lords over a ₹5,400 crore business employing over 7,000 people. Its strong brands, large distribution network and diverse product portfolio will be its key strengths driving its growth internationally.

Source: Annual Reports of Havels India

Functional Strategy

Functional strategy is the approach a functional area takes to achieve corporate and business unit objectives and strategies by maximising resource productivity. It is the game plan to manage a principal subordinate activity within a business. Functional strategy is concerned with developing and nurturing a distinctive competence to provide a company or business unit with a competitive advantage. Just as a multidivisional corporation has several business units, each with its own business strategy, each business unit has its own set of departments, each with its own functional strategy.

The orientation of the functional strategy is dictated by its parent business unit's strategy. For example, a business unit following a competitive strategy of differentiation through high quality needs a manufacturing functional strategy that emphasises expensive quality assurance processes over cheaper, high-volume production; a human resource functional strategy that emphasises the hiring and training of a highly skilled, but costly, workforce; and a marketing functional strategy that emphasises distribution channel "pull" using advertising to increase consumer demand over "push" using promotional allowances to retailers. If a business unit were to follow a low-cost competitive strategy, a different set of functional strategies would be needed to support the business strategy.

Functional strategies, while being narrower in scope than business strategy, contain relevant details to the overall business game plan by setting out the actions, approaches and practices which are to be employed in managing a particular function.

Just as a competitive strategy may need to differ from one regime of the world to another, functional strategies may need to differ from region to region.

One major responsibility for conceiving for each of the important business functions and processes lies with those who are charged with managing the functional area in question. It is the functional managers who establish performance objectives and strategies that will promote accomplishment of business level objectives and strategy. Compatible, collaborative, mutually reinforcing functional strategies are essential for the overall business strategy to have maximum impact. Furthermore, functional strategies should be in sync rather than serving their own narrower purposes. Coordination and consistency among the various functional strategies can be accomplished in the best possible manner during deliberation stage.

Implementation Planning

Implementation planning—an integral component of strategic management system, is a way of operationalising strategic decisions. It is concerned with the operational aspect of strategic management with a view to translating strategic plan into action and achieving the desired results.

Implementation planning involves creating organisational arrangements that allow the firm to pursue its strategy more effectively through committing the people and the resources to the strategic choice. While creating organisational arrangements, implementers must keep in mind, objectives, strategies and capabilities of the enterprise for carrying into effect the strategic plans.

Strategic success calls for simultaneous viewing of planning and doing. Greater the overlap, greater the probability of success.[15]

Successful implementation planning is a key to sustained competitive advantage of a firm. A brilliant strategy, a block buster product, or a breakthrough technology can put a firm on the competitive map, but only a solid execution can hold it there for long. The firm will have to be able to deliver on to its intent. Unfortunately, the majority of companies are not very good at it, by their own admission.[16]

In recent years, corporate management has begun to realise that effective execution is a competitive business advantage. Companies are now seeing that if they execute better, they perform better. If they integrate long-term and short-term objectives, if they consider incentives, controls and feedback, they execute better.

It should, however, be noted that making strategy work is more difficult than setting a strategic choice. It is for the fact that implementation is the result of thousands of decisions made everyday by employees acting according to the information they have and their own self interest. Thus, there are more people involved in executing strategy today and execution takes longer than people expect. Political and organisational problems typically surface. So, once a strategy is developed, the management has to go throughout the organisation and through dozens of planners to make sure it is carried out. Once execution starts, it could be one or two years or even require a three-to-five year time frame.

Since implementation planning is action focused, action planning or operational strategy forms an important part of implementation planning. Action planning represents planning of detailed and specific actions needed to achieve organisational goals. In fact, action planning seeks to decompose long range plans into actionable programmes. Action plans are essentially operational, more people and force oriented. Such plans, while of lesser in scope, add further detail and completeness to functional plans. They provide the basis for detailed specification of various activities to be carried out by the enterprise in a synchronised manner on a time-bound basis throughout its subsystems. Through such plans, the management can allocate tasks and resources to managers, supervisors and rank and file personnel at the operating level. They serve as a means of pinpointing responsibility, delegation of authority and imposition of accountability for results at various operating levels in the organisation.

Effectiveness of strategy implementation calls for determining clearly to what extent the organisation will have to change so as to translate the strategy under consideration and manage the change process, manage the organisational structures, manage the culture of the organisation and choose a suitable approach to implement the strategy. All these tasks can be performed successfully with least problem if the organisation has adept managerial leadership who can build consensus on how to move ahead, inspire the people and secure their commitment and cooperation.

Responsibility for formulating action plans is assigned to front-line managers, subject to review and approval by higher-level managers. There has to be a logical flow of strategic information between the upper and lower levels in terms of strategy and tasks and there has to be accountability along the way.

Monitoring

Strategy cannot be said to be successful in achieving the desired objectives unless management ensures that the actual performs conforms to the desired performance. This calls for evaluation of corporate activities and performance results with the planned results. If it is found that the actual performance does not match the planned performance, corrective action is taken to enforce a strategy that is not being followed or to modify a strategy that is not working. Thus, monitoring is an important ingredient of strategic management system.

Figure 2.3 shows dimensions of strategic management system.

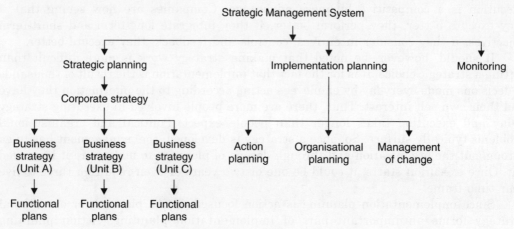

Figure 2.3 Dimensions of strategic management system.

SIGNIFICANCE OF STRATEGIC MANAGEMENT SYSTEM

Strategic management—the top management function—charts the firm's direction, develops competitively effective strategic moves and business approaches and pursues what needs to be done internally to produce good day-in, day-out strategy execution and operating excellence. Strategic management system provides the management a powerful mechanism to cope with highly complex environment characterised by diversity of cultural, social, political, technological, competitive and economic forces existing in different markets of the country and abroad. The mechanism includes objectivating, linking and balancing. **Objectivating** refers to the ensuring of proper objectivity where documents are prepared and where alternatives are compared. **Linking** brings together various activities such as selling, distributing, financing and manufacturing. **Balancing** means reaching an equilibrium between the requirements of customers and the resources of the plants and the suppliers. By means of effective planning the management develops and improves its capability to cope with the volatile external environment forces. It enables the management to prevent impending crisis which may irrevocably narrow the firm's freedom of action in future.

Strategic management system offers way of thinking, a discipline and a technique to manage changes. By this, a management is totally prepared to anticipate, respond and influence the firm's destiny regardless of the developments taking place in the business world. By constant surveillance of various external forces and a thorough capability analysis, it can discern the new opportunities for their timely exploitation and impending threats that need to be minimised, and modify or revise the existing product-market strategy.

Another significance of strategic management approach is that it provides a dual approach to problem solving: (i) exploitation of the most effective means to overcome problems and face competition and (ii) deployment of limited resources among critical activities as well as among different regions. It furnishes the most scientific technique with which the management can make investment decisions in order to achieve the objective of maximising wealth with minimum loss.

A company having no clear direction, vague or unchallenging performance targets, a muddled or a flawed strategy or no competence to execute its strategy effectively is likely to be facing grim financial problems and its business is at a long-term risk as its management is sorely lacking. In contrast, a company having skillfully crafted strategy and prudently executed the same will lead to greater cohesiveness of the initiatives and activities of different divisions, departments, managers and work groups.

In a rapidly changing and fiercely competitive environment, there is considerable scope for an analytical and integrated approach through forecasting and planning. The very complexity and uncertainty of the future environment make strategic planning more necessary than ever before. Organisations, which do not keep abreast of environment changes, will underutilise and waste their resources, miss opportunities and fail to withstand seemingly relentless forces. It is through comprehensive planning programmes that a firm can not only cope with external environmental changes for its survival but also open the door for expansion, growth and diversification, adoption of new markets and so forth.

While there are significant external forces which necessitate planning, there are also forces within an organisation which relate to the day-to-day work of an enterprise and which have a major contribution in its success. Strategic planning process handles these forces very effectively, particularly by establishing organisational objectives, measuring accomplishments and coordinating efforts within an organisation.

Strategic management process leads to better decisions because it focuses attention on all factors which influence decision-making and insists on the identification of myriad product-market options, their evaluation and selection of the best alternatives for the achievement of corporate objectives. It provides the objective criteria for making sound decisions on commitment of resources and on major directions of the enterprise for specified period in the future. It encourages the management to choose the best course of action to realise its objectives. Without corporate planning system, a management might not have been able to achieve all these.

Once the course of action has been decided it is imperative to communicate the same to the managers so that they may make their contribution towards the job to be performed. The strategic management process provides a channel of information flows. It serves as a means of communication among all levels of management regarding objectives, strategies and detailed operational plans. As plans are in the process of development, common understanding is generated among all levels of management about opportunities and threats important to individual managers and to the organisation. Once plans are completed and put on record, vital decisions are made, such as who is going to implement them and how they should be carried out.

Strategic management system brings about improved performance. The entire process is based upon the basic objectives and goals of an enterprise. Thus, the very act of strategic planning focuses attention on these objectives. Because of the emphasis on establishment of objectives at all levels of management, managers are forced to think of planning for results rather than merely planning activities. To ensure that objectives are realistic, managers are required to think of the way they will accomplish the given tasks, the organisation and personnel they will need to perform them and the resources they will require. It also elicits the commitment of managers for satisfactory performance. Individual managers equipped with clearly defined objectives and goals set their goals and thus get an opportunity to put their ideas into planning programmes. It is because of the involvement of down-level managers in decision-making that strategic planning serves as a motivating force. Everyone has a clear idea of what the company is setting out to achieve and is, therefore, encouraged to help the organisation achieve its aim. This is why a strategy-focused organisation is more likely to be a strong bottom-line performer.

Strategic management system provides an objective basis for measuring performance. Since most people seek a sense of accomplishment in their work, there must be some means by which their performance can be evaluated. People want to know what it expects, how they will be evaluated and when the evaluation will take place. Clearly defined goals and establishment targets provide the framework for measurement and, thus, the potential for feeling a sense of accomplishment. An effective planning system readily identifies individuals or units within an organisation, who or which fail to meet desired goals. This enables the organisation to assess the impact of failure on other units and to take appropriate action. In this way, a well-conceived planning system not only permits managers at all levels to control the performance of their subordinates but also serves as a means of improving their performance.

In brief, a company having conceived good strategy and highly competently executed its strategy will be an outstanding performer in the market place.

PITFALLS OF STRATEGIC MANAGEMENT SYSTEM

The foregoing account of the utility of strategic management system should not give one the impression that it is a fool proof managerial approach bereft of any limitations. In fact, it suffers from certain pitfalls, as enumerated below:

Lack of Accuracy

Strategic management is not an exact approach, since it is founded on forecasting of future events, which are uncertain and hazy. Plans are based on various assumptions and parameters. If they do not hold true and future events do not occur as expected, the whole system will fail. Unexpected and unpredictable developments may result in failure despite sophisticated planning.

Danger to Rigidity

In many instances, managers, particularly lower level managers, may regard budget estimates as the rigid dictates of policy, and business operations are performed according to the original estimates. While adopting a planning programme, the management should remember that the business situations can never be static and accordingly the programmes must be continually adapted to incorporate changing conditions within the firm.

A Complex Exercise

Strategic management system involves complex and cumbersome exercise, which requires a high level of imagination, foresight, analytical ability, creativity and fortitude to identify alternatives and choose the most suitable strategy for direction and collection of resources. The central management must exert pressure to demand the best efforts from managers and staff. If this is not done, preparation and maintenance of a high standard planning schedule is difficult to achieve. Besides, a comprehensive understanding of the fundamental principles of the planning process and an ability to apply appropriately and adroitly, many new techniques developed to facilitate planning are other requisites of successful planning programmes.

A Costly Exercise

A comprehensive strategic planning exercise calls for considerable time, money and effort for special research studies and information pertaining to the economic, social, political, technological and competitive aspects of the business environment and their likely effect on the future of the enterprise. If the potential benefits from such an exercise do not match the cost, the planning effort will be a waste. However, it is not possible to measure precisely because a strategic planner is always in a 'either/ or' situation. Likewise, it is difficult to compute the cost of any planning exercise undertaken by the management. It is, of course, the incremental cost over an informal planning approach that is relevant.

However, various research studies have come to the conclusion that planning does pay off and there is no better way to run an organisation.

BUILDING BLOCKS OF SUCCESSFUL STRATEGIC MANAGEMENT SYSTEM

Success of strategic management system of an organisation depends on various critical factors, such as the following:

(i) Strategic management as a philosophy of management requires the management dedication to acting on the basis of the contemplated future, a determination to plan regularly and systematically as an integral part of management. Top managers must not only have an innate desire for planning but also back their wishes by positive action. Genuine ownership of the strategy by the top of management is vital to its success. They are expected to establish a planning climate which stimulates managers and employees at all levels of the organisation to practice the planned approach. They should make others feel that they insisted on seeking new methods, new tools and new procedures to improve the entire planning process.

(ii) Management at all levels must be concerned with the long-term results of all decisions. Current decisions are taken about the product-market path which the enterprise will follow in the long run. Every manager should take time off from his daily routine to assess the outcome of his decisions.

(iii) Strategic management system based on rational decision-making should always be a choice of probable product-market options and an objective exercise to select according to the management's emotions and desires. It should be based on an objective consideration of all possible alternatives and definitions of all the practical ways of solving each particular problem. Thus, the entire decision-making in the strategic planning system should be based on available facts and suitable management techniques should be employed in the decision process.

(iv) The strategic management system must continually be reviewed and its result appraised so as to confirm that the standards set are being achieved and also to incorporate new environmental developments in the planning system. Proper recording of the expected results is, therefore, an essential principle of strategic planning. Such recording also leads to clearer thinking and better decision-making.

(v) The entire strategic management system presupposes the team approach to decision-making and action. This implies involvement of all managers and employees throughout the organisation in developing strategic plans and their implementation. The chief executive should provide an opportunity to every executive to participate in discussions leading to any decision so that plans have both the involvement of all those responsible for them, and the approval of the man whose duty is to set the overall pace of the organisation. Team approach to planning creates a congenial atmosphere for the discussion of problems and encourages the growth of creative ideas, which serve as a diet needed for the successful survival on an enterprise. The overall approach should be to involve senior managers, particularly, in developing strategy for the organisation and to have a wider participation of junior level executives and employees in formulation and implementation of plans.

In sum, for strategic management system to be successful the chief executive must buy the proposition that planning as such is an identifiable, controllable function essential to sound health of the enterprise and sell it to everyone in the enterprise. The chief executive is responsible for planning the progress of the company in the same way as every line manager is responsible for planning his own operations.

MANAGEMENT POLICY AND STRATEGIC MANAGEMENT

The chief executive of an organisation and his team need guidance to incorporate the strategic direction of its strategies. This involves definition of purpose and mission, choice of objectives, interpretation of the environment, selection of strategies, implementation of specific plans that are developed from those broader perspectives, and the integration and coordination of strategies in operational activities. Management policy furnishes such guidance.

Although management policy is considered a guidepost to thinking and action, it has been interpreted by the management experts in different ways. Thus, some experts including William Glueck regard management policy, long-range planning and strategic management as the same thing.[17] However, this view is not correct inasmuch as while management policy provides a basic framework defining fundamental issues of a company, its purpose, mission and broad business objectives, and a set of guidelines governing the company's conduct of business within its total perspective, strategy delineates critical courses of action toward the attainment of company objectives, and defines the means of deploying resources to exploit current and future opportunities and combat present and impending threats.

Some scholars like Frank T. Paine and William Naumes and Robert Murdic, consider policy as the rule for executing strategy.[18] This concept of policy is too restrictive. It lays stress on only one aspect of policy, and ignores the strategic dimension, which is the nerve centre of the management policy.

There are others such as Robert Mockler, Trewatha and Newport and the one contained in the policy manual of General Electric Company who consider policy to be the bench guides for determining the future destiny of an enterprise.[19] The viewpoints of the experts in this category are quite comprehensive as they focus on different dimensions of policy. It is appropriate to state that policy establishes guidelines for decisions and actions pertaining to every area of the company's operations. It provides general framework for decision-making.

The differences in the views of the management scholars stem out of the fact that policy is all encompassing and relates to the entire process of management. Hence, the management policy is composed of myriad of policies formulated at different levels of management for directing executives. Thus, policy defining the fundamental character of a company, its purpose and broad business objectives and a set of guidelines governing the company's conduct of business within its total perspective is more strategic in nature and is developed at the top level. In order to execute strategy, detailed guidelines are constructed to direct lower-level executives. These are more tactical in nature. Besides, certain minor policies are also laid down to help executives to deal with specific repetitive situations, as for example overtime reimbursement, leave travel concession, educational refund and inventory evaluation policies. Such policies are nothing but contingent decisions. Ansoff interpreted policy in this sense.[20]

It will, therefore, be in fitness of things to consider management policy as an explicit statement of fundamental criteria by which future decisions are to be judged. These criteria serve as guidelines in taking decisions regarding the nature and scope of business of the company, the long-term course of action to be pursued in attaining the objectives and the procedures and rules concerning the implementation of plans.

It may be made clear at this stage that the management policy and business policy are not the same, as is commonly understood. In fact, the management policy is an explicit statement of basic guidelines within which future decisions are to be made by the organisation—both profit-making and non-profit organisations. In contrast, business policy contains major guidelines that serve as parameters within which profit making business organisations are supposed to take decisions. Thus, the management policy is a broader term, of which business policy is a part.

As opposed to the management policy, in strategic management, decisions are made regarding the long-term course of action to be followed to achieve the firm's objectives and resources are deployed accordingly. These decisions are made within the overall framework of the management policy. In short, while the management policy contains guideposts, actual decisions are made in strategic management.

While highlighting relationship between the management policy and strategic management, it has been rightly observed that strategic management system emerges out of the management policy and the management policy emanates from strategic management system. Thus a policy that gives birth to strategic management is strategic policy, which contains broad guidelines regarding the dimensions of the strategic management programmes and the levels of management of which these will be chalked out, methodology to be followed for the formulation of strategy and guidelines along which operating strategies will be developed to effectuate overall corporate strategy. It also defines the way in which people will participate in strategic management programmes and also the way changes in the programmes will take place.

It is also pertinent to point out that policy emerges out of the strategic management system. Once corporate strategy and supporting strategies are developed, these need to be translated into action, for which detailed and specific guidelines are necessary. For instance, a company may pursue a strategy of locating a plant in a minority area or poverty pocket so as to mitigate the problems of squalor of the nation. To give shape to this strategic decision, the general manager of a major division of the company may establish a policy that every effort should be made to subcontract work from the plant so long as certain quality and cost standards are met. Departmental managers might set up policies to determine the quality and costs which are acceptable. Then policy in regard to hiring and promoting minority groups might be formulated.

It is, thus, paradoxical to observe that the management policy while guiding strategic planning programme is also derived from it. This is because of the existence of policies at all levels of management. A management policy that directs strategic planning programme is a basic policy, whereas one that emerges from strategic planning programme is an operating policy.

COLLABORATIVE STRATEGIC MANAGEMENT

In today's business world characterised by rapid, unpredictable change and higher competition, organisations to survive and thrive will have to be agile and nimble, create not only new products but also new market and do so faster than their competitors ever imagined possible. It's not enough to be first to market, or to double the firm's revenue overnight; it's also important to be able to reduce its presence in one part of globe at the same time it is established in another within a short period of time. This demands pursuing collaborative strategic approach to management that acknowledges and leverages the growing interdependence of human resources (HR), corporate real estate (CRE) and information technology (IT). This process is called **collaborative strategic management**.

According to Charles E. Grantham and others, collaborative strategic management focuses on alignment of HR, CRE and IT with one another, and with the organisation's broader strategic goals. Each of the functional areas has its own disciplines, its own values and its own challenges. Yet no business can operate effectively unless they are integrated. Businesses today desperately need a clearly defined methodology that allows them to align their HR, IT and CRE strategies, and thus achieve that all-too-elusive corporate agility.[21]

Collaborative strategic management approach—based on systems perspective —demands functional managers to look at a particular problem from the viewpoint of the organisation as a whole and also consider the interests of other functional areas and arrive at the solution. This approach is based on the premise that with the advent of truly global markets, the continuing information technology, the globally distributed workforce, and the growing worldwide human talent gap, senior managers have to understand that they can no longer hit their own targets without strategic cooperation of the company's other business units and those unable to adapt their management practices to the growing interdependence of IT, HR and CRE will soon find themselves marginalised by their more strategically coordinated competitors.

The methodology that is usually followed in this approach is that the CEO of the company constitutes a task force comprising senior executives from all critical functional departments to consider a particular issue of corporate wide implications. What is more important is that everyone in charge has a complete understanding of the company's core business plan, its financial strategies—both short-term and long-term—and its product development and marketing strategies. Besides, those heading the task force need an understanding of the market forces that drive the industry and an awareness of the competitive atmosphere, both local and global, within which the company operates.

Having understood the corporate as well as financial strategies and the decision rules, the task force must focus on strategic alignment of the objectives and plans. It is imperative that any workplace strategy be completely aligned with the corporate vision and business mission and plan. The task force should also acquaint itself with product development plans, workforce staffing plans, financial policies and strategies, and branding programme of the company for the next-five-years and how the technology deployment plan will support all these.

After reviewing the present and future state of affairs of the company, the task force need to interact with the external team to get insight into issues as business drivers, competitive threats, strategy development and decision process.

After reviewing and interacting, the task force should come out with the statement of the business problem and specification of the results desired. This is followed by reformulation of suitable corporate strategy along with business and functional plans.

Once recommendations are made, the task force must carefully coordinate the implementation of its recommendations with the top management.

Summary

The concept of strategic management as an approach of managing enterprises is subtle and dynamic. The present concept of strategic management has evolved through four phases, viz., forecast-based long-range planning, economic planning, strategic planning and corporate and integrated planning. In the context of increased uncertainty and business complexity and ferocity of competition due to globalisation, technological advancement and fast changing human values focus of strategic management system shifted from strategic planning to scenario and contingency planning.

Strategic management as a modern approach of managing corporate enterprises has certain unique attributes. Thus, this approach is highly organised and systematised, comprising strategic planning and strategy execution. This approach is primarily concerned with the futurity of the present decisions. The process of strategic management is highly dynamic in character and involves continuous review to accommodate changes in the external as well as internal environment. The time span of strategic planning is long-range. The basic task of long-range planning is to visualise the enterprise, as it could be 5 to 10 years hence. However, no organisation should be dogmatic about the time spectrum of the strategic plan.

The strategic management system is composed of strategic planning and implementation planning. Monitoring of plans is also an integral part of the strategic management approach. Strategic planning refers to strategic thinking and not strategic programming, as is actually practiced. Strategic planning is done at the corporate, business unit and functional levels. Implementation planning is concerned with operational aspect of the strategic management with a view to translating strategic plan into action and achieving the desired results.

Strategic management approach plays crucial role in achieving sustained success of an enterprise. A company's performance in the market place is directly contingent upon the calibre of its strategy and its proficiency with which the strategy is executed.

However, effectiveness of the strategic management system depends primarily on the top management support and commitment to acting on the basics of the system and involvement of different levels of management in strategy making. There is a strong need to continually review and rejig the system so as to ensure that the targets are achieved and also to incorporate emerging environmental developments.

Key Terms

Business strategy	Forecasting	Monitoring
Collaborative strategic management	Functional strategy	Scenario and contingency planning
Corporate planning	Implementation planning	Strategic programming
Corporate strategy	Integrated planning	Strategic thinking
Economic planning	Long-range planning	

Discussion Questions

1. "Concept of strategic management is subtle and dynamic". Discuss this statement and bring out various phases of strategic management system.
2. In what way should strategic management system be considered? What are its distinguishing features?

3. "The strategic management as a management philosophy is reflected in the structure of plans". Comment.
4. Discuss the components of strategic management system in proper perspective.
5. What is strategic thinking? How is it different from strategic programming?
6. What is corporate strategy? What are its salient ingredients?
7. What is business strategy? How is it different from corporate strategy? What are the major forces that render a business strategy effective in achieving sustainable competitive advantage?
8. Why has strategic management become so important for today's organisations?
9. Why are strategic decisions different from other kinds of decisions?
10. What are the pre-requisites that render strategic management as an effective approach to managing modern business?
11. What is collaborative strategic management? How is this model worked out?

References

1. *Stocks, Bonds, Bills and Inflation: 1997*, year book, Ibboston Associates, Chicago, 1997.
2. Nohria, Nitin, William Joyce, and Bruce Roberson, "What Really Works", *Harvard Business Review*, July, 2003.
3. Clausewitz, Carl Von, *On War*, Edited and translated by Michael Howard and Peter Paret, Princeton University Press, Princeton, NJ, p.128, 1984.
4. Chandler, Alfred D., Jr., *Strategy and Structure*, MA: MIT Press, Cambridge, 1963 and scale and scope, MA: Harvard University Press, Cambridge, 1990.
5. Steiner, George A., *Top Management Planning*, The Macmillan Company, London, p. 34, 1969.
6. Glueck, Frederic W., Stepher P. Kangman and A. Steven Walleck, "Strategic Management For Competitive Advantage", *Harvard Business Review*, USA, p. 5, 1985.
7. Vaghefi, M.R. and A.B. Huellmantel, "Strategic Leadership at General Electric", *Long Range Planning*, April, pp. 184–200, 2000.
8. A Growing Focus on Preparedness, *Harvard Business Review*, July–August, 2007.
9. Kotler, P. and James L. Heskett, *Corporate Culture and Performance*, Free Press, New York, pp. 17–36, 1992.
10. Montgomery A. Cynthia, "Putting Leadership Back into Strategy", *Harvard Business Review*, January, 2008.
11. Ansoff, H.I, *Corporate Strategy*, McGraw-Hill, p. 17, 1968.
12. Hussey, David, *Corporate Planning—Theory and Practices*, Pergamon Press, Oxford, p. 3, 1976.

13. Singh, B.R., "Corporate Planning—An Analysis of Practices of Selected Large Companies in India", Ph.D. thesis (unpublished), Banaras Hindu University, 1983.

14. Mintzberg, Henry, "The Fall and Rise of Strategic Planning", *Harvard Business Review*, January–February, 1994.

15. Hrebiniak, Lawrence G., "Good Strategy? Try Implementing It", *Indian Management*, July, 2005.

16. Neilson L. Gary, Martin L. Karla and Elizabeth Powers, "The Secrets to Successful Strategy Execution", *Harvard Business Review*, South Asia, June, 2008.

17. William Glueck, *Business Policy—Strategy, Formulation and Management Action*, McGraw Hill Kegakuska Ltd., 1976.

18. Paine, T. and W. Naumes, *Strategy and Policy*, The Driden Press, New York, 1982 and Murdic Robert G., "Nature of Planning and Plans", *Advanced Management Journal*, Vol. 30, November 4, 1965.

19. Mockler, Robert J., *The Business Management Process*, Shoal Greek Publishers Inc, Texas, 1973, Trewatha and Newport; Management—Functions and Behaviour, *Business Publications*, Texas, 1976 and *The Policy Manual*, General Electric Company, 1953–55.

20. Igor H. Ansoff, *Corporate Strategy*, McGraw Hill, 1968.

21. Grantham, Charles E., James P. Ware and Cory Williamson, *Corporate Agility*, PHI Learning, New Delhi, pp. 2–3, 2008.

Internet Resources

- *http://Knowledge.wharton.upenn.edu*
  This website of Wharton School Publishing contains an article on 'Good Strategy. Try Implementing It" by Lawrence G. Hrebiniak.

3

Strategic Management Process
A Synoptic View

LEARNING OBJECTIVES

The present Chapter aims at:
- Providing a vivid view of various phases entailed in strategic management system.
- Acquainting readers with how strategic planning function is organised.

INTRODUCTION

Strategic management, as explained in the preceding chapter, is about defining the company's purpose and objectives, determining the most profitable way to deploy resources to exploit present and future opportunities, implementing, monitoring, recycling and reformulating plans. Formulating a strategy, that is planning on an effective guidance to action, is both an art that individual managers must develop and a process that a well managed firm must execute.

It is important to note that strategy is developed and executed within a firm. However, decisions pertaining to strategy making are shaped by the history of the firm, the processes it has in place for making the decisions and the interests and perspectives of the top management. Typically, these factors come together in a "strategy process"—a process through which strategy is defined and developed, implemented and evaluated by the management.

Every firm has some set of routines for making the decisions central to its overall direction. Some have elaborate strategic planning processes in which managers throughout the firm contribute to an annual strategic planning document. Others rely on a small group of senior managers to make these decisions without any well-defined planning process. Still others do not follow planning process, responding instead to the tempo of market changes. Thus, there may be a wide array of strategy processes, each firm laying down its process distinct from others. This is because environmental forces—external and internal—of firms that bear upon strategy processes differ. Thus, a small and well focused firm may have effective formal strategy processes which might not be found purposeful to a large firm diversified in different lines of business located in various regions of the world. A firm competing in e-commerce cannot afford to wait for the next annual planning cycle to make changes in strategy, since its market changes dramatically every month. An organisation in a stable external context with a successful strategy in place might devote fewer organisational resources to strategy process than a firm experiencing a radical strategic change.

Despite wide variations in strategy processes adopted by firms, there are certain activities which every firm has to undertake to develop strategy and translate it into action. These activities, for convenience of presentation, may be categorised into four broad phases, viz., identification, development, implementation and monitoring. The following section delves into these strategic activities:

PHASES OF STRATEGIC MANAGEMENT PROCESS

The phases of strategic management process are as follows:

Identification Phase

Strategic management process begins with identifying occasions that trigger review of existing strategies. This trigger could be the existence of the gap between the expected and the actual performance, change in ownership of top management, acquisition of new skills, newly emerging buyers' preferences and requirements, the initiatives of rival firms to grab increased market share, emergence of new opportunities and threats in the wake of radical changes in government or governmental policies, technology and social conditions.

At times, dramatic changes in product-market strategy are required particularly when external developments affect the firm's strategy or when a rival firm makes radical move to attract customers or when technological advancements are very rapid. Recent outbreak of grim financial crisis around the world following the sub-prime crisis of the US and Euro debt crisis have forced almost all the corporate enterprises across the world to rejig their current strategies and make requisite adjustments therein or pursue new strategy away from the existing one to cope with the perilous challenges.

It is thus normal to change strategies—sometimes gradually and sometimes swiftly, sometimes reactively and sometimes proactively. Changes in strategic moves may not only be necessary to counterbalance the economic challenges but also to sustain competitive advantage in future and to cope with the waves of change in the market place.

Before the central management could think of the ways to solve the problem and exploit the opportunities, it would be pertinent to diagnose the current situation. A good diagnosis includes both the reasons leading upto need for decision and obstacles standing in the way of achieving the objectives. To find the causes of a problem, the management must build up both a good database on business activities and trends and a continual monitoring of the environment confronting the firm with a wide scanning for possible signals. Illustrative Capsule 3.1 explains Philips Electronics new ventures.

ILLUSTRATIVE CAPSULE 3.1

PHILIPS ELECTRONICS ON A REJIG TO MOVE FROM CONSUMER ELECTRONICS

In a shift in its Indian strategy, Philips Electronics has decided to move away from consumer electronics to medical, health and wellness products.

The management has noted that there is buoyancy in the health care space across the country. They believe that as much as 35%–40% of the total investment into setting up of a hospital is on the equipment. This gives a huge untapped market opportunity.

The medical equipment business in India is estimated to be ₹28,000 crore and growing annually at 12%–15%. Philips has a 50% critical share in the diagnostic imagery and critical care arena.

The company also plans to evolve its lifestyle business into four categories including healthy living, home living, interactive living and personal care.

Mr. Elwin de Valk, Senior Vice-President and Cluster leader (Growth Cluster), Philips Consumer Lifestyle said that the company is mapping various consumer insights to develop products customised especially for the Indian market.

Source: Press Conference of *Business Standard* by Mr. Elwin de Valk, SVP on June 30, 2009.

Development Phase

Once a firm has spelt out its purpose and objectives, it knows where it intends to go. The question is how best to get there. The firm, therefore, needs a grand design, a general programme of action for achieving the corporate objectives. The strategy should focus on providing a product or service that is superior to that of competing rivals or developing unique capabilities which the rivals cannot match.

Based on scanning of environment and penetrating analysis of Strengths, Weaknesses, Opportunities and Threats (SWOT), the management must construct a strategy. A strategy must be formulated that matches the external opportunities contained in the environment with the firm's internal strengths.

Developing strategy demands identifying strategic options and evaluating each of them. A strategic option should be a coherent, self-contained strategy with the four elements of purpose, mission, objectives and competitive advantage. Each option should be evaluated in terms of its effectiveness to seize fresh opportunities and availability of the resources. The chosen strategy should exploit the opportunities for which the firm's strengths and resources are well suited.

Ansoff suggested a "cascade approach" to choose the most suitable strategy. Cascade approach is a multi-stage approach of formulating rules in gross terms and then successively refining alternatives through several stages as the generation of a solution proceeds.[1]

While evaluating strategic options, three important factors should be kept in view. The first one is suitability of the option. This is to be judged in terms of its potentiality to exploit opportunities and overcome threats. Feasibility is another factor to determine as to what extent a chosen option can be put into effect. In other words, availability of requisite resources at the right time and in the right place needs to be examined. Finally, acceptability of the alternative by the stakeholders merits consideration. For example, if a company is mulling to bring about substantial change in product range and store design, the management must examine if this course of action will be acceptable to the unit level managers and other executives.

Ultimate choice of strategy is a matter of management judgement. It is notable that the selection process cannot always be viewed or understood as a purely objective, logical act. It is sternly influenced by values of managers and other groups with interest in the organisation and finally may very much reflect the power structure in the organisation.

Implementation Phase

The strategic management system does not stop with the choice of strategy. The strategic plan so developed must be executed to achieve the desired results. Strategy implementation is action-oriented activity which is concerned with putting the selected strategy into operation. While executing strategy, the management must factor in objectives, strategy and capabilities of the enterprise for carrying into effect the strategic plans. The task of executing strategy involves assessing what must be done to develop organisational capabilities and to reach the desired goals in time.

Implementation measures include the following:

 (i) Organising the firm's tasks.
 (ii) Building an organisation capable of carrying out the strategy successfully.
 (iii) Developing budgets to steer ample resources into those value chain activities that are critical to strategic success.
 (iv) Establishing operational policies and procedures.
 (v) Instituting best practices and mechanism to perform core business activities and to push continuous improvement.
 (vi) Installing support systems that enable company personnel to carry out their strategic roles successfully day in and day out.
 (vii) Tying rewards and incentives to the achievement of performance objectives and good strategy execution.
 (viii) Creating performing culture to ensure successful strategy execution.
 (ix) Developing effective leadership to push implementation of strategy and to keep improving on how strategy is being executed.

Monitoring Phase

Monitoring—the last but the most critical phase of strategic management process—involves checking if the strategy is purely a matter of "hot air" or whether it is actually having an effect upon the activities. This requires that various relevant aspects of performance be measured and compared with corresponding aspects of the plan. If the firm is not attaining its objectives, the management must ferret out the causes for the gap. The causes could be poor strategy, poor strategy execution or both. The change in the industry environment within which the firm may adversely affect the adequacy of the strategy. Thereafter, the management will take corrective steps in terms of modification of the firm's strategic vision, mission, objectives and strategy.

So as to ensure effective monitoring of strategy, it would be in fitness of things to install suitable mechanisms so that potential environmental changes are monitored timely and managers are alerted to send and respond the developments that require a change in strategy and implementation practices.

A bird's eye view of the strategic management process can be hogged from Figure 3.1.

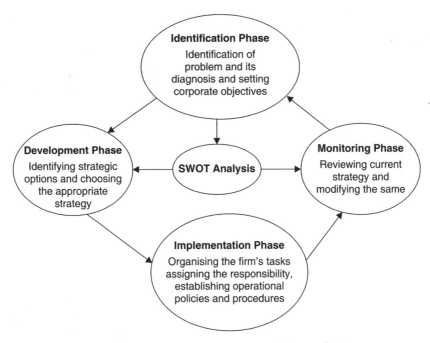

Figure 3.1 Strategic management process in a firm.

At this juncture, it must be noted that strategy making is typically an ongoing process but not a regular, continuous process. It is most often an irregular, discontinuous process, proceeding in fits and starts. There are periods of stability in strategy development, but also there are periods of flux, of groping, of piecemeal change, and of global change[2]. As such, managers are obligated to review adequacy of the existing strategy from time to time, refine and recast it as situations warrant. Illustrative Capsule 3.2 explains Dr. Reddy's Laboratories' strategy making.

ILLUSTRATIVE CAPSULE 3.2

STRATEGY MAKING BY DR. REDDY'S LABORATORIES IN TOUGH CONDITIONS

Exploit more, and explore less, has been the strategy of ₹6,944 crore pharma major, Dr. Reddy's Laboratories, to face challenges thrown up by the global economic slowdown.

The company has over the past one year (2008–09) revisited its strategy to come up with this approach. The company is focused on consolidating its position in more significant markets. Accordingly, the company has exited several small, distribution driven markets, whose contribution while insignificant, added to the complexity of operations.

The entire organisation design has been reworked to respond comprehensively to the changing business landscape.

The company now has a global generics business, a pharmaceutical services and active ingredients business and proprietary products business.

In recent times, the company embarked upon structural changes involving merging discovery research and Aurigene and the alliance with GlaxoSmithKline, which will enable full realisation of the huge potential of product pipeline in high growth emerging markets.

The company's strategy for the future is in place. It is now focused on executing it.

Another top priority of the company is to make the German subsidiary Betapharm profitable and contribute to growth.

Source: Chairman's speech in Annual General Meeting held on July 22, 2009.

It is also important to remember that the issues that corporate managers will encounter while conducting the strategic management process differs from firm to firm depending on its competitive environments, the firm's internal strengths and weaknesses and the number of other businesses being carried by the firm. Accordingly, each firm has to tether its strategic management to the situations best suited to the firm. Here is an example of Hindustan Unilever as given in Illustrative Capsule 3.3.

ILLUSTRATIVE CAPSULE 3.3

CHOOSING STRATEGY BY HINDUSTAN UNILEVER DURING ECONOMIC SLOWDOWN

The robust expansion is the offtake of Fast Moving Consumer Goods (FMCGs) of Hindustan Unilever (HUL) even as most other sectors of the economy grappled with the slow down and the company's ability to outperform others with strong topline and profit growth made the company darling of the investing community.

However, after a smooth sail through the initial phase of the slowdown, HUL's topline growth began to decelerate towards the end of 2008. After expanding its overall net sales by nearly 20% in each of the first three quarters of 2008, HUL saw the growth rate dip to 16.8% in December 2008 quarter and further to 6% in March quarter of 2009. That was even as the FMCG market actually picked up.

HUL's volume growth has been on a downhill journey since 2008, decelerating steadily from a 10% growth in March 2008 to low single-digits by end-2008. It actually slid into negative territory by March, 2009. HUL's key businesses—home and personal care and foods—have shown a sequential deceleration in growth in recent quarters. HUL's slowing growth rate can be traced to its decision to take larger price increases than its competitors on some of its key segments in 2008.

The period from January to June 2008 saw a sharp upward spiral in the prices of key inputs such as LAB, petroleum derivatives and palm oil, which contributed to sharply escalating costs for soaps and detergents.

HUL made the strategic choice of passing on these input costs almost entirely to its customers by taking substantial price increases spanning these portfolios.

The higher realisations shored up margins and helped HUL close the year ended March 2009 on a strong note. It managed a 15.5% growth in net sales, a higher profit margin (14.5% against 13.1% the previous year) and a net profit growth of 15%.

However, with a slowdown in consumer spends over the past six months, staple FMCG categories such as soaps and detergents have begun to show signs of downtrading by consumption.

Given the tilt in HUL's product mix towards mid-market and premium brands and its significant price hikes in 2008, HUL's brands have borne the brunt. Between March 2008 and March 2009, HUL lost market share in six out of key segments in which it operates and ceded more than 2% points in market share in personal wash (54% to 48.2%), skin care (55.4% to 52%) and toothpaste (29.5% to 28%).

The past quarter has seen an active strategic exercise by HUL to regain market share by reducing prices, increasing grammage on its products and rolling out promotional offers.

The company has also decided to reactivate more brands to reestablish a presence across price points. That prices of key raw materials such as palm oil, LAB and packaging materials have dipped 25%–40% below the last year's levels may also help.

Source: Business Line, July 12, 2009

ORGANISING STRATEGIC PLANNING FUNCTION

Efficiency of strategic management as an approach to manage business in highly complex, competitive and discontinuous environment depends, inter alia, on how the function is organised and what are the tasks being performed by different levels of management in making and executing strategic decisions.

The pattern of organising strategic management function in a firm hinges on the following factors:

- Forms of organising strategic planning function.
- Forces influencing the choice of pattern of strategic planning organisation
- Size of planning staff
- Task of different levels of management in making and executing strategy.

Forms of Organising Strategic Management Task

Corporate enterprises may have different forms of organising strategic planning functions; prominent among these are outlined in the following:

(i) An enterprise may not have a separate strategic planning department to carry out functions of formulating and implementing strategy. Each executive is entrusted with the responsibility of planning his operations and executing the same.

(ii) An enterprise may have organised planning functions in critical areas such as finance, marketing, production, research and development, human resource management, and the like. No formal strategic management process is done at the corporate level.

(iii) An enterprise may have strategic planning organisations in different business units and/or in divisions but no strategic planning organisation at the corporate level. In this set up, the chief executive serves as a focal point for making strategy and is assisted by the key functional executives at the corporate level.

(iv) An enterprise may have a full-fledged department entrusted with the responsibility of formulating strategy and executing, but does not have a planning staff at the unit or division level. This is an example of centralised planning structure. A majority of Indian corporate organisations have this type of structure.

(v) An enterprise may have a decentralised structure with central department at corporate level to perform the task of formulating strategy and planning organisation at the levels of functional divisions. Such a pattern usually exists in multinational and multi-divisional companies. In such a structure, the divisional planning staff plays an active role in establishing divisional objectives, goals and strategies, and operating plans in their respective areas within the overall strategy framework evolved by the central department. In a decentralised structure, strategic department at the corporate level plays an active role in integrating business unit strategies and functional plans crafted at unit and divisional levels.

Forces Influencing the Choice of Pattern of Strategic Planning Organisation

There is no standard pattern of strategic management organisation to meet the needs of all kinds of business enterprises. Every company has to organise its planning functions in such a way as to suit its requirements. This is why in real life we find considerable differences in the organisational pattern of planning function in different enterprises. As a matter of fact, a myriad of factors bears upon the choice of a particular pattern. Among these, the size of a company, autonomy, nature of its products, and attitude of its top management are important ones.

Size of organisation is one such very important variable. In a small company, its president may himself do all kinds of planning. As the company grows in size, the chief executive may be assisted by his key executives in formulating strategies and executing them. In contrast, large companies may have a full-fledged strategic planning department. Multi-nationals and multi-divisionals have planning departments both at the corporate level as well as division levels.

The degree of autonomy given to divisions and units also influences the overall planning programme. Where top executives are reluctant to part with planning function to departmental and divisional managers, there will emerge a centralised structure. In a sharper contrast to this, decentralised structure will be favoured in an organisation where top managers are prepared to involve managers at all levels in the planning function.

Nature of product is another factor that influences the organisational pattern of strategic planning. Organisations engaged in manufacturing automobiles or aircrafts will have a planning structure different from the one producing consumer goods, such as readymade garments. This is because of the demand of high and complex technology, burgeoning capital investment and long development cycles.

The attitude of top executives also influences the type of planning organisation a company has. Thus, a company with a chief executive who believes in doing his own planning will have a centralised planning set up.

Where a company is just beginning to do formal planning or has had much experience with the process will affect its planning organisation structure. The planning organisation will differ between a company in financial crisis and one enjoying great success as a result of past planning.

Size of Strategic Planning Staff

There is no rigid role to govern the number of corporate planners which an organisation should have to manage the strategic planning task. However, it must be noted that this number should be kept as low as possible. With growth in size of the firm in terms of product variety, operation variety and market structure, size of the planning staff tends to increase.

It is also pertinent to note that size of the planning department should not be decided exclusively on the basis of the initial work-load which the firm has to carry at the time of installation of strategic planning system. Initially when the planning system is designed and introduced, strategic planning department is bludgeoned with variety of functions and responsibilities. But once the formulation and implementation stages are over and strategic planning comes into existence as a continual function, the burden tends to be lesser and steadier. It would, therefore, be a folly to decide the size of planning staff on the basis of the initial stages of planning. In fact, size of the planning staff should be determined on the basis of normal work load of planning in the organisation. The firm may, if necessary, call upon the services of outside consultants.

In India majority of large enterprises have a planning staff of more than ten people. However, there are only a few enterprises having planning staff of more than twenty. These enterprises are mostly diversified, decentralised and multi-divisional in character.[3]

Task of Different Levels of Management in Making and Executing Strategy

This section seeks to delve into the various levels of management of an enterprise involved in the task of strategic management and the part played by the functionaries at each level in this process.

Generally, in large organisations there are five responsible units—Board of Directors, Top Executives, Planning Staff, Committee and Line Managers. Figure 3.2 exhibits this structure. Medium-sized organisations have relatively fewer levels of management associated with the activity of strategic planning and management.

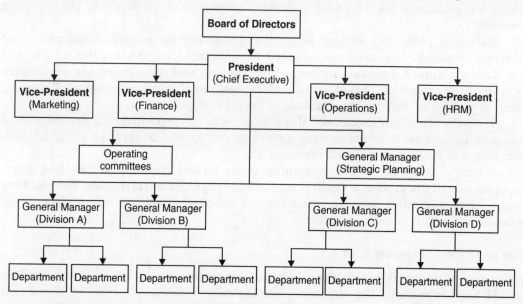

Figure 3.2 Strategic planning organisational structure in a large organisation.

Board of Directors: Board of Directors is the apex body in an organisation. It is supposed to discharge the responsibility of performing strategic management task. The Board normally carries out three major functions in this regard, viz., (i) guiding the establishment of corporate objectives, corporate and business strategies and broad policies of the enterprise; (ii) asking discerning questions regarding plan proposals; (iii) selecting the chief executive of the organisation.

The Board is supposed to scan strategic plan proposals submitted to it by the chief executive and approve, disapprove or modify the same. Besides, it has to review previously accepted strategies and question their continued validity.

The Board of Directors has to ensure that all proposals have been adequately analysed and considered and that the proposed strategic actions are superior to available alternatives; flawed proposals are customarily withdrawn for revision by management.

Further, the Board has to evaluate the calibre of the chief and other senior executives' strategy making and implementing skills. They have to determine the effectiveness of the current chief executive in performing strategic management task. In recent years, the Directors of General Motors, IBM, Goodyear and Compaq Computer noted that the executives were not adapting their company strategy fast enough to cope with environmental changes affecting their markets. They forced the chief executives to resign, and installed new leadership to give fillip to the task of strategy making and executing.

In India, the Board of Directors' role in strategic management process has been found to be very limited.[4] In some cases, the Directors do not involve themselves in reviewing of strategic plans or approval of corporate objectives. This is, perhaps, due to non-professional background of the Board members. In those organisations where the Board members have professional background, their involvement in the planning process is high.

Top executives: The chief executive (Chairman or President) of a company is next to the Board in the management hierarchy. He represents the central authority of the organisation commanding overall control over strategic management process. It is he who coordinates the objectives and plans of various business units and divisions of the organisation and arbitrates conflicts within the group. It is at this level that corporate-wide decisions are made which are binding on managerial units at lower levels.

In recent years, tasks and responsibilities of chief executives have increased tremendously due to growing size of organisations, increasing complexities of business, fast changing technological developments, turbulent changes in business environment and growing complexity of relationship between the firm and its environment. As a result, the traditional structure of a single key executive as the chief of the enterprise has been found to be inadequate for managing the decision workload which devolves on the corporate office. It has been felt that the top management job is such that one man cannot perform it efficiently.

Simultaneous demand for broad range of critical skills and talents further exposed the limitation of one man chief executive concept. Hence, the recently emerging concept of top management is a corporate office consisting of several key executives, each authorised to make major decisions and all somehow managing to make these coherently and consistently with one another. The concept of a chief executive team rather than a single chief executive has received wider acceptance in the business world because it is quite unlikely that one man will possess the diverse skills and temperaments which the job requires. In the real world, we find that the chief executive appoints a few key executives to help him in the discharge of his diverse duties.

Thus, the modern concept of the top management is a team of a few key executives, say two or three or even more, each endowed with independent authority for taking decisions in their specified activities. In a multidivisional organisation where independent divisions are headed by general managers or divisional managers, the top management team comprises, besides the chairman and vice-chairman, general managers and divisional managers also.

Top executives play the role of entrepreneurs and innovators when they determine the destiny of the enterprise. It is they who have to decide, "what is our business and what it should be"? Picking up the right mission and objectives obviously is crucial because they provide a basic sense of direction to the company's activities and serve as a criteria for all subsequent managerial decision-making. By setting the overall objective in terms of production, profitability, growth, market, leadership, technology, and so on, chief executive assigns values which the firm uses as a guide for future decision-making. These values are spelt out in qualitative terms.

The top management's role in setting corporate objectives is integrating and synthesizing the diverse interests and goals of all the stakeholders. They are supposed to possess the skill of finding the right mix of corporate objectives towards which the individuals having conflicting interests can be simulated to coordinate their diverse interest in a cohesive way.

After establishing the corporate purpose and objectives, the top executives guide the functional managers in establishing supportive objectives within the framework of the overall basic objective.

Above all, the top executives serve as custodians of corporate objectives. They have to defend these objectives against superficially attractive diversification or corporate growth that glitters like fool's gold.

In order to achieve the overall objective of the company, the top management has to choose a course of action which will yield best results. For this purpose, they have to identify different alternatives, evaluate each of them and select the most suitable one. This calls for a detailed investigation of different external forces with the intention of assessing business opportunities, and corporate competence analysis to discern corporate strengths and weaknesses. They have to take the help of the planning staff in this task. A corporate planning staff gathers all the relevant information pertaining to environment in the country and abroad, and makes forecasts about markets, quantity of sales, prices, products, technical developments, costs, tax rates and policies. On the basis of these forecasts and keeping in mind the corporate capabilities and limitation, the chief executive or his team chooses a strategy that suits the enterprise. Choosing strategy is such an important decision that they should not entirely depend on the corporate planner and other executives.

In making strategy, the top management plays the role of an architect of strategy because they react to the environmental forces and respond to the diverse needs of society while formulating the strategy for the organisation.

Since corporate strategy determines broad directions, major thrusts and over-riding priorities, the top management have to play an active role in laying down comprehensive operational policies with the intention of guiding the execution of strategy by foreign subsidiaries. Such a role is inescapable as it will ensure that the intent of corporate strategy as well as sub-strategies is correctly interpreted by those charged with the responsibility of executing these strategies.

Policy guidelines are generally laid down regarding product lines, customers, sales promotion, production, procurement, research and development, human resource areas, finance, and so on. These policies indicate the direction and degree of emphasis these and other sensitive fields should receive in order to effectively project company strategy. They permeate the numerous daily activities of subsidiaries and help establish a normal and predictable pattern of behaviour.

Besides laying down guidelines, the executives play a crucial role in bringing the corporate strategy into effect. Although they do not directly get too deeply involved in the development of operational plans of their different subsidiary units, they have to see that these plans are co-terminus within the overall corporate objectives and strategy. This is done by a coalition team consisting of the chief executive, other key executives at the corporate level and manager of multinational affiliates. This task is important as well as complex. It is important because it affects the operations and profitability of the entire business both immediately and for the future. While a certain percentage of error in planning at lower levels is less consequential because of the relatively smaller size and more limited activities of the subsidiaries, the same amount of error at the topmost level can create severe and long-lasting difficulties. Planning is complex and cumbersome in the sense that the top executives have to balance and integrate conflicting and competing goals and plans, diverse preferences, and values of the overseas managers and also give due attention to the social expectations. They serve as the ring masters in keeping all the operations and efforts of the company within and outside the country headed in the same direction. They may help the overseas management in the formulation of their strategic plans. However, their major concern must be to ensure optimum coordination and continuity.

Besides playing the role of an integrator and coordinator, the chief executive must also see that the plans so finalised are translated into action. He has to present the plan in a way that appeals to the imagination and elicits the support of all those, whose efforts are essential for the success of the plan. He has to design an appropriate organisation structure, keeping in mind the needs of corporate strategy. The task of identifying key organisational activities, grouping them into departments, delineating authority and responsibility and establishing working relationship among the group that will enable both the company and the individuals to realise mutual objectives rests with the chief executive. The organisational structure should be such as to secure the whole hearted cooperation of individuals to the satisfaction of all, although this task, at times, becomes impossible. Integration of differences can be easily achieved if the members are committed to a common purpose.

It is the major responsibility of the chief executive and other key executives to maintain a conducive climate in the organisation where there is no political manoeuvering for positions and prejudices, where high value is assigned to interpersonal amity and tolerance of individual members, acceptance and encouragement of innovation with consequent freedom to act upon ideas, and where there is a clear-cut provision of rewards for accomplishments and penalties or failures.

Another major task of the top management is to ensure that strategies are put into action and actual performance in different units, departments and divisions conforms with the plans. For effective review and evaluation, a comprehensive mechanism at the corporate level must be designed and clear standards and policies which serve as evaluation criteria must be developed and made known to all the line executives. Once this is done, the chief executive with or through his line of vice-presidents receives performance reports, reviews the same and evaluates the plans. He has to find out whether and to what extent actual performance is in conformity with the expected or planned performance. The causes of deviations, if any, are investigated and identified.

Monitoring may reveal that deviations have occurred because standards were improperly set. In such a case, standards need to be revised. In some situations, correction of deviations may not be feasible immediately but could be done at later date. Deviations may also be traced to the aberrations in human behaviour, either willingness or inability. In such an eventuality, motivation and training devices are to be set in motion to set right human behaviour. Deviations may also have their sources in resource, deficiencies, process defects, structural shortcomings, environmental forces and even imperfect measurement techniques and instruments. It is, therefore, necessary to identify and isolate the exact cause of deviations and initiate appropriate corrective actions.

It is not possible for the chief executive and his team to watch and control all aspects of the activity. He should, therefore, concentrate on a few key or strategic areas which are critical for the survival and success of the organisation. Key areas for control in a business enterprise are to be identified in manufacturing, purchasing, marketing, finance, personnel, R&D and so on. For example, in marketing, the key result areas are market share, order position, customer complaints and gross margin percentage. Thus, the top management also plays the role of an evaluator and a controller.

The planning staff: The strategic planning department headed by strategic planner constitutes the third link in the management hierarchy. It is worth stating that strategic planner plays the role of a staff authority while dealing with the top management and other levels of management. However, his role in relation to his planning staff is that of a line authority.

The planning staff's role and tasks are to help the management in setting corporate and business objectives and goals and determining organisational directions. This help is rendered by way of fundamental studies of external as well as internal environment and their implications for corporate objectives and strategies. The planning staff gathers and evaluates information for corporate and divisional use. It provides the basic economic, political and competitive intelligence to the top management. It also identifies and measures new opportunities and threats to the enterprise and lends factual support for new ventures. It also undertakes studies of new methods, techniques and procedures, that will improve planning within the organisation, reduce costs or improve product quality and acceptance.

Strategic planners are supposed to help managers in crystallising the strategic issues which ought to be addressed; in addition they have to provide data, help analyse industry and competitive conditions, and distribute information on the company's strategic performance. But strategic planners should not make strategic decisions or make strategic action recommendations that usurp the strategy-making responsibilities of managers incharge of major operating units. Giving planners' responsibility for strategy-making and line managers' responsibility for implementation makes it how to fix accountability for results.[5] It also includes line managers into thinking that they should not be held responsible for crafting a strategy for their own organisational unit or for devising solutions to strategic problems in their area of responsibility. Further, line managers, not actively involved in strategy making, will not take much interest in implementing the strategy.

Executive committee: Executive committee forms the fourth link in the organisational chain. This committee deliberates upon strategic proposals of different divisions and functions and finalises them. It also reviews strategic plans and oversees its implementation and recycling. Executive committee provides an opportunity for consultative information exchange and group thinking. The committee consists of key executives with the chief executive as its chairman and corporate planner as the secretary. This committee, if necessary, appoints ad-hoc committees or task groups to undertake special studies on problems such as acquisitions, diversification or venture development.

Line management: The last link in planning organisational set up is line management. Line executives play a very crucial role in the formulation and execution of strategy. Strategic management process can yield positive results only when it is effectively implemented. For this purpose, involvement of line executives from the very beginning of strategy formulation is inevitable. It is the primary responsibility of the top management to see that line managers actively participate in all strategic decisions pertaining to their areas.

Involvement of line executives in India has been very limited. The top management has not been very enthusiastic about securing the commitment and participation of middle and lower level executives in the planning process. They do not seem to have felt the need for sprucing up the organisational process, adjusting the management style and building up the awareness for encouraging greater involvement of line executives. This is a most intriguing phenomenon of the strategic planning system in Indian organisations.

Summary

Strategic management approach of managing business involves process of identifying environmental opportunities and discerning threats, assessing corporate strengths and weaknesses, developing strategic options and evaluating each of them to choose the most suitable strategy, taking measures to execute the strategy and monitoring plans so as to ensure that the firm is moving forward in the desired direction.

The process of strategy making is typically an ongoing process but not a regular, continuous process. It is most often an irregular process in fits and starts.

The effectiveness of strategic management approach depends, inter alia, on how strategic planning function is organised and what tasks and responsibilities are performed by different levels of management in making and executing corporate strategy.

Key Terms

Acceptability of option	Identification phase	Purpose
Cascade approach	Implementation phase	Scanning of environment
Competitive advantage	Line management	Suitability of option
Development phase	Mission	SWOT analysis
Executive committee	Monitoring phase	Top management
Feasibility of option	Objectives	

Discussion Questions

1. Putting yourself in the position of a corporate planner, formulate a strategic plan of your firm.

2. Why should an existing strategy be revisited? What major factors need to be factored in?

3. What are the steps involved in developing strategy for an enterprise?

4. Discuss, in brief, various measures which management should take to execute strategy effectively.

5. "Strategic management process is continuous but irregular". Comment

6. How should strategic planning function be organised? What variables should be kept in view while organising strategic planning function of a firm?

References

1. Ansoff, Igor H., *Corporate Strategy*, McGraw-Hill, p. 17, 1918.

2. Mintzeberg, H., "Planning on the Left Side and Managing on the Right", *Harvard Business Review*, July–August, p. 56, 1976.

3. Singh, B.R., "Corporate Planning—An Analysis of the Corporate Planning Practices of Selected Large Size Companies in India", *Ph.D. Thesis* (unpublished) Banaras Hindu University, pp. 115–119, 1983.

4. Ibid.

5. Arthur A., Thompson and A.J. Strickland, *Strategic Management*, Richard D. Irvin, Inc., p. 18, 1995.

4

Corporate Governance in Corporate Enterprises

LEARNING OBJECTIVES

The present Chapter aims at providing an:

- Overview of emergence of corporate governance philosophy in corporate world.
- Understanding of nature and objectives of corporate governance.
- Insight into the fundamentals of corporate governance in a corporate enterprise.
- Understanding of the codes of effective corporate governance for a corporate enterprise.

INTRODUCTION

The term corporate governance is much in use these days; everybody and anybody having anything to do with the corporate sector talks of good corporate governance. Certainly, corporate governance is not just a buzz word or management fad but has become need of the hour for every organisation if it is to survive and grow successfully and achieve competitive edge over its rivals in fast paced and brutally competitive, landscape and enhance its legitimacy in highly awakened society.

The concept of corporate governance has come to the fore in the wake of major corporate debauches, corporate failures, collapses and financial irregularities in countries such as the US, the UK, Canada, France and Australia in the late 1980s and early 1990s causing shareholders, banks and other investors to worry about their investments. Scandals plagued such companies as Adelphia Communications (family misuse of corporate funds), Enron (off balance sheet activities and the use of fictitious corporate entities), Health South, Tyco International (alleged CEO expropriation of corporate loan and cash for personal use), Martha Stewart Living Omnimedia (CEO indicted for lying to federal investigation regarding personal stock sales), WorldCom (one of the biggest bankruptcy in the US corporate history and falsified accounting records), Imclone Systems (CEO's blatant insider trading of company stock), Qwest Communications (improper accounting and revenue recognition) and Lehman Brothers (biggest bankruptcy in the US financial market due to bad mortgages against housing loans), to name just a few.

Recent failures of top management of Indian organisations, as evidenced by the indifference of ITC Board toward evasion of excise duties and violation of the Foreign Exchange Regulators Act (FERA) for years, lapse of the Shaw Wallace Board in detecting financial profligacy, and mute watch of the Bata Board members to its Chairman frittering away the Company's brand equity among middle class customers, connivance of top management of BPL, Sterlite Industries and Videocon International with big bull Harshad Mehta in rigging the prices of their shares and spate of other corporate scandals including the latest financial fraud committed by Satyam erstwhile Chairman B. Ramlinga Raju bear sufficient testimony to the Boards being decorative and decorous baubles behaving like anesthetized witnesses, and rubber stamping the decisions already made by the Chief Executive.

As a matter of fact, the Board members have been found shying away from discharging their legitimate responsibilities. It is only when the organisation and its Chief Executive's performance are berated and proscribed in public that the Board members wake up from slumber and come into action to stem the organisation and its Chief out of the crisis. In fact, well-functioning Boards are more than an exception than the norm, as the spate of resignations (340) by independent Directors in the wake of the Satyam episode goes to show. This phenomenon has been global, as evidenced by the study of the *Business Week of American Companies* in 1996 showing the existence of different degrees of quality of corporate governance ranging between 9.9 and 97.8 (out of score of 100) and desperate attempts to rehaul the functioning of corporate boards in the US and the UK—best symbolised by the now famous recommendations of the Cadbury Committee and the Greenbury Committee on corporate governance that the UK-based corporations are adopting and by the lead set by the General Motors.

Thus, emergence of competitive environment with customers—both external and internal—dictating the organisations to perform best in their interests and maximise their value, and highly awakened investors demanding greater transparency and adoption of international standards of disclosures have forced organisations to practice good governance for sake of existence and hence the emerging concept of governance. As a matter of fact, organisations are increasingly realising that good governance can be a source of competitive advantage. A firm can build an inherently powerful corporate brand on that basis. Customers and business partners will find it economically beneficial to do business with such firm.

In recent years, the tide of the boardroom activism has been steadily rising and some events of recent years suggest that the Boards taking exception to their CEOs are becoming the rule.

Nature and Objectives of Corporate Governance

The concept of corporate governance is subtle and elusive. It has been defined differently by managerial scholars and management practitioners. The Cadbury Committee defined corporate governance as the system by which companies are directed and controlled, thus placing the Board of Directors of a company at the centre of the governance system.[1] In Canada, the Toronto Stock Exchange's guidelines defined corporate governance as "the process and structure... to direct and manage the business and affairs of the corporate with the objective of enhancing the shareholders' value, which includes ensuring the financial viability of the business."[2] The OECD'S *Business Sector Advisory Group Report*, however, takes a much more pragmatic view on the subject: "Corporate governance comprehends that the structure of relationships and corresponding responsibilities among a core group consisting of shareholders, board members and managers designed to best foster the competitive performance required to achieve the corporate's primary objective."[3] In India, the *Kumar Mangalam Birla Report* asserts that the "the fundamental objective of corporate governance is the enhancement of the long-term shareholders' value while at the same time protecting the interests of other stakeholders."[4]

Thus, corporate governance is all about the affairs of an organisation in such a way as to ensure fairness to customers, employees, investors, creditors, vendors, the government and society at large. Corporate governance is about culture. It is about mindset. It is about the honesty and willingness of the management and the shareholders at large.

Corporate governance, in fact, is a philosophy of management by which owners and managers are expected to be perennially responsive to other entities such as minority shareholders, promoters, institutional shareholders, depositors, creditors, customers, employees and institutional lenders. Corporate governance has its in-built interest in overall employee involvement for quality and cost, empowerment and accountability towards the stakeholders. The essence of corporate governance is a framework in which owners and managers are expected to be perennially responsive to the stakeholders. It is all about conducting the company's affairs in such a manner as to ensure fairness to customers, employees, investors, creditors, vendors, government and the society.

Corporate governance provides a set of systems and processes which ensure that a company is managed in the best interest of all the stakeholders. Although the issue of corporate governance focuses on enhancing shareholders' value and protecting interests of employees, creditors and customers and holding management accountable for their performance, it would be a pity if corporate governance acquires a restrictive definition of improving shareholders' lot by way of adequate return. A company is no longer responsible simply for making a profit or producing goods but for simultaneously contributing to the solution of extremely complex ecological, moral, political, racial and social problems.

Corporate governance is, thus, an instrument for benefiting all the stakeholders of a corporate entity. It entails driving the corporation's strategy and overseeing the day-to-day business with each process through creation of checks and balances. In its wide sense, corporate governance is almost akin to a trusteeship. It is about creating an outperforming organisation which leads to increasing customer satisfaction, shareholders' value and safeguarding interests of other stakeholders.

Corporate governance has as its backbone a set of transparent relationships between an institution's management, its board, shareholders and other shareholders.

It should, therefore, take into account a number of aspects such as enhancement of the shareholders' value, protection of their rights and compensation and role of PRO and of directors' integrity of accounting practices and disclosure norms and internal control system. As far as the banking industries are concerned, corporate governance relates to the manner in which the business and affairs of individual banks are directed and managed by their Board of Directors and senior management. It also provides the structure through which objectives of the institution are set; the strategy of attaining those objectives is determined and the performance of the institution is monitored.[5]

It is useful to recognise that corporate governance is a dynamic concept in terms of scope, thrust and relevance. For example, the issue is approached very differently today compared to original view of the Cadbury Committee on the subject. East Asian crisis and global financial disaster have a new dimension to corporate governance in the context of financial stability. In the US, regulatory regimes, post-corporate scandals are very different from those of the early 90's. The OECD set out its corporate governance principles in 1999 but revised them in 2004. The Basel Committee on banking supervision published guidelines on corporate governance in banks in 1999. As an update in July 2005, the Basel Committee issued a Consultative Document on enhancing corporate governance for banking operations on boards of the banks. Thus, corporate governance should be viewed as an ongoing process subject to rapid changes based on experiences, developments and policy setting.[6]

In a service industry like banking, corporate governance relates to the manner in which the business affairs of individual banks are directed and managed by their Board of Directors and senior management.

Unlike manufacturing concerns, where corporate governance is concerned with safeguarding and maximising the owners' value, in banking organisation, corporate governance has to focus on minimising the depositors' risks and preventing the possibility of contagion. Further, the involvement of the government is discernibly higher in banks due to importance of stability of financial system in the larger interests of the public. A large part of the Indian banking institutions is mostly government-owned and interests of other stakeholders appear more important to it than in the case of non-banking and non-finance organisations.[7]

According to N.R. Narayan Murthy, Chairman Emeritus of Infosys Technologies, "Corporate governance is not just filing up check list, it is about culture. It is about mindset. It is about who you are. It is about the honesty and the willingness of the management and the shareholders at large".[8]

In India and so also in other countries, banks and other financial institutions can succeed in deregulated environment only if they manage public savings operations with integrity and responsibility and adopt sound business practices. Irregularities on the part of the financial institutions may lead to mistrust among public. If they have to attract local and foreign capital, they have to demonstrate better standards of governance and place greater emphasis on their financial soundness and viability. Once this is assured, the shareholders' value will not only be retained but also enhanced. A sound corporate governance culture enforces better discipline upon corporate management and ensures maximum value to the shareholders, keeping in view the interests of other shareholders such as conditions, customers, employees and above all, the society at large.

Broadly speaking, corporate governance has two components: one is preventing the downside—that is, a firm wants to create transparency, ensure internal controls to decrease the probability of fraud, ensure regulatory compliance. The other is more about creating an upside and the role the Board can play in collaborating with the CEO and through that process, enabling the company to make the right strategic decisions and choices.

Unfortunately, company management and members of Boards often do not have a basic understanding of what corporate governance is. At a recent colloquium on the Board leadership, the participants who were Directors or belonged to senior management of medium-sized companies were asked to write down anonymously on a piece of paper what each one understood by corporate governance. Surprisingly, corporate governance meant different things to different people. Less than half the class believed that corporate governance meant leadership; several referred to Clause 49 as "imposed" by SEBI and several others were honest enough to proclaim their belief that business was all about money, control and power.

Before we delve into the fundamentals, let us have some glimpses of corporate failures and lapses in corporate history (Illustrative Capsules 4.1 and 4.2).

ILLUSTRATIVE CAPSULE 4.1

CORPORATE GOVERNANCE FAILURES

Enron: Enron, known for off-balance sheet activities and the use of fictitious corporate entities, moved away from its core business (electricity and natural gas) to trading in derivatives. It believed that the profits from derivatives could be used to mask the losses of its primary business. Enron started incurring massive debt. Though its derivatives related asset yields grew by good number, liabilities also piled up rapidly.

Trouble began in 2001. To hide bad investments in derivatives as well as its poorly performing assets in the energy business, it created multiple special purpose vehicles.

It started avoiding millions in tax dues by using its stock options. Its financial conditions were sustained by institutionalised, systematic and creatively planned accounting fraud. In the meantime, it lost exclusive rights to its pipelines.

For the third quarter of 2001, Enron reported a huge $618 million loss and on November 4, 2001 the company told its investors that they were restating profits for the last four and a quarter years. Finally, on December 2, 2001 the company filed for bankruptcy. The scandal created such waves in the auditing community that it led to the dissolution of Arthur Anderson, one of the World's top accounting firms.

WorldCom: WorldCom—known for one of the biggest bankruptcy in the US corporate history and falsified accounting records—was the US's second largest long distance phone operator between 1998–2002. During the 1990s, WorldCom was involved in acquisitions and completed several "mega deals" which later backfired. In the year 1989, revenue growth stalled. The Company started borrowing money to cover up losses. By March 2002, the Securities and Exchange Commission requested for information from WorldCom suspecting fraud, as AT&T was losing money even as WorldCom was not. In July, the company announced bankruptcy and later that month it declared that it had been inflating profits by $3.8 billion over the previous five quarters. The Company inflated profits by classifying routined expenses as investments and long third operators to carry Traffic.

Under CEO Bernie Ebbers, WorldCom was accused of falsifying as much as $9 billion in earnings going back to 1999.

Xerox: In June 2002, shortly after the WorldCom scandal broke, office equipment maker, Xerox admitted to overstating its revenues and profits for the years 1997–2001. This allowed the company to meet profit expectations.

The Securities Exchange Commission began an investigation that exposed the fact that over 5 years the company had improperly classified over $6 billion in revenue, leading to an overstatement of earnings by nearly $2 billion.

Tyco International: The CEO of Tyco International Dennis Kozlowski, lived a life of luxury in large part using corporate funds. Kozlowski grew Tyco's revenues over 10-fold from 1992 to 2001, and he expanded the company through conglomerate-like acquisitions of hundreds of different businesses. By the time Kozlowski's excesses were discovered, Tyco had become a major player in such disparate areas as health care, security systems, electronics, plastics and engineered products. Although Kozlowski generally acquired solid businesses, Tyco fell under a huge debt load, and rumours about impending bankruptcy became widespread in late 2002. Although the new CEO Ed Bree has stabilised Tyco's shaky earnings, Kozlowski himself was indicted and tried for conspiracy and grand larceny changes.

America Online (AOL): AOL—the internet service provider—was accused of playing around with its financials even in the early 1990s. In these years, changing its amortisation policies and capitalising revenue expenses was a commonly followed practice. The magnitude of fraud began to increase with competition. From January 2002, the company indulged in material misstatements of its financial results, including overstatements of operating income and free cash flow, overstatements of net income, understatements of net losses and total debt. The intention was to report that it had met its new subscriber targets, an important metric the market used to evaluate AOL. Meanwhile Times Warner had taken over AOL. This resulted in Times Warner playing $300 million to Securities Exchange Commission as civil penalties.

ILLUSTRATIVE CAPSULE 4.2

SATYAM COMPUTER SERVICES—AN EPITOME OF GOVERNANCE LAPSE

Bursting of the news of gigantic fraud committed by B. Ramalinga Raju, the erstwhile chairman of Satyam Computer Services, known for his talent, dedication and great purpose and his confessions of defrauding the company of over ₹700 crore gave a rude shock to the corporate world.

Raju began his entrepreneurial journey in software way back in 1987. Earlier, in 1982, Raju's family had established Sree Satyam Spinning and Weaving Mills. In 1984 Satyam Construction was set up (subsequently renamed Maytas Properties in 1998). Later in 2005, Maytas Infra was founded. Both Maytas Properties and Maytas Infra were founded by Raju and his brother Rama Raju and by Raju's two sons—B. Rama Raju and Teja Raju. Raju had floated no less than 327 companies to buy land.

While Raju's family (the three brothers and their families) assumed the stewardship of the business of Sree Satyam Spinning and Weaving Mills, Satyam Impex (exporter of shoe uppers) and oceanic farms (into aqua culture), Ramalinga Raju opted to be different. Charmed more by cyber space than spindles, and IT being his hobby, he decided to set up computer services.

In five years of its listing—by 1995—Satyam Computer began attracting attention. It had posted a 122-fold rise in net profit on a top line that had grown over 20-fold since incorporation. Within ten years, the soft-spoken shy US-returned son of a successful farmer (Raju's father Byrrasu Satyanarayana was a group farmer) metamorphosed Satyam into one of the fastest-growing companies in India. India's fourth largest IT Services with revenue of $2.14 billion and 51,217 people for the year ended March 2008, had operations in 66 countries, 690 clients, 228 development centres around the world. Over 90% of the revenues were from export services the income from which was tax free. In 14 years, it got listed on the New York Stock Exchange and subsequently staked claim to join the billion-dollar club by 2006.

Raju had strong liking for land. In fact, he liked land more than the code. Over the years, Satyam shed most of its other businesses, except Satyam Construction. Raju's accumulated land holdings, estimated at around 6800 acres were held by the Maytas firms. Maytas Properties was into development of urban infrastructure such as master-planned integrated township, special economic zones, hospitality, retail and entertainment businesses. Questions are now being asked on the sources of funds for acquiring these lands and whether there was any nexus with politicians. Acording to E.A.S Sarma, former Secretary, Economic Affairs, Government of India, "the way valuable chunks of land were doled out to Satyam and Maytas violated the law of the land and the way in which project after project was awarded to Maytas showed that there was a close nexus between the promoters and the political leadership. We have been questioning these deals but the officials and the politicians chose to remain indifferent".

Those who have worked with Raju says that: he was all along a meticulous strategist, focused and hardworking and had the ability to take risks and move at a fast pace. He had included in his Board the people with an impeccable track record and were very close to him, viz., Krishna Palepu, Harvard University Professor and Corporate governance expert, T.R. Prasad, former Cabinet Secretary, Vinod Dham, Co-father of the Pentium Processor and M. Rammohan Rao, Dean, Indian School of Business, Hyderabad. Even when hiring key people, he would always spend time to get to know them.

Raju was always ambitious. Way back in the mid-90s, he would tell his employees—then just a few hundreds—that the company would need to aim at touching a figure of 10,000 people by year 2000. And it was not just the company scaled new heights; Raju himself reached the high table when he shared the podium with the former US President Bill Clinton during the latter's visit to Hyderabad. Being a skillful networker, Raju was known to be politically savvy. He was as comfortable sharing the dais with TDP supremo and former Andhra Pradesh Chief Minister N. Chandrababu Naidu as with the Chief Minister Y.S. Rajasekhar Reddy's son. He would typically talk to them about big projects like the creation of a million jobs. In the words of late Rajasekhar Reddy, "he used to come up with some really innovative ideas like that of EMRI or the 108 ambulance service (108 replicate, the US 911 emergency service; it began with initial funding from Satyam)".

Raju and his family had held 25.6% ownership of Satyam communication in March 2001 which over the years dwindled to 8.74% in March 2008. Early this year (2009), their holding came down to a 2.3% without anybody raising finger. In 2006, Raju's family had transferred their shares to the family's company SRSR Holdings Pvt. Ltd. from which he took out loans, using the shares as collateral.

On December 16, 2008, Satyam Board in the presence of independent Directors and members of the Company's audit committee decided to pursue diversification strategy and okayed $1.6 billion acquisition plan involving 100% stake in Maytas Properties and 51% in Maytas Infra. The Board felt that "the two companies being acquired in the challenging market offer potential for significant upside in the future". The Board agreed to pay $1.3 billion (₹65,00 crore) to buy all of Maytas Properties and pay $300 million to buy 51% of Maytas Infra. Some brokerage firms estimated the net worth of the company to be $225 million (₹1,125 crore). The deal translated into valuation of ₹1 crore per acre while the average market rise of the land ranged between ₹25–50 lakh.

In the shareholders' meeting on December 17, duly approved acquisition proposals were rejected by the investors which included Foreign Institutional Investors, mutual funds and insurance companies who owned a little over 60% of Satyam. They were quick to protest what they interpreted as sheer brazenness of the promoters to push through non-synergistic acquisitions of family-promoted companies.

On December 25, nine days after Satyam announced its aborted acquisition bid, Dr. Mangalam Srinivasan—an independent Director who had been on the Board of Satyam since 1991 quit the Board.

On December 29, after reports surfaced that the Satyam promoters had pledged their shares, the company issued a press release as follows: "The promoters informed Satyam that shares in the company were pledged with institutional lenders and that some may exercise or may have exercised their option to liquidate shares at their discretion to cover margin calls". Following this belated disclosure, three independent Directors, Vinod Dham, Krishna Palepu and M. Rammohan Rao resigned.

In September 2008, global brokerage CLSA had noted, "with almost $1.2 billion of cash, we find it intriguing that Satyam closed 2007–08 with $56 million of debt". None of the independent Directors or auditors had even raised questions about this. CLSA had originally put out a report way back in 2001 on Satyam's dubious accounting practices. In 2003, then RPI MP Ramdas Athawale had accused Raju and gang of tax fraud and insider trading. But it failed to invoke any reaction from the independent Directors, the external auditors, the banks and the stock exchanges.

In a dramatic letter released on January 7, 2009, Raju admitted to non-existent cash balances, fake interest proceeds and grossly overstated revenues that totalled $1.4 billion, amongst other things. In it, he also reported a 'real' operating margin of 3% for the second quarter of 2008–09, which is what forced him to pump the numbers. The financial analysts were of the view that this figure was absurd, considering that Infosys Technologies had reported a 33% operating margin and the two firms competed for similar kinds of business in similar geographical locations. He solemnly pledged that neither he nor his brother Rama Raju took a paisa from the company and that they did not sell "any shares in the last eight years—excepting for a small proportion declared and sold for philanthropic purposes".

Many industry observers suspected that Raju just removed all the cash that he now says never existed from the bank accounts over the last three months of 2009. Several bank statements crucial for investigating the fraud are missing. According to the analysts, the ₹400 crore capital expenditure which Satyam had reported for the April–September quarter of 2008–09 could have been cooked up since the employee count had not changed. IT companies have little need for capital expenditure other than rent for office buildings and equipment for employees.

Earlier in 2005, Satyam had spent $160.4 million on the acquisition of six companies that many on Dalal Street questioned. CLSA reported in August 2008: "There has been little articulation of any follow-on wins, thanks to these assets and the scale of acquisitions continues to raise doubts on whether they can truly move the needle for a $2 billion top-lone company". Accounting experts say that it is common for Indian promoters to overpay for acquisitions in order to siphon out money from their companies and then pay a commission to the sellers of the acquired companies. They feel that it is quite likely that Raju was using this technique to divert the fund.

While tendering resignation to the Board in its meeting held on January, 2009 Raju wrote."It was like riding a tiger, not knowing how to get off without being eaten". He said the balance sheet, as of September 30, 2008, carries "inflated (non-existent) cash and bank balances of ₹5,040 crore (as against ₹5,361 crore) reflected in the books. The balance sheet also carries an accrued interest of ₹376 crore which is non-existent, an understated liability of ₹1,230 crore on account of funds arranged by me, an overstated debtors position of ₹490 crore (as against ₹2,651 crore reflected in the books)". He further said: "What started as a marginal gap between actual operating profit and the one reflected in the books of accounts continued to grow over the years. It has attained unmanageable proportions as the size of the company operations grew significantly.… "The aborted Maytas acquisition deal was the last attempt to fill the fictitious assets with real ones". He reiterated this during Central Investigation Department (CID) interrogation soon after his arrest on January 9, 2009. After prolonged interrogation, Raju finally admitted to diverting funds to his family firm and this was going on since 2004.

Sensing the seriousness of the fraud, the case was handed over to the Serious Fraud Investigation Office and subsequently to the Central Bureau of Investigation (CBI) to investigate the matter threadbare and unearth the magnitude of the financial fraud committed by Raju and his family.

The CBI in its report observed that Ramalinga Raju, his brothers and their spouses have acquired 1,065 properties with a registered value of ₹350 crore. The CBI had come out with evidence that Raju and his associates had created seven fake foreign customers for whom forged and fabricated invoices were raised to the tune of ₹430 crore.

Besides Raju and his family, the CBI has discovered that former chief finance officer of Satyam, Srinivas Vadlamani, acquired 20 properties in his and in the name of his family members. These acquisitions were made from the wrongful games earned by setting Satyam shares during the period the accounting fraud was perpetuated in the company.

On the whole, the CBI found that Raju, his family members and the front companies floated by them have received ₹2,700 crore by selling shares and also by pledging shares with non-banking financial corporations.

FUNDAMENTALS OF CORPORATE GOVERNANCE

Corporate enterprises aspiring to catapult themselves on global marquee and sustain their competitive superiority must lay down their governing structures along the following fundamentals:

(i) Good corporate governance is all about commitment of a company to run its businesses in a legal, ethical and transparent manner, and that the tone must be set at the top. The top management must have strong conviction that if it runs its business in a legal, ethical and transparent manner, it is following principles of good governance. For the believers, governance is a necessary requisite for long-term sustainable growth. They believe that one can progress by doing good. They look beyond compliance and are able to make good governance their competitive advantage. Illustrative Capsule 4.3 gives some of the successful corporate goverance practices.

ILLUSTRATIVE CAPSULE 4.3
GOOD GOVERNANCE PRACTICES

Practice 1: A very successful family-owned business was started in Kolkata in a small way as a symbol of the nationalist spirit, about eight decades ago. Since then the business has grown from strength to strength through diversification into multiple product lines, modernisation and innovation. It is still growing. Though ownership and control still remain with the family and none of the businesses are listed on the stock exchanges, the family felt persons of great eminence had to be inducted into the Board so that they could give the best possible advice on the business. They also believed in the fidelity of financial numbers and felt that they needed to get their books audited by a reputed auditing firm. They believed that the growing complexities of business and international competitiveness demanded that the Chairman and the CEO positions be better left to outside experts. They voluntarily accepted Clause 49 as the benchmark for corporate governance standards and incorporates systems and procedures which would ensure compliance, as these would be in the best interest of business. They even called outside experts from time to time to check if the Company's governance was on the right track. If one enters the company and talks to the C-suite, one can easily feel and see how shared practices and beliefs permeate across the organisation.

Practice 2: A Corporate Group began practising corporate governance and environmental and social governance from 1912. The Group began its journey in the Victorian period, inspired by the spirit of nationalism, to become an international business conglomerate with its footprints across constituents. The companies in the group grew all along with a shared belief in a common value system and a common purpose of improving the quality of life of the community it catered to and returning wealth to the society it served.

Practice 3: A group in South India began in a small way as a money lender in 1900 to become a $3 billion business by 2008. During this period, the group grew by managing generational transitions within the family smoothly, carrying out organisational and entrepreneurial changes through transparency and without operational disruption. The family-managed group successfully converted into a professionally managed corporate house, engaging outside experts for restructuring and implementing succession plans and even handing over reins of the Chairman and CEO positions to experts outside the family. A common value system was shared by the family and, from the family there was osmosis into the business. Times changed but the values did not. For the family, business interest and the interest of those who manage the business were paramount and the family was secondary. They always wanted business to grow on the strengths of integrity and transparency. If they had brought outsiders into the Board, it was because they felt that complexity of business needed such people to steward the business.

Source: Press Conference of *Business Standard* by Mr. Elwin de Valk, SVP on June 30, 2009.

The code of a company like GE is a case study in itself. Its code of business conduct and ethics, known very symbolically as "The Spirit and Letter" has a tag line: "Unyielding integrity", which is a musing of what GE has been standing for 125 years. The code expresses GE's commitment to perform with integrity "Everywhere", "Everyday" and for "Everyone". The code expects all employees "to obey applicable laws and regulations governing their worldwide business conduct; to be honest, fair and trustworthy in all their GE activities and relationships; to avoid all conflicts of interest between work and personal affairs; to foster their employment practices, to strive to create a safe workplace and to protect the environment and through leadership at all levels, sustain a culture where ethical conduct is recognised, valued and exemplified by all employees. The Tatas have an elaborate code of conduct predicated on the concept of *"Humata, Hukta, Huvarashta"* from which follows the five Tata core values of integrity, understanding, excellence, unity and responsibility. This code provides the guidelines by which the group conducts its businesses. Infosys has a detailed code based on core values C-LIFE: Customer delight, Leadership by example, Integrity and transparency, Fairness and pursuit of Excellence. These companies believe in these principles, live by them and conduct businesses. It is evident that not only the tone has been set on top, but it has permeated throughout the organisation, and has been imbibed in everyday business of these companies.

(ii) Corporate governance implies self-regulation. As suppliers, potential collaborators, investors and customers start rewarding companies with good governance practices, companies realise that good governance can be a powerful source of competitive advantage. This is why code of governance should not be thrust on companies. Every company has to evolve its own code to subserve the interests of its stakeholders.

(iii) Corporate governance is about a set of management systems comprising structure and processes. While structure defines relationships between a company's management, boards, shareholders and other stakeholders, management processes spell out how things are done in the organisation. Management systems need to be designed and developed, keeping in view the vital interests of the company's stakeholders. This can best be done by the Board of Directors of the company. As representative of the shareholders, the Directors have the authority and responsibility to establish basic corporate policies and to ensure that they are followed. This signifies that the company is fundamentally governed by the Directors overseeing the top management with the concurrence of the shareholders.

(iv) Corporate governance, based on agency theory, which defines the relationship between principals (the owners/shareholders) and their agents (top management), is greatly concerned with how effectively interests of the two are synthesized so that the overall objective of the company is achieved. The top management—represented by the Board of Directors—is expected to make strategic decisions and execute them in the best interests of the principals as also other stakeholders. This is why corporate governance focuses on issues like size and composition of the Board, professional competence of the Directors, and their role and responsibilities.

(v) Good governance does not restrict the management to comply with regulatory laws. It expects the management to take strategic decisions in the long-term interests of the company and its stakeholders, keeping in view socio-economic, political, technological and competitive environmental developments. These decisions need to be taken with the concurrence of the owners.

(vi) The basic premise of corporate governance is that effectiveness with which the Board of Directors discharges its responsibilities determines a company's competitive position in the market. This is why good governance provides an architecture of accountability and autonomy. Independent Directors are supposed to play active role in governance of the company. In recent years, greater emphasis is being lend not only on clear-cut division of responsibilities at the top level of a company so as to ensure a balance of power and authority among them, but also on inclusion in the board of large number of external experts having dexterous competencies in the required field, their qualifications, and other eligibility criteria for their appointment.

(vii) Transparency has come to be regarded as the golden rule for the orderly behaviour of the corporate business. There are several reasons for this development. First, transparency backed by prudent supervision enhances the accountability of the system. This, in turn, builds and reduces the probability of failures and systematic risk. Secondly, it provides a payment and settlement system to the economy and has important linkages with the rural sector. Shareholders get all the relevant information necessary to judge whether their interests are being taken care of. Transparency and disclosures also serve as an important adjunct to the supervising process as they facilitate market discipline of the banks. They also facilitate translation into allocative efficiency and a clear perception of the risk-return trade-off embedded in investment proposals.

CORPORATE GOVERNANCE PRACTICES IN THE INTERNATIONAL ARENA

In the wake of the heightened competitiveness following the adoption of the policy of liberalisation, privatisation and globalisation across the globe in the 1990s, need for improving corporate governance practices was strongly felt in different countries of the world. Various countries constituted expert committees to study existing governance practices and suggest ways and means to improve the corporate governance system.

Corporate Governance in France

In France, focus of corporate governance is on initiative and enterprise. This system strengthens the institutional shareholders who can access the information they need from the company. President of the organisation enjoys absolute power. Government plays significant but informal role in corporate governance. Only nationalised industries have employees' representation on their Boards; private sector companies do not.

A sort of code of best practices is recommended vide the Vienot Report of 1995 in France.

(i) Elimination of 'cross share holding' when companies hold shares in each other and Directors sit on each others' Board thereby exchanging favours.

(ii) Banning of the CEOs of companies sitting on the remuneration committees of others' Boards.

(iii) Limiting individual Directors board members, thereby exchanging favours.

(iv) Allowing direct access to Audit the Committees, to the people drafting financial statements.

Corporate Governance in the United Kingdom

The *Cadbury Committee Report* in the UK forms the cornerstone in the development of corporate governance norms not only in Britain but also all over the world. Concerned with the hostile takeover in the 80s. The committee on corporate governance was set up in May 1990 with Sir Adrian Cadbury as its Chairman. At the heart of the Report is the code of best practice, which refers to Board structure, non-executive Directors, executive Directors and reporting and controlling systems. Major recommendations of the Committee were:

There should be a clearly accepted division of responsibilities as the head of a company (i.e., the appointment of Chairman and the Chief Executive should be held by two different people) (Cadbury Code 1.2).

(i) The pay package of the Chairman and the highest paid company Directors should be disclosed in the annual accounts, and split into salary and performance related pay (Cadbury Code 3.2).

(ii) The Board of Directors includes atleast three non-executive Directors, two of whom are independent of management and free of other business link with the company (Cadbury Code 1.3 and Note 1).

(iii) The Board should have an audit committee comprising of atleast three non-executive Directors (Cadbury Code 4.3).

(iv) Each Board should have a remuneration committee consisting of wholly or mainly non-executive Directors (Cadbury Code and Note 6).

The Greenbury Committee on the role of remuneration committees, the Hampel Committee and the latest Turubull Report followed the Cadbury Committee to indicate the degree of seriousness with which the corporate governance is taken in the UK. In 1995, the London Stock Exchange made statements of compliance or failure to comply with the Cadbury Code, a condition of listing.

Corporate Governance in the United States

The Thrust of corporate governance in the US is on minimum state interference and minimisation of conflicts of interest between owners and managers. Codes of corporate governance in the US are Business Round Table and General Motors BoDs Code—

Reports and legislation from Investor Responsibility Centre (RRC) 1999, Report of the NACD Blue Ribbons Commission 1997 and Global Corporate Governance Codes.

There are very limited legal or constitutional provisions which the companies in America are bound to follow. The US companies are striving to set trends of corporate governance which others would follow. This will lead to further enhancing the company's image and the shareholders' confidence in it.

Corporate Governance in Canada

In Canada, guidelines on corporate governance are derived from the Toronto Stock Exchange (TSE) guidelines contained in the TSE Report. As per the guidelines, the TSE requires listed companies incorporated in Canada or a province of Canada to disclose on an annual basis, their approach to corporate governance with reference to the guidelines and an explanation of the difference between the companies' approach and the guidelines. The code does not insist them as mandatory because they feel that every company is unique and every company should bring its own approach to corporate governance.

The guidelines in TSE require the Board of Directors to assume responsibility for the stewardship of the corporation including strategic planning, risk management, succession planning, communication policy and integrity of the internal control system. Here comes in the role of non executive Directors who can ensure objectivity.

The Board of Directors should be composed of individuals with diverse backgrounds, but balanced against favouritism to specific constituencies. A majority of the Board of Directors should be 'unrelated', i.e., independent of management and free from any interests that could interfere in its abilities to act in the interests of the corporation. The Directors' independence also signifies being independent judgement. The guidelines lay stress on performance evolution and emphasise that the Board of Directors must develop and implement a process for assessing the effectiveness of the Board of Directors Committee and contributions of the individual Directors.

Corporate Governance in Japan

Corporate governance in Japan is not focused on the Board of Directors of the company. The Japanese concept of obligation to company and country, and their willingness to follow a consensus make the system's accountability easier and trust based. In fact, the Japanese sense of nationalism and devotion to duty and family environment in workplace lead to involvement in the business and its growth and they don't need a code to further improve their business practices of the Board of Directors.

The Japanese companies with corporate governance have to do with the appreciation in the value of Yen and to reduce the risks borne by the banking system. The legal structures of corporate control in Japan are akin to those of other countries. However, the role of corporate and financial institutions is considerably high in view of their high stake in the companies.

In Japan, few institutional shareholders exercise direct control, aided by stable and concentrated shareholding. The 'Main Bank', being the prominent one, plays crucial role in corporate governance. The most important feature of the Main Bank system is that it provides a type of contingent governance. When performance is good, corporate affairs are left to the incumbent management. When it deteriorates, the Main Bank, as a lender and shareholder, intervenes in the management of companies to supervise downsizing reorganisation, where necessary. Such reorganisations could occur at times through the appointment of bank Directors to the Board of the company.

Corporate Governance in Australia

As per the Australian Investment Manager's Association, the Board of Directors of a listed company should prominently and clearly disclose in a separate section of its annual report, its approach to corporate governance issues specific to the company so that public investors understand how the company deals with those issues. In terms of this, the responsibilities of the Board of Directors include adoption of a corporate strategy, control of succession and training provision of an investor relations programme, management of information and internal control and establishment of performance hurdles for the Directors' remuneration.

As per the guidelines, the Chairman should be an independent Director. Where the Chairman is not independent, the independent Director must appoint a lead director who serves as an acting non-executive Chairperson. Thus, the importance of independent Directors in corporate governance is emphasised. Further, the shareholders of the company will evaluate governance disclosures. The onus of responsible and positive communication lies upon the shareholders who hold obligation to have some familiarity with concepts of corporate governance, the Australian rules and continuous disclosure laws.

Corporate Governance in South Korea

The Korean Stock Exchange sponsored committee of corporate governance issued in 1999 the code of best practices for corporate governance. The code prescribes norms and guidelines for Korean companies to adhere while framing their internal governance structure and processes. The focal points of the code are on the mission of the Board of Directors, appointment and orientation of Directors, role and responsibilities of executive Directors, and independent Directors, their compensation, their performance assessment and the like.

Corporate Governance in Germany

In Germany, a two-tier dual Board system is required by law. One is a Management Board and the other is a supervisory Board. The supervisory Board is composed of non-executive Directors and a significant percentage must be employee representatives.[9] The supervisory Board even appoints the Management Board and approves the company's strategy.

CORPORATE GOVERNANCE IN INDIA

The Indian corporate governance code (Clause 49 of the Listing Agreement) requires a company to lay down procedures to inform the Board members about the risk assessment and minimisation procedure. These procedures should be periodically reviewed to ensure that executive management control risks through means of a properly defined framework. Besides, the Companies Act, 1956 covers corporate governance widely through its various provisions such as inclusion of the Directors' responsibility statement in the Directors' report under Section 217 (2AA), constitution of Audit Committees under Section 292 A, fixing maximum ceiling on remuneration that can be drawn by a Director under Schedule XIII, and those relating to oppression, mismanagement, and so on. Further, environmental and other pieces of legislation also protect different stakeholders' interest ensuring, in the process, good corporate governance.

However, these provisions failed to curb the Securities scam in 1992 in which Harshad Mehta could convert various companies into diverting hard-earned money of small savers to make quick gains in speculation; ITC scam where senior managers and even the Chairman were arrested for their involvement in violation of Foreign Exchange Regulation Act (FERA) regulations. Shaw Wallace in India was involved in a case where it tried to evade excise duty and its top management was involved. These and many other scandals eroded the shareholders' confidence in the governance of their companies and they felt insecured investing their hard-earned savings in them.

In view of the above, it was strongly felt to strengthen governance mechanism.

The CII made several useful recommendations for improving corporate governance to develop a high level of public confidence in business and industry. The CII feels that there is no need for the adoption of two-tier boards where the Management Board is composed of executive Directors and the supervisory board of non-executive Directors and nominated by the owners and employees. The CII's recommendations cover the role of the non-executive Directors and measures to make them more responsive and alacre to corporate issues. It talks of the incentives like stock options, commissions, and so on. The recommendations also focus on reappointment of Directors, accounting and information flows, audit committees, and the like.

Another landmark development in the evolution of corporate governance in Indian corporate sector is the report of the *Kumar Mangalam Committee* of the Stock Exchange Board of India (SEBI) in 1999. This report is fairly exhaustive and is considered by the SEBI and others as a definitive statement on corporate governance in India. The Committee acknowledged the fact that the code of corporate should be dynamic, keeping in view the expectations of all the stakeholders and not merely the shareholders.

The Committee noted that the objective of corporate governance is the enhancement of long-term value of shareholders, while protecting the interests of other stakeholders. Practices are more important than formulations of codes. This is something, the Committee felt, which only those in the Board of Directors can do if they feel strongly enough for it. Compliance, the Committee emphasised, should be sought in letter, and spirit and interpretation of codes should focus on substance rather than form.

Some of the recommendations are mandatory while others are not. These recommendations include those regarding the composition of the Board, its accountability, personal characteristics and core competencies. In the context of involvement of financial institutions in India, a noteworthy point in this report is that it categorically states that financial institutions should have no direct role in managing, should not have Nominee Directors and should instead use voting power or market mechanism to achieve their ends and to discipline the Board and the management team, if and when necessary.

The *Kumar Mangalam Committee* has acknowledged the role played by the main group in the business of corporate governance, viz., the Board, those responsible for financial management including the internal auditor and the external auditor and has recommended the constitution of audit committees to promote the credibility of financial disclosure and transparency of dealings. One of the major recommendations of the Birla Committee was that on a Board with an executive Chairman, atleast half the members should be independent. In case of a non-executive Chairman one-third of the Board members should be independent.

The issue of the Board's remuneration and disclosure relating to it has also been covered by the Report. This Report has also sought to highlight what the functions of the management should be and has made it mandatory for the Board to define the role of management, the shareholder's right and their specified role. In view of the legal and regulatory framework in vogue in the country, it has been felt that some changes in these are called for so as to ensure better compliance.

In May 2000, the Department of Company Affairs came out with a Report on how to achieve excellence in corporate governance.

Naresh Chandra Committee, which submitted its report in December 2002, made no distinction between a Board with an executive Chairman and a non-executive Chairman. The Committee noted that the trend towards separation of roles has never been mandated by the legislation, which is exactly as it should be. Instead, the companies define the roles and responsibilities of their Chairman and the CEO on their own. At times, financial institutions as investors in the companies play crucial role in deciding the composition of the Board and articulating the roles and tasks of the Chairman and the CEO.

The Committee recommended that all listed and unlisted companies with a paid-up capital and free reserves of over ₹10 crore or a turnover of atleast ₹50 crore should have a Board of at least 7 Directors with 4 members as independent Directors. It also recommended that the audit committee of such companies should comprise only independent Directors. Regarding appointment of auditors in companies, the Committee recommended rotation of audit parties every six years to discourage formation of affinity between controlling shareholders or promoters or management.

In a bid to strengthen corporate governance across India Inc., the Government of India came out on December 21, 2009 with a set of voluntary guidelines for the industry, making significant recommendations like separation of offices of the Chairman and the CEO and a cap of seven on the number of directorships an individual can accept. Other important recommendations are rotation of audit firms every five years and an annual review of the effectiveness of the company's internal controls.

To prevent unfettered decision-making power with a single individual, there should be a clear demarcation of the roles and responsibilities of the Chairman of the Board and of the MD/CEO. The roles and responsibilities should be separated, as far as possible, to promote balance of power.

Guidelines were aslo sought to fix six-year tenure for independent Directors emphasising that there should be a lapse of three years before such an individual is inducted in any capacity.

On auditors, the recommendations sought a three-year term for an audit partner and five years for audit firm to get a 'fresh outlook' on the audit exercise.

Regarding internal controls, the company Board should conduct an annual review of their effectiveness.

CODE OF EFFECTIVE CORPORATE GOVERNANCE PRACTICES FOR CORPORATE ENTERPRISES

Code of corporate governance refers to the rules prescribed for different functionaries of the organisation to achieve the necessary high standards of corporate behaviour. These rules should set norms on the size of Board of Directors, composition of the Board, roles and responsibilities of the Directors, Chairman and executive committee of the Board, role and responsibilities of the Audit Committee, conduct of Annual General Meeting and disclosure standards and transparency.

Although several models of corporate governance such as Cadbury model, Greenbury model, CII model, Stock Exchange Board of India (SEBI) model and World Bank model, International Corporate Governance Network and ICICI model have been formulated as reactions to corporate disasters so as to guide the conduct of the affairs of the enterprises in the best interests of the stakeholders, no single model can, however, work necessarily for all the companies. In fact every organisation has to evolve its own code of corporate governance, keeping in view the fundamentals of governance thus enumerated above, the special conditions under which the organisations function in India, and the veritable fact that it has to be such as to serve as a source of competitive advantage to the organisation in highly competitive and unforgiving society.

Size of the Board of Directors

Although there is not optimal size of the Board, a large number of Directors provide greater opportunity for variety in terms of Directors' background, contacts, and expertise and also provide ample manpower to staff increasingly important board committees. However, a large Board makes it more difficult for a dissident Director to muster support for honing his position, because a dissident shareholder must then win over more individuals to gain support for a controversial proposal.

Various studies on the optimum size of the Board have been undertaken in the US and the UK. One conclusion emerging from these studies is that a Board should ideally have 12 Directors. This, of course, does not take into account the peculiarities, which a banking company may have, warranting a variation from this number. The Companies Act of 1956 also talks of a maximum number of 12 Directors. In the Discussion Paper, Shri S.H. Khan, former Chairman, IDBI, observed that the Board of Directors of any institution may ideally consist of 12 to 15 Directors.

In fact, the size of the Board should be such that sufficient non-executive Directors exist to perform the assigned function to oversight committees.

The State Bank of India (SBI's) Board consists of 11 members and Bank of Baroda 14. Private sector banks such as ICICI Bank and HDFC Bank have 16 and 12 members in their Boards respectively.

COMPOSITION OF THE BOARD

In view of the growing competitive pressure, the task of the Board of Directors has become formidable inasmuch as it has to steer clear the organisation through turbulent times, make crucial decisions pertaining to product pricing and develop competing strategies and execute them to meet the challenges posed by the new players.

Composition of the Board should be decided, keeping in view the above tasks. Further, while determining the Board composition, the focus should be on balancing independence, expertise, knowledge and business experience of the individual Directors as also the diversity of backgrounds likely to make the Board most effective. In India, regulation enforced through Clause 49 of the Listing Agreement makes it mandatory for listed companies to have atleast a third of their Boards made up of independent Directors.

In recent years, proportion of outside Directors, relative to the inside, has been increasing. While in 1960 fewer than half of all Directors were outsiders,[9] this proportion had increased to 75% by the early 1990s.[10] Recent legislative and regulatory changes in different countries suggest increasing proportion of outside Directors on the Board.[11] It is due to the fact that outsiders have been found helpful to the Boards in promoting the shareholders' interests. It is believed that companies with good governance have independent Directors who are held accountable and who can add value through experience and expertise. Many Boards today are cosmetic ones with Directors adding little or no value to the company and are just irrelevant to the specific field of the company. The Satyam Board certainly had familiar well-known names that were seen to lend credibility, but failed to navigate Satyam into clear waters. Most of the independent Directors and not just in the case of Satyam Computers tend to go along with the promoters who appoint them.

The Board should also be diverse. Empirical results suggest that board diversity has a positive relationship with shareholders' value. Board diversity can help corporate management broaden their perspectives, which might become overly narrow with a homogeneous Board. A diverse Board may strengthen the ability of the entire Board to act more independently, since the Board members with non-traditional backgrounds might be considered the ultimate outsiders.[12]

Responsibilities of the Board of Directors

The governance of a firm rests with the Board of Directors. Accordingly, conceptualising the future and seeing what others cannot see has to be the hallmark of the Board of Directors of an organisation. The Directors are expected to conceive the vision and share it with employees, customers, suppliers, collaborators, investors and other enlightened groups of the society and solicit their opinion which will enable them in turn to crystallise it in terms of corporate purpose and mission. Sharing of the vision generates excitement, brings order out of chaos and builds confidence and trust among the employees who will work harder to make it succeed.

Based on the SWOT analysis, the Board has to evolve strategic policy guidelines in respect of nature and scope of business, approach to growth, development of resource plan, structuring of organisation, and the like. The Board of Directors has to play actively the role of change agent, entrepreneur, facilitator and coordinator to enable the organisation to cope with competitive challenges through strategy building and restructuring.

The Board of Directors has to assume mantle of translating the strategy into action. It must have a game plan that takes care of the overall picture, with each piece of the picture well defined, well thought, and well put. It is the ultimate responsibility of the Board to see that the operational plans are tethered to the overall objective and strategy. The Directors have to oversee the operational guidelines formulated by the senior executives to serve as guideposts for the development of functional tactical strategies.

In its efforts to execute the strategy, the Board of Directors has to strive for developing organisational structure which is proactive and responsive to the market place and which reconfigures resources to address emerging opportunities. Creation of self-managed teams with focused objectives and tasks is the demand of the day.

The Directors are, therefore, expected to guide the managers in designing and developing lean, thin and flat structure so as to enhance organisational responsiveness, augment productivity, reduce costs and improve quality. The roles and responsibilities of executives in organisational hierarchy need to be clearly defined and the same be communicated to all concerned.

The Board should ensure that the firm is run with integrity, complies with all legal requirements and regulatory standards, and conducts its business in accordance with high ethical standards.

The Board has also to ensure that proper control systems exist and are functioning the right way, and that the operations of the firm are conducted with due regard to assurance that necessary provisions are made.

The independent Directors are expected to function in a fiduciary capacity protecting the rights and interests of the minority shareholders. Besides their regulatory role as a watchdog for minority shareholders, their oversight extends to items where there is a potential conflict of interest, especially in related party transactions.

Role and Responsibilities of the Chairman

The Chairman of a company is next to the Board in the management hierarchy. As a top executive of the organisation he represents the central authority who has overall control and accountability for effective functioning and performance in terms of a set of norms for coordination of the product businesses within the firm and the various functional managers. It is the Chairman of the firm who has to ensure that the collective ability of the Board provides both the leadership and the checks and balances which effective governance demands. He has also to ensure that the non-executive Directors receive timely and relevant information tailored to their needs and they are properly briefed on the issues arising at meetings so as to make them effective Board members.

Role and Responsibilities of Non-executive Directors

Among the non-executive Directors are independent directors who have a key role in the entire mosaic of corporate governance. According to the Kumar Mangalam Committee, independent Directors are those who apart from the Directors' remuneration do not have any material pecuniary relationship of transactions with the company, its promoters, its management or its subsidiaries, which in the judgement of the Board may affect their independence of judgement. About the role of independent Directors, the Committee is of the view that non-executive Directors including the independent ones help bring an independent judgement to bear on the Board's deliberations, especially on issues of strategy, performance, management of conflicts and standards of conducts. The independent Directors are not expected merely to provide functional expertise in finance, law, business management, and so on or knowledge of the industry. They must also be a moral check, built into the system of corporate governance, to sense when promoters and managers are failing in their responsibilities to society, and to correct them.

Role and Responsibilities of Nominee Directors

In recent years, financial institutions in India have nominated their executives in the Boards of companies assisted by them. In many cases it has been found that these nominees have remained content with safeguarding the interests of the institutions *vis-à-vis* of the company.

There is a general impression that whenever a conflict arises between the interest of the financial institutions and that of the company, the nominees invariably safeguard only the interests of their institutions. This impression is wholly erroneous. What is good for the company should be good for the financial institutions too. If the Nominee Directors ensure that things happen in the best interests of the company, rarely will the interests of financial institutions be jeopardised. After all, in the ultimate analysis, only if the company does well, the investments of the financial institutions will be protected.

The Nominee Directors should exercise their influence for maintaining high standards of corporate governance. They should encourage regular and systematic contacts at senior executive level to exchange views and information on strategy performance, the Board membership and quality of management. They should also play a significant role in the appointment of non-executive Directors of the requisite calibre, dexterity, experience and objectivity.

Personal Competencies and Skills of Individual Directors

To be an effective member on the Board of an organisation, besides stature and eminence, he/she must be honest, above the Board, trustworthy and possess appropriate skills and experience. A Director, apart from having an independent mind, should have a close insight into how firms operate, what the statutory requirements are under the Companies Act and what the economic scenario is in and outside the country. Besides, a Director should also be able to think in a top of the line manner. He should be well-versed in the macro economic trends as well as specific trends in the industry. Personal attributes like ability to listen, being open minded and being articulate will go a long way in making a bank Director quite effective.

In order to have competencies and skills in an ever-changing environment, it is important that the Directors also undergo exposure programme especially with respect to latest developments in economic and industrial fields both at the domestic and global levels.

Audit Committee of the Board of Directors (ACBs)

The Audit Committee of the Board acts as an important link in the corporate governance of a commercial bank. This body provides direction and function in the organisation. As per the guidelines laid down by the Reserve Bank, the ACB should review various aspects of the internal inspection/audit function including the system, its quality and effectiveness in terms of follow-up. It is also supposed to evaluate the inspection reports of specialised and extra large branches and all branches having unsatisfactory ratings. While reviewing inspection reports, focus should be on certain areas such as inter-branch adjustment accounts, unreconcited long entries in inter-bank accounts, arrears in balancing of books at various branches, frauds and all other major housekeeping. The ACB may also, if necessary, seek the assistance of the outside consultants for assessing the effectiveness of the total audit function.

The ACB is expected to closely monitor the impact of the domestic and global financial crisis on the bank's earnings, cash flow, liquidity and compliance with debt covenants and monitor key indicators of trouble.

The ACB should also pay serious attention to the area of disclosure standards. No doubt, the RBI prescribes disclosure standards to be followed by every bank while preparing financial statements and other reports. There is, however, an ample scope for improving upon them. Adoption of international standards of disclosures and transparency can facilitate the organisations in accessing global financial markets and getting their shares listed on the international stock markets. Audit Committees have to act independently and should not be under the thumb of the management, as was in the case of Satyam. Audit Committees should pay attention to information sources. Getting the right information is essential to providing effective oversight of the company's financial reports, its risks and internal controls.

Role and Responsibilities of Secretary of the Board

The Secretary of the Board has to play significant role in corporate governance. It is his responsibility that all the agenda items are properly placed before the Board and its various committees, so as to discharge his responsibilities properly. Thus, only a qualified Company Secretary with adequate experience and legal background should be appointed.

Unfortunately, there is no system of recruiting a professional person for this purpose. This system has got to be changed and a Chartered Accountant or Company Secretary should be appointed as the Secretary of the company. A professionally qualified Secretary will also acquaint the non-executive Director with details of the functioning of the Board.

Remuneration of CEO and Directors

The Chief Executive Officers' (CEO) compensation has always been a hotly debated topic in the US. Of late, the debate has spread to India. A study by XLRI found that in the past eight years, CEO pay in India has risen faster than profits, the average employee pay, the return on capital employed or even the return on equity. The study showed that between 1992–93 and 2000–01, the top management salaries grew by 33.1% while the compounded annual growth rate of sales was 11.52%, of PBDIT 13.84% and of pay for themselves was 9.81%.

According to CII, Indian CEOs cannot pay themselves too much. It feels that Indian Corporates cannot follow the US model of paying the CEO excessive amounts. Indian CEOs should have some limits in mind in terms of personal emolument structure. It emphasised that companies should bridge the salary gap between the CEO and the second rung of command. There is not much difference between what Infosys's Narayan Murthy and Nandan Nilekani earn and for that matter between CEO A.M. Naik and President M. Karmani at L&T.

At a conference on CEO pay, Narayan Murthy reiterated that CEO compensation should not be more than 15–18 times the pay of the lowest level of employee in the firm.

The Companies Act currently puts a lid of 11% of a company's annual profits as the remuneration for all Directors put together. For an individual CEO the figure is 5%. Where there is no profit, the pay is linked to something akin to the company's net worth.

The Indian Government is seriously mulling capping the Directors' remuneration, as CEOs and Directors are exorbitantly paid. A quick study by FICCI suggests that instead of being "vulgar", CEO salaries in some of India's largest corporations mostly account for a fraction of net profit.[13]

It would be more useful if the CEOs compensation is determined by the Board of Directors and approved by the shareholders in the general body meeting. Like everything in life and business, the emoluments of CEOs have to be reasonable keeping in mind market conditions and performance of the organisation. However, it should be good enough to attract, and retain highly proficient persons and motivate them to contribute their best to the organisation.

It is also imperative that a company must have credible and transparent policy in determining an accounting for remuneration of the Directors. The overriding principle in respect of the Directors' remuneration is that of openness and the shareholders are entitled to a full and clear statement available to the Directors. This is important for the fact that currently the information disclosed represents only the base amount and constitutes a mere fraction of the money and perks that the CEOs' compensation under accounting heads.

Disclosure Standards and Transparency

Transparency, as observed earlier, is an important element of corporate governance. This is why the Cadbury Committee emphasised on openness and transparency because it feels that "the life blood of markets is information and barriers to the flow of relevant information represent imperfections in the market." The Committee further added; "the cardinal principle of financial reporting is that the view presented should be true and fair. The Board should aim for the highest level of disclosure consonant with presenting reports which are understandable and avoid damaging to their competitive position. They should also aim to ensure the integrity and consistency of their reports and they should meet the spirits as well as the letter of reporting standards".

The Basel Committee on Banking Supervision in its *Report on Enhancing Bank Transparency* (September 1998) recommended that banks in their financial reports must provide timely information which would facilitate market participants' assessment of banks. Accordingly, a bank should furnish details of its working results as well as of its subsidiaries. There should also be information on allocation of capital to different business groups or activities within the banks so that activity-wise/business group-wise return on capital is revealed.

Besides, the bank should also disclose information about the Directors' experience, qualifications and other positions held by them in order to guard against conflicts of interest.

Summary

Effective corporate governance is necessary for organisations if they have to grow and successfully compete on sustained basis in liberalised environment. Mere compliance with regulatory requirements is not adequate for good governance.

Strong corporate governance is based on a set of systems and processes built up in the interests of the stakeholders, separation of ownership from management, independence, disclosures and transparency, accountability and self-regulation. In fact, good governance goes beyond regulations and laws.

In view of the recurrence of large scale corporate scams and frauds in recent years leading to failures of large number of corporate enterprises across the world, increasing competitiveness and growing awakening of the stakeholders, need for improving good governance system in the organisations was felt and various countries constituted expert committees to study existing governance practices and suggest ways to improve corporate governance system.

Every organisation has to evolve at codes of governance taking into consideration the existing demands and effectively act upon it so as to maximise the value of the stakeholders. In fact, corporate governance goes beyond regulations and laws.

Key Terms

Accountability	Kumar Mangalam Birla Committee
Audit Committees	OECD's Business Study Advisory
Cadbury Committee	Self-regulation Group Report
Disclosures	Systems and processes
Governance structure	Transparent relationship

Discussion Questions

1. What is corporate governance? Why is the concept of corporate governance gaining prominence across its world in recent years?

2. Discuss the nature and objectives of corporate governance.

3. Discuss, in brief, the fundamentals of corporate governance.

4. Briefly outline corporate governance practices in different countries of the world.

5. What steps have been taken in India in recent years to improve corporate governance practices?

6. What are the major recommendations of the Kumar Mangalam Birla Committee to improve corporate governance practices in the company?

7. What should be the broad codes of corporate governance which a company should adopt to ensure equity and fairness to the stockholders and other stakeholders?

8. Discuss the roles and responsibilities of the Board of Directors in a large organisation.

9. What role the audit committees are supposed to play to protect the interests of the stakeholders of a company?

References

1. "The Report of the Financial Aspects of Corporate Governance," *The Cadbury Committee Report*, 1992.

2. Guidelines for Improved Corporate Governance in Canada, TSE, 1994.

3. Corporate Governance: Improving Competitiveness and Access to Capital Global Markets, *Report of the Ira Millstein Committee*, 1988 OECD.

4. *Report of the Kumar Mangalam Birla Committee on Corporate Governance*, SEBI, 2000.

5. *Report on Trend and Progress of Banking in India*, p. 28, 2001–02.

6. Reddy, Y.V., Conference on Corporate Governance for Directors of Indian Banks, *The Indian Banker*, January, 2006.

7. RBI, *Report on Trend and Progress of Banking India*, p. 294, 2007–08.

8. *Business Line*, January 8, 2009.

9. Vance, Stanley C., *Boards of Directors*, University of Oregon Press, p. 19, 1964.

10. Monks and Minow, *Watching the Watchers*, p. 170, 1981.

11. Bhagat, S. and B. Black, "The Uncertain Relationship Between Board Composition and Firm Value", *Business Lawyer* 54, pp. 921–963, 1999.

12. Fields, M.A. and P.Y. Keys, "The Emergence of Corporate Governance from Wall Street to Main Street: Outside Directors, Board Diversity, Earnings Management and Management Incentives to Bear Risks," *Financial Review*, 38, pp. 1–33, 2003.

13. *Business Standard*, October 7, 2009.

SECTION II

Scanning Business Environment
Processes and Techniques

5

Scanning
Macro Environment

LEARNING OBJECTIVES

The present Chapter aims at:

- Providing an apt understanding of dynamics of business environment.
- Assessing utility of environmental scanning in strategy making.
- Discussing how various macro environmental forces can be scanned.
- Describing, in brief, major techniques of environmental scanning.

INTRODUCTION

A business enterprise, being a subsystem of the overall environmental system, has to operate within an environmental framework. Although both the social environment and the enterprise affect each other, the influence of the former on the latter is relatively much more pronounced and prominent. According to the open-system perspective, an enterprise in order to survive successfully has to constantly interact with the social environment in which it operates and the forces acting to reshape this environment. The management must, therefore, understand the dynamics of business environment in proper perspective. They must be able to perceptively diagnose the firm's external environment along with the firm's own internal environment so as to evolve at a strategy which is an excellent match to the firm's situation, is capacious to build competitive advantage and improves long-term performance of the firm. This is possible only when the management has a deeper understanding of the dynamics of macro environment. They have to undertake perspicacious analysis of various environmental forces and discern the emerging opportunities, and isolate impending threats. They need to be familiar with the techniques which can be parlayed to monitor the macro-environment. The following paragraphs are devoted to analyse these aspects.

Dynamics of Business Environment

Business environment refers to external environment which comprises all the relevant factors and forces that are outside the firm's boundaries but bear upon strategic decisions. According to Gerald Bell, "an organisation's external environment consists of those things outside an organisation such as customers, competitors, government units, suppliers, financial firms and labour pools that are relevant to an organisation's operations".[1]

External environment of a firm comprises two major components, viz., macro environment and the industry-specific, competitive environment. Macro environment consists of the totality of all such forces as are external to and beyond the control of individual business enterprises and their management.

Macro environmental forces are essentially the 'givens' within the firm and their management have to operate. For example, the value system of the society, the rules and regulations laid down by the government and its fiscal policy, the monetary policy of the central bank, the institutional set up of the country, the ideological beliefs of the leaders and their attitude towards foreign capital and enterprise, and so on, constitute the environmental system within which a business enterprise has to operate. Macro environmental forces are general in nature inasmuch as they directly or indirectly impact every firm and every industry. These forces influence the long-term as well as short-term environment in which all firms operate. Forces like aging of the country's population, the incorporation of new technology to transform products, and the growing pressure of foreign competition have long-term consequences on product-market options of the firms. There are other factors such as interest rates, changes in household purchasing power and exchange rates which have short-term impact. Nevertheless, a macro environment creates ripple effect on all firms within and across industries and these effects benefit some firms while others may feel hurt.

Another component of external environment is industry-specific competitive environment which represents forces and conditions which are directly relevant to the firm's immediate industry and competitive environment. In view of the fact that industries differ widely in their economic characteristics, competitive feature and profit prospect, it would be pertinent for the firm to concentrate the environmental analysis on the industry specific forces.

Figure 5.1 shows the relationship between the macro environment, the competitive environment and the organisation. A granular look into the exhibit shows that industry-specific environment has the most powerful direct and immediate effect on the organisation.

A salient feature of the external environment is that it is dynamic and ever-changing[2]. Some of the environmental forces such as technological and competitive environment are changing faster than the political environment. Further, the degree of environmental volatility is greater for some organisations than for others. For example, the rate of change in technological and competitive environments in pharmaceuticals,

The External Environment

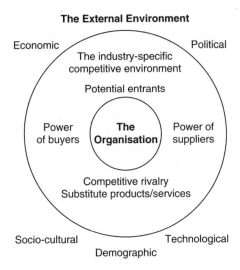

Figure 5.1 The organisation and its external environment.

chemicals and electronic industries is faster than in the machinery, autoparts, and confectionary industries. Furthermore, environmental changes can be more sharp for some sub-units of an organisation than others. For example, R&D department of many organisations faces high volatility because it has to keep pace with newly developing technological applications. In contrast, production department may deal with a relatively slow-changing environment characterised by a steady flow of raw materials and labour.

The business environment is complex because of myriad of external forces to which the organisation must respond and also to the variety within each factor. Among the environmental forces, technological developments, government rules and regulations, labour environment and competitive environment are considered relatively more complex. The environment for all organisations is expected to be more complex and uncertain in years to come because of increasing globalisation of national markets and pathbreaking technological developments. As more and more markets are becoming global, number of factors a firm must consider in any decision became huge and more complex. With new technologies being discovered every year, markets change and products must change with them.

In the wake of cataclysmic change in economic and financial policies of countries across the world and technological advancements at breakneck speed, the entire world has turned into global village resulting in increased interdependence, free movement of capital and know-how, decreasing trade barriers, instantaneous worldwide communication, emerging global financial system, spreading of free enterprise system and fast changing personal, social, familial and cultural values, growing sophistication and awareness of customers and their aspirations for better lifestyles and better value for their money. In the changed milieu, thinking globally is no longer a luxury but a pre-requisite for success. Customers around the world are growingly demanding the same high levels of quality and service we take for granted. Globalisation is no longer a phenomenon or same passing trend but an overarching international system shaping the international politics and foreign relations of almost all countries. Globalisation can be increasingly empowering and growingly coercive. It can democratise opportunity and democratise panic. It is also enabling people to share their unique skills farther and wider. The environmental forces generally differ from country to country. The pattern of business environment that exists in India may not be the same as in the US, the UK, Russia, Germany and Japan. Nevertheless, same forces may be alike, the order and intensity of the environmental forces do vary among different countries. For instance, sub-prime crisis in the US leading to global financial meltdown badly affected economies of different countries across the globe, but the degree of impact has been different. India, China and other emerging countries have not been so severely affected as developed countries like the US, Japan, the UK and France. Even within a country, different regions may have diverse magnitude and direction of environmental forces[3].

International macro environments vary so widely that a company's internal environment and strategic management process must be highly flexible. Differences in macro-environments strongly affect the ways in which a Multi National Company (MNC) conducts its marketing, financial, manufacturing and other functional activities. For example, the existence of regional associations like the European Union, the North American Free Trade Zone, and Mercosur in South America has a significant impact on the competitive "rules of the game" both for those MNCs operating within and for those MNCs intending to enter these areas.

What is most interesting to note that environmental forces are interdependent and affect each other. For example, sociological environment affects and gets affected by economic environment of business. The social attitude towards business and management determines how many people get attracted to private business as an activity and to management as a career. If business gets a social sanction as a respectable profession, the occupational structure of a country will reflect a sizeable category of professional managers. On the other hand, if more and more of active labour force join professional management, the social attitude towards business and its management also changes.

Likewise, a social trend of healthier eating and consumers' increasing distaste for factory farming may signal to supermarkets a change in consumer, behaviour and spending patterns.

The political and economic environments are also inter-dependent. In a state of political stability, a large number of business enterprises come up for operation, and different sectors of the economy rev up, foreign investments increase and economic prosperity grows. This is what Indian economy experienced boom during the last decade having average growth rate of Gross Domestic Product (GDP) of over 7% when there was political stability. Where there exists political instability, business uncertainties multiply, and entrepreneurs are loath to set up projects. The gloomy state of West Bengal is a case in point. Likewise, the ideology of the ruling party influences the economic system. The interests of private sector business enterprises are likely to be adversely affected if the ruling party, as in the distant past, in India believed in using socialism as a strategy and nationalisation of enterprises as a tactic to strengthen the economy. On the other hand, at times a series of fiscal measures may be necessary to cope with the changes in economic milieu. For example, to overcome recent economic crisis and industrial recession due to global meltdown, the Government of India, like other countries' government have, of late, provided economic stimulus to corporate sector.

Political-legal environment does influence competitive environment in an industry. For example, the government policy of privatisation allowing private fuel retail outlets in 2002 led to entry of private sector enterprises like Reliance, Essar and Shell to enter the market and compete with public sector giants like IOC, HPC and BPCL.

Similarly, the educational-cultural environment influences and is influenced by the economic environment. The state of economic development acts as a decisive factor in the choice of a system of education. For example, only a relatively high-income country can afford to import costly higher education in service and technology. The system of education, on the other hand, may be responsible for a given economic environment. For example, the emphasis on education in 'arts' and the absence of vocational courses may be held responsible for the problem of unemployment in many countries.

UTILITY OF ENVIRONMENTAL SCANNING IN STRATEGY MAKING

Environmental scanning in strategy making, also referred to as the basic monitoring system, is the process of monitoring economic, competitive, technological, socio-cultural, demographic and political settings with the sole purpose of detecting the signals that will act as a signpost for future changes in the organisation's industry as also to discern patterns and trends that are beginning to form and try to forecast the future direction of these trends. Such an analysis involves information compiling, processing, forecasting the above conditions, and discerning opportunities and threats.

Scanning of environmental forces is a stupendous task in view of their complex, turbulent and tumultuous character. Even then this exercise should be undertaken by every firm if it has to survive successfully and grow amidst highly volatile and dynamic environment. Failure to monitor and evaluate the external environment in today's harsh business world can have serious and very negative consequences. NIRULA's failure to scan business environment is a case in point (Illustrative Capsule 5.1).

ILLUSTRATIVE CAPSULE 5.1
NIRULA'S FAILURE TO SCAN BUSINESS ENVIRONMENT

If one turns the corner at L-block in Central Delhi, Rajiv Chowk, one will run into a Haldiram's food outlet, which for many Delhiites, is a jarring realisation of the changing times. This, after all, was the flagship location of the legendary eating establishment NIRULA, which Delhi residents regularly flocked to for mouth-watering savouries or ice creams. NIRULA's other immensely popular location near the Chanakya cinema hall also no longer exists. These were leased properties and NIRULA lost the leases. But it has three new homes in Connaught Place alone.

That may be so, but it could also be a metaphor for what has happened to NIRULA. In the past 15 years or so, Indian consumers have become increasingly younger and are armed with more disposable income than ever, they have become Kungry for food outside home, frequenting fast food chains such as McDonald's, Domino's, Pizza Hut, KFC and others, indeed fuelling the rise of formidable domestic players such as Haldiram's and Bikanerwala's. Yet, NIRULA's has atrophied, unable to read this demographic trend and exploit, despite its brand name and once loyal fan following, having ceded acres of ground to its more agile fast-food competitors.

This ultimately culminated in the sale of NIRULA's to NAVIS Capital for ₹90 crore three years ago.

Source: www.businesstoday.in

A firm can set its future direction and targets of performance and formulate the most suitable strategy only when it has been able to visualise and perceive the opportunities and constraints in store for it. Visualisation and perception of business opportunities and threats arising out of developments inside and outside the country call for comprehensive environmental scanning because both favourable and unfavourable components are inherent in the overall environment. Macro-environmental analysis can act as an early warning system by giving opportunities and threats and develop appropriate responses.[4] It enables the organisation to discern changes, however small, that have the potential to disrupt its competitive environment.

The environment may offer major profit opportunities due to anticipated economic, socio-political and industrial trends and new opportunities in the market/product/customer segments which the company can readily exploit particularly in the case of technological advances. In the same vein, an economic downturn, an adverse social or political condition, structural changes in the industry, market decline or product obsolescence, competitive threats and above all tight financial market can pose considerable threats that greatly limit a company's range of choices.

The entire environmental framework and its component parts, as noted above, are dynamic and the pace of changes is tumultuous and such a change affects the market for the firm's present products, the prospects for future products, success of products and market choices. The environmental changes may pose threat on the established strategies and call upon the management to be alert to the possibility that the opportunity they have seized will soon expire. They may also provide new opportunities in terms of new market needs which the management can satisfy. No firm can remain oblivious to these environmental developments which are relevant to its own sphere of operation. It has got to adjust itself in consonance with environmental changes. In order to respond to the environment, the management should attempt to sense and predict changes in different environmental forces and discern the opportunities and threats emanating to bring about necessary changes in the organisation. The more time and energy a firm devotes for environmental appraisal, the greater is its capacity to survive.

Environmental appraisal enables the firm to get clear idea about the existing competitors, their current operations, and future plans. This is inevitable if the firm has to formulate strategy to counteract the competitors' moves. If the competitor is on something, it needs to be investigated, otherwise the competitor's move could lead to his pulling ahead, growing faster and becoming more profitable. Assessment of foreign competitive situation is also important when considering any foreign environment. It will always be in the interest of a firm to ascertain how many local rivals are there and how good they are. If the rivals are very efficient and their products excellent and their marketing perfect, then the situation is much different than if there are no competitors or if the firms in the country are inept and inefficient. A multinational firm scanning alternative possibilities might well avoid a country, at least temporarily, that offers strong domestic or other foreign competition. This is especially true if the market is relatively small or saturated.

Environmental appraisal enables the management to predict future development, to make the invisible more visible and thus, lessen the uncertainty about the future in the face of spectacular, powerful and rapid environmental changes. Those who foresee the critical changes that effect the firm will have a far better chance of being successful than those who will not be able to do so.

Thus, the management has to search the environment to determine which factors pose threat to the firm's present product-market strategy and accomplishment of objectives, and which environmental forces present opportunities for greater accomplishment of objectives by adjusting the firm's current strategy. No organisation can afford to ignore changes in technology, competitive environment, government policy or changes in social values. If it does not react to the demands of the environment by changing its strategy, it is counting its decline or oblivion. Companies that are winning today collect, analyse and respond to information as living beings do, in real-time. Dell, Wal-Mart, Toyota, SAP, Infosys, Wipro, Tata Motors are giants as far as this strategy is concerned. At the core of their success lies a remarkable ability to sense and respond to change and move from its core business to new business. Transformation of Bharat Forge Ltd. from auto sector to non-auto sectors is a case in point (Illustrative Capsule 5.2). They are the adaptive enterprises of the present century. These enterprises have the smartness to foresee that gearing up for ever-shrinking response times and ever-changing competitive landscape needs more than tweaking its own internal systems.

ILLUSTRATIVE CAPSULE 5.2

BHARAT FORGE LTD.'S TRANSFORMATION IN RESPONSE TO ENVIRONMENTAL CHANGE

Bharat Forge Ltd. (BFL)—the world's largest forgings company—was set up in 1961 by Babasaheb Neelkanth Kalyani's father to meet the forging needs of the fledgling Indian automotive industry. Over the 60's and 70's, BFL did its bit amidst a bevy of other forging companies in India to foster industrialisation in socialist environs. In 1971, Neelkanth Kalyani took over the reins of the company. With change in leadership, BFL's penchant for technology came to the fore. Archaic processes were mothballed and a bloated work force was replaced by a more skilled one. In the last decade, Kalyani's international aspirations were noticed. Since 2004, BFL has made a string of international acquisitions, including that of Carl Dan Peddingaus GMBH, one of the largest forging companies in Germany. The company has been growing in the region of 20%–22%. Automotive component sector accounted for close to three-fourths of revenues.

However, in 2008 BFL decided to make a crucial strategic shift to derisk the business model and increase the non-auto share when it found that automobile sector started collapsing in the wake of the recession triggered by the sub-prime crisis in the US.

The shift towards non-auto was inevitable because the flagship business was under pressure, more overseas than at home (global operations accounted for close to 70% of BFL's business). BFL turned into red since June 2009. Overseas sales started falling and came down to more than half since the period July–September in 2008.

The downturn accelerated BFL's push towards creating a larger non-auto footprint, as evidenced from its increasing contribution to 32% in April-June, 2009, up from 28% for 2008–09. The company has targeted to hit 40% by 2012 and go up to 75% by 2015. The management has decided to use the company's manufacturing capabilities to become an engineering conglomerate.

One non-automotive industry that Kalyani is betting big is energy, right from wind to thermal to nuclear. Realising that he needs to build competencies to become a full solution (rather than just a supplier of components) in the energy sector, Kalyani has embarked on a string of joint ventures with Indian and global majors.

Aerospace is another business which BFL has embraced and started manufacturing of structural components. Kalyani is keen to make engine components but admits that it is years away. Likewise, the company is looking at various components in transportation (railways and marine), and oil and gas.

Source: www.businesstoday.in

Input-output relationship between a firm and environment also necessitates environmental scanning. A firm, in order to function, must procure various inputs such as human, capital, managerial and technical from the environment. These inputs are then converted into goods and services and made available to those living in the environment. Thus, a firm's operations regarding acquisition of quantum and kinds of inputs and distribution of output are subject to environmental influences.

The management must also scan the environment so as to find out what the diverse claims are and the expectations of different sections of the society which the firm has to fulfil in order to be socially acceptable. These claims need to be accorded due weightage while formulating overall objectives, policies and strategies.

Above all, environmental scanning has emerged as a potent source of building and sustaining competitive advantage in global market. In the changed environment, issues such as—how to successfully penetrate foreign markets? how to explain diverse capabilities and take advantage of regional cost advantages? how to coordinate competitive activity on a global basis? and how to develop, source, manufacture and distribute products and services for world markets?—have become the key to building and sustaining competitive advantage.

Environmental scanning ensures long-term successful survival and research has found a positive relationship between environmental scanning and profits.

All these are possible if dispassionate scanning of the environmental developments across the country and outside of it is done on a continuous basis.

While scanning environment the management should remember that such an appraisal facilitates spotting of opportunities at the level of an industry rather than at a firm's or its product's level. As a result of this aggregation, management decision loses the sharpness needed for choosing a particular product-market. Furthermore, environmental analysis fails to answer whether the desired economic and technological potentials existing within a particular industry will be available to the firm. The prospects of an industry as a whole are not necessarily the same for an individual firm particularly when the total industry capacity substantially exceeds the demands. Along with this, the determination of opportunities or threats is often as much a function of the perception and the attitude of the managements as it is of the factor itself. For example, there are two factors, viz., increased government interference and competition increasingly centered on technical specification of the control system as well as on the machine. To a management wedded to the philosophy of no-governmental intervention of any type, both factors appear to be a threat. However to a management with less rigid attitudes, a great opportunity is opened up in terms of a chance to break into an existing competitor's historical preserve by product innovation for which the government subsidises part of the cost and also mitigates the risk through adverse orders for prototypes for trial in factories. Thus, both factors seem equally valid and yet the same basic factors are merely viewed with different attitudes. To an enterprising management, all changes offer new opportunities and the chance to generate new alternatives for growth and restructuring of an existing business.

PROCESS OF SCANNING MACRO ENVIRONMENT

The principal objectives underlying scanning of macro environment are to identify current and potential changes taking place in the environment, to gain deep insight into the important intelligence for strategic decision-making and to facilitate and foster strategic thinking in the organisation. As such the management must be familiar with the present and future changes in various environmental forces in the country as also in those countries where the organisation is intending to conduct business and discern long-term opportunities and threats present therein.

While scanning environment forces, focus of the planner should be on identifying current and forthcoming changes and evaluating these changes in terms of business opportunities and threats and assessing their likely impact on extant product-market strategy of the organisation and possibility of changing the present strategy to improve its competitiveness.

The following paragraphs are devoted to provide an incisive account of important variables of economic, technological, political, demographic and socio-cultural environment of the country, and assess the implications of these variables for large organisations.

Economic Environment

The economic environment is by far the most significant and pervasive component of the external environment inasmuch as it affects the very survival of a business organisation. It is concerned with the analysis of all such economic developments as directly and indirectly affects the product-market complexion of the enterprise.

A study of economic trends such as size of the economy, income levels, pattern of income distribution, pattern of personal consumption, growth and stability patterns, inflationary trends, institutional financing system, debt pattern, price levels, employment levels, agricultural and industrial production, exchange rate levels, and the like provide deep insights into the existing economic situations and changes that are likely to take place in the state of the economy as also the purchasing power of the people. This will facilitate the management to foresee demand behaviour of the products of the industry to which the firm belongs.

The size of the economy is a basic measure of a country's potential as a market for the products of an enterprise. It is generally measured by the Gross National Product (GNP) which shows the total level of economic activity in a country. A country with substantially large GNP is considered highly potential for marketing of the products by an organisation because of the people's high earning capacity.

However, study of the GNP should be undertaken along with size of population so as to determine the per capital income of a person which, in turn, will help the management in deciding the nature of the potential a country offers as a market for different types of goods.

The per capita income of a person must be determined so as to ascertain his purchasing power. This can be done by forecasting the gross national product and size of population. Per capita income should be studied along with changes in the price level because that has bearing on real purchasing power. For instance, there has been a rise in per capita income of the people in India during the plan period but real purchasing power of the people has eroded substantially because of rise in the inflation rate exceeding the money-income growth rate, hovering of unemployment and increase in the tax burden. There is little possibility to any improvement in this situation in the near future. In view of the global economic recession in the recent past leading to slowdown of development in advanced and emerging economies including India, level of national income, employment, and wage and consumption decelerated, seriously affecting the economic and industrial development of both developed and developing countries and so also manufacturing, service and financial sectors. However, emerging countries like India, China, Brazil and South Africa are showing signs of recovery and foreign investors are evincing keen interest in these countries. Even the US, Germany and France are reported to be out of the economic recession. These trends augur well for the economies and for different organisations and sectors.

The corporate planner should also pay attention to the pattern of income distribution in the country because that determines the type of products needed by people of different income groups. In India, income distribution is pronouncedly skewed. At the top of the income pyramid, there are a small number of wealthy consumers whose expenditure patterns are not affected at all by changes in price levels. These consumers constitute a major market for luxury products. The upper middle-class which is also omitted in number will have to exercise some expenditure restraint but are able to afford expensive clothes, shoes, toiletries, and so on. The vast majority of the Indian population comprising the bottom of the income pyramid will have to pay dearly for the necessities of life, husband their resources and try hard to meet their day-to-day needs.

Income levels and growth rates also vary regionally. They are affected by the level of local economic activity and employment, the rate of in and out migration and wage rates. There may be certain regions where entrepreneurs get all sorts of facilities to carry out their business activities while they have to encounter several hardships in other regions. This results in the concentration of industrial activities in certain regions. The level of economic growth in these regions will be relatively more pronounced in comparison to other regions. Thus, the pattern of demand for products will differ in different regions. This is why the management must take geographical income differences into account while formulating strategy.

The demand for a product is also influenced by savings and debt patterns. Where consumers have a reservoir of purchasing power to supplement their income, their demand for goods will expand. Consumers can also increase their purchase through borrowing.

Management must also predict change in expenditure patterns of consumers due to changes in the level of income. It was stated by the German Statistician Ernst Engel in 1857 that with the rise in the level of income, the proportion spent on food tends to decline, the percentage of spending on housing and household operations tends to remain constant and the expenditure on clothing, transportation, recreation, health and education and savings tends to increase. An enterprise engaged in manufacturing a product falling in the category of food should endeavour to analyse the demand behaviour in this respect with change in the level of income.

Also, a company contemplating to foray into foreign markets should take into consideration additional factors such as currency convertibility. Without convertibility, a company operating in Russia cannot convert its profits from roubles to dollars. Exchange rate stability is another critical variable that merits serious consideration.

Technological Environment

Corporate planners must scan the changes in technological environment and assess their impact on product-market strategy of their organisation. Rapid technological developments including the internet, use of sophisticated software, genetic engineering and nano technology are changing the way we live and work.

Rapid advancement of technology is also changing the quality of lives through improvements in products and services. The days of maddening commute through endless streams of traffic congestion are going to be over for many people. Flexi working schedule, emergence of the fully equipped home office and new forms of communication are making new lifestyles possible. New technological developments have profound effect on the efficiency with which products can be manufactured and sold. They must be able to perceive how technological changes will affect customers' demand for products.

Impact of technology is all pervasive because it affects the economic, social, cultural and demographic conditions of human beings. This effect is perceptible because technology has increased the ability to generate, store and distribute energy, increased the ability to design new materials and changes the properties of others, brought about significant changes in processes and methods of production, increased the ability to master time and distance for the movement of freight and passengers, extended human ability to sense things, increased understanding of individual and group behaviour and how to deal with it, and increased the understanding of diseases and their treatment. All these changes have their bearing on development, production and distribution. New technology may result in the creation of entirely new products or new uses for existing products, changes in the processes of production or alter the way in which the existing product is made and packed. Thus, the production line, magnitude of operation, production quality and control and cost structure of business enterprises are influenced significantly by technological development. Market structure and even organisational structure may change phenomenally due to change in technology. Recent technological changes have also changed the dynamics of industries such as banking, financial services and insurance, allowing the new entrants to enter the market at a lowest cost base than the incumbents, thereby offering more competitively priced products and services and gaining more market share in the process.

An organisation must, therefore, monitor changes in the technological environment before taking decisions regarding new investments, modifications, by-products and waste control and removing bottlenecks. Any investment decision without consideration of technological factor may spell the quick demise of the organisation. However, before adopting new technology, the management must match the benefits with the problems associated with it.

Political Environment

Another component of the external environment that has an impact on the operations of a business organisation right from its incorporation to liquidation is political environment which is concerned with the study of attitudes and actions of political and government leaders and legislators. The major factors that affect virtually every enterprise and almost every aspect of life are the political system existing in the country, roles played by the government and pressure groups. The management must interact with these forces in order to seize the opportunities offered by the government and minimise the risks inherent in the environment.

The political atmosphere of a county is significantly relevant to business organisations. No organisation can think of expanding or diversifying its activities if the political atmosphere is charged with turmoil and instability. Where the ruling party is strong and stable and relations between the Central and State Governments are cordial and role of opposition party is constructive, decision-making powers are reasonably distributed among different social groups and the government has clear-cut fiscal, financial and trade policies, business organisations will find it conducive to expand their operations. The political climate in our country presents a mixed picture. On the one hand, we have the democratic and federal system of government in which there is strong and stable Central Government with equally strong State Governments working in harmony with each other, and businessmen have freedom to operate within the prescribed limits. These aspects are quite encouraging for the growth of private sector business enterprises. However, emerging regionalism at the political level, occasional communal disturbances, linguistic problem and politicalisation of trade unions present threats to business enterprises.

Government policies also impact the business climate of a country. Recent policy of globalisation of Indian economy and liberalisations and delicensing backed by fiscal, financial and infrastructural support have created invigorating climate for private sector investment in the country. Foreign multinationals are foraying in every sector of the economy on a large scale and forming alliances with Indian partners to do their business in the country.

For large and multinational enterprises, study of political environment at the international level is equally important while deciding the growth profile and direction of their business. With growing political turbulence in the world, particularly in the third world nations, business organisations are exposed to greater political risks of confiscation of property expropriation with compensation, restrictions on market shares, employment policies, locally shared ownership, loss of freedom, repatriation of earnings and capital, breaches or unilateral revision of contracts and agreements, damage to property and person due to riots, insurrections, revolutions and wars.

The government's foreign policy is another important factor for such organisations. A positive political relationship between a foreign country and the Government of India enables Indian organisations to engage in a smooth trade, and set up operations in that country. However, political instability in a foreign country may render business difficult or impossible regardless of the amicable relationship between that government and the Indian government. Therefore, a management must also monitor the international environment regularly and adjust their strategy accordingly.

Through their diverse roles the government influences pricing, employment practices, production, competitive and other decisions of business organisations. In a democratic country like ours, the government plays three major roles, viz., regulatory, participative and promotive.

Through its regulatory role, the government enacts various laws. In India as well as in other democratic countries, owing to social and political pressures and growing complexity of technology and business practices, the government has enacted a web of laws and regulations to constrain and regulate business activities. Some of these laws currently in vogue in India are the Industries (Development and Regulation) Act, Competition Act, Contract Act, The Companies Act, Imports and Exports (Control) Act, Foreign Exchange Management Act (FEMA) and Essential Commodity Act. Besides, there are innumerable labour laws, taxation laws, banking laws and local laws.

Some laws have been enacted to protect companies from unfair competition between them. Some laws are designed to protect workers, consumers and communities from business firms. Some laws are intended to make contract enforceable and to protect property rights. Many are designed to regulate the behaviour of managers and their subordinates in business and other enterprises. Remarkable changes in these laws are now being made following the policy of liberalisation.

The role of a welfare government is not restricted to mere regulating and constraining business activities but extends much beyond it to promotional activities whereby it promotes and stimulates business organisations by dispensing fiscal and financial assistance. For instance, the Government of India's frantic efforts to foster balanced growth of industries and to strengthen development of basic industries as well as small and cottage industries. It has been offering from time to time various incentives such as subsidies, tax exemptions and concessions, liberal financial, managerial and technical facilities, provision of developed industrial plots and sheds, incentives for exports and relaxation of import controls and the like. Perceptive managers are always on the lookout for these incentives and make necessary changes in their strategies to capitalise the incentives provided by the government. It may be noted that a number of leading organisations such as Reliance Industries, Tata group of companies, Kumar Mangalam Birla group of companies, Bajaj Industries, Hindustan Levers, Philips India, Dunlop India and other companies have been making changes in their investment strategies from time to time to take maximum advantage of fiscal incentives of the government.

Finally, the government also plays a participative role to undertake industrial activities particularly in those fields that cannot be carried on by private business entrepreneurs, viz., war and defence, public works, public services and to provide competition to private sectors. For instance, the Government of India has established public sector organisations in the field of basic and heavy industries so as to provide basic inputs for the development of the country further. However, participative role of the government is tending to decline since the adoption of the policy of privatisation, encouraging private sector enterprise to enter into infrastructure sector as also in defence sector.

As such, companies need to undertake scanning the political environment for signs of change in government policy and business laws which might impact their industry. Without adequate knowledge of the major policies and laws and changes therein from time to time it would not be possible to formulate realistic plans.

Organisations intending to embrace overseas business must have a deep understanding of the form of government, political ideology, tax laws, political stability, government attitude toward foreign companies, regulations of foreign ownership of assets, strength of opposition groups, trade regulations, foreign policies, terrorist activity and legal system of country/countries when they are planning to enter into.

Demographic Environment

Corporate planner should also study the demographic environment and identify the broad characteristics of the population that affect the organisation. An alert management will have plenty of advance notice of potential changes in demographic factors and can start searching for new product lines and more attractive markets.

The major factors in the demographic environment relevant to business organisations are trends in size, aging, geographical shifts and literacy of population.

Growth in population has significance for the government as well as for business organisations. A growing population means increasing human needs which, in turn, results in the expansion of product markets if there is sufficient purchasing power. Where growth size of population exceeds the availability of food supply and resources there will be rise in costs which will, in turn, depress profit margins of businessmen.

The ageing pattern of the population should also be analysed as it affects product demand. For instance, an increase in the population of the age of 18 to 24 will result in surging sales for electronic goods, motor cycles, sports products, clothes and accessories, cosmetics, magazines, and the like. Shrinking population of old persons is likely to result in decline in the demand of certain medical goods and services, certain magazines read exclusively by older people and so on.

Geographical shifts of population also affect business enterprises. Migration of people from rural areas to urban areas will result in the rise in demand of consumable products in urban areas. Organisations engaged in production of such goods after estimating these changes will adopt the expansion strategy so as to exploit the opportunities.

Owing to the development of quick modes of transportation, sizeable sections of the working population may move from their places of work to the suburbs. This will certainly increase the demand for station wagons, home workshop equipment, garden furniture, lawn and gardening tools and supplies and outdoor cooking equipment in addition to consumer goods of daily use.

In the last few years, people, particularly young ones, have been tempted to settle in metropolitan cities because of superior cultural and recreational facilities. This means strong opportunities for multi-storey apartment construction and retail outlets in these cities.

Trends in the educational pattern of the population should also be visualised because it has bearing on business activities. Rising population of educated persons implies increasing demand for quality of goods, books, magazines and travel, and fall in television viewing because educated persons tend to watch television less than their counterparts.

In recent few years, there has been a tremendous change in global level demographics, as manifested in increased participation of women in the workforce, postponement of marriage, more divorces, small families. Thus, emergence of a more varied lifestyles and the gradual aging of population have far-reaching implications on product-market posture of business organisation. For example, massive increase in number of senior citizens—the result of lower birth rates, advances in healthcare and a host of other social factors—creates enormous opportunities for organisations attuned to this trend. In view of these changes, there is a likelihood of substantial increase in demand in coming years for specialised products and services targeted at senior citizens—such as healthcare, forms of transportation and a whole array of specialised financial services.

In view of far-reaching ramifications of demographic changes, it will always be desirable to monitor this aspect of external environment closely and regularly and assess their implications on the firm's product-market strategy. Let us study about a silent revolution in this sphere in Illustrative Capsule 5.3.

ILLUSTRATIVE CAPSULE 5.3

A SILENT REVOLUTION IN DEMOGRAPHIC ENVIRONMENT IN INDIA

Demographic environment in India is undergoing extraordinary changes in recent years, having many interesting implications for the country and society and, of course, businesses and potential entrepreneurs. One of the most important implications will be on account of a rapid increase of women in the workforce in the coming years, resulting in an unprecedented economic and social empowerment for them and thereby a dramatic redefinition of their roles and influence.

India already has, next to China, the largest number of women workforce. About 30%−35% of the estimated 480 million jobs are being performed by women, with a very large proportion actually in rural India.

Till recently, most of these jobs were largely relating to physical, menial labour such as on farms, on construction sites and as domestic help, and in relatively low-wage manufacturing such as apparel manufacturing. Most of these jobs, rather than helping in the empowerment or emancipation of women, added to their exploitation. However, with gradual transformation of Indian economy following tectonic policy reforms leading to liberalisation, privatisation and globalisation and technological development at a blistering pace during the last 15 years, there has been remarkable change in the role of women in every field of activity.

The IT and ITe/Bussiness Process Outsourcing (BPO) sector, created the first relatively higher paying, socially much more aspirational and respected career-oriented jobs for hundreds of thousands of women from the less privileged strata of society. Modern retail too is doing the same for women in a more influential way. Many other sectors such as aviation, travel and hospitality, financial services, growing and personal care, healthcare and education are now poised to induct a very large number of women in career-oriented jobs. Indeed, of the estimated 90 million or more new jobs expected to be created in India in the next five years, almost 45 million are likely to be in services alone, out of which as many as 20 million could be taken up by women.

The percentage of women enrolled for higher education has also risen to about 40% of all enrollments and hence there will be no shortage of better educated and better skilled women in the workforce in the ensuing years.

The increase in the number of women in white-collar jobs will lead to re-allocation of the roles. There will be a very rapid increase in dual-income households, particularly in urban area. Women who have lesser time to be home makers, will lead to the emergence of new needs such as ready-to-cook or ready-to-eat meals, availability of third parties who can take up routine housekeeping roles, enhanced requirement for household helps, nannies and baby-sitters, and for goods and services that can be home delivered on the orders placed over phone or through internet. Thus, modern retail also is likely to get a big boost.

Another important implication will be reflected in greater financial freedom of women, and their increased confidence. They will increasingly demand more products and services specifically created for them and directly marketed to them.

Almost certainly, more and more women will choose to marry late and have fewer children much later in life. This will have a very pronounced impact on birth rates and population growth rates in the future as well as on the dynamics within the family and on the behavioural patterns of society.

Source: www.business-standard.com

Socio-Cultural Environment

A business organisation can survive in the long run only when it is responsive to the socio-cultural environment of the society in which it operates and aims at promoting social welfare. The management must, therefore, understand the existing environment of the society and visualise future changes therein before long-range plans are formulated to accomplish corporate analysis.

The socio-cultural environment is concerned with analysis of the attitudes, values, desires, expectations, degrees of intelligence and education, beliefs and customs of people in a society, traditions and social institutions, class structure and social group pressure and dynamics. Some of the beliefs and values are much more important to people. For example, most Indians believe in work, getting married and living a simple life. These beliefs shape and colour more specific attitudes and behaviours found in everyday life. People also hold secondary beliefs and values that are liable to change in the wake of new social forces. For example, belief in early marriage is a secondary one. Management must note that it would be unwise to change the core beliefs and values and should avoid formulating a business strategy that violates these beliefs.

Some of the beliefs and attitudes of great relevance for managerial decisions are expectations from certain products, their quality, price and social welfare activity, attitudes towards the importance of work, workers' attitudes towards organisational climate, expectations of workers and executives from the organisation, employees' attitudes towards authority structure, responsibility and organisational positions, peoples' belief in customs, traditions and conventions and their belief in science and technology, belief in competition and in the importance of change and experimentation to find better methods of doing things and in the general attitude towards education.

The socio-cultural beliefs bear upon the operations of a business organisation in different ways. They directly affect corporate purpose and objectives by prescribing the norms of corporate behaviour. A major socio-cultural influence has been an increased emphasis on the concept of social responsibility, a subject we shall discuss later.

Socio-cultural factors also influence the products to be manufactured by an organisation. An organisation has to produce that type of product which meets the requirements of the people. A demand for high quality readymade garments will lead to modification of product strategy by those in the business. Increasing awareness of better standard of living and good nutrition have brought about a proliferation of products and services such as high quality products, vitamin supplements, efficient automobiles, decent housing and better educational facilities.

In order to survive successfully in the long run, the management must consider the socio-cultural factors while formulating objectives and product-market strategy. It must be able to anticipate the changing expectations of different sections of society and serve them more effectively. The organisation itself has to change in consonance with the new environment.

MNCs conducting business abroad must be familiar with customs, norms and values of the country/countries where they are planning to enter into or expand their operations. Besides, various social institutions, lifestyles of the people, their religious beliefs, attitude towards foreigners, literacy level, human rights, and the like merit serious considerations.

TECHNIQUES OF ENVIRONMENTAL SEARCH

Collection of information and its proper interpretation provide a sound basis for environmental search. With adequate information, strategic planners can analyse the opportunities and threats in the environment. According to Glueck[5], the three major search techniques are: Information gathering, Spying and Forecasting. Of late, 'Bench Marking' has emerged as another technique of environmental search. We shall now discuss each of these in the following paragraphs:

Information Gathering

A management can learn a great deal about national and international environmental forces by gathering verbal as well as written information. Verbal information is obtained by hearing reports from different sources both informally and formally. The main sources of verbal information are radio and television, firm's employees including executives and subordinates and from outside the enterprise including the customers, wholesalers, brokers, suppliers, competitors and their employees, bankers, stockbrokers, stock analysts, consultants, researchers and the like. By interacting with these people during various meetings and conferences, the management can get first-hand information about environmental developments.

Written information can be gathered from various publications such as reports of the government and its agencies, commercial publications, research publications and publications of leading organisations who have separate research division to conduct studies from time to time about economic, technological and political environments and publish them.

The methodology an organisation follows to undertake the analysis of economic environment differs depending on the purpose of the analysis and the situation of the firm. For instance, if a foreign firm has a local subsidiary in the country and the objective of the analysis is to plan for further expansion, or diversification into new industrial activities, a two-tier analysis is carried out. At the first tier, the local subsidiary gathers and processes all the available local data and passes on the resulting information, along with its own assessment of the situation and prospects, to the home office overseas. The home office—the second tier—then scans the information of the subsidiary and makes its own assessment, keeping in view its global corporate and strategic goals, as well as the opportunities and threats existing all over the world. The home office usually has an independent economic research division or economic analysts to generate independent information that is compared with that supplied by the subsidiary and used for support of contest.

In contrast, where the firm is contemplating to enter a country for business purpose, it may have a consultant who is an expert on the particular country to do comprehensive economic analysis. Information is also gathered from the available materials, such as government publications, country studies, commercial publications, and so on. At times, local consultants are hired because of their intimate knowledge of the local environment and better access to relevant information. Another option is the employment of international consultants who utilise local associates and sources of information; while the latter supplies vital contacts and information, the former integrate and analyse the data and prepare the formal report on the country study.

Competitive Intelligence

Competitive intelligence technique is about gathering information on a company's competitors. This information pertains to potential products under development, new technologies that may be incorporated in existing products, new markets to enter, service quality and responsiveness. Continuous intelligence gathering can be extremely useful to firms in understanding better their environment, and their competitors, in identifying new opportunities for future improvements as well as possible threats to a firm's competitive position.

In this method, the top executives employ an individual or individuals to gather trade secrets. An employee of the competitor or his supplier or customer can also be engaged to solicit regular information about the competitors' activities.

Until recently, very few Indian companies had employed this technique. As against this, all Japanese companies involved in international business and most large European companies have active intelligence programmes.[6] This situation is, however, changing. Competitive intelligence is now one of the fastest growing fields within strategic management.[7] According to a recent survey of large US corporations, more than 75% of the employees reported competitive intelligence activities within their firm.[8]

Forecasting

Forecasting technique is concerned with estimating those events that may occur in the future and would have a significant impact on the work to be performed by the management and on the objectives to be pursued by them. In effect, it anticipates probable occurrences rather than waiting for them to happen and merely reacting to them later. Forecasting is directed to reduce the uncertainty surrounding the future.

There are myriad techniques of forecasting and it is not feasible to discuss all of them here. We shall, therefore, discuss briefly only the most commonly used techniques such as extrapolation, factor listing, time series analysis, casual modelling, jury of opinion, sales force composite, customer expectation method, Delphi technique, brainstorming and scenario writing.

Factor Listing Technique

This is a very popular method of forecasting upward or downward movement. In this method, favourable and unfavourable factors that affect operations of the firm are discerned and on that basis the firm's future is predicted for the ensuing year. However, no explanation is given in this method. No quantitative evaluation of the factors which affect the business is made. It is, thus, an intuitive method which involves a lot of guess-work.

Time Series Analysis

This method provides a quantitative base for the forecaster to make better judgements about the future. This technique seeks to identify historical patterns or tends and extends them into the future. The analysis is based on the assumption that what has occurred in the past is a good indication of what will occur in the future. Time series analysis is often useful for projecting demand for goods and services, projecting inventory needs, and predicting sales patterns and personnel needs. The most important component in time series analysis is probably the trend because it is the basic factor used in understanding the behaviour of the variables. For any time series where trend growth is fairly constant and there is no visible reason to think that the trend will not continue, this method can be very useful in making a first approximation of a forecast.

For this analysis, past events are plotted on a graph or by means of a table. Figure 5.2 illustrates the use of time series analysis to assess sales of automobiles for 2010 based on sales between 2003 and 2009.

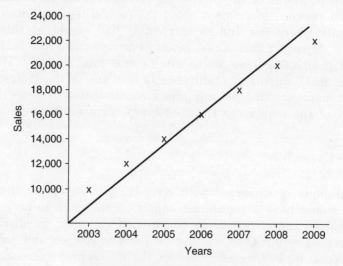

Figure 5.2 Time series analysis.

Time series analysis forces the forecaster to consider the underlying trend, cycle and seasonal element in the sales series. It provides a systematic means of making quantitative projections. However, the basic premise on which this technique is based— that historical patterns of change in sales components will continue in the future also—may not always be true. This technique is also not satisfactory for short-term forecasting. Furthermore, it may be difficult to get useful results from this technique in cases where fluctuations are erratic and irregular.

Casual Modelling

Casual modelling is the most sophisticated and mathematically complex quantitative forecasting technique in use today. It is used to forecast what will occur in a particular situation by studying the statistical relationship between the factor under consideration and other variables. For example, the future demand for new, single-family houses essentially depends on personal income, population changes and the interest rate for mortgages. A casual method, after studying the behavioural relationship between demand for new housing and the three major variables, might reveal that each time demand for new housing decreases with an increase in the mortgage rates.

Statisticians consider this relationship as a correlation. The more perfect the correlation, the better the model's ability to forecast. A perfect correlation (1.000) is one in which historically the relationship has always held true. For example, if the demand for colour television sets always declined by 10% when national income decreased by 5%, one could reasonably forecast that this would occur again in the future.

The most sophisticated of all casual models are the economic models developed to predict movements in the economy.[9] These models explain past economic activity and predict future economic activity by deriving mathematical equations which will express the most probable inter-relationship between a set of economic variables. Economists predict by means of mathematical models the future course of variables such as income, money supply, government expenditure and private expenditure on the basis of the "establish relationship". With the help of a full-time research staff and a sophisticated computer, these models, to be meaningful, must be revised periodically to provide for the changing weights of the parameters in the equations so that the real world is reflected in them.

Econometric models are superior to other quantitative techniques of forecasting because they are more analytical, process-oriented and sophisticated, and also because they seek to establish positive and accurate relationships between the cause and effect over a period of time. However, the cost of developing these models is so high that even a large firm subscribes to an existing model rather developing its own.

The various techniques thus discussed require sufficient information to establish a trend or a statistically valid relationship between variables. When the amount of information is not sufficient or the management does not understand the sophisticated technique or when a quantitative model is too expensive to be used by the firm, the management parlays qualitative techniques for forecasting.

Four widely used qualitative forecasting techniques are: a jury of opinion, the sales force composite, customers' expectation method and the Delphi technique.

Jury of Opinion

In this method, the opinion of experts in relevant areas are pooled and averaged. The actual process can take different forms. Usually executives from different areas of the organisation—production, marketing, finance and administration—are provided with all the background information available and the firm seeks their opinion of probable sales and profit margins. An informal variation of this method would be a group brain storming session in which members first try to generate as many ideas as possible. After getting all the ideas, an analysis is made to form a firm opinion. This can be a time-consuming process but is often helpful when the organisation needs many new ideas and alternatives.

This method provides forecasts easily and quickly. It does not require the preparation of elaborate statistics, but brings a variety of specialised viewpoints together for a pooling of experience and judgement. In the absence of adequate data this method may be the only feasible means of forecasting. However, this method is inferior to more factual bases of forecasting since it is based on opinions. It is not necessarily more accurate than other methods because opinion is averaged, responsibility is dispersed, and good and bad estimates are given equal weight. This method is not more reliable for developing forecasts by products, time intervals or markets for operating purposes.

Sales Force Composite

This is the so-called **grass-root method** in which the forecast is based upon data collected by sales representatives. Sales personnel are provided with standard forms to prepare their sales forecasts for the coming year. These forecasts are then discussed with the sales managers. Modifications are made and the results are complied and sent to district and regional managers who aggregate the district and regional estimates and send them to the head office. At the head office, a staff group may make a separate forecast and compare it with those arriving from district and regional offices. At this level, changes in the forecast may be made as a result of a decision taken by the management to increase or decrease advertising, to modify a particular product, to abandon a product and so on. Such a review completes the forecasting process.

This method has an advantage in that it forces different levels of management to examine their estimates on these fronts. The method uses specialised knowledge of the sales representatives who are close to the market. Further, a grass-root forecasting procedure results in estimates broken down by product, territory, customer and sales representatives. However, sales forecasts made by the sales force must be used very cautiously in view of the fact that sales representatives are biased observers, often being either unduly optimistic or unduly pessimistic. Furthermore, salesmen are often unaware of broad economic developments shaping further sales and are thus incapable of forecasting trends for extended periods. They may also be inclined to understate demand so that the company will set a low sales quota. Since sales forecasting is a subsiding function of the sales force, sufficient time may not be available for it.

Customer Expectation Method

This method, as the name implies, makes forecasts on the basis of a survey of the organisation's customers. A list of all potential buyers is prepared; each buyer is approached personally and asked to estimate his own future needs and requirements and a proportion of it which would be bought from the firm. By assembling all the information, the management can forecast the overall demand.

However, this method is difficult to employ in markets where users are numerous or are not easily located. Further, it is doubtful if the buyers freely report their buying intentions. It also requires considerable expenditure of time and manpower. The cost can be reduced by taking a probability sample of customers and also by substituting telephone or mail interviewing for personal interviewing. In short, this method is most suitable where the buyers are few, cost of reaching them is low, buyers have clear intentions and they are willing to reveal products, for consumer durables, for product purchases when advanced planning is required and for new products where past data does not exist.

Delphi Technique

The Delphi technique is a more formal version of the *jury of opinion* method. It was originally developed by the Rand Corporation to forecast military events.[10] This technique is basically a procedure to systematically enable a panel of experts to arrive at a consensus instead of taking one man's opinion or indulging in an open discussion to reach a consensus. Experts from a wide variety of related fields from both inside and outside an organisation's ranks are approached to fill out a detailed questionnaire about the problem under consideration without disclosing their identity. These opinions are then compiled and the summary of the responses is sent again to the experts and the experts are asked to reconsider and possibly revise their estimates and if it is out of line with others, to explain why. This process is repeated several times until a consensus prediction is arrived at. When a convergence of opinion begins to occur, the results are then used as an acceptable forecast.

The anonymity of the experts is an important element. It helps to avoid the possibility of a group's thinking status-consciousness, inter-personal conflict or social needs to colour the expert's opinion. This technique has come to be widely used successfully to forecast everything from future sales of a product to changes in complex phenomena such as social patterns and advanced technology.

Brainstorming

In this technique, persons equipped with good understanding of the scenario to be predicted assemble. It starts with someone proposing without first mentally screening them. Others then offer their ideas which are built on previous ideas and this process goes on as long as the consensus is reached. There is no place for any criticism in this technique. Brainstorming has found favour with operating managers who have conviction in "gut feel" and are loath to use quantitative "number crunching techniques".

Scenario Writing

Scenario writing is another widely employed technique, originated by Royal Dutch shell, where descriptions of different likely future scenarios are presented in a narrative fashion. The scenario may be merely a written description of some future situation in terms of key variables and issues or it may be generated in combination with other forecasting techniques.

When future scenario about a particular industry is forecasted and described in a narrative way, it is known as Industry Scenario. Such a scenario is developed by analysing the likely impact of future societal forces on key groups in a particular industry.[11]

Summary

In a highly dynamic and competitive environment, a firm, while formulating product-market strategy, must scan the macro-environment and discern opportunities emerging out of changes in the external environment which can be squeezed for improving competitiveness of the firm and identify impending threats to the firm.

In view of globalisation and liberalisation of economic system during the last three decades, leading to the emergence of global village, the management should analyse both local as well as global environment even though the firm may work locally.

Though a myriad of environmental forces—both direct and indirect—affect product-market options, the management should focus on economic, competitive, technological, political and socio-cultural factors. It is important to note that these forces are complex and inter-related.

While scanning economic environment the management needs to appraise how the economy and its various components are likely to behave and assess their implications on the firm's future. In this process, it would be pertinent to monitor secular trends in general economic condition, state of industries and supply of essential resources.

In view of rapid advancement of technology and its far reaching impact on efficiency of manufacturing and distribution and also the day-to-day lives of the people, it is always imperative to prognosticate the future changes in technology and determine their effect on the firm's product line, magnitude of operations, production quality and control and cost structure.

In studying behavioural changes of the political environment, the focus should be on current political system of the country, and the roles played by the government and the pressure groups. The management must interact with these forces to seize the opportunities offered by the government and minimise the risks inherent in the environment.

Corporate strategist should assess the demographic environment and identify broad characteristic of the population that affect the firm. An alert management will have plenty of advance notice of potential changes in demographic factors and can start searching for new product lines and more attractive markets.

An enterprise, to survive and succeed in the long run, needs to sense and respond to the changes in the socio-cultural environment of the society in which it is operating and/or in which it intends to operate in future. While analysing the socio-cultural environment, the management should factor in attitudes, values, desires, expectations, degrees of intelligence and education, beliefs and customs of people, traditions and social institutions, class structure and social group pressure and dynamics, and attempt to assess their implications on the firm's business.

The management can make use of a slew of techniques to undertake effective appraisal of the environment. Among these, the important ones are factor listing, time series analysis, casual modelling, jury of opinion, sales force composite, customer expectation methods, Delphi, brainstorming and scenario writing.

Key Terms

Brainstorming	Economic scanning	Legal environment
Competitive intelligence	Environmental scanning	Political environment
Customer expectation method	Industrial scenario	Scenario writing
Delphi technique	International macro-environment	Socio-Cultural environment
Demographic environment	Jury of opinion	Technological environment

Discussion Questions

1. What do you mean by external environment? Discuss the major components of external environment.
2. Bring out the distinguishing characteristics of a macro environment.
3. "Environmental forces are interdependent and effect each other". Elucidate this statement with suitable examples.
4. Discuss the significance of environmental scanning in strategic decisions.
5. How can a strategy maker identify strategic factors in the corporation's domestic as well as international environment?
6. What are the macro-environmental forces that the management of an enterprise should scan and monitor for strategy formulation?
7. "Major firms cannot survive and thrive without analysing their general environment and acting upon the trends identified. Scanning and monitoring are activities they cannot afford to ignore". Comment.
8. What aspects of economic environment should a corporate planner scan for his firm?
9. Discuss the relevance of socio-cultural environment scanning in strategic decisions of a firm.
10. What effect does a political environment have on the strategic making of a firm? How can a planner respond to these influences?
11. "The fortunes of a business depend, to a large extent, on its external environment". Discuss this statement and show how the macro environment can be effectively monitored.
12. Discuss in brief the various techniques of environmental search.

References

1. Ginter, P. and J. Duncan, "Macro Environmental Analysis for Strategic Management", *Long Range Planning*, 23(**6**), pp. 91–100, 1990.
2. Thomas, J.B., S.M. Clark and D.A. Gioia, "Strategy Sense Making and Organisational Performance: Linkages Among Scanning, Interpretation, Action, Outcomes," *Academy of Management Journal*, April, pp. 239–270, 1993.
3. Mercer, D., *Marketing Strategy: The Challenge of the External Environment*, Open University, Milton Keynes, 1998.
4. *Business Standard*, November 19, 2009.
5. Glueek, William F., *Business Policy and Strategic Management*, McGraw-Hill, Kogakusher, Tokyo, pp. 48–51, 1970.
6. Kahaner, L., *Competitive Intelligence*, Simon & Schuster, New York, 1996.
7. Shaker, S.M. and M.P. Gembiki, *War Room Guide to Competitive Intelligence*, McGraw Hill, New York, p. 10, 1999.

8. Vedder, R.G., "CEO and CIO Attitude about competitive intelligence", *Competitive Intelligence Magazine*, October–December, pp. 39–41, 1999.

9. Elien, "Textbook of Econometrics and Powell", *Econometrics of Macro and Monetary Relations*, Wiley, New York, 1973.

10. North, H.Q. and D.L. Pyke, Probes of the Technological Future, *Harward Business Review*, 47(**3**), May–June, pp. 69–81, 1969.

11. Porter, Michacl E., *Competitive Advantage*, Free Press, New York, pp. 448–470, 1985.

Internet Resources

- *www.businesstoday.in*
- *www.business-standard.com*

6

Scanning
Competitive Environment

LEARNING OBJECTIVES

The present Chapter aims at:
- Providing a critical view of Porter's 'five forces framework'.
- Furnishing vivid view of the impact of collective strength of the five competitive forces.
- Bringing out significance of co-opetition in competitive environment.

INTRODUCTION

In view of the increasing ferocity of competitive pressure across the globe in recent few decades due to incredible policies of liberalisation, privatisation and globalisation and technological advancements at breakneck speed, leading to integration of world economies, growing similarity of countries in terms of available infrastructure, fluid global financial markets, changing attitude of MNCs from the US and Japan from rivalry to alliances, it would be pertinent for the top management of a company to scan and monitor competitive environment of the industry within which the company operates and assesses its impact on its current product-market strategy, and also to assess how it can achieve competitive advantage. Such an analysis has even become more important in India which has, of late, witnessed an unprecedented change in the consumer and the market place and an acceleration of competitive intensity.

The nature of competition in an industry is contingent essentially upon developments taking place in the competitive environment. The competitive environment and the level of competition should be analysed from the viewpoint of all such forces as affect the fierceness of competitive behaviour. These forces have been logically identified and discussed by Michael Porter in his epoch making treatise, "Competitive Strategy:

Techniques for Analysing Industries and Competitors".[1] The collective strength of these forces, according to Porter, determines the ultimate profit potential in the industry, where profit potential is measured in terms of long-run return on invested capital.[2]

The **Five Forces Framework** of Porter should be undertaken from the perspective of an incumbent organisation. However, it can also be gainfully used by a firm outside an industry to determine whether it should enter the industry. In such cases, the barriers to entry which may be protecting the incumbents is an additional cost that outsiders must factor into their analysis of whether to enter the industry.

PORTER'S FIVE FORCES FRAMEWORK: AN OVERVIEW

Porter's five forces model, depicted in Figure 6.1, is a powerful analytical technique that can be employed to diagnose systematically the major competitive pressures in a market and assess how strong and important each one is. It enables an organisation to determine the attractiveness of a particular industry by examining the interaction of five competitive forces.

The five forces are: (1) threat of new entrants, (2) bargaining power of buyers, (3) bargaining power of suppliers, (4) threat of substitute products or services, and (5) intensity of rivalry among firms in an industry. By analysing these forces, an organisation can gain insight into how effectively it can compete in an industry. The five forces framework is founded on an economic theory on '**The Structure-conduct-performance (SCP) model**' which states that the structure of an industry determines an organisation's competitive behaviour (conduct) which, in turn, determines its profitability (performance).[3]

Figure 6.1 Forces driving industry competition.

With the help of five forces framework, an organisation can make informed decisions, given its resources, about whether competitive rivalry, bargaining power of suppliers, bargaining power of buyers, threat of new entrants and threat of substitutes make the industry an attractive and profitable one to compete in. The decision to continue or exit the industry can be objectively made on the basis of the Porter's model. Use of this model can aid an organisation to improve its competitive position in relation to industry trends. For instance, an awareness of a trend toward consolidation among suppliers (leading to strengthening of supplier power) might suggest the management to further deepen its relationship with the existing suppliers to escape from downward pressures on its profit margins. Thus, prognosticating future trends in the five forces provides an insightful indication of future profits in the industry.

While assessing the five forces, strategists should remember that each competitive force will have different impact on their industry. They should, therefore, try to understand the relative impact of each of the five forces on their industry structure. This will enable them to determine their ability to influence the forces with the greatest impact on their industry structure through their strategy formulation.

A strategist can analyse any industry by rating each competitive force as high, medium or low in strength. For example, the Health and Wellness segment of Food and Beverage industry and skin products industry in India could be currently rated as under: rivalry is high; threat of potential entrants is high; threat of substitutes is high; bargaining power of suppliers is medium but rising (suppliers are gaining in size); bargaining power of buyers is high. Based on the current trends in each of these competitive forces, the industry appears to be increasing in its level of competitive intensity, signifying falling profit margins in the industry.

Analysing the Five Competitive Forces

1. Threat of New Entrants

Attractiveness of an industry depends, inter alia, on the opportunity to new companies to enter the business. Where firms in an industry are raking earnings in excess of their cost, it will be tempting for new entrepreneurs to enter the industry. This will lead to more intense competition, thus posing challenge to existing firms. It will, therefore, be in fitness of things for the existing firms to analyse the threat of entry barriers, which act to prevent an influx of firms into an industry whenever profits, adjusted for the cost of capital, rise above zero. Entry barriers exist whenever it is difficult or not economically viable for a new entrepreneur to replicate the incumbents' position. Where entry barriers are high, the threat of entry of new firms in the industry will be low.

Some of the possible barriers to entry are economies of scale, product differentiation, capital requirements, switching costs, access to distribution channels, cost and resource advantages independent of size and government policy.

Economies of scale deter entry by forcing the entrant to come in as large organisations or come in at a small scale and accept a cost disadvantage. For instance, scale of economies in operations, research and marketing and service are probably the main barriers to entry in the mainframe computer industry, as Xerox and General Electric discovered.

Product differentiation is another potent barrier to entry when incumbent firms have well-established brand names and clearly differentiated product, forcing entrants to spend heavily on advertising and promotion, to overcome present customer loyalties. For instance, in electronics and automotive industry, Japanese consumers have strong preference for Japanese brands. A potential entrant may, therefore, find it uneconomical to undertake the marketing campaign necessary to introduce its own products effectively. Further, it may take years for the entrepreneur to build reputation for product quality, no matter how large its initial advertising campaign is.

High capital investment required to compete successfully in the market creates an obstruction to entry particularly if the fund is required for risky or unrecoverable up-front advertisements or research and development. For example, entry barrier is very high in the oil industry because huge capital investments are involved in exploration and in plant and machinery.

Switching cost is another source of entry barrier. Switching cost is one time cost which arises out of switching over by the buyer from one supplier's product to another's. Where these switching costs are high, the new entrants must offer a major improvement in cost of performance so as to entice the buyer from an incumbent.

Access to distribution channels may prove to be an obstacle to new entrants, especially in consumer goods industry, in gaining access to consumers because supermarket retailers are not keen to provide shelf space to new products from small producers who may not have sufficient resources to advertise their products effectively. The new entrant may have to persuade the channels to accept its product through price breaks, cooperative advertising allowances and the like, which reduce profit margin.

Cost advantages to incumbent firms independent of their size may at times limit the prospects of entry by new firms. For instance, Tata's *Nano* car at the global cheapest price because of adoption of new technology and new business model has created formidable problem for new entrants in small car field.

The **existing policy of government** is yet another source of entry barrier. Government can limit or even foreclose entry of new firms to industries by clamping such as licensing requirements and limits on access to raw materials. More subtle government restrictions on entry can stem out of controls such as setting air and water pollution standards and producing safety and efficiency regulations. The Government policy of denying Chinese telecom companies from selling equipments in India on security ground is a case in point.

2. Bargaining Power of Buyers

Competitive pressure in an industry can be exerted by buyers through their ability to squeeze industry margins by forcing companies to either reduce prices, or increase the level of service offered without recompense or to provide higher quality and to play competitors off against each other.

Bargaining power of buyers is dependent on a host of characteristics of the market situation and on the relative importance of its purchases to the industry compared to its overall business. Probably, the most important determinants of buyers' power are concentration of buyers and the volume of purchase of any one buyer. Buyers' power is strong where there is a concentration of buyers in relation to the number of suppliers. Automakers have historically enjoyed considerable leverage in dealing with steel makers. They have a strong bargaining power in negotiating for buying original equipment tyres from Firestone, Continental, Good year, and so on.

A buyer making large purchases like Wal-Mart, can exert tremendous pressure on its suppliers' margins.

Buyers are also powerful if they have the potential to integrate backward by producing the product itself. For example, a newspaper chain could make its own paper.

The buyers' power increases where alternative suppliers are plentiful because the product is standard or undifferentiated. Motorists, for example, can choose among many petrol retail outlets.

Where the costs to the buyer in switching over suppliers is low or entails less risk, the buyers' power is enhanced.

A buyer making low profits will always scout suppliers selling required quality goods at lower costs and therefore, be sensitive to costs and service differences. Where buyers are highly profitable they will generally be less price sensitive.

Where the quality of the buyer's final product is not significantly affected by the industry's supplies, the buyer will be more price sensitive and therefore, in a better bargaining position.

Well-informed buyers are in a better position to negotiate a better deal from suppliers.

Where demand of a product is declining, the bargaining power of the buyers is strengthened. On the contrary, strong demand creates sellers' market weakening the power of buyers.

Buyer bargaining position can obviously be offset in situations in which competitors are themselves concentrated or differentiated. Both these conditions have helped manufacturers of stainless, especially steels, achieve higher rates of profitability than large, integrated steel makers.

3. Bargaining Power of Suppliers

Suppliers can exert bargaining power on participants in an industry through their ability to raise prices or reduce quality of purchased goods and services. Powerful suppliers can thereby squeeze profitability out of an industry unable to recoup cost increase in its own prices. A supplier can enjoy the commanding position where:

(a) the suppliers' industry is dominated by a few companies and is more concentrated than the industry it sells to;
(b) there are few or no substitute supplies available;
(c) the buyer does not represent significant proportion of the suppliers' sales;
(d) the suppliers' product or service is unique and/or it has built up switching costs (as in the case of word processing software);
(e) the suppliers' products constitute an important input of the buyers' business; and
(f) there is a threat of forward integration and the suppliers have power to integrate forward into the buyers' industry and compete with the buyers.

4. Threat of Substitutes

Product substitutes limit the expected returns of an industry by placing a ceiling on the prices firms in the industry can profitably charge. The threat that substitutes pose to an industry's profitability depends on the relative price-to-performance ratios of the different types of products or services to which customer can turn to satisfy the same basic need. The threat of substitution is also affected by switching costs—i.e., the costs in areas such as retraining, retooling or redesigning, incurred when a customer switches over to a different type of product or service.

Substitute materials that are exerting pressure on the steel industry include plastics, aluminium, and ceramics. The industry must also reckon with the substitution threat associated with less-intensive use of steel in the end-products such as cars. Aluminium's lighter weight and superior lithographic characteristics enable it to take volume away from steel despite higher prices.

It is important to note that any analysis of the substitution must factor in all products that perform similar functions for customers, not just at physically similar products.

Analysis of the substitution possibilities open to buyers should be supplemented by taking into consideration the possibilities available to suppliers.[4] Supply side substitutability influences suppliers' willingness to provide required inputs, just as demand-side substitutability influences buyers' willingness to pay for products. For example, integrated steel makers who mix steel scrap with iron ore as inputs into their production processes, have not been able to hold down swap prices because of growing demand for scrap from mini mills, which use it as their primary input.

5. Intensity of Rivalry among Existing Competitors

A firm's ability to earn profits in excess of its cost also depends on degree of intensity of rivalry among the existing competitors arising out of the pressure on profit margin and/or opportunity to improve position. Moves and countermoves by competitors and use of tactics like price competition, advertising battles, product introductions and enhanced customer service for outsmarting the rivals are very likely to affect all firms in the industry culminating in the exit of marginal firms. Rivalry among existing competitors can best be understood from Illustrative Capsule 6.1.

ILLUSTRATIVE CAPSULE 6.1

RIVALRY AMONG EXISTING COMPETITORS

Nokia cut the profit outlook recently for its key phone unit as the world's top cellphone maker struggles in the market for more expensive handsets, sending its shares sharply lower.

Nokia still lacks top-range model to challenge Apple's iphone three years after its launch. Its last high-end hit phone was the N95, which was unveiled in 2006.

"Everyone wants an iphone and their competitors have now made it impossible for them", said David Buik, partner at BGC Partners.

Shares in Nokia were 12.7% lower at £9.85 by 1036 GMT, dragging the STOXX Europe 600 Technology Index 3.4% lower.

Apple's quarterly results blew past Wall Street expectations on the back of record iphone sales earlier in the last week of April, 2010 and the company gave a strong revenue forecast, sending its shares to an all time high.

The smart phone market continued to expand through the economic downturn helped by cheaper models, and research from Gartner has forecast that it will grow a whopping 46% this year.

Nokia is benefiting from growth among cheap smart phones, and with analysts at Goldman Sachs estimating Nokia has a 70% market share in that segment.

However, average sales price of a Nokia smartphone dropped 17% from the quarter January–March 2010 to just £155 ($208.4).

Nokia also delayed the renewal of its Symbian Software-seen as crucial to improve its position in the high-end of the market—from April to July, 2010.

The degree of rivalry among firms is an outcome of host of factors such as number of and type of competitors, industry growth rate, fixed costs, degree of differentiation, scope of capacity augmentation, and diversity of competitors.

Existence of a large number of competitors or relatively few firms but balanced in terms of size and perceived resources paves way for instability in the industry because the firms may be prone to outbeat each other and manage resources to ensure sustained and aggressive tight. Conversely, when the industry leader is dominated by a few firms and every firm is aware of each other's relative strength, the industry leader is likely to impose discipline as well as play a coordinating role in the industry through devices like price leadership.

Rivalry in an industry tends to be more unstable if a number of firms have high stakes in achieving success there. For example, a diversified firm may accord greater value to achieving success in a particular industry so as to further its overall corporate strategy or a firm in its endeavour to build global prestige or technological credibility may perceive a strong need to establish a solid position in a foreign developed market. Under the circumstances, the goals of the firms might not only be diverse but even more destabilising because they are expansionary and involve potential willingness to sacrifice profitability.

Slow growth rate increases intensity of competition in the industry while rapid growth rate opens opportunity to every firm in the industry to improve its performance just by keeping pace with the industry.

High fixed costs in relation to value added and not as a proportion of total costs create strong pressure for all firms to utilise full capacity which is likely to lead to rapidly calculating price cutting.

Absence of product differentiation results in intensity of price and service competition which is generally volatile.

Where scale of economies warrant capacity addition to a large extent, such capacity additions may lead to volatility to the industry supply/demand balance, especially when there is a threat of bunching capacity additions.

Intensity of rivalry among the competitors and so also pressure on profitability will tend to be high where competitors have differing strategies, origins, personalities and relationships to their parent organisations as also varying rules of game for the industry. Illustrative Capsule 6.1 gives idea about rivalry of some companies.

The existence of high exit barriers may hinder firms needing to exit the industry. Decrease in demand will result in creation of excess capacity in the industry and consequent reduction in profit margin within the industry. For example, in case of firms engaged in producing highly specialised products, it will be very difficult to produce alternative goods.

Critical Evaluation of Porter's Five Forces Framework

Porter's five forces analysis has been subject to a slew of criticisms. These criticisms emanate mainly out of different perspectives on how sustainable competitive advantage might be achieved. Some of these criticisms are discussed below:

(i) Porter's assumption that five forces framework involve a zero-sum game, i.e., the competitors can only succeed at the expense of other players in the industry, does not always hold true because organisations being aware of the added value that other players such as suppliers can create, may forgo alliance with these suppliers which benefit both parties. Toyota and Honda, for example, closely work with their suppliers to ensure availability of the parts and equipments at the right prices, at the right time and of the specified quality so as to reduce inventory and associated costs.

Porter admits that there is always a possibility of emerging strategic move in every company. However, he points out that a company needs to see the design, see how pieces fit together, and make interdependent choices consistent for making strategy a success.

(ii) Another criticism of the Porter's analysis is that it is not a dynamic analysis and throws little light on how players in the industry interact with each other in rapidly changing environmental conditions. According to C.K. Prahlad,[5] strategy is not about positioning the company in a given industry space but about influencing, shaping and actually creating industry space. He argues that there is need for a new paradigm which embraces disruptive competitive changes. Likewise, D'Aveni[6] argued that in hyper competitive environment, organisations would not tolerate existence of any competitors and would employ all the tools to destabilise a competitor's competitive advantage through creating constant disequilibrium and change.

Brandburger and Nalebuff[7] used the concept of co-opetition to show how organisations can collaborate and compete with their competitors to create a larger industry in which everyone gains.

In response to this criticism, Porter observed that the five forces model applies at any point of time. In fact, this model, he contended, helps to reveal whether changes in the industry are important. However, Porter admits that there is room for more research work to be done to understand how the elements of industry emerge and the linkage between organisational behaviour and industry structure.

(iii) According to the Porter's model, competitive strategy is the outcome of deliberate assessment of the attractiveness of the industry and the position a firm occupies against five competitive forces. However, in real life, unexpected changes in the external environment, according to Mintzberg and Waters,[8] may compel organisations to make ad hoc decisions to cope with any unforeseen situation. Thus, in this case, the strategy being followed is not planned but is allowed to emerge in response to changes in the competitive environment. Furthermore, in emerging industries where it is not easy to identify who the rivals are, use of the five forces framework will not be helpful.

DETERMINING THE IMPACT OF COLLECTIVE STRENGTH OF THE FIVE COMPETITIVE FORCES

After discerning the specific competitive pressures comprising each force and assessing if these competitive pressures constitute a strong or weak competitive force, a strategic manager needs to evaluate the combined strength of the five forces and determine the impact of state of competition on profit margin of the industry.

Generally speaking, there exists negative correlation between state of competition and profit margin of the industry. The higher the degree of competition of the five competitive forces, the lower the profit margin of the players in the industry. An industry will be competitively unattractive when there is low entry barrier, rivalry among sellers is vigorous, competition from substitutes is intense, and is able to exert considerable bargaining power with buyers and suppliers. Even intense competitive pressures from just two or three of the five competitive forces may be strong enough to affect adversely the overall profitability of the industry, forcing marginal firms to exit the business. This is true especially in the case of tire manufacturing and apparel industries where profit margins have historically been low.[9]

Conversely, an industry will be competitively attractive and the participants can expect reasonably high profit margin if the collective impact of the five competitive forces is moderate to weak. The competitive environment for raking high profits will be ideal when there exists high barriers to prevent further entry of new players, when rivalry among the players is not intense, and when both buyers' and suppliers' bargaining positions are weak. In case a company is not making good profits even when the state of competition is weak, it is indicative of the company's weak competitive position.

Competitive pressure on Coca-Cola India can be illustrated through Illustrative Capsule 6.2.

ILLUSTRATIVE CAPSULE **6.2**

COMPETITIVE PRESSURE ON COCA-COLA INDIA

The cola war is passe; it is time now for the battle over nimbu paani. A year after its arch rival launched and made a huge success of *Nimbooz*, a lemon-based drink, Coca-Cola has finally got into the act.

Coke's *Nimbu Fresh*, launched in January 2010 under the Minute Maid brand will be initially available in 35,000 outlets in Tamil Nadu and will be rolled out nationally later in 2010. The plan is to reach 90,000 outlets by 2010 itself.

Coca-Cola in India currently enjoys market leadership in the juice drink segment with brand *Maaza* and *Minute Maid Pulpy orange* and the company hopes *Nimbu Fresh* will further extend its leadership in this fast growing segment.

Analysts, however say that Coke's delay in entering the lime-based drink market is surprising. Even Parle Agro has got a head start with *LMN* as lemon is the most popular flavour with a share of 49% of the total juice-based drink market. Of the total packaged juice market of 90 million cases (one case is around 5–6 litres of beverage), juice-based drinks account for about 90%.

However, Coca-Cola India's Vice-President (Marketing) says the company is not in a race with its competitors and is rather interested in launching the best product. But the Cola major was obviously conscious of the fact that it is a late entrant and has to do something to make up for lost time. That explains its move to price *Nimbu Fresh* aggressively. While *Nimbooz* is available in 200 ml and 350 ml plastic bottles at ₹10 and ₹15, respectively, a 400 ml *Nimbu Fresh* will cost ₹15. There will also be a one-litre bottle for ₹40.

The positioning of the lemon-based drinks by all the three players is almost similar. They are looking at making a dent in the large unorganised segment with each claiming that their products taste closest to home-made lemonade drink. While Pepsi is marketing *Nimbooz* with the promise that it tastes as good as the original 'nimbu paani', Coke is playing on the theme—'*Bilkul Ghar Jaisa*' (just like home), as its punchline.

Both Coke and PepsiCo have lime offerings already—*Limca*, *Sprite*, *7UP* and so on. But company's executives say these are carbonated beverages and would not compete with the nimbu paani offerings.

Though the earlier examples of trying to introduce packaged drinks like tender coconut have not succeeded, Pepsi and Parle have already hit on the Jackpot with *Nimbooz* and *LMN* with sales much above their own expectations. Technology had played a big role to play in this. While nimbu paani made at home does not have much shelf life, Pespi had used a technology called 'hotfill' that increases the shelf life of *Nimbooz* as much as four months.

Industry experts estimate the nimboo paani market to be atleast around a billion cases by volume in 2010. The juice and juice drinks market is pegged yearly at ₹1,500 crore or 500 million cases by volume. According to an industry expert, 90% of consumption of packaged juice and cold drinks is out of home, giving companies a great opportunity to grow.

CO-OPETITION AND COMPETITIVE ENVIRONMENT

Porter's five forces framework provides seering insight into the impact of each of the five competitive forces on attractiveness of industry. According to Porter's analysis, in a highly competitive environment where there is low entry barriers, rivalry among sellers' vigorous, there is threat of substitution, and both buyers and sellers are able to exert high bargaining power, profitability of the industry will be low, forcing the exit of marginal firms. However, this does not always hold true in dynamically changing competitive conditions when certain organisations may embark on 'co-opetition' strategy to create value for the industry as a whole which may be beneficial to all the players in the market. Thus, Brandenburger and Nalebuff was[10] of the view that some organisations in their attempt to create value for the entire industry produce products and services which complement (or support) those of other organisations and therefore, add value within the industry. Such organisations which supply complements to the industry and in so doing create value for the industry and affect its dynamics through their bargaining power, are termed as *complementors*. Instead of win-lose, there will exist an explicit recognition that a sustainable strategy can involve both cooperation and competition. There is cooperation among suppliers, organisations and customers to create value, and competition, on how this value is divided up. Thus instead of viewing substitutes as inherently adversarial and complements as friendly, an organisation can have elements of cooperation in its interactions with its substitutes and competitive elements with complementors.[11] Figure 6.2 clearly explains this idea.

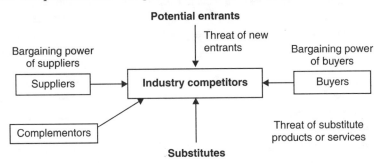

Figure 6.2 The inclusion of complementors within Porter's five forces framework.

If we look at the relationship between Microsoft and Intel, it becomes apparent that this is not one of customers and suppliers but one of complementors, i.e., the dual-core microprocessors provided by Intel allow the software provided by Microsoft to run more quickly and efficiently without Intel's innovative processors and Microsoft's upgraded software. Similarly, without Microsoft's upgraded products which require faster processor speeds would be less reason to buy Intel's improved processors.[12] The recent tie up of Tata Tea with its competitor PepsiCo (Illustrative Capsule 6.3) is a case in point. Bharti Airtel, which aquired Zain Telecom's assets in 16 African countries in 2010 has, of late, decided to pursue strategy of co-opetition to reduce capital cost and improve profitability. It has now started collaborative discussions with all its key competitors—MTN, Voda com, Orange, Millicom and Etisalat for sharing tower infrastructure and back-end fibre networks. These competitors are very eager to share tower and fibre infrastructure so that the costs can come down.

ILLUSTRATIVE CAPSULE 6.3

CO-OPETITION OF TATA TEA WITH PEPSI CO

Tion, the cold beverage from the Tata Tea, which has extracts of tea, ginseng and fruit, was launched with much fun fare in 2009. But a year on, the product exists in two states only—Tamil Nadu and Kerala.

In competitive segments such as fruit drinks, which estimated to be ₹2,500 crore in size, growing at a steady clip is not enough, say experts. According to them, one needs to have the wherewithal, the muscle power and the strength to carry on in a competitive segment such as this. Tata Tea has been tad slow even in launching the product in a few regions before going in for a full-blown national launch. In fact, *Tion* is hardly visible in the market place.

This piecemeal approach to the brand, according to experts, lies in the company's inability to compete with the like of PepsiCo and Coca-Cola in a segment that they clearly dominate. *Nimbooz*, a lemon flavoured drink launched by PepsiCo in 2009 is said to be clocking sales of over 2,00,000 bottles per day or 70,00,000 bottles per month. Coca-Cola's *Minute Maid Nimbu Fresh*, launched a few months earlier, is also doing sales of above 2.5 million bottles per month. As against this, *Tion*, is now doing sales of about 20,00,000 per month in the 250-ml segment, while the larger 400-ml variant with sales of about 2,00,00 bottles per month.

Under the circumstances, Tata Tea decided recently to tie up with its competitor PepsiCo, signing a memorandum of understanding with the latter for a new non-carbonated beverage entity.

Tying up with PepsiCo will allow Tata Tea to leverage the latter's skills in the non-carbonated beverage business—something it needs badly if it has to emerge as a well-rounded beverage major.

Health and wellness is a market too hard to resist, given that overall beverage consumption is moving there, whether in India or abroad. According to a recent report prepared by the Tata Strategic Management Group, health and wellness beverages in India are likely to grow at 22% year on from 2014–15. The market at the moment is about ₹6,200 crore in size including fruit juices, cold drinks, energy and sports drinks, and so on. Worldwide, the health and wellness market (including food and beverages) is already over $460 billion in size.

PepsiCo knows well the implications of playing in this market. It already has a $10 billion health-drink business worldwide. The company plans to triple its health-drink business over the next 10 years. Tie-ups in the area are likely to help further the cause as PepsiCo looks to shed its image as a make of Cola drinks alone. The MOU with Tata Tea in the Indian market is yet another step in this direction.

So *Tion* and other products like it do have a future in the end.

Thus, to survive successfully on a sustainable basis in competitive environment, an organisation has to create value for the industry as a whole and create larger market which can at best be done by cooperating with customers and suppliers. At the same time, an organisation needs to be concerned with how this large market is to be divided, i.e., its competitive position.

In view of the above, a complementary as sixth force needs to be included in the Porter's five competitive forces so as to make the model more logical in the dynamically changing competitive environment. In that case, the six-force model will evolve, as shown in Figure 6.2.

Summary

The competitive environment and the state of competition need to be analysed from the viewpoint of all such forces as to affect the ferocity of competitive behaviour. These forces have been forcefully identified and discussed by Michael Porter. Porter's five forces model is a powerful analytical tool that can be employed to diagnose systematically the major competitive pressures in a market and assess how strong and important each one is. The five forces are threat of new entrants, bargaining power of buyers, bargaining power of suppliers, threat of substitute products and intensity of rivalry among firms in an industry. Given its resources, a firm can take a decision as to which industries it can most effectively compete in and position itself to reduce the adverse effects of these forces.

Porter's model has been questioned on its static nature which is contested by Brandenburger and Nalebuff. In a dynamically changing competitive environment, an organisation, to survive successfully on sustainable basis, has to create value for the industry as a whole and create a larger market by cooperating with customers and suppliers and at the same time competing with the other players on how value is to be divided. Thus, Brandenburger and Nalebuff introduced the concept of co-opetition and value net in assessing the competitive environment. They hold the view that Porter's five force model should be supplemented by sixth force as complementary.

Key Terms

Complementor	Entry barriers	Switching costs
Co-opetition	Entry threat	Threat of substitution
Disruptive competitive change	Intensity of rivalry	Zero-sum game
Economies of scale		

Discussion Questions

1. Why is it pertinent for a company to assess competitive environment of the industry?
2. Critically examine Porter's five forces model for studying competitive environment of an industry.
3. Why is it important to analyse entry threat? How should threat of new entrants be assessed?
4. How does bargaining power of buyers exert competitive pressure on suppliers?
5. How can bargaining power of suppliers influence competitive environment of the industry?
6. To what extent does intensity of rivalry among existing competitors affect the state of competition in the industry?
7. How should combined strength of the five competitive forces be evaluated and its impact on profit margin of the industry examined?
8. What is co-opetition? Discuss its significance in the analysis of competitive environment of an industry?
9. "Inclusion of complementor as sixth force in Porter's Five Forces Framework would render the model more useful in studying the state of competition in an industry". Discuss.

References

1. Porter, Michael E., *Competitive Strategy: Techniques For Analysing Industries and Competitors*, Free Press, New York, 1980.
2. Ibid, *Competitive Strategy.*
3. Henry, Anthony, *Understanding Strategic Management*, Oxford University Press, New Delhi, p. 70, 2008.

4. Brandenburger, Adam and Stuart W. Harborne, Jr. "Value-Based Business Strategy", *Journal of Economics and Management Strategy*, (5) pp. 5–29, 1996.

5. Prahlad, C.K., "Changes in the Competitive Battlefield", in *Mastering Strategy*, T. Disckson (Ed.), Prentice Hall, Harlow, pp. 75–80, 2000.

6. D'Aveni, R.A., *Hyper Competition: Managing the Dynamics of Strategic Manoeuring*, Free Press, New York, 1994.

7. Brandenburger, Adam, and B.J. Nalebuff, "Co-opetition: Competitive and Cooperative Business Strategies for the Digital Economy", *Strategy and Leadership*, 25(**6**), 30, 1995.

8. Mintzberg, H. and J.A. Waters, Of Strategies, deliberate and emergent, *Strategic Management Journal*, 6(**3**), 257–72.

9. Thompson, Arthur A., Jr. and others, *Crafting and Executing Strategy*, McGraw Hill, New Delhi, p. 67, 2008.

10. Brandenburger, Adam, and Nalebuff, Co-opetition, *Currency Doubleday*, New York, 1996.

11. Brandenburger, Adam and Nalebuff, "Co-opetition of Competitive and Cooperative Business Strategies for the Digital Economy", *Strategy and Leadership*, 25(**6**), 30, 1997.

12. Henry, Anthony, *Understanding Strategic Management*, Oxford University Press, New Delhi, p. 84, 2008.

Internet Resources

- *www.business.standard.com*
- *www.business.standard.com*

7

Scanning
Internal Environment

LEARNING OBJECTIVES

The present Chapter aims at:

- Providing a resource-based view of internal environment.
- Sensitizing readers to the process of scanning internal environment.
- Dilating upon the strategic issues involved in internal environmental scanning.
- Acquainting readers with the core competence and leveraging of resources.

INTRODUCTION

In a fiercely competitive environment, a company to survive and grow successfully, must have competitive advantage. A company has sustainable and profitable competitive advantage when it has edge over its rivals in attracting customers and defending against competitive forces. Where there is a match between the distinctive competencies of a company—a unique strength that allows it to achieve superior efficiency, quality, innovation or customer responsiveness, and to create superior value—and the factors critical for success within its industry that permits the company to outperform competitors, competitive advantage is said to exist. For example, Bharti Airtel's "least-cost business model", where just about every activity from network operations to IT is outsourced, provides the company sustainable competitive advantage (Illustrative Capsule 7.1).

Breakthrough innovations in everything from wind turbines to X-ray machines to new-age locomotives provide GE a competitive superiority over its rivals.

Likewise, superior technology and competitive prices give Exide a huge scope to compete and grow (Illustrative Capsule 7.2).

ILLUSTRATIVE CAPSULE 7.1

BHARTI AIRTEL'S COMPETITIVE ADVANTAGE

Bharti Airtel's "least-cost business model", where just about every activity from network operation to IT is outsourced, has got the cellular phone operators setting up and taking note. The management believes that in Indian telecom, which has the highest competitive intensity, lowest tariffs and infrastructural problems, innovation is more of a necessity and survival issue. Over the years, Airtel has brought to the market a number of innovative products and services such as Hello Tunes, Easy charge and Blackberry services. Airtel has a big portion of innovation portfolio in breakthrough projects. This is because its leaders want to take chances and make mistakes.

Airtel has gone to villages where there is no road, no bridge, no water, but there is Airtel with its "four-pillar strategy", covering—Network, Distribution, Service and Brand-building.

ILLUSTRATIVE CAPSULE 7.2

COMPETITIVE ADVANTAGE OF EXIDE INDUSTRIES

Kolkata-based Exide Industries is a leader in lead-acid storage batteries for the automotive and industrial sectors.

Although Exide has no control over sales of cars, about 77% of new cars sold in India come fitted with Exide batteries and need a replacement after two years. Recently, Exide has increased its presence by entering smaller Tier II and Tier III towns. From 30 locations in early 2008, it has over 200 across the country today.

Greater focus on replacement market is the result of robust demand in this market. The company's superior technology and competitive prices give it a huge advantage to compete and grow.

At the back end, Exide cuts costs by reducing its dependence on lead imports and acquiring two smelters. Exide has ensured that its lead requirements come from its own sources; against 28% in 2007–08, savings on raw materials cost was 8% in 2008–09.

Exide prefers to focus on below-the-line public utilities and product innovation.

So as to determine if a company possesses competitive advantage to compete in its markets and industries, it would be imperative to scan its internal environment. Scanning and analysing the external and competitive environment does not throw light on competitive advantage of the company. Contrary to the assertions of Michael Porter, Rumelt argues that the defining factor in differential firm performance is not the industry structure within which the company finds itself. Rather it is more with factors at the individual company level such as its resources that determine if the company will be able to take mileage of opportunities while avoiding threats.[1] This is why strategic management as a discipline is becoming increasingly concerned with the internal environment of the company.

Scanning internal environment, also known as **organisational analysis**, internal capability analysis, profiling the organisation or resource audit, is the process of assessing a company's posture relative to its current position, competition within and outside the industry, overall performance and its capability in terms of strengths and weaknesses.

Since internal environmental analysis is essentially concerned with identifying and developing a company's resources, it is characterised by the resource-based view of internal environment.

RESOURCE-BASED VIEW OF INTERNAL ENVIRONMENT

Resource-based view held by Prahalad and Hamel[2], Rumelt[3], Barney[4] and Peteraf[5] takes an inside-out approach. Since an enterprise is composed of resources and competencies, which can be configured or reconfigured to provide it with competitive advantage, the resource-based perspective becomes inside out. Thus, according to this approach, it is the internal resources that determine the strategic choices the company makes in competing in its external environment.

In contrast to Porter's argument that it is the industry structure within which organisations compete and how they position themselves against that structure which determines how profitable individual organisations will be, the resource-based view of competition holds that it is a cluster of resources and capabilities of an organisation that determine its competitive performance.

Thinking behind the resource-based perspective is that in real business world, variation of profit levels in firms within industries is as great as that between industries. If we compare the performance of IT firms including TCS, Infosys, Wipro and other firms, we find a great divergence in profitability among these firms that compete in the same industry.

According to this approach, competitive advantage of a firm is best sought by an examination first of its existing resources and competencies; then an assessment of their profit potential in relation to congruent opportunities presented by the market and the choice of strategies based upon possibilities this reveals. The task is then to fill whatever resource or competence gap is identified by stock taking of existing resources and competencies in relation to the perceived profit potential of a given opportunity. This will lead to emergence of a set of decisions to build competencies internally, to form alliances with other firms with complementary competencies or to acquire a firm with such competencies.

Thus, the resource-based view of competition points not to industry but to the resources and capabilities that a firm possesses or it might want to develop in order to achieve a sustainable competitive advantage.

Resources are regarded as inputs with which a firm carries out its activities. They do not create value for the firm themselves. It is only when they are put to some productive use, value follows. Resources of a firm may be tangible and intangible.[6] **Tangible resources** represent physical assets which a firm possesses and comprise physical resources such as buildings, machinery, materials and productive capacity, financial and human resources. **Intangible resources** refer to intellectual and technological resources and reputation and include firm's ability to innovate the speed with which innovation takes place. Firms equipped with precious tacit knowledge, which cannot easily be transferred because it is deeply rooted in employee experience or organisational culture and processes.[7]

Although existence of resources is important, they themselves do not confer any benefit on an enterprise. In fact, it is the efficacious configuration of resources that provides an enterprise with competencies or capabilities. A competence is the attribute that a firm requires so as to be able to compete in the market place. Usually a firm's competence emanates from deliberate efforts to develop the organisational ability to perform constructively. These efforts entail choosing talented people, upgrading and developing existing skills of the individuals and moulding the efforts and work product of individuals into a cooperative group effort to create organisational ability. Competence is, therefore, about the firm's skills at coordinating its existing resources and directing them to a productive use. With growing experience in performing the activity consistently well and at a reasonable cost, the firm's competence gets honed.

Competence is a prerequisite for a firm to compete in an industry. Competence of a firm, as noted above, is derived from its systems and processes. For example, an automobile company to compete in the market place must possess knowledge and skills about designing an engine and its body manufacture without which the company would not be effective in outbeating its rivals. Maruti Suzuki, in its efforts to combat intensive competitive pressure in the compact car segment in India, has, of late, decided to develop more fuel efficient engines which would offer a mileage of more than 20 km to a litre of fuel and bring about differentiation in its products. As such, a company to be distinctive, must have both resources and competencies.

While scanning internal environment of a firm, a strategist has to determine if the existing resources and capabilities of the firm are its strengths or weaknesses. A resource is a strength if it provides a firm with a competitive advantage. A strength is something a firm is good at doing or a characteristic that gives it an important capability. Strength can be in the form of skill or expertise of low-cost manufacturing, technological know-how, improved production processes, a proven record of defect-free manufacturing, excellent customer service, superb merchandising skills or unique advertising and promotional talents.[8] Hero Honda's biggest strength is its wide product range catering to all segments. Major strengths of Nestle—the world's biggest food company—are the trust of customers, passion for quality and clear business processes. The entire organisation is aligned behind these. Valuable physical and human assets as also valuable organisational assets and precious intangible assets such as powerful brand name, image of technological superiority as that of Sony and Dell and strong buyer loyalty and goodwill are strengths of an organisation. Worldwide trading infrastructure of Wal-Mart is its distinguished strength.

A weakness is something a company lacks or does poorly (in comparison to others) or does not have the capacity to do while its competitors have the capacity to do, putting it at a disadvantage. Relatively poor customer service of Citi Bank and ICICI Bank has been a great weakness of these banks adversely affecting their competitive position in the market.

PROCESS OF SCANNING THE INTERNAL ENVIRONMENT

Internal environmental analysis entails construction of capability profile of the company and comparing it with the profile of successful competitors in the industry so as to develop a pattern of company's strengths and weakness in relation to its current product-market strategy. It will be in fitness of things to assess the company's strengths not only in relation to the competitive rivals of the industry to which the company belongs but also with the industries into which it seeks to diversify. The organisation's deficiencies should be compared with those of its successful rivals.

Thus, the process of appraisal of corporate competence involves identifying strategic factors which are crucial to the success of an organisation such as those relating to marketing, operations, finance, human resources, R&D and management, and determining the importance of each of these factors, especially in terms of the amount of contribution which each factor makes to the organisation in the attainment of its desired objectives, determining the strengths and weaknesses of the organisation in each of these factors by comparing with the firm's own past results, comparing with what they ought to be and finally preparing a strategic advantage profile for the firm and comparing it with the profiles of successful competitors in the industry.

Analysing the Strengths and Weaknesses of an Organisation

We shall now discuss the factors of a business organisation which should be appraised to determine its strengths and weaknesses, and how this appraisal should be made. As indicated earlier, the management should confine the competence analysis to those crucial factors, which contribute to the accomplishment of the overall desired result of the organisation. These factors might be traced in functional areas such as marketing, operations, finance, human resource, research and development and management systems because activities of these areas have their bearing on the overall performance of the enterprise. Their contribution may be positive or negative.

Marketing

Assessment of the marketing position of a firm is the most vital task in the analysis of its capability. This task relates the enterprise to the outside world and is a vital force in securing competitive advantages.[9]

In determining marketing strengths and weaknesses of the organisation, the management should study its competitive position, product mix, product life cycle, marketing research, channels of distribution, sales force, pricing and promotional efforts.

The first important aspect which the management has to investigate while assessing the marketing position of the enterprise is its competitive position in different product lines and outside the country. A distinct measure of the competitive position of the firm is the percentage of industry sales and major competitors' sales in the total company sales. Analysis of trends of these percentages indicates share of the market the company presently holds in a particular country and how firmly it is, whether the company is so big that its activities are likely to bring prompt responses from other leading companies in the country or the company may be small enough to enjoy independent maneouverability. Hero Honda's biggest success has been its ability to nudge market share upwards—from 52% to 57% in 2008–09. Of course, to be most meaningful, these percentages should be computed separately for product lines and type of customers.

Product-wise analysis of competitive position shows whether the company is the market leader in one product or more than one product or several products. Where the company is market leader in more than one product, it will be regarded as strength of the company. On the contrary, heavy dependence of the company on a single product for its earnings is a clear symptom of its weak marketing position particularly when the product life is in the declining phase.

Appraisal of the marketing position of an organisation from the geographical viewpoint discloses whether the company is selling its products to different regions of the country and also to different parts of the world. If the company's sales are widely diffused among different regions of the country, its position will certainly be stronger than the one which is almost a regional organisation and depends essentially on a particular region. This is due to the fact that there exists wide regional differences in resources, industrial structures, climatic conditions, fiscal, monetary and commercial policies and political, social and other environmental factors. Any adverse condition in a particular region will expose the enterprise of that region to a greater risk than the one whose sales are widely diffused.

Similarly, if the company's sales are confined to a few big customers in the country, it is always exposed to a greater risk because fall in demand of even a single customer or diversion of a customer to some other organisation will land it in a crisis. Hence, it would be considered as a weakness of the organisation. However, this problem does not arise in the case of company having a large number of customers who are widely dispersed all over the country.

The strength or weakness of a company from the marketing point of view can also be determined by identifying the stage at which the company's product is in or may be heading toward in the country. A company, dealing in a product which is in the growth stage, is very strong but its position will be weak if it is dealing in a product which has reached maturity. A company dealing in a mature product should soon abandon it in order to stave off the impending crisis.

An efficient and effective market research system is a source of strength because it enables the management to take marketing decisions in the light of the economic, competitive and other environmental developments.

The relationship between a company and the distribution system is another vital aspect of the marketing position. Efficient channels of distribution help the organisation in taking the goods at the customer's point and thus, increase the marketability of the product. Further, the company gets feedback periodically about the product and its utility. This information is very useful in revising its strategies. Therefore, a company with efficient and effective channels of distribution will be much more stronger than the one devoid of it.

Marketing factors also need investigation because they affect the demand of a company's product. Here, the major thrust is on ascertaining whether pricing of a product suits the market it serves and is competitive with other firms. Highly competitive price of a product and its suitability to the market will be a plus point for the organisation.

A company's sales force and its capability directly influence the distribution of a product and also the level of sales. A dynamic, efficient and strong sales force having close ties with a large number of customers in the host country is definitely an asset to the organisation. Such an organisation will be more effective in the market than the one where sales representatives confine themselves to a few customers.

The market standing of a company is also dependent upon the extent of promotional and publicity efforts undertaken by it. Sales promotion comprising a wide variety of tactical promotion tools of a short-term incentive nature, is designed to stimulate earlier and/or stronger target market response. A company with efficient promotional efforts will be stronger than the one whose promotional efforts are not so effective.

An international organisation providing efficient and effective after-sales service for a long period of time throughout the host country will attract more customers than the one which does not provide such a service or provides it for a short period of time. Hence, the former will be considered stronger than the latter.

The existence of an efficient and effective system of evaluation of marketing policy and strategy is a distinct capability of an international enterprise because it provides an opportunity to the management to review the company's objectives, policies, strategies and programmes and ascertain whether they match the market environment. Such a periodic review is inevitable because of rapid obsolescence of the company's products in view of turbulent environmental developments. Against this background the product-market strategy is modified or overhauled to suit the new developments.

More intangible but no less significant are the relative standing of company products and their reputation in the market. Market reputation is tenacious. A company with a high reputation of quality, service, price and sharp dealing will continue to remain effective in the long run and will help the company in augmenting its sales. On the other hand, the poor image of an enterprise in terms of quality and service will be an obstacle in its programme of improving its market standing.

Thus, relative share of the market, comparative quality of production, reputation with consumers, its distribution system, promotion and publicity of products are vital aspects of marketing which define the marketing strengths and limitations of a company.

Manufacturing

Another crucial area, which has to be examined for the purpose of preparing the capability profile of an organisation, is manufacturing. Manufacturing activity comprises all such activities that contribute to the conversion of raw materials into finished products. Thus, various factors such as availability of materials, production technology, operation procedure, cost of production, inventory control system, location of facilities, capacity utilisation, degree of vertical integration, rationalisation of resources and patents of products, need detailed examination to determine the manufacturing strengths and weaknesses of the organisation.

Availability of inputs is a crucial factor which influences the operations of an organisation. Ready and inexpensive access to raw materials in the country is a major asset for companies using bulky products. Ownership or long-term contracts with those who own raw materials may assure their continuous supply at a low cost. In the event of scarcity of supplies, this arrangement ensures uninterrupted production and so it becomes an added advantage to the organisation.

Further, if the company has easy access to a number of suppliers of good quality of raw materials it can continue its production activity uninterruptedly. This is the strength of the organisation. At the same time, heavy dependence on a particular supplier, who has been erratic in supplying materials, will be regarded as a limitation on the organisation's efficiency.

Use of effective and efficient production technology considerably influences the operating efficiency of an enterprise. In this respect, the management must see the extent to which the latest developments in technology have been assimilated in the past and the viability of its various plants and processes. A company, with a full-fledged R&D department in the country, engaged in a product development and innovation programme based on the needs defined by market research has its distinctive advantage.

Efficient and effective operation procedures in the form of production design, scheduling, output and quality provide a strategic advantage to the firm because they are greatly helpful in increasing its production.

An assessment of cost of production and its components provides an insight into the operating efficiency of a firm. A company with higher cost of production in comparison to other firms in the same line of business because of higher cost of raw materials or higher labour cost and establishment charges is a great handicap to the organisation in its endeavour to compete with other firms. If the management control over the factors contributing to high cost of production is lax there is little possibility of any improvement over the current state of affairs. The organisation will then fail to meet the challenge of its competitors.

Efficient inventory planning and control bring, down the cost of production by reducing the costs of carrying materials and improves profitability of a firm. A company with an elaborate and effective inventory control system is always superior to the one having a poor system of inventory control. The effectiveness of inventory control system can be adjudged with the help of inventory turnover ratio. High turnover ratio is indicative of efficient utilisation of stock, and a low ratio may reveal inefficiency.

The capability of a firm should also be visualised from the location point of view. Usually, a firm sets up its factory near the place where raw materials and labour are abundantly available. This becomes more important if raw materials cannot be easily transported. Such a locational strategy not only assures uninterrupted production due to continuing supply of materials but also cuts down the cost of production. The location factor is receiving increasing attention from the management in recent years in our country because of the fiscal and financial incentives package being provided by Government of India and several State governments to increase growth speed in the backward areas.

Fuller utilisation of production capacity cuts down the cost of production and improves profitability. Hence, it is a source of strength to the organisation. Such an organisation will have an edge over its competitors who have a poor capacity utilisation.

Operating efficiency of an enterprise also depends on the extent to which the resources have been rationalized. This becomes more significant in multi-divisional organisations because in such organisations there is considerable scope for avoidance of duplication of efforts and facilities. Profitability of a firm improves to the extent the management has been able to minimise overlappings.

A company having patent right and legal production for manufacturing products will have a distinct advantage over other firms, which are devoid of such facility.

Finally, degree of vertical integration determines capability and competitive position of an enterprise. A company, which has acquired ownership or increased control over supply systems or distribution systems, enjoys higher growth or profit as compared to others who lack such control. Management must, therefore, assess the extent of control, which the enterprise has over supply as well as distribution systems.

Finance

The key to an enterprise's success is in its financial strength. In determining financial strengths and weaknesses of a firm, the management must analyse all aspects of financial management such as financial planning, acquisition of funds, utilisation of funds, management of income and profitability.

Designing optimal capital structure is an important aspect of financial planning. The finance manager has to plan the pattern for capital structure in such a way as to minimise the overall cost of capital and financial risk and maximise the stockholders' interest. In order to know whether the capital structure of a firm is optimal, the finance manager must analyse the trends of debt-equity ratio of the firm and its cost of capital, and compare it with other firms in the same line of business. Low cost of capital and high equity base are indicators of sound capital structure and strength of the organisation. In contrast to this, high debt-equity ratio and high cost of capital are financial weaknesses of a firm.

Funds have to be employed in different assets in such a way as to maximise profitability without jeopardising the firm's liquidity. High turnover of cash, receivables and inventories are indicators of efficient allocation of funds, which in turn, results in high profitability. The management can ascertain effectiveness and efficiency of utilisation of funds by calculating the firm's liquidity ratios, turnover ratios and profitability ratios.

Management of income is another crucial financial aspect, which influences the success of an enterprise. Availability of internal resources to finance modernisation and expansion programmes for the enterprise and its ability to attract external funds depend on how efficiently the management has designed the dividend policy. Sound dividend policy is one which enables the firm to retain adequate funds without adversely affecting the dividend payments to the owners. Adoption of a stable dividend policy is an index of efficient management of income.

In financial management, taxation influences investment, financing and dividend decisions. A firm, which constantly takes the taxation provisions into consideration and assesses their implications while making financial decisions and brings about necessary changes therein so as to avail of tax incentives offered by the government, will be financially stronger than the one which does not engage in tax planning exercise.

Human Resource

One of the hallmarks of a successful enterprise over a period of time is its human resource. Long-term productivity and profitability of an enterprise depends upon the state of human resource in the enterprise. Existence of highly talented people, and their commitment to the organisation, sense of responsibility, morale, feeling of autonomy, sense of security and safety, and amicable labour-management relations are the major characteristics of good organisational climate and the basic factors behind the success of an organisation.

The most important human resource element to be assessed for strategy making is the organisational climate. A healthy status is a firm's major strength because it secures the commitment of employees to the firm's aims. How far the firm's employees are willing to contribute to its goals and programmes is a factor to be probed into by the corporate planner. High morale of the employees, their unflinching commitment and ability are great assets to the organisation.

Management

A more subtle factor in corporate competence is management capability and attitude. Appraisal of managerial competence of an enterprise helps the present managerial team in sensing changes, anticipating possible outcomes, exploiting opportunities and circumventing impending dangers in the environment. The major thrust in the analysis of managerial competence is on technical acumen, human and conceptual skills and attitude. Thus, highly technical and organisational acumen of managers, their willingness to risk profit and capital, their high urge to gain personal prestige through corporate growth, their keen desire to ensure stable employment for present workers are the strengths of an organisation, because with such a managerial team it can face any challenge in the future. Furthermore, outstanding research capability or willingness to take risks might be the key to success of a growing organisation.

Unstinted commitment of executives to corporate goals and programmes is undoubtedly an asset to the organisation. However, if they are so committed to the existing corporate strategy that they show reluctance to change or are not capable of change, it will be a great managerial deficiency on the part of the organisation, as this sort of commitment restricts the strategic options that can be realistically considered. Executives of competing firms may likewise have strong commitments that shape their range of possible actions.

In analysing managerial attitude, the analyst should try to find out the executives' views regarding delegation, participative decision-making, communication channels and control. Whether a particular style of leadership is a strength or weakness to the organisation will depend on the situation. In situations where the group does not respond positively except to autocratic methods, the latter leaders are less effective in sustaining productivity and ensuring the satisfaction of their group. On the other hand, democratic management style is a strength to an organisation in most of the situations because their long-term success depends essentially on commitment and a sense of belonging of the employees who feel more secured and motivated under democratic management.

In the modern business world which is characterised by turbulent environmental developments offering greater opportunities, and also posing threats to business organisations, entrepreneurial and aggressive managers are much more successful than the conservative managers who are very often unable to capitalise on favourable situations. Another important management strength in highly competitive landscape relates to its capability of forming inter-dependent vertical and horizontal clusters for performing chain of production and distribution utilities. Where the management has organised the entire business of the company along the entire chain of production, and its control transcends the legal confines of the organisation, it will be a great source of strength to the organisation as it will minimise cost of operations and improve quality.

Preparing the Capability Profile

After scanning crucial aspects of corporate competence and perceiving the strengths and weaknesses therein, the top executives construct a capability profile for the organisation, as shown in Table 7.1. In this profile, each factor is assigned due weight. Weighing indicates whether the degree to which the factor is evaluated is an advantage or disadvantage. Significance of the factor to the organisation has been expressed in terms of '0' (for neutral) '_' (for negative) and '+" (for positive).

Table 7.1 Capability Profile of a Large Organisation

Factor	Weighing Factors				Significance to the organisation
	Strong	Very strong	Weak	Very weak	
Marketing:					
• Total market share			✓		0
• Market share in the region	✓				+
• Product-service line and service	✓				+
• Channels of distribution				✓	−
• Pricing		✓			0
• Product life			✓		+
• Promotion of products		✓			+
• Product image		✓			+
Operations:					
• Raw materials		✓			+
• Facilities			✓		−
• Cost of production			✓		−

(Contd.)

Table 7.1 Capability Profile of a Large Organisation (*contd.*)

Factor	Weighing Factors				Significance to
	Strong	**Very strong**	**Weak**	**Very weak**	**the organisation**
• Product technology		✓			+
• Inventory control				✓	–
Finance:					
• Capital structure	✓				0
• Liquidity		✓			+
• Profitability	✓				+
• Tax planning			✓		+
Human Resources:					
• Quality of Employees	✓				+
• Personnel relations			✓		0
• Commitment of employees				✓	–
Management:					
• Capability, skill and experience	✓				+
• Attitude towards exploitation of opportunities and avoidance of threats	✓				+
• Product life	✓				+

Strategic advantage profile exhibits, in relative terms, the strengths and weaknesses of the firm in various strategic areas. In assigning the relative ratings, some organisations may prefer to use a simple two-valued strength or weakness classification. Others would rank the capabilities as outstanding, average or weak; still others may construct bar-chart profiles.

Another approach to summarise the analysis of the strategic internal factors in terms of strengths and weaknesses is the 'Internal Factor Analysis Summary' (IFAS). IFAS organises the internal factors into strengths and weaknesses and analyses how effectively the firm is responding to these specific factors in the light of the perceived importance of these factors to the firm. IFAS Table (as contained in Table 7.2) involves the following steps:

- Column 1 lists the most significant strengths and weaknesses of a firm.
- Column 2 contains weights assigned to each factor from 1.0 (most crucial) to 0.0 (insignificant) on the basis of the impact of each factor on the firm's strategic position. More important factors are assigned higher weight. All weights must total 1.0 irrespective of number of factors.

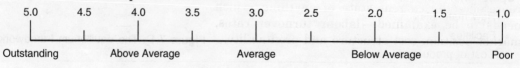

Table 7.2 Internal Factor Analysis Summary: Tata Motors

Internal Factors (1)	Weight (2)	Rating (3)	Weighted Score (4)	Comments (5)
Strengths:				
S.1 Experienced & committed management	0.05	3.0	0.15	Proven experience and loyalty
S.2 Vertical integration	0.03	2.0	0.06	In-house assembly
S.3 Product innovation	0.05	4.0	0.20	Focus on innovation
S.4 Current asset management	0.10	2.0	0.20	Effective inventory control system
S.5 Distribution network	0.10	3.5	0.35	Strong distribution capability
S.6 International orientation	0.15	3.5	0.52	Quick expansion in foreign countries.
S.7 Work culture	0.13	3.5	0.45	Leadership creates a culture where people are encouraged to question entrepreneurial beliefs from time to time.
Weaknesses:				
W.1 Global positioning	0.15	0.05	0.75	Not very strong
W.2 Product portfolio	0.10	0.3	0.30	Lack of synergies due to unrelated diversification
W.3 Profit margin	0.14	4.0	0.56	Low profit margin of two premium international care brands
Total scores	**1.00**		**3.54**	

- Column 3 embodies rating assigned to each factor from 5.0 (outstanding) to 1.0 (poor) keeping in view the management's response to each factor.
- Column 4 displays weighted score which is obtained by multiplying the weight in column 2 for each factor times its rating in column 3.
- Column 5 contains comments, explaining why a particular factor was selected and how it was rated.

Still another way of analysing corporate capability is **Equilibrium approach**. In this approach, key result areas are identified and managers of the firm are invited across a wide front to discern various factors contributing positively as well as negatively to each of the critical result areas and consider them together to arrive at a particular conclusion. Thus, equilibrium analysis is based on group discussions focusing attention on:

(i) achieving a common understanding of strengths and weaknesses;

(ii) identifying strengths as well as weaknesses;

(iii) deciding priorities for corrective action;

(iv) to identify corrective action.

Figure 7.1 displays the basic framework of the equilibrium approach. The horizontal line represents the current state of anything, which needs to be examined—labour turnover rates, market position, cost structure and profitability.

Figure 7.1 The equilibrium framework.

The equilibrium analysis begins with the question—why is our profitability 16%? The base line then represents this state, a profitability rate of 16%. The answer could be that—it is as high as 12% because certain positive features support it. It is as low as 16% because certain negative features hold it down.

In order to identify the positive as well as negative factors, meeting of executives who have a detailed knowledge of the situation should be convened. Positive and negative factors thus identified should be recorded respectively at the top and bottom of the diagram. If a large number of weaknesses have been identified, one may challenge the profitability figure of 16%. Conversely, if too many strengths are identified, one may again be tempted to ask why the profitability rate of 16% has not gone up, to say 25%.

Once factors constituting strengths and weaknesses have been pinpointed, the management should then rate the significance of these factors, as shown in Figure 7.2.

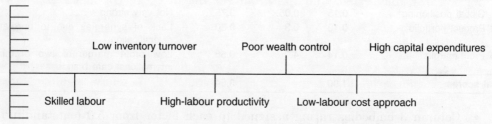

Figure 7.2 The equilibrium approach factors.

On the basis of the above, the top executives can decide if the existing position of the organisation can be improved by strengthening a positive factor or removing a negative one. They can also determine the relative significance of the factors, which enable them to contemplate ways of strengthening them if these are positive, and minimising the influence of factors if these are negative.

Thus, equilibrium approach presents a complete picture about corporate competence by involving all the managers of an organisation. On this basis, suitable strategic action can be taken.

STRATEGIC ISSUES IN INTERNAL ENVIRONMENTAL SCANNING

While analysing internal environment of an organisation, in order to determine its resources and competences as also strengths and weaknesses vis-à-vis its rivals, the strategist should be concerned with certain strategic issues which are of great significance to the future success of the organisation. This is for the fact that an organisation's competitive edge is grounded in its skills and capabilities relative to its rivals and more specifically in the scope and depth of its ability to perform competitively crucial activities along the value chain better than its rivals. Strategic issues that merit the concern of top management are:

(i) Are the firm's competencies appropriable?

(ii) Are the firm's competencies durable?

(iii) Are the firm's competencies replicable?

(iv) Are the firm's competencies competitively superior?

(v) Do the firm's competencies provide access to a wide variety of markets?

(vi) Do the firm's competencies make a significant contribution to the perceived benefits?

Let us analyse each of these:

(i) Are the firm's competencies appropriable?

So as to sustain its competitive edge and profits derived therefrom, a firm must have competencies that have the lower degree of appropriability. A competence or an asset is difficult to appropriate if it is deeply embedded in the firm's culture and system and the profits of the firm can confidently be ascribed to the routines and team excellence developed by a wide range of managers and staff within the firm. When a firm has been performing excellently over a period of time, the competence may even transcend individuals or teams, and become a competence of the firm itself in an organisational learning way. Low appropriability of the strategic competence, therefore, signifies superior competitiveness and high profit sustainability.

(ii) Are the firm's competencies durable?

The strategist should also examine the durability of the resources and competencies of the firm. The longer the competitive value of a competence lasts, the greater is its value. Here, durability of intangible resources instead of physical resources needs to be analysed. Shortening product and technology life cycles due to pathbreaking technological developments during the last decade has rendered intangible resources less durable than they were even a decade earlier. However, there are certain assets of a firm which have a longer staying power. A firm's reputations do not decay with the years as long as they do not show visible decline in their essential perceived innovative, productive and high quality initiatives. Similarly, leading brand names prove remarkably durable. As products come and go, such household names as Kellogg's, Nestle, Du Pont, Dell, GE and Tata Motors continue with undimmed reputations in public eyes. However, any one of these can lose its image with no more than a year of poor performance. The recent diminishing reputation of IBM and Bajaj Electricals is a salutary illustration of this. The more durable the core competence, the higher the profit sustainability.

(iii) Are the firm's competencies replicable?

A firm, to enjoy sustainable competitive advantage in the market place, should have skills and competencies that cannot be initiated or difficult and costly to imitate. The easier the replicability, the lower the strategic importance of the resources and competencies. For example, competitors are finding it difficult to copy the *Nano* technology of Tata Motors. Likewise, Wal-Mart's super-efficient state-of-the-art distribution and store operations competencies are such that its rivals have failed miserably to match them.

(iv) Are the firm's competencies competitively superior?

In order to stay competitively superior to its rivals, the firm will need to consist of a 'portfolio of competencies' rather than 'portfolio of business' and this portfolio of competencies should excel that of the competitors. P&G's competencies in superior marketing distribution and R&D in five technologies— fats, oil, skin, chemistry surfactants and emulsifiers—are certainly superior to its competitors.

(v) Do the firm's competencies provide access to a wide variety of markets?

Sustainable competitive prowess is contingent upon such competencies of the firm as making it capable of infusing products with irresistible functionality or better yet, creating products that customers need but have not yet even imagined. Canon's competencies in three areas—precision machines, fine optics and micro electronics—have acquired leadership in a host of products in the areas of cameras, video cameras, copiers, coloured copiers, faxes, laser faxes, printer and laser beam printers.

(vi) Do the firm's competencies make a significant contribution to the perceived benefits?

A firm will have a competitive advantage when its competencies are such as produce goods and/or services with which it creates more value for its customers than do rivals through low cost and differentiation. Honda's engine expertise is a case in point.

In a nutshell, a firm to achieve competitive edge over its rivals and derive competitive advantage on an enduring basis, must have competencies unique and distinct from others. C.K. Prahalad and Gary Hamel have termed such kind of competence as core competence.[10]

CORE COMPETENCE

Concept of Core Competence

So as to ensure that the organisation is capable enough to offer new products and services unexpected by the customers, it should be endowed with core competencies. Core competencies, according to Prahalad and Hamel, are "the collective learning in an organisation, especially how to coordinate diverse production skills and integrate multiple streams of technologies". Sony's core competence is its capability to miniaturise. To bring miniaturisation to its products, Sony has ensured that technologists, engineers and marketers have a shared understanding of customer needs and of technological possibilities. The skills that together constitute core competencies, Prahalad and Hamel observed, must coalesce around individuals whose efforts are not so narrowly focused that they cannot recognise the opportunities for blending their functional expertise with those of others in new and interesting ways.[11]

Honda's core competence in engines and power trains gives it a distinctive advantage in car, motorcycle and generator business (Illustrative Capsule 7.3).

Illustrative Capsule **7.3**

HONDA'S CORE COMPETENCY

Honda is known as a leader in engines. They leverage their core competency to create excellent products in a variety of markets—all built on their excellence in engines. Honda produces small snow-blower engines, lawn-mower engines, truck engines, and race-car engines. A lot of small to medium–sized businesses try to do everything they do as best they can. They tend to realise where their profits come from and feel that everything else is just the cost of doing business and they need to handle it internally, which may cost them a majority of their profits. They say "there is no other way". They also want full control and feel that they can do it cheaper in-house. Companies should put more focus on the customer and improve their abilities to add value.

Core competence is a corporate thinking of creating new products to serve customers by optimising the use of existing skills in an innovative way. Core competence approach is a way of managing the numerator's growth through new product and business development, and through prospectives for new markets.

In sum, core competence is the managerial capability to consolidate corporate-wide technologies and production matter into competencies that enable the organisation to bring out innovative products of world class standards at competitive prices to cater to the ever changing needs of customers.

A core competence can relate to any of several aspects of a company's business, viz., excellent skills in manufacturing a high quality product in superior cost-cutting skills, outstanding marketing and merchandising skills, meticulous capability to provide better after-sales service, remarkable ability to respond quickly to changes in customer needs and searching new market trends, superb know-how in creating and operating a system for filling customers' orders accurately and swiftly, usually effective sales force, extraordinary skills in working with customers on new applications and uses of the product and unique expertise in integrating multiple technologies to create whole families of new products. A company may have more than one competency in its resource portfolio, but hardly there are a few like Canon and Proctor & Gamble that can legitimately claim more than two or three core competencies.

By focusing on its core competencies, firms stand to gain since they do those things at which they are the best.

It is important to note that while core competency of a company may change, the core business remains the same. For example, core competence of Indian Railways till 1980s was handling steam engine business technology where after it embraced diesel engine and then electric engine-based technology but the core products—transportation for goods and passengers—remain the same.

With companies increasingly competing globally as corporation rather than as business, the development of core competence has become a key element in building a long-term strategic advantage. It is, therefore, pertinent for an organisation to identify if it possesses core competency. For this, a fair understanding of distinguishing features of core competency is necessary.

Immanent Features of Core Competence

(i) A core competence relates to a set of skills, expertise in performing particular activities or a company's scope and depth of technological know-how. It transcends organisational boundaries and is more than skills.

(ii) A core competence resides in a company's people, their mindsets and creativity and not in assets on the balance sheet. Thus, core competence lies outside the existing tangible resources of the company. Furthermore, a core competence is more likely to be grounded in cross-department combinations of knowledge and expertise rather than being the product of a single department or work of group.

(iii) A core competence is the one that provides potential access to a wide variety of markets. It is a corporate-wide thinking of creating new products to serve customers on an ongoing basis by optimising the use of existing skill in an innovative way. Core competence enables the management to conceive synergies among related as well as dissimilar products so that the organisation brings out new and innovative products to cater to the existing as well as prospective market requirements. Figrue 7.3 shows how Honda uses its core competence to create end-use products for a wide variety of markets.

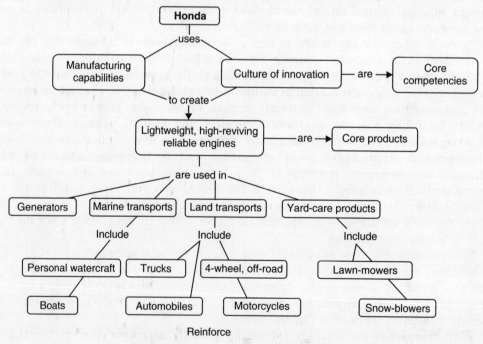

Figure 7.3 Honda's core competencies.

(iv) A core competence is one that should make a significant contribution to the perceived customer benefits of the end product. Tata *Nano's* core competence of designing, manufacturing and distributing and servicing, in radically new way, has allowed it to produce high quality cheapest car for the middle class people (Illustrative Capsule 7.4).

ILLUSTRATIVE CAPSULE 7.4

TATA NANO'S CORE COMPETENCIES

Tata's *Nano* is the world's most inexpensive car. Its closest competitor, the *Maruti 800* sells for roughly twice as much. The price of the entire *Nano* car is roughly equivalent to the price of a DVD player option in a luxury western car. This could be possible because of the *Nano's* competencies in innovative designing, manufacturing, distributing and servicing.

It started by looking at everything from scratch, applying what some analysts have described as "Gandhian engineering" principles—deep frugality with a willingness to challenge conventional wisdom. The car is smaller in overall dimensions than the Maruti, but it offers about 20% more seating as a result of its designing such as placing the wheels at the extreme edges of the car. The *Nano* is also much lighter than comparable models as a result of efforts to reduce the amount of steel where possible. The car currently meets all Indian emission, pollution and safety standards. The fuel efficiency is attractive—50 miles to a gallon.

The most innovative aspect of the *Nano* is its modular design. The *Nano* is constructed of the components that can be built and shipped separately to be assembled in a variety of locations. In effect, the *Nano* is being sold in kits that are distributed, assembled and serviced by local entrepreneurs. As Ratan Tata, Chairman of the Tata group of companies, observed in an interview with the Times of London: "*A bunch of entrepreneurs could establish an assembly operation and Tata Motors would train their people, would oversee their quality assurance and they would become assembly operators for us. So we would create entrepreneurs across the country that would produce the car. We would produce the mass items and ship it to them as kits. This is my idea of dispersing wealth. The service person would be like an insurance agent who would be trained, have a cell phone and scooter and would be assigned to a set of customers*".

In fact, Tata envisions going even further, providing the tools for local mechanics to assemble the car in existing auto shops or even in new garages created to cater to remote rural customers. This is an "open distribution" innovation because it mobilises large numbers of third parties to reach remote rural consumers, tailor the products and services to more effectively serve their needs, and add value to the core product or service through ancillary services. These innovations in products and processes come together to support "open distribution". Increased modularity (both in products and processes), aggressive leveraging of existing third-party, open non-commercial institution in rural areas to more effectively reach target customers, creative use of information technology carefully integrated with social institutions to encourage use and deliver even greater value. Modular designs combined with creative leverage of local third-party institutions help participants to get better faster.

(v) A core competence is one which competitors find it difficult to imitate. If core competence of a firm is harmonisation of complex individual technologies and production skills, it will be difficult for a competing firm to copy. A rival might acquire some of the technologies that comprise core competence but will not be simple to duplicate the more or less comprehensive pattern of internal coordination and learning. For example, Toyota's core competencies that derive from its ability to blend core competencies across the whole organisation are difficult to be copied by the rivals.

(vi) Core competencies emerge from a company's experience, learned skills and focused efforts in performing one or more related chain components. These competencies are built through a process of continuous improvement and enhancement that may span a decade or so. A company that has failed to invest in core competence building will find it very difficult to compete in global market. Merck and Glaxo, two of the world's most competitively capable pharmaceutical companies, built their strategic positions around expert performance of a few key activities such as extensive R&D to achieve first discovery of new drugs, a carefully constructed approach to patenting skill in gaining rapid clinical clearance through regulatory bodies and unusually strong distribution and sales force capabilities.

(vii) Core competence of a firm is like the root system that provides nourishment, sustenance and stability to the firm like a tree which grows from its roots. Core products are nourished by competencies and engender business units whose fruits are end products. Management looking at fruits of a tree as its end products can miss the strength of competitors (Figure 7.4). As such, for competitive edge, the company should nourish and strengthen its roots.

(viii) Core competence does not diminish with use. Unlike tangible assets, which do deteriorate over time, core competencies are enhanced as they are applied and shared. But competence skill need to be nurtured and protected, for knowledge fades if not used. Competencies are the glue that binds existing businesses. They are also the engine for new business development and act as guideposts for patterns of diversification and market entry.

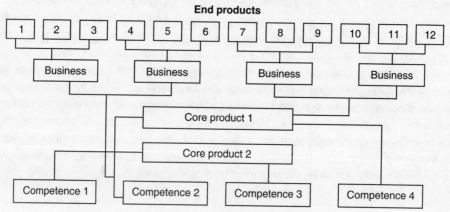

Figure 7.4 Core competencies: Roots of competitiveness.

CORE COMPETENCE AND LEVERAGING OF RESOURCES

In the changing milieu, corporate management must concentrate on the development of a few essentials skills of the organisation so as to innovate products of world-class standards, develop infrastructure network for global expansion and competence of the management. Core competence concept is based on the philosophy that an organisation with limited resources should focus on doing more with less, and investing on core competencies where management feels it has the potential to become world order. This is what is ingrained in the concept of 'Leveraging' and 'Stretch'. The basic premise of the concept of Stretch is that copious resources cannot guarantee continued industry leadership and conversely modest resources cannot be deterrent to future leadership. General Motors, Philips and IBM with burgeoning resources at their command were found on the defensive with Honda, Sony, HP and Dell. NEC succeeded in gaining market share against AT&T. IBM challenged Xerox in the computer business but failed, while Canon, a company with only 10% of the size of Xerox in the mid-1970s, eventually displaced Xerox as the World's most prolific copier manufacturer.

As such, the focus of an organisation should be on leveraging its existing resources. Resources of an organisation can be leveraged through concentrating, accumulating, complementing, conserving and recovering.[12]

Leveraging through Concentration

Leveraging through concentration demands convergence and focus. The organisation should confine deployment of its limited resources in a few strategic areas identified by the management to realise the vision. NEC is the only company in the world that is one of the top five producers of both computer and communication equipment. The company achieved this through its strategic focus on the purpose of becoming a leader in both computers and communication and elaboration of that purpose in terms of the skills and capabilities required for it and pursuing its ambition unswervingly for the next decade and a half. On the other hand, IBM with stupendous resources at their command lost leadership both in computers and telecommunication business because of absence of strategic focus on any of its business. Thus, convergence prevents the diversion of resources overtime.

Further, an organisation should prevent the dilution of its limited resources at any given time by focusing on a few key-operating goals at one time. It must specify and prioritise on the improvements the company will pursue.

It is true that companies which concentrate their resources on core business fare better than their counterparts. However, companies must branch out into new businesses to compensate for the declining prospect of creating value in older ones.

Leveraging through Accumulation

Routes to leveraging through accumulation of resources are extraction and borrowing. The thrust of extraction is on making maximum use of reservoir of experiences and insights gained by organisational people in the past about customers, competitors, suppliers, and technologists for developing new products at reduced cost. However, extraction calls for the capacity to learn which, in turn, is dependent upon the knowledge of employees, invigorating organisation people, empowering them to perform and continuous benchmarking.

Borrowing the resources of other companies is another device of accumulating resources. The philosophy of borrowing is summed up in the remark of a Japanese manager that, "you (in the west) chop down the trees and we (in Japan) build the houses." This signifies that while Americans do hard work of discovery, Japanese exploit those discoveries to create new products and markets. Sony was one of the companies to commercialise the transistor and the charge-coupled device technologies pioneered by AT&T's Bell Laboratories. The organisation should, therefore, tap into the global market for technology for leveraging the resources. It should also ensure that the skills borrowed are internalised. Internalisation is often a more efficient way to acquire now skills than acquiring an entire company. NEC relied on hundreds of alliances, licensing deals and joint ventures to bolster its product development efforts and to gain access to foreign markets.

Leveraging through Complementing

Leveraging through complementing is done by way of blending and balancing. Blending demands integration of diverse functional skills like R&D, production, marketing and sales. GM or Ford could not beat Honda in the field of all-round engine performance because the former were less capable of harmonisation of their diverse technologies than Honda. Another form of blending is a company's ingenuity in dreaming up new product permutations. Sony and 3M, for example, have demonstrated great imagination in combining core technologies in innovative ways. Sony's 'Walkman' brought together well-known functional components—headphones and an audiotape playback tap device—and created a huge market, if not a new life-style.

Balancing is another approach to complementing resources. A company is like a stool which must have atleast three legs—a strong product development capability, capacity to manufacture its products or deliver its services at world-class levels of cost and quality and a sufficiently widespread distribution, marketing and service. If any leg is weaker or shorter than the others, the company will find it difficult to optimise the investments made in its areas of strengths. By deploying resources in the weak or missing skills, it can multiply the earnings on its assets.

Leveraging through Conservation

Conserving resource is another device of leveraging. Two major ways of conserving resources are recycling and coopting. More often a given skill is used, the greater the scope for the resource leverage. The common saying in Japan is that 'no technology is ever abandoned; it is reserved for future use'. Japanese companies like Sharp and Honda are the strong advocates of this maxim. Sharp exploits its liquid-crystal-display competence in calculators, electronic pocket calendars, mini TVs, large-screen projection TVs and laptop computers. Recycling is not limited to technology-based competencies; brands can also be recycled.

Co-option provides another route to conserving resources. Organisations should make efforts to entice a potential competitor into a fight against a common enemy, work collectively to establish a new standard or develop a new technology, and build a coalition around a particular legislative issue. The underlying idea behind all these is to co-opt the resources of other companies and thereby extend one's own influence. Nokia and Microsoft, at one time fierce rivals in the mobile telecommunications business, forged alliance in May 2010 to break the dominance of Research Motion's Blackberry in wireless services for corporations.

Leveraging through Recovering

Recovering resources as rapidly as possible is yet another source of leverage. A company, that can do anything twice as fast as its competitors by shortening product development, ordering processing and product launch times, or by building global brand and distribution positions that allow the company to preempt slower levels, enjoy competitive advantage.

SIGNIFICANCE OF INTERNAL ENVIRONMENTAL SCANNING

An objective and dispassionate analysis of internal environment of an organisation is significant in as much as it forms the cornerstone of strategy and basis for creating competitive advantage. Such an analysis has a crucial role in strategic planning. Without such an exercise it will not be possible to formulate economic strategy for an organisation on an objective basis. As a matter of fact, it provides the platform from which a strategic plan emerges. It establishes whether or not a company is ready to risk a bold step into the future or is at a point of impending troubles.

An over-ambitious management swayed by personal values and initial success may be tempted to choose a path of expansion without perceptive and penetrating enquiry into the company's past performance and present capabilities. Such premature and over ambitious growth can bring untold sufferings. Attempting to plan without carrying out this fundamental step is rather like trying to reach the top floor of a building without using the stairs or the lift; the ascent is possible, but highly dangerous and calls for more effort. Ignorance of this basic step may lead the company to adopt the wrong strategy to take decisions, which, at best, restrict its achievement of its highest potential and, at worst, lead to ruin.[13]

Corporate appraisal also helps a management in choosing the most suitable niche for the organisation. The management of a company aspiring to grow may identify an array of opportunities during environmental surveillance. This may help it to penetrate the existing market, to enter into new markets, to develop products related to its original product, to expand geographically and also to diversify its product line in a number of countries. To decide on the best among several opportunities, identified by appraising diverse external environmental forces, is more than environmental appraisal. If the difficulties inherent in adopting a new product-market posture in a swiftly changing world are to remain manageable, then some criteria of choice of alternatives besides the opportunity for profit and growth must be observed.

Economic opportunity may abound in different parts of the world but not the ability to prosecute. Opportunism without competence is a garden path.[14] Thus, for instance, an organisation engaged in a country for making profit in computer manufacturing but it did not have the requisite ability to do this work, even then it went ahead. The result was—early demise of the business. Thus, the fact that there is greater scope of profit in the new field does not mean that an organisation with the ability to do a different kind of business should enter the new field. What is necessary is to appraise strategic advantages of the organisation and match them to opportunities so as to narrow down to a range of alternative courses of action and to evaluate these alternatives to select the most suitable one for the organisation. Position audit of an organisation highlights its distinctive capabilities.

Every organisation has some distinct capabilities in contrast to others. Some firms can serve customers and markets which others cannot. Similarly, some firms have excellent product facilities but are not so strong in the marketing. Some firms may have well-known brands but do not have strong research and development organisations. Such an analysis focuses sharply on the areas where it is strong and can operate most effectively. With this kind of analysis, the management can decide on the type of business the company should engage in a country and the type of business to abandon.

Corporate capability appraisal also provides an insight into the weaknesses of an organisation. Identification of weaknesses—which may be serious limiting factors to the organisation's long-range plan—is the first step towards their removal. Obviously, not all the weaknesses are rectifiable and these are some that every organisation has to live with. But with this knowledge, management can safely avoid capturing a business opportunity where the organisation lacks. It takes adequate steps to remove the weaknesses of the organisation in the long run. The ways of doing this may be built into the long-range plan. While this is so in some, other organisations concentrate only on those areas where they are strong, and avoid frittering away their resources on removing weaknesses. Much would depend on the views of the top management and the personnel of the organisation.

The competence profile of an enterprise provides opportunities to the management to measure synergistic benefits, those arising out of combined performance of two product-market entries. Such a measurement contributes a lot in deciding whether to acquire a new organisation or make a new market entry.

An analysis of the core competence of an organisation guides the management in deciding about the business it should embrace and the investments to be made in skills which can make it globally competitive.

In sum, carrying out a detailed appraisal of the current background of a company is a complex but very useful exercise.

Summary

In a brutally competitive environment, a firm must have sustainable competitive advantage. So as to determine if the firm possesses such advantage, it should scan its internal environment. Internal environmental analysis is characterised by resource-based perspective of internal environment. According to resource-based approach, competitive advantage of a firm is best sought by an examination first of its existing resources and competencies; then an assessment of their profit potential in relation to congruent market opportunities and the choice of strategies based upon possibilities this reveals.

Resources of a firm may be tangible and intangible. Although, existence of resources is important, they themselves do not confer any benefit to an enterprise. In fact, it is the efficacious configuration of resources that provides an enterprise with competencies. Usually, a firm's competence emanates firm deliberate efforts to develop the organisational ability to perform constructively. Competence of a firm is derived from its systems and processes.

While scanning internal environment of a firm, a strategist has to determine if the existing resources and capabilities of the firm are its strengths or weaknesses. A resource is strength if it provides a firm with a competitive advantage. A weakness is something a company lacks or does poorly (in comparison to others) or does not have the capacity to do while its competitors have the capacity to put it at disadvantage.

Internal environmental analysis involves identifying strategic factors, which are crucial to the success of an organisation, determining the importance of each of these factors, determining the strengths and weaknesses of the organisation in each of these factors and finally preparing a strategic advantage profile for the firm and comparing it with profiles of successful competitors in the industry.

In doing this exercise, the management should also determine if the firm's competencies are appropriate, durable, replicable and superior so as to ascertain how far the firm can perform competitively crucial activities along the value chain better than its rivals. In other words, a firm, in order to achieve competitive edge over its rivals and derive competitive advantage on an enduring basis, must have unique competence which Prahalad and Hamel have termed as core competence-capability to consolidate corporate-wide technologies and production matter into competencies that enable the organisation to bring out innovative products of world-class standards at competitive prices to cater to the ever-changing needs of customers.

Core competence is about corporate-wide thinking of leveraging resources through concentration, accumulation, complementing, conservation and recovery.

Key Terms

Appropriability of competence
Capability profile
Competitive advantage
Core competence
Durability of competence
Equilibrium approach

Financial strength
Human resource strength
Intangible resources
Internal factor analysis summary
Leveraging
Managing strength

Marketing strength
Perceived benefits
Replicability of competency
Stretch
Tangible resources

Discussion Questions

1. Why should a firm undertake internal environmental analysis?
2. What is the resource-based view of the firm? Discuss its relevance in strategy making.
3. What do you believe is the contribution of the resource-based view to strategic management?
4. Bring out the steps involved in internal environmental analysis.
5. How would you prepare capability profile of an organisation?
6. How would you evaluate functional strengths and weaknesses of a firm?
7. How is competence analysis made under Internal Factor Analysis Summary Table?
8. Discuss equilibrium approach of assessing competence of a firm.
9. What is core competence? Discuss its distinguishing features.
10. Why is core competence analysis important in today's competitive environment?
11. "Core competence is about corporate wide thinking of leveraging resources". Comment upon the statement with suitable examples.

References

1. Rumelt, "How Much Does Industry Matter?" *Strategic Management Journal*, 12(**3**), pp. 167–85, 1991.
2. Prahalad, C.K. and G. Hamel, "The Core Competence of the Corporation", *Harvard Business Review*, 71(**2**), pp. 75–84, 1993.
3. Rumlet, R.P., op. cit.
4. Barney, J., "Firm Resources and Sustained Competitive Advantage", *Journal of Management*, 17(**1**), pp. 99–120, 1991.
5. Peteraf, M., The Cornerstones of Competitive Advantage: A Resource-based View, *Strategic Management Journal*, 14, pp. 179–91, 1993.
6. Collis, D.J. and C.A. Montgomery, "Competing on Resources: Strategy in the 1990s", *Harvard Business Review*, 73(**4**), pp. 118–28, 1995.
7. Polanyi, M., *The Tacit Dimension*, Routledge & Kegan Paul, London, 1966.
8. Hussey, David E., *Introducing Corporate Planning*, Pergamon Press, Oxford, p. 58, 1985.
9. Quinn, James Brian, *Intelligent Enterprise*, Free Press, New York, p. 76, 1992.
10. Prahalad, C.K. and Gary Hamel, "The Core Competence of the Corporation", *Harvard Business Review*, May–June, 1990.
11. Ibid.
12. Hamel, Gary and C.K. Prahalad, "Strategy as Stretch and Leverage", *Harvard Business Review*, March–April, 1993.

13. Prahalad, C.K., "Growing Competencies", *Business Today*, January 7–21, 1994.

14. Thompson, Arther A., Jr. and A.J. Strickland III, *Strategic Management*, 8th ed., Richard Irwin, Chicago, pp. 94–95, 1997.

Internet Resources

- *http://www.opexcanada.com/learning/keytoprofit-corecompetencies.html*
- *http://www.cmap.bradercomm.net.8001*
- *www.business-today.com*
- *www.business-standard.com*
- *www.soundknowledegstrategies.com*

8

Value Creation
and Competitive Advantage

LEARNING OBJECTIVES

The present Chapter aims at:

- Providing a vivid view of value creation through value chain analysis.
- Discussing how value chain linkages are managed.
- Describing new paradigms of value creation.

INTRODUCTION

In bruising, discontinuous and competitive environment unleashed by the adoption of the policy of liberalisation, privatisation and globalisation by governments across the globe and consequent integration of world economies, proliferation and convergence of informational and communicational technologies and fast changing personal, familial and social values, the biggest problem, as noted in the first chapter, plaguing organisations all over the world is how to cope with the fast changing business milieus and complex competitive challenges in their field so as to ensure their sustained success. In such an environment being better or bigger is not good enough.

Even the excellent companies listed by Tom Peter and Robert Waterman in their book *In Search of Excellence* and James Collins and Jerry Porras in their book *Built to Last* lost their halo. Of late, General Motors—100-year old legendary auto giant of the US and Japanese Airlines—the Asia's largest airline by revenues, had to opt for bankruptcy. What made these companies go from good to great and then slide back to so-so or also-ran was that they did not transform themselves according to the environmental developments.

The key to long-term success in an environment of discontinuity and high degree of competitiveness is resilience. The organisations must have capability to constantly check to see how the environment is changing, and how things could be different tomorrow. They have to face the inevitability of strategy decay and prepare alternative routes to success. They must be able to reinvent business models and redefine core businesses faster than the change in circumstances so that they achieve superior performance and provide products or services that customers will pay more than what it costs the firm to provide them. In this way, the company must be able to create value. Value creation, in fact, is at the heart of any successful strategy.

Concept of Value

Competitive advantage grows fundamentally out of value a firm is able to create for its buyers that exceeds the firm's cost of creating it. Value is what buyers are willing to pay, and superior value stems from offering lower prices than competitors or providing unique benefits that more than offset a higher price.[1]

Customer value can be conceptualised by the following equation:

$$V = \frac{Q + F}{P}$$

where

V = Customer value
Q = Product quality
F = Product features valued by the customer
P = Price of product to the customer

An increase in the numerator factors of quality and features (as defined by the customer) will increase value. Similarly, a decrease in the denominator factor of price will also increase value. The value (margin) of a product produced by a company represents the amount of revenue it earns over the cost. The total revenue of a product is calculated by the price of the product (service) multiplied by the quantity consumed. If we know the total cost of each product, then the difference between the total revenue and total cost is the profit margin for the company. A company can create more value for its customers either by lowering the cost or by making the product more attractive through superior design, functionality and the like so that customers place a great value on it. A company will have a competitive advantage when it creates more value for its customers than to rivals through low cost and differentiation.[2]

However, value creation is not enough. In order to survive and thrive, the company must be capable of capturing the value it creates. It is not usual for a company to retain all the value it generates and increase its profits commensurately. For example, competition may allow a company's customers to capture some of the value it creates. A famous example of this unhappy phenomenon is the invention of the Computed Tomography (CT) scanner.[3] EMI invented this technology and brought the first product to a market where demand was high. But EMI earned little of the tremendous value it created. While it initially dominated this market, EMI abandoned it seven years after it sold its first scanner. EMI found that it could not compete with firms like General Electric (GE), which rapidly copied the innovation and had the complementary resources for on-going product development, marketing, service and distribution. GE captured some of the value created by EMI.

Thus, to create and capture value consistently, the company must have distinctive competence; otherwise a rival could replicate what the firm does, and the ensuing competition would sharply limit the firm's ability to capture value.

The management is keen to create and enhance value as also to retain the same for the consumers of its products, be they the end consumer or an intermediate such as a distributor. It must know where and how much value each activity adds, how this value can be added further by reconfiguring parts (or all) of the value added process and by co-opting its suppliers, customers and distributors.[4] Value chain analysis has come to be recognised as a basic tool of strategic cost analysis for determining whether a company's prices and costs are competitive and thus conducive to winning in the market place.

CONCEPT AND CONSTITUENTS OF VALUE CHAIN ANALYSIS

Value chain analysis is a tool, devised by Michael Porter in 1985, to analyse activities, which a firm performs to design, produce, market, deliver and support its product so as to understand the behaviour of costs and the existing and potential sources of differentiation. The chain of value creating begins with the procurement of raw materials and continues on through parts and components production, manufacturing and assembly, wholesale distribution and relating to the ultimate end-user of the product or service.

Value chain, according to Porter, represents total value, which consists of value activities and margin. Value activities are physically and technologically distinct activities a firm performs. These are the building blocks by which a firm creates a product valuable to its buyers. The chain includes a profit margin, because a mark-up over the cost of performing the firm's value creating activities is customarily a part of the price borne by buyers.

Porter, therefore, stressed that rather than cost, value must be used while analysing competitive position, since firms often deliberately raise their costs so as to command a premium price via differentiation.

An organisation is a collection of activities, which aid in the design, production, marketing and support of its product. All these activities can be captured using value chain analysis. Porter divides value chain activities into two broad categories—primary activities and support activities.

Primary Activities are those activities that are directly involved in the physical creation of the product and its sale and transfer to the buyer as well as after sales service. There are five generic categories of primary activities involved in competing in any industry, viz., inbound logistics operations, outbound logistics, marketing and sales and service.

(i) *Inbound Logistics* are the activities concerned with receiving, storing and distributing inputs to the product division, such as material handling, warehousing, inventory control, vehicle scheduling and return to suppliers.

(ii) *Operations* represent activities associated with transforming inputs into the final product form, such as machining, packaging, assembly, equipment maintenance, testing, printing and facility operations.

(iii) *Outbound Logistics* refer to activities associated with collecting, storing and physically distributing the product to distributors such as finished goods warehousing, material handling, delivery vehicle operations, order processing and scheduling.

(iv) *Marketing* and *Sales* are the activities designed to make consumers aware of the product/service and are able to purchase it. These include advertising, promotion, channel selection, channel relations and pricing.

(v) *Services* represent activities designed primarily to provide service to enhance or maintain the value of a product such as installation, repair, parts supply, training and product adjustment.

Each of the categories may be vital for a company to gain competitive advantage, depending on the nature of its business. A service rendering company like bank's main value adding activities are marketing and sales. For a supermarket like *Reliance Fresh*, the core activities are procurement, inbound logistics and outbound logistics. A hotel's most important activities and costs are in operations — check-in and check-out, maintenance and housekeeping, dining facilities, room service, conventions and meetings. Among the manufacturing industries, importance of value chain differs. For example, in the soft-drink industry, important primary activities are processing of basic ingredients, and syrup manufacturing, bottling and can filling, wholesale distribution, advertising and retail merchandising; while for the computer software industry major primary value adding activities are programming, disk loading, marketing and distribution.

Support Activities lend great support to primary activities so as to improve their efficacy in reducing cost and improving product differentiation. Support activities comprise four types of activities, viz., procurement, technology development, human resource management and a firm's infrastructure. It is important to note that while the first three activities can cut across with specific primary activities as well as support the entire chain, infrastructure supports the entire chain of primary activities.

(i) *Procurement*: This refers to the function of purchasing inputs used in the firm's value chain not to the product inputs themselves. Purchased inputs include raw materials, supplies and other consumable items as well as assets such as machinery, laboratory equipment, office equipment and buildings.

    A given procurement activity can normally be associated with a specific value activity or activities which it supports. The cost of procurement activities themselves usually represents significant position of total costs, and thus, has a large impact on the firm's overall cost and differentiation. Improved purchasing practices can strongly affect the cost and quality of purchased inputs, as well as of other activities associated with receiving and using the inputs and interacting with suppliers.

(ii) *Technology Development:* This covers a company's 'know-how', its end procedures, use of technology that has an impact upon process and resource developments.

(iii) *Human Resource Management:* Given that there are no activities, which are completely independent of humans, the process of acquiring, training, evaluating, compensating and developing human resources is present in all the five primary activities. Given the impact that capable and motivated people can have on all activities of a firm, human resource management is potentially the key support activity.

Human resource management affects competitive advantage in any firm through its role in developing the skills and motivation of employees and the cost of hiring and training. In some industries it holds the key to competitive advantage.

(iv) *Firm's Infrastructure:* Firm's infrastructure consists of a number of activities including general management, planning, finance, accounting, legal, government affairs and quality management. Infrastructure, unlike other support activities, usually supports the entire chain and not individual activities.

Firm's infrastructure is something viewed only as "overhead" but can be a powerful source of competitive advantage. Proper management information systems, for instance, can contribute significantly to cost position, while in some industries the top management plays a vital role in dealing with the buyers.

Just as each of the primary activities has associated costs, so do the support activities. The support activities enhance the firm's positioning and profitability to the extent that they contribute to value primary activities and the final product or service purchased by the customer. Figure 8.1 portrays the generic value chain.

The dotted lines in the figure reflect that procurement, technology development and human resource management can be associated with specific primary activities as well as support the entire chain. Firm's infrastructure is not associated with particular primary activities but supports the entire chain.

A perspicacious examination of individual value activities within value chain analysis in the figure involves:

(i) An identification of centre of gravity in the value chain.
According to Galbraith, a company's centre of gravity is usually the point at which the company started its business. Once a company successfully established itself at this point by obtaining a competitive advantage, one of its strategic interventions is to move forward or backward along the value chain in order to reduce costs, guarantee access to key raw materials or to guarantee distribution.[5]

In the textile industry, for example, Arvind Mills' centre of gravity is in the raw materials and primary manufacturing segments of the value chain. Arvind Mills' expertise is in spinning and weaving, which is where the company

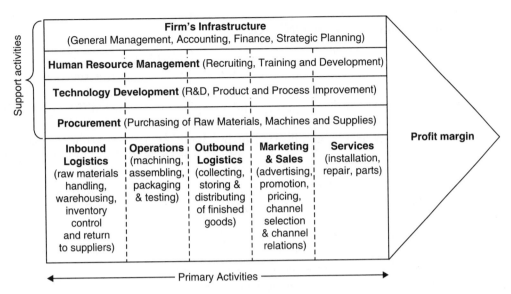

Figure 8.1 The generic value chain.

Source: Competitive Advantage: Creating and sustaining superior performance by Michael E. Porter.

started. It integrated further by using its fabric to make garments, but its greater capability still lay in getting the highest return from its fabrics. In contrast, Zodiac clothing is primarily an apparel company in the industry and its expertise is in producing the product, and in the market distribution segment of value chain. Zodiac sources the required fabric and garment for sale through both its own retail outlets and distributors. But Zodiac's strongest capabilities have always been in the demonstration activities, viz., product marketing and development and management.

(ii) Determination of each product line's value chain in terms of the various activities involved in producing that product or service and assessment of core and distinct competencies or weaknesses so as to ascertain magnitude of competitive advantage of each activity.

(iii) Assessment of the linkages within each product line's value chain so as to understand the relationship between these value activities.

(iv) Analysis of the potential synergies among the value chains of different product lines or business units with a view to optimalising the use of resources deployed in each value activity. For example, if a particular product in value chain is not being produced at a high enough level to achieve economies of scale in distribution, another product could be used to share the same distribution channel. This is an example of economies of scope, which occurs when the value chains of two separate products or services share activities, such as the same marketing channels or manufacturing facilities. This leads to derivation of synergistic advantage in terms of lower cost of joint production of multiple products than the cost of production of individual products.

VALUE CHAIN ANALYSIS AND LINKAGES

In its endeavour to enhance competitive advantage and achieve competitive edge over the rivals, the corporate management must identify linkages within the firm's value chain, between supplier's value chain and the firm's and buyer's value chain and exploit them as they reduce cost, improve quality and bring about product differentiation.

Although value activities are the cornerstones of competitive advantage, the value chain, it must be noted, is not a collection of independent activities but a system of inter-dependent activities. The value chain of a firm is composed of a networked system of interdependent activities connected by linkages. Linkages are relationships between the way a value activity is performed and the cost of performance of another activity. Identifying linkages is a process of searching for ways in which each value activity affects or gets effected by others.

Linkages can lead to competitive advantages in two ways: **Optimisation** and **Coordination**. Linkages often reflect trade-offs among activities to achieve the better result. For example, a more costly product design, more stringent materials specifications or greater in-process inspection may reduce the amount of resources needed for after-sales service and therefore reduce the overall cost of the product.

Linkages may also reflect the need to coordinate activities. On time delivery, for example, may require coordination of activities in inbound logistics, operations, outbound logistics and service. The ability to coordinate linkages often reduces cost or enhances differentiation. Better coordination, for instance, can reduce the need for inventory throughout the firm.

Linkages within the value chain may be numerous and some are common to many firms. Thorough inspection of incoming parts, for example, may reduce quality assurance costs later in the production process, whereas better maintenance often reduces the downtime of a machine. Thorough inspection of finished goods often improves the reliability of products in the field, reducing servicing costs. Quicker deliveries to buyers may reduce inventory and accounts receivable. There also exists linkages between support activities and primary activities represented by the dotted lines on the value chain (Figure 8.1). For example, product design affects the manufacturing cost of a product while procurement practices often affect the quality of purchased inputs and hence production costs, inspection costs and product quality.

Linkages among the value activities arise from a slew of reasons, the important ones being:

(i) Performance of the same function in different ways—for example, conformance to specifications can be achieved through purchase of high quality inputs or 100% inspection of finished goods.

(ii) Improvement of cost of performance of direct activities by greater efforts in indirect activities—for example, better scheduling (on indirect activity) reduces sales force time or delivery vehicle time (direct activities).

(iii) Reducing the need to demonstrate, explain or service a product about activities performed inside the firm—for example, cent-percent inspection can substantially affect reduction in service costs in the field.

(iv) Performance of quality assurance functions in different ways—for example; incoming inspection is a substitute for finished goods inspection.

Though linkages within the value chains are crucial to competitive advantage, they are often subtle and go unrecognised. For example, the importance of procurement in affecting manufacturing cost and quality may not be obvious. Similarly, the link between order processing, manufacturing scheduling process and sales force utilisation may not be recognised.

MANAGING LINKAGES WITHIN THE VALUE CHAIN SYSTEM

A company's value chain is embedded in a large system of activities that include the value chains of the upstream suppliers and downstream customers or allies engaged in getting its product/service to end-users.[6] In most industries, organisations do not undertake all the activities constituting the value chain system but focus on a specific number of activities where it has superior competency and has the ability to outsource the remaining activities backward or forward or both ways. How an organisation manages the linkages between its own chain and value chains of suppliers and distributors and customers bears upon how value is created and enhanced. The extent of such linkages will obviously be an important source of competitive advantage and hence the need to understand the entire value delivery system, and not just the company's own value chain. This means consideration of the value chains of suppliers and forward channel allies (Figure 8.2).

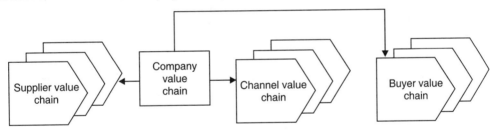

Figure 8.2 Value chain system in a firm.

Source: *Competitive Advantage: Creating and Sustaining Superior Performance* by Michael E. Porter.

The supplier value chains are relevant to a company because the way the suppliers perform their activities impacts upon cost and/or differentiation capabilities of the company. Also, they are relevant because suppliers carry out activities and incur costs in creating and delivering the purchased inputs used in the company's own value chain; the cost and quality of these inputs bear upon the company's competitive advantage. If a company helps its suppliers in reducing their cost or improving their effectiveness, it will certainly improve its own competitiveness. For example, a firm's procurement and inbound logistics activities interact with a supplier's order entry system, whereas a supplier's application engineering staff works with a firm's technology development and manufacturing activities. A supplier's product characteristics as well as its other contact points with a firm's value chain can significantly affect a firm's cost and differentiation. For example, frequent supplier's shipments can reduce the firm's inventory needs, lower handling cost through appropriate packaging of supplier's products while supplier's inspection can remove the need for incoming inspection by the firm.

Thus, linkages between supplier's value chain and a firm's value chain provide opportunities to the firm to increase its competitive advantages. Both the firm and its supplier can be benefitted by influencing the configuration of the supplier's value chain to jointly optimise the performance of activities or by improving those areas in which both the supplier and the firm gain. For example, by agreeing to deliver bulk chocolates to a confectionary producer in tank cars instead of solid bars, an industrial chocolate firm saves the cost of inbound handling and melting. The proportion of the benefits of coordinating or optimizing linkages between a firm and its suppliers is a function of supplier's bargaining power and is reflected in the supplier's margin. Japanese automobile manufacturers are a good example of managing supplier's value chains in order to facilitate just-in-time deliveries of parts which can be put to immediate use rather than being tied up in expensive and unproductive inventory. The American retailer Wal-Mart is also known for the manner it manages the linkages between itself and its suppliers. This enables Wal-Mart to leverage its massive buying power while at the same time provide its suppliers with scale economies for their products through Wal-Mart stores. Tata's *Nano* is also managing its suppliers' channels in as much as the latter have been permitted to set up their plants within the campus of the assembly plant, facilitating supply of equipments, parts and other facilities as and when required without holding any inventory and warehousing, and promoting close collaboration of part design and production scheduling.

A company should also study downstream distributors' value chains because the costs and margins of downstream companies are a part of the price the ultimate end-user pays, and the way the activities are performed by them affects the end-user's satisfaction. Channel linkages can lower cost or enhance differentiation through coordinating and jointly optimising with channels. Channels have value chains through which a product passes. Channels perform such activities as sales, advertising and display that may substitute for or complement the firm's activities. There are also multiple points of contract between a firm's and channels' value chain activities such as the sales force, order entry and outbound logistics. Exploitation of channel linkages is contingent upon affective information system.

Corporate management should also understand buyer's value chain and identify linkages between the buyer's value chain and the firm's value chain so as to enhance the firm's competitive advantage.

Buyers have value chains and a firm's product represents a purchased input on the buyer's chain. It is easy to comprehend the value chains of industrial, commercial and institutional buyers because of their similarities to that of a firm. However, the same is not true in respect of households because they engage in a wide array of activities while products purchased by them are used in conjunction with this stream of activity. For example, a car may be used for a trip to work, shipping and leisure, while a food product can be consumed as a part of the process of preparing and eating meals. It is not practically possible to prepare a chain for these activities which are relevant to know how a particular product is used. Chains need not be constructed for every household. But chains for representative households can be helpful in product differential analysis.

With buyers, the key for organisations is to construct a value chain for them, based on the activities that are relevant to how the product is used. This is for the fact that the consumers of the product will assess that organisation on the benefits they derive from it. An organisation's ability to differentiate its offering will be a product of how its value chain relates to the buyer's value chain. Value for the customer is created when a company is able to lower the buyer's costs or improve differentiation for the buyer. The buyer's perception of the value to be derived from a product will determine the company's ability to charge a premium price.

UTILITY OF VALUE CHAIN ANALYSIS IN STRATEGY MAKING

Value chain analysis is one of the most powerful strategic tools in the hands of corporate management to assess competitive advantage of a firm. By analysing each value activity separately and by determining each activity's cost and contribution, corporate managers can judge the value of each activity to the firm's search for sustainable competitive advantage. By disaggregating a firm's operations into strategically relevant activities and business process, value chain analysis makes it possible to better understand the firm's cost structure and to see where the major cost elements are. This will, in turn, enable the company to compare its cost position with that of its rivals in terms of individual items in product line, customer group and geographical market. Each activity in the value chain incurs costs and ties up assets; assigning the firm's operating costs and assets to each individual activity in the chain provides cost estimates for each activity. This facilitates the management to know if a particular activity will enable the firm to achieve competitive advantage in terms of lower cost or product differentiation.

Value chain analysis calls upon managers to think innovatively about how the firm goes about its activities affect each other. The managers are expected to reconfigure the firm's activities and operations so that the latter can produce or render services that are viewed as being of comparable value to those of its competitors, but to do so at the least cost. Alternatively, the firm may configure and perform its activities in a way that results in its products or services being viewed as differentiated from those of its competitors so that the buyers are willing to pay a premium for them.

With the aid of value chain analysis, a firm can gain competitive advantage by finding new ways to arrange the value chain activities, new procedures for getting things done, new technologies or new inputs to its various processes.

Further, value chain analysis points to the need for comparing the degrees of upstream and downstream linkages and their effectiveness in terms of cost savings and/ or product differentiation with those of the rivals. This will enable the management to make necessary adjustments for differences, if any, in the scope of activities performed. In fact, competitiveness of a firm is dependent not only upon how effectively its value chain activities are performed but also upon the efficacy of the performance of the activities by suppliers or by forward channel allies. Suppliers or forward channel allies may have excessively high cost structures or profit margins, which jeopardise a firm's cost competitiveness even though its costs for internally performed activities are competitive.

Value chain analysis also suggests when competitive advantage of a firm is sustainable. Where competitive advantage is a result of the configuration of many different activities, stemming out of creativity and innovativeness of the management, ostensibly it will be more difficult to imitate and therefore more sustainable. Competitive strategy then can be seen on how a firm configures its range of activities *vis-à-vis* its competitors.

While scouting for reducing cost and improving quality through establishing fruitful linkages with suppliers and distributors, a firm must also examine if it will be in its vital interest to undertake all the activities of the product or service itself or outsource some of the activities in the value chain to those who have requisite expertise and can do the job more efficiently and responsibly. This is more important when the firm competes on price. In their drive to reduce cost and improve operational efficiency, nearly 80% of big European companies are outsourcing bigger portions of their logistics operations to outside contracts that have expertise to handle the job more efficiently and economically. In India too, a large number of manufacturing and IT companies have outsourced the logistics operation to be managed by service providers who design, deploy and manage virtual private networks, freeing companies to focus on core tasks. Value chain analysis helps the firm to understand where it can add value in its activities and where its costs may exceed its value. Both financial considerations and the firm's strategic capability need to be factored while addressing the make or buy decision. If an activity underpins an organisation's capability, i.e., its ability to compete successfully in the market place, it should retain that activity. Where an activity is not cost effective or not competitive in terms of differentiation, the same should be outsourced. However, it would be unwise on the part of the organisation to outsource what may constitute the source of its competitive advantage.

NEW PARADIGMS OF VALUE CREATION

Although, Porter's value chain analysis is significantly useful in analysing value creation activities of a firm and identifying sources of its competitive advantage, this concept epitomises the unilateral role of the firm in creating value, where the firm and the customer have distinct roles of production and consumption, respectively. Implicit in this view are designing products, developing production processes, crafting marketing messages and controlling sales with little or no interference from consumers. Customers get involved only at the point of exchange. Firms aggregate consumers into 'meaningful segment' for ease of exchange.

This concept of value creation is now being challenged by the emergence of highly connected, informed, active and empowered customers.

Thus, the approach of value creation based on Porter's value chain analysis is the firm's centric where a firm can unilaterally create value for its customers through its activities. Value creation is associated with products and services. This approach is founded on the premise that firms have more information and knowledge than the customers and value is exchanged with those customers who represent passive demand for the firm's offerings.

In an emerging democratisation of business, firms are no longer repositories of information and knowledge about products and markets, and individuals have a new fond for freedom that liberates, than being mere targets to be of companies. Currently, there are 4.7 billions of people online, and millions of individuals offline who have contributed materials to the 'Net': from product reviews to e-Bay ratings. At *Amazon. com*, thousands of individuals share information, write buyer's guides and recommend products and services. Further, through their cellphones and other ways of 'voicing', consumers can communicate with other consumers. This enables them to learn much more rapidly about experiences others have had with products and services. New communication technologies like blogs and facebooks are fundamentally challenging the nature of relationship between institutions and individuals. As individuals become far more informed, they have the means and motivation to take control of the value creation process from the citadel of command and control by the corporation.[7] Individuals are now seeking to exercise their influence in every part of the business system. Informed consumers have the power to pick and choose and put together their own solutions, depending upon their level of sophistication, skills and knowledge. Further, consumers have become more finicky, more skeptical, cynical and jaded about claims made by companies and the variety of products and services continue to proliferate, creating more confusion. These customers are no longer satisfied with making yes or no decisions on what a company offers. Under the circumstances, organisations across the globe are realising the imperativeness of co-opting customers' experiences in value creation activities if they have to grab market opportunities and grow successfully. And hence the evolution of the concept of co-creation of value as a new paradigm of value creation.

CO-CREATION OF VALUE

Concept of Co-creation of Value

Concept of co-creation of value was introduced to the business world by C.K. Prahalad and V. Ramaswami through their article "Co-opting customers' competence" in *Harvard Business Review*, 2000. They developed their arguments further in their book published by Harvard Business Press, *The Future of Competition.*

According to them, co-creation is the corporate approach of developing systems, products or services through collaboration with the stakeholders including customers in order to unlock value creation opportunities and execute them. Co-creation is an active and creative process based on collaboration between producers and users that is initiated by the firm to generate for customers. Value, according to them, will be increasingly co-created by the firm and the customer, rather created entirely inside the firm. Co-creation not only describes a trend of jointly creating products but also describes a movement away from the customers buying products and services as transaction to those purchases being made as a part of an experience. Consumers today, the authors held, seek freedom of choice to interact with the firm through a range of experiences. They want to define choices in a manner that reflects their view of value, and they want to interact and transact in their preferred language and style.

Immanent Features of Co-creation of Value

(i) Co-creation is a systematic and structured process based on collaboration with outsiders to generate value for the firm as well as for the customers.

(ii) It is a creative and innovative way of changing the business in fundamental ways.

(iii) Co-creation is a customer-centric approach of value creation facilitated by technological and social infrastructure. Companies need to interact with the customers so closely that they "co-create" value with them on an individual basis ($N = I$). Google has over 100 million customers all of whom can, for example, create their own music portfolios. These are products that allow customers to use and customise them for their own individual purposes. At the same time, companies will source the goods and services needed to develop new offerings from anywhere in the world ($R = G$). Amul has a highly interactive, super efficient supply chain. It distributes seven million litres of milk sourced from 2.2 million suppliers everyday and thus is a classic case of personalised globalisation.

The first equation, $N = I$, calls for a level of customer intimacy that can only be achieved with extensive use of deep analytical technology. The second, $R = G$, requires supply chain and logistics expertise that allows companies to source goods and services efficiently from anywhere.[8]

(iv) In co-creation, concept of value is based on the customer's view and not that of the company's.

(v) Co-creation signifies joint problem definition and problem solving. Customers have a say in this process.

(vi) The new locus for creating value with customers signifies going beyond products and services to innovating 'experience environments' for co-creating value. This is at the crux of the emerging new opportunity space.[9]

Experience Environments for Co-creating Value

An experience environment, which can be anywhere in the business system, is centered on individual-centric interactions with the company's products, processes and people as well as customer communities. Experience environments imply the ability of an organisation to accommodate a wide spectrum of context specific experiences of heterogeneous individuals. The focus in innovative experience environments is not only on products, processes, employees and customers, but also it enables customers to 'lay design' to engage in a co-creation of co-constructing experiences of value through a series of high-quality interactions in the experience environment. Companies need to build platforms that enable experience environments. The experience environments are not just about hardware; the flexibility for a variety of experiences derives from sophisticated use of software. A deep and imaginative understanding of the enabling technologies is a must.

In co-creation, direct connections with consumers and consumer communities are critical. Customer experiences and shifts in needs and wants are best understood by being there, co-creating with them.

The basis of value for the customer shifts from a physical product (with or without ancillary services) to the total co-creation experience, which includes co-designing as well as all the other interactions among the consumer, the company and the larger community of the company's product users.

As such, the co-created experience outcome depends on the nature and level of access to the company's employees and extended community, as also the level of participation of all the parties. For this to take place, the management must thoroughly design and develop the technology platforms and information infrastructure in such a way as to support compelling experience environments. Apple's latest iTunes service is a case in point.

Through its iTunes service, customers have been able to download over 350 million songs of their choice, after listening to samples of the songs. In order to make Apple's iTunes even more powerful, the company has now unveiled the iCloud—a web-based service. At the centre of the iCloud is a new version of iTunes that will allow users to download on any device any song they have ever bought. Songs on a person's iTunes library, that were not bought from Apple, can be added for $25 a year.

The success of the iPod lies in the fact that Apple understood and focused on the 'user experience' that results from user interaction with the iPod. Working 'backwards' from the user experience, Apple designed the interface—right down to the scroll wheel—to facilitate a compelling experience environment of accessing and listening to music. Besides the physically 'cool' design, this meant paying a lot of attention to the underlying software. According to the late Steve Jobs—the Chief Executive Officer (CEO) of Apple—the software is the user experience.[10] In other words, the software enables individuals to scroll through their library quickly, construct playlists on the go, and/or simply play user-defined playlists. Moreover, at the Apple stores, individuals visit and learn about how to actually get music into the iPod (from their own music collections), download songs from iTunes, and get answers to simple questions such as: How do I get music into my iPod? Thus, the Apple store is a 'learning environment', apart from being a 'sales environment'. The individual's interactions with knowledgeable people at the 'genius bar' (including consumers from Apple user groups) support his/her learning experience.

Value creation, based on customer experience, can be illustrated with the help of the Illustrative Capsule 8.1.

ILLUSTRATIVE CAPSULE 8.1

MODERN HOUSEBOAT COMPANY

Modern Houseboat Company is engaged in building customised houseboat. A customer accesses the manufacturing plant and tracks the progress of a boat. While tracking the construction of the boat, an idea cropped up in the mind of the customer. He wanted the boat to have a moving dining table for four feet. The company asked the engineers to discuss this with the customer—the pros and cons of doing that—and take joint decisions about the changes through the principle of informed choice, recognising the cost, quality and safety implications of the choice made.

The company also arranged a meeting of the customer with the community of houseboat users so that the customer could evaluate his choices as he goes along, as well as learn about the possible use of a houseboat that he could not have imagined.

This co-creating process gives the customer a greater level of knowledge and experience about houseboats and with it great degree of self-esteem.

Dialoguing with the company's employees and tracking the progress of the boat along the factory floor creates a sense of emotional bonding with the product and the company (an outcome of value to the customers).

The company's transparency and willingness to dialogue enhances the customer's readiness to trust the company and believe in the quality of its product. Access to the community of the company's customers increases the customer's enjoyment of the houseboat.

The basic building blocks of co-creation are: Dialogue, Access, Risk management and Transparency (DART).

Dialogue encourages not just knowledge sharing but also a shared understanding between companies and customers. It also provides opportunity to individuals to interject their view of outcomes of value into the process of value creation.

Access to knowledge, tools and expertise helps individuals construct their own experience outcomes. Access also challenges the notion that ownership is the only way for consumers to experience value. By focussing on access to experiences at multiple interaction points, as opposed to mere ownership, companies can broaden their view of business opportunities.

Risk management assumes that if consumers become co-creator of value, they will demand more information about potential risks of goods and services, but they may also have to bear more responsibility for dealing with those risks.

Transparency of information in the interaction processes is necessary for individuals to participate effectively in a co-creation mode and to build trust between companies and individuals.

Thus, the new approach to value creation is customer-centric (Figure 8.3), as opposed to firm's centric in traditional approach. In the new approach, firms must seek to co-create value with customers through an obsessive focus on individual-centric interactions between the customer and the company. This requires managers to escape from their product and service centered thinking and focus on the experiences that customers want to co-create. Individual's experiences are associated with interactions and outcomes with products, processes, employees and customers. The process of value creation, as against the traditional model, is a co-creation of experiences with communities of customers and networks of firms. Firms need to engage customers on their terms.

Relationship between firms and customers has, thus, witnessed a fundamental change, as evidenced from the following (Table 8.1).

Table 8.1   Change in Relationship between Firms and Customers

From	To
• One way	• Two ways
• Firm to customer	• Customer to firm
• Controlled by firm	• Customer to customer
• Customers are 'Prey'	• Customer can hunt
• Choice—Buy/Not buy	• Customer can impose his/her view of choice
• Firm segments and targets customers; customers must fit into firm's offerings	• Customers are empowered to co-construct a personalised experience around himself/herself, with firm's experience environment

CO-CREATION PRACTICES IN THE CORPORATE WORLD

After the publication of *The Future of Competition*, a large number of companies applied the principles of the Prahalad Ramaswamy research to a broader range of business activities. Companies engaged customers in the delivery of their experience, including Harley Davidson (bikers riding together and customising their motorcycles), Scion car dealerships (customisation of cars at the dealer and dealer events) or Apple Inc. (exchange of play lists through *iTunes*). Co-creation played an even bigger role in companies such as Cisco and GoldCorp where executives involved outside resources, such as researchers, academics and customers, to actually change and redesign the ways things are done inside the firm. Customer-facing functions such as sales or customer collaboration were also opened up to co-creation at the companies including Star bucks and Dell Computer.

Co-creation has now become global, as practices reached senior managers at the companies in Europe and Asia including Linux (open software), Procter & Gamble's Connect & Develop (dramatically improved research productivity platform with people outside P&G), and Innocentric (research collective in the pharmaceutical industry).

In India, Tata Motors was the first amongst a few corporate enterprises to have adopted co-creative approach to reinvent new business model in letter and spirit. Launching of the *Nano* at the cheapest price is the outcome of the new approach.

The top brass at Frito-Lay, the foods division of PepsiCo India—the largest leader with a market share of around 48%, is taking the co-creating concept very seriously. Frito-Lay's latest campaign for *Lay's*—"Give us your Delicious Flavour"—is giving consumers an opportunity to co-create the flavour they like for *Lay's*. The winners were promised mega prize of ₹50 lakh plus 1% of the sales turnover from the new flavoured snacks, which was launched at the end of May, 2010. Consumers were made to send in their entries by post, drop boxes, email, website and SMS. Frito Lay had also launched a similar campaign in 2009 asking consumers to vote for the flavour of their choice between the new launches—(Spunky Pimento) and (Balsamic Blast).

Introduction of *ChotuKool* by Godrej & Boyce is again the outcome of the firm's adoption of co-creation model of value creation (Illustrative Capsule 8.2)

ILLUSTRATIVE CAPSULE 8.2

GODREJ'S *CHOTUKOOL*

The bullock cart stops in one of the dusty alleys in Osnamabad, a small town in the Marathwada region of Maharashtra. And two village girls, dressed in traditional Marathi kasta saree, step out in style with the products they have helped co-create with the engineers at Godrej & Boyce.

The quality of the sales pitch of the class 10th passed girls would do an MBA proud. For, they know the products well, as the company involved them right from the conception stage to designing and marketing its 'nano' refrigerators named *ChotuKool* (Little cool). The refrigerators are set for a nation-wide commercial launch in March, 2010.

For *ChotuKool*, the Godrej group has junked the traditional model of a proprietary channel with a sales force and a distributor-dealer chain and has joined hands with micro-finance institutions.

Besides trying out unique experiment of the new distribution system, Godrej has brought about a change in module of the product. *ChotuKool* does not have a compressor. It looks like a 43-litre cool box, which is loaded from the top and can run on battery. The refrigerator weighs only 7.8 kg, runs on a cooling chip and a fan similar to those used to cool computers. Given the power shortage in the country side, it also uses high-end insulation to stay cool for hours without power. The operational cost is low: The refrigerator consumes half the power consumed by regular refrigerators.

But the clear winner is its cost. At ₹3,250, it costs almost 35% less than the cheapest category of refrigerators available in the market today. Apart from involving village girls in selling the products at a commission of ₹150 per product sold (something that the company claims will reduce the distribution and marketing costs by 40%), Godrej has gone in for several engineering innovations to keep the price low. The size is small and the number of parts in *ChotuKool* has been reduced to just 20 instead of 200 that go into regular refrigerators.

The idea to target the bottom of the pyramid customers was given shape at a workshop with Clayton M. Christensen, a Harvard University Professor, best known for his ideas on disruptive innovation. The idea discussed in the workshop was to involve villagers, right from the design to selling of the product. The company did that in right earnest ever since it unveiled the first prototype of *ChotuKool* in September 2009. The product went in for several alterations after every little detail, including pricing and colour was discussed with a select group of villagers and micro-finance institutions.

The Godrej group is betting big on *ChotuKool*. The group has lost its leadership position to Korean giants, LG and Samsung and Whirlpool of the US a few years ago. Godrej & Boyce is currently fourth largest player in the over three million units market.

ITC—one of the largest FMCG companies in India—co-created with the farmers to expand their business through its Trail blazing's e-choupal initiative (Illustrative Capsule 8.3). Through this initiative the ITC has been able to successfully connect subsistence farmers to regional markets and build an overwhelming trust between a large firm and small farmers leading to an active collaboration. Further, it is to be noted from the case that the ITC could also build capabilities of the farmer community through learning by doing.

ILLUSTRATIVE CAPSULE 8.3

CO-CREATION OF VALUE—A STUDY

ITC—one of the largest Fast Moving Consumer Goods (FMCG) companies in India—partnered the Indian farmers for close to a century. The company is currently engaged in elevating this partnership to a new paradigm by leveraging information technology through its trail blazing—the e-choupal–initiative. The e-choupal was set up along the model of a hub and spoke. Each e-choupal was run by a Sanchalak to cater to the needs of several villages nearby. With the massive government investments in rural roads, connectivity between villages has improved. This enabled ITC to potentially add more spokes to each of its hubs. Initially, the e-choupal's (Version 1) key business was sourcing farm produce. Through the e-choupals, ITC is significantly widening its farmer partnerships to embrace a host of value-adding activities; creating livelihoods by helping poor tribals, make their wastelands productive, investing in rainwater harvesting to bring much-needed irrigation to parched dry lands; empowering rural women by helping them evolve into entrepreneurs; and providing infrastructural support to make schools exciting for village children.

ITC reached 40,000 villages by 2006, benefiting about 40 lakh farmers and hundreds of thousands of poor tribals. The Company set up the Choupal Saagars for catering all the needs of the rural community. A choupal saagar is a permanent and multiple rural services facility that includes an agri produce warehouse, retail hypermarket and a fuel station.

In its drive to seize new opportunities, ITC found many—some emerging from the adversities that have got it rethinking, leading to adoption of Version 2 of the e-choupal. In e-choupal's Version 2, it provided services to the farmers in the form of information about weather, prize, and so on, knowledge regarding farming methods, soil testing, purchase of seed, and fertiliser for the farmers and purchase of farmers' crops, cattle care, water harvesting, women employment, and the like.

Services like weather agri inputs and pricing were provided through the Sanchalaks through multimedia presentations made on village computers, but these services were customised only for crops and regions. No money was charged for these services.

In its endeavour to deepen its reach to the farmers and provide them personalised services, ITC has now embarked on Version 3 of the e-choupal. Under Version 3, the plan is to deliver personalised agri services to individual farmers via mobile phones. Accordingly, ITC has recently signed a memorandum with Nokia for this. The company already powers some of Nokia's "Life Tools" meant for farmers. Right now the information dissemination is limited and one-way from the company to the farmer. ITC plans to make the information flow two-way. A farmer will be able to provide information on, say, the type of soil, the date of sowing and the kind of crop to the company. The company can then process these inputs and give him very specific advice.

Apart from creating economic value by offering personalised services to the farmers, the data thus, generated could be of immense value to companies selling farm inputs (for example, seeds, fertilizers, pesticides), financial firms and government planners. Thus, personalised agri business will add a second anchor to the e-choupal.

With rural youth, especially in villages closer to towns, shunning agriculture and farm labour, ITC sees vast opportunities in using the e-choupals as centres for information on job vacancies and – eventually—providing skills that help increase the employability of rural youth.

On August 11, 2009, the e-choupal in alliance with Monster India, the leading online career and recruitment resources, has launched Rozgarduniya.com, a website to enable job seekers in rural India to access and apply for jobs through the e-choupals. In less than a month of the service, over 1,200 job openings from 52 companies were made available through this channel.

With the farmers around the e-choupal diversifying their produce, ITC decided to plan for forward integration in more ways than one. The company moved into the 'Choupal Fresh' through forward integration with the horticulture farmers. Choupal Fresh (it is still in a pilot phase with six outlets in Hyderabad) is more "fresh" than other chains since vegetables and fruits make an 80% of products sold through its outlets. The forward integration is also evident in the export of processed foods and fruits.

Many of ITC's products and businesses have backward integration with the *e-choupals*. Bingo, for instance, is made from potato sourced entirely through the *e-choupals*. Similarly, the export of processed foods and fruits is dependent on the *e-choupals* now.

Since mid-2008 ITC has entered personal care products in a big way. The *e-choupal* network is a platform to take these products to consumers in the countryside.

These branded products will also be introduced at the Choupal Haats which are going to be launched over the next couple of months. The *Sanchalaks* will be the key men in organising the Choupal Haats.

By personalising its relationship under the *e-choupal's* Version 3, ITC hopes to increase its reach from 40 lakh farmers to 160 lakh even adding any village to its network.

The ITC has, of late, laid the foundation for building unique personalised experiences for individual farmers. This will obviously help the company to improve the farmers' economic opportunity as well as experiences.

Summary

In excruciating environmental scenario and complex competitive landscape, a firm, to survive and succeed enduringly, has to be resilient to constantly sense the impending changes and respond to the same by reinventing business models and redefine core business faster than the change in circumstances so that it achieves superior performance and provides value to the customers higher than what its competitors deliver.

A firm can create more value for its customers either by lowering cost or by making the product more attractive. Besides, the firm must be able to retain the value for a long time. To create and capture value consistently, the firm must have distinctive competency. It should also know where and how much value each activity adds, how this value can be added further by reconfiguring parts (or all) of the value added process. Value chain analysis has come to be recognised as a basic tool of strategic cost analysis to determine precisely if the firm's prices and costs are competitive.

A firm's value chain represents total value consisting of value activities and margin. According to Porter, a firm's value chain consists of primary activities and support activities.

A perspicacious analysis of value chain of a firm provides valuable information about the firm's centre of gravity, value addition of each of the product line, linkages within each product line's value chain and potential synergies among the value chains of different product lines or business units.

In its attempt to enhance competitive advantage and achieve competitive prowess, the management must identify linkages within the firm's value chain, between supplier's value chain and the firm's value chain and the buyer's value chain and exploit them as they reduce cost, improve quality and bring about product differentiation. Linkages can lead to competitive advantage through optimisation and coordination.

Besides aiding the firm to reduce cost and improve quality through establishing fruitful linkages with suppliers and distributors, the value chain analysis can aid the firm in making optimal 'make or buy' decisions.

Nevertheless, Porter's model of value chain analysis provides an incisive view of value adding activities of a firm and impact of their linkages on its competitiveness, the model no longer remains very much relevant in today's competitive environment where individual customers are well connected and informed and have become finicky and aspire to be actively involved in all such decisions as influence value creating activities. They are not prepared to accept the product/service offerings created by the firm unilaterally without interacting with them. Thus, the changing profile of customers led to the evolution of the concept of 'co-creation of value' by Prahalad and Ramaswami. Co-creation of value, according to them, is the integrated approach of designing and developing systems, products and services through collaboration with various stakeholders including customers so as to unlock value creation opportunities and exploit them.

Thus, co-creation model of Prahalad and Ramaswami is customer-centric where individual customers play dominant role in the process of identification of the problem and finding solution. The boundary for co-creating value goes far beyond products and services to encompass innovating 'experience environment' for enhancing value for the customers and thereby maximising value of the firms.

A large number of MNCs such as Apple, Google, CISCO, Starbucks and Dell Computer have applied the co-creation model to gain competitive edge in the market place. In India too, companies like Tata Motors, PepsiCo India, Godrej & Boyce, ITC and Coca-Cola India have co-opted customers to create value with a view to improving their market share.

Key Terms

Centre of gravity	Customers' experience environment	Support activities
Co-creation of value	Distinctive competency	Value chain
Competitive advantage	Primary activities	Value chain analysis
Core business	Resilient	Value chain linkages

Discussion Questions

1. What is value chain analysis? Bring out its major components.
2. How can a firm create value for itself and for the customers through value chain analysis?
3. Assess the significance of linkages in value chain analysis.
4. What is the utility of value chain linkages in strategy making?
5. Discuss the utility of value chain analysis in strategic decisions.
6. How can value chain analysis aid a firm in gaining and sustaining competitive advantage over its rivals?
7. To what extent can value chain analysis be useful to corporate organisations in creating value for its customers who are well connected, informed and empowered and who are not co-opted by them?
8. What is co-creation of value? Discuss its redeeming features.
9. How is value created through co-option of customers?
10. What is experience environment? What are its building blocks?
11. Distinguish between Porter's model of value chain analysis and Prahalad and Ramaswamy's model of co-creation with respect to creation of value.

References

1. Porter, Michael, *Competitive Advantage—Creating and Sustaining Superior Performance*, The Free Press, New York, 1985.

2. ———, *Competitive Advantage*, Ibid.

3. Introduced by EMI in 1972, the CT scanner was initially used for brain scans. Innovations by EMI in 1974 above are estimated to have added about $7 billion (1980 dollars) in value. EMI's profits from the technology were modest at best. *See* Manual Traitenberg, *Economic Analysis of Product Innovation: The Case of CT Scanners*, Cambridge, MA, Harvard University Press, 1990.

4. Galbraith, J.R., "Strategy and Organizing Planning", in *Strategy Process: Concepts, Contents.*

5. Brandenburger, A. and B.J. Nalebuff, *Co-opetition*, Doubteday, New York, 1996.

6. Prahalad, C.K. and Gary Hamel, "The Core Competence of the Corporation", *Harvard Business Review*, May–June, 1990.

7. Holf, Robert, "The Power of US", *Business Week*, June 20, 2005.

8. Prahalad, C.K., "Companies Need Continuous Changes—Not Episodic Breakthroughs", *Indian Management*, May, 2008.

9. Prahalad, C.K. and Venkat Ramaswamy, *The Future of Competition: Co-creating Unique Value with Customers*, Harvard Business School Press, 2004.

10. Schlender, Brent, "How Big can Apple Get?" *Fortune*, February 7, 2005.

11. *See* Prahalad and Ramaswamy, Supra.

Internet Resources

- *www.business-standard.com*
- *www.business-today.com*

SECTION III

Dynamics of Strategy Making

9

Formulating Corporate Objectives

LEARNING OBJECTIVES

The present Chapter aims at:

- Providing conceptual exposition of corporate objectives.
- Familiarising readers with redeeming features of corporate objectives.
- Focusing on the need to set objectives for a firm.
- Explaining the process of setting different levels of objectives and the forces interacting with these objectives.

INTRODUCTION

Objective setting is the first and foremost step in strategy making as it serves as a beacon and creates sense of purpose for an organisation, and provides yardsticks for evaluating actual performance. Despite its overwhelming significance, management scientists have not been unanimous in understanding the term corporate objectives. For the sake of convenience, these views have been categorised into two major groups, viz., narrow view and broad view.

Narrow View

In this category we include the viewpoints of all those scholars who either regard objectives as statements that give indication of what the company as a whole is trying to achieve and to become alongwith what the company hopes to attain or who considers objectives as the company's targets. The definition provided by Scott, Brickner and Cope, Massie and Douglas, Argenti and Ansoff, given below, fall in the category of narrow concept.

Objectives are the statement of planning purposes developed within any kind of business plan. They are established within the framework of planning and they normally evolve from tentative idea to more specific declarations of purposes.

—B.S. SCOTT[1]

Basic objectives mean the long-term aspirations of an organisation. They represent the direction of growth. Normally, they are statements of values and expectations for the long range.

—WILLIAM H. BICKNER & DONALD M. COPE[2]

Objectives are ideas and statements that give the direction and goal to behavior and effort... Objectives answer the questions of what we are doing and where we are going.

—JOSEPH L. MASSIVE AND JOHN DOUGLAS[3]

An objective is something fundamental to the nature of a company and which distinguishes it from other types of organisation. It is the reason for the very existence of the company, that for which it came into being... It is a permanent unalterable purpose, or raison d'etre.

—JOHN ARGENTI[4]

Objectives are decision rules which enable management to guide and measure the firm's performance towards its purpose.

—H. IGOR ANSOFF[5]

According to the above definitions, objectives are long-term purpose and mission which state the reason for the existence of an organisation and declare what it wants to achieve in the long run. These definitions do not throw any light on the acquisitive and retentive character of objectives nor do they differentiate between performance and stylistic objectives.

Further, short-term objectives expressed in quantitative terms have not been recognised as part of corporate objectives.

In a striking contrast to the above, there are scholars who have viewed objectives only in the sense of targets. The definition given by Trewata and Newport, therefore, falls in the second category of the narrow concept.

Objectives may be defined as the targets people seek to achieve over various time periods.

—ROBERT L. TREWATHA AND GENE NEW PORT[6]

According to this, objectives are the goals expressed in terms of targets for specified time periods. However, this view fails to recognise the strategic component of objectives.

Broad View

In this category, views of those scholars can be included who consider objectives as statements of purpose of the existence of the organisation, desired future positions and specific time-bound targets to be achieved in the pursuit of its long-term mission.

Definitions proffered by Ackoff Rheuman, Mockler and Husse belong to this group.

Objectives are states or outcomes of behaviour that are desired. An organisation may desire either to obtain something that it does not currently have or to retain something it already has. Hence, objectives may be either acquisitive or retentive.

—RUSSELL L. ACKOFF[7]

Objectives can be divided into two categories: external institutional objectives— those which define the impact of the organisation on its environments; and internal institutional objectives—those which define how much is expected of the resources of the organisations.

—ERIE RHEUMAN[8]

The overall corporate objectives define the kind of company the owners.. have determined will most profitably put their resources to use in exploiting available market opportunities over the long run... The way in which a corporate objective is stated varies from one company to another.

—ROBERT J. MOCKLER[9]

Corporate objectives are the general reason for the company's long-term existence; they are what the company is trying to achieve; they are the targets for strategic decisions... Objective is a generic term which embraces a fairly wide range of targets of various types.

—D.E. Hussi[10]

The broader concept of corporate objectives includes purpose, mission, long-term objectives and short-term goals of the organisation.

In view of varying interpretations of objectives, it becomes pertinent to find a common basis from which to begin our consideration of the problem of establishing corporate objectives. This common basis can be traced what Drucker[11], Humble[12], Reddin[13] and Meckoney[14] opine that objectives form a hierarchy within an organisation and take the shape of a pyramid. Thus, at the top of the pyramid exists the purpose and mission of a business. At the next level of the hierarchy the objectives in key result areas are stated. These objectives are further translated into division, department and unit goals down to the lowest level of the organisation. It will, therefore, be more appropriate to say that purpose, mission, objectives, goals and standards are different elements of corporate objectives. We shall now explain the meaning of each of these elements and the difference between them.

ELEMENTS OF CORPORATE OBJECTIVES

Vision

Strategy making in an organisation begins with the visualisation of vision. Vision of an organisation is about what is our present business and where we are headed. Vision provides road maps, which enable people to see the direction in which the organisation should be heading. Through vision statement, an organisation expresses how it intends to position itself and what it aspires to do to excel locally and compete globally. Through vision, an organisation conceptualises its future. An organisation's vision reveals the corpus, the quintessence of being, the values and philosophy of actual working. It is something that organisational people can relate and that which sets the direction for the organisation not only in the long-term but also in daily working.

The following are vision statements of some leading organisations.

"To become the world's best at bringing people together, giving them easy access to each other and to the information as and when required?"

—**AT&T**

"We are in the business connecting people."

—**Nokia**

"To be a world class oil and natural gas company integrated in energy business with dominant Indian leadership and global process."

—**ONGC**

"To become one of the world's largest and best power utilities."

—**NTPC**

"To light up people's lives"

—**Eveready**

"To become one of the top ten global IT services firm."

—**WIPRO**

"To strengthen our position as a premium aluminium company sustaining domestic leadership and global competitiveness through innovation, quality and value added growth."

—**Hindalco**

"To create a world-class car company."

—**Tata Motors**

"To be the most respected software services company in the world."

—**INFOSYS**

"To grow into India's largest independent power producer, to become the largest private infocom player, to retain leadership in petrochemicals, and to become a significant player in petroleum and gas exploration business."

—**Reliance**

"To be the most preferred and significant software engineering led global IT services provider in our chosen markets."

—**HCL Technologies**

"We want to be a market leader in each of the businesses we are in."

—**ICICI Bank**

Thus, vision is a mental journey from the known to the unknown, creating the future from a montage of current facts, hopes, dreams, dangers and opportunities. Management has to draw up a futuristic vision, articulating fundamental line of future business of an organisation.

In conceiving vision, management should always think unreasonably because the unreasonable person has to make the world respond to him while reasonable person responds to the world.

Conceptualising the future or seeing what others cannot see is the hallmark of a strategic manager. Vision not only provides driving fuel, direction to the business strategy but also helps managers evaluate management practices and make decisions. The ignited soul is the most powerful resource of a firm. It ignites thinking among organisational people. It serves as the beacon that motivates and energises an organisation and industry. Penetration of vision shall, therefore, become an important and integral part of a management in the future.

What is crucial about a vision is not its originality but how well it serves the interests of the important constituents—customers, shareholders, employees—and how easily it can be translated into a realistic competitive strategy.[15]

Strategic vision of a firm focuses on its nature and scope of business, providing a clear indication as to what activities to pursue, what not to pursue and what kind of long-term competitive position to build vis-à-vis both customers and competitors.

The strategic vision should be clearly spelt out so as to make the people in and outside the organisation aware, what the latter wants to do. It is crystallised in terms of corporate purpose and mission.

The terms corporate purpose and mission are statements of the strategic vision of an organisation and are, therefore, used as interchangeables. However, some scholars find some difference between the two terms. *Mission*, according to them, tends to be more concerned with the present (what is our business?), whereas vision decides the future long-term direction (where are we headed, what kind of company are we trying to become, and what sort of long-term market position do we aspire to achieve?)[16]

There is a general feeling that there does not exist any difference between purpose and mission except that the former is generally used by profit-seeking organisations while non-profit organisations like hospitals, temples and churches, educational institutions use the latter term. However, there is a conceptual difference between the two. Corporate purpose accords to clear recognition to what the company is and desires to be. It states the overall reason for the existence of an organisation. It is the definition of the fundamental line of business which it wishes to pursue. Corporate purpose, in fact, is a continuing aim lasting throughout the life of an enterprise.

Mission

While corporate vision provides an overview of nature of business of an organisation, corporate mission defines the scope of business, establishing the principal concentration of company efforts in terms of customers, products and business areas. A mission statement provides the basis of awareness of a sense of purpose, the competitive environment, the degree to which firm's mission fits its capabilities and the opportunities, which the environment offers.[17]

A mission provides the basis of awareness of a sense of purpose, the competitive environment, the degree to which the firm's mission fits its capabilities and the opportunities which the government offers.[18]

Thus, mission of a firm spells out the scope of operation in terms of products and markets of service and client. Through its mission statement a company indicates what it is trying to achieve and in what field.

The following are mission statements of some leading organisations:

"To take over everyone's digital life through all kinds of services over the net—from entertainment and games to business."

—MICROSOFT

"To pursue creation of value for our customers, shareholders, employees and society at large."

—HINDALCO

"To achieve and maintain a leading position as suppliers of quality, systems and services to serve the national and international markets in the field of energy. The areas of interest would be the conversion, transmission, utilisation and conservation of energy for applications in the power, industrial and transportation fields."

—BHEL

"Dedicated to excellence by leveraging competitive advantage in R&D and technology with involved people:

- Imbibe high standards of business ethics and organisational values;
- Abiding commitment to health, safety and environment to enrich quality of community life;
- Foster a culture of trust, openness and mutual concern to make working a stimulating and challenging experience for our people;
- Strive for customer delight through quality products and services;
- To be a competent, prosperous and socially conscious team of professionals;
- To create a wealth for the company shareholders and employees by legal and ethical means.

—ONGC

"To realise imagination through

the power to be free

the power to guard your space

the power to negotiate

the power to manage

the power to reach-out."

—HCL TECHNOLOGIES LTD.

A close scrutiny of the above vision and mission statements clearly reveals that vision and mission represent highest level of the corporate objectives which define, in qualitative terms, the kind of activity in which the organisation aspires to be involved. Ackoff refers to such kind of objectives as stylistic objectives.[19]

It may further be noted that the corporate vision and mission are more ethical and philosophical in character and reflects the top management values.

Objectives

Objectives refer to the ultimate end results, which a firm desires to accomplish over a specified period of time. Objectives represent desired results an organisation intends to attain through its operations. They indicate specific sphere of aims, activities and accomplishments. Business organisations are generally concerned with a particular type of goods and services within specific cost and profit constraints. This concern is reflected in their objectives for such areas as profitability and productivity.

In a highly competitive environment, the ultimate objective of a firm is to survive and grow successfully and outbeat the rivals. For this purpose, the firm should aim at competing for opportunity share and not the market share. This requires the firm to aim at achieving sustainable competitive advantage in terms of cost saving and differentiation and create value for the organisation and the shareholder. No organisation can attain all these objectives if its focus is not on creating value for customers.

Thus, while setting the objectives for the firm, an array of aim needs to be established to provide the basis for strategy making and execution.

Profit objective is the most important objective for any business enterprise because this is the only way by which an organisation can protect its capital. In order to earn a profit, an enterprise has to set multiple objectives in key result areas such as market share, new product development, quality of service, management training and selection, finance, physical facilities and even social responsibilities. Objectives set in these areas are the values which the enterprise uses as guideposts to direct its destiny and as criteria to evaluate its performance. Ackoff calls them *performance objectives*.[20]

Objectives are long-term ends, which are expressed qualitatively as well as quantitatively. For instance, profitability objectives may be stated in terms of profits, return on investment, earning per share, or profit-to-sales ratios, among others. More precisely, this objective may be expressed as "to increase return on investment to 15% after taxes within 10 years" or "to increase profits from ₹10 lakh today to ₹80 lakh ten years hence".

Marketing objective may also be described in a number of different ways. They may be expressed as, "to increase market share to 20% within 5 years" or "to increase total company sales by 10% from now".

Productivity objective may be expressed in terms of ratio of input to output (for example, "to increase number of unit to 'x' amount per worker per eight-hour day"). This objective may also be stated in terms of cost per unit of production.

Product objective may be spelt out in terms of product improvement such as, "to introduce a product in the middle range of our product line within 3 years" or "to phase out the rubber products by the end of next year".

In the same vein, **finance objective** includes objectives relating to cash flow, debt equity ratio, new issues of common stock, working capital, dividend payments, collection period and comparable financial matters. They may be described as, "to increase the collection period to 26 days by the end of next year" or "to reduce long-term debt to ₹10 lakh within 5 years".

Human resource objective may also be described in terms of absenteeism, tardiness, number of grievances and training. It may be stated as attempts "to reduce absenteeism to less than 5% by the end of next year" or "to conduct a 20-hour in-house management training programmes for 100 frontline supervisors within 5 years at a cost not exceeding ₹200 per participant".

Social objective may be outlined in terms of types of activities, number of days service or financial contribution, for example, "to hire 200 unemployed persons from the host country within the next 5 years," or "to set up a 100-bed hospital in the host country within the next 2 years" or "to set up a degree college in the host country with the next 5 years".

Thus, the objectives of an enterprise are more specific and less philosophical than its vision and mission. The objectives focus on results, which an organisation seeks to achieve from the business activity.

The main objectives of Microsoft, for instance, are to deliver world-class e-business solutions to its existing and future customers, to continually advance and improve software technology and to make it easier, more cost-effective and more enjoyable for the people to the computers and to strengthen R&D efforts.

Infosys sets out its objectives as to:

- be a world-class software house in the global market;
- be a recognised and respected name for software solutions;
- create a competent, focused, prosperous and socially conscious team of professionals;
- create a wealth for the company shareholders and employees by legal and ethical means.

HCL Technologies Ltd.'s objectives are to:

- build a strong marketing network;
- emphasise on offshore centric revenue;
- emphasise on moving up the value chain to become significant on the overall business plans of their customers;
- pursue strategic alliances.

Goals

Goals are the short-term objectives whose attainment is desired within a specified time period covered by the plan. They are the quantified objectives expressed in a specific dimension. They are usually very specific and concrete. Time dimension of goals is not more than one year. Goals are, thus, quantifiable in terms of specific levels of achievement desired. For example, "obtain 5% of the country's eastern market for watches by the end of this year". It is worth stressing that goals are always time-oriented. For example, "to bring out the new product by January 2011".

They are established wherever and whenever the top management wishes to guide activity, set standards for performance and measure performance. They also form a network covering the entire business at all levels and including all individuals. Although for any one subunit in the company or any individual, the total number of goals may be less than the number of objectives set for the business as a whole, in the aggregate there will be, of course, far more short-range goals than the company objectives.

Goals for the company as a whole for each of the key result activities such as "increase sales by 5% in each calendar quarter of the next year", "raise earnings per share to ₹2 for the year", or "hire a new chief economist this year". Similarly, for each division and department there should be goals covering very important activity for which performance is to be evaluated. Each subsidiary unit should also set goals for its initial activities.

Generally, goals are set forth in the budgeting process. However, individual goals are mostly quantifiable which they themselves establish or which may be developed for them or in participation with higher-level management. They may, at times, be personal and non-quantifiable in nature, for example, instituting a training programme at an institute of management, improving staff work, or developing better relations with union leaders.

Goals set at the individual level partake the character of standards of performance.

Objectives and goals conceptually differ in terms of time spectrum, specificity, focus and measurement. Thus, objectives have long-term time range; sometimes they are timeless and impending. But goals are time bound. They have a short span of time. In goals even the date of accomplishing the target is specified. Further, objectives are less specific than goals and focus more on the external environment of the enterprise whereas goals are expressed in terms of conditions existing within the enterprise. This is because goals imply commitment of resources of the organisation in order to accomplish specified target. Finally, accomplishment of goals can be measured more objectively than the objectives because the former are comparatively more specific and quantitative.

Although we can draw conceptually clear-cut distinctions between vision, mission, objectives and goals, it may not be always necessary to find such distinctions nor always desirable because they are so interwoven and interrelated with each other that no management can afford to ignore one for the other without risking the life of the organisation.

CHARACTERISTICS OF CORPORATE OBJECTIVES

A discussion of the major features of the corporate objectives will provide insight into the substantive nature of these objectives. Further, it will provide an idea about the attributes which objectives need to possess if they have to make a genuine contribution to organisational success.

Objectives from a Hierarchy

The objectives of an enterprise exists in a hierarchy according to their relative importance. The hierarchy begins with a broad statement of vision and concludes with very specific goals. Objectives are arranged in such a manner that each sub-objective is arranged in the form of a pyramid, as shown in Figure 9.1.

Figure 9.1 Hierarchy of objectives.

Thus, at the top of the pyramid, a company has a broad vision of providing the cheapest and most convenient means of recreation to people. This is followed by a corporate mission which states the fundamental objective and the line of business which the organisation seeks to pursue. Around this are developed long-term objectives of the company in key result areas. Within the parameters of long-term objectives, short-term goals of the company and its different divisions and departments are determined. At the bottom of the objective hierarchy, the company has a standard of performance which constitutes the targets set for individuals. It is interesting to note that the objectives at the upper levels tend to be less specific and quantified than those at the lower levels. The higher level objectives are broader in scope and have long-term duration. They serve as a foundation for setting objectives at lower levels.

The objective hierarchy can also be explained by way of ends-means analysis. According to this analysis, subordinated objectives provide the means for achieving higher order objectives. Thus, each objective in the hierarchy is the sub-objective of a unit which must be accomplished. This sub-unit objective serves as a means for attaining a higher objective. For example, the top management of a multinational organisation considers manufacturing and selling novelty items in international markets as the main objective of the organisation. Objectives set by marketing and production managers become the means for achieving the objectives established by the top management. This sort of analysis continues until the objectives of each individual in the organisation are set forth in quantitative terms. Table 9.1 will explain this analysis:

Table 9.1 Means-ends Chain of Objectives

Objectives	Sub-objectives			
• Major objective	Manufacture and sell novelty items			
• Means for achieving objective become department goals	Sales department		Production department	
	Sell 25,000 items to earn ₹1,00,00,000		Produce 25,000 items by 31st December, 2011 at variable cost of not more than ₹100 per unit	
• Means for achieving goals become unit subgoals	Direct mail order sales	Sales to jobbers	Purchasing	Product planning control
	Priced at ₹500 each	Priced at ₹300 each	Obtain price, compare bids, place order for raw materials	Schedule runs for greater productivity of labour and equipment
• Means for achieving units' subgoals are individual objectives	Individual employees objectives			

The objectives of business units and sub-objectives should be closely related because there is a close inter-relationship among the major economic objectives. For example, an objective to maintain or increase return on investment equal to or above the industry average must be pursued in the light of sales objectives, financial objectives and objectives pertaining to efficient use of resources. One cannot be established without relation to others. In relating the network of aims one can start with any one major objective and develop sub-objectives from it. There should be a reasonable meshing of objectives and sub-objectives. Figure 9.2 exhibits the inter-relationship among objectives.

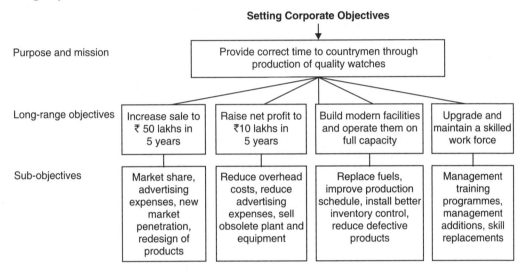

Figure 9.2 Inter-relationship among objectives.

Objectives should be Multiple

Objectives at every level have to be multiple because forces influencing the very existence of an enterprise are many and the management cannot afford to ignore any of them with impunity. Thus, even broad major enterprise objectives are multiple. A business enterprise might have four basic objectives, viz., to fulfill the human and economic needs of society through the production of goods or services, to maximise opportunity share, to maximise earnings on shareholder's investment and to retain global business leadership. Similarly, the enterprise might set multiple long-term objectives in critical areas for guiding and measuring the performance, such as "to increase rate of return on investment by 10% over a 5-year period", "to cut down establishment expenses by 2% during a 5-year period", "to reduce absenteeism by 10% during the next 5 years" or "to replace the obsolete plant and machinery during a 10-year period". In the same way, short-term goals of the organisation as a whole as well as those of divisions, departments and units are likely to be multiple and diverse so as to cover each and every activity of the enterprise whose performance will affect its survival and success.

It is impossible to identify even one major objective that would cover all possible relationships and needs. Organisational problems and relationships cover a multitude of variables and cannot possibly be explained by a single objective. Similarly, sub-objectives and sub-goals have to be multiple so as to guide and measure the performance of every sub-activity. What is very important for the management is to ensure that the diverse objectives fit within the environmental constraints and not be at cross purposes with one another. If all the objectives are not integrated with one another, they can be detrimental to the survival of the organisation. Thus, the task of balancing objectives becomes one of the essential activities of the top management. Failure to make the objectives mutually supportive tends to cause conflict between the units of the organisation responsible for attaining the inconsistent objectives.

Objectives should be Specific and Quantitative

Although objectives can be expressed qualitatively or quantitatively or both, it will be more useful if they are specific and quantitative so as to provide a clear reference point for subsequent decisions and for evaluation of progress. The objective—"to increase net profit after taxes by 10% during the next two years by increasing sales from ₹10,00,000 to ₹12,00,000 during the period"—is more specific and verifiable than the objective—"to increase net profit after taxes during the next 2 years by increasing production". With such objective it is easy for the top management to know exactly how well the organisation is doing. The value of this becomes obvious during the control function.

Objectives should be Time-oriented

A specific time horizon is another characteristic of effective objectives. They should not only specify what the organisation wants to accomplish but also when the result is to be attained. It will be more meaningful to state the objective "to increase sales by 20% during the next 3 years" than "to increase sales by 20%".

Objectives should be Attainable

Since an objective can and should serve as a strong motivational tool for the individual manager, it must be one that is within reach and is challenging for the employees. An objective that is well beyond reach can soon create a defeatist attitude on the part of the manager. It should not be too easy to accomplish because that can also create the same kind of a defeatist attitude. Therefore, the objectives should strike a balance, requiring a stretch of effort on the part of the manager and his subordinates while still assuring the probability of success with such an effort. Objectives which challenge rather than frustrate individuals are preferable.

Objectives should be Accountable

For effective achievement of the corporate objectives it is necessary to fix accountability. It will, therefore, be necessary to split the corporate objectives into those to be attained by the top management, those to be attained by the managers of subsidiaries, those by the functional managers, and those by individual, departmental and unit managers.

Need for Setting Objectives

The following factors motivate organisations to set objectives:

Objectives Serve as a Means of Legitimacy

By defining what kind of business the company is in and what it wants to do, corporate purpose conveys to insiders as well as outsiders the environment in which the company is going to operate, opportunities which will be seized and threats which will be combated. In this way it justifies its activities and its existence in a particular country to such groups as customers, politicians, employees, stockholders and society at large. Through a well-conceived and clear-cut vision, a business enterprise can build its image of business acumen, dynamic growth, trend-setter or public responsibility in the eyes of the government, customers and society at large and also in the eyes of employees and accordingly affect their behaviour.

Objectives Provide Basis for Decision-making

The vision and its supportive objectives serve as criteria for all subsequent managerial decision-making. Setting objectives for different departments, units and sub-units prescribe the direction according to which managers have to take decisions and execute them. If the managers did not know what their organisation's basic purpose was, they would have no logical reference point for deciding which alternative is best.

Objectives also help in coordinating decisions of different executives and departments and units because they know what the business objectives demand of them in terms of performance and how best they can contribute to the total success of the enterprise. They know the areas of discretion and adjust to the need of others. Peter Drucker rightly observed that objectives in the key result areas are the instrument panel necessary to pilot the business enterprise. Without them, the management lacks direction—without landmarks to steer by, without maps and without having flown the route before.

Objectives Serve as a Motivating Force

Objectives motivate the employees to work with zeal and zest for the accomplishment of targets particularly when they actively join their superior in setting the objectives and elicit their commitment for performance. They feel overwhelmed with a sense of satisfaction when they achieve the targets they set for themselves. They no longer wait for guidance and decisions because they have clearly defined purpose before them and they were party to its determination. They also feel inspired to do their best for the attainment of the goals of the organisation because by doing so they would achieve some of their personal objectives.

Objectives Provide Yardsticks to Measure Performance

Verifiable objectives provide a sound basis for evaluating the performance of the organisation. Short-term goals furnish milestones for measuring progress towards long-range objectives. All managers can see how step-by-step achievement of short-term targets can lead to the accomplishment of ultimate ends. Goals also provide precise standard with which performance of managers at different levels can be evaluated.

PROCESS OF SETTING CORPORATE OBJECTIVES

Setting Corporate Objectives involves the following process:

Articulating Corporate Vision and Mission

Objective setting begins with the articulation of suitable vision and mission for the organisation. Vision is something that cannot be finalised and written in a day, sitting in a room. It is something that has to evolve.

Vision, as noted earlier, is a mental construct of some desired future state. The top management has to create a grand vision—a purpose, which is noble, lofty and aspirational. It is a dream that should excite and energise everybody in the company. For instance, Infosys' vision is so powerful as to make everyone in the organisation feel proud to belong to it and will work hard to make it a better one.

Four important aspects involved in establishing well-conceived strategic vision and expressing it in terms of the corporate purpose and mission are[21]:

(i) Defining what business a company is really in and what business it intends to be in;

(ii) Establishing relationship between present and future product-market complexion of the company;

(iii) Sharing the vision, purpose and mission;

(iv) Deciding when to change the company's strategic direction.

Defining the Business

Through the strategic vision, purpose and mission, a firm decides what business it is in and intends to be in. In order to arrive at a sound concept of business, the management must factor in three crucial factors, viz., customers' needs (or what is being satisfied), customers' groups (or who are being satisfied) and the technologies used and functions performed (or how customers' needs are being satisfied).

Defining a business in terms of customers makes complete definition. Products or services per se are not important to customer; a product or service becomes a business when it satisfies a need or want. Customers' groups are relevant because they indicate the market to be served—the geographical domain to be covered and the type of buyers the company is going after.

Technological and functional aspects of business are important because they indicate how the company will satisfy the customers' needs and how much of the industry's production-distribution chain, its activities will span. For instance, a company's business can be specialised, concentrated in just one stage enterprise as it focuses on the retail and of the consumer goods business; it does not manufacture the items it sells. Exxon and Mobil are fully integrated, leasing drilling sites with wells, pump oil, transport crude oil in their own ships and sell gasoline and other refined products through their own networks of branded distributions and service station outlets.

Between these two extremes, the organisations can engage in partially integrated business. Good year, for instance, both manufacture tyres and operate a chain of company-owned retail tyre stores, but it has not integrated backward into rubber plantations and other tyre-making components.

The corporate purpose and mission of an organisation should never be expressed in terms of profitability because it is the outcome of business activity. Profit is not the explanation, cause or rationale of business behaviour and business decisions but the test of their validity. Because an organisation is an open system, it can only survive in the long run by satisfying some need outside itself. A firm can earn profit only when it survives. It should look to the environment in which it operates for a customer. The purpose of a business must, therefore, be outside of it.

It is the customers who determine the purpose and mission of a firm. In setting realistic purpose and mission for the firm, the top management must make conscious efforts to ascertain existing needs, values and expectations of the customers and the potential gap in the light of future economic, industrial, technological, political, social and competitive developments. Diamler India Commercial Vehicle (DICV)—a subsidiary of the German auto giant Diamler AG—has set its aim as "to sell trucks that are made in India, for India and by Indians". The company entered India in 2006 to study the market for the last 4 years and gain customers' insight. Its first product will hit the market only in 2012—a good 6 years after its entry in India (Illustrative Capsule 9.1).

ILLUSTRATIVE CAPSULE 9.1

CUSTOMISATION OF VISION BY DIAMLER INDIA COMMERCIAL VEHICLES (DICV)

Diamler AG—the largest German truck maker in the world with a presence in over 150 countries—decided to capitalise on the tremendous market opportunity which the country offers in terms of significant increase in demand of trucks from the current 2.02 lakh units per annum to over 5 lakh units by 2018, and set up its subsidiary, Diamler India Commercial Vehicle (DICV), at Chennai with an investment of ₹4,400 crore to manufacture and sell light, medium and heavy-duty trucks. It has plans to hit the market in 2012 by rolling out over 70,000 units a year.

Nevertheless, the truck industry in India is highly competitive because of the presence of leading players like Tata Motors and Ashok Leyland who controlled 85% of the commercial vehicle market, for Diamler AG India is a very crucial market to squeeze the burgeoning market opportunity in future and capture the market by identifying the existing gaps and fulfilling these gaps. The management set its strategic vision as "to sell trucks that are made in India, for India and by Indians".

One of the earliest decisions the management took was to tailor a product for India rather than rushing in with a detro-fitted model drawn from its vast product portfolio. The management believes that, "We need to have an in-depth understanding of the needs of the Indian consumers, which will enable us to design products that are suited to this market". The company has been studying Indian market for the last 4 years. DICV is not banking just on market research for its success. It is also imbibing the local culture. "We do not need Diamler culture, we need Indian culture and the resultant local creative solution", says Marc Llistsella, CEO of DICV.

To start with, three German executives from Diamler AG interacted with the drivers at the Chennai's Koembedu vegetable and fruit market—one of the biggest markets in Asia—what they thought about collapsible steering, air bags or honey comb paneling for the front of the truck which will collapse on frontal impact and thus save the driver. What they learnt stunned them. Indian drivers have little interest in these features and prefer to leave their safety to the lemon and green chilly they string and hang in front of the truck and an idol of their favourite deity they place in the dashboard. Back home, the Germans tweaked the dashboard design for all the Diamler vehicles that will be manufactured and sold in India to include a flat surface to mount God's idol, apart from incorporating the various safety features.

India, the management feels, is one of the most demanding markets when it comes to truck performance. The total cost of ownership—fuel efficiency, product reliability cost of spares and resale value—needs to be the best. "India may be a developing economy, but commercial thinking in the trucking sector is First World. I have not seen the cost consciousness that Indians exhibit everywhere else in the world. We need to offer a highly efficient and a very reliable product at a very competitive price", says Marc Llistosella. Adds Cakmaz, Vice President (Product Engineering): "We have to be very precise in India. Life cycle costs are calculated very meticulously here".

That is not all. India has an unusually high proportion of first-time users and small fleet operators which call for product offerings that are tailored very differently from what global players are used to.

Thus, Diamler's focus is to have high localisation levels for all vehicles. The trucks will have localisation upto 85%, including frames, engines and axles among other crucial components. Also, DICV is tapping heavily into Indian talent to design the right product for India. Of the 500 employees, it has today, only 30 are expats.

The company has also taken care not to let its pedigree come in its way and has chosen to adapt to the Indian market in every possible way. "We have chosen to unlearn whatever we know about trucks and learn trucking the Indian way", says Llistosella. All senior managers including expats, routinely visit major trucking sites to meet the stakeholders. Some even travel in a truck for days to experience first hand the Indian way of trucking. These efforts have helped DICV appreciate and adopt certain Indian practices that may not be a part of Diamler's system.

Source: *Business Today,* June 13, 2010.

It is noteworthy that the market-based definitions of a business are superior to product or technology-based definitions because products and technologies are transient. The basic market needs generally endure for a longer time. A radio manufacturing company will go out of business as soon as transistor and television are invested. However, the same company defined as recreational will experience no difficulty in switching from radio manufacturing to television manufacturing.

Sharing the Strategic Vision

The corporate management should not only conceive the vision but also share it with employees, customers, suppliers, collaborators, investors and other enlightened groups of the society to solicit their opinions which will enable him to crystallise it in terms of purpose and mission. Sharing of the vision generates excitement, brings order out of chaos and builds confidence and trust among the employees who will work harder to make it succeed. People are proud with a company having a worthwhile vision and are trying to be the world's best at something competitively significant. An exciting vision brings the workforce together, galvanises people to act, stimulates extra effort and arouses people to live in the business instead of just coming to work.

It is worth noting that vision and mission should be expressed in simple and concise language. Managers need to communicate the vision in such a way as to arouse a strong sense of organisational purpose, build pride, generate enthusiasm for the firm's future course and elicit personal effort and dedication from everyone in the organisation. A crisp, clear and inspiring strategic vision has the power to turn heads in the intended direction and begin a new organisational march.

When to Rejig and Alter the Vision

The emergence of new scenario and the concomitant change in business milieu render it imperative for the management to continuously rejig the company's current product-market position and future prospects, always checking when it is time to steer a new course and adjust the vision. Sapient entrepreneurs, for instance, have a sharp eye on changing customers' wants and needs, emerging technological development, fast changing trade conditions and other important symptoms of growing or shrinking business opportunity. These entrepreneurs quickly respond to users' problems and complaints with the industry's current products and services and bring about change in vision and adopt new business model.

In recent years, for instance, the organisations engaged in consumer electronics and telecommunications have come to believe that their future products will have to incorporate microprocessors and other elements of computer technology to offer multipurpose mobile devices. Accordingly, they are changing their vision to broaden their business horizon, and embrace new business model to squeeze emerging opportunities and improve their market share. Nokia, for instance, has transformed itself from lumbering business into telephony business and has now become a giant MNC offering voice-optimised phone, and multimedia devices or computers. Some of these devices are almost like Swiss Army Knives, because they offer many solutions to finicky customers. Nokia's mobile phones have inbuilt camera, music, navigation and other devices enabling the company to add value to the telephony industry.

Vodafone, in its strive to cope with bruising competitive challenges and economic downturn across the globe, has decided to focus on looking at the business and economics, listening to its customers daily and then try and adapt very quickly to the new changes. In economic crisis, Vodafone and others in the industry went from a growth model to a stable one.

In finalising the corporate mission, the top management should keep in view the firm's capabilities and resources. Although the firm may be in a position to accomplish many things, it should aim at the activity which it can do best. Likewise, it should set a mission which it can achieve with its existing resources.

Determining the Objectives

Within the broad framework of the corporate vision and mission, a firm has to build up a spectrum of specific objectives. Setting objectives translates the strategic vision and directional course in desired outcomes and performance milestones. The objective-setting is a call for action: what to achieve, when to achieve it and who is responsible to achieve. It is, therefore, essential to express the objectives in quantifiable or measurable terms and a time for achievement. This means avoiding as far as possible generalities, like maximising profits, reducing costs, becoming more efficient or increasing sales.

Objectives have to be set for each key result areas. Broadly speaking, two types of key result areas standout: those relating to financial performance and those relating to the strategic performance. Achieving acceptable financial performance is necessary for the survival of an organisation. Achieving acceptable strategic performance is essential for sustaining and improving the firm's long-term market position and competitiveness. Examples of financial objectives and strategic objectives are brought out in Table 9.2.

Table 9.2 Financial and Strategic Objectives

Financial Objectives	Strategic Objectives
• Increase in revenue	• Higher opportunity
• Decrease in cost	• Higher product quality
• Increase in earnings per share	• Higher productivity
• Higher return on invested capital	• Superior customer service
• Rise in stock price	• Expanded growth opportunities
• Stable earnings during recessionary periods	• Total customer satisfaction

For strategic thinking and action to permeate organisation behaviour across the firm, the objectives must be established not only for the organisation as a whole but also for each of the organisation's separate business, product lines, functional areas and departments. Only when every manager from the CEO to the lowest level manager is held accountable for achieving specific results and when each unit's objectives support achievement of the company objectives, the objective setting process is said to be complete enough to ensure that the whole organisation is headed down the chosen path and that each part of the organisation knows what it needs to accomplish.

We shall now discuss how objective in different areas are established for guiding and for measuring performance of the organisation and its parts.

Profit Objectives

The most important yardstick of profitability is 'Return on Investment' (ROI). This ratio can be obtained by relating net profit after tax to total investments. The expected net profit figure can be ascertained by estimating expected revenues and costs. However, their profitability rate suffers from the drawback of the time factor. It does not distinguish between the value of present earnings, value of earnings two years hence, value of earnings four years hence and so on. It will, therefore, be more useful if the profitability rate is expressed in terms of 'Discounted Rate of Return' or 'Internal Rate of Return (IRR)'. Discounted rate of return is that earning rate which discounts all the future cash earnings from capital investment to the level of investment outlay. Thus, anticipated total profits over the life of the investment are reduced to their present cash value, rather than as an annual rate of return.

Another yardstick of profitability is profit as a percentage of sales. This ratio helps to measure the operating efficiency of the company.

Now the question arises: what should be the profitability rate? It must be such as to ensure the company's survival. This can be only when the profitability rate is not less than the industry average.

Marketing Objectives

Profit objective is supported by marketing objective. Marketing objective has to be stated in terms of the market standing, which the organisation aims in national and foreign markets. Marketing objectives should be spelt out in terms of desired standing of the existing products in their present market expressed in absolute as well as relative terms; abandonment of the existing products; introduction of new products in the existing markets: the number of products, their properties, volume and the desired market shares; introduction of new products in new markets expressed in absolute as well as in relative sense; and the distributive organisation desired to accomplish the marketing goals and the pricing policy appropriate to them. The service objective will also form part of the marketing objectives. Here the organisation states how well it will render services to the customers' satisfaction.

Marketing objectives should be established after a thorough survey of what its market is, who the customer is, where he is, what he is, what he buys, what he considers value and what his unsatisfied wants are. The marketing objective has to ensure continued growth of sales atleast at the pace of the industry to enable the firm to retain its share of the market.

Innovative Objectives

A company must also spell out its innovative objective so as to ensure its successful continuance in the environment and maintain its current market share. Innovative objective receives added emphasis where technological changes are turbulent. This objective may be expressed in terms of new products or services needed to achieve marketing objectives, product improvement needed to attain marketing objectives, new processes or modification in old processes needed to satisfy market objectives, and innovation and improvements in other major areas so as to keep abreast of the advancement in knowledge and skill.

For developing innovative objectives, forecasts have to be made about the innovations needed to reach marketing goals according to product lines, existing markets, new markets and services requirements. Appraisal of technological development and its effect upon different areas of business should also be undertaken. The forecasts have to be made on short-term as well as long-term basis.

Productivity Objectives

The productivity objective should be stated in order to gauge managerial competence and allow comparison between managerial efficiency of different units within the enterprise and of different enterprises. The only yardstick available to precisely measure productivity is 'contributed value'. Contributed value is the difference between the gross revenue received by a company from the sale of its products or services rendered by outside suppliers. Thus, contributed value considers all the costs of factors of production that contribute to the final product. The productivity objective can be expressed as 'increase in the ratio of contributed value to total revenue'.

Objectives Relating to Employees

Employees' objectives must receive managerial attention because of greater consciousness among employees regarding their rights and prerogatives and the realisation that overall productivity and profitability of an organisation depend on their efforts.

These objectives—generally stated as 'to improve industrial relation', 'to promote employees' welfare' and 'to develop human resources'—are qualitative in character. This hardly provides any guidance because they do not provide a way of determining one's degree of success in the pursuit of the objective. Yet attempts should be made to quantify them. For example, the objective of improving labour-management relations can be quantified by way of expressing this objective in such terms as reduction in absenteeism, labour productivity, and so on. With these standards, the extent to which the organisation has been able to achieve the objective can be measured.

Similarly, the employees' welfare objective can be specified in terms of specific welfare programme and quantum of facilities to be given to the employees.

In emerging economies, there has been increasing awareness among the business houses regarding employees' welfare because of their realisation that improved industrial relations are necessary for the success of the organisations.

Social Objectives

A business enterprise being a socio-economic unit has a responsibility towards society. The society provides a conducive environment for the operation of enterprises and incurs several costs for them. It, therefore, becomes the moral responsibility of the top management to consider the interests of the society. This is also necessary for the survival of the enterprise. No organisation can exist without social acceptance.

It is, therefore, essential to set social objectives as a part of the corporate objective. However, the task is bewildering. Even within the same country the domestic firm may face the dilemma of striking socially responsible behaviour satisfying to all in view of varying expectations of different stakeholders.

Even then, the management should set the social objectives and the key to conflict resolution is to maintain a balanced unbiased perspective. These should be determined keeping in view the cost-benefits of the social operations and overall policies of the firm.

Determining Divisional and Departmental Goals

For implementation of the corporate objectives, it is necessary to articulate goals for every division and department. These goals are set by divisional/departmental managers in consultation with their subordinate executives. These goals have to be set up within the framework of the corporate objectives. There are three approaches adopted by an organisation in this regard, viz., centralised approach, decentralised approach and mixed approach. In the **centralised approach**, the top management designs the overall corporate objectives as well as divisional objectives and then directs them to chalk out their programmes accordingly. Complete integration of divisional goals with corporate objectives is a great advantage of this approach. However, it does not leave any room for divisional autonomy. Too much centralisation smothers initiative, innovative urge and creativity of the individuals and groups which are necessary for the success of an organisation.

In the **decentralised approach**, divisional/departmental managers are given autonomy to evolve their own objectives and goals. Each division holds a conference of its managers and works out the objectives. The top management helps them in integrating these divisional objectives into the corporate objectives.

In the **mixed approach**, divisional objectives are worked out independently within the overall framework of the corporate objectives. Divisional objectives are finalised by a committee consisting of the top management team and divisional managers.

The commitment of departmental executives to the accomplishment of the corporate objectives is a pre-condition for the translation of the objectives into action. For this purpose, departmental goals must be split into performance norms or targets for lower management levels. Here too, there may be several approaches. In one approach, departmental managers, in consultation with line managers, fix the norms for their performance. In another approach, individuals are requested to develop their performance norms which are refined and integrated into departmental goals. There may be another approach where departmental managers set the targets for individual executives without consulting them.

Among the different approaches, the one where targets are set jointly by the departmental manager and the concerned executives is most useful since it involves the direct participation of those who have to achieve goals. It also motivates the employees to do their best for the organisation because from time to time they get feedback about their performance. Linking the performance with a suitable incentive system will further inspire the individual employees to contribute their best to the organisation.

FORCES INTERACTING WITH CORPORATE OBJECTIVES

A business enterprise, being a sub-system of overall social system, cannot choose its objective in a vacuum. Realistic objectives cannot be arbitrarily decreed in a smoke-filled boardroom. They must be developed through a continual interaction with various forces. These forces can be categorised as external environmental forces, forces within the firm and value system of the firm's management.

Forces in the Environment

A business organisation, in order to survive, must dispassionately consider the developments likely to take place in the economy in general and industry in particular, technological changes, and competitive environment within the country as well as of those countries where the firm's subsidiaries are operating, government policy, political conditions existing in the country and abroad and the likely changes therein, and changes in human values and preferences because they affect the targets which the organisation is going to set regarding profit, market standing, innovation, productivity, and the like. For instance, the top management aspiring for maximising profit for the enterprise may have to modify it because of government policy regarding pollution controls, excess profit tax, pricing and others. Trade unions may require higher than market wage rates, more holidays and other benefits. Competitors may sell other products or services at unrealistically low prices and spend excessive amounts on advertising. Suppliers may feel that they have a monopoly and begin to charge outrageous prices.

In short, selecting objectives is part of a process of establishing a favourable balance between a firm and environmental relations. At one extreme, the environment has total control over setting a firm's objectives. At the other extreme, an organisation has total control over its environment. Most organisations are in between, and depending upon which is more powerful at the moment, objectives are either modified or remain unmodified. Much of the success of firms like Tata Motors, Mahindra and Mahindra, TCS, Wipro, Infosys, ITC and Reliance Industries can be attributed to their ability to respond to the environment and adjust their objectives to what they perceive.

Forces within the Firm

Another force influencing the formulation of objectives is the nature and make-up of an organisation's resources and internal power relationship. The management should assess the firm's resources before establishing objectives to seize upon environmental opportunities. Larger and more profitable firms have more resources with which to respond to forces in their environment than smaller or poorer firms.

Internal power relationships also influence selection of objectives. Different groups and individuals within an organisation have varying interests that they attempt to promote through the selection of organisational objectives. Accordingly, the nature of an organisation's objectives is influenced by continued bargaining among various individuals and groups attempting to ensure that their differing interests are represented. For instance, stockholders bargain with employees over the relative division of profits and departmental units bargain with one another for greater prestige and status. As a consequence of such exchanges, the organisational objectives represent compromises reflecting the relative power of various organisational coalitions.

Value Systems of Management

A third factor which influences the choice of the objectives is the values and preferences of the managers. Managers' beliefs and preferences emanate from their education, experience and the information they receive. So each manager's values are his own. An enterprise having high value system or ideologies will attract and retain managers having similar values. Venturesome executives usually assign high priority to innovative objective which promises large profit with high risks, while conservative executives want to tread on a risk-free path. There are also some executives who have a sense of personal obligations to serve society. They believe that their firms should be responsible. They expect that the organisation spells out its determination to promote community welfare. The influence of the personal values of executives on the choice of objectives is far reaching. Executives with certain values would be inclined to emphasise one set of objectives while another group of executives will like another set of objectives. The final objectives emerge out of the managers' attempt to satisfy the needs of all the groups which are involved with the enterprise.

BALANCING CORPORATE OBJECTIVES

A formidable challenge which the top management of an organisation generally faces regarding strategic management lies in the formulation of general and specific corporate objectives and ranking them according to their importance to the organisation. This is due to the fact that, the organisations do not have objectives, only people have objectives. Thus, the corporate objectives are derivatives of objectives and goals of all such individuals and groups, which have direct and indirect interest in the organisation. Within the organisation, these individuals include shareholders, executives, employees, creditors and outside the organisation, customers, suppliers, government and society at large are the prominent participants in the organisation. These participants have diverse goals because of their varying notions, preferences, attitudes and values. Their expectations from the organisation are different.

For instance, the shareholders are interested in the maximisation of wealth and hence they would like their organisation to operate for achieving the objectives of wealth and profit maximisation, even though it may require the management to adopt diversification strategy or to undertake innovation of product and service, exposing the organisation to risks. However, the top management will have the goals of protecting their private sphere of influence rather than maximise shareholders' wealth and they may be reluctant to take decisions which pose a threat to their survival. Such type of management is more willing to be satisfied with maintaining the status quo rather than go in for maximising wealth.

Different executives in the organisation may have varying objectives because of differences in their values and perceptions about opportunities in the environment and the way of seizing them. For example, the finance manager in his endeavour to maintain profitability of the firm may wish to establish the objective of restricting capital expenditures during the period of next two years. However, the production manager may insist on the objective of innovation so as to install a new production process for increasing production of the firm. Likewise, employees of the organisation, who are more concerned with continuity in employment, adequacy of their income, good promotion opportunity and other benefits, will expect the organisation to set employees' welfare as its chief aim.

Similarly, the creditors are always keen on the solvency of the firm and hence they dictate the objective of high liquidity even at the expense of profitability. This is not compatible with the owners' objectives of high profitability. Customers of an organisation expect that it should supply goods according to their tastes at reasonable price. No organisation can afford to ignore the customers' expectations.

Society expects an organisation to provide employment opportunities to all eligible unemployed people, impart free education and medical facilities to the local people, ensure a pollution-free environment, provide infrastructure facilities, and so on. The organisation cannot afford to ignore the society because they are the ultimate consumers and also because they are affected by its operations. But the objective of fulfilling the society's expectations may counterbalance the firm's objective of profit maximisation, especially in the short run.

An enterprise, in order to function effectively, must, therefore, take cognisance of the multiplicity of interests so as to accommodate the variety of preferences among individual members. One of the genuine skills of strategic management is to find the right mix of objectives within which individuals having conflicting interests can cooperate and be stimulated to coordinate their diverse interest in a cohesive way. If conflicts stemming out of the pursuit of inconsistent multiple objectives are not resolved, the managers should endeavour to cope with the conflicting pressures on them, which may not always be in the best interest of the company. A satisfactory trade-off should, therefore, be struck.

The whole approach of synthesizing the varied interests of the stakeholders should be based on problem-solving rather than on normative decision theories based on the statistical decision theory and theories of individual choice because of their inadequacies. The problem-solving approach is based on the premise that the managers do not maximise but select aspiration levels which are attainable. The starting point is that an organisation is a coalition of individuals. Despite diversity in their values, aspirations and notions, individuals stay together because they share some aspirations which are, by implication, of greater significance to them than those they disagree with; otherwise they would part with the company.

The interest of all the individuals and groups lies in the survival of an organisation. There will, therefore, be no conflict among the different interest groups about the firm's objective of survival and for that matter, the objective of earning minimum rate of return.

Once the overall basic objective is established, the next step is to decide the supporting objectives in such a way as to accommodate the interests of all the stakeholders. It should, however, be recognised that all these objectives cannot be pursued with the same amount of emphasis. Attempts should be made to assign priorities to such objectives as can make substantial contribution to the overall objective. The basic problem arises regarding the priorities assigned to the objectives of different individuals. Every individual wants his objective to be accorded top priority. It is here that the top management, as the strongest group in the coalition, has to play a crucial role in reconciling the conflicts among individuals. They bargain with the various groups and try to produce a commonly agreed set of objectives and provide ranking to each of these objectives to the satisfaction of majority of stakeholders.

Inconsistencies among the objectives can be resolved by rating them. In this regard, the management must remember that they cannot settle the conflicts once and for all. There will only be a quasi-resolution. They should, by 'muddling through' approach, evolve at the current set of objectives and set their priorities to the satisfaction of as many demands and desires as possible. The objectives and their priorities should be periodically reviewed in the light of environmental changes, corporate resources and constraints. This approach can be gainfully employed to harmonise objectives and goals at every levels of management.

Many times when it becomes almost impossible to evolve commonly agreed objectives, the top management exercises its formal authority to accomplish this. Such an action is relatively quicker and more decisive. However, there will be no room for flexibility in this action, and commitment to the objective on the part of executives and employees will be a far cry. It will, therefore, be more useful if formal authority is exercised for developing cooperative relationships.

Conflicts may also arise between long-term objectives and goals. The management must take into account short-term goals for the long-term future. If long-term needs of the firm are not given due consideration while developing short-term targets, the future of the firm may not be so bright. In balancing the short-term and long-term objectives, the management has to decide how much immediate results should be sacrificed for the sake of long-term growth or how much the long-term growth should be jeopardised for the sake of short-run results. For example, the short-term objective of expanding sales is not compatible with the long-term objective of increasing the profitability rate. To increase sales means sacrificing immediate profit. But to earn higher profit means sacrificing long-term sales. A proper trade-off has to be struck between growth and profitability objectives. There is no reliable formula for doing this; each business requires its own balance and even the same organisation may require a different balance at different times. Balancing is not a mechanical job, it is a risk-taking decision.

Summary

Formulating the objectives for an organisation is the first and foremost step in strategy crafting. The corporate objectives are composed of vision, mission, long-term objectives, goals and standards of performance. Vision states how organisation will position itself, and what business it will engage in, while mission spells out the scope of business, long-term objectives articulate anticipated end results over a period of time, and goals state short-term targets. Thus, the corporate objectives are multiple and form a hierarchy.

Every organisation has to formulate its objectives with a view to conveying to the outside world about its legitimacy, providing basis for decision-making and yardsticks for assessing performance.

The corporate purpose and mission should always be customer-oriented with focus on product class, technology, customer's group and market need. The corporate objectives—both long-term and short-term—need to be expressed in terms of opportunity share, profitability, liquidity, productivity, human resource development, R&D and social aspects.

Key Terms

Acquisitive objectives
Departmental objectives
Divisional objectives
Financial objectives
Goals
Innovative objectives
Marketing objectives

Mission
Muddling through
Opportunity share
Performance objectives
Productivity objectives
Profitability objectives
Purpose

Retentive objectives
Social objectives
Strategic objectives
Stylistic objectives
Vision

Discussion Questions

1. How do you define corporate objectives? Distinguish between vision, mission, objectives and goals.
2. 'Corporate objectives form a hierarchy'. Comment on the statement with the help of suitable examples.
3. 'Outcomes of behaviour that are desired by organisations are stated as purpose, mission, objectives and goals'. Comment.
4. Discuss the redeeming features of corporate objectives.
5. 'Objectives form a network'. Explain.
6. Why should an organisation formulate its objectives?
7. Imagine you are the owner of a firm. How would you determine objectives for your firm?
8. What are the principal forces with which corporate management has to interact while formulating the firm's objectives?
9. 'A single objective, however specific it may be, is not adequate'. Do you agree with this statement? What, in your opinion, should be the pattern of corporate objectives?
10. 'The basic problem facing corporate management while formulating firm's objectives is to strike satisfactory trade-off among conflicting objectives of different stakeholders'. Comment and suggest how such conflicts can be resolved.
11. What is stylistic objective of a firm? How is it different from performance objectives?
12. Distinguish between strategic objectives and financial objectives. Are they related?
13. Outline the process of formulating corporate vision and mission, giving suitable examples.

References

1. Scott, B.W., "Long Range Planning in American Industry", *American Management Association*, 1965.
2. Brickner, William H. and Donal H. Cope, *The Planning Process*, Winthrop Publishers Inc., New York, p. 50, 1977.

3. Joseph and Massie, and John Douglas, *Managing—A Contemporary Introduction*, Prentice-Hall Inc., p. 274, 1977.

4. Arganti, A.J., *Corporate Planning: A Practical Guide*, Allen and Unwin, 1968.

5. Ansoff, Igor H., *Corporate Strategy*, op.cit.

6. Trewatha, Robert L. and M. Gene, *Management—Functions and Behaviour*, Business Publications Inc., New Port, p. 137, 1976.

7. Ackoff, Russel L., *A Concept of Corporate Planning*, Wiley Interscience, New York, pp. 23–25, 1970.

8. Rheuman, Erle, *Organisations Theory for Long-range Planning*, Wiley Publication, New York, 1973.

9. Mockler, Robert J., *The Business Management Process—A Situational Approach*, Austin Press, New York, p. 101, 1973.

10. Hussey, D.E., *Introducing Corporate Planning*, Pergamon Press, Oxford, pp. 33–35, 1985.

11. Drucker, P.F., *Managing for Results*, Heinemann, London, 1970.

12. Humble, J.W., *Management by Objectives*, Gover Press, Epping Essex, 1972.

13. Reddin, W.J., *Effective Management by Objectives*, Prentice-Hall, Englewood Cliffs, 1976.

14. Meckney, D.D., *Financial Management by Objectives*, Prentice-Hall, Englewood Clliffs, 1976.

15. Chany, Y.N. and Fileman Campo-flores, *Business Policy and Strategy*, Good Year Publishing Company Inc., California, p. 77, 1980.

16. Thompson, Arthur A., Jr. A.J. Strickland III, *Strategic Management*, Richard Win, Chicago, p. 23, 1995.

17. Ibid.

18. Harvey, David F., *Business Policy and Strategic Management*, Charles F. Mernill Publishing Company, Columbus, p. 16, 1982.

19. Ackoff, R.L., op. cit., p. 25.

20. Ibid.

21. Abell, Devek F., *Defining the Business: The Starting Point of Strategic Planning*, Prentice-Hall, Englewood Cliffs, NJ, p. 169, 1980.

22. Levitt, Theodore, "Marketing Myopia", *Harvard Business Review*, July–August, pp. 45–46, 1970.

23. Ansoff, Igor H., op. cit., p. 69.

10

Developing Competitive Strategy for a Firm

LEARNING OBJECTIVES

The present Chapter aims at:

- Providing a searing insight into Porter's model of generic competitive strategies.
- Discussing a resource-based approach to strategy making.
- Providing an insight into the mechanism of developing competitive strategy in turbulent and hyper competitive environment.

INTRODUCTION

An enterprise, to maximise its opportunity share and so also its corporate value in today's intensifying competitive environment, must have a sustainable competitive advantage in its activities. A sustainable competitive advantage, as noted in the previous chapter, is about performing different activities or performing similar activities in different ways on an enduring basis. For this, the firm needs to develop a competitive strategy. Competitive strategy is the search for a favourable competitive position in an industry, the fundamental arena in which competition occurs.[1]

Competitive strategy is concerned with how to create competitive advantage in each of the business in which a company competes. It focuses on improving the competitive position of a company's business unit's products or services within the specific industry or market segment that the company or business unit serves. Competitive strategy aims at establishing a profitable position against the forces that determine industry competition.

Competitive strategy examines the way in which a firm can compete more effectively to strengthen its market position. The rules of the game cannot achieve their intended effect unless they anticipate correctly how business responds strategically to competitive threats and opportunities.

The crux of competitive strategy is to provide buyers with what they perceive as superior value—a good product at a lower price or a better product that is worth paying more for. A case study on *Thums Up* illustrates this point. (Illustrative Capsule 10.1)

ILLUSTRATIVE CAPSULE 10.1

THUMS UP'S SUCCESSFUL COMPETITIVE STRATEGY

Thums Up is possibly India's most resilient iconic brand. While legions of companies pumped large sums of money into their brands in the hope that they attain 'iconic status', *Thums Up* has done so with minimal fanfare. Launched by the Chauhan brothers Ramesh and Prakash in order to fill the gap that Coca-Cola left when it exited India in 1977, *Thums Up* introduced a bold new flavour that Indian customers instantly took to. "We first tried variants that tasted like *Pepsi* and *Coke*, then launched our version with an orange base and more fizz", says Ramesh. Apparently, colas have a base fruit flavour in the concentrate. *Pepsi* and *Coke* are, according to Chauhan, lemon-based. "In our minds we had an image of a man with an eye-patch. We wanted a different taste that would be the hook and the differentiator for our brand", he adds.

The stronger, fizzier carbonated beverage has ruled the ruthlessly contested cola category for much of its existence. At first, *Thums Up* faced-off against local competitors such as *Campa Cola*, *Double Seven*, *Duke's McDowell's* crush and *Double Cola*, amongst others. When the Chauhans sold *Thums Up* to *Coca-Cola* in 1993 upon the cola giant's re-entry, it was forced to share shelf space with both *Coke* and *Pepsi*.

In 1993 when Coke entered India, *Thums Up* had a 36% market share versus 36% for *Pepsi*. But subsequently *Thums Up's* market share began to take a precipitate dive, resulting in Coke India ceding ground to *Pepsi*.

Thums Up is once again a kind of the cola hill, with a 16% share and *Sprite* and *Pepsi* trailing it with 15% and 13%, respectively. *Thums Up's* remarkable resilience has been its clever and constant advertising. In the 1980s, *Thums Up* ads featured a hummable jingle—"Happy Days Are Here Again"—innocuous enough, but in reality, this was a coded message that not only announced the availability of Cola, but also signaled the end of Emergency. This was followed by "Taste the Thunder" tagline in the 1990s which is in existence till today.

More importantly, *Thums Up's* "taste profile has resonated well with the Indian palette. It offers a masculine appeal and its taste becomes biologically coded with this appeal after sometime", observed former Head of Mc Cann Erickson. Still, the question is, can *Thums Up* continue to attract the Gen Next audience who are so completely familiar with *Pepsi* and *Coke*? "I do believe that it will survive and thrive", says marketing expert Harish Brijon.

Still, Coke's *Sprite* has quickly become the No. 2 brand in the country and is within spitting distance of *Thums Up*. Under the circumstances, *Thums Up* needs a strategy to compete with not just colas, but other flavours in the sparkling category as well if it wants to continue tasting the thunder.

The Essar group promoted Loop Mobile in its strive to increase its revenue share to around 15% in the next 18 months, from 9% on August 1, 2010 and has decided to launch new value added services (Illustrative Capsule 10.2).

ILLUSTRATIVE CAPSULE 10.2

LOOP MOBILE LAUNCHING NEW VALUE ADDED SERVICES

The Essar group promoted *Loop* Mobile, which owns mobile telephony licenses in 21 states, is on an overdrive to launch new value added services, improving internet access and e-mail access in order to increase its market share to around 15% in the next few month from 9% on August 1, 2010.

In July 2010, *Loop* Mobile introduced a new SMS scheme called "Reply all", allowing consumers to SMS to up to seven people at the cost of one SMS. If one of the consumers in the group replies, the response will be sent to all the users, allowing a chat conversation in a group, giving the same utility as a reply-all-email. Around 40,000 consumers used the application during one month and 2.4 million SMSes had been sent, with an average of 7–8 SMSes per conversation. This is for the first time that any mobile telephone company has launched such a scheme.

Loop Mobile is also introducing a new tariff concept called 'smart paid'. Targeted at the loop-end of the market, these pre-paid recharges will offer more minutes to the consumer with larger recharges. The recharge will come bundled with a combination of SMS, Internet download and calling minutes. The recharge will also have voice mail services and missed call alerts.

Loop Mobile is also planning to come up with a recharge coupon for post-paid connections. This is aimed at consumers who stay away from billing centres and those whose usage breaches monthly usage limits regularly. With this scheme, consumers can take the advantage of paying parts of their bill in the form of pre-paid connections, which are available at various retail outlets. At present, the company is in discussions with retailers over margins of this scheme.

The telecom operator is also in the midst of a network upgrade where it is improving its network coverage in connectivity, call quality, and the like. It is adding new cell sites to expand its network, and replace its existing network equipment.

Loop Mobile intends to become the best network in Mumbai.

FOUNDATIONS OF COMPETITIVE STRATEGY—PORTER'S VIEW

According to Michael Porter, choice of competitive strategy is the function of attractiveness of the industry it competes in and its relative position within that industry. Both industry attractiveness and competitive position can be shaped by a firm, and this is what makes the choice of competitive strategy both challenging and exciting. While industry attractiveness is partly a reflection of factors over which a firm has little influence, competitive strategy has considerable power to make an industry more or less attractive.[2]

Competitive strategy is supposed not only to respond to the environment but also to attempt to shape that environment in a firm's favour.

Thus, the essence of formulating competitive strategy lies in relating a firm to its environment. The key aspect of a firm's environment is the industry or industries in which it competes. Given the industry structure, a firm's performance is determined by the competitive positioning that it adopts with respect to its competitors.

Keeping in view the five forces that determine industry's competitiveness and profitability, (already discussed in Chapter on "Assessing competitive environment"), Porter held that the firm should develop approaches to defend itself against those five competitive forces. This is what should be provided for in competitive strategy. These approaches are in respect of positioning, influencing the balance and exploiting change.

The first approach to competitive action is matching the company's strengths and weaknesses with the structure of the industry. The thrust should be on building defence against the competitive forces or as finding positions in the industry where the forces are weakest. The corporate management must have comprehensive idea about the areas where the organisation should confront competition and where avoid it. Where the enterprise is a low-cost producer, it may decide to sell to powerful buyers. However, it should see that it sells them only products not vulnerable to competitions from substitutes.

The organisation may pursue offensive approach to focus on altering the causes of the competition. This may include marketing innovations, substantial capital investments in large-scale facilities or vertical integration. The balance of forces is the function of external as well as internal forces.

Another approach to counteract competitive forces should be to pursue strategy appropriate to the new competitive balance with the objective of exploiting change. With the growing maturity of an industry, its growth rate changes, product differential is said to decline, the companies tend to integrate vertically. While analysing the changes, the management should try to ascertain if they affect the sources of competition, and forecast the magnitude of each underlying cause and then construct a composite picture of the likely profit potential of the industry.

PORTER'S GENERIC COMPETITIVE STRATEGIES

While recognising that the best strategy for a firm will actually be unique and reflect its individual circumstances, Porter developed three generic competitive strategies, viz., cost leadership, differentiation and focus, to help an organisation outperform rivals within an industry and so successfully position itself against the five forces.[3] These strategies are shown in Figure 10.1. Each of the generic strategies involves entirely different routes to competitive advantage, combining a choice about the type of competitive advantage to be achieved. While cost leadership and differentiation strategies seek competitive advantage in a broad range of industry segments, focus strategies try to achieve cost advantage (cost focus) or differentiation advantage (differentiation focus), in a narrow segment. The specific measures required to implement each generic strategy vary widely from industry to industry.

	Low-cost position	Uniqueness perceived by the customer
Industry-wide	Overall cost leadership strategy	Broad differentiation strategy
Particular segment or market niche	Focused low-cost strategy	Focused differentiation strategy

Figure 10.1 Generic strategy choices.

The basic premise of the concept of generic strategies, according to Michael Porter, is that competitive advantage is at the heart of any strategy, and achieving competitive advantage demands a firm to make a choice about the type of competitive advantage it seeks to attain and the scope within which it will attain.

Cost-Leadership Strategy

A firm pursuing cost-leadership strategy strives to be the overall low-cost provider so as to outperform competitors by doing everything it can to produce goods or services at a cost lower than theirs. Cost-leadership aggressively exploits opportunities for cost reduction through economies of scale and cumulative learning in purchasing and manufacturing, tight cost and overhead control, avoidance of marginal customer accounts and cost minimisation in areas like R&D, service, sales force and advertising.[4]

Some companies, which are successfully following cost-leadership strategy, are Nirma, Bharti Airtel, Spice Jet and Indigo Airlines, Timex and Ghari. Bharti Airtel has pursued cost-leadership strategy to minimise its operational cost and emerged telecom leader in India.

The thrust of cost-leadership strategy is on cost minimisation. The firm pursuing this strategy chooses a low level of product differentiation and strives to achieve and maintain a level of a company that competes by spending resources on product development.

To gain low-cost competitive advantage and leadership, a firm's cumulative costs across its value chain must be lower than its competitors' costs. There are two ways to achieve this:

(i) Do a better job than rivals of the performing internal value chain activities efficiently and manage the factors that drive the costs of the value chain activities;

(ii) Revamp the firm's value chain to bypass some cost producing activities altogether.

Successful cost leaders usually derive their cost advantage from multiple sources within the value chain. Cost-leadership requires an evaluation of every activity in a firm for opportunities to reduce cost, and the consistent pursuit of all of them.

A firm can potentially gain competitive advantage over its rivals by controlling the cost of significant value activities. The major cost drivers that come into play in determining a firm's costs in each activity segment of the value chain fall into two categories: (i) structural determinants of the cost that depend on the fundamental economic nature of the business, and (ii) executional cost determinants stemming directly out of the management of internal activities.

Structural cost drivers are economies or diseconomies of scale, learning and experience curve effects, linkages with other activities in the value chain, sharing opportunities with other business units within the enterprises, the benefits of vertical integration versus outsourcing and controlling location.

Executional cost drivers include timing considerations associated with first mover advantages and disadvantages, the extent of capacity utilisation and strategic choices and operating decisions.

A firm can also achieve dramatic cost advantages through reconfiguring value chain in such a way as to make it significantly different from its competitors. Reconfigured value chains may be in the form of a different production process, differences in automation, direct sales instead of indirect sales, a new distribution channel, a new raw material, relocating facilities closer to suppliers, customers or both to curtail inbound and outbound logistics achieving a more economical degree of forward or backward vertical integration relative to competitors, new advertising media, and the like.

Thus, cost-leadership strategy requires pursuing cost savings throughout the value chain, leaving no potential area overlooked. Low-cost leaders have cost conscious culture that are champions of frugality, intolerant to wastes and are aggressive in committing funds to projects that have potentials to minimise costs (Illustrative Capsule 10.3).

ILLUSTRATIVE CAPSULE 10.3

LOW-COST AIRLINES

Recent news about continued operating losses by India's premier air carriers, viz., Air India, Jet Airways and Kingfisher as against the profits made by low cost airlines, Spice Jet and Indigo, is quite amusing.

Although Spice Jet and Indigo have been facing handicaps everyday, such as lack of options for airports and landing strips resulting in record 30-minute average turnaround times and high aviation prices—driven up by taxes of upto 34% which is as much as double elsewhere in the world such as Dubai and Singapore, they have developed knacks to operate at lower cost.

Sensing India's demographies—the value-conscious business travellers and an increasingly mobile young population—the management of Spice Jet and Indigo firmly believe that low-cost airlines are the models best suited for the country. Accordingly, their focus is on cost reduction and cost savings in every activity right from procurement of aircraft to day-to-day operations.

Both Indigo and Spice Jet have taken initiatives to leverage several cost advantages. Indigo, for instance, counts its large order book for planes as a big differentiator among airlines in India. It has, on order, 100 Airbus, A 320 planes for delivery until 2015, some 27 of which have been delivered by May, 2010. Such a large order—second only to Air India—gives the airline not just big leverage while negotiating purchases (10%–15% discounts are normal in such deals) but also sweet heart arrangements on spares supplies and maintenance.

Both Spice Jet and Indigo could increase their passenger traffic by over 44%, more than double the industry average. At least half this growth could be possible on account of "sweating their asset more than usual" by increasing aircraft utilisation. According to Sanjay Aggarwal, former CEO, Spice Jet was able to raise aircraft utilisation to 12.5 hours a day from 10.5 hours in 2008–09—significantly higher than Kingfisher's 9.5 hours, Jet's 10.5 hours and Air India's 8.5 hours—by focusing attention on ground-handling and refueling times and re-jigging airline schedules. As a result, Spice Jet's cost per available seat km (a measure of per seat operation costs) is ₹2.30, much lower than that of Kingfisher and Jet's which have around 60% of their capacity in low-cost operations.

For Spice Jet, focusing on costs often entails more than just cutbacks. Although, Spice Jet took such obvious steps as freezing salaries and curtailing non-essential expenditure, it also focused on maximising cost benefits. In India, where fuel cost accounts for about 40% as against roughly 25% in foreign countries, due to higher local taxes, managing fuel consumption is critical to profitability. Spice Jet's solutions for achieving this were unique. One of the ways the Spice Jet did this was by focusing on what Aggarwal calls "smart flying". This involves getting pilots to adjust ascent and descent profiles to yield significant cost benefits. Pilots are encouraged to climb slowly after take off, request air traffic control for ideal cruising altitudes, and start their descent earlier so that gravity helps save fuel. Result: A 2% saving on cost or ₹20 crore on a ₹1,000 crore annual fuel bill at Spice Jet.

Indigo and Spice Jet tank up fuel airports in states where the tax rates are as low as 4%—Hyderabad in Andhra Pradesh, Jaipur in Rajasthan or Nagpur in Maharashtra. Since this is an option with full-service carriers too, the low-cost duo gets discounts from oil marketing firms who have had a bad experience with the likes of Kingfisher, Jet and Air India over unpaid fuel dues.

"Cost avoidance", as Aggarwal puts it, also helped. For instance, Spice Jet saved about ₹1 crore by relocating its training simulators from Hong Kong and Dubai and signing a three-year maintenance repair and overhaul (MRO) contract with Malaysian Airlines instead.

The results are revealing; at Indigo, revenues for fiscal 2010 closed at around ₹2,500 crore with "net profitability in the 15% to 20% range"—₹375–500 crore, which puts it ahead of even Spice Jet by a yard. "Indigo is a debt-free company, has, on a cumulative basis, returned the money of shareholders". In 2008–09, Indigo had reported profits of ₹82.6 crore.

Spice Jet declared a ₹61 crore profit for the year ended March, 2010 on revenues of ₹2,242 crore—considerable improvement over the results the company had been posting in the two preceding years. In fiscal 2009, the airline had a net loss of ₹352.5 crore and lost ₹133.4 crore in the year prior to that.

But, there is a looming challenge: Jet and Kingfisher are quick studies and are scrambling to adapt and adopt from their lost cost competitors.

Cost-Leadership Strategy and Porter's Five Competitive Forces

Cost-leadership strategy provides to the firm strong defenses against the five competitive forces. Thus, the low-cost company is in a best position to meet the challenges from rivals on the basis of price, to defend against price war conditions, to use the appeal of lower price to grab sales and improve market share and to earn above average profits. As a matter of fact, low-cost strategy in the event of price competition is the most powerful defensive weapon.

Low-cost strategy provides a firm defence against the power of buyers with partial profit margin protection. Firm with low-cost strategy enjoys relatively greater bargaining power over its suppliers. In the event of arrival of substitute products in the market, the low-cost leader can reduce its price to compete with them and retain its market share. This is what Hindustan Unilever (HUL) has recently done. In its strive to regain its lost market share in its FMCG products, HUL adopted the strategy of reducing cost of sales and distribution and cutting prices by shedding its profit margin obsession.

Low-cost strategy also acts as a barrier for new entrants. The low-cost leader can use the price falling to make it difficult for a new rival to win customers.

Cost-leadership strategy can be more fruitful to a firm in achieving competitive prowess over its rivals where the degree of competition among the competitors on price front is vigorous, industry's product is standardised, buyers are large in numbers and have strong bargaining power.

However, there are risks inherent in cost-leadership strategy. One such risk arises due to fast changing technological developments that may help the competitors to produce the goods at relatively lower cost and beat the cost leader at its own game. Another danger of this strategy is that the rival firms may easily imitate the cost leader's methods of production and thereby outsmart the latter.

At times, the cost leader is so obsessed with cost minimisation devices that it might lose sight of changes in customers' tastes and preferences like growing interest in added features or services, and declining buyers' sensitivity to price. This is likely to affect the market share of the firm.

A firm pursuing cost-leadership strategy may be required to continuously update and streamline its production process so as to minimise the cost without affecting quality. This will obviously lead to rise in capital cost of the firm.

It is important to note that the cost leader, while pursuing cost minimisation strategy, should not be tempted to compromise with quality of the offerings.

Differentiation Strategy

In this strategy, a company offers a product as unique in industry by proving that it provides a distinct advantage over other products by setting it apart from other competitors' brands in some way or the other, besides price. Products sold by two different companies may be exactly the same, but if customers believe the first is more valuable than the second, then the first product has a differentiation advantage. Thus, the existence of product differentiation, in the end, is always a matter of customers' perception. But firms can take a variety of actions to influence these perceptions.

The differentiation strategy adopted by the firms needs to possess sufficient skills and abilities to differentiate the product from that of the competitors based on some attributes that allow the consumers to perceive the product as different from that of the competition. Such firms have access to advanced scientific research, a highly skilled labour force, and effective communication strategies. Airtel is providing free digital EPABX with free leased lines (no connectivity charges). So the firm is providing latest EPABX to the consumer which is costing about ₹50,000.

Indian FMCG companies like Marico, Dabur and Emami have successfully managed to ring-fence themselves from the onslaughts of foreign competitors such as Nestle, Procter and Gamble and Hindustan Unilever by dint of their ability to differentiate products on ayurvedic formulations. In order to push its sales into malted food drinks market, HUL adopted differentiation strategy and offered a differentiated offering that caters to health-conscious customers. The sale of the product has grown considerably over the last few years.

Companies in India have adopted different methods for differentiation of their product/service offerings, as evidenced below:

Differentiation based on Ingredients

- TTK group launched its *Prestige* range of non-stick frying pans.
- Dabur tweaked its *Chyawanprash* brand—a health tonic—to provide it in different flavours.

Differentiation through additional features

- Godrej with its 300 ltrs and 390 ltrs refrigerators targeting high lifestyle people.
- Coca-Cola India is offering an entire range of its chilled soft drink products to markets deep in the hinterland, even where there is no electricity through 'eko cool', a chest cooler developed internally.

Differentiation in packaging

- *Brylecreem* in handy tube.
- *Hit* for cockroaches with sleek nozzle for hidden areas.

Differentiation by design

- Kinetic *Honda* with electronic ignition to avoid kick-start.

Differentiation by positioning

- Dominos *Pizza* with their 30-minutes home delivery or free concept.
- Maggi with their '2-minutes noodles'.

Differentiation strategy of Nirma is contained in Illustrative Capsule 10.4.

ILLUSTRATIVE CAPSULE 10.4
DIFFERENTIATION STRATEGY OF NIRMA

Nirma is one of the few names which is instantly recognised as a true Indian brand, which took on mighty MNCs and rewrite the marketing rules to win the heart of the consumer. India being one of the largest consumer economy, with an upcoming middle class, and a widespread, diverse market place, *Nirma* aptly concentrated all its efforts towards creating and building a strong consumer preference towards its 'value-for-money' products.

Nirma's vision was to make consumer products available to masses at an affordable price. Distinct market vision, infrastructure, good distribution network, umbrella branding and low profile media promotions allowed it to offer quality products, at affordable prices. *Nirma* has been a huge success story. It has a good hold into the FMCG market but has been recently crowded out by HLL and other major players.

According to a research study, a differentiation strategy is more likely to generate higher profits than a low-cost strategy because differentiation creates better entry barriers. A low-cost strategy is more likely, however, to generate increase in market shares.[5]

It may be noted at this juncture that focus on developing uniqueness in product does not mean that the cost control is not necessary. Nevertheless, differentiation is usually costly but differentiation expects the firm to keep the cost somewhere near that of the cost leader. Efforts need to be made to control all costs that do not contribute the firm's differentiation advantage so as to ensure that the price of the product does not exceed what customers are willing to pay. Since bigger profits are earned by controlling all costs and by maximising revenues it pays to control costs. So as to gain sustainable competitive advantage on score of product differentiation, a firm's source of uniqueness must involve barriers. Proprietary learning, linkages, interrelationships and first-move advantages tend to be more sustainable drivers than simply a policy choice to be unique in an activity. The firms should have sustainable cost advantage in performing activities that result in differentiation.

Henkel India's differentiation strategy can now be studied as Illustrative Capsule 10.5.

Illustrative Capsule **10.5**

HENKEL INDIA'S DIFFERENTIATION STRATEGY

Henkel—a multinational corporation—entered in the detergent market in India in 1994 and is rallying behind its detergent brand, *Henko Stain Champion* (*Henko*). The market of ₹13,000 crore is highly competitive. Hindustan Unilever with a market share of 37.5% has recently lost ground and the second-largest player, Procter and Gamble (16.5%), has not made new inroad either. The other pan-India players are Nirma and Jyothi Laboratories. Henkel's value share, which had hovered around 6.3% from January to March, 2010 went up to 6.9% in April, 2010, while volume share during the period went up from 7.6% to 8.3%.

In 2009, *Henko* was launched with neem—a plant with anti-bacterial properties—as an ingredient. Henkel now wants to differentiate its product based on this trait, as opposed to just stain removal and whitening. The management felt the need to make the germ-kill properties more salient, and decided to get it endorsed by a celebrity in order to create more awareness. Actor Irfan Khan was roped in because of his no-nonsense persona. The company wanted to avoid a pompous tone and be more sincere.

The company launched the product in 2009 after its survey with over 3,000 respondents revealed that 85% of consumers felt that owing to pollution, there was a need to make clothes germ-free, while 95% were wary of skin infections from clothes that had germs even after a wash. *Henko's* research also reveals that *Henko* has 10 times more disinfecting power than other fabric-washes. The management believes that since *Henko* is not in the mass segment of detergents, rather than freebies and discounts, an additional characteristic of the product for the same price could sway the consumers.

Henkel has not thought to stir up the sort of hornet's nest that Hindustan Unilever's ad targeting Procter and Gamble has done earlier in 2010. In a head-on battle, the two companies not only fought on prices but were also locked in a legal battle. Thereafter, the company has pursued a sales reorganisation strategy to consolidate its strongholds in the southern and north-eastern markets through trade promotions and activations. In markets such as Kerala, *Henko* enjoys as much as 20% of volume share; it has similar numbers in the north-east.

Detergent brands have traditionally harped on their ability to remove stains, preserve colours, add brightness to whites and emit fragrance. Henkel too has trodden on the same path. In 2005, it launched a fragrant version of the product, and in 2007, it claimed *Henko* had active oxygen which tackled tough stains. Will its latest positioning as a germ-killer work?

Differentiation Strategy and Porter's Five Competitive Forces

A differentiation strategy improves competitive position of a firm by enhancing customers' loyalty to the firm's brand or model and greater willingness to pay a little more for it. Further, effective differentiation strategy creates entry barriers in the form of customers' loyalty and uniqueness that new comers find it difficult to handle. It also reduces buyers' bargaining power for the fact that the products of the rival firms are less attractive to them. A firm with differentiation strategy can fend off threats from substitutes devoid of matching features. Such firms are in stronger position to withstand the efforts of powerful suppliers to get a higher price for the items they supply. In sum, effective differentiation creates lines of defence for dealing with the five competitive forces.

However, the differentiation strategy has inherent risks. This strategy may not always be useful, particularly when it does not reduce buyer cost or raise buyer performance as perceived by him. If buyer perceives little value in uniqueness, a low-cost strategy can easily overtake a differentiation strategy. The objective of differentiation strategy will also be defeated if their rival firm can quickly imitate most of the firm's products. Thus, to be successful at differentiation, a firm must have long-term capability to maintain uniqueness and accordingly ferret lasting sources of differentiation, which may prove to be burdensome to the rivals to pursue.

Creating unnecessarily higher level of differentiation relative to what buyers need may boomerang, resulting in the firm's vulnerability and a lower price.

Differentiation approach may also create problem and the firm pursuing a differentiation strategy may experience decline in the market share if the premium charged by it is too high to justify the degree of uniqueness.

Furthermore, a firm focusing on intrinsic product attributes to achieve differentiation without considering its contribution to value addition to buyers is likely to face tremendous challenges even from such rivals who may not have degree of differentiation in their product but have deep insights into the buyers' predilections and buying process.

Finally, firms who perceive differentiation only in terms of the end physical product and do not explore the possibility of exploiting differentiation opportunities existing in various value activities both at the primary and supporting levels are bound to lose market leadership to rival firms in the long run. Likewise, if a firm fails to take cognizance of the existence of buyer segments and its strategy does not satisfy the needs of any buyer very well, it is likely to be outsmarted by its rivals.

Focus Strategy

Unlike the low-cost and differentiation strategies which aim at the entire industry, a focus strategy is aimed at serving a segment (or segments) within an industry. A firm pursuing focus strategy selects a segment or group of segments in the industry and tailors its strategy so as to serve them better than their competitors. Thus, a focus strategy concentrates on catering to a particular market niche, which can be defined geographically, by type of customer or by segment of the product line. The focus strategy is based on the premise that the organisation is able to serve its narrow strategic target more effectively than its rivals. As a result, the organisation attempts to do so either through differentiation or a low-cost approach.

Thus, there are two variants of focus strategy—cost focus and differentiation focus. In cost focus, an organisation seeks a cost advantage in its target market while in differentiation focus, an organisation seeks uniqueness in its target segment.

A cost focused strategy is suited to a segment of buyers who are cost conscious while a differentiation strategy is most suitable to the buyer segment who is quality and differentiation conscious. A firm pursuing focus strategy however can achieve competitive advantage by dedicating itself exclusively to a particular segment of buyers.

Thus, a focused firm may have exclusive focus on differentiation or cost leadership, depending on the segment of buyers it intends to reach. A firm parlaying a focused low-cost strategy likes to compete its rivals in the market segments where it will have no cost disadvantage. Where a firm employs a focused differentiation approach, it has access to all the means of differentiation to compete its rivals in only one or in just a few segments. Focus strategy of Bajaj Auto is a case in point (Illustrative Capsule 10.6).

ILLUSTRATIVE CAPSULE 10.6
BAJAJ'S FOCUS STRATEGY

'The more, the merrier' has been the theme song of Bajaj Auto for many years. But not any more.

India's second largest two-wheeler company, which had bombarded the market with multiple brands to break the market with multiple brands to break the near-monopoly of market leader Hero Honda in the economy segment, has withdrawn all but two of its brands.

In the changing market dynamics, Bajaj has now decided to focus on just two brands—*Discover* and *Pulsar*. *Discover* is clearly positioned for the commuter segment and the *Pulsar* as the 'sporty' option. While the *Pulsar* has held its own over the years in the power and performance segment, *Discover* is the pivot in the commuting category. According to Bajaj Auto Managing Director Rajiv Bajaj, *Pulsar* is for sporty, young and those who want to have some fun with the bike. The *Discover* buyer is more sober and an economy-conscious person who wants to take a safe decision and higher mileage.

The company recently changed its strategy from a product to a brand-led company as it believes that the product game will not go anywhere and it is only brand that will make all the difference.

Presently, about 70% of the company's sales come from the *Discover* and *Pulsar* segment, both of which share seven models between them—up from just 3% about three years ago. The company reported its highest ever number in May, 2010. It aims to sell one million Pulsar units every year, starting 2010.

Bajaj Auto, which had a 20.47% market share in the two-wheeler category in May, 2010—up from 19.05% in the previous month—is working on adding yet another model under the *Pulsar* category in the coming months. It also launched in May, 2010 a new 150CC bike under the *Discover* brand. The company intends to focus on just these two brands till the market is mature enough for more.

Focus Strategy and Porter's Five Competitive Forces

Focus strategy, based on either cost or differentiation, will be useful to a firm if the target segment is big enough to be profitable, the segment has good growth potential, and is not crucial to the success of major competitors, the focusing firm has core competencies and resources to serve the segment effectively and the focuser is in strong position to defend itself against the rivals on the customer goodwill it has built up and its superior ability to serve buyers in the segment.

A firm using focus strategy and fulfilling the above conditions defends itself from competing rivals against the five competitive forces which multi-segment rivals may not have the same competitive capability to challenge the firm's competence in serving the market niche. This raises entry barriers, thus making it harder for firms outside the niche segment to enter. It also lessens the threat from substitute products. The bargaining power of powerful customers is thwarted somewhat by their own unwillingness to shift their business to rival firms less capable of meeting their expectations.

The protection from the five competitive forces allows the firm to earn above average returns on its investments. Focus strategy also enables the firm to stay close to its customers and to respond to their changing needs.

However, a firm using focus approach to gain competitive edge faces certain operational risks. One such risk which a focuser encounters with is on cost score. Since such firm produces a small volume, its production costs generally exceed those of a low-cost firm. Higher costs will obviously reduce profitability if the focuser is constrained to invest heavily in developing distinctive competency, such as costly product innovation, so as to compete with a differentiated firm. This disadvantage is increasingly reduced in view of development of flexible manufacturing systems which have made it possible for focused firms to produce even small level of production at a lower cost.

A focused firm may be in trouble if competing firms find out effective ways to match the former in serving the niche segment.

Technological change or change in buyers' tastes may result in sudden disappearance of niche market of the focused firm who finds it harder to shift toward the new niche segment.

An erosion of the differences across buyer segments minimises entry barriers into a focuser's market niche and opens the doors for competitors in adjacent segments to begin competing for the focuser's customers.

Another risk associated with focused strategy is that the segment becomes so attractive that it is soon crowded with competitors resulting in splintering of segment profits.

Hybrid Strategy

At times, firms may pursue hybrid strategy to create and sustain competitive advantage. In the present hyper competitive market, large business units are found combining the strategy of low-cost with some form of differentiation. Toyota, for instance, is known for cost reductions while at the same time its cars are differentiated from other major automakers. There is also constant cola war between MNCs—Coca-Cola and Pepsi Cola—both on price and quality scores. Even smart mobile phones of MNCs like Microsoft, Apple, Google and Sony Ericsson are trying to outsmart each other by reducing cost while at the same time adding new functions and features in their models.

Even local Indian brands—Micromax, Spice and Karbonn—according to the Voice & Data annual telecom survey raised their share of the market from 2% in 2008–09 to 11% in 2009–10 at the expense of Nokia whose share fell from 64% to 52% by managing to sell their products at low prices—30% to 40% below comparable multinational models and also adding new features in their models.

Firms may compete with hybrid strategy for either proactive reasons (attempting to modify some segment of their environment to enhance their effectiveness) or for reactive reasons (responding to environmental change to sustain their competitive advantage).

It is generally found that firms using cost-leadership strategy without sacrificing differentiation have an edge over their rivals. Firms find no problem in simultaneously accomplishing cost-leadership and differentiation where competitors are stuck in the middle and none is well positioned to force a firm to the point where cost and differentiation become inconsistent.

Breakthrough technological advancements have helped firms in achieving advantage of lower cost and at the same time enhance differentiation. However, the ability to be both low-cost and differentiated is a function of being the only firm with the new innovation. The moment competitors also begin launching the innovation, the firm will have to make a trade-off to maintain leadership position.

A firm, not keen to forego differentiation, has to aggressively pursue all cost minimisation opportunities. Likewise, a firm should also pursue all differentiation opportunities which are not costly. This is exactly what FMCG firms, mobile phone makers and auto players are doing in recent times. Beyond this point, a firm will have to choose what its ultimate competitive advantage will be and resolve to strike trade-offs accordingly.

COMPETITIVE STRATEGY—GRANT'S RESOURCE-BASED VIEW

R.M. Grant, through his epoch making article in 1991, challenged Porter's premise of competitive strategy by arguing that a focus solely upon the external environment may not provide a sufficient basis for long-term strategy.[6] When the external environment is in a state of flux, the firm's own resources and capabilities may be a much more stable basis on which to define its identity. Hence, a definition of a business in terms of what it is capable of doing may offer a more durable basis for strategy.[7]

Grant further argued that even the choices articulated by Porter competing on cost or differentiation within a broad or narrow market, are themselves predicated upon the resources within the organisation, since no organisation can hope to follow an overall cost leadership strategy if it does not possess economies of scale and technology proficient plant and machine.[8]

According to Grant, strategy making at the business unit level involves four stages, viz., identifying resources and appraising strengths and weaknesses in relation to competitors, identifying the firm's capabilities, appraising the rent generating potentiality of resources* and capabilities and choosing a strategy that best exploits the firm's resources and capabilities relative to external opportunities. A detailed discussion on these aspects has already been made in Chapter 7.

Thus, the key to a resource-based approach to strategy making is understanding the relationship between resources, capabilities, competitive advantage and profitability... this requires the design of strategies which exploit to maximum effect each firm's unique characteristics.[9]

Resource-based approach has been criticised on the ground that it is unclear how resources and capabilities evolve overtime.[10]

---

* Rent generating potentiality of resources refers to the potentiality of generating surplus that is left over when the inputs to a productive process, which includes the cost of capital being employed, has been covered.

However, the overall purpose of developing strategy remains the same in both Porter's and Grant's perspective. It is how the organisation gets to this position that generates contention. Empirical study conducted by Henderson and Cockburn suggests that both these views should not be seen so much as incompatible but more as occupying different positions on the same continuum.[11]

COMPETITIVE STRATEGY—KIM AND MAUBORNE'S BLUE OCEAN VIEW

According to W. Chan and Renee Mauborne, organisations to succeed in competitive market, need to create and capture blue oceans of uncontested market space.[11] Based on a decade-long study of 150 strategic moves spanning more than 30 industries and over 100 years (1880–2000), they noted that companies have long engaged in head-to-head competition in search of sustained, profitable growth. They have fought for competitive advantage, battled over market share, and struggled for differentiation. Yet in today's overcrowded industries, competing head-on results is nothing but a bloody "*red ocean*" of rivals fighting over shrinking profits. According to them, tomorrow's leading companies will succeed not by battling competitors, but by creating "*blue oceans*" of uncontested market space ripe for growth. Kim and Mauborne believe that in formulating business strategy, the analysis of neither the company nor the industry will lead to the creation of blue oceans and sustained high performance. What is important is the strategic move representing 'the set of managerial actions and decisions involved in making a major market creating business offering'. Thus, BOS or **Blue Ocean Strategy** is the systematic pursuit of new market and new demand creation through the simultaneous pursuit of higher value and lower cost. It is called "*blue ocean*" because of its focus on creating unknown market space where a firm does not compete head-to-head against the competition but rather outcompete them by creating new markets where no competition exists.

The three key conceptual building blocs of BOS are: value innovation, tipping point leadership and fair process. Value innovation is the simultaneous pursuit of differentiation and low-cost. It focuses on making the competition irrelevant by creating a leap of value for buyers and for the company, thereby opening up new and uncontested market place. A cardinal feature of value innovation is a belief that market boundaries and industry structure are not given but they can be reconstructed by the actions and beliefs of industry players.[12] Tipping point leadership, contrary to the conventional theory of organisational change, focuses on transforming the extremes: the people, acts and activities that exercise a disproportionate influence on performance (instead of changing the mass). By transforming the extremes, tipping point leaders are able to change the core fast and at low-cost to execute their new strategy. Fair price builds execution into strategy by creating people's buy-in upfront. Three mutually reinforcing elements that define fair process are engagement, explanation and clarity of expectation.

Kim and Mauborne further emphasise that in order to strengthen their competitive position and improve profitability, companies have to maximise the size of their "*blue oceans*" by concentrating on non-customers and building on powerful commonalities in what buyers value. This will allow companies to reach beyond existing demand to unlock a new mass of customers that did not exist before.

Although the universe of non-customers offers big *"blue ocean"* opportunities, Kim and Mauborne have noted that few companies show keen insight into who non-customers are and how to unlock them. To convert this huge latent demand into real demand in the form of thriving end customers, companies need to deepen their understanding of the universe of non-customers. There are three tiers of non-customers that can be transformed into customers. They differ in their relative distance from the market. The first tier of the non-customers is closer to the market. It has buyers who minimally buy an industry's offering out of necessity but are mentally non-customers of the industry. They are waiting to jump ship and leave the industry as soon as the opportunity presents itself. The second tier of non-customers consists of those who have seen the industry's offerings as an option to fulfill their needs but have voted against them. The third tier of non-customers is farthest from the market. It has non-customers who have never thought of the company's offerings as an option. By focusing on key commonalities across these non-customers and existing customers, companies can understand how to pull them into their market.

As an integrated approach to competitive strategy at the system level, BOS requires organisations to develop and align the three strategy propositions: value proposition, profit proposition and people proposition.

Thus, value innovation argument goes against Porter's assertion that an organisation can pursue either differentiation or a low-cost strategy.

It must, however, be noted that companies seeking to create and capture *"blue oceans"* must possess requisite capabilities and organisational support.

A few Indian Companies such as HCL Technologies and Fertilisers and Chemicals, Travancore have adopted BOS.

Blue ocean strategy has been criticised on several grounds. Criticisms include claims that no control group was used, that there is no way to know how many companies using this strategy failed, that a deductive process was not followed and that the examples given by the authors were selected to tell a winning story. It is also argued that rather than a theory, BOS is an extremely successful attempt to brand a set of already existing concepts and frameworks with a highly "sticky" idea. The concepts behind the BOS, such as competing factors, the consumer cycle, non-customers, and the like are not new.

SHAPING COMPETITIVE STRATEGY IN TUMULTUOUS AND HYPER COMPETITIVE ENVIRONMENT

In today's business world where changes are discontinuous and partake the character of earthquakes that quickly take the low ground all the time and raise it high and at the same time, submerge some mountain peaks below ocean because of competence-enhancing or competence-destroying disruptions arising out of fast and frequent changes in customers' tastes, technological substitution or obsolescence of a competence, crafting business strategy to achieve sustainable competitive advantage is not possible. The reason being the practices and business models that constitute advantages for today's most successful companies only do so because of particular factors at work under particular conditions at a particular time.[13] Both Apple and Google have challenged the hegemony of Microsoft in computer industry through their disruptive innovations. Similarly, competence-enhancing disruptions by PepsiCo in competitively priced products including *Kurkure* and *Aliva* have helped the PepsiCo India overtake Nestle India as No. 1 among Indian branded and processed foods and beverage companies.

Under such turbulent conditions, strategists need to get to grips with why and under what conditions certain practices lead to competitive advantage. Christension rightly points out that even tacit knowledge, which is normally difficult to imitate, confers only a temporary advantage because of continuous technological developments at blistering pace, leading to replication of the knowledge.

A close and continuous monitoring of environmental developments and a deeper understanding of the strategies of dominant incumbent players and those of challengers who are seeking to disrupt environment is inevitable so as to assess adequacy of the firm's existing competitive advantages in the changing scenario and imperativeness to hone the advantages accordingly. Through continuous and concerted programmes, organisations need to reduce their costs and find new ways to add value to the product. This is why MNCs in computing and communication industry like Microsoft, Apple, Google, Research in Motion, Palm and Symbian and others are relentlessly engaged in refining their product offerings to retain their competitive advantage.

In hyper competitive environment characterised by frequent and discontinuous disruptions and leaders engaged actively in creating new competencies and deliberately disrupting themselves, before their rivals do as in the case of Apple and Google, there is no such thing as a sustainable competitive advantage, and successful strategies typically last only months to a few years. The only way in this kind of dynamic environment to sustain any competitive advantage, according to D' Aveni, is through a continuous series of multiple short-term initiatives aimed at replacing a firm's current successful products with the next generation of products before the competitors can do so.[14] The aim of industry leaders and challenges in each environment, according to D' Aveni, is to achieve supremacy of trying to control the degree and pattern of turbulence. By understanding the pattern of turbulence in the current competitive environment, managers can develop better strategies that lead to and maintain strategic supremacy.[15] It is interesting to note that MNCs in FMCG, computing, IT and telecommunication sectors around the world are continuously and ceaselessly monitoring the pattern of turbulence in the environment and closely watching the strategic moves of their rivals in order to retain and improve their market share, capture more control over the assets and activities which are most valuable to their core business.

In the absence of certainty and risklessness in the environment, it may be desirable for the company to go for adaptation strategy. However, the company with this move may not always be able to encash the emerging market opportunities. Under the circumstances, it would be in fitness of things for the management to revisit their current business strategy and proactively adopt new business model suited to the new developments so as to sustain their competitive advantage.

According to John Hagel III, John Selly Brown and Lang Davison, in highly uncertain and disruptive environment, it would be pertinent for the top management to have long-term perspective of the industry and or market and identify the potential opportunities and impending challenges accordingly. On the basis of such scanning, it should redefine the terms of competition in the industry and convey them to all concerned about the benefits that can be availed through adoption of the new terms.[16] This is what Indian organisations like Hindustan Unilever, Dabur, Coca-Cola India, PepsiCo and Glaxo Smithkline in the FMCG sector and Tata Motors, Mahindra & Mahindra (M&M) in automotive sector are now doing. These organisations have upended prevailing perceptions of risk and reward. This is likely to lead to slow action or no action. So as to motivate a large number of players to engage in disruptive innovations to satisfy the fast changing customers' needs and thereby encash market opportunities, a market leader should rejig the calculus by diminishing perceived risks and maximising perceived rewards.

Three elements of a shaping strategy are: a shaping view, a shaping platform and shaping acts and assets.[17]

The first step in shaping an industry or market to one's advantage is to change the way potential participants perceive market opportunities. This calls for a clear and compelling long-term view of the relevant industry or market. This view provides a clear perspective on the direction of the relevant market or industry and articulates the value creation implications for all companies involved.

The second component of shaping strategy is the shaping platform, spelling out a set of clearly defined standards and practices that help organise and support the activities of many participants and enable the participants to leverage their resources. Shaping platforms typically offer one or two forms of leverage. Some provide **development leverage**, derived from new technologies, that reduces the investment required to build and deliver products or services. For example, *salesforce.com* has provided a platform (*force.com*), which enables third party developers to easily create application services for the company's market.

Another type of shaping platform provides interaction leverage. This form of leverage seeks to reduce the cost and effort required for a large number of participants through coordination of their activities. To facilitate the coordination, thrust is on designing a set of standardised protocols and practices. Li & Fung (L&F) provides an example of a shaping platform that relies primarily on telephone and fax—simple, low-cost technology easily available to its partners. A rich set of protocols coordinates complex supply chain activities across a global network that L&F configures and reconfigures to serve consumer goods companies.

The third element of the shaping strategy is the strength of the shaping company in terms of its acts and assets which can enable the company to counteract the threats from a powerful shaper. Robust acts and prudent application of the shaper's assets can assuage such threats. The assets of the shaping company can also become potent factors in cajoling the potential participants. A shaper with burgeoning assets will obviously have an edge over others as it adds to the credibility of the shaping view and platform. Google—an established company with massive assets but having limited experience in the telephone industry—has gained credibility for its mobile phone platform, the Android operating system; by announcing the open Handlet Alliance.

Summary

Competitive strategy is concerned with how to create competitive advantage in each of the business in which it competes. According to Porter, choice of competitive strategy is the function of attractiveness of the industry it competes in and its relative position within that industry.

While recognising that the best strategy for a firm will be unique and reflects its individual circumstances, Porter developed three generic competitive strategies: cost-leadership, differentiation and focus to help an organisation outperform its rivals within an industry and so successfully position itself against the five forces.

Organisations pursuing cost-leadership strategy seek to offer their products or services at a lower price than their rivals. With a differentiation strategy, the organisation delivers a product which consumers perceive to be of better value than the product offerings of rival firms, and thus charges a premium price. Unlike these two strategies which are aimed at the entire industry, a focus strategy is aimed at serving a segment (or segments) of the market. At times, large firms employ more than one generic strategy to trounce their competitors.

Porter's competitive strategy model was challenged by Grant on the ground that long-term business strategy cannot be solely dependent upon external environment. In his view, it is capability of the firm that offers a more durable basis for a strategy. Empirical study conducted in this respect suggests that both these views should not be seen so much as incompatible but more as occupying different positions on the same continuum.

Kim and Manborne hold that organisations need to create "*blue oceans*" of uncontested market space and for that matter, have to make a set of managerial decisions in order to make a major market-creating business offering. They are of the view that the firms should shift their focus from trouncing the competition to making the competition irrelevant by placing equal emphasis on both value and innovation.

In a fast changing business environment and a hyper competitive landscape, organisations can better tailor their strategies to the environment by better understanding the interaction between strategy and the environment. However, in the sustained disequilibrium of today's business environment, it would be pertinent, according to John Hagel III and others, to shape the turbulence around us by creating an effective management ensemble that moves beyond adaptation to a shaping aspiration. More fundamentally, we need to understand how we can turn the instability created by digital infrastructures to our advantage by mobilising many other participants to shape a more rewarding future.

Key Terms

Blue ocean view	Cost-leadership strategy	Hyper competitive
Competence-destroying disruptions	Differentiation focus	Rent
Competence-enhancing disruptions	Differentiation strategy	Resource-based approach
Cost focus	Focus strategy	Shaping strategy

Discussion Questions

1. Discuss generic competitive strategies formulated by Michael Porter. What are the basic premises of these strategies?
2. What is cost-leadership strategy? How can it enable a firm to defend against the competitive forces?

3. What is a differentiation strategy? How is it different from cost-leadership strategy?

4. How can differentiation strategy defend a firm from competitive forces?

5. Discuss focus strategy. What are its implications on cost and differentiation planks?

6. Is it possible for a firm to follow a cost-leadership strategy and a differentiation strategy simultaneously?

7. Discuss, in brief, Grant's view of competitive strategy.

8. Discuss Kim and Mauborne's *"blue ocean"* view of competitive positioning.

9. How can organisations compete within hyper competitive markets that are characterised by constantly changing industry rules?

10. Discuss, in brief, elements of shaping strategy and their significance in enabling organisations to sustain their competitive advantage.

11. Is it possible for a firm to have a sustainable competitive advantage when its industry becomes hyper competitive?

References

1. Porter, Michael E., *Competitive Advantage*, op.cit., p. 1.

2. Ibid.

3. Porter, Michael E., *Competitive Strategy: Techniques for Analysing Industries and Competitors*, Free Press, New York, 1980.

4. Ibid.

5. Carves, R.E. and P. Ghemawat, "Identifying Mobility Barriers", *Strategic Management Journal*, January, pp. 1–12, 1992.

6. Grant, R.M., "The Resource-based Theory of Competitive Advantage, Implications for Strategy Formulation", *California Management Review*, 33 (spring), pp. 114–35, 1991.

7. Ibid.

8. Ibid.

9. Porter, M.E., "Towards a Dynamic Theory of Strategy", *Strategy Management Journal*, 12, (special issues) pp. 95–117, 1991.

10. Hunderson, R. and I. Cockburn, "Measuring Competence? Exploring Firm Effects in Pharmaceutical Research", *Strategic Management Journal*, **15** (special issues), pp. 63–84, 1994.

11. *Business Standard*, July 2, 2010.

12. Kim, W.C. and R. Mauborne, "Blue Ocean Strategy", *Harvard Business Press*, Boston, MA, 2005.

13. Ibid.

14. Christensen, C.M., "The Past and Future of Competitive Advantage", *Academy of Management Executive*, 9(**4**), pp. 49–61, 2001.

15. D' Aveni, R.A., *Hyper Competition*, The Free Press, pp. xiii–xiv, 1994.

16. D' Aveni, R.A., "Strategic Supremacy through Disruption and Dominance", *Sloan Management Review*, 40(**3**), pp. 127–35, 1999.

17. Hegel III, John, John Seely Brown and Lang Davison, "Shaping Strategy in a World of Constant Disruption", *Harvard Business Review*, South Asia, October 2008.

18. Ibid.

Internet Resources

- *www.coca-colaindia.com*
- *www.spicejet.com*
- *www.indigoairlines.com*
- *www.nirma.co.in*
- *www.henkelindia.com*
- *www.bajajauto.com*

11

Crafting Corporate Strategy

LEARNING OBJECTIVES

The present Chapter aims at:

- Providing a searing insight into dimensions of directional strategy.
- Furnishing a vivid view of portfolio strategy and its utility in allocation of funds.
- Discussing corporate parenting as an approach to creation of added value across the organisation.

INTRODUCTION

Conceptual clarity of strategy, as noted earlier, is extremely helpful in crafting strategy for an organisation and in its execution.

The late Mike Rukstad identified three critical components of a good strategy statement—objective, scope and advantage. He rightly believed that executives should be forced to be crystal clear about them.[1] Any strategy statement must begin with definition of the ends that the strategy is designed to achieve. Since most organisations compete in a more or less unbounded landscape, it is also crucial to define the domain of the business—the part of the landscape in which the firm will operate.

Once the objectives and domain of the business are articulated, the top management should clearly spell out the means by which the firm will achieve its objective. The management should decide how the firm can deliver a unique value to meet an important set of needs for an important set of customers. Strategy has to do with what will make the firm unique.[2] The firm's competitive advantage, as noted earlier, is the essence of its strategy. This advantage has complementary external and internal components: a value proposition that explains why the targeted customers should buy the firm's product above all the alternatives and a description of how internal activities must be aligned so that only the firm can deliver the value proposition.

A successful company is one that has found a way to create value for the customers— that is, a way to help customers get an important job done. By 'job' we mean a fundamental problem in a given situation that needs a solution. The better a firm's solution is than existing alternatives at getting the job done (and, of course, the lower the price), the greater the Customer Value Proposition (CVP).[3] CVP by Tata *Nano* is narrated in Illustrative Capsule 11.1.

ILLUSTRATIVE CAPSULE 11.1

TATA NANO'S CUSTOMER VALUE PROPOSITION (CVP)

Tata *Nano's* customer value proposition can be summed up as "offering an affordable, safer, all-weather alternative for scooter families whom Ratan Tata saw carrying entire family members on their motor scooters snaking precariously on a Mumbai road on a rainy day".

When Ratan Tata looked out over this scene, he saw a crucial job to be done: providing a safer alternative for scooter families. He understood that the cheapest car available in India cost easily five times what a scooter did, and that many of these families could not afford one. So, offering a car at an affordable price was a powerful value proposition, one with the potential to reach tens of millions of people who were not yet part of the car buying market.

For fulfilling the requirements of its CVP and profit formula, Tata Motors had to reconceive how a car is designed, manufactured and distributed. Tata built a small team of fairly young engineers who dramatically minimised the number of parts in the vehicle, resulting in a significant cost saving. Tata also reconceived its supplier strategy choosing to outsource a remarkable 85% of the *Nano's* components and use nearly 60% fewer vendors than normal to reduce transaction costs and achieve better economies of scale.

At the other end of the manufacturing line, Tata envisioned an entirely new way of assembling and distributing its cars. The ultimate plan is to ship the modular components of the vehicles to a combined network of company-owned and independent entrepreneur-owned assembly plants, which will build them to order. The *Nano* will be designed, built, distributed and serviced in a radically new way.

Thus, in a competitive environment, a successful company has to find a way to create value for its customers on an enduring basis. For this, the management must keep up with best practices while solidifying, clarifying and enhancing the company's unique value proposition.

Basic Issues in Crafting Corporate Strategy

A company to create value for customers and so also to maximise its value needs to craft overall strategy that focuses on the scope of industries and markets within which the organisation competes for attaining its aims. In fact, the corporate strategy of an organisation is essentially about the choice of direction in which it will move. This is where the organisation is small, dealing a single business with only one or a few products or a large multinational, multi-product corporation. Where an organisation is made up of many businesses operating in different markets, the corporate strategy is about managing various product lines and business units for maximum value and allocation of resources across the business units. The corporate level strategy, therefore, involves decisions regarding the flow of financial and other resources to and from a company's product lines and business units.

Based on the concept of fit and stretch, an organisation's corporate strategy deals with three major issues:

(i) The organisation's overall orientation toward growth, stability, retrenchment or liquidation;

(ii) The industries or markets in which the organisation competes through its products and business units;

(iii) The manner in which the management will coordinate activities, transfer resources and cultivate capabilities among product lines and business units.

The first issue concerns with formulating directional strategy while the second key issue deals with drawing portfolio strategy. In large organisations having different business units handling diverse products and services there is a need to coordinate activities and strategies of different business units so that the organisation as a whole succeeds as a "family". Through a series of coordinating devices, corporate head office plays the role of organisational "parent" in dealing with various products and business unit "children"[4] and transferring skills and capabilities developed in one unit to other needy units so as to obtain synergies among numerous product lines and business units and enhance the value of the corporate as a whole higher than the sum of its individual business unit parts.[5] As such, a third dimension of the corporate strategy is developing suitable parenting strategy.

The following paragraphs are devoted to dilate upon these crucial issues of the corporate strategy.

DIRECTIONAL STRATEGY

In its endeavour to increase opportunity share of the organisation and maximise its value, the top management must decide whether the organisation should:

(i) grow, cut back or maintain status quo;

(ii) confine itself within the existing industry or diversify into other industries; or

(iii) expand organically or inorganically.

In the present chapter, we shall discuss the first dimension of directional strategy, i.e., growth strategy, stability strategy, retrenchment strategy and liquidation strategy. The remaining two aspects will be examined separately in the next two chapters because of their strategic importance in the present scenario.

Growth Strategy

Of all the strategies, growth strategy is the most important strategic option which a firm pursues to achieve its objective of increase in sales, market share, assets and profits. A growth strategy is one that a firm pursues when it increases its level of objectives upward in a significant increment much higher than an extrapolation of its past achievement level.[6] Thus, growth contemplated in growth strategy is different from normal expansion which a firm can achieve through its normal learning curve. According to the normal curve concept of growth, organisations grow in terms of sales and profits by dint of experience. The growth rate in the initial stage is slow and steady. After organisations reach a certain level of maturity, their sales and profits tend to stabilise. In contrast to this, growth strategy is adopted to accelerate the rate of growth of sales, profits and market share faster than the previous years by entering new markets, acquiring new resources, developing new technologies and creating and honing new managerial skills.

The strategic run for growth is designed to allow the firm to maintain its competitive position in rapidly growing national and overseas markets and to ensure its successful survival and growth. A firm that does not plan to grow will be thrown out of the markets where the environment is highly competitive and volatile.

Forces in Making Growth Strategy

While planning for growth of business enterprise, management needs to assess profit opportunities in a contemplated move and availability of financial and managerial resources. Traditionally, organisations have been organising their companies into business units and geographic regions and then holding those entities accountable for performance. Over the past two decades, however, advances in information technology have made it feasible both to target ever-finer-grained market segments and to measure the sources of growth in an increasingly detailed way. So far, few organisations have figured out how to turn the oceans of data available to them into islands of insight about their best opportunities for growth. Even fewer have attempted to structure and manage themselves with sufficient granularity to match the texture of the markets in which they play.[7] Thus, there lies untapped potential for companies to accelerate their growth and separate from competition.

In order to exploit the untapped potential and quicken the pace of growth, a new approach, viz., **Granular approach** has been recommended.[8] According to this approach, companies can develop far better growth strategies by looking microscopically at their markets and their current performance in relation to their rivals. Thus, the firm needs to identify micro segments of customers, geographic regions and products with the strongest market momentum.

Another factor that must receive serious attention while mapping growth strategy is that the firm possesses the needed requirements to meet the immediate investment requirements and is prepared to develop additional capacity to satisfy increased obligations and anticipated requirement in case of unexpected business downturn without exposing itself to additional risk.

Further, the top management must ensure that the company has acquired sufficient managerial skills to handle effectively the more demanding tasks of managing growth. It should also be ensured that the company has the capability to cope with changes in organisational structure and human resources to handle a more complex business operation. If necessary, it may acquire new skills from outside the country.

For better allocation of resources across the firm's portfolio of business, the management need to assess dispassionately the current performance of the firm in meeting the customers' demand and its capability to cope with emerging opportunities particularly in high growth pockets. Furthermore, the management should opt for zero-based budgeting (budgeting a fresh), requiring managers to justify each and every expense instead of incrementally increasing the budgeted amount year after year. With this exercise, the management can correct the past misallocations. At times, one may go for divestment and acquisition initiatives for reconfiguration of resources.

It is noteworthy that accelerated growth on a sustainable basis in escalating competitive environment as in computational and communicational industries and also in FMGS where companies are engaged in price wars to increase their share of the market, requires persistent efforts to cost reduction. Maruti Suzuki, in its drive to maintain the tempo of growth has recently asked its 200 odd vendors to cut costs of components by 3%. LG India has also planned to reduce the cost of manufacturing new products through use of new technology.

Approach to Growth Strategy

Growth of a business enterprise implies realignment of its product-market environment. This is sought to be achieved through the basic growth approaches of intensive expansion, integration (merger and acquisition), diversification and international operations. Table 11.1 shows these basic approaches.

Table 11.1 Basic Growth Approaches

Approach	Elements	Scope	Chief Means
Intensive expansion	Product, product lines, market	Within industry	Market penetration, Market development, Product development
Integration	Product, market, business area	All-inclusive	Backward integration, Forward integration and Horizontal integration
Diversification	Business area	Within and outside industry	Concentric, Horizontal, conglomerate diversification
International business	Product, market, business area	Across the globe	Exporting, foreign licensing, direct investment

Intensive expansion approach: This approach is pursued for expanding a firm's product-market complexion with a view to augmenting the sales, market share and profits of the current product-service at a rate faster than what it has been in the past. Intensive expansion move can be fruitful to firms who have not exploited to the fullest, the untapped opportunities existing in the current products and markets. Ansoff has presented vividly a product-market matrix to explain the approach (Table 11.2).

Table 11.2 Product-Market Matrix

Market \ Product	Existing	New
Present	Market penetration	Product development
New	Market development	Diversification

Intensive expansion of a firm can be accomplished in three major ways, viz., market penetration, market development and product development.

Market penetration: When a firm believes that there exists ample opportunities for its current products in its current domestic and overseas markets which if exploited through more aggressive efforts can augment its sales and market share, it pursues the market penetration approach. This approach is, thus, followed in order to increase significantly and permanently the firm's market share. The content of this move is determined by the newness of the product or service compared with its competitors and the rate of technological change in product design.

The thrust of the move may be as under:

(i) The firm can motivate existing customers to buy its product more frequently and in larger quantities. This can be done with the help of new releases, price promotion, advertising, publicity and wider distribution.

(ii) The firm can augment its efforts to attract customers of competitors. For this purpose, the firm must develop significant competitive advantages. The types of competitive advantages available are usually dictated by the stage of product and market evolution. Attractive product design, high product quality, attractive prices, stronger advertising, and wider distribution aid an enterprise in gaining the upper hand over its competitors. All these require heavy investment which only well endowed firms can afford. Firms less well endowed may search for customer groups. Many small time manufacturers have survived by searching out and cultivating profitable niches in the market. Less well-endowed firms may also gain a share with a narrow focus on customer functions or technologies for which they have special expertise or strength. There are a variety of possibilities to look for, such as location, cost, speed or distribution credit, and service arrangements, manufacturing capability and so on. Working closely with significant customers to find what they value, management may develop an appeal to the quality conscious, the performance-oriented or those with special requirements.

(iii) The firm can increase its sales by attracting those persons in its current market areas who are not the users of its products. Price concessions, better customer services, more publicity and similar other steps can be useful in this endeavour.

In view of vast opportunities in rural India due to growing prosperity of the rural folks, MNCs operating in India and Indian corporates in electronic and telecommunication fields as also in FMCGs are penetrating aggressively in rural markets to exploit untapped opportunities for improving their market share and profits.

Bharti Airtel—India's largest mobile telephony player—pursued penetration strategy to encash a material opportunity across many categories in rural India and its salience is on the increase driven by a wide range of stimuli. For this purpose, Airtel created a two tiered structure with Rural Super stockists and Rural Distributors under them. Another iconic example of penetration strategy is that of ITC which has penetrated in more than 40,000 villages through its network of e-choupals providing all kinds of value added services to the villagers.

Market development: In the market development approach a firm seeks to increase the sales by taking its product into new markets. This effort offers two possibilities:

(i) The firm can move its present product into new geographical areas of the country escalating coverage to adjacent territorial areas for regional or national distribution. This can be done by enlarging its sales force in the country as also outside of it or acquiring additional channels of distribution, sales agents or manufacturing representative; and by franchising its operation through a chain of franchisers who, by contract, act as retailing outlets, and have made the same product/market commitment.

(ii) The firm can expand sales by attracting new market segments. This can be done by introducing minor modifications in the product that appeal to these segments, entering other channels of distribution or advertising in other media.

A large number of multinational corporations have, of late, adopted the market development strategy to exploit vast potentials of Indian market. Thus, IBM joint venture with Tata Information Systems Ltd., computer giant Hewlett Packard Ltd.'s alliance with HCL, tie-up of Black and Decker, the world leader US multinational in electrical power tools and household appliances with Bajaj Electrical Ltd., General Electric Appliances' joint venture with Godrej and Boyce are intended to sell the joint venture products in Indian market.

Likewise, many Indian companies in their bid to squeeze emerging opportunities in European and South Asian countries forged alliances with multinationals. For instance, Tata Tea entered into joint venture with US multinational Teteley Inc. to spearhead its entry into the world market of packet teas. Ranbaxy has set up joint venture with a US based pharmaceutical company Eli Lilly & Company to market Lilly products in India, Sri Lanka, Bhutan and Nepal. Blue Star constituted a new company, viz., Blue Star Middle East LLC in 1993 to produce and market sophisticated industrial air conditioners in six countries of the Gulf region. Arvind Mills also negotiated with a large European Process house and producer garments for the manufacture of cotton shirting for marketing in international markets.

Product development: Expansion through product development consists of the development of new or improved products for its current markets. This effort offers three possibilities:

(i) The company can expand sales through developing new products;

(ii) It can create different quality versions of the product;

(iii) It can develop additional models and sizes of the product to suit the varied preferences of the customers.

Product development has, of late, been the epicentre of growth strategy of MNCs operating in India as well as of Indian corporates. PepsiCo India, for example, has been fiercely engaged successfully in launching a slew of new products such as *Aliva, Lays, Kurkure, Nimbooz*, each with unique taste suited to Indian consumers, in order to sustain surging growth and improve its market share. In automobile industry, Tata Motors in its attempt to squeeze market opportunities in domestic and offshore markets has the distinction of having a portfolio of vehicles from the entry level low-cost car *Nano* to the highest echelon represented by the *Jaguar* to cater to the needs of diverse consumers groups. The company is constantly engaged in launching new quality versions of these cars, keeping in view changing preferences of the consumers of India and abroad. The company also has a joint venture with Fiat in India for the manufacturing and distribution of Fiat cars in India like the *Palio* and *Stile*. Lately, Tata Motors is gearing up to launch the electric version of the *Indica* in the UK and Denmark in 2011.

In mobile telephone segment of telecom industry, MNCs like Nokia, Sony Ericsson, Research in Motion, Apple are vying with each other to manufacture and distribute several models of internet-connected gadgets smartphones imbedded with unique features of high quality screen, better battery life, video chat via Wi-Fi and a gyroscope sensor for improved game. There has also been mad rush among them to bring new quality versions of smartphones, keeping in consideration the tastes of the consumers.

Basic considerations in intensive expansion strategy: While taking strategic decisions regarding internal expansion of the enterprise, the management should keep in mind number of factors. Some of the important factors are:

(i) There exists adequate business opportunities for the firm's current products and markets to maximise wealth of the owners. For this purpose, future net cash inflows associated with expansion must be matched with cost involved in financing it. An expansion project with higher net cash inflows will be useful to the organisation. Where there are a number of expansion options, the one with the highest net present value will be a natural choice provided, it does not add to the existing risk exposure of the firm.

(ii) Competitive behaviour should be prognosticated in order to determine now, and when each competitor will expand the capacity.

(iii) Assessment of the economic condition in general and condition of industry in particular should be made in the manner discussed earlier to determine demand of the product and product price.

(iv) The firm must assess its strengths and weaknesses against its competitors to ascertain its competitive advantages.

(v) The firm must have adequate financial, technological and managerial capacity to support the proposed expansion programme.

(vi) The management should also ascertain if the host country government permits the firm to expand the way it chooses.

(vii) Technological changes that are likely to take place in future and its impact on current capacity addition and markets must be closely winnowed so that adequate provisions are made at the time of capacity additions. This exercise is very necessary, particularly in highly technological industries such as electronics, chemicals, and the like.

Integrative expansion approach: Integrative expansion approach is about inorganic way to expand the business by acquiring other firm—domestic or international. Broadly speaking, integration move may be vertical or horizontal.

In **vertical integration**, firms engaged in successive stages of production in an industry join to reduce costs, gain control over a scarce resource, guarantee quality of a key input or obtain access to potential customers. Vertical integration may be backward or forward. **Backward integration** refers to going backward on an industry's value chain. Acquisition of oil fields of De Company of Columbia by ONGC, General Chemicals Ltd., US by Tata Chemicals, Mount Gordon Copper mines of Australia by Hindalco, and Carborough Downs Coal project in Australia by Tata Steel are examples of backward integration. The Vijay Mallya-owned United Breweries Ltd. —the market leader in India's beer industry—is planning to embark on a massive backward integration initiative to control the huge spendings on barley—the main agri-commodity in brewing beer. **Forward integration** is about going forward on an industry's value chain. Motorola, for example, forged alliance with Bharati Teletech to use the latter's network of its distributors and retailers in the country for selling its handsets and accessories.

A company seeking to strengthen its competitive position in a highly promising industry (especially when technology is predictable and markets are growing) should pursue vertical growth strategy.[10]

Horizontal integration refers to the combination of firms engaged in the same activity. Acquisition of UK's *Tetley* Tea by Tata Tea, National Steel Singapore by Tata Steel, UK's Corus by Tata Steel, Korea's Daewo Motors by Tata Motors, Algoma, Canada by Essar Steel, Betapharm, Germany by Dr. Reddy's Laboratories and US's Novelis HINDALCO are illustrious examples of horizontal integration. Horizontal integration option is driven by the objectives of accessing new markets, achieving cutting edge technology, developing new product mixes, enhancing market share and improving operating margins.

Other routes to growth of a company are diversification, and international business expansion. We shall discuss each one of them separately in the subsequent chapters. Illustrative Capsule 11.2 gives the growth strategy of Britannia.

ILLUSTRATIVE CAPSULE **11.2**

BRITANNIA'S GROWTH STRATEGY

In mid-April 2010, Nusli Wadia, Chairman, Britannia Industries, through one of his group companies, acquired 25.48% stake of French giant Group Danone in Britannia and got complete control of the 117-year old firm and the opportunity to make up lost ground in the ₹9,000-crore organised biscuit market.

Over the last couple of months, Wadia along with Britannia's Managing Director, Vinita Bali, put in place a blueprint to regain market share lost to competitors—the firm's share was as high as 46% in 2003, but was down to around 35% in 2009.

Britannia is already aware that it has to operate in an environment of high degree of competition not only from its erstwhile partner Danone but from a whole host of competitors—domestic and international, including Kraft Foods. The latest global threat is in the shape of Pepsi, which has launched a baked savoury snacks called *Aliva*. The company has also noted the legion of local competitors which range from the big boys like ITC and Parle to regional lynchpins like Priya gold, Anmol and Haldiram priced at ₹5, which has enabled the company to make its products an impulse buy on railway platforms. Britannia has added transit points such as bus stops and small shops to its distribution network.

Along with the buyout of Danone, another acquisition within an existing joint venture that came as a shot in the arm for Britannia was Fonterra's stake in Britannia New Zealand Foods. Britannia now appears well-poised to target profitable growth in the two new segments of bread, cakes and rusks and dairy products to offset the slowdown in biscuits.

Britannia set up two Joint Ventures in West Asia, with Khimjo Ramdas Group and Strategic Foods International. Bali says, with this presence in the Persian Gulf region, Britannia can target 30–40 countries in the geography. The company does not believe in going into mature markets since there is little growth there.

The top management has also been working non-stop behind-the-scenes to streamline Britannia's operations. In West Asia, the company has merged two of its biscuit factories into one and put together a single distribution network in the region. Its Chennai R&D lab engineers have been able to reduce ₹200 crore off Britannia's expenses by recessing of exhaust gases, evening out thickness of biscuits and doubling packing from 70–90 packets to 150 a minute.

During the last couple of months, Nusli Wadia along with Britannia's Managaing Director, Vinita Bali, put in place a blueprint to regain market share which the company lost to its rivals—the company's market share was as high as 46% in 2003 which plunged to around 35% in 2009. Broadly, the blueprint addresses three key areas: competition, both from domestic and international players, products and product innovation, and inorganic growth through strategic acquisitions and joint ventures.

Britannia has strengthened its chocolate portfolio, upgraded packing and added new flavours. "Chocolate is an important flavour in the food industry across confectionary, malted drinks and biscuits", says Neeraj Chandra, Britannia's COO. The company has upgraded and re-packaged key products in this segment including *Bourbon* and *Pure Magic*. It has made more incremental innovations than anyone else, claims Chandra.

One of the key success stories for Britannia has been the out-of-home package for biscuits.

Stability Strategy

An Overview

A company is said to have opted for stability strategy if:

(i) It decides to serve the same category of customers with the same products;

(ii) It continues to pursue the same objectives, adjusting the level of achievement by about the existing annual growth rate;

(iii) Its strategic thrust is on incremental improvement of functional performance; and

(iv) It concentrates its resources in the existing product-market scope for developing a meaningful competitive advantage.

It is mistaken if it is believed that stability strategy does not provide for any improvement in a present level of performance. As a matter of fact, stability strategy focuses on continuance of the improvement of a company's business without any significant change in the direction. It may be appropriate for a successful company to pursue stability strategy in a reasonably predictable environment. This is more so when the management feels that the company is performing extremely well.[11] At times, the management may feel contended with the status quo because the company can retain its distinct competence based on specialisation and continued evolution within it.

In a number of organisations, stability strategy is adopted because the management is averse to take risk. Such risk-averse managers prefer to avoid taking such decisions as can expose the company to additional risk.

Stability strategy is also pursued by those organisations which have been aggressive in the past and as a result grew up so fast and to such an extent that it has now become imperative to stabilise for a while, otherwise the organisation will become unmanageable and inefficient, rendering the cost of production too high to compete with other firms in the same line.

Stability strategy is popular among small organisations which have found a niche and are happy with their success and the size of their firms.

In an environment of economic slowdown, organisations are interested in retaining their volume growth and so also market share. For that matter, they may opt for stability strategy. The case with Hindustan Unilever (Illustrative Capsule 11.3) sheds lurid light on stability strategy pursued by it.

In a nutshell, stability strategy can be very useful in the short run but it can be dangerous, if followed for too long.

ILLUSTRATIVE CAPSULE **11.3**

HINDUSTAN UNILEVER'S STABILITY STRATEGY

Market dynamics changed rapidly in the FMCG business in early 2008 when consumer non-durable companies were grappling with a sharp increase in raw material prices like oil and packaging material on the one hand, and drop in sales volumes as modern retailers were tightening their product portfolios and downsizing existing inventory, on the other hand. However, towards the end of 2008, raw material and packaging material prices started sliding. Consumer non-durable companies soon passed the benefits on to the consumers by paring product prices. FMCG's roller-coaster ride seems to have come to an end.

Such a rapid cycle made it tougher for FMCG behemoth Hindustan Unilever Limited (HUL) to navigate the market conditions. HUL volumes dipped 4% towards the end of March 2009. However, lower raw material costs helped boost margins by two percentage points.

HUL has been losing some ground to small and mid-sized companies in recent years and lost market share in March 2009 in some key product categories. For instance, in soaps, market share in value was down to 47.5% in March 2009 from 53.4% during the same period last year. In shampoos, HUL's market share dipped to 45.9% from 47.3%. In toothpaste and detergents, too, HUL slipped. In tea, however, HUL managed to buck the trend and increased its share from 22.6% to 23%. Price hikes and the downstocking in big retail had an impact on HUL's sales. HUL has now corrected its product pricing and is working to regain market share in the ensuing period.

The business environment remains challenging for FMCG companies as the economy is not out of the woods. So, HUL's focus was on retaining volume growth in 2009–10 by fine-tuning its pricing and packaging of its products. Cost control and managing marketing networks were other thrust areas. The company has also been working on reducing its execution cycles so as to better respond to marketing changes. It is streamlining distributor network sticking to a fewer big distributors, and through the use of technology, seeks to reduce inventory levels. As a result, it will lead to quicker response to fickle consumers.

HUL now is gearing up to take on competition with new price points and a streamlined distribution.

Considerations in Making Stability Strategy

While deciding to go for stability strategy for the company, the top management must factor in certain fundamental considerations. The first such consideration is with respect to maintaining the current rate of return on capital employed and cash flow. This is necessary to sustain the existing operations.

Continued availability of human resources is another essential requirement for the success of stability strategy. Unless the terms and conditions of employment and remuneration are acceptable, the rate of output will be less than the desired one, with adverse consequences for both cost flow and profitability.

These considerations may be enough for no-growth survival if the overall performance is upto the level of satisfying the current expectations of the owners and if the owners' present controlling power is not in peril and above all, if the environment—both socio-economic and technological—remains sufficiently stable. However, in real life, these conditions do not exist in the long run. Real life business situations may in fact force even risk averse managers to scan the environmental developments continually so as to perceive the threats to their ability to continue the existing product-market posture.

It must be noted that pursuing stability strategy over a long period of time demands sufficient investment in capital equipment and human resources so as to survive. The company must rejig its plan to keep pace with continually rising expectations of productivity and of income to be drawn by those whom it employs. At the same time, it must maintain and hone its human capital including its managerial, technical and task skills.

Although the company may acquire these skills from outside, they may take time to assimilate and develop. Technological improvements and innovations will have to be made even if there is no remarkable change in direction or emphasis. For this, a dispassionate appraisal of technological and human resource environment is essential.

Thus, continuous short-term and long-term review of the environmental developments in and outside is necessary to assess adequacy of the current strategy. Inherent in stability strategy is the need to sharpen the company's competitive advantage. For example, a company might seek to continue outperforming its rivals on the score of innovative customer services. For this purpose, alterations in deployment of resources may be required to break its competitive records already set by the organisation. This again calls for constant monitoring of the environment which focuses on the trends that signal potential for developing new competitive strengths or altering existing ones.

Approaches to Stability Strategy

There are various approaches to stability strategy. The management has to choose the one that best suits the corporate objectives. Some of the more popular of these approaches are incremental growth, harvesting, pause and no change.

Incremental growth approach: A company seeking to achieve what it has accomplished in the past, after adjusting for inflation, pursues an incremental growth approach. In this approach, the company concentrates on one product or service line. It grows slowly but surely, increasing its market penetration by steadily adding new products or services and continuously expanding its market.

Harvesting approach: This approach is most suitable to a company whose principal objective is to generate cash. Even market share may be sacrificed to earn profits and generate funds. A host of ploys such as selective price increases, and reducing costs without reducing price may be used for the purpose. In this approach, selected products are milked rather than nourished and defended. Hindustan Unilever's *Lifebuoy* soap is an example in point. It fetched large profits under careful management.

Pause approach: This approach is adopted when a company needs a breathing spell. It is conceived as a temporary move to conduct the business smoothly until a particular environment becomes more hospitable. A company having grown so fast for a long period needs to consolidate its resources as otherwise it will become inefficient and manageable. This strategy was followed by Dell in 1993 after its growth strategy had resulted in more growth than it could handle.

No change approach: In this approach, the company decides to do nothing new but to continue its current operations and policies for the foreseeable future. This approach will be useful for a company if there is no imminent change in its situation. The relative stability created by the company's modest competitive position in the industry facing little or no growth encourages the company to continue on its current course of action, making only minor adjustments for inflation in its sales and profit objectives.

Retrenchment Strategy

An Overview

A company having not performed satisfactorily in its operations in terms of sales and profits for a number of years may pursue retrenchment strategy so as to put a great deal of pressure to improve its performance. Retrenchment strategy may also be followed by companies which have not been able to achieve their objectives by adopting growth or stability strategy and there is tremendous pressure from stakeholders to arrest deterioration in the performance.

Retrenchment strategy calls for immediate functional improvement through cost reduction, market and product reduction. Many Japanese companies such as NEC Electronics group, Mazda Motor and Nissan Motor, having suffered adverse financial performance in the recent past, adopted retrenchment strategy to affect more staff cuts, cut product lines, trim executive salaries and abandon their growth plans. The IBM adopted retrenchment strategy in December, 1992 to overcome the continued decline in sales due to global economic slowdown and a rapidly changing computer market. Tatas adopted this kind of strategy in 1993 and divested TOMCO—a loss making company having incurred losses.

RPG Enterprises led by Harsh Goenka had to pursue retrenchment strategy recently when it suffered financial losses (Illustrative Capsule 11.4).

ILLUSTRATIVE CAPSULE 11.4
RETRENCHMENT STRATEGY OF RPG ENTERPRISES

When RPG Enterprises suffered operational losses in their tyre business in 2008, the top management got quickly seized with the matter to find out whether their group was on the right track and whether the strategies at their various group companies would stand upto the challenge of economic slowdown.

While contemplating measures to address the problem, several thoughts came to the management's minds—Was there too much manpower? How do we cut costs? Should we liquidate inventory aggressively?

The management felt that at the outset it must be recognised that there was a serious problem and everyone has to put their heads together. Accordingly, a cross-functional team was set up. The top management realised that knee-jerk reactions would not help. In the past, they were perpetually behind in the run rate on profit before tax to sales vis-à-vis the top three in the business, and things were getting worse by the time the first half financial year 2009 ended.

The management believed that cost-cutting alone would not be the solution. A clear brief was, therefore, drawn up. They decided to cut cost by ₹50 crore in the second half over the first half. A plan was to be developed which would make CEAT competitive on a sustainable basis. Thus, Project XL was born.

Project XL had some clear ground rules. The top management, particularly the Managing Director, will be on line and the finance department would ratify all the numbers. The management decided to snatch the "low hanging fruit:"—reduce scrap, use better-price-fabric, negotiate hard on rents and commissions. It was also decided to reduce inventory, check receivables carefully, reduce foreign exchange losses by stopping position taking and keep a close eye on operating expenses. The company moved from a monthly to a weekly to eventually a daily planning "bucket", with dynamic planning and monthly reviews. The idea was to make every ball count change the product mix and the market mix to become more profitable.

The share of the lucrative replacement market moved up from about 67% in October, 2008 to as much as 76% in September, 2009. The less profitable original market share fell from 15% to 9% and exports from some 19% to 15%. On the product mix side, the share of the premium tyres rose from 40% to 46% and the economy tyres share fell from 60% to 54%.

There was strict budgeting, and low-profit products were knocked off. The plan was working. Costs were kept low, and there was a manpower optimisation initiative alongside.

The management also kept a regular connects with critical talent, since they believe critical talent wins matches.

The result: Against the ₹50-crore savings target, Project XL managed to achieve ₹58 crore by the second half of financial year 2009. By the first half of financial year 2009, as against a ₹30 crore target, the actual savings was of ₹40 crore.

Thus, the management came to the conclusion that a company cannot achieve turnaround by cutting costs alone. The approach must be holistic in nature, and sustainable. There should be—in a positive sense—a paranoid mindset, where achievement of the objective is paramount.

It must be realised that the devil is in the detail and that one must address those details. The entire organisation must embrace it. And there must be regular communication between the team and the top management, with reviews on a regular basis.

There are things that are now a way of life at CEAT and most of RPG companies.

To be effective, retrenchment strategy calls for scanning future environmental changes, delineating courses of actions, specifying methods of resource deployment and outlining contingency plans to handle unexpected changes in external and internal situations.

Phases of Retrenchment Strategy

A well-conceived retrenchment strategy has three phases, viz., the contracting phase, the improvement phase and the recovery phase.

The **contracting phase** is characterised by reduction in personnel, administrative and functional costs. Such a cost reduction is sought to be achieved by hiring freeze, across-the-board personnel reduction, scheduled department layoffs, cutbacks in budgetary expenditures relating to general administration, overheads, R&D, advertising, supplies and services and saving of production, marketing and financial costs. The contracting phase lays down the path for subsequent recovery and growth by getting rid of surpluses without adversely affecting the basic functioning of the organisation and arousing excessive hostility among employees. This is followed by a structured plan to direct cost savings during the consolidation phase when the objective is to augment sales, improve profit and increase productivity.

The **improvement phase** of retrenchment strategy focuses on profit improvement by embarking on programmes of improving marketing, production, R&D, purchasing and finance activities. The content and intensity of these programmes depend essentially on state of general economy and ability of the organisation to reach the point of internal stabilisation.

The **recovery phase** places emphasis on offensive approach which involves market intensification through product modification and concentrated advertising. This is possible when financial position of the company is strong.

Variants of Retrenchment Strategy

Retrenchment strategy may take various forms ranging from turnaround to divestment and liquidation.

Turnaround strategy: When company is suffering business losses since long due to continued decline in sales, it takes recourse to turnaround strategy to arrest and reverse the declining performance of the business. Turnaround strategy with its basic philosophy of holding the present business and cut the cost is a critical move which stops just short of selling the hibernation, or degenerating into insolvency. Such a course of action should be resorted to only when the business is worth saving. It would, therefore, be pertinent to determine the company's future earning power and compare the same with the estimated liquidation value. If the firm's future earning power is higher than the liquidation value, it will be worthwhile to continue the operation of the firm.

Turnaround strategy demands strong managerial actions. Decision in this regard must be taken after diagnosing the present problem and careful analysis of costs and prices and detailed evaluation of internal operations, alongwith making cash flow projection.

Cost cutting strategy should start with pruning R&D expenditures followed by reduction of market expenditures. Expenditure on customer services and product quality can also be trimmed if the situation so demands. However, it should be ensured that existing customers do not switch over to the rivals.

In addition to cost paring move, the management may also consider the options of augmenting revenue, disposition and divestiture. Sales revenue may be increased through promotion or price reduction. Disposition of surplus assets including inventories, equipment, plants, and so on and pruning marginal products and workforce can help cash savings which can be used to reduce the level of outstanding short-term debt and to reinvest in securities to increase cash inflow.

Once the company's financial stability is restored, it should launch a well-planned and aggressive marketing campaign and production activities to ensure adequate managerial and financial wherewithal for recovery and growth.

Bata India's turnaround strategy (Illustrative Capsule 11.5) throws lurid light on how the company suffering from loss became profit-making organisation by dint of its prudent planning.

ILLUSTRATIVE CAPSULE 11.5

TURNAROUND STRATEGY OF BATA INDIA

When Thomas Bata hand-picked old loyalist Marcelo Villagram in February 2005 from Bata's thriving subsidiary in Chile to steer Bata India, the shoe major was scuffed and worn out. The balance sheet was splattered with red ink, shareholders were disgruntled, workers were unhappy— and India shining was no longer thronging the outlets of the country's largest shoe maker.

Villagram took the helm as Managing Director with an unenviable mandate of stabilising a ship that was almost sunk.

Indeed, Bata India's ₹62.7 crore losses in 2004 appear a distant memory today. The turnaround began to get reflected in the 2005 numbers itself, thanks to some desperate measures that included retrenchment (via retirement schemes and attrition). Some 1,467 left in 2004 itself, and in 2006 another 946 bailed out. This was just one prong of the turnaround trick.

Villagram adopted three more strategic moves to improve performance of the company. The first and the biggest hurdle was the footwear collection. It was good but it was not giving any margins for profits, recalls Villagram and adds, "So we did a lot of re-engineering with the shoes and designs".

Bata doubled the number of people preparing the collection, cut costs by outsourcing a lot of operations and refreshed the collection with chic designs without increasing the price so that "Bata continued to remain very affordable". Bata has been importing parts on a large scale from China", admits Chairman Bata India, Priya Mohan Sinha.

Expanding the number of stores came next. "We started generating good cash flow and were capitalised in 2005, so it was possible for us to expand. The primary focus was the expansion of big-format stores", says Villagram. While the format was international, Villagram kept a hawk's eye on the tiniest detail, like displaying shoes in pairs.

"We are the only one to have thought of doing so", says a beaming Villagram. The segmentation highlights the chic and trendy designs.

"Specialisation was third on our list. Bangalore does school shoes, Hosur deals with *Hush puppies* and the one in Kolkata manufactures sports shoes and sandals. This specialisation has helped us in improving the quality and reducing costs", Villagram says.

"The turnaround was not so much from the point of marketing but was more closely linked to sales, quality and manufacturing capacity", says Sinha.

Besides cost-saving measures, Bata India tied up with retailing chain Shopper's Stop for shop-in-shops across cities. An alliance with Reliance Retail was also forged. The 262-acre township in Kolkata has been developed by Riverbank holdings between Bata India and the Calcutta Metropolitan Group.

Bata also introduced a Commissionaire system, wherein Bata will provide space, furniture and products to those wanting to take up the deal who, in turn, earn a commission on sales and are free to recruit as many people as they require. Bata had around 70 stores in 2007 under this system.

The results of the above: sales shot up from ₹729 crore in 2004 to ₹1,024 in 2008 and loss of ₹63 crore in 2004 turned into profit of ₹61 crore in 2009.

Divestment strategy: Divestment strategy seeks to sell or spin off its business which has not been performing satisfactorily for several years and has proved to be a drag on competitiveness of an organisation. Divestment may also be due to the simple fact that present level of business has become unmanageable.

The sell out strategy makes sense if the management can manage to obtain a good price for the shareholders and the employees can keep their jobs by selling the entire company or its division to another firm in the hope that the latter will have the competence and grit to run the business successfully. The sale of Tata Oil Mills (TOMTO) to Hindustan Unilever Ltd. (HUL) is a case in point.

Hindustan Unilever Ltd. (HUL) also followed divestment strategy to exit out of the low margins commodities market when it decided to divest its edible oil business to American company 'Bunge Co.'.

Success of divestment strategy depends on the ability of the management to accurately spot the industry decline before the problem becomes alarming and to sell out while the company's assets are still valued by others.

However, great care needs to be taken while deciding about divestment move as there is a risk of losing forever any opportunities that may arise in that area. Further, it may have far-reaching adverse effects on personnel due to redundancy and re-deployment which may cause hostility among employees.

It would, therefore, be pertinent to prepare a profile of environmental opportunities, threats and strategic advantages for each business unit/division. Steps must be taken to see that the assets are disposed off in a profitable way and divestment has the least detrimental effect on the company's overall earnings.

Liquidation Strategy

Liquidation strategy is about closing down a firm. A company is constrained to take such an extreme course of action under the following circumstances:

(i) The business condition of the company is serious with no hope of recovering from the present crisis;

(ii) The company is suffering from a business crisis and does not have adequate resources to ride over the crisis;

(iii) The company's position is so grave that no one is keen to buy it;

(iv) The liquidation value is higher than the future earning power of the company.

It is generally observed that even when things are going terribly wrong, the top management may be loath to liquidate the organisation so as to escape from the blame and avoid the curse of the shareholders to come forward and ask the management to wind up the organisation and quit. Paramount Airways—the poster boy in Indian aviation until recently is heading towards liquidation (Illustrative Capsule 11.6).

ILLUSTRATIVE CAPSULE 11.6

PARAMOUNT AIRWAYS HEADING TOWARDS LIQUIDATION

Among a dozen airlines and service variants, Paramount Airways was the lone all-business class carrier flying domestic skies. It was the only airline to fly Embraer-made jets. It was a regional operator long before the nomenclature became common. Paramount Airways flew its five planes with the highest passenger occupancy among all peers. It had profits three years on the trot in an industry which in 2008–09 alone accounted for some ₹10,000 crore losses.

Paramount Airways seemed to have got everything right. Its medium-sized planes with a capacity of 70–75 seats qualified for a waiver of landing fees at airports and paid just 4% sales tax on fuel (versus upto 34% for larger jets); its ticket yields were a healthy ₹4,200 (at par with Kingfisher and a third more than Spicejet), and had a loyal following, won over by gourmet on-board meals and on-time performance. "Paramount was the model to emulate", recalls Ankur Bhatia, Executive Director, Bird Group, a travel services company.

Paramount continues to be the odd man out today. It is an airline with no planes. Almost between December, 09 and May, 2010, the airline's two lessors—GE Capital Aviation Services (GECAS) and EEC Leasing Company—have taken back or are in the process of doing so the five planes the Paramount had leased from them. Reason: Non-payment of lease rentals and dues, and suspicion that Paramount was cannibalising spare parts from one plane to keep others airworthy.

In September, 2009 Paramount promoter M. Jhiagarajan, a lanky 32-year old with the demeanour of a techie, had planned to expand to North India from the South where the airline flew between cities such as Madurai, Chennai, Bangalore, Thiruvananthapuram, and Coimbatore. His model worked splendidly: With just 1% aircraft seat capacity nationally, he commanded a market share double that by flying his planes more and fuller. His share in the Southern market was 26%.

However, everything was not honky dory in recent months. The Paramount's cash flow problems aggravated and the airline had difficulties with its payroll. In October, 2009 the cash flow problems compounded when GECAS hauled Paramount before DGCA to deregister three Embraer jets the airline had leased. Pending payments from Paramount had amounted to $8,21,213.42 (about ₹3.7 crore) by July 2009, prompting the lessor to send a grounding notice on July 20, 2009. The amount was paid, but a series of defaults followed. A lease termination notice was served on October 14. Three Embraer planes from GECAS no longer fly on Paramount's deep blue colours.

Even ECC Leasing has terminated its lease on its two planes rented to Paramount and is pursuing deregistration of the two aircraft leased to the airline with the DGCA. It is also pursuing a legal process in India to recover its aircrafts due to events of default on lease payments.

A combative Thiagarajan says, "GECAS has $49 million from Paramount in maintenance claims, a caution deposit and a maintenance deposit". According to Thiagarajan, "we told GECAS in September–October, 2009 that *you owe us a lot of money, so adjust it against the lease rentals payable*, because we had no intention of renewing the lease of the three jets set to expire in October, 2010. So, we stopped paying lease rentals from October, 2009". According to Thiagarajn, he may prefer to lease aircraft from elsewhere a make outright purchases. "With several aircrafts grounded, there are opportunities to get them either on rental or on purchase at cheaper prices", he says. But it will be difficult for Paramount to find leasing planes, because the world of aircraft lessors is a close-knit with airline reputations marked and checked closely, thus leaving it with only expensive purchase options.

According to experts, it is the steep lease rentals and fuel costs that aid Paramount in and offset all gains from lower sales taxes on fuel and exemptions from landing and parking charges at airports. According to an analyst, "An airline can hope to make profits if it can keep its lease rentals at around 15%–16% of its revenues. But in case of Paramount, it was at an unsustainable 37% in 2007–08, 30% in 2008–09 and about 20% in 2009–10".

Experts point out that a more fundamental reason for Paramount's troubles was its flawed business model. Thiagarajan used long-haul, small commercial jets to fly short routes. The reason behind this argument becomes clear when one looks at one measure of airline performance with 'Cost per Available Seat Mile' (CASM). Embraer E-170 planes operated by Paramount do not compare favourably with ATR turboprops used by Jet Airways and Kingfisher even though both types of aircraft carry around 70-odd passengers. Data from the US and Europe show Embraer jets have a 20%–25% higher CASM.

Paramount has also been suffering because, on shorter routes, the Jet's speed advantage gets negated and they waste fuel in taking-off and landing. Worse, because most of Paramount's routes were in the 500 km range, which again guzzled fuel.

The road back to business is going to be very arduous for Thiagarajan. The Paramount brand has suffered with cancellations and safety scrutiny of the regulator. He has very few options: pump in substantially more than the $100 million he has already invested, or, close shop and let Paramount be another casualty of the dogfight that Indian aviation is. Sadly, both choices are painful.

PORTFOLIO STRATEGY

As noted in the preceding Chapter, a company can gain competitive advantage by using competitive and cooperative strategies. However, for boosting overall performance of a firm and sustaining its competitive prowess, companies with multiple product lines or business units need to address the singular issue as to how resources are to be allocated across their product lines and business units to achieve the corporate objectives. Portfolio strategy can aid the management in this regard.

According to the portfolio approach, a company engaged in different product-market areas has to formulate a strategy that would build an effective mix of markets and products to achieve the corporate objectives. The thrust of portfolio strategy is on portfolio analysis which allows the management to assess the competitive position and identify the rate of return it is receiving from its various product lines/business units. The management is supposed to constantly juggle the portfolio of investments comprising the product lines/business units so as to ensure the best return on the company's investments. This the management can do efficaciously by disaggregating the organisation into its individual business units and deciding about which markets and products to be built, maintained, phased down and phased out, keeping in view relative attractiveness of each of the markets and products in terms of their future prospects for growth and profitability. Thus, the primary objective of formulating strategy, according to the portfolio approach, is to keep refreshing the company's portfolio of business by flushing out the poor ones and adding promising new ones in order to ensure that corporate resources are channeled in a most profitable business. A host of portfolio models has been developed to undertake portfolio analysis. Amongst these, Boston's Portfolio model and GE Business screen model are widely used by the organisations.

Boston's Portfolio Model

This model, developed by the Boston Consulting Group (BCG)[12], uses the growth-market share matrix concept on which the portfolio of business operated by a company can be positioned. BCG model evaluates a company's products, business units and/or profit centres as separate entities. Decisions are made for each entity pertaining to its market share and existing or potential growth rate for the industry.

Figure 11.3 displays growth-share matrix and the corporate portfolio. As evident from the figure, the BCG matrix plots an organisation's business units according to (i) its industry growth rate, and (ii) its relative market share. Industry growth rate can be determined by reference to the growth rate of the overall economy. As such, if the industry is growing faster than the economy as a whole, it is regarded as a high growth industry and vice-versa. A business unit's relative market share (or competitive position) is defined as the ratio of its market share in relation to its largest competitor within the industry. A firm having market share above 1.0 is the market leader.

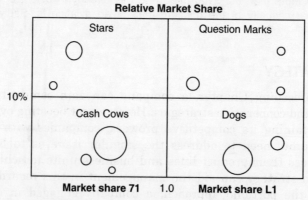

Figure 11.1 The BCG growth-share matrix.

It may be noted from the above that the critical element of the BCG matrix is market share. The matrix relies largely upon the experience curve which suggests that a high market share is a function of cost-leadership achieved through economies of scale. In this figure, each business unit (or product) is represented by a circle and plotted on the matrix according to its relative market share and industry growth rate. The area of the circle represents the relative significance of each business unit or product line to the company in terms of revenue generated.

The lines dividing the portfolio into four quadrants are somewhat arbitrary.[13] A high industry growth rate is placed at 10%, whereas the lines separating relative market share are set equal to the largest competitor which is 1.

A business unit can fall within one of the four strategic groups in which it will be characterised as a star, question mark, cash cow or dog. These classifications can be gainfully used for funding decisions.

Stars

Star businesses in the upper-left quadrant have high growth and high market share and are the business leaders, generating large amount of cash. Such businesses require substantial amount of investment to maintain their competitive position. As such, such businesses should be maintained and strengthened as a first priority for investment.

Cash Cows

When star businesses mature, they become low-growth, high share operations or cash cows, where the opportunities for reinvestment are too limited to absorb the cash generated. Hence, cash cows generating high cash flows can serve as the principal source of funding those businesses that are expected to grow.

Question Marks

Question marks (also called *wild cats*) in the upper-right quadrant of the matrix represent high-growth, low-share businesses. Such businesses have high funds requirements, because they are in-growth industries, but do not generate enough cash due to their low market share. Question marks require the most difficult decisions, as to which wild cats are to be divested and which are to be continued. These decisions must be made keeping in mind the market potential and cost of penetration of risks of future. If a wild cat has a probability of success with the allocation of proper resources, it should receive adequate support. Wild cat with low growth prospects should be abandoned.

Dogs

Dogs represent businesses with a low market share within a low-growth industry. As a result, the cash needed to maintain their competitive position will be in excess of the cash generated by them. Under the circumstances, dogs should either be sold off or managed carefully for the small amount of cash they can generate.

Thus, BCG model helps the management in constructing a balanced portfolio along the following lines:

(i) Invest heavily in stars because of higher probability of future success;

(ii) Maintain cash cows because they provide resources for future growth;

(iii) Selective resource allocation for wild cats to convert them into stars;

(iv) Liquidate or divest dogs.

However, the BCG model may not always be practically useful in view of its certain premises. For instance, the four-cell matrix is based on the classification of businesses into high-low. In real world, growth rate and market share of business units may vary between the two. It would, therefore, have been more meaningful if businesses were classified into high, medium and low.

Further, the matrix has accorded due considerations to only two factors, viz., market share and growth rate of sales, and thus ignored equally important factors such as product life cycle, market evolution, strategic fit among different businesses, presence of competitive advantages, impending threats and opportunities, size of the market, capital requirements, and the like.

Another limitation of the BCG model is that it assumes that long-term profitability and liquidity of a firm are the function of growth and market shares. In real world, this may not be always true. In many industries, firms with low share in a large and growing market are able to make high earnings. Likewise, business with high market share in low growth industry may not generate high cash surplus in view of fierce competition.

General Electric-Mc Kinsey Portfolio Model

Another pioneering effort in the field of Portfolio analysis was made by General Electric Company and Mc Kinsey Company of the US. This model, displayed here as Figure 11.2, is a 3X3 matrix with relative business strength and industry attractiveness as the parameters.

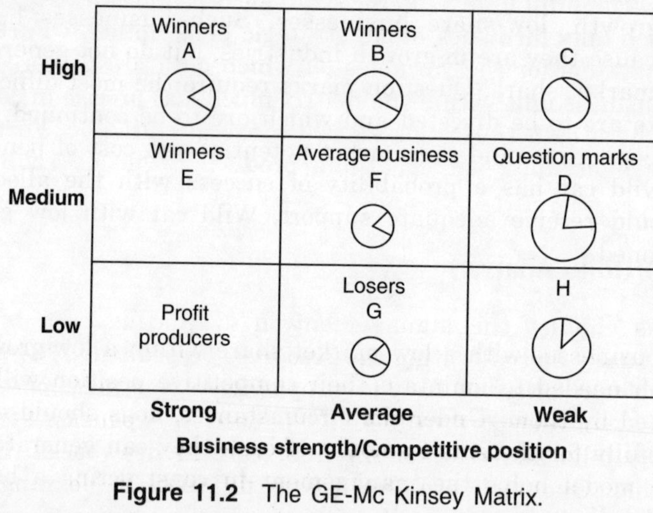

Figure 11.2 The GE-Mc Kinsey Matrix.

The vertical axis of the matrix represents business strength which is judged on the basis of a number of variables such as product strengths and weaknesses, market share, relative market price, marketing expense level, rate of new product innovation, raw material position, productivity, capacity utilisation and relative cost and financial performance. On the horizontal axis is shown industry attractiveness which is determined on the basis of a compendium of factors including demand characteristics, trends in distribution channels, buying decision motivation, changes in product and process development, cost factors of production and marketing, trends in investment, competitive behaviour in the industry and socio-economic, political and technological environments.

The individual product lines or business units are identified by a letter and plotted as circles on the GE Business Screen. The area of each circle corresponds to the size of the industry in terms of sales. The pie slices within the circles depict the market share of each product line/business unit.

Each business unit is evaluated on the basis of the above two parameters and plotted on the portfolio matrix where both business strength and industry attractiveness are classified into high, medium and low. Thus, there will be nine strategic options if both the parameters are combined.

According to this model, a firm should adopt growth strategy for those businesses which have industry attractiveness and strengths or which have high industry attractiveness although strengths are medium, or which have medium industry attractiveness but high strengths. In contrast, the firm should pursue divestment strategy for those business units which have low industry attractiveness and strengths. However, the firm will have to be choosy where opportunities and strengths are medium or the former is low and the latter high or vice-versa.

The GE Mc Kinsey model is an improvement over the BCG growth-share matrix inasmuch as many more variables are factored in assessing the performance of business units.

However, it is doubtful if any specific strategic decision can be taken with the help of this model which only furnishes broad strategic prescription.[14] Further, there is no specific weighing system for the variables on which data are gathered, rendering the positioning of a business unit within the matrix much less precise in comparison to the Boston's model where both the major variables are quantifiable. Further, this model cannot effectively depict the positions of new products or business units in developing industries.[15]

Evaluation of Portfolio Analysis

Portfolio analysis enables the management in evaluating each of the company's businesses individually and allocating the resources accordingly. The management can make use of externally oriented data to supplement their judgement. This approach focuses on the issue of cash flow availability for use in expansion and growth.

However, portfolio analysis suffers from certain drawbacks, limiting its uses in strategy making. One such problem lies in difficulty in defining product/market segments. It suggests the use of standard strategies that can miss opportunities. The value-laden terms like cash cow and dog can lead to self-fulfilling prophecies.

A firm following portfolio approach in making strategic decisions faces a lot of problems in implementing them. One such problem pertains to creating organisational structure in conformity with Strategic Business Units or SBUs as per the portfolio approach. Hardly, the SBU of a firm is found to conform to its formal structure. It may at times be found that elements of a SBU are located in two or more product or geographic divisions of a firm. Further, there is a possibility for the top management to evaluate a corporate portfolio in the context of the formal structure rather than account separately for divisional business. This may result in serious aberrations.

CORPORATE PARENTING

A crucial issue at the forefront of the corporate strategy in a multi-business organisation is how to manage and coordinate its businesses for adding value to the organisation as a whole. This task is enjoined upon the corporate headquarters who are expected to perform the role of a parent. A corporate parent is, therefore, concerned with managing and coordinating the flow of financial and other resources to and from the company's product lines and business units in such a way as to obtain synergistic advantages among numerous product lines and business units so that the corporate whole is greater than the sum of its individual business unit parts. For example, Mahindra & Mahindra brought together its automotive and tractor businesses in April, 2010 and placed under Pawan Goenka, President, Automotive and Farm Sector, with the sole objective of driving maximum synergies between the two. The development and sourcing functions have also been merged. The technical expertise required for both the product categories is the same. More than half of the 500-odd vendors for the two lines are the same. Combined orders will certainly drive down prices. According to Goenka, the company can save up to 1.5% of its costs through the various synergies.

Corporate parenting perceives the company in terms of resources and competencies that can be employed to build business unit value as well as generate synergies across business units so that these units perform better collectively than they would as stand-alone units. According to Campbell, Goold and Alexander, "Multi-business companies create value by influencing-or-parenting-the businesses they own. The best parent companies create more value than any of their rivals would if they owned the same businesses. Those companies have what we call parenting advantage.[16] By establishing a good fit between the parent's skills and resources and the needs and opportunities of the business units, a corporate parent is likely to create value. If, however, there is not a good fit, it is likely to destroy value.[17]

Thus, corporate parenting approach to corporate strategy is significantly useful in deciding what new businesses to acquire and also in choosing how each existing business unit should best be managed. The secret to the success of GEC under CEO Jack Welch in adding value to the organisation was imposing tough standards of profitability and disseminating knowledge and best practice quickly around the GE empire. If some manufacturing trick cuts costs in GE's aero-engine repair shops in Wales, he insists it be applied across the group.[18]

In brief, the primary job of a corporate parent is to obtain synergy among the business units by providing needed resources to units, transferring skills and capabilities among the units, and by coordinating the activities of shared unit functions to attain economies of scope.[19]

Making Investment Portfolio Decisions

While deciding about businesses which the corporate parent should include in its portfolio, each business unit should be assessed in terms of areas in which the performance can be improved. For example, two business units might be able to gain economies of scope if their sales forces are combined. In another instance, a parent company having world-class manufacturing and logistics skills may improve the performance of a unit which lacks in these skills. The corporate parent could also transfer some people from one business unit endowed with the desired skills to another in need of those skills.

Further, there is a need to analyse how well the corporate parent fits with the business unit. For this, corporate headquarters must be familiar with its own strengths and deficiencies in terms of resources, skills and capabilities and ascertain if they are adequate to squeeze opportunities of each business unit.

This is why, Campbell, Goold and Alexander recommended the use of a parenting-fit matrix that emphasises upon the fit between parent company skills and needs and opportunities of each business. The parenting mix, depicted in Figure 11.3, comprises two dimensions: the positive contribution that the parent can make and the negative contribution by the parent. The combination of these two dimensions creates five different positions with its own implications for strategic decisions.

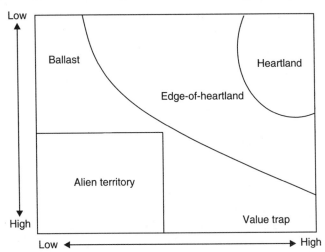

Fit between parenting opportunities and parenting characteristics

Figure 11.3 Parenting-fit matrix.

Figure 11.3 is divided into four quadrants. A business will occupy one of these quadrants according to how well there is a fit between its needs and opportunities and the skills of the corporate parent.

According to Campbell, Goold and Alexander, business units that lie in the top right corner of the matrix should be at the heart of the company's future because **heartland businesses** have opportunities for improvement by the parent and the critical success factors of these businesses are understood by the parent who can add the value to the business.

Edge-of-heartland businesses represent those business units whose needs and opportunities do not fit fully the parent's characteristics or the parent may not really understand all of the unit's strategic factors. For example, a business unit may be very strong in creating its own image through advertising—a critical success factor in its industry (such as in performance). However, the corporate parent may not have core competence to support this success factor. In case the parent forces the business unit to abandon its own creative endeavour and adopt the former's favourite ad agency, the latter may flounder.

In such cases, it would be pertinent for the parent to know when to interfere in the business unit's activities and strategies and when to keep at arm's length so that these businesses do not suffer and can be transformed into **heartland businesses**.

Ballast businesses occupying top left corner of the matrix refer to those which are well understood by the corporate parent but contain very few opportunities, leaving little scope for the parent to improve. Although there is a fit between the parent and the business, the question to be considered is the opportunity cost involved in squeezing opportunities of the business unit. The corporate parent may contemplate using ballast businesses as cash cows as important sources of stability and earnings. But the crucial issue that needs to be addressed carefully is, should ballast businesses be continued or divested?

Alien territory businesses represent those business units which have little opportunity to be improved by the parent and there exists a misfit between the parenting characteristics and the unit's critical success factors. There is limited scope for value creation but great possibility of value destruction by the parent. Such business unit should be divested at the earliest.

In case of **value trap businesses**, which appear attractive to the corporate parent on the surface, the parent has no understanding of the unit's strategic factors because of which the former is likely to make wrong decisions for improving the performance of the latter. For example, a parent may destroy value of its unit whose critical success factors have been product development and niche marketing expertise, when it decides to make the unit a world-class manufacturer (because the parent is endowed with world-class manufacturing skills).

In brief, the best corporate parents are those who create added value to the business units by dint of their skills and resources which fit well with the unit's needs and opportunities. They focus primarily on those businesses where their parenting characteristics can create substantial value (heartland businesses). But they are discreet in investing time and resources in businesses, which fall outside the heartland, such as ballast businesses.

Summary

The corporate strategy of a company is about the choice of direction in which it will move. In a multi-business company it is about managing various product lines and business units for maximum value and allocation of resources across the business units.

A company's corporate strategy concerns with formulating directional strategy, portfolio strategy and corporate planning strategy.

In its attempt to enhance opportunity share of the organisation and maximise its value, the top management must decide if the organisation should grow, cutback or maintain status quo. Growth strategy is the most important strategic option which a firm pursues to achieve its objectives. A host of factors should be factored in while deciding about the growth of the firm. The growth of a firm may be achieved through intensive expansion, integration, diversification and international expansion.

A company is said to follow stability strategy if it decides to serve the same category of customers within the same products and its strategic thrust is on continuation of the improvement of its business without any significant change in the direction. It may be appropriate for a successful company to pursue stability strategy in a reasonably predictable environment. This is more so when the management feels that the company is performing extremely well.

A company not having performed satisfactorily for a number of years may follow retrenchment strategy. This strategy calls for immediate functional improvement through cost reduction, market and product reduction. There are three phases of retrenchment strategy, viz., the contracting phase, the consolidation phase and the recovery phase. Retrenchment strategy may take various forms ranging from turnaround to divestment and liquidation.

For boosting overall performance of a firm and sustaining its competitive edge, the management should address a crucial issue: how best the resources are to be allocated across the company's product lines/business units? Portfolio strategy is crafted for this purpose. According to portfolio approach, a company has to build an effective mix of markets and products to achieve the corporate objectives. The main thrust of portfolio strategy is on portfolio analysis. The BCG Portfolio model and GE model are the most popular models used by corporate enterprises across the globe for building investment portfolio for allocation of funds.

An organisation to achieve its objective of creating added value must manage and coordinate its product lines/businesses effectively. This task has to be performed by the corporate headquarters who have to play the role of a corporate parent to coordinate the flow of financial and other resources to and from the company's product lines and business units in such a way as to obtain synergistic advantages among product lines/businesses, so that corporate whole is greater than the sum of its the individual unit parts.

Key Terms

Alien territory	Divestment strategy	Liquidation strategy
Backward integration	Edge-of-heartland	Pause approach
Ballast	Forward integration	Portfolio strategy
Competitive advantage	Growth strategy	Retrenchment strategy
Corporate parent	Harvesting approach	Stability strategy
Corporate parenting strategy	Heartland	Synergistic advantage
Customer value proposition	Horizontal integration	Turnaround strategy
Directional strategy	Intensive expansion	Value trap

Discussion Questions

1. Discuss the major issues which the corporate strategy of a company should address.
2. What are the basic considerations that influence formulation of growth strategy of a company?

3. Discuss, in brief, various approaches to growth strategy.

4. What do you understand by intensive expansion? Outline the major considerations involved in intensive expansion.

5. What is integrative expansion? Discuss the various issues involved in formulating integrative expansion strategy.

6. What do you mean by stability strategy? Under what circumstances should firms pursue stability strategy?

7. What are the different approaches to stability strategy?

8. Under what circumstances should a firm adopt retrenchment strategy? Discuss the different phases of retrenchment strategy.

9. What is turnaround strategy? How is this strategy formulated?

10. Why should a firm pursue divestment strategy? What precautions should be taken while drawing up divestment strategy?

11. Under what circumstances will adoption of liquidation strategy be in the interest of the firm? What considerations should be factored in while taking liquidation decision?

12. Discuss the portfolio approach to strategy making.

13. Discuss the BCG model. How is it different from the GE-Mc Kinsey model?

14. If an organisation's portfolio of business comprises some dogs, what are the options open to it according to the BCG model? State the circumstances in which an organisation might be prepared to tolerate dog businesses.

15. Discuss the role that a corporate parent is expected to play in creating added value across the organisation.

16. What parenting strategy should corporate headquarters follow to create added value across different businesses of the organisation?

References

1. *Harvard Business Review*, South Asia, p. 64, April, 2008.

2. *Business Line*, Sunday, January 8, 2007.

3. Johnson, Mark W., Clayton M. Christensen and Hemming Kagermann, Reinventing Your Business Model, *Harvard Business Review*, South Asia, December, 2008.

4. Campbell, A., M. Goold, and M. Alexander, "Corporate Strategy: The quest for Parenting Advantage", *Harvard Business Review*, March–April, pp. 120–132, 1995.

5. Porter, Micheal E., "From Competitive Strategy to Corporate Strategy", in *International Review of Strategic Management*, Vol. 7, edited by E. Hussey, John Wiley & Sons, p. 29, 1990.

6. Glueck, William F., Business Policy-Strategy Formulation and Management Action, 2nd ed., McGraw Hill, Koga Kusha, Tokyo, p. 117.

7. Baghai, Mehrdad, Smit, Sven and Patrick Viguerie, "Is your Growth Strategy Flying Blind?" *Harvard Business Review*, South Asia, p. 66, May, 2009.

8. Ibid.

9. Ansoff, Igor H., *Corporate Strategy*, McGraw Hill, New York, 1968, pp. 112–113.

10. Slocum, J.W., Mc Gill, M. and D.T. Lei, "The New Learning Strategy: Anytime, Anything, Anywhere", *Organisational Dynamics*, Autumn, p. 36, 1994.

11. Inkpen, A. and N. Choudhary, "The Seeking of Strategy Where it is Not: Towards a Theory of Strategy Absence", *Strategic Management Journal*, pp. 313–323, May, 1995.

12. Gerald, Allan, "A Note in the Boston Consulting Group Concept of Competitive Analysis and Corporate Strategy", *Inter-collegiate Case Clearing House*, June 9, 1976.

13. Hedley, B., Strategy and the Business Portfolio, *Long Range Planning*, 10(1), pp. 9–15, 1977.

14. Allen, M.G., "Diagramming GE's Planning for What is What" in R.J. Allio and M.W. Pennington (Ed.), *Corporate Planning Techniques and Applications*, New York, AMA. Com., 1979.

15. Hofer, Charles W. and Dan Schewnel, *Strategy Formulation, Analytical Concepts*, St. Daul Minn, West, 1978.

16. Op. cit., Campbell, A, Goold, M. and M. Alexander, p. 121.

17. Ibid.

18. "Jack's Gamble", *The Economist*, October 28, pp. 13–14, 2010.

19. Collis, D.J., "Corporate Strategy in Multi Business Firms", *Long Range Planning*, June 1996.

Internet Resources

- *www.tatamotors.com*
- *www.britannia.co.in*
- *www.hul.co.in*
- *www.rpggroup.com*
- *www.bata.in*
- *www.paramountairways.com*

12

Devising Strategy
for a Diversified Company

INTRODUCTION

In tumultuous and turbulent environment rife with risks and offering little opportunity for growth in the existing business, the organisations aspiring to survive successfully, maintain market share, improve profit margin, remain resilient and de-risk the business against the business oscillations may decide to expand through diversification route which moves them away from their current products and markets and into new product lines and new markets. New business may be related with the expanding business and major skills and resources required for the former may be matched with the latter. At times, they may diversify into unrelated business with a view to reducing business risk and/or overcoming financial problems.

Whatever be the motive underlying the diversification move, the end objective should be to create added value to shareholders higher than what they can capture through diversifying their investments on individual basis.

CRITICAL ISSUES IN DIVERSIFICATION MOVE

While contemplating to diversify its current business, the corporate management should focus on the following critical issues:

280

- Why should a company diversify?
- Which way should a company move?
- What strategic considerations should be factored in while deciding about diversification move?

Why Diversify?

A company may be driven to depart from the current business and move into new business because of myriad of forces. Some of these forces can be discussed now.

Accelerate Growth Rate and Improve Profitability

The most crucial factor prompting a company to diversify in new product lines is to achieve growth rate faster than the present growth rate. When the management believes that in the current and forthcoming economic landscape, growth opportunities for the existing business in the country are very low, it may decide to enter into new products and new markets.[1] For example, Bharat Forge—one of the top names in the world of automotive components—made a strategic move to enter into non-automotive business to arrest the declining growth rate in the main business due to economic slowdown in 2005–06 and to maintain growth rate of the company. As a result, Bharat Forge today, besides automobile, makes forgings for the energy (for hydro and wind turbines), railway (axles for high speed trains in Europe, crankshaft for locomotives) and marine (ship components) sectors. The whole game plan of India bulls group to get into businesses ranging from retail to special economic zones to power was to grow and chase high growth sectors.

Tata Global Beverage presently engaged in bouquet of tea, non-tea, non-carbonated beverages and mineral water, among others, intends to foray into food and fortified health drinks with a view to growing revenues more than three-fold and enhancing profitability.

Another significant factor that has prodded organisations to diversify is to bag business opportunities so as to improve their performance and strengthen competitive position in domestic and world markets. For example, during the last decade, MNCs—both global and Indian—have been found moving into new businesses—both related and unrelated—to capture a tsunami of opportunities, particularly in FMCG and telecom sectors. Among the global MNCs, Dell, the Computer giant, Sony—leader in entertainment industry—and Microsoft and Oracle—the software Goliaths—forayed into mobile telephony business. Among Indian MNCs, Tata, Birla, Godrej, ITC, Mukesh Ambani Group entered into FMCG and telecom sectors to squeeze enormous market opportunities in these sectors in India.

In its drive to strengthen its competitive position, PepsiCo India silently transformed itself from a sweetened, fizzy, water company to the one that produces and sells healthier products to cater to the growing consumption of Indian consumers. As a result, around 37% of PepsiCo India's revenue until September, 2009 came from snacks and foods.

Apollo Group, which has tyres as its main business, chose to get into logistics simply because of tremendous opportunity fuelled by the booming exports and retail sectors.

The 117-year-old Chennai-based Amrutanjan Health Care Ltd. (AHCL) has, of late, decided to go off the beaten track by becoming a health and wellness company so as to increase its turnover to ₹250 crore in the next two years from ₹89 crore in 2010–11. The company has already forayed into fortified fruit drinks. It is also planning to foray into ready-to-eat segment under the brand *Kitchen Delights*. Next in line is a foray into sanitary napkins and hand sanitizers where manufacturing would be done through third party.

De-risk Business

A large number of organisations pursue diversification strategy to de-risk their business from many events such as cyclical, seasonal and secular shifts in demand, changes in the life cycles of different products of the line, the impact of variations of raw material prices on finished goods prices and demand, or delays in getting component parts.[2] In order to minimise the risk arising out of the recent currency impact on export dominated business, many export-oriented industries and textiles in India including Gokaldas Exports have tweaked their business model to enter into new segments such as suiting business, denim business and industrial garments.

Achieve Higher Utilisation of Resources

At times, the organisations are driven to diversify into new businesses just to make fuller use of their existing resources and skills and thereby reducing the operating costs and increase their efficiency. To realise the synergistic benefits, a company may diversify into new activities to add new product lines and new markets. For example, Videocon Group having a large network of dealers and distributors in its consumer durables business and having ownership of 17 million new houses, decided to provide telecom services and avail the synergistic benefits.

Piramal Group led by Ajay Piramal has utilised its resources fully to make forays into spheres as diverse as pharma and glass from a family business focused on textiles. It is also entering into retail market and intends to become number one in the country.

Likewise, Bharti Airtel diversified into primary sector to grab enormous business opportunities across the world and to use its burgeoning resources—managerial talent and capital—in a more efficient manner.

Gain Financial Strength

At times, financial considerations spur companies to diversify into new businesses. For example, Mahindra and Mahindra (M&M), the diversified business group with significant interest in automotive and information technology, entered into non-banking financing business to provide financial support to its domestic as well as global entities.

Biyani of Future Group business model is to hawk financial products through the 400-odd retail outlets of flagship Pantaloon Retail. The finance arm of the Group will drive consumption by providing customers with the means to finance their purchases at the site where consumption decision is made.

State-owned power companies are planning to foray into the banking business in order to access cheaper funds.[3]

Gain Access to Latest Technology

More often than not, companies may diversify into new businesses for accessing latest technology cheaply. For example, Jenson & Nicholson India—leading paint manufacturer in the country—decided to diversify into industrial electronics and for that purpose forged alliance with Carl Schevek AG of Germany and got access to modern technology for manufacturing its electronic products.

Widen Market Base

A host of organisations harbouring the ambition of widening their market base to become leading player in the global marquee enter into new businesses. Most illustrious examples of this kind are Mukesh Ambani's Reliance Industries, Bharti Group and Vedant Resources.

Recently, Reliance Industries decided to enter into telecom business and is betting big on wireless broadband.

Bharti Group in an endeavour to ramp up its business and widen market base moved into primary sector because Sunil Mittal, its Chairman, saw food as the largest globally outsourced product out of India in a few years, adding upto as big an opportunity as business process outsourcing. Further, it forged a joint venture with global leader Wal-Mart to set up Bharti Wal-Mart store in the country.

Of late, Vedanta Resources Group, that rode the global commodity boom, decided to foray into oil and gas exploration business, and for that matter, took over the country's third largest oil and gas exploration company, Cairn India. If the regulators clear the deal, Vedanta will join BHP Billiton, the world's largest resources company, and Brazil's Vale to have interests in oil and gas.

Which Way to Diversify?

Broadly speaking, there are two routes to diversification, viz., concentric and conglomerate. The management has to decide which one will be most suited to the company under the current and ensuing circumstances.

Concentric Diversification

A firm is said to have pursued concentric diversification strategy when it enters into new product or service area belonging to different industry category, but the new product or service is similar to the existing one with respect to technology, customers and marketing.

Concentric diversification strategy will be most suited to the organisations who have strong competitive position but industry is becoming unattractive. Such organisations may use their strengths as their means of diversification. They attempt to secure strategic fit in an industry where their existing product knowledge, manufacturing capabilities and the marketing skills can be put to good use.[4]

Thus, in concentric diversification move, the company's products, processes and the customers' groups are related to the new ones in some way, and they possess some common thread and provide enough scope for realising synergistic benefits leading to cost reduction and product differentiation.

Entry of Dell, Microsoft and Sony in telephony mobile business is an instance of technology related concentric diversification. Very recently, Bharti Airtel announced its entry into the fast-growing mobile handset business as the group firm Beetel launched in September 2010, eight handsets in the price range of ₹1,750–₹7,000. This is again an illustrious example of concentric diversification.

Addition of non-beverage foods and snacks to the product portfolio of PepsiCo India and sports drink called *Stamina* to the portfolio of Amul are vignettes of product and marketing related diversification. Foray of Tata Global Beverage into food and fortified health drinks is also a burning example of product and customer-related diversification. Entry of commercial banks in insurance mutual funds and security investment business is yet another example of product-related diversification.

Illustrative Capsule 12.1 vividly narrates how Simplex Infrastructure made entry into new but related businesses successfully.

Illustrative Capsule 12.1
CONCENTRIC DIVERSIFICATION BY SIMPLEX INFRASTRUCTURE

In recent years when Indian Corporates including those engaged in construction business have been facing problem of tight credit and bear market and rate of return on construction projects has been showing decline, Simplex Infrastructure chose to de-risk its business model by focusing on new areas within the ambit of construction. According to Director Amitabh Mundhra, "We decided to diversify our operations from just three segments to eight segments."

Before 2002, Simplex's activities consisted of piling work, and setting up industrial and power plants. In the subsequent years, it stretched its wings into areas like urban infrastructure, real estate, railways, roads and water. This was accompanied by geographical diversification too, with Simplex entering markets in West Asia like Dubai, Doha and Oman.

The benefits of Simplex's diversification are evident today. Example: Although real estate is in the doldrums, power is holding its own. Also, today its biggest order is just 5% of the order book, which makes the company less susceptible to orders getting cancelled.

Simplex's order book stood at a healthy ₹10,200 crore as of end December, 2008. These orders have to be completed over the next 30 months. The worry, however, is on the profitability front. Although growth rate at the bottom-line level is still in double digits, net profits, which rose by 47% in the September—ended quarter, were up by just 15% three months later. "After a period of high growth, profit numbers get into consolidation phase, after which they once again begin rising", explains Mundhra. He says, in times of huge growth, the company gets conservative in taking orders. Mundhra adds that margins have come down because of higher depreciation provisions for machinery and equipment purchased during 2007.

More than anything else, what generates confidence about Simplex is its uninterrupted track record of profit-making and dividend-paying since 1924.

Conglomerate Diversification

In conglomerate type of diversification, a company adds new products that are entirely different from present product line and/or markets, and that use technologies different from the current line. Absence of any tenuous link between existing markets and products and the diversified industry is a redeeming feature of conglomerate diversification. It may be that the company has copious management skills and financial resources to provide it with core competence that can gainfully be leveraged across different business units. This has been the most important factor that contributed to the success of India's most venerated business houses like Tata, Birla, Godrej, Jindal, Essar, Reliance and Wipro who diversified in wide range of unrelated businesses (Illustrative Capsule 12.2).

ILLUSTRATIVE CAPSULE 12.2

TOP CONGLOMERATE CORPORATE GROUPS IN INDIA

Tata Group: Salt, Beverages, Foods and Fortified health drinks, Telecommunication, Software, Textiles, Automobiles, Construction equipment, Power, Chemicals and fertilizers, Retail.

Birla Group: Textiles, Cement, Aluminum, Fertilizers, Telecommunication, Mines, Finance, Retail.

Jindal Group: Steel, Power, Cement, Infrastructure, Aluminum & IT.

Essar Group: Oil refineries, Oil distribution, Minerals, Telecom, Consumer durables retailing.

Reliance Industries: Oil exploration, Production and distribution, Textiles, Telecommunication, Retail, Power, Dairy business.

Godrej Group: Steel furnitures and locks, Soaps and detergents, Edible oils, Beverages, Feminine hygiene, Household insecticides, Shoe shine, Hair cream, Toiletries, Processed poultry.

Wipro: Vegetable oils, Computer hardware, Software, Medical equipment, Hydraulic cylinders, Consumer care products, Lighting, Furnitures and storage, Financial services, and so on.

This route of diversification is suited to the organisations who are experiencing decline in a demand of their products and future growth opportunities in the existing business are almost negligible and they have sufficient financial and managerial resources to manage new businesses belonging to different industries offering fantastic opportunities. ITC Limited diversified into paper products, hotel business, and agro products mainly due to the constant threat to its cigarettes business (Illustrative Capsule 12.3).

ILLUSTRATIVE CAPSULE 12.3

CONGLOMERATE DIVERSIFICATION BY ITC

ITC, the company once known as Imperial Tobacco Company, is one amongst the few companies in India having transformed itself from tobacco and cigarettes business into non-tobacco business with a view to minimising the adverse impact of constant regulatory threat to its core business and to rev up the overall performance of the organisation.

ITC's diversification strategy aims at creating multiple drivers of growth. Accordingly, it has diversified into a wide range of activities including tobacco and cigarettes, hotels, paper boards and packaging, agri-business, packaged foods and confectionary, information technology, branded apparel, personal care products, greeting cards, safety matches and incense sticks. What is more important than just a diversified presence is how the group has tapped synergies among its various divisions to carve a commanding presence in all the segments it is present in.

ITC has leveraged its expertise in the tobacco, hospitality and IT sectors to build apparently unrelated businesses. For instance, the company uses its agri-sourcing network to source raw materials for its biscuits and atta businesses and also uses the e-choupal network to distribute products in areas where other channels do not exist. Similarly, ITC Hotel—the second-largest hospitality chain in the country-tapped the expertise of its master chefs to help the Foods Division create 16 distinct taste platforms for *Bingo* and a number of other branded packaged foods. Its diverse knowledge base, the synergies between its different divisions, an unmatched distribution reach, massive brand building capabilities and efficient supply chain management have enabled it to emerge as the leader or challenger in all the FMCG and lifestyle segments.

The management belief that by not having all their eggs in one basket (focusing on one market or product range) they can diversify their risk, also prompt the organisation to pursue conglomerate path. In case an organisation handles many different businesses, failure of one business as a result of adverse economic conditions may not land it in crisis.

Another patent cause for conglomerate diversification might be regulatory factor which may look upon vertical and horizontal integration as uncompetitive, and thus discouraging any move for concentric diversification.

Both concentric and conglomerate diversification moves have the potential for improving competitive position of an organisation. However, a concentric path, which is comparable to a conglomerate diversification in economic prospects and flexibility will usually be more profitable and less risky because of synergistic factor. While this is true that conglomerate diversification does not offer any synergistic advantage, a well-planned and developed conglomerate strategy does have a sense of direction expressed through competitive advantage, product-market scope and objectives.

Strategic Considerations in Deciding Diversification Move

Decision about foray into new business activity is an integral part of strategic management. As such, primal considerations that are factored in while deciding about new enterprise do apply to diversification strategy also. Since these factors have already been broached in greater detail in the preceding chapters, let us have their semblance in the following paragraphs:

Identification and Evaluation of Environmental Opportunities

So as to determine the routes of diversification, it would be ineluctable for the management to undertake penetrating appraisal of current and future environmental developments and choose the most promising and attractive industries that will further improve competitive position of the firm.

Assessing Organisation's Resources and Their Compatibility

Once the most potential industry is identified and chosen, its feasibility study must be made in terms of availability of managerial, financial and other resources and their compatibility with the resource requirements of the new businesses.[5] Diversification in new business areas is more likely to enhance the shareholders' value when the company has sufficient resources that fit in with managerial and resource requirements of the new business. This is more so in case of unrelated businesses. The broader the diversification, the greater the concern about whether the company has gargantuan managerial resources, as that of Tata Group to cope with the diverse range of operating problems which its future wide business lineup presents.

Undertaking Risk Analysis

Since the above strategic decision is being made under the conditions of partial ignorance, a risk analysis must be made, particularly for the one involving large investment. For each of the strategic variables (total market potential within chosen geographic area, the market share, net price per unit, raw material cost per unit, production cost per unit, marketing cost per unit, total overhead and total investments), uncertainty ranges are estimated on the basis of the best judgement available, and probabilities are assigned to each range on a subjective basis. Different opportunities, of course, result in varying profitability ranges. The most probable central value is then calculated for each of them. The one promising the highest profitability value is chosen.

Summary

To encapsulate the corporate organisations, in their endeavour to sustain competitive advantage and improve performance in murky and morose environment, opt for diversification route to expand their business. Thus, the main driving forces underlying the choice of path of diversification are: achieving higher growth rate, minimising business risks, accessing latest technology, widening market base and utilising resources.

There are two routes to diversification: concentric and conglomerate. A firm is said to have pursued concentric diversification strategy when it enters into new product or service line which is related to the existing one. On the contrary, in conglomerate diversification, a company adds new products that are entirely different from the present product line.

While choosing the path of diversification, the management should factor in a host of crucial forces, viz., identification and evaluating of diversification opportunities, assessment of the organisation's resources and their compatibility with the resource requirements of the new businesses and analysis of risks involved in diversification decision.

Key Terms

Concentric diversification

Conglomerate diversification

Resource compatibility

Synergistic advantage

Discussion Questions

1. What prompts an organisation to choose the path of diversification?
2. What is concentric diversification? How is it different from conglomerate diversification?
3. Under what conditions will the choice of conglomerate diversification route be most suited to an organisation?
4. List out the five celebrated Indian corporate houses who have successfully pursued conglomerate diversification strategy.
5. What strategic considerations should a management factor in while deciding about diversification of the firm's business?
6. "Diversification strategy brings about more drastic changes in product-market orientation than the expansion strategy but it involves greater risks". Comment.

References

1. Markidls, C., "To Diversify or Not to Diversify", *Harvard Business Review*, 75(6), November–December, pp. 93–99, 1997.
2. Drucker, Peter F., *Management: Tasks, Responsibilities and Practices*, Harper & Row, New York, 1973.
3. *Business Standard*, August 26, 2010.
4. Ilinich, A.Y. and C.P. Zeithaml, "Operationalising and Testing Galbraith's Centre of Gravity Theory", *Strategic Management Journal*, June, pp. 401–410, 1995.
5. Op. cit., Campbell, Michael Gould and Marcus Alexander, "Corporate Strategy: The Quest for Parenting Advantage", *Harvard Business Review*, USA, pp. 120–32.

Internet Resources

- *www.simplexinfrastructures.com*
- *www.itcportal.com*

13

Making Strategy for Mergers and Acquisitions (M&As)

LEARNING OBJECTIVES

The present Chapter aims at:

- Providing insightful view into forces driving for mergers and acquisitions.
- Providing vivid discussion of how mergers and acquisitions can be managed.
- Discerning the critical factors for the success of mergers and acquisitions.

INTRODUCTION

There are two routes to business expansion, viz., organic (internal expansion) and inorganic (external expansion). A company may grow externally by acquiring another company by buying the assets or stocks of the latter or by combining with the latter. Thus, acquisition of an organisation can be accomplished either through the process of merger or through the takeover route.

Merger is a combination of two or more companies into a single company where one survives and others lose their identity, or a new company is formed. The survivor acquires the assets as well as liabilities of the merged company. Shareholders from each company become shareholders in the new combined company. If, as a result of a merger, one company survives and others lose their independent entity, it is a case of 'absorption'. Merger of TOMCO with Hindustan Lever Limited (HLL) is a case in point. But if a new company comes into existence because of merger, it is a process of 'amalgamation', or 'consolidation'. For example, Nalco Chemicals was formed in 1987 with Nalco Chemical Company in the US and ICI India Ltd., each holding 40% of the equity.

Takeover is the purchase by one company of a controlling interest in the share capital of another existing. In takeover, both the companies retain their separate legal entity.

TRENDS IN MERGERS AND ACQUISITIONS (M&As)

The corporate organisations across the world pursued collaborative approach since the early 1970s in their frenetic bid to cope with increased business complexities and combat ferally competitive challenges and to become globally competitive in terms of cost, quality and services. With the increasing globalisation of business and concomitant surge in competitive pressure, M&As all over the world have been on the rise. The total global acquisition deals spiraled from 30,639 valuing $2.99 trillion in 2005 to 31,858 deals worth $4 trillion in 2006. However, there has been a continuous deceleration in M&As since 2006 touching an all round low level of M&A deals at 9,400 worth $1,800 billion in 2009. This dramatic decline can be explained mainly by global liquidity crisis affecting the economies of both developed and emerging markets.

Indian organisations, which until recently loathed to do business jointly, have also begun jumping on to the bandwagon of M&As in the domestic market and abroad in recent years.

Till 2003, M&A deals remained exceptional whereafter wind of acquisitions started blowing across the country. Thus, it may be noted from Table 13.1 that the total number of M&A deals in 2004 which stood at 40 valuing over $2 billion, skyrocketed to 661, valuing $51 billion in 2007. What is more important to note is that during the period of two years (2006 and 2007), overseas M&A deals were higher (more than two-thirds of the total) than domestic acquisitions, indicating irresistible appetite of Indian corporates to reach out to the world.

Table 13.1 M&As by Indian Organisations

Year	No. of M/A Deals	Value of Deals (US $ billion)
2004	40	2
2005	329	17
2006	480	32
2007	860	59
2008	433	32
2009	650	20

Year 2007 was an exceptional year when a slew of Indian companies exercised their ambitions of domestic and global acquisitions. Three deals alone involving Tata-Corus, Vodafone-Hutchinson-Essar and Hindalco-Novelis amounted to $29 billion. These were amongst the biggest deals India has ever seen.

There was, however, a precipitating fall in M&A activities during the next two years due to liquidity crunch faced by the corporate world in the wake of global financial crisis and concurrent business risks.

With the economy on the rebound after the year-long slowdown that started mid-2008, more companies started going shopping abroad leading to a phenomenal spurt in M&A deals to touch a record value of $48.6 billion upto June 28, 2010.

Examples of prominent takeovers by Indian organisations are listed in Illustrative Capsule 13.1.

ILLUSTRATIVE CAPSULE 13.1

RECENT TAKEOVERS BY INDIAN CORPORATE BEHEMOTHS

Acquirer	Acquired
Mahindra & Mahindra	Punjab Tractors Ltd.
Tata Tea	Glaceu, US
Tata Steel	National Steel, Singapore
VSNL	Teleglobe, US
ONGC	Imperial Energy, Russia
Tata Steel	Corus Group, UK
Hindalco	Novelis, Canada
Tata Motors	Jagaur Land Rover, UK
Suzlon Energy	Repower System, Germany
Dr. Reddy's Laboratories	Betapharm, Germany
Wipro	Unza, Singapore
Tata Chemicals Ltd.	General Chemicals Industries Products, US
Essar Steel	Algoma, Canada
Reliance Industries	Reliance Petroleum Ltd.
HDFC Bank	Centurian Bank of Punjab
Bharti Airtel	Zain Telecom, Africa
Mahindra & Mahindra	Ssang Yong, Korea
Reliance Industries	Infotel, India

DRIVING FORCES FOR M&As BY INDIAN CORPORATES

Forces that triggered Indian corporate enterprises to opt for inorganic route to expansion are too many to be detailed in this section. However, major considerations underlying M&A deals are discussed in the following:

Gain Scale and Improve Presence in Global Market

A flurry of M&As by Indian companies has been spurred by their ravenous appetite to ramp up their business in new markets and enhance their position in international market, taking advantage of buoyancy in the world market on the one hand, and outstanding managerial capabilities, on the other. As a result, many of them find themselves in the rarefied top echelons of world rankings. For instance, Bharat Forge is today the second largest forgings company in the world after acquiring Germany's forging company CDP in 2000. Videocon became the world's third largest television picture tube maker after it acquired the operations of France-based Thomson SA. Tata Tea emerged as the second largest branded tea company after it bought UK's Tetley; Tata Steel has catapulted to 5th position in steel making in the world from 56th after acquiring Corus in 2007 and Hindalco, ranked at 13, has emerged as one of the five integrated aluminium company in the world after taking over a Canadian aluminium sheet manufacturer Novelis in the same year.

Dr. Reddy's Laboratories acquired one of the world's largest generic drug makers, Betapharm of Germany, for gaining strong presence in all key pharmaceutical markets of the globe.

Recent acquisition of Korean automaker Ssang Yong Motor Company by Mahindra & Mahindra was aimed at becoming a global utility vehicle major.

Voracious appetite for global expansion through acquisitions has also been noticed among several small and middle sized companies such as Havel, Essel Packaging, Amtek Auto, Sundaram Fasteners, Subex, United Phosphorus Ltd., Rain Commodities, and so on. Godrej's recent acquisition drive bears eloquent testimony to the hunger of the group for global expansion (Illustrative Case 13.2).

ILLUSTRATIVE CAPSULE 13.2

GODREJ'S OVERSEAS ACQUISITIONS

Godrej—a leading conglomerate corporate group of India with a Total asset of about ₹12,000 crore—decided in 2005 to straddle the emerging markets in Africa, Asia and South America with its hair colours, household insecticides, soaps and so on which the group has done well in the domestic market.

Since 2005, Godrej Consumer Products Ltd. (GCPL) has made seven international acquisitions. In 2008, the Group set itself a target of tripling its growth in the FMCG business in three-four years. "There was a realisation that if we had to make that kind of growth happen, it would have to be inorganic and we would have to lose outside India", explains Mahendran, the Managing Director of GCPL. In fact, Godrej had little option but to go in developing markets where some of its niche products were pretty relevant because the domestic market was heavily penetrated and highly competitive. And then began the slew of acquisitions mostly in Africa, followed by Latin America and Asia.

Over the last few years, "we have followed a very disciplined and focused approach to identify acquisitions that represent a strong fit with our business, both strategically and operationally", said Chairman GCPL, Adi Godrej. For the company, there is method in the madness. "It is our '3 by 3' matrix strategy", says GCPL Managing Director, Dalip Sehgal. The company will operate in three continents (Africa, Asia and South America) in three categories: Hair Care, Home Care and Personal Care. These are the markets where MNCs like Unilever, Procter and Gamble and L'oreal don't have an overbearing presence; this leaves ample scope for smaller companies and regional brands to grow.

According to investment analysts, Indian companies like GCPL have realised the worth of emerging markets and are thus in hurry to expand there. The focus of the company on emerging markets is recent one. The most preferred continent of the company is Africa which is the most densely populated and houses 13% of the population. Its economy was anticipated to grow at 4.3% in 2009–10. GCPL, therefore, acquired two hair care companies—Rapidol and Kinky—which together control the entire hair care market of South Africa. Sensing huge opportunity of personal wash in the continent, GCPL acquired Tura. It gave GCPL roads into West Africa, particularly Nigeria.

GCPL bought an Indonesia maker of household insecticides, viz., Megasari Makmur along with its distribution company. Its acquisition has given GCPL a strong hold in Indonesia which is one of the largest markets in the region. Megasari Makmur has 35% of household insecticides market. The acquisition comes with six factories, 11 branches and 74 regional distributors.

The 14-year joint venture Godrej Sara Lee—now in the GCPL fold—has been sold in Asia. Its products are sold in 51 countries, most of it in the Indian sub-continent. It has full-fledged operations in Sri Lanka and Bangladesh and is now setting up a plant in Nepal. In India, of course, it straddles the whole spectrum of household insecticides and mats, coils, lotions and acrosols.

Recently, alliance with Sara Lee has been restructured with GCPL buying out the Godrej Group's 49% in the venture. This has come at a time when Sara Lee Corporation has decided to exit its consumer products business of around $2 billion per annum to focus on foods. Godrej has the right to buy it out of the joint venture. According to Mahendran, the Godrej Sara Lee is looking for the acquisitions of strong local household insecticide brands in markets like China and Indonesia.

"GCPL's international acquisitions have changed the scale it operates drastically. It catapulted itself to the top 3 consumer companies rather smartly", says Nikhil Vora, Managing Director, IDFC Securities.

Gain Synergistic Benefits

Quite a large number of Indian organisations have, of late, embarked on the acquisition drive to derive synergistic advantages leading to cost reduction, improved efficiency and higher utilisation of resources. Merger of Reliance Petrochemicals with Reliance Industries was aimed at enhancing the shareholders' value by realising significant synergies of both the companies. Mergers of Indian Airlines with Air India, and Air Sahara with Jet Airways were prompted to avail operating economies and reduce overlappings.

Acquisitions of Corus and Novelis respectively by Tata Steel and Hindalco were driven by synergistic consideration. Corus having strong R&D capabilities and strong presence in the high end of the market has created synergies that add $300–350 million a year to the bottom line of the integrated entity.

Likewise, the combination of the Hindalco having a strong presence in the upstream aluminium business with Novelis—the largest producer of aluminium flat rolled products in the world—was aimed at establishing a global integrated aluminium producer with low-cost aluminia and aluminium production facilities blended with high end aluminium rolled product capabilities, thus producing synergy that Birlas were looking for in the flat products segment.

In its endeavour to leverage the value of the entities and increase cost efficiency, Tata Group has recently decided to merge Tata Coffee and Mount Everest Mineral Water with Tata Tea; Rallies with Tata Chemicals; Tata Teleservices (Maharashtra) with Tata Teleservices; and Tata Sponge Iron with Tata Steel. This consolidation move is also intended to ring-fence businesses from economic instabilities. The merger initiative will help the major Tata companies scale up operations and enhance bargaining power.

Recent takeover of South Korea's car maker Ssang Yong by M&M is another illustrious example of synergy factor behind the move. Ssang Yong's strong competencies in R&D and technology will help M&M to acquire marquee global Suv brand. Mahindra's focus on alternative fuels and electric vehicles will further strengthen Ssang Yong's brand value and take it to new geographies.

Lately, ADAG-promoted Reliance Power and Reliance Natural Resources have been merged for gaining synergistic advantages.

Capture Opportunities

Another important consideration motivating Indian business entrepreneurs to take over offshore companies has been to grab surging opportunities in some countries against saturating domestic market. Recent acquisition of Zain Telecom of South Africa by Bharti Airtel is a glaring case in point (Illustrative Capsule 13.3). Bharti Airtel has roped in IBM to strengthen its infrastructure in Africa and achieve its goal of bringing affordable and innovative mobile services to remote locations in Africa.

ILLUSTRATIVE CAPSULE 13.3
BHARTI AIRTEL'S OPPORTUNITY GRABBING ACQUISITION OF ZAIN

On March 30, 2010 Bharti Air-India's largest Telecom operator, acquired Zain Telecom's operation in 15 African nations with a customer base of over 42 million to become the world's fifth largest mobile operator with 180 million subscriber in 18 Asian and African nations—the second largest population coverage among Telecompanies globally. It was a $10.7 billion (about ₹50,000 crore) deal of which $9 billion was payable in cash and $1.7 billion through debt while a payment of $700 million has been deferred for a year.

Earlier in 2008, Bharti Airtel, tried to enter into deal with MTN—the largest telecom operator in Africa—twice, but talks failed on management control and brand issues. Without expressing regret over the fallout of the deal, Sunil Mittal, Chairman, Bharti Airtel observed that "MTN was the first opportunity that was available at that time. In MTN's case, we would have had Board control but no management control and no change in brand. Zain is the second largest operator in Africa. We will have full control and our own brand. We are fortunate that we got the second chance and got much better deal".

According to Sunil Mittal, the deal is a landmark for global telecom industry and game changer for Bharti. "More importantly, this transaction is a pioneering step towards cooperation and strengthening of ties between India and Africa. With this acquisition, Bharti Airtel will be transformed into a truly global telecom company, fulfilling our vision of building a world-class multinational. We are excited at the growth opportunities in Africa, the continent of hope and opportunity. We believe that the strength of our brand and the historic Indian connect with Africa coupled with our unique business model will allow us to unlock the potential of these emerging markets.

For Mittal, "The deal is not a faddish, nor fashionable. Africa's size excites me. It has a population of over 1 billion people like India, but the geographical territory is 10 times larger. That resulted in very poor spread of networks there. The beauty of Africa is that spectrum is not a problem there. Unlike India where one is starved for spectrum, there are dallops of spectrum in Africa, which makes a big difference.

With this deal, Mittal believes that "we will have an unparalleled footprint in one at the fastest developing regions in the world. We are looking at more opportunities as we build more rollouts in Africa."

This acquisition deal is expected to result in combined revenues of about $13 billion. Bharti Group's global telecom footprint will expand to 21 countries along with operations in Seychelles, Jersey and Guernsey.

Access to Latest Technology

At times, Indian organisations have allowed foreign companies to acquire their shares in lieu of the latest technology so as to rev up their production and improve earnings. Recent $7.2 billion deal by Reliance Industries Ltd. (RIL) with the UK based BP Plc for the sale of 30% stake in 23 oil and gas sharing contracts being currently operated by the RIL is a case in point.

This tie up will enable the RIL to access BP's technical expertise that will help the RIL to ramp up the gas output by resolving complexities in the KGD6 block, wherein gas production has slipped from 60 mm sc md in June 2010 quarter to about 55 mm in December 2010 quarter (compared to target levels of 90 mm sc md). Further, with BP on board, RIL could also speed up exploration in other key blocks. For BP, the deal marks an easy entry into India's exploration sector.

Speed-up Diversification

Many companies join together to reduce business risk through diversification of their operations geographically and product-wise. Reliance Industries Ltd. has, of late, taken over Infotel just to re-enter into telecom industry. Proposed acquisition of Cairn India for $8.48 billion by Vedanta group has been triggered to enter into new business of oil production and distribution. Case Study of United Phosphorus Ltd. (UPL), which has acquired 26 companies across 23 countries since 1994, amply explains the hunger of a medium-sized company for acquiring overseas companies for diversifying its operations (Illustrative Capsule 13.4).

ILLUSTRATIVE CAPSULE 13.4
UNITED PHOSPHORUS'S AGGRESSIVE ACQUISITIONS FOR DIVERSIFICATION

Raju Shroff is one amongst a very few entrepreneurs who looked overseas way back in the mid-1950s when India's first industrial policy was announced in 1956. He set up a chemicals plant in the UK for his family business. In 1969, Shroff founded agro-chemicals and seeds firm—United Phosphorus Ltd. (UPL). It was not until the early 1990s—when Indian businesses were finally opened up—that Shroff looked outbound again. Since 1994, UPL has made 26 acquisitions of companies and products. The acquired firms belonged to 23 countries. These acquisitions have enabled UPL to address customers in 86 countries.

The buyouts have been across the world, right from developed countries like the US, the UK, Japan and France, to developing ones like Argentina and South Africa. "An entry into the US from India is very difficult, but with acquisitions, it is much easier", explains Shroff, the Chairman and Managing Director, UPL. Many of UPL's purchases have been from leading global players like Syngenta, Bayer and DuPont.

The common triggers for most of these takeovers were access to geographies and addition of new products to the portfolio including agro-chemicals, seeds and biotechnology.

Often, an acquisition has helped UPL enter areas where it did not have a presence, and where creating one would have been time and resource-consuming. Jai Shroff, the CEO, UPL gives the example of the buyout of Dutch seed maker Advanta, which was triggered by the impact of biotechnology on the agro-chemicals sector.

UPL acquisitions, according to analysts, have helped it to become a global major in generic crop protection, with a diversified geographical and crop presence. "Such a diversification helps UPL smoothen the volatility inherent in a business dependent on weather patterns", says a Kotak Securities report. The report adds that UPL's low-cost of manufacturing, the significant entry barriers it has built in developed markets in the form of registrations, and increasing global footprint are the company's three distinct edges.

UPL's guiding principle while making acquisitions is "that the investment needs to be recovered in three years. If it can't, the acquisition does not make sense."

Over the past five years, in which UPL has made 16 acquisitions, revenues have increased 4.3 times to ₹3,761 crore as of 2007–08. Net profit has jumped 6.7 times to ₹281 crore. Profitability at its two largest acquisitions, Cerexagri and Advant, has improved.

Access to Funds

The target company might be setting on a pile of funds, which it might not need immediately. TDPL merged with Sun Pharma since it did not have the funds to launch new products.

Strengthen Controlling Power

Acquisition of profit-making companies by Indian business entrepreneurs like Kumar Manglam Birla, Ratan Tata, Mukesh Ambani, R.P. Goenka, Piramals, Ruias, Khaitan and Mahindras took place to get hold of the controlling interest through open offer of market prices.

MANAGING MERGERS AND ACQUISITIONS

Despite humungous potentialities of M&A route in aiding the acquirer to access new geographical markets, new technologies and brands, develop new product mixes and new distribution channels, to achieve exponential growth at less risk, and cost, improve competitive share and operating margins and thereby catapult the firm to the global marquee, the general conclusion from multiple global studies is that a significant portion of M&As (about two-thirds) have failed to add shareholders' value. Whereas the objective of M&As is to make one plus one produce three, the reality is that they mostly produce even less than two.[2] A plethora of factors both on planning and execution fronts have contributed to this.

Inadequate planning, as reflected in the absence of focused vision and objectives of the M&As and strategy based on environmental opportunities and core competencies of the acquirer, discerning of complementary strengths of the target firm and identification of the concomitant revenue and cost synergies and improper valuation of the acquired firm in terms of intended benefits have been the major causal factors for failure of M&A deals. Lack of proper understanding of cultural differences and ineffective mechanism to overcome them have also contributed to the failure of M&A deals.

On the execution side, ineffective organisational arrangements and inefficacious communication system and failure to manage people belonging to different cultures have been responsible for the failure of M&A deals.

Thus, the kernel of success of M&A deals lies in how dexterously they are managed. Sapient management of M&A deals calls for mapping out comprehensive strategy and evolving effective structure and mechanism to affectuate the deal.

Planning for M&A Deals

Strategy making in respect of the acquisitions demands sketching of basic business plan of what the acquiring firm aspires to achieve. The top management has to identify on the basis of environmental scanning which products, activities or services are suitable for collaborative approach and will meet the firm's vision and objectives, and which markets are suitable for development or penetration.

For choosing a market or product or both, the management should make dispassionate winnowing of the firm's existing core competencies and assess their adequacy in capturing new businesses or products and identifying competencies that will be needed to encash emerging business opportunities and achieving sustainable competitive edge.

Another strategic aspect of acquisition planning is to identify and choose the most potent target firm. While doing so, due diligence is needed to determine the target firm's expectations, business processes, financial, technological, managerial and marketing strengths, present and future growth rate, and to ensure that the target firm's business fits in with the business strategy of the acquiring firm.

At this stage, it would also be relevant to assess precisely the complementary strengths of both the firms that must be pulled in to the enterprise to achieve the vision. The analysis should extend to an appreciation about what is required from both parties to enable these strengths to come into the venture.

In cross-border acquisitions, the matters to be covered in the due diligence also include appraisal of the social, economic and political milieu of the country where the target firm is operating and determining the risks and growth opportunities in the country so as to identify the value drivers that need to be protected.

Cultural aspects of the target firm need to be perspicaciously looked into so as to ascertain conflicts in the culture of the acquiring and the target firm and take corrective measures to prevent them. One way to stave off cultural conflicts is to perform cultural due diligence. Network analysis maps, which describe the connections among people in an organisation, provide some insight into the similarities between culture of the acquiring firm and that of the target firm.

Proper comprehension of vital differences in processes across diverse cultures eases the post-merger integration. Successful cross-border negotiations require developing a clear map of the players who are likely to influence the formal—informal decision process. Only when these players are known, the acquirer can develop a strategy that takes care of their interests. Building consensus among different players is critical not only to reaching an agreement but also to making it work.

Once the acquiring firm finds the suitable target firm, it is ineluctable to hammer out meticulously the details of the deal directly with the target firm. The deal should aim at evolving shared vision and objectives and developing strategies therefor. At this stage, an agreement has to be made about the assets to be acquired, liabilities to be cleared and financial and human resources to be deployed for implementation of strategies. Issues like ownership and management should be settled unambiguously in order to avoid any possibility of breakout of the deal. Specific agreements need to be made about the continuing independence for the two firms. This will obviously maintain and deepen the relations.

With a plethora of factors to be factored in during an acquisition, valuation exercise is the single most important but complex task which has to be performed very carefully. A slew of variables such as industry sector dynamics, competitive environment, market sentiments, quality of management, financial health of the target firm, potential liabilities such as environmental claims, tax demands and off-balance sheet liabilities, operating synergies and their effect on cost and revenue in the event of the merger play decisive role in determining the value of the target firm.

While finalising the deal, the acquiring firm must ensure that the deal in the Earning Per Share (EPS) is accretive. Ideally, the target company should also add the EPS of the acquiring firm. An acquisition of a loss—making company can affect profitability of the parent. This is witnessed in several large acquisitions such as Tata Motors and Jaguar Land Rover.

Executing M&A Deals

For carrying out the above tasks and executing the M&A deals, it would be in fitness of things to install clearly defined stage gate system.[3] This system involves three separate phases of review and evaluation. At the strategy approval stage, the business-development team (which includes one or two members from both the business unit and corporate development) evaluates the targets outside. A subset of the team then derives the process and assigns key roles to the team members. The crucial decision at this point is whether a target firm is compatible with the corporate strategy, has strong support from the acquiring firm and can be integrated into it.

At the approval-to-negotiate stage, the team decides on a price range, keeping in view above variables pertaining to the target firm. A vision for incorporating the target firm into the acquirer's business plan, a clear operating programme, and an understanding of the acquisition's key synergies are important as well. At the end of this stage, the team is supposed to produce a non-binding term sheet or letter of intent and a road map for negotiations, confirmatory due diligence and process to close.

The Board of Directors must endorse the definitive agreement in the deal approval stage. While vetting the agreement, the focus should be on issues of valuations, integration, deal's execution risk, and the like.

Each stage should be tailored to the type of deal at hand. Small R&D deals, for example, need not have to pass through a detailed Board approval process but may instead be authorised at the business or product unit level. On the contrary, large deals that involve huge risks and require significant regulatory scrutiny must pass through the Board.

As companies adapt to a faster-paced, more complicated era of M&A deal making, they must fortify themselves with a menu of process and organisational skills to accommodate the variety of deals available to them.

Further, fast, flexible and flat structure that meets the needs of the deal and not the needs of the individual firms, has to be built. It would be germane to build empowered team comprising of talented persons who are gravid with skills and experiences and are committed to the job, a part-time assignment is a recipe for failure. It would also be pertinent to define and communicate required roles and associated responsibilities of the two organisations.

It would also be in fitness of things to evolve an objective system to communicate 'why' and 'what' of the acquisition deal to all functionaries and solicit their support.

Developing a measurement framework to generate a realistic progress report is equally useful. Creating performance metrics and communication processes, which can be used to benchmark the deal, will also be meaningful.

PRE-REQUISITES TO THE SUCCESS OF M&As DEALS

Completion of M&A deal does not guarantee its success in achieving the desired result because of various challenges that the acquiring firm has to encounter during the post-merger including integration. The write down of German firm Betapharm's assets by Dr. Reddy's and the not-so-impressive performance of Ranbaxy's acquired Romanian subsidiary, Therapia, are often highlighted as instances where the acquisition and subsequent integration were not all that smooth. The top management should address these challenges along the lines suggested below:

Complete Integration

Both the acquiring and acquired firms need to be carefully integrated as part of a broader transformation strategy. This is possible if there is cultural compatibility between the two firms. Organisations have to encourage a high degree of cultural cohesiveness by focusing on common ground to nurture a spirit of collaborative activity. It would be useful to establish a process along with the common vision for periodically checking into the progress of integration on all fronts.

One powerful means to foster integration of the two different units, which is being successfully employed by Tata Group, A.V. Birla Group and, the M&M Group is 'partnering'.[4] The partnering approach entails keeping an acquisition structurally separate and maintaining its own identity and organisation. The acquirers retain the senior executives, particularly the CEO, of the forging corporations they buy and give them the same power and autonomy they used to enjoy. The new products simply lay down their values to serve as a beacon and create a fresh sense of purpose in their organisations. Partnering approach was summed up in 2004 by Tata Group's Chairman when South Korea's Daewoo Commercial vehicle company was acquired: "Tata Motors will operate Daewoo as a Korean company in Korea, managed by Koreans. But it will work as part of a global alliance with its Indian counterpart".

A bird's eye view of how Tata Group integrated the operations of Tata Chemicals and those of the acquired Brunner Mond in the UK and its Kenyan subsidiary, Magadi Soda, can be had from a perusal of a case study on Tata Chemicals's integration approach (Illustrative Capsule 13.5).

ILLUSTRATIVE CAPSULE 13.5

INTEGRATION OF TATA CHEMICALS WITH BRUNNER MOND AND ITS SUBSIDIARY MAGADI SODA

Soon after the acquisition in December 2005, senior Tata Chemicals executives held one-on-one meeting with key Brunner Mond and Magadi Soda managers. In the meeting they assured them that they would retain all senior executives and employees, and would not change the companies' names, identities, or reporting set up. The acquired firms' executives were also informed that Tata would seriously consider issues related to Brunner Mond's pension plan liabilities—then a major concern of the acquired company's employees. It was also decided that the post-acquisition decisions would be guided by a "best of three" evaluation philosophy, taking into account best practices, processes, and ideas from all the three companies.

In February 2006, senior executives from the three companies met in Mumbai to develop a 100-day plan. Teams made up of managers from all the three companies identified 35 primary tasks, including:

(i) Harmonising the strategic planning process.

(ii) Developing plans for servicing top global accounts.

(iii) Aligning HR best practices and policies.

(iv) Establishing commercial and PR protocols.

Before the meeting, Tata chemicals issued the following communications guidelines for its executives:

(i) Talk about the Tata Code of Conduct and Business Excellence Model at every opportunity.

(ii) Convey the group's core business values and commitments to society.

(iii) Do not interact solely with Tata chemicals people; make sure you mingle with your new colleagues

(iv) Avoid terms like "acquisition" and "ownership"; speak of "coming together" and "parentage".

(v) Avoid terms like "you" and "us", say "we".

After the first 100 days, Tata chemicals took some organisational steps:

(i) It set up a Global Chemical Advisory Council, chaired by the Managing Director of Tata Chemicals and including eight senior members drawn from all the three companies to guide strategy and operational policies.

(ii) It constituted a three-member Business Heads Council, which is chaired by rotation. This group is responsible for coordinating operations, sales and marketing strategies.

(iii) The three companies have started sharing data, especially when they approach global customers.

(iv) Tata Chemicals is helping the two companies' source equipment from Indian suppliers.

(v) Tata Chemicals innovations centre in India and Brunner Mond's new-ventures team are working together to find new business opportunities in Europe.

M&M Group has also pursued partnering approach for integration process, as is evident from its case study (Illustrative Capsule 13.6).

ILLUSTRATIVE CAPSULE 13.6

M&M's MODEL OF INTEGRATION

The merger and acquisition team comprising senior managers of the company submits to the Board of Directors, docket before any acquisition plan.

The plan lays down to the last detail how the integration can be achieved as quickly and smoothly as possible. Once the acquisition is closed, a 100-day integration plan is rolled out. Its progress is monitored by a cross-functional steering committee.

The plan for each acquisition is different. But there are some common strands. First, none of the integration plans is radical. Most western companies bring in abrupt changes: new enterprise resource planning, new systems, new organisational structures and often, large layoffs. "Indian DNA is different. We want people (in acquired companies) to feel important, that they can embrace our core values", says Mahindra Group CIO and Executive Vice-President (Finance and M&As), V.S. Parthasarthy.

Secondly, the brands of the acquired company—provided they enjoy good equity—are rarely killed. Punjab Tractors, for instance, continues to sell under the Swaraj brand. Though, it has been merged into M&M, the Swaraj Team has its own identity and, according to Parthasarthy, it will not play second fiddle to the Mahindra Team. Similarly, M&Ms Chinese tractor companies have continued with their brands (Jinma and Feng Shou), though some have started using the Mahindra Prefix.

Third, the old management is usually retained. Thus, the CEOs of the forging units in Europe have continued in their job, though the scale of operations has increased substantially. Maini also continues to serve as the chief of technology and strategy at Mahindra Reva, M&M knows that Maini drove Reva single-handedly and is crucial for its success in the days to come. So, his family still holds 30% in the company, and he continues to be closely involved in its affairs. Similarly, the current management of recently acquired company, Ssang Yong, will remain the same; replacing them could cause disruptions as M&M does not have the managerial bandwidth to run a business of that scale. The Korean staff will train in India, so that they know what M&M wants. Something similar was done when the Chinese tractor companies were acquired. Instead of ramming any particular ethos down their throats, employees were exposed to the M&M way of work in India over-time. This helped transfer the M&M culture from India to China without disruption.

Managing People

In a knowledge-based economy it is the people—the repository of intellectual capital—who contribute to the success of M&A deals. As such, for complete integration of the two units on sustained basis, managing people belonging to different cultures will help quell insecurities about job-loss or working styles and ensure effective use of the human capital. There has to be total transparency on the part of the two firms, sharing all relevant information to the people and involving them in decision-making and its execution. Effective communication system should be developed to address all issues relating to the acquisition and ensure speedy, timely and clear flow of information to all those concerned. Suitable incentive system need to be established to foster speedier integration.

In any M&A deal, human resource initiative should be at the heart because human resource manager and his team play two roles—one is at the due diligence stage, i.e., before an M&A is formalised, assessing cultural fit and synergies as well as understanding how effective the integration might be based on leadership ability of the target, policies and processes, and so on. The second role of the HR team relates to alignment of compensation and benefit plans, organisational structure, and so on—all critical to post M&A finalisation. Post M&A, HR plays the crucial role of bringing the two firms together through organisation of regular employee engagement activities and allowing all employees to share their opinions.

Trust and Commitment of Management

Overarching elements of long-term relationship between the two firms are mutual understanding, trust, respect for each other and unflinching commitment of the management to honour the deal. Lack of such commitment may lead to fall out of the deal on discordant note, as, of late, has been witnessed in case of Sun Pharma-Taro acquisition (Illustrative Capsule 13.7).

ILLUSTRATIVE CAPSULE 13.7

SUN PHARMA-TARO DEAL FIASCO: INDIA'S LARGEST PHARMA COMPANY BY MARKET CAPITALISATION

Sun Pharmaceutical Industries entered into a merger agreement with an Israel firm Taro Pharmaceuticals on May 18, 2007. Accordingly, Sun agreed to acquire Taro for $454 million. On February 19, 2008, Sun hiked its stakes in Taro to 36%.

The merger agreement failed to materialise when the Levitt, family-promoters of Taro unilaterally terminated it after a year and sent the notice to that effect on May 21, 2008. This was because Taro's fortunes turned around to post-profits.

On May 29, Sun sued Taro in the US for not honouring the deal and launched a hostile open offer to acquire the remaining shares, invoking provisions of the merger agreement.

Taro questioned the validity of the Special Tender offer in an Israeli court on June 24, 2010 which ruled in favour of Sun Pharma.

On June 26, 2008 a Sun subsidiary bought the 12% promoters' stake.

Taro filed an appeal to block the domestic company's efforts to acquire Taro's outstanding shares. The Supreme Court dismissed the appeal on September 7, 2010, allowing Sun Pharma to acquire Taro's outstanding shares for $7.75 per share.

Sun Pharma, which owns 36% in Taro, will now acquire 12% shares from the promoter to ramp up its holding to 48%.

Establishing Monitoring Team

So as to ensure that both parties' needs are being respected, each other's capabilities are leveraged effectively, the capabilities that one party brings in are not being smothered by the other, and to ensure that existing vision, objectives and strategies are adequate enough in the changed business milieu, high-power team comprising the top managers of the two firms should be constituted. This will go a long way in preventing occurrence of any problem at the initial stage, on the one hand and deepen the relationship between the two, on the other.

Summary

A company may expand its business through acquisition of another company. Forces that usually prompt a company to opt for the inorganic route include enhancing appetite for speedier growth, gaining global scale, capturing market opportunities, deriving synergistic advantages to reduce cost and improve efficiency, de-risking business and strengthening controlling power.

Despite tremendous potentialities of M&A route to growth, studies show failure of significant portion of M&A to add value. This is ascribed to inadequate planning and ineffective execution.

It would, therefore, be pertinent for the acquiring firm to draw business plan on the basis of environmental scanning and the firm's core competencies. Further, strategic decision has to be taken about the target firm, keeping in view its strengths complementing to those of the acquiring firm. Cultural aspects of the target should also be looked into so as to identify conflicts in the culture of the two firms and take necessary steps to minimise them.

Once decision about the target firm is made, it is ineluctable to frame details of the deal including valuation of the target firm.

For carrying into effect the deal, suitable process, structure and communication system need to be established.

The management of acquiring firm must remember that success of any M&A deal hinges how effectively operations and cultures of the two firms are managed and also upon the commitment of the top management to the deal.

Establishing a high powered monitoring team to assess the post-merger progress will go a long way in preventing any problem at the initial stage and strengthening the relationship between the two firms.

Key Terms

Absorption

Amalgamation

Core competencies

Environmental scanning takeover

Partnering approach

Reference call forecasting synergy

Stage gate system

Discussion Questions

1. What forces have prompted Indian corporate to expand through acquisition route? Illustrate your answer with suitable examples.

2. "Pursuit of synergy is the only reason for acquiring business." Comment.

3. Why have significant portion of M&As across the globe failed to add value to the shareholders?

4. "Success of M&A deals depends on how efficiently acquisition strategy is formulated and executed". Discuss.

5. What important considerations should an acquiring firm factor in while choosing a target firm?

6. What is the significance of cultural factor in acquisition of overseas firms? How should cultural conflicts between the two firms be resolved?

7. What is partnering approach to integration of firms? How has this approach been adopted by Indian corporates? Explain with examples.

8. "Completion of M&A deal does not always guarantee its success". Elucidate this statement and throw light on the forces that bear upon the success of an M&A deal.

References

1. *Business Standard*, June 28, 2010.

2. *Times Business*, March 4, 2010.

3. Uhlaner, Robert T. and Andrew S. West, Running A Winning M&A shop, *Indian Management*, April 2008.

4. Kale, Prashant, Habir Singh and Anand P. Raman, "Don't Integrate Your Acquisition, Partner with Them", *Harvard Business Review*, June, 2010.

Internet Resources

- *www.godrej.com*
- *www.airtel.in*
- *www.uplonline.com*
- *www.tatachemicals.com*
- *www.mahindra.com*
- *www.sunpharma.com*

14

Designing Strategy
for Entering Overseas Market

INTRODUCTION

In the wake of rapidly increasing pace of globalisation of the world economy, the organisations in their endeavour to create added value and achieve sustainable competitive advantage are harbouring the rapacious ambition of capturing leadership not just in domestic market but also in world market. The overall philosophy underlying the organisations' aspirations is ingrained in the Theory of Comparative Advantage propounded by Adam Smith in his historical title *Wealth of Nations*. According to this theory, "if a foreign country can supply us with a commodity cheaper than we ourselves can make it, better buy it from them with some part of the produce of our own in which we have some advantage".

FORCES TRIGGERING COMPANIES

Based on this fundamental principle of international business, a volley of proactive forces have triggered companies to move into overseas markets and pursue, by and large, inorganic route to enter into foreign countries speedily with relatively less cost and inconvenience. Besides these, certain reactionary forces have also forced organisations to go abroad. Let us now study the positive forces.

Positive Forces

Following are the most important forces which have motivated organisations to ramp up their foreign business:

Access to New Markets

Organisations, especially in emerging countries, are driven to go global, to penetrate into overseas markets and encash profusely available opportunities. Indian corporate behemoths such as Tatas, Birlas, Mahindra & Mahindra, Bharti Airtel, Sun Pharma, Dr. Reddy's Laboratories, Wipro and Godrej have moved into foreign markets, particularly European and African markets, for grabbing abundant opportunities and thereby enhancing their market share and accelerating growth rate. Even global MNCs like IBM, Nokia, Dell Computers, Du Pont, Nestle, LG Electronics, HUL, P&G and GE are moving aggressively in the emerging markets of India and China to tap the ocean of market opportunities and to acquire global leadership.

Now Toyota Motor Corporation—the world's biggest car maker—has decided to enter into the emerging markets of China, India and Brazil with its low-cost car for boosting the growth of its turnover in these markets.

These organisations believe that global presence is necessary not only to squeeze the existing opportunities but also to beat the competition by understanding the dynamics of local market situations.

Access to Low Cost Inputs

Availability of various inputs-natural resources, technologies, skilled personnel and other materials in certain countries at lower cost and difficulty in transporting these resources have spurred many domestic organisations to set up their operations in these countries so as to gain economies of scale and cost-competitiveness. For example, Hindalco quietly bagged the Mount Gordon Copper mines of Australia while Tata Steel acquired Carborough Downs Coal project in the same country for expanding its business in the country.

London-based Vedanta group has in recent years entered India and acquired companies engaged in aluminium, power generation, iron-ore production and oil exploration to access plentitude of natural resources of iron ore, manganese, chromite, bauxite and coal sprawling in different parts of the country.

During the last few months, Reliance Industries Ltd. (RIL) has moved into the US to exploit vast tract of shale gas and has since April, 2010 struck three deals including the latest one in September with the US based Carrizo Oil & Gas which will give RIL access to about 62,600 acres of underdeveloped lease hold in the core area of Marcellus Shale with an expected resource potential of two trillion cubic feet equivalent. The RIL will also acquire advanced technological capabilities for operating their assets and leveraging these skills to capitalise on the potential shale gas exploration in India.

Derive Low Labour Cost

Rising labour cost in the US, Japan and European countries have pushed global MNCs to go abroad. Many Japanese and the US firms, especially in electronic and automobile fields, are setting up their plants in India and China primarily because of low cost of skilled labour.

Access to Low Cost of Funds

More often than not, cost of doing business including interest rates and taxes varies from country to country because of fiscal and financial policies, business environment and infrastructure forces. Through their access to international financial markets, MNCs are in a unique position to minimise their cost of capital and thereby maximise their value. Dominance in more than one country increases the ability of a company to control cost. This is considerably helpful in a cyclical industry like automobiles. Tata Motors is a burning example in this respect.

Capitalise on Its Core Competencies

A company, blessed with unique competency in its product/service line, may take mileage of this strength to expand its business in foreign markets and gain competitive advantage. Global MNCs like Honda, Nokia, Apple computers, Google, Sony, Coca-Cola, GE, Nestle and other global organisations have gainfully leveraged their core competencies and nationally recognised brand name into marketing, production and distribution efficiencies that are unavailable in foreign markets.

Minimise Business Risks

At times, organisations may be tempted to move into a number of foreign countries to spread the business risks which are involved in depending on domestic market. Recently, quite a large number of American and European companies have entered in the African and Asian markets to pare the risks due to severe financial crisis.

Take Advantage of Diverse Economic, Demographic and Cultural Factors

Existence of different levels of economic and industrial development and diverse lifestyles, customs and conditions across the globe provides enough driving force for foreign entrepreneurs. A mature product in a declining market at home, for example, may be an innovative product in a growing market in some countries. Likewise, outdated technology at home may be appropriate for foreign locations.

Attractive demographic factors such as large populations, growing size of middle income group and rising per capita income, as in China and India, are providing an irresistible lure to global MNCs.

Emerging countries such as China, India, Brazil and Africa have, of late, emerged as the hub of foreign direct investment and MNCs because of their enabling monetary, fiscal and trade policies.

Reactionary Forces

At times, domestic companies may be constrained to enter into foreign markets because trading partners, who are customers with their products or services, clamp trade barriers in the form of tariffs, quota, and the like resulting in making their products or services more expensive and thus, rendering them unattractive in internal turf especially when local product is not subject to such trade barriers.

Where a company's customers happen to be internal, it has to follow the lead to retain them as customers. Many foreign companies prefer to deal with a small number of suppliers worldwide, because if a supplier cannot meet their needs in foreign locations, it may lose the business as a domestic supplier.

Regulations and restrictions imposed by the domestic government (as in case of India during pre-liberalisation era) may also compel the domestic companies to move into these countries where environment is business friendly. Adoption of policy of liberalisation and globalisation by the Government of India after 1991 has resulted in arrival of large number of global MNCs in different spheres of business in the country and massive surge in Foreign Direct Investments (FDIs).

Thus, ferociously changing global environment has offered incredible opportunities to organisations to expand and diversify their operations across the world, to access latest technology and cheap finance. However, these organisations face enormous challenges in encashing the opportunities because of myriad of forces such as greater susceptibility to economic, financial and political crisis experienced by other countries leading to volatility in global market place and increased exchange rate risk. Differences in cultural and competitive environment, financial markets, legal, accounting and tax environment, varying marketing and distribution channels, personnel management and differences in corporate governance practices in cross border countries add to the problems of the organisations intending to do foreign business. To cope with these problems and the concurrent business risks and capture business opportunities, organisations need to be managed relatively more astutely and all the strategic issues involved therein should be dexterously addressed.

STRATEGIC ISSUES IN OVERSEAS BUSINESS

So as to evolve an integrated strategy for a company's offshore business, the management needs to consider the following three major issues threadbare:

- Choosing product offering for offshore markets.
- Choosing countries for investment.
- Choosing mode of entry into overseas markets.

Choosing Product Offering for Offshore Markets

One of the strategic issues that merits serious attention of an organisation contemplating to pursue operations abroad is products/services to be offered. As a matter of fact, a firm's product defines its business.

The major challenge before a firm with global horizons is to develop a product policy and strategy that is sensitised to market needs, competition and the firm's resources so as to achieve sustainable competitive edge across the globe. There may be several product options before a firm such as broad-line global product, globally standardised product and localised product. Choice of a particular option, a mix of the two or more than two must be preceded by evaluation of these options and its contribution to the enhancement of the competitive advantage of the firm.

Broadline Global Product Option

This strategic option requires production of a wide range of products or services in one or more industries. The two corporate leviathans of India, viz., Tatas and Birlas, as noted earlier, are engaged in manufacturing a wide range of products in a number of industries and their distributions in various markets. Among global MNCs, IBM in computers competes in the segments of mainframes, minicomputers, personal computers and software. On the contrary, most of its rivals concentrate on only one of these segments (Apple in micros and mobile phones and Microsoft in software). Firms with substantially large resources can only afford to offer a wide range of products because of huge capital cost requirement and susceptibility to competition from focused companies in individual industry segments.

Firms with strategy to produce a wide range of products would have advantage of such major competitive strengths as physical and financial economies of scale and possession of a multi-country production and distribution network resulting in improved cost competitiveness. Such firms can also take advantage of transferring experience curve gains accruing from production and sales of one product to other products. Finally, firms selling products spanning from low-cost to highly specialised items may achieve greater sales and profits than a rival that focuses on only one end or segment of the market.

This strategy should, however, be pursued so long as it keeps the firm ahead of its rivals.

Globally Standardised Product Option

This strategic option signifies worldwide concentration on one or a few products for a worldwide competition. Firms pursuing this option generally standardise the core product or large parts of it, while customising peripherals or other parts of the product.[1] For example, electronic and telecommunication firms like Sony, Philips, Motorola, LG, Samsung and Nokia have pursued this strategy to manufacture standardised products imbedded with certain features suited to local styles and tastes. Airbus—a European Company—pursues the standardised product option, and recently it has enlarged its industrial and engineering footprint outside Europe. According to its President and CEO, Thomas Enders, this expansion strategy is not just about reducing cost but also about tapping into the increasing pool of skilled engineers around the world.

Globally standardised product strategy has the advantage of enabling the firm to achieve scale economies at every stage of value chain activities and opens up opportunities for tax savings, servicing and transfer pricing. It can also be helpful in improving the quality of the products and ensuring better management of resources. This is why, product standardisation strategy has been popular until the recent past. Most Japanese firms lacking in resources focused on small number of globally standardised products to conquer foreign markets initially through cost and then through superior quality.

However, the strategy of standardisation is gradually losing its sheen because of growing differences in the usage of product in different countries due to cultural differences, and geographical factors of climate and terrain, increased green environmental concerns of different countries and consumers becoming much more discerning and making high expectations of all the elements of the augmented product as also their varying perceptions of the value and satisfaction of products and concurrent differences in their acceptability from country to country.

As such, global firms should offer products/services to satisfy the most common needs of the most important markets.[2]

Localised Product Option

Thrust of localised product option is on national responsiveness. Companies following this strategic option address local tastes and government regulations. In view of fast changing dynamics of world economy, escalating competitive environment and emergence of African and Asian countries as epicentres of burgeoning market opportunities, MNCs are increasingly pursuing localised product strategy to offer products to customers suited to their tastes.

FMCG giant, PepsiCo through its subsidiary PepsiCo India has in recent years, sought to offer customers locally relevant tastes, flavours and ingredients in innovative and healthy manner. Likewise, Nestle—the world's biggest food company—has adopted localised product strategy and set up 450 factories in 84 countries including India to use local raw materials for making products that are made to local tastes and are sold in the country.

GE India has pursued this strategy to resurrect its fortunes (Illustrative Capsule 14.1).

ILLUSTRATIVE CAPSULE 14.1

GE INDIA'S STRATEGY TO LOCALISE OPERATORS

In his letter to the shareowners in the 2009 annual report, General Electric (GE) Chairman of the Board and Chief Executive, Jeffrey Immelt, had said that GE had a $38-billion business in growth markets, which include resource and people-rich regions like West Asia, Latin America, China and India. We sought out pockets of growth wherever we could find them. We deepened our position in fast-growing markets in Australia, Brazil, China and India.

Till recently, GE honchos would often talk of a turnover of $8 billion in India by 2010. GE had ended 2008 with $2.8 billion. Sensing shortfall of its target, GE appointed John Flannery as the President and CEO of GE India who joined the company in January, 2010. His brief, before he winged his way to India, from Immelt was three-fold: "Grow GE's presence in multiple dimensions, localise it and transform the organisation for the long haul".

According to John Flannery, macroeconomic opportunity in India still excites GE. "The opportunities in GE's core areas of infrastructure (power, railway, water treatment and so on), oil & gas and finance continue to remain huge. These (growth) markets are investing trillions of dollars in infrastructure and favour a multi-business company that can bring solutions. This allows us to form a 'company-to-country' approach in countries where government and business work together to solve infrastructure needs", Immelt has said in his letter to the shareowners.

John Flannery noted that, ever since GE set up shop in India, all the business lines reported to their global business headquarters. Key decisions on products, distribution and investments were taken outside India. Thus, GE's business in India was not looked as a single profit & loss centre. He further noted that all management thinkers have stressed the need for multinational corporations to think local. Those who listened carefully to the Indian customers have gained immensely; those who didn't have failed miserably. The success of LG and Samsung of Korea and Suzuki of Japan can largely be attributed to strong local product development, manufacturing and distribution. All of them empowered their local employees to take important decisions.

After joining GE India, Flannery changed GE's reporting structure in India. GE India has now become a standalone profit and loss account. Business lines of all report directly to Flannery. "I will be able to control the vast majority of decision-making", says Flannery.

Realising the importance of localisation of operations, Flannery decided to localise GE's business. This means sending people out to the market to gather what products and services are required, designing and manufacturing those products in India, and finally distributing them in India. For design, Flannery is planning to leverage the skills sets of GE's Bangalore Technology Centre. So far, this centre has focused on GE's global requirements. To save cost and time was the first brief to the centre. The centre will now work on products that could be relevant for India. "The brief is changing as we speak in an incremental and supplemental way. It will continue to be a key base for GE's global operations; that won't stop. But we will add resources to go local; some resources may be shifted", say Flannery. "For the past 18 months, there has been in-country, for-country team at work for India-specific products and designs". In fact, some products developed at Bangalore centre have already found their way to the Indian market.

Elaborating on the Indian strategy, John L. Flannery observed that "localisation of the company has been our main focus area, starting from marketing and manufacturing to what the customer needs". He has targeted that the localisation levels will go up from 10% to 20% currently to 60% to 70% in the next five years. "The company will be setting up a manufacturing site of over 5,00,000 square feet with shared facilities, manufacturing multiple products."

Also, plans are on the anvil to get into more joint ventures with local manufacturers, which could also include sourcing agreements to produce products catering to specific needs in the country.

This is based on what Immelt had outlined as the strategy in his letter: "Our focus is on introducing more new products at more price points. We are deriving management practices to capture new opportunities, called reverse innovation. Essentially, this takes low-cost, emerging-market business model and translates it to the developed world. To this end, we have developed a full line of high-margin, low cost health care devices, designed in China and India and now marketed successfully in developed world".

Choice of a particular product strategy for overseas markets is contingent upon a host of external and internal forces such as physical characteristics of the host country market, competitive and cultural forces, demographic and regulatory factors existing in the host country and competence of the firm to produce quality goods at relatively low cost. Above all, overall corporate philosophy and top management policy with respect to foreign business influence the firm's decision regarding a particular product option.

Choosing Countries for Investment

Once a company has decided to go abroad with products/services to offer, it has to decide what world markets are to be tapped. The management should not be swamped along by growth and cost reduction opportunities, competitive and technological advantages leading to high profit margins, for the fact that the foreign investment is usually vulnerable to several risks arising out of exchange rate fluctuations and diverse and dynamic socio-economic, political and cultural conditions existing in different countries of the world. Nevertheless, investment in several countries allows an organisation to more effectively bear the risks by offsetting the loss from one country by gains in other countries and impart flexibility in its operations; there still remains the need to watch for the possibilities of dramatic loss by expropriation, devaluation or some other national setback. As such, it would be pertinent to make incisive analysis of all the relevant issues for choosing a suitable country.

This analysis should cover the following:

(i) Determining the Firm's Needs and Objectives
(ii) Assessing Business Climate of Off-shore Countries
(iii) Assessing Country Risk
(iv) Assessing the Firm's Capabilities

Determining the Firm's Needs and Objectives

A firm's product strategy is the nucleus of its core business and hence the overseas investment. Thus, firms aiming at the production of mass consumption goods will be on the lookout of global markets with substantially large demand. On the contrary, those with localised product strategy, say for example, to cater to the vast needs of consumer electronics and cellular products in the emerging countries will have to concentrate on these countries only.

Assessing Business Climate of Off-shore Countries

Keeping in view the firm's needs, the management should identify the countries and then assess their business climate in terms of pace of economic development, growth opportunities, competitive position, availability of infrastructure facilities, state of financial markets, cultural factors, and political environment so as to determine precisely the investment opportunities existing in different countries and accompanying business risks.

Countries promising high economic and industrial growth opportunities provide conducive environment for foreign companies to invest. With the help of typical indicators such as the GDP and its growth, per capita income and its distribution, size of population, balance of payments position and exchange rate levels, and its socio-demographic make-up, consumption pattern and inflationary trends, size of the market and its growth potentiality and demand behaviour of the products which the firm is intending to produce can be determined. For instance, macro level analysis of various countries may reveal that Japan offers great market opportunity for diamond and other precious metals, marine products, garments, granite and leather goods. India has tremendous potential market for household necessities, consumer durables, electronic and telecommunication products. Australia and South Africa with rich natural resources can serve as a rich source to MNCs who depend heavily on natural resources. Germany offers tremendous opportunities for textile and leather goods, readymade garments, beverages and tobacco and vegetable and foodstuffs. There exists vast market for mass consumption goods in Hong Kong, Taiwan, Bangkok, Thailand and Indonesia.

Competitive position with respect to different industries and product lines in the countries having large markets and high growth potentials should be assessed by identifying the local rivals, their market share, technological excellence, marketing strengths, and the like. A firm should avoid those countries that offer strong competition. For instance, Indian firms may not find it easy to grab opportunities in Japan in the field of readymade garments, leather goods and fabrics in view of the presence of strong players like Korea, China, Taiwan and Hong Kong. However, they can capitalise on great market potentials in marine products, gems and jewellery and granite, in view of their strong competitive strength vis-à-vis other players.

Availability of infrastructure facilities, raw materials and skilled labour at reasonable price is another important consideration that merits attention of the aspiring entrepreneurs. Global MNCs are taking lots of interest in emerging countries especially Korea, India, Brazil, Taiwan and China not only because of large market opportunities but also due to availability of cheap labour.

Financial factors should also be factored in to ascertain availability of funds at a reasonable price. Thus, countries where firms can have easy access to ample sources of funds at relatively cheaper cost, will obviously have an edge over other countries.

Scanning of socio-cultural environment of the potential countries is inevitable to determine, particularly the attitudes of host country workers towards work, management and their authority, their attitude towards change and achievement. It would be useful to get an insight into the structure and attitude of the local trade unions, their record for restrictive practices, unofficial disruptions and strikes and their ability to maintain discipline amongst their members.

Assessing Country Risk

Before taking a final decision to set up a business in a country to take advantage of the opportunities, the management must assess country risk which may arise due to the unexpected change in the characteristics of the environment of the host country, affecting adversely the organisation's cash flows.

Two dimensions of country risk, which are of great relevance to organisations planning to move overseas markets, are political risk and financial risk. Political risk is caused by uncertainty about political or policy changes ranging from the outright expropriation of foreign assets to unexpected changes in tax laws, labour laws and other laws that hurt the profitability and viability of the foreign project. Financial risk occurs due to unexpected developments in the financial or economic environment of the host country, affecting the value of the company's business.

As such, while assessing political risk in the host country, the management should attempt to ascertain degree of political stability which in itself depends on the political and governance systems of the country, philosophy and ideology of political parties, government policy towards integration into the global system, ethnic and religious stability and attitude of host country consumers, and so on. At the same time, business risk arising out of expropriation, blockage of funds, loss of intellectual property rights, and the like, need to be minutely looked into.

Likewise, analysis of various financial risk factors such as current and potential economic health of the host country, its financial state, monetary and fiscal policies, and splurging of government spending needs to be perspicaciously made so as to determine the level of financial risk in the country.

Assessing the Firm's Capabilities

Organisations intending to move abroad must have to ensure that they possess certain critical strengths including technological, marketing, financial and managerial strengths. Companies having core competency in R&D and innovative skills such as, Microsoft, Dell Computers, Hindustan Petroleum (HP) and CISCO have always the advantage of entering and exploiting the overseas markets with their new products and processes to establish their supremacy in foreign markets mainly because of their strong managerial competence. Likewise, Nestle has emerged as the world's biggest food company by dint of its leadership and management principles and simpler and clearer business processes.

Strong and stable financial health of the organisation provides added strength to it, particularly when it is seeking entry in an emerging country suffering from funds inadequacy.

Based on the above analysis, the management should opt for a country (/countries), promising highest return with minimum risk.

Choosing Mode of Entry into Overseas Markets

When a firm chooses a particular country/countries for conducting overseas business, it has to make decision simultaneously about the route to enter in the country. Choice of mode of entry in an offshore market is one of the most important international decisions the firm makes. It is something like the marriage decision for an individual which involves certain commitments and hence cannot be easily reversed.[3] Further, such decision bears directly upon the firm's objectives of achieving high degree of competitiveness in foreign markets.

There are various entry modes in foreign markets, important amongst them being exporting, licensing, franchising, management contracts, turnkey projects, and strategic alliances and mergers. We shall discuss, in brief, the strengths and weaknesses of each of these modes and the specific conditions in which they may prove most useful:

Exporting

Exporting is the most traditional mode of entering in an international market. In this method, a firm uses its domestic plant to produce goods and export the same to overseas markets when it finds that the domestic market is too small to absorb the volume of production or an elastic demand curve that prevents raising prices sufficiently to cover costs.[4]

Exporting as a route to foreign business is relatively less expensive and less risky. It is most suited to firms capable of using domestic production to cater to foreign markets and thus, augmenting sales and reducing inventories. The exporter is not to bother about the problems inherent in foreign operating environment. Exporting also provides a unique opportunity to develop contacts with local people and exploit the market potentials. In case of failure of export business in a particular country, the firm will just stop exporting any more in that country without any long-term loss of capital.

However, exporting may not be adequate enough to penetrate the existing markets effectively and counteract the local competitors. Cost of exporting per unit may at times be higher than other methods of overseas investment. Further, exported goods may lack features appropriate to specific offshore markets. At times, the exporting firm may not be able to capture lucrative market opportunities because of clamping of new tariff barriers and other constraints by the host country government. In such cases, the firm may think of other entry routes.

Effectiveness of exporting as a mode of entry into the foreign markets depends, in the main, on cost-competitiveness of the exporting firm and the host country trade rules. A company, not exposed to foreign environment, may find exporting as an excellent initial strategy to enter a foreign market.

Licensing

Licensing is an easy way of entering into the foreign markets without any investment. Under international licensing, a firm in one country (Licensor) permits a firm in another country to use its intellectual property (such as patents, trademarks, copyrights, technology, technical know-how, marketing skill or some other specific skill) for a certain period of time in lieu of a fee or share of profits.

Companies, endowed with great knowledge and expertise on products and manufacturing capabilities but do not want to manage them directly via own manufacturing/own sourcing, may find licensing as quicker, convenient and less risky entry route in overseas market. It becomes more attractive if the host country clamps restrictions on direct investment. Italy's fashion brand, Paul & Shark, has granted licensing rights to Reliance Brands—a subsidiary of Mukesh Ambani led Reliance Retail.

However, the licensor may risk losing its competitive edge to its licensee in the long run. Many American companies complain about their licensing experience with Japanese firms; a common refrain being, "We gave our best R&D and know-how to Japan for only 5% of sales. In less than a decade, they come back and beat us in our own market". Further, by licensing the rights, the licensor loses its grip over the quality of its products, processes, the use and misuse of these assets and even its corporate image.

As such, the licensor should take all precautionary measures to guard itself against the above ills.

Franchising

In franchising, the franchisor grants another independent entity (the franchisee) the right to use brand name of its product technology and trademark and expertise and assists it in its operations by supplying requisite inputs, like the Coca-Cola supplying the syrup to bottlers.

Many overseas companies have established a strong presence in the Indian markets through franchising. In the hospitality and food service industries, this has been the preferred means for starting operations. Success stories include those of Hertz, AVS & Budget car rental, Radisson, Best Western & Quality Inn Hotels, Kentuchy Fried Chicken, Dominos Pizza, TGI Friday's, Ruby Tuesday, Subway & Baskin Robin's for food.

Beverage companies have always considered franchising for their expansion plans, especially bottling plants. Some popular examples are Coke, Pepsi and even the once independent Cadbury Schweppes, which explored this option. Instead of setting up manufacturing plants globally, Coke and Pepsi only produce syrup concentrate which is then sold to various bottlers throughout the world who hold a Coca-Cola and Pepsi franchise rights with their respective territories. Coca-Cola and Pepsi bottling franchises, which hold contacts with the company, produce finished product in cans and bottles from the concentrate. Their bottling partners are local companies and so they are rooted in their communities, thinking and acting locally.

India has been the favoured destination for multinational companies (MNCs) to use franchising an excellent way to expand their business because of lower capital requirements, vast Indian market of over 120 billion people and easy access to local market knowledge. Indian master franchisees offer the foreign franchisors direct access to substantial market knowledge and a considered and sophisticated approach to its exploitation. Further, franchising well suits the entrepreneurial side of Indian culture. Indian business people are fiercely proprietary and feel a need to have ownership and control over their business operations which they can pass on to future generations. However, at the same time, they are keen to benefit from the goodwill and technology that can be provided by the foreign franchisor. Franchising allows them to reconcile these conflicting ambitions.

With large and inherent entrepreneurial talent, franchising is poised to help spur Indian economy as it is an excellent way of encouraging private enterprise and fulfilling the growing need for connecting the customer through self-driven localised partners and helping in the establishment of global standards products and services. This is why, the practice of franchising is fast catching up in India, as reflected in the increasing number of examples we see around us in diverse fields such as in Aptech & NIIT in computer education, McDonald's and Dominos Pizza in Food, ABF and Others in entertainment, DHL and Blue Dart in couriers, and many other examples in health care fitness centres and the like.

Management Contracting

In countries where government insists on complete or majority ownership by the local entrepreneur, organisations take recourse to management contracting as an alternative route to enter into these countries. In management contracting, the supplier brings together a package of skills that will enable provide an integrated service to the client without incurring the risk and benefit of ownership.

Management contracts bring in all the benefit of foreign investment. A large number of organisations, especially in service sector, are employing them as a profitable opportunity to sell valuable skills and resources.[5] The entire benefits are without the need to find the capital for investment and exposure to investment risks. This mode of entry is acceptable to all countries of the world including those having clamped prohibition on foreign investment.

Examples of management contracting by TCS and Reliance Global Com can be found in Illustrative Capsule 14.2.

ILLUSTRATIVE CAPSULE 14.2

MANAGEMENT CONTRACT BY TCS AND REL GLOBAL COM

Tata Consultancy Services (TCS): On September 29, 2010, software firm, TCS, announced that it bagged a five-year IT services contract worth more than 50 million AUD (about ₹218 crore) from Australia's renewable energy company AGL Energy. Under the contract, the company will manage and provide infrastructure management services to AGL Energy. "We expect the new deal to similarly enhance our experience, further strengthening our strategic relationship", Owr Coppage, Chief Information Officer & Group General Manager—Customer Operations at AGL, said in a statement. Prior to this contract, TCS has been executing a number of programmes at AGL, covering advanced metering, gas trading, pricing engine and multiple SAP project, and over 650 TCS consultants are delivering these engagements for AGL.

According to TCS General Manager (Australia & New Zealand), Varun Kapur, "Technology provides AGL with a strong competitive advantage. We are confident AGL will continue to experience delivery certainty with TCS and our strategic partner, BMC Energy and Utilities, is a big focus area for TCS and we are proud to have AGL as our showcase client".

BMC Software Inc. is a multinational corporation specialising in Business Service Management (BSM) offering software solutions across distributed, virtual and cloud environments. "We partnered with TCS to move AGL from a silo-based support structure to BMC's value-based approach with our BSM offerings. Given the delivery capability of TCS and solution capabilities of BMC, we look forward to several other clients benefiting from this strategic partnership", BMC (Asia Pacific) Chip Salyards said.

Rel Global Com: On September 30, 2010, Anil Ambani Group Firm said in a statement that it has bagged contracts worth $100 mn (about ₹449 crore) between April and early July, 2010. The company operates spanning 65,000 kms, seamlessly integrated with Reliance Communications, connecting 40 key business markets in India, the Middle East, Asia, Europe and the US. The company in its statement said that Reliance Global Com has been developing processes specifically designed to centrally manage multi-carrier networks, and streamline network, billing and contract management, developing truly global business scalability for customers. "Enabling our customers to grow their business regardless of geographic or business, boundaries, requires us to understand our customer needs and provide management processes which achieve their objectives. Our recent results prove that we are delivering exactly that", Reliance Global Com President & CEO, Punit Garg said. Contract renewals with existing customers were also strong throughout 2010, with major enterprise customers looking at further increasing the efficiency of their internal resources and reduce the total cost of ownership of their networks. Reliance Global Com's customer base has expanded significantly since April 2010, with several new multi-million dollar contracts signed. The company serves over 2,100 enterprises, 200 carriers and 2.5 million retail customers in 163 countries across 6 continents.

Turnkey Projects

This mode of foreign entry permits a foreign client to acquire a complete operational system to install and operate a project together with skills investment sufficient to allow unassisted maintenance and operation at the system following its completion.[6] In turnkey operation, there is an agreement by the seller to supply a buyer with a facility fully equipped and ready to be operated by the buyer's personnel, who will be trained by the seller. A good example of turnkey projects is that of BHEL (Illustrative Capsule 14.3).

ILLUSTRATIVE CAPSULE 14.3
THE BHARAT HEAVY ELECTRICALS LIMITED'S (BHEL'S) TURNKEY PROJECTS

BHEL has recently secured two turnkey power projects worth ₹2.2 billion ($4.5 million): One project has been secured from Power Grid Corporation of India for setting up a 220 KV substation at Kabul and second project has been secured from Water & Power Consultancy Services (WPCOS) India, for supply and installation of electro mechanical packages for 42 MW Salma Hydroelectric Power Plant in Afghanistan. BHEL's scope of work for the Kabul substation project includes design, manufacture, supply, erection and commissioning, besides civil works. For the Salma Hydro Project, the scope of work will be similar for the 3 × 14 MW Francis-type hydro turbines with matching generators and micro-processor based control and excitation equipment.

BHEL has also bagged a ₹55 crore contract for setting up a substation in Bangladesh. The contract entails supply and installation of a new 230 KV substation and the expansion of an existing substation. BHEL is involved in design, supply, construction and commissioning of the 230 KV substation of Bangladesh.

BHEL has also bagged a ₹46 crore order to set up two substations in Ethiopia. The work includes design, supply and commissioning of the Semera & Dichoto substations in Ethiopia.

Strategic Alliances and Joint Ventures (JVs)

In the wake of bruising competitive and uncertain environment in recent times, strategic alliances, joint ventures (JVs) and mergers and acquisitions (M&As) (already discussed in the preceding chapter) representing collaborative approach have become the most potent and powerful route to enter into the foreign markets, minimise business risks, share the cost of large scale investments and inject new found entrepreneurial spirit into businesses.[7]

Strategic alliances are a specific type of partnering arrangements between two or more companies to form a new joint organisation for manufacturing, marketing and distribution, research and development and other specific activities and range widely in scope from an informal business relationships based on a simple contract to formalised inter-organisational relationships such as joint venture agreements as also a fully integrated merger of two companies.

In Joint Venture (JV) form of collaborative arrangement, the parties agree to create a new entity by both contributing equity and then sharing in the revenues, expenses and control of the enterprise. The venture can be for one specific project only or a continuing business relationship such as the Sony Ericsson joint venture. Ownership of the companies in their respective fields remains intact. This is in contrast to M&As which represent permanent, structural changes in how the company exists including change in ownership and management control.

A slew of forces have triggered organisations across the globe to form a JV and other alliances. The main reason for a JV has always been an entry strategy. Joint Venture (JV) provides a lower risk option of entering into a new country. For Fiat, Pepsi, Ford, Xerox, Suzuki, and the like, the JV is an ideal way to enter into Indian markets and establish itself as a leader ahead of other competitors.

Of late, Nippon Steel Corporation of Japan entered into JV agreement with Tata Steel, Japan (Illustrative Capsule 14.4) to address the local needs of Indian automotive customers for high quality steel sheet.

ILLUSTRATIVE CAPSULE 14.4

JOINT VENTURE BETWEEN TATA STEEL AND NIPPON STEEL CORPORATION OF JAPAN

Earlier 2010, the Tata Steel Board approved a joint venture between Tata Steel and Nippon Steel for the production and sale of automotive cold-rolled flat products at Jamshedpur to address the localisation needs of Indian automotive customers for high-grade cold-rolled steel sheets.

Tata Steel holds 51% in the venture, while Nippon Steel has 49%. The JV aims to capture the growing demand for high grade automotive, cold-rolled flat products in India by setting up a continuous annealing and processing line with a capacity of 6,00,000 tonnes. Nippon Steel would transfer its technology for producing high-grade cold-rolled steel sheet for automotive application, including skin panels and high tensile steels.

The target for start of operations is March 2013.

Another reason that has made JV an attractive route to offshore business is that it enables both the partners to further strengthen their core competencies and improve their earnings. The JV between Modi group and Xerox is a case in point. While Xerox could get early lead in the photocopier market due to the JV, the Modi group's photocopier business became significantly profitable. Recent deal between JFE Steel Corporation of Japan and JSW Steel of India has not only enabled the latter to access the former's superior production process technology but also to get much needed funds to minimise its debt burden and meet its short-term and long-term capital needs.

Joint Venture (JV) agreements between Maruti and Suzuki, Caltax and IBP, Tata Telecom and AT&T facilitated the partners to access latest technology which reduced their production cost and also improved quality of the product leading to improvement in their competitive position in the overseas market.

Another immanent advantage flowing from a strategic tie up is that a partner gets the opportunity to learn about the skills of the other partner, as witnessed in the case of Modi-Xerox JV. Xerox learnt a lot about distribution channels and copier usage model from Modi group. Likewise, TVS learnt a lot from Suzuki about making motorbikes.

Joint Venture (JV) has also the advantage of minimising costs and risks involved in the business. Nokia and Siemens merged their networks business primarily to lessen the impact of growth slump in European market by sharing high fixed research and development costs and reducing overheads.

At times, strategic alliance is stuck to escape from the rigorous rules and regulations of the host country preventing the entry of foreign players. For example, Indian government laws preventing foreign retailers and insurance companies from foraying in Indian market forced the formation of JVs between Tata & AIG, ICICI and Lombard, Bajaj and Allianz, and Bharti Wal-Mart.

Another advantage of JV is that the partners can access to financial and other resources easily and economically. At times, companies in emerging economies lack capital to expand. A JV or a strategic investment will infuse capital to the local operations and make it more profitable. In an emerging economy, a local partner provides distribution network, human capital and government links as its investment in the JV, while the foreign partner provides the capital and knowledge.

The greatest advantage of a JV is that complementary strengths of the partners help them in bolstering their competitive position in the offshore market, as is manifest from the alliance between Sanyo Electric Company Ltd. of Japan and BPL Ltd. of India (Illustrative Capsule 14.5).

ILLUSTRATIVE CAPSULE 14.5

JV BETWEEN SANYO ELECTRIC COMPANY LTD. AND BPL LTD.

On July 27, 2004 BPL Ltd. announced a landmark partnership with Sanyo Electric Company Ltd. of Japan to create a JV for the colour television business in India. As per the agreement, BPL would transfer its existing colour television business undertaking to this JV, constituting the BPL brand for CTV business, manufacturing, sales, service, marketing and distribution infrastructure. Both BPL and Sanyo would be equal equity partners in the JV with the intention to create one of India's leading and most technologically advanced consumer electronics company.

On the signing of this partnership, BPL CMD announced, "We have cemented our close long-term relationship with Sanyo through this agreement and believe that Sanyo and BPL, working together, will create an impressive platform of global, technologically advanced products for the Indian consumer."

He further said, "The rapid growth in the CTV market in India offers a great opportunity to BPL with its brand, sales, distribution, marketing, service and manufacturing infrastructure and Sanyo's state of art of technologies and R&D capabilities to enhance the product offering, increase the market share and achieve number one status in the Indian market".

The two JV partners have had a relationship since 1982 and Sanyo provided latest technologies to BPL for colour televisions, refrigerators, compressors, washing machines, alkaline batteries, and so on.

Sanyo believes that its entry into India in a strategic alliance with BPL is a major step in Sanyo's strategy to enter new international markets. Thus, with BPL, it desires to achieve number one status in the Indian consumer electronic market.

A granular view of prominent strategic alliances and JVs forged recently between Indian and foreign organisations may be had from Illustrative Capsule 14.6.

ILLUSTRATIVE CAPSULE **14.6**

MAJOR STRATEGIC ALLIANCES AND JOINT VENTURES BETWEEN INDIAN AND FOREIGN COMPANIES FORGED RECENTLY

BHEL, Toshiba tie up for power distribution business (Feb 17, 2010)

Nissan to build ₹2.5 lakh car with Ashok Leyland (March 03, 2010)

Reliance tie up with US Sports Co. IMG Worldwide (March 15, 2010)

Bharti tie up with Dow Jones (March 18, 2010)

Airtel tie up with Apple for 3G phone (March 20, 2010)

Rolls-Royce, HAL tie up to form engine parts venture (March 31, 2010)

Infosys signs 3-year services part with Microsoft (April 15, 2010)

SAIL tie up with POSCO (May, 2010)

LIC mutual tie up with Nomura for fund management (May 29, 2010)

Tata Comm joins hands with Google (July 16, 2010)

BHEL, GE unit sign pact for oil, gas compressors (July 22, 2010)

NSE tie up with London Stock Exchange of cross listing (July 29, 2010)

ITC Infotech, Oracle join hands (August 19, 2010)

RCom joins hands with Nokia for Ovi Life Tools (August 21, 2010)

Kingfisher, British Airways sign code-sharing pact (September 05, 2010)

Wipro tie up with Oracle (September 11, 2010)

Managing Strategic Alliances and Joint Ventures (JVs)

Despite humungous potentiality of alliances and JVs as entry strategy in foreign markets and improving competitive position of the partners, large scale failures (over 53%) are reported[8], culminating in the fall out of the JV earlier than expected. The main reason why a JV fails is changes in partner's strategy. Often either one of the partners changes its strategy which makes this JV redundant. For example, in Ford-Mahindra JV, Ford wanted to expand the operations, but Mahindra wanted to focus more on SUV segment and did not want to invest for the expansion, thus forcing Ford to go alone. Likewise, Renault-French automaker—having forged partnership with Bajaj for the production of ultra low cost cars—seems to have decided to go solo on the project when its country head, Marc Nassif, sounded non-committal on the project in May, 2011 at the launch of the Fluence Sedan saying, "It may pull out if the car being developed and manufactured by Bajaj will not meet its expectations".

Very often, changes in conditions such as government regulations, access to technology or capital or gaining sufficient confidence by a partner to go alone subscribe to the failure of a JV. For example, TVS-Suzuki JV fell apart when TVS learnt how to design motorbikes on its own. TVS designed *Victor* on its own and it was a success.

Another popular cause why a JV falls apart is when the JV is successful. In such a circumstance, the JV becomes a cash cow and both the parties now want greater control over it. This often results in a nasty fight for control and in the process the JV falls apart. Alternatively, when a JV is not doing well, the partners start blaming each other and want to take over control to avert further deterioration.

In view of the above, success of a strategic alliance and joint venture hinges on how effectively long-term partnering relationships are managed. Managing strategic alliances involves two major stages, viz., pre-alliance tasks analysis, negotiation and decision-making and the post-alliance tasks of coordination, integration and adaptation. A detailed discussion in this respect has already been made in the preceding chapter.

Choice of mode of entry into a foreign market depends essentially upon the size of the firm and its exposure to international business, product life cycle, return on investment, level of risk and corporate policy of the firm.

Summary

In recent years, organisations across the globe are expanding their business abroad so as to penetrate in overseas markets and capture plethora of opportunities and gain market leadership. Besides, a host of other forces such as to access low cost financial and other resources, minimise business risks, capitalise on the core competencies and diverse economic, demographic and cultural factors, have spurred companies to move overseas.

However, foreign business in the fast changing global environment is susceptible to variety of problems and risks which need to be addressed prudently. Three strategic issues that merit serious attention while planning for foreign investment are: choosing product offering, choosing countries for investment and mode of entry.

There are three major product options, viz., broad-line global option, globally standardised product option and localised product option. Choice of a particular product strategy for overseas markets rests upon a host of factors including physical characteristics of the host country market and competitive, cultural, demographic and regulatory forces in the country. Above all, the corporate philosophy of a company also influences this decision.

While choosing a country for foreign business, the management need to consider a number of factors such as the firm's need, business climate of offshore countries, country risk and the firm's capabilities and its preference for a country promising highest return with minimum risk.

Another crucial decision regarding foreign business pertains to the mode of entry in foreign markets. There are several entry routes; the most prominent are export, licensing, franchising, management contracting, turnkey projects and strategic alliances, joint ventures and mergers and acquisitions. Choice of mode of entry depends, in the main, upon size of the firm and its exposure to international market, product life cycle, return on investment, level of risk and corporate policy of the firm.

Key Terms

Broad-line global product option	Licensing
Country risk	Localised product option
Export franchising	Management contract
Globally standardised product option	Strategic alliances
Joint venture	Turnkey project

Discussion Questions

1. Why should an organisation move abroad?
2. What are the strategic issues which need to be addressed before deciding to conduct foreign business?
3. Discuss, in brief, the various product options for a firm contemplating to enter into foreign markets.
4. Distinguish between globally standardised product option and localised product option.
5. What are the strategic considerations influencing a firm's decision to choose a foreign location?
6. How would you access the business climate of cross border countries?
7. What are the various modes of entry into foreign markets? Evaluate, in brief, the utility of each of these entry routes.
8. Why are strategic alliances and joint ventures (JVs) becoming more popular means to enter into overseas market? Illustrate with suitable examples.

References

1. George, Yip S., *Total Global Strategy*, Prentice-Hall Inc., New Jersey, 1995, p. 76.
2. Ibid, p. 83.
3. Terpastra, Vern, *International Dimensions of Marketing*, 2nd ed., PWS-Kent Publishing Company, Boston, p. 108, 1988.
4. Daniels, John D., Earnest W. Ogram Jr. and Lee H. Ralebaugh, "International Business: Environments and Operations", *Reading Mass*, Addison Wesley, pp. 371–75, 1976.
5. Brooks, Michael Z., *Selling Management Services Contracts in International Business*, John Wiley and Sons, New York, pp. 3–22, 1988.
6. Wright, Richard W. and Colin Russel, "Joint Ventures in Developing Countries: Realities and Responses", *Columbia Journal World Business*, 10, Spring, pp. 74–80, 1975.
7. Bamford, James, David Ernst and David G. Fubini, "Launching a World-class Joint Ventures", *Harvard Business Review*, February, p. 91, 2004.
8. Mc Cann, J.E., III, "The Growth of Acquisitions in Services", *Long Range Planning*, December, pp. 835–841, 1996.

Internet Resources

- *www.ge.com*
- *economictimes.indiatimes.com*
- *www.businessline.com*
- *www.business-standard.com*
- *www.bplworld.com*
- *www.thehindubusinessline.com*

15

Strategy and Corporate
Social Responsibility

LEARNING OBJECTIVES

The present Chapter aims at:

- Providing a succinct view of changing perceptions of Corporate Social Responsibility (CSR).
- Elucidating the fundamentals of CSR philosophy.
- Familiarising readers with the broad areas of CSR.
- Providing acquaintance with process of formulating strategy for social responsibility and its execution.
- Highlighting major CSR practices of Indian organisations.

CHANGING PARADIGMS OF CORPORATE SOCIAL RESPONSIBILITY (CSR)

Corporate social responsibility (CSR) has in recent years, emerged as an epicentric theme in the business community around the world and is gradually being mainstreamed that the corporate strategy, howsoever carefully crafted, will be of little help in a company's long-term survival and success if it is not tempered by a sincere and unswerving concern for public interest and social good. However, the overall philosophy of CSR as "doing good" to the society or "giving back" to the society originated in the corporate world way back towards the end of the 19th century. As Europe and America started spawning industrial giants, hundreds of trusts cropped up to use part of the corporation's profits to help the underprivileged and making the world a better place. The origin of the concept of CSR in India can be connected to the thinking of the founder of the Tata Group—one of the oldest and most respected business houses in India—Jamshedji N. Tata that "in a free enterprise, the community is not just another stakeholder in business but is, in fact, the very purpose of its existence".

Over the years, approach to CSR and so also its contours have undergone metamorphic change and CSR is coming out of the purview of doing social good and is fast becoming a business necessity. This is because of the increasing role of business enterprises, particularly in the day-to-day life of the people at large and the growing awareness of the scale of ecological problems and of the limits to natural resources caused by national and multinational companies that have made often the target by various pressure groups for anti-pollution measures, environment protection and conservation. There has also been growing realisation of the organisations in recent few years to employ CSR as a strategic tool to enhance their credibility in the society and improve competitive advantage. To cope with the backlash against globalisation, more and more MNCs are now adopting strategies that go beyond short-term profit maximisation. One such strategy is to embrace social business enterprise approach that broadly conflates the interests of MNCs with socio-economic development. Thus, there has been a paradigm shift in the approach to CSR from 'profit only' point of view and philanthropy to 'triple bottom line and humanity-oriented perspective'.

For effective enmeshing of the CSR with corporate strategy, it would be germane for the corporate management to have deep insights into various approaches to CSR.

APPROACHES TO CSR

Let us study the different approaches to CSR.

Profit Only Point of View

According to this viewpoint, there is one and only one social responsibility of business: to use its resources and engage in activities designed to increase its profits so long as it stays within the rules of the game. Adam Smith was an early proponent of this view. He opined that, "by directing the business in such a manner as its produce may be one of the greatest value, businessman intends only his gain... By pursuing his own interest, he frequently promotes that of the society more effectively than he really intends to promote it".[1]

Adam Smith's emphasis on the pursuit of self-interest does not result in a conflict but in cooperation because he believed that perfect competition in a market, while satisfying the interest of the businessman, would further the common good. The market mechanism, according to Smith, is capable of responding automatically to changes in society needs.

A similar view was held also by Milton Friedman who believed that the business entrepreneurs have only one social responsibility: to use their resources and engage in activities designed to increase their profits—engage in open and free competition without deception or fraud.[2] Friedman's contention was based on a laissez-faire worldwide economy. In his view, a business person who acts 'responsibly by cutting the price of the firm's product to prevent inflation or by making expenditures to reduce pollution, or by hiring the hard-core unemployed is spending the shareholders' money for a general social interest. By taking on the burden of these social costs, the business becomes less efficient—either prices go up to pay for the increased social costs or investment in new activities and research is postponed. These results negatively affect—perhaps fatally—the long-term efficiency of a business.[3]

Thus, according to the above view supporting the economic role of a business enterprise, the socially responsible business is one which is concerned primarily with efficiency and providing its owners with the best possible return on investment within the parameters established by law and ethical conduct. According to the proponents of the profit viewpoint, by making a profit, a company creates thousands of jobs. It imparts valuable skills to its employees. It pays crores in taxes and improves the lives of millions of satisfied customers with its products and services. This is an enormous service to society. If some shareholders get rich on the way, so what? Thus, a company's social responsibility is to make profits legally, not to harm nature, and uphold the highest standards of governance.

Philanthropic View

According to the Steward principle, it is the moral responsibility of the business community and other wealthy people to consider themselves as the stewards (caretakers) of the society's wealth and manage it prudently to multiply this wealth.[4]

In today's corporate world, Bill Gates and Warren Buffet of the US have emerged as the giant philanthropists who contributed more than 90% of their funds to the Bill and Melinda Gates Foundation for the social cause. They are currently on their mission to appeal to all rich individuals around the world to contribute atleast half of their wealth for the welfare of the society. In India, Tatas, Birlas, Godrej and Wipro have been exemplary philanthropists.

The $72 billion Tata group sowed the seed of constructive philanthropy—from setting up an endowment fund to improve education—in 1892 for building prominent educational institutions, hospitals and performing art centres in the country. For the Birlas, philanthropy dates back to 1940s when G.D. Birla espoused the trusteeship concept of management. Lately, Wipro Chairman, Azim Premji, made philanthropic contribution of $2 billion to his trust for improving school education in India. In case of Godrej, 25% of the shareholding of Godrej group's holding company, which owns a large part of the shares of all its companies, is held for many decades by the Pirojsha Godrej Foundation where the main philanthropic activity is aimed at education, health care and environment.

However, philanthropic view of social responsibility should not be misconstrued as alms-giving. In fact, philanthropic initiative spotlights long-term interests of the organisation.

Triple Bottom Line (TBL) Perspective

This concept of social responsibility is represented by economic success, environmental responsibility and social commitment. Since inception, the Tata Group had placed equal importance on maximising financial returns as on fulfilling its social and environmental responsibilities. Through its TBL initiative, the Tata Group aims at harmonising environmental factors by reducing the negative impact of its commercial activities and initiating drives for encouraging environment-friendly practices.

While carrying forward the philanthropic philosophy of Birla Group, Aditya Birla weaved in the concept of 'sustainable livelihood' which transcended cheque book philanthropy. He was of the view that channelising resources to ensure that people have the wherewithal to make both ends meet would be more productive. Kumar Manglam Birla institutionalised the concept of TBL accountability, texturing the interests of all the stakeholders into the Group's fabric.

Quality of Life Perspective

In recent years, a new concept of social responsibility, known as "Quality of Life", has come into vogue. This concept of social responsibility goes beyond mere trusteeship and accountability. According to this view, business is a partner with government, education and other social institutions in solving society's problems and creating a better quality of life for everyone.

The essence of this approach is "what is good for society is good for the company".[5] Enlightened self-interest is the crux of the approach. It can be described as the socially responsible actions of the firm that cannot be justified on the basis of economic cost and revenue alone.

Keeping in view Quality of Life perspective, Archie Carrol proposes that business organisations have four responsibilities:[6]

(i) *Economic responsibilities:* To produce goods and services of value to the society so that the firm can repay its creditors and shareholders.

(ii) *Legal responsibilities:* To obey government laws.

(iii) *Ethical responsibilities:* To follow the generally held beliefs about behaviour in a society.

(iv) *Discretionary responsibilities:* These are purely voluntary obligations a firm assumes, such as philanthropic contributions, training the unemployed and providing day care centres.

Carroll lists these fours responsibilities in order of priority (Figure 15.1). A business firm must first make a profit to satisfy its economic responsibilities. To continue in existence, the firm must follow the laws, thus fulfilling its legal responsibilities. According to Carroll, the firm should look to fulfilling its social responsibilities which include both ethics and discretions, but not economic and legal responsibilities.

Economic (Must do)	Legal (Have to do)	Ethical (Should do)	Discretionary (Might do)

Figure 15.1 Components of business social responsibilities.

Social Business Enterprise Perspective

In the wake of globalisation of business and growing influence of MNCs in day-to-day lives of the people, an innovative perspective of social responsibility, based on humanity-oriented decision-making approach, is now being pursued by the MNCs to escape from the wrath of the society.

Drawing cue from late C.K. Prahalad's theory of the **Bottom of the pyramid** which advocated that the poor have the right to be treated as consumers and that it made good business sense than charity if businesses targeted the poor as a market. MNCs have, of late, adopted the strategy of business of humanity which broadly conflates the interests of MNCs with socio-economic development. Humanity in business decision-making focuses on safety, quality, diversity, environment, social sustainability, gender equality and integrity and draws attention to the bottom of the pyramid.

At a recent meeting of the Business of Humanity Forum, the need to shift the primary focus of business decisions from making short-term accounting profits to putting human beings back into the equation, an approach better for business and humanity in general, was emphasised.

Coca-Cola's strategy to become water-neutral in its operations on a global basis is a case in point. This strategy signifies returning water used in the manufacturing process back to the environment in a form that sustains aquatic life and helps protect watersheds where the company operates.

Thus, over the years, concept of corporate social responsibility has transformed from philanthropy and charity to the strategy of business of humanity which encompasses all those actions that would maximise the probability of the company's long-term survival and sustained growth. A peep into the fundamentals of Corporate Social Responsibility (CSR) philosophy will further make the conceptual understanding of CSR crystal clear.

FUNDAMENTALS OF CSR PHILOSOPHY

(i) Organisations, like individuals, depend for their sustenance and growth on the support and goodwill of the communities of which they are integral part and must pay back this generosity in every way they can.

(ii) CSR is about legitimacy and responsibility of an enterprise towards its various stakeholders and society at large. An enterprise is said to be legitimate if it is responsive and sensitive to social issues.

(iii) CSR is about enterprise behaviour towards safeguarding interests of different stakeholders. As a matter of fact, it signifies commitment of the organisation to the society beyond the basic economic functions of producing and supplying goods and services.

(iv) CSR is self-regulatory in nature and calls for more than complying with the legal requirements. It expects the organisation to own moral responsibility to serve different stakeholders to the best of its competence.

(v) CSR initiative is proactive and structured with well-defined policies, strategies, and set goals and sanctioned budgets for carrying into effect CSR programmes.

(vi) CSR is a never-ending process. It is not an occasional act of charity or one-time token financial contribution to a local school, a hospital or an NGO.

AREAS OF CSR

Corporate organisations have a responsibility towards their direct stakeholders, viz., employees, suppliers and vendors, dealers as well as shareholders, and indirect stakeholders, viz., communities living near the product facility, consumers and others whose livelihood could be influenced by the operations of the company. A company to ensure sustained growth must identify major areas of CSR and take suitable measures.

Consumers

Organisational practices affect consumers in several areas including pricing, advertising and performance of products. Although many laws and regulations govern managerial actions in these areas, these have not been effective to satisfy the consumers' expectations. A company is expected to charge reasonable price from the consumers and refrain from deceptive advertising. It should guarantee its product performance.

Employees

To employees, an organisation has the duty to provide fair compensation and safe working conditions and to provide avenues for promotion. These benefits are generally sought to be ensured through labour legislation. However, the extent of these rights in employees' organisational setting is not only a matter of law, but is also a matter of ethics and social responsibility.

Suppliers

A firm is also responsible to those who supply raw materials, machines and equipment and finances. It is expected to ensure timely payment of the dues. To the suppliers of funds, the firm has responsibility for payment of interest and dividend regularly. They also expect high degree of transparency in the firm's operations.

Community Development

Corporate organisations have to play active role in national building and socio-economic development. They should proactively promote public interests by contributing to development of community, particularly in the areas of health, education, and infrastructure development (supplying potable water, constructing roads, setting up schools and hospitals and basic housing). They are expected to build the capacities of the poor of the communities and provide suitable opportunities to them to improve their quality of life.

Environment

In view of increasing global warming and environmental degradation caused by carbon emissions by two critical sectors of the economy—energy and transport—and fast depleting forestry resources, corporate organisations are expected to be environmental friendly. They must accept the responsibility to ensure that their activities do not adversely affect the environment and also take various measures to mitigate carbon emissions and focus on sources of renewal energy such as solar energy, wind energy, nuclear, retrofitting, and building all coal-based power plants with a still experimental technology of carbon capture and storage. Companies should proactively engage in reforesting of the forestland so as to replenish the forest resources. So as to reduce cost involved in developing clean energy, corporate organisations should pursue collaborative approach.

Rightfully, national governments along with MNCs have, of late, focused their attention on low carbon development and 'sustainability', and efforts are on to evolve clear development technology.

STRATEGY FOR SOCIAL RESPONSIBILITY

Corporate social responsibility is not a cosmetic; it must be rooted in a company's values. It must make a difference to the way it does business. Responsible business, as noted earlier, is a form of corporate self-regulation which has to be integrated into the business model. Whatever companies intend to do for the society, have to be related to their core business. It is, therefore, imperative for companies to adopt strategic approach involving the employees in long-term process of positive social transition. The following strategic steps should be taken:

Assessment of Economic and Social Environment

Ideally, CSR policy should function as a built-in self-regulating mechanism in which companies would monitor and ensure their support to law and ethical standards. The management should, therefore, make critical evaluation of the impact of its activities on the community where it has its unit or is planning to set up. It should also scan the environment existing in the community where the company intends to operate. In this scanning, attempt should be made to determine social activities not required or suggested by the government and which are not directly linked to enhancing the efficient operation of the company.

Survey of the values, notions and preferences of policymakers and stakeholders including government, politicians, workers, managers, union leaders, suppliers, customers and community leaders, business leaders, media people, academics, and the like should be undertaken to determine precisely their attitudes towards the company.

Appraisal of the Company's Policies and Competencies

The management must make dispassionate assessment of the company's policies, procedures and practices including the management of the public affairs function, management accountability and rewards for social programmes. The company's existing skills in managing public affairs and internal communications need to be scanned so as to determine their adequacy to undertake social programmes.

Formulating CSR Objectives and Strategies

Based on the above, the corporate management should articulate vividly vision and mission of the organisation to indicate: what it intends to do to foster the welfare of the society, what will be the thrust areas, what it wants to achieve and how its objectives will be achieved. CSR vision and mission of Aditya Birla Group are, "to actively contribute to the social and economic development of the communities in which they operate. In so doing, build a better, sustainable way of life for the weaker sections of the society and raise the country's human development index".

Once vision and mission of the company are spelt out, the management should formulate long-term specific plan to achieve the company's objectives. For example, Tata Motors laid down a detailed plan for protecting environment and reducing pollution with a focus on soil and water conservation, extensive tree plantation, setting up effluent treatment facilities in its plants, conserving resources and recycling materials, developing alternative fuel engine technologies. Tata Motors has directed all its suppliers to package their products in alternative materials instead of wood (Illustrative Capsule 15.1).

ILLUSTRATIVE CAPSULE 15.1

CSR PHILOSOPHY, AIMS, THRUST AREAS AND STRATEGY OF LEADING CORPORATE ORGANISATIONS OF INDIA

TATA STEEL

Philosophy of CSR

J.N. Tata: "In a free enterprise, the community is not just another shareholder in business but is in fact the very purpose of its existence".

J.R.D. Tata: "What came from people has to go back to the people many times."

"No success in material terms is worthwhile unless it serves the interests of the country and its people"

Aim of Tata's CSR Initiatives:

To be socially and morally responsible to consumers, employees, shareholders, local community & society with a view to improving quality of life in the communities.

Thrust Areas of CSR:

- Reducing pollution through (i) Introduction of cleaner engines; (ii) Setting up effluent treatment facilities.
- Environmental protection through (i) Soil and water conservation programmes; (ii) Extensive tree plantation drives.
- Community development through (i) Self-initiated cottage industries; (ii) Providing self-help groups.
- Providing service to society at large.

CSR Strategy

Integrating social responsibility with corporate strategy and business processes.

ADITYA BILRA GROUP

Philosophy of CSR

G.D. Birla: "Trusteeship Concept"

Aditya Birla: "Concept of Sustainable Livelihood"

Kumar Mangalam Birla: "Concept of Triple Bottom Line"

Aim of Birla Group CSR Initiatives:

To build a better, sustainable way of life for the weaker sections of society and raise the country's human development index.

Focus is on the all-round development of the communities around the plants.

Thrust Areas of CSR:

- Rural development through
  (i) Education
  (ii) Health & Family welfare
  (iii) Sustainable development and livelihoods
  (iv) Water conservation

- Community development through
  – Construction of roads, dams, community centres, houses, electricity

- Social causes: widow/dowry-less marriages, women empowerment.

CSR Strategy:

CSR is imbedded in corporate strategy of the Group carried out under the aegis of the Aditya Birla Group Centre For Community Initiatives & Rural Development. All Group Companies are implementing bodies.

Follows collaborative approach, partners in development are govt. bodies, district authorities, village panchayat and the end beneficiaries.

Collaboration with UNICEF, World Bank, Care India, Habitat for Humanity International.

ITC

Philosophy of CSR

Wants to be one of the major economic engines in the Indian society and make a positive contribution.

Aim of CSR Initiatives

To position as a most valued and admired corporation that serves all stakeholders—the nation, its people, partners (farmers, tribals, distributors, stockists and vendors), customers and shareholders.

Thrust Areas of CSR:

- Rural development through
  (i) Helping 40 lakh farmers and many tribals and disadvantaged farmers in turning their barren lands into productive source of income;
  (ii) Empowering rural women;
  (iii) Support to make schools exciting for village children.
- Environment protection
  ITC is water-positive, carbon positive and a zero solid waste producer.
- Water conservation & recycling

- Conserving energy through
  - (i) Reducing specific energy consumption;
  - (ii) Undertaking initiatives to use renewable energy such as bio-mass, wind and solar power.

CSR Strategy

ITC has woven its corporate social responsibility initiatives into its business plans.
CSR at ITC is not seen as a cost centre.

RELIANCE INDUSTRIES

Philosophy of CSR

Organisations, like individuals, depend for their survival, sustenance and growth on the support and goodwill of the communities of which they are an integral part, and must pay back this generosity in every way they can.

Aim of CSR Initiatives

To bring about qualitative changes and support the underprivileged.

Thrust Areas of CSR:

- Community development through close and continuous interaction
  - (i) Drinking water
  - (ii) Improving village infrastructure
- Environment protection
  - (i) Effluent treatment
  - (ii) Treatment of hazardous waste
  - (iii) Tree plantation
- Education
  - (i) Professionalised and Institutionalised Training
  - (ii) Skill development of local youths
  - (iii) EDPs
- Health
  Health centres at most of the manufacturing plants to address various health problems. It operates Dhirubhai Ambani Hospital at Lodhival and renders quality medical services to the rural population and highway accident victims.
- Women empowerment
  Conduct training programmes to help rural women to be self-sustaining and generate income for themselves and support their families.
- Rural development
  By RRDT
  Acting as an exemplary NGO to improve the rural infrastructure under the Govt. of Gujarat's rural development plans through:
  - (i) Construction of roads
  - (ii) Anganwadis
  - (iii) Drinking water facilities

CSR Strategy

CSR is integrated into the very core of business objectives and strategy.
Environmental protection is an integral part of the planning, design, construction, operation and maintenance of all the projects.
CSR teams at all manufacturing divisions.
All social responsibility activities are planned and monitored by Dhirubhai Ambani Foundation.

Dr. REDDY'S LABORATORIES

Philosophy of CSR

Do what you want to do the most now
"Give back to society".

Aim of CSR Initiatives

To:

alleviate hunger,
create livelihoods,
provide education,
access to safe drinking water,
pull back children from hazardous industries.

Thrust Areas:

- Training and development through livelihood advancement business school
- Safe drinking water
- Create women entrepreneurs
- Assist schools to provide education to poor students

CSR Strategy

Reddy's philanthropic initiatives are ventures that he or his family has funded out of personal money. In some cases supplemented with donations from Dr. Reddy's Laboratories and other large companies and individuals.

Dr. Reddy is planning to put in place an institutionalised structure and corpus to keep these activities going. Also planning to set up Kallan Anji Reddy Foundation to which all or part of his 10% stake (about ₹100 crore) will be transferred.

ONGC

Philosophy of CSR

The company would have an abiding commitment to health, safety and environment to enrich quality of community life.

Thrust Areas of CSR Initiatives

At Corporate Level:

(i) Disaster relief management
(ii) Water management

At Plant Level:

(i) Environment protection
   - Through reduction of pollution
   - Conservation of resources through utilisation of waste
(ii) Safety
   Set up the Institute of Petroleum Safety, Health and Environmental Management in 1980 with the objective of improving the safety, health and environment standards in the Indian Petroleum industry.
(iii) Other CSR Initiatives
   Promoting games and sports.

CSR Strategy

ONGC formulated a corporate citizenship policy in 2004 to provide direction to its CSR initiatives.

Executing Strategy

So as to execute the CSR strategy, the top management should draw up operational plans, stating the targets and specific programmes. For example, Reliance Industries has laids down detailed programmes for regions where it has its plants regarding drinking water, construction of schools and hospitals, development of village infrastructure, effluent treatment, tree plantations, teachers' training programmes, and so on (Illustrative Capsule 15.1).

After specifying programmes, a budget for each activity will have to be prepared showing resources to be allocated for different programmes. It should also state anticipated results. Accountability will have to be fixed to senior executives to achieve the results.

The task of organising social programmes may be assigned to public relations department consisting of senior executives and some specialists.

MONITORING CSR STRATEGY

Constant surveillance by the top management of corporate strategies and operational plans as also executive actions with business ethics should also be undertaken. The focus of the monitoring should be on identification of the gaps, if any, between the action plans and the actual results, and the gaps, if any, between current public welfare policies and the expectations of the various interest groups. Monitoring Committee comprising top executives should be constituted to perform this job.

A bird's eye view of the CSR strategy may be had from Figure 15.2.

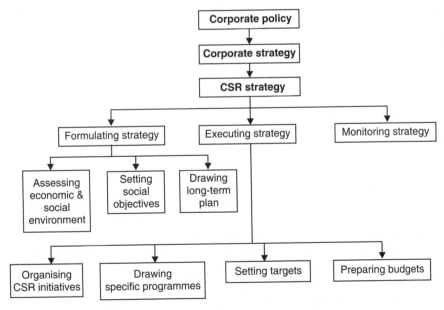

Figure 15.2 The CSR strategy of a firm.

HIGHLIGHTS OF CSR PRACTICES IN INDIA

Nevertheless, CSR is not new to India, and the track record of corporate India in this sphere has been less than exemplary. Barring a few notable and enlightened business houses including Tata, Birla, ITC, Godrej and Oil & Natural Gas Commission (ONGC), CSR initiatives are ad hoc and chief executive driven rather than integrated with the corporate strategy.

Corporate India investment in socially-oriented programmes is woefully low, ranging between 0.1% and 2% with an exception of 19% by Tata Steel as against the standard norm of 3%–5% of the profits.

CSR in India is still one of the least understood initiatives in the corporate sector. It is mostly philanthropic in nature and not business-centric. Because of accent on philanthropy and absence of well-planned process, implementers are not accountable to their stakeholders and CSR initiatives lack transparency.

What is most important to note is that public sector undertakings are paying greater attention to socially responsible projects than their private counterparts. Further, older companies and those with higher turnover have been found relatively more socially responsible.

Preferred areas for CSR in India have been meeting environmental standards, adhering to labour standards and donating money to social causes. The other activities taken up included education and health, natural resource management, infrastructure development, community support and livelihood-based activities.

Prominent focus targets for the most significant activities of the companies are economically weaker sections of the society, company employees, children, rural communities, people affected by natural calamities, disease-affected people and community work near company's plants.

It is revealing to note that in India there is absence of negative impact on a company, if it does not actively give back to society. This is in sharper contrast to what exists in advanced countries where CSR activities are typically focused more around limiting the negative impacts of industrial and corporate activities and/or there is strong business motivation.

Illustrative capsule 15.1 provides a glimpse of CSR philosophy, aims, thrust areas and strategy of some of the illustrious corporate organisations of India.

Summary

Corporate social responsibility (CSR) has, of late, emerged as an epicentric theme in the business world. The concept of CSR has recorded cataclysmic change over the years and is fast becoming a business necessity. CSR is, in fact, about legitimacy and responsibility of an enterprise towards its various stakeholders and society at large. Compliance with laws and regulations is not a part of CSR initiative. It is doing something voluntarily for social development. CSR initiative needs to be productive and well-planned. It is about integrating with business plans of the enterprise. It is, therefore, imperative for companies to adopt strategic approach involving the employees in the long-run process of positive social transition.

Making strategy for social responsibility calls for assessment of economic and social environment to ascertain the likely impact of the company's operations on the community it plans to operate and also the expectations of the policy framers and stakeholders. The company should also scan its competencies to carry out the expected social programmes. Based on the assessment, the management formulates strategies of the company and draws out specific time-bound programmes to satisfy the needs of the society. The task of organising social programmes may be assigned to the public relations department of the company. Constant surveillance by the top management of social responsibility programmes is necessary in order to ensure that progress is made as per the schedules, and the gaps, if any, are corrected without loss of any time.

Nevertheless, CSR is not new to India, and the track record of corporate India has been less exemplary. Barring a few notable and enlightened business houses including Tata, Birla, ITC, Reliance and ONGC, the efforts have largely been limited to setting up a hospital or two, a school or a college, a few scholarships, adoption of a few villages to provide some business amenities or launching a few public communication campaigns. While all of these efforts are laudable, they are not enough to make a visible impact on India. With global warming and environmental degradation engaging national and international attention, many large businesses have, of late, focused their attention on 'sustainability'. With many Indian companies now reaching billion or multi-billion dollar revenue scale, they should consider deploying some of their formidable innovation, product development, manufacturing, distributing, marketing and managerial skills towards coming out with truly revolutionary, paradigm-altering products and services providing effective solutions to hundreds of millions of Indians at the bottom of the pyramid. Merely allocating a few crores of rupees or a couple of million dollars for product R&D will, sadly, not be enough.

Unfortunately, CSR in India in most of the cases is even today regarded as a price of rhetoric intended to placate environmentalists and human right campaigners. To make companies realise that CSR should form normal facet of business, the proposed amendment of the Companies Bill is including provisions to mandate companies to invest atleast 2% of their average net profits in CSR. Of course, a rule-based approach to CSR has its advantages, but few would disagree that CSR ultimately depends on the personal integrity of the people who manage a company.

Key Terms

Charity principle

Philanthropic view

Profit-only point of view

Quality of life perspective

Social business enterprise perspective

Stewardship principle

Trusteeship concept

Discussion Questions

1. How has the concept of corporate social responsibility (CSR) changed over times?

2. Outline different views about a firm's social responsibility. What is your perception of social responsibility of a business organisation?

3. "CSR is coming out of the purview of doing social good and is fast becoming a business necessity". Comment.

4. Discuss triple bottom line perspective of CSR.

5. What are the contours of social business enterprise perspective of CSR?

6. "The economic role of a business organisation does not conflict with its social responsibility". Comment.

7. What are the fundamentals of CSR philosophy?

8. Discuss relevant areas of CSR.

9. How should strategy for CSR be formulated? What measures need to be taken to ensure its effective execution?

10. Critically evaluate CSR practices in Indian organisations.

References

1. Smith, Adam, *The Wealth of Nations*, The Bobbs-Merril Book Company, New York, 1961, Chapter 2.

2. Friedman, Milton, *Capitalism and Freedom*, University of Chicago Press, Chicago, p. 133, 1962.

3. ———, "The Social Responsibility of Business is to Increase its Profits", *New York Time Magazine*, 13 September, 1970.

4. Frederic, William C., *Corporate Social Responsibility and Business Ethics*, Lexington Books, Lexing Pon, MA, USA, pp. 142–161, 1987.

5. Ibid.

6. Carroll, A.B., "A Three-Dimensional Conceptual Model of Corporate Performance," *Academy of Management Review*, October, pp. 497–505, 1979.

7. *Business Standard*, June 10, 2010.

8. World Business Council for Sustainable Development, "Corporate Social Responsibility: Making Good Business Sense", www.wbscd.ct, January, p. 7, 2000. (accessed October 10, 2003).

SECTION IV

Strategy Implementation and Strategic Audit

16

Strategy Implementation
A Synoptic View

LEARNING OBJECTIVES

The present Chapter aims at:

- Providing an insight into strategy implementation as a source of organisational success.
- Acquainting readers with process of implementing strategy.
- Familiarising them with basics of strategy implementation success.
- Providing an understanding of various approaches to implementation of strategy.
- Creating an awareness of problems in strategy implementation.

STRATEGY IMPLEMENTATION AS CONCOMITANT TO COMPETITIVE ADVANTAGE

Importance of strategic management cannot and does not come to an end with articulation of vision and objectives and formulation of strategies to achieve the objectives. A corporate strategy, howsoever sound it may be, will be of little value to an enterprise if it has not been properly implemented. In fact, the first attribute tested by Thomas Peters and Robert Waterman as distinctive of excellent and innovative companies is related to the corporate view of implementation. They contend that excellent companies have a bias for execution for getting on with the job.

Strategy implementation denotes putting the selected strategy into action. It is concerned with operational aspect of strategy management for achieving the desired results. It has been considered by many management scholars as a management activity involving organisation and execution[1] of a complex problem-solving process of group interaction[2] and combination of sub-activities of the organisation structure and organisational process involving motivation and control.[3]

Strategy implementation is about aggregation of the activities and choices required for putting strategy into action. It is the process of translating strategic plan into action through development of programmes, budgets, and procedures and through creating organisational arrangements that allow the firm to pursue its strategy most effectively.

Thus, strategy implementation is action focused, making things happen, and a task that tests the management's capability to enforce the strategic plan.

Strategy formulation and strategy implementation are inseparable aspects of strategic management and are interdependent upon each other. Formulation and implementation merge into a fluid process of learning through which creative strategies the evolve.[4] Changes in current strategy to achieve the desired results demand changes in the organisation structure, new leadership style, new culture and new process. Likewise, the strategy implementation bears upon the strategy making process. At times, the companies tend to adopt a strategy which can be effectively executed with the help of the present structure and process.

In escalating competitive and complex business environment, the key to success of an organisation hinges essentially on how speedily and efficaciously it can execute its strategy. A brilliant strategy, blockbuster product or breakthrough technology can put a firm on the competitive map but only solid execution can hold it there firmly.[5] Absence of execution is the single biggest obstacle to success and the cause of most of the disappointments that are mistakenly attributed to other causes. Excellence in the execution of a strategy in terms of articulation of objectives and goals, putting in place right infrastructure, people and resources, alignment of the entire organisation to corporate objectives and goals, ensuring continuous free flow of information across organisation boundaries, creating people friendly environment and always remaining focused on the strategy execution, irrespective of changing circumstances can be a powerful source of competitive advantage inasmuch as it leads to cost reduction, product differentiation, improved performance and consequent higher consumer satisfaction. Inept and delayed execution of a project may not only cause enormous losses but at times be responsible for the decay of the organisation. Around 90% of organisations have been found either stagnating or decaying due to poor execution.[6] Air India, which was once the most effective and trusted airline services in the country, lost its sheen during post-liberalisation period mainly due to its inefficacious execution of the strategy including extraordinary delay in procurement of fleets, less utilisation of its aircraft, high operating costs and ineffective human resource management.

Likewise, Haldia Petro Chemicals in West Bengal is a classic case of delay in execution, costing the government and investors thousand crores of rupees; the project cost having soared from ₹2,000 crore when it was originally conceived to over ₹10,000 crore when it got implemented. National Highway Corridor Plans and Bangalore International Airport are other two important examples of delayed execution costing the exchequer avoidable enormous loss.

Very lately, improper execution of strategy including structural issues like raw material procurement has landed Ispat Industries in bankruptcy like situation forcing it to sell its 41.29% stake to JSW steel.[7]

In refreshing contrast to this, timely and meticulous execution has enabled organisations to reap fruitful results. Reliance Industries's Jamnagar Refinery project is an illustrious example of effective execution. The project got completed in 24 months making it a record of sorts in the petrochemical industry worldwide. It turned out to be a giant masterstroke that helped Reliance Industries grow leaps and bounds in revenues and profits and emerge eventually as an undisputed leader in the private sector in the country.

In the domain of public property management, one example of executive excellence is that of the Cochin International Airport (Illustrative Capsule 16.1).

ILLUSTRATIVE CAPSULE 16.1

COCHIN INTERNATIONAL AIRPORT—A CASE OF EXCELLENT EXECUTION

Cochin International Airport is a novel project in the history of Indian civil aviation built outside the ambit of the governanment. The airport was owned by Cochin International Airport Ltd. (CIAL), a public limited company in which the government of Kerala was the single largest shareholder. The airport required ₹23 billion and a span of six years to be completed. The traffic was a mere 76 flights a week when it started its operations in June 1999.

The passenger traffic stood at 4,86,000 in 1999–'00. It went up to 13,30,000 in 2003–04. CIAL had declared its maiden dividend of 8% in June 2004 and became the first companys in the country's infrastructure sector to declare a dividend within such a short period of operations. This was because of concerted efforts made by the government and the management.

Many private sector organisations such as Bata India, Dalmia Cement Ltd. and Dr. Reddy's Labs could successfully turnaround their business due to effective execution including restructuring management set up.

It is also important to note that strategy can never be sustainable strategy unless it is backed by successful execution. Lessons learnt during the initial stages of execution should be used as inputs to alter/modify/overhaul strategy. An interesting example is the bitter lessons learnt by organised Indian retail in the last few years (Illustrative Capsule 16.2).

ILLUSTRATIVE CAPSULE 16.2

ORGANISED INDIAN RETAIL'S FAILURE TO INCORPORATE EXECUTION LESSONS

Indian organised retail story took off with a bang with the launch of Reliance Retail, followed by a slew of other big retail players like Aditya, Birla, Bharti, Wal-Mart, Tatas, and so on.

Indian retail strategists opined that retail was getting organised, threatening the business of the neighbourhood store which would not be able to compete on scores of economies of scale and a whole new customer experience.

Customers did throng the stores, especially when their unique promotions were launched like Big Bazaar during days 'mahabachat' (massive saving), but they continued to patronise their neighbourhood shops.

Unorganised retailers in the vicinity of organised retailers did experience a decline in their volume of business and profit in the initial years after the entry of large organised retailers. But the adverse impact in sales and profit weakened over-time.

Big Indian retailers failed to take notice of this. Customers kept flocking to organised retail but repeat buying was not robust. Any business, which does not generate robust repeat sales, is a leaking pot. But oblivious to this, big retailers continued scaling up, implementing their staggering targets of reaching an X number of outlets.

Size and scale, the strategy proclaimed, will bring volumes. It did not.

The neighbourhood unorganised retailer would suffer badly as customers will plumb for great shopping experiences. This did not happen.

Besides the proximity, which is a major comparative advantage, the unorganised retailer displayed significant competitive strengths that included consumer goodwill, credit sales, amenability to bargaining, ability to sell loose items, convenient timings, and home delivery.

By the time big retailers started realising that numbers were not coming in and the strategy was not sustainable, a lot of money had already gone down the drain. Reliance had around 700 outlets, while Subhiksha was refuting sell-off rumours in media.

Big retailers failed to realise that the day they start executing strategy, they should immediately be open to learning lessons and incorporating them back. Unless the execution lessons are incorporated, a closed loop between strategy and execution is fully in place, it is the duty of the strategist to remain fully involved.

It may not be out of place to note that making strategy work is more difficult and time-consuming than strategy making. It is rather easy for a firm to design where they intend to go. The hard part is to get the organisation to act on the new priorities. It involves a wide range of managerial activities that needed to be addressed. It is so difficult for the companies to grasp this because there are more people involved in executing strategy today and execution takes larger than people expect. Political and organisational problems typically surface. When a strategy is developed, the management has to go throughout the organisation and through dozens of planners to make sure it is carried out. It takes time, one or two years or even more.

PROCESS OF STRATEGY IMPLEMENTATION

Once the strategy has been formulated, it has to be translated into action to achieve the desired results. For that to happen, specific goals related to critical processes and to the people, the technology and the organisational climate and culture need to be determined and communicated freely to all those to be involved in strategy execution.

This is to be followed by identifying and authorising resources for a portfolio of strategic initiatives intended to help achieve the strategy's objectives. A strategic initiative is a discretionary project or programme of finite duration designed to close a performance gap. It might focus on, say, developing a customer loyalty programme or training all employees in the six sigma quality management tools. Achieving an objective in the customer or financial realm generally requires complementary initiatives from different parts of the organisation such as human resources, information technology, marketing, distribution, and operations.

With strategic metrics, targets and initiative portfolios in place, the company next develops an operational plan that lays out the actions which will accomplish its strategic objectives. This stage starts with setting priorities for process improvement projects followed by preparing a detailed sales plan, a resource capacity, and operating and capital budgets.

The managers need to deconstruct each strategic process to identify the critical success factors that the employees can focus on in their daily activities. They must also identify the resources that will be required to implement their strategic plan. Before that, they need to deconstruct their overall sales target into the expected quantity, mix and nature of individual sales orders, production runs, and transactions.

Armed with data about expected increase in productivity from process improvement and estimated sales numbers, the management have to determine what resources they would need in the ensuing years to execute their strategic goals. The most powerful tool which can be used for this purpose is 'Time-Driven Activity-Based Costing' (TDABC). This tool measures the cost and profitability of processes, products and customers, besides the ability to easily translate future sales numbers into a forecast of required resource capacity. This tool seeks to describe how various transactions and demands consume the capacity of resources such as people, equipment and facilities.

Once the managers have determined the authorised level of resources for the future period, operating and capital budgets need to be drawn up. In operating expenditure budget is shown as the expected cost of hiring additional human resources and meeting other establishment expenses is shown. Capital expenditure budget will exhibit incremental expenditure on installation of additional equipment and other infrastructure facilities.

After determining operating and capital expenditure and thereby computing total incremental cost to be incurred in procuring the required resources for incremental production, the company can ascertain profit for each product, customer, channel and region simply by subtracting the additional cost from the expected sales revenue.

Having determined precisely product-wise, customer-wise and region-wise incremental profit expected to be earned during the ensuing period, the top management need to design suitable organisational structure for dividing and coordinating the tasks of the members of the organisation and to develop organisational skills to implement the plan.

Robert S. Kaplan and David P. Norton have provided a powerful conceptual framework, known as Balanced Score Card (BSC)[8]. BSC offers a four-layered perspective of the state of strategy implementation as it cascades down (Figure 16.1). At the top layer is the financial perspective which lays down the financial expectations of the shareholders that the strategy must meet. In the next layer is the customer perspective which asks: What are the customers' expectations that must be met or exceeded so that the financial objectives are attainable? At the third level, the BSC looks at the internal processes that a company must develop to deliver customer value. The fourth layer is about learning and growth which addresses issues pertaining to organisational competencies, skills and systems that the company must create to motivate the workforce that will ultimately enable the achievement of its overall vision and objectives.

Thus, BSC is a strategy map that figures out various critical aspects of the strategy and contains guidelines for its effective implementation.

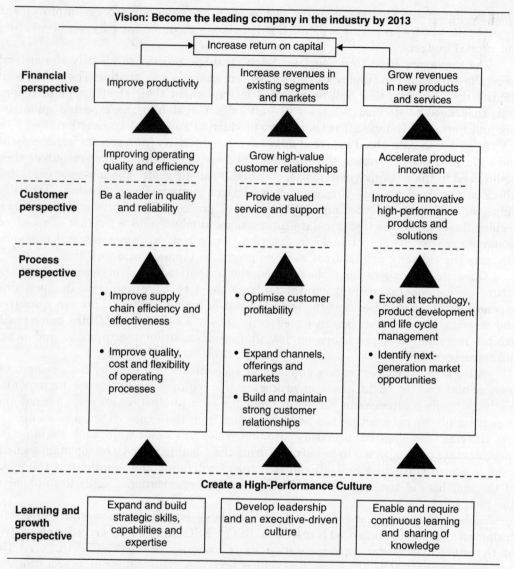

Source: *Adopted from BSC Strategy Map developed by Kaplan and Norton.*

Figure 16.1 BSC strategy map.

FOUNDATIONS OF STRATEGY IMPLEMENTATION SUCCESS

Successful implementation of business strategy of an organisation hinges essentially on four factors, viz., clarification of decision rights, designing effective information system, developing suitable structure and creating an invigorating ambience.

Clarification of Decision Rights

For robust execution of a strategy, it would be pertinent for the top management to spell out in unambiguous terms the roles and responsibilities of the managers at various levels of the organisation and report relationships.[9] While defining the tasks of the managers and their decision-making rights, the needs of the respective departments and divisions should be kept in view. This will help in building the cross-departmental and divisional links which will be fruitful for developing the global capabilities of the organisation as a whole. Furthermore, it should be ensured that roles and responsibilities of the managers at the departmental level are compatible with those of divisional managers.

Designing Effective Information System

Another pillar of effective strategy implementation is efficacious information system. The management should design and develop information system of the organisation in such a way as to ensure the flow of accurate and up-to-date information, especially about the current and future competitive environment from the grass-root level to headquarters quickly and uninterruptedly so that the latter can play powerful role in identifying the emerging business models and practices and adopting them across the business segment and geographical regions of the organisation. In case the information system of the organisation fails, the management at the corporate level will very likely impose its own agenda and strategies that may not always be customer friendly.

The top management has also to ensure that the information flows freely across organisational boundaries. When the information does not flow horizontally across different parts of the company, the units behave like silos, forfeiting economies of scale and the transfer of best practices. Moreover, the organisation as a whole loses the opportunity to develop a cadre of up and coming managers well versed in all aspects of the company's operations.

It is also important to ensure that the field and line employees usually have the information they need to understand the bottom-line impact of their day-to-day choices. Rational decisions are always bounded by the information available to employees. If the managers do not understand what it will cost to capture incremental revenue, they will pursue the latter. They can hardly be faulted, even if their decision is, in the light of full information, wrong.

Developing Suitable Structure

Before plans can lead to actual performance, a company should be appropriately organised, programmes should be adequately staffed, and activities should be directed toward achieving the desired objectives. A detailed discussion on structure is made in the chapter to follow.

Creating an Invigorating Ambience

A company must also create an ambience where employees feel enthused and enthralled in doing their best for the organisation, and where talents bloom and blossom. It has to design and develop a system that helps unleash the employees' potential, and builds in a reward and recognition system that provides value for people. Fostering an invigorating culture of mutual trust and confidence between the management and the employees through high degree of empowerment and recognition, openness, authenticity, internal and external equity and collaboration is imperative for execution excellence.

APPROACH TO IMPLEMENTATION OF STRATEGY

There are five fundamental approaches to implementing strategies. These are: commander approach, organisation change approach, collaborative approach, cultural approach and crescive approach.

Commander Approach

In this approach, the manager is concerned with the formulation of suitable strategy while its execution is done by his subordinates. This approach provides opportunities to the managers to concentrate on strategy making and pass on doing work to their subordinates. It motivates ambitious managers who feel pride in that their thinking and decision-making can affect the organisation and its people.

However, the main drawback of this approach is that it fails to inspire employees who feel that they have no say in decision-making. This may lead to strangulating intrapreneurship and creativity in the organisation.

Organisational Change Approach

The thrust of this approach is on how to get organisation members to implement strategy. The managers function as an architect, designing administrative systems for effective effectuation. They view their job as getting the company moving towards new goals. This is sought to be achieved through behavioural interventions such as changing the organisational structure, revising planning and control systems and invoking other organisational change techniques.

This approach is more effective than the commander approach, for the fact that it uses behavioural tools. However, it does not handle political and personal agenda, resulting in subjectivity among strategists. Absence of motivational content is another drawback of this approach because the strategy is thrust upon the middle level management.

Collaborative Approach

Under this approach, the task of strategy formulation is done by the manager in consultation with the executives. The executives are encouraged to contribute their ideas and views on strategy making with the manager acting as a coordinator, who ensures that all good ideas are discussed at length and decisions are made by consensus.

This approach has the greatest merit of getting useful information from the executives who are closer to operations and providing forums for free and frank exchange of opinions. This obviously improves the quality of strategic decisions, leading to efficacious strategy implementation.

However, strategy making process in this approach is time consuming because strategy has to be negotiated among the managers with different points of view and goals. As a result, the organisation may miss crucial opportunities and fail to react quickly to changes in the environment.

Cultural Approach

Under this approach, the top management provides direction to the organisation by articulating vision and mission and communicating the same to the executives who are given full freedom to design and develop their own activities to achieve the vision and mission. Once the strategy is formulated, the executives are guided and encouraged by the management to make decisions on how best to execute the strategy.

The greatest advantage of this approach lies in involvement of all levels of organisational people in both formulation and implementation of strategy. HP—an electronic company—is an illustrious example where employees shape and share a strong company vision and mission. They are well aware that the "HP Way" encourages product innovative at every level. Likewise, TCS and Tata Motors, Wipro and Infosys involve their executives in making strategic decisions and execution thereof.

However, this approach can be a success in organisations with informed intelligent people. Organisations with substantially large resources to absorb the cost of building and maintaining supportive value system can make use of this approach to execute the strategy.

Crescive Approach

In this approach, the tasks of strategy formulation and implementation are carried out simultaneously. The managers encourage their subordinates to design, develop and execute strategies on their own. This approach is distinct from other approaches in the sense that strategy making process moves upward from the doers and bottom level executives. Further, corporate strategy is a reflection of the individual proposals that surface throughout the year. Further, in this approach, the top management acts as an evaluator to screen the proposals instead as a master strategist.

Crescive approach has manifold advantages. In the first instance, it provides opportunities to middle and low level executives to formulate suitable strategies and to implement them. Secondly, strategies developed by those who are closer to realistic world are more operational and hence readily implementable.

However, the success of this approach calls for dispensing adequate amount of funds to individuals to develop good ideas unencumbered by bureaucratic approval cycles.

This approach can be gainfully employed by large and complex organisations where it is difficult for the Chief Executive to know and understand all the strategic and operating forces that affect each division. The 3M has used this approach to implement its strategy. The top management sets a target for the percentage of each division's revenues from new products. Accordingly, divisional managers develop their strategies and take steps to execute these strategies so as to achieve the targets. A divisional manager in 3M in his attempt to accomplish the target went to the extent of restructuring his division into cross-functional teams to bring new products to market more quickly.

It is important to note that strategic success really demands a simultaneous view of planning and doing. The greater the overlap of doers and planners, greater the profitability of success. It is so important for the managers to be thinking about execution as they are formulating the plans. It is a mistaken belief that execution is a lower-level responsibility[9]. Involving people from all organisational levels in the formulation and in the implementation of strategy tends to result in better organisational performance.

IMPEDIMENTS TO STRATEGY IMPLEMENTATION

According to a survey of 93 Fortune 500 US firms[10] and survey conducted by Goodward Insurance[11], organisations fail to effectuate strategy because of the following problems:

   (i) Implementation takes more time than originally planned.
  (ii) Unanticipated major problems arise.
 (iii) Information does not flow freely across organisational boundaries.
  (iv) Important information about the competitive environment do not get to headquarters quickly.
   (v) Competing activities and crisis take attention away from implementation.
  (vi) The involved employees are not adequately trained.
 (vii) Key implementation tasks and activities are poorly defined and communicated. As a result, no one has a good idea of the decisions and actions for which he or she is responsible.
(viii) Departmental managers lack in leadership and direction.

The top management should take appropriate steps proactively to stave off the occurrence of the above mentioned problems.

Summary

Strategy implementation is about translating strategic plan into action. It is action-oriented, making things happen.

In fiercely competitive and complex business environment, success of an organisation depends, in the main, how effectively it executes its strategy. In fact, excellence in execution can be a powerful source of competitive advantage of an organisation. Inept and delayed execution of a project may result in enormous losses to the organisation, as witnessed in the case of Air India and Haldia Petrochemicals.

It is notable that making strategy work is more difficult and time consuming than strategy making because the former involves wide range of managerial activities that need to be addressed and more people are involved in it.

In order to implement a strategy, a company has to set specific goals for each critical process and for the people, technology and the organisational climate and culture, and communicate the same to all those involved in strategy execution. This is to be followed by identifying and authorising resources for a portfolio of strategic initiatives. The management then develops an operational plan, laying out the actions which will accomplish its strategic objectives. The managers have also to deconstruct each strategic process to identify the critical success factors that employees can focus in their day-to-day activities. They must identify the resources required to implement their strategic plan. The most useful tool for the purpose is TDABC.

To carry into effect the above plans and programmes, the management need to organise the company's tasks and design suitable structure, and build strategic competencies.

As a guidepost to effective strategy implementation, Kaplan and Norton developed a strategy map known as BSC.

Four fundamental building blocks on which excellence of strategy implementation depends are: clarification of decision rights, designing effective information system, developing suitable structure and creating an invigorating ambience.

There are five basic approaches to strategy implementation, viz., commander approach, organisation change approach, collaborative approach, cultural approach and crescive approach.

A company has to face host of problems in implementing its strategy effectively. These problems include interrupted information flows, lack of training of the involved employees, lack of proper definition of roles and responsibility and their communication to the people concerned. The management is, therefore, advised to take suitable measures to prevent the occurrence of these problems.

Key Terms

Balanced score card	Cultural approach
Capital budget	Operating budget
Collaborative approach	Organisational change approach
Commander approach	Strategic initiatives
Crescive approach	Time driven activity-based costing

Discussion Questions

1. Why is strategy implementation so significant for corporate success?
2. "A brilliant strategy can put a firm on the competitive map but only solid execution can keep it there". Comment.
3. How can excellence in strategy implementation serve as powerful source of competitive advantage?
4. Discuss, in brief, the process involved in strategy implementation.
5. What are the basic foundations of strategy implementation success?
6. Give a brief outline of balanced score card.
7. Discuss various approaches to strategy implementation.
8. What bottlenecks come in the way of effective implementation of strategy?

References

1. Newman, Willliam H. and James P. Logal, *Strategy, Policy and Central Management*, South Western Publishing, Cincinnati, Ohio, pp. 9–11, 1971.

2. Paine, Frank T. and William Naumes, *Organisation Strategy and Policy*, Saunders, Philadelphia, pp. 38–41, 1978.

3. Chrintenson, Roland C., Andrews, Keneth R. and Joseph L. Bower, *Business Policy, Text and Cases*, Irwin, Homewood, III, p. 674, 1978.

4. Ackoff, Russell E., "Management Misinformation Systems", *Management Sciences*, December, p. 154, 1967.

5. Neilson, Gary L., Karla L. Martin, and Elizabeth Powers, "The Secrets to Successful Strategy Execution", *Harvard Business Review*, South Asia, June p. 37, 2008.

6. *Indian Management*, June, 2006.

7. Ibid.

8. Kaplan, Robert S. and David P. Norton, "Mastering the Management System", *Harvard Business Review*, South Asia, January, pp. 54–58, 2008.

9. Herebiniat, "Good Strategy? Try Implementing It", *Indian Management*, p. 79, July, 2005.

10. Alexander, L.D., "Strategy Implementation: Nature of the Problem", *International Review of Strategic Management*, Vol. 2(1), D.E. Hussey (Ed.), John Wiley & Sons, New York, pp. 172–184, 1991.

11. Neilson, Gary L. and Elizabeth Powers, op.cit.

17

Organising for Competitive Advantage

LEARNING OBJECTIVES

The present Chapter aims at:

- Providing an incisive view of strategy and structure relationship.
- Presenting a vivid account of various strategic issues involved in organising activities.
- Familiarising readers with emerging trends in organisational structure.

INTRODUCTION

Matching the structure of an organisation with its objectives and strategy enables it to achieve enduring success in the fast changing competitive milieu. This is for the fact that each and every facet of organising—identification and classification of required activities, grouping of activities necessary to attain objectives, assignment of each grouping to a manager with the authority necessary to supervise it and provision for coordination horizontally and vertically[1]—is impacted by the company's overall objectives and strategy.

Since corporate strategy determines basic long-term objectives of the enterprise and adopts courses of action and allocates resources necessary for carrying out these objectives, the structure should be so designed as to achieve organisational objectives and strategy.

It would, therefore, be in the vital interest of an enterprise that corporate strategy shapes its organisation structure. Thus, while identifying activities to be organised, it would be in the fitness of things to undertake a critical inquiry into the corporate objectives and strategy of the enterprise as it provides the management an adequate clue about the activities to be organised, the decisions to be made and the relations to be formalised with the organisation.

STRATEGY AND ORGANISATION STRUCTURE FIT

After organising the critical activities, their grouping into departments along functional regions, product, customer and other bases would depend mainly on the size of the company and the characteristics of the external environment. Thus, if the company is small and deals in a single product or market space and operates in a relatively stable environment, it should have a functional structure. In contrast, a large sized enterprise operating in dynamically changing environment should have divisional and adaptive structure so that the company adjusts itself in sync with environmental developments.

Another critical aspect of organising—assignment of tasks and responsibilities to functionaries and delegation of authority—is influenced by a myriad of forces including corporate strategy of a company. A company having embarked on the growth strategy needs to delegate more powers to its employees so that they make quick decisions to capitalise on the opportunities. Tendency to decentralisation will be more pronounced where companies are planning to diversify their operations. Likewise, firms planning to expand through acquisition will have to decentralise their authority structure because often the top management finds itself not so capacious in managing the acquired operations. However, the management has to centralise decision-making authority in the event of the company having adopted retrenchment strategy to overcome the problem.

At times, a company may intend to venture into unfamiliar areas of business involving greater risks. In such cases, close and direct control of the top management becomes necessary. Hence, the adoption of centralised organisation structure will be useful.

Further, strategy, operating policies and rules of a company facilitate coordination of activities of various divisions and departments. They tie together and structure the range of recurring and day-to-day action initiatives, methods of performing work and modes of required behaviour among the functionaries of the company.

In a continuously changing environment, a company may change its objectives and strategy from time to time to exploit business opportunities and stay ahead of its competitors. For that, it may have to perform new or different key activities requiring different skills and capabilities and different organisational arrangements. If such organisational adjustments are not made, the resulting mismatch between the strategy and structure can open the door to execution and performance problems,[2] as could be evidenced from Illustrative Capsules 17.1(A) and 17.1(B).

ILLUSTRATIVE CAPSULES 17.1(A) AND (B)
MISMATCH BETWEEN STRATEGY AND STRUCTURE

(A) A company dealing in single product with significant market share decided to diversify into related multi-product business in order to exploit tremendous growth opportunities. Leveraging its existing distribution and retail network to sell the associated products was another trigger to the diversification strategy. All the additional product categories showed strong demand growth. Initial response to these products was good and some market share accrued within a year. However, in early 2007, as sales were gaining momentum, signs of a slowdown in market growth emerged. Revenues fell and the organisation started losing market share as other competitors introduced upgrades to their products and it was unable to respond swiftly; problems in product commercialisation and product launch coordination became evident. Competing product priorities within each function paralysed the company. Lack of a coherent response to a product across functions drive up costs, and different units worked at cross-purposes so that no one seemed to be in charge for any of the product lines. The company finally restructured itself as a strategic business unit. This resulted in a clear profit and loss focus around each product. Over a period cf time, it improved the company's capability to manage multiple product lines.

(B) A company in its attempt to grow significantly and enhance its market share, pursued geographical expansion strategy. It empowered geographical divisions to move accordingly. For a couple of years, they made good progress, but as the downturn set in, competition started dropping prices to gain market share and the organisation found its products becoming increasingly uncompetitive. The fundamental issue was an expensive and unproductive duplication of resources and lack of standardisation. Each location created its own ways of working and functional expertise deteriorated. This weakened the control of work cultures across geographic divisions, forcing the organisation to embark on an initiative to centralise and focus it on standardisation of products and processes.

Alfred Chandler was the first management authority who, on the basis of empirical study of 100 US firms from 1909–1959, proved that authority impacts the structure of a company. Chandler's research revealed that changes in a company's strategy bring about new administrative problems, which, in turn, require a new or refashioned structure for the new strategy to be successfully implemented. He noted that the increased activity of an organisation with several products tends to require more independence within the organisation, leading to adoption of divisional structure with its emphasis on accountability, decentralisation and the efficacious allocation of functional resources. This is why Chandler coined the now famous maxim: **structure follows strategy.**[3]

However, it is important to observe that strategy-structure relationship is two-way. It is not always that strategy always influences structure but at times, structure does impact strategy making decision. For instance, a company intending to expand may opt for a concentric diversification route because it makes use of existing production facilities, technological skills and capabilities. Likewise, a company is constrained to acquire another firm because it is felt that the present management skills of the company are adequate to manage both the organisations effectively. A company can gain synergistic advantages and accomplish optimum results if it factors in organisational structure aspect while crafting its strategy. Miles and Snow, therefore rightly observed, that strategy shapes structure and process and structure constrains strategy in that an organisation is seldom able to veer away substantially from its current course without a major structure process alterations.[4]

As such, the top management needs to address various strategic issues pertaining to organising and organisational structure so as to ensure efficacious effectuation of strategy in a fast changing and highly competitive and complex business environment.

STRATEGIC ISSUES INVOLVED IN ORGANISING ACTIVITIES

(i) Identifying activities to be performed internally
(ii) Choosing right kind of structure
(iii) Delegation of decision-making power
(iv) Deciding about degree of flexibility

Identifying Activities to be Performed Internally

Before making any decision on building a structure for the firm, it would be pertinent for the management to identify which activities in the value chain are to be performed by it. According to the core competency perspective, a firm must focus only on that segment of business where it has core capability and can get out of everything else. This is based on the premise that a firm cannot be an outstanding performer and cost-effective in all the activities. If a firm concentrates all its investments and energy on the one thing it does best and farms out everything else, it can achieve unprecedented level of efficiency, speed and quality.

As such, to improve the firm's competitive advantage in terms of cost, quality and speed on a sustainable basis it has to outsource all those activities, which cannot be performed better, to those specialised agencies who are adept and skilled in doing them. Outsourcing enables a firm to concentrate on core operations and achieve excellence therein and farm out other activities to outside vendors having specialised expertise. These vendors can perform certain specialised activities economically and better than a company that performs these services only for itself. Besides reducing internal hassles and lowering costs, outsourcing support-activities can aid the firm in decreasing internal bureaucracies, flattening the organisation structure, speeding decision-making, heightening the company's strategic focus, improving its innovative capability and enhancing competitive responsiveness.

It should, however, be noted that outsourcing can be considerably useful to a firm if it concentrates its resources and energies on those activities for which it can create unique value to make it different from others. In its strive to achieve maximum benefits out of outsourcing, a firm must have strategic control to build core competencies, achieve competitive advantage and manage key customer/supplier/distribution relationships.

In view of the above, outsourcing has emerged as a powerful business model in corporate world to achieve sustainable competitive edge during the last three decades. Almost all the organisations, both the big and small, in different business segments have embraced this model. However, excessive outsourcing may boomerang on the future of the firm. A firm that goes overboard on outsourcing can hollow out in knowledge and capabilities, putting itself on the mercy of outside suppliers and leaving it short of the resource strengths to be master of its own destiny. This is why, prudent organisations have been outsourcing strategic-critical activities more judiciously and with safeguards against losing control over the performance of key value chain activities and becoming excessively dependent on single suppliers. They have also been evaluating regularly their suppliers' overall performance and also whether they should switch to another supplier or even bring the activity back in-house. To avoid loss of control, companies need to work closely with major suppliers. This will ensure that the suppliers' activities are closely integrated with their own requirements and expectations.

Another business model embraced by corporate enterprises during the post liberalised period across the globe to look outside for carrying out their business effectively is partnering arrangement with other organisations through forging strategic alliance. The strategic alliance, representing cooperative arrangements between organisations belonging to the same country or different parts of the world or different ends of the supply chain, are unique partnering relationships to serve the basic objective of maximising corporate value through product innovation and development or through diversification.[8] These alliances may range widely in scope from an informal business relationships based on a simple contract such as networks, subcontracting, licensing and franchising to formalised inter-organisational relationships such as joint ventures.

So as to improve their performance and enhance competitiveness through cost reduction and increased competencies, collaborative arrangements are made in the entire gamut of the value chain. At times, competitors turn collaborators for gaining synergistic benefits. Alliance between Kingfisher Airlines and Jet Airways is a case in point (Illustrative Capsule 17.2).

ILLUSTRATIVE CAPSULE 17.2

KINGFISHER AIRLINES-JET AIRWAYS—COMPETITORS TURNED COLLABORATOR

Since the takeoff of its first flight in 1932, the Indian Aviation Industry has been shaped by a series of events. While the deregulation in 1991 ended the monopoly of the state players, the repeal of the Air Corporation Act in 1994 witnessed the rise of private players' dominance. However, with the introduction of Low-Cost Carriers (LCCs), air fares dropped to as low as train fares and passenger traffic shot up recording 25% annual growth. To attract more passengers, fares were decreased and capacity was increased. Added to this, cost of Aviation Tribune Fuel (ATF) was increased exorbitantly.

With the fall in the revenues and increase in the costs, players were unable to break-even. As a solution, players increased fares, indulged in consolidation and pleaded the government for a bailout. However, with the failure of all the measures and the losses mounting by the day, on October 13th, 2008 arch-rivals Jet Airways and Kingfisher Airlines announced to form an alliance in eight major areas. With the two having different aircrafts and a large-scale route overlap, they expected major synergies out of the alliance.

Very recently, Tata Steel has tied up with its competitors, SAIL and Nippon Steel, for accessing more raw materials and strengthening technical relationship (Illustrative Capsule 17.3).

ILLUSTRATIVE CAPSULE 17.3

TATA STEEL PARTNERING WITH SAIL, NMDC AND NIPPON STEEL

Tata Steel has fully integrated iron-ore resources and 60% security in cooking coal. Still the company is actively looking for more raw materials. It is in two joint ventures with SAIL and NMDC, both government-owned entities. The joint ventures with SAIL and the MoU with NMDC to scout for raw materials are both long-term initiatives for the company.

Although, SAIL and Tata Steel might be competitors in steel, both companies have similar requirements and objectives in raw materials, especially in coal and that is why they have tied up.

Tata Steel has a long standing relationship with Nippon Steel Corporation of Japan—the world's fourth largest producer.

In early 2010, the Tata Steel board approved a joint venture between Tata Steel and Nippon Steel for the production and sale of automotive cold-rolled flat products at Jamshedpur to address the localisation needs of Indian automotive customers for high grade cold-rolled steel sheet.

Tata holds 51% in the venture, while Nippon Steel has 49%. The Joint Venture aims to capture the growing demand for high-grade automotive, cold-rolled, flat products in India by setting up a continuous annealing and processing line with a capacity of 6,00,000 tonnes. As per the agreement, Nippon Steel would transfer its technology for producing high-grade, cold-rolled steel sheet for automotive application including spin panels and high tensile steels.

The target for start of operations is March, 2013.

Choosing Right Kind of Structure

Corporate managers must remember that there can be no standard structure for a firm to organise its business which may always be useful to it because the structure of an organisation evolves as the firm grows and changes over time. In fact, choice of optimal structure at a particular time depends upon a slew of factors including external environment, corporate objectives and strategy, size of the firm and its resources, the geographical dispersion of the firm's operations and the range of its business.

However, historical review of the evolution of multiple structural variations in business world reveals emergence of a pattern. In his new-classical study, Chandler found that company typically began with a simple structure and a single product. It specialised in what it did best: manufacturing and selling a product. To do this successfully, a company used a centralised, simple structure to execute a narrowly focused strategy. However, as the company grew, it was noted that a new strategy required a new structure if the enlarged enterprise was to operate effectively. The increased activity with several products tended to require more interdependence within the organisation and hence the adoption of functional structure with centralised control. With growing success and pursuance of diversification strategy, companies tended to have a multidivisional structure with emphasis on accountability, decentralisation and efficient allocation of functional resources, as the functional structure was found inadequate for the task of coordinating across units making radically different products.

With growing business complexities following diversification of operations according to product, location and customers, firms felt the exigency of adopting matrix structure so as to maximise the benefits of organisational flexibility without sacrificing functional specialisation.

However, in the wake of tectonic changes in the economic structure of the country, increased ferocity of competitiveness and growing expectations of consumers, corporate entrepreneurs have adopted lean, mean and flat structure, and thus network structure is gaining prominence in recent years in the business world.

A brief discussion of redeeming features of basic forms of the organisation structure and their strengths and weaknesses will indubitably furnish invaluable guidelines to the management in choosing a particular structure under the given circumstances. Broadly speaking, these may be categorised into three groups: simple structure, hierarchical structure and network structure.

Simple Structure

This hierarchiless structure (Figure 17.1) revolves around the entrepreneur with no functional or product categories in a centralised structure in which the entrepreneur makes all strategic decisions and undertakes exclusive responsibility of executing the decisions and monitoring operations of the firm. High centralisation, low formalisation, and low complexity are unique features of this structure.

Figure 17.1 Simple structure.

The greatest strengths of this type of structure are effective control and coordination of operations, flexibility and dynamism. The firm gets energised by unabashed drive of the entrepreneur.

However, weakness of the simple structure begins to surface when the firm expands its business and the entrepreneur finds it too difficult to attend the problems single-handedly, which may culminate in floundering of the firm. Greiner labels this as a **crisis of leadership**.[10]

Hierarchical Structure

Hierarchical structure with its immanent characteristics of high job specialisation and top-down authority structures came in vogue at the beginning of the 20th century when the US business sector was thriving and industry was shifting from job-shop manufacturing to mass production and management thinkers like Frederick Taylor and Henri Fayol noted that addition of hierarchical structure would be most useful for the greatest efficiency and productivity.

Hierarchical or pyramidal structure with the President or other executive at the top, a small number of vice presidents or senior managers, under the President and several layers of management below this, having the majority of employees at the bottom of the pyramid, can be represented in a graphical form by an organisational chart.

Hierarchical structure may be Functional, Divisional, Strategic Business Units (SBUs), and Matrix.

Functional structure: Tasks in this kind of organisation are grouped according to functional specialisation such as marketing, production, finance, human resources and R&D (Figure 17.2).

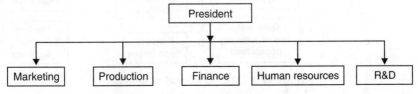

Figure 17.2 Functional structure.

A manager having expertise and experience in a particular function is assigned the responsibility of heading the concerned functional department. He/she reports directly to the President.

Functional structure with inbuilt specialisation promotes efficiency and fosters the development of greater expertise. It requires little coordination and a few interpersonal skills. Clear definition of roles and responsibilities of the managers renders monitoring of operations easier. There is a high degree of centralisation with each functional head reporting to the President.

However, the greatest weakness of functional groupings is that people with the same skills and knowledge may develop a narrow departmental focus and have difficulty in appreciating any other view which is important to the organisation. This may lead to the development of a departmental subculture values which may not be co-terminus with those of the firm.

Other weaknesses of functional structure such as delay in decision-making, and problems in fixing accountability and coordination arise as the organisation grows and its range of products expands. Speed of decision-making in functional groupings is slowed down as the manager has to seek approval of the CEO before moving ahead. At times, it becomes harder to determine accountability and judge performance in a functional structure. For example, if a new product fails, it may be very difficult to blame a particular department. In addition, coordination of work across functional boundaries can become a difficult task.

As such, this kind of structure is most suited to firms with focus on simple competencies, limited product line and growing market.

ITC has adopted a functional structure, as can be glanced from Figure 17.3.

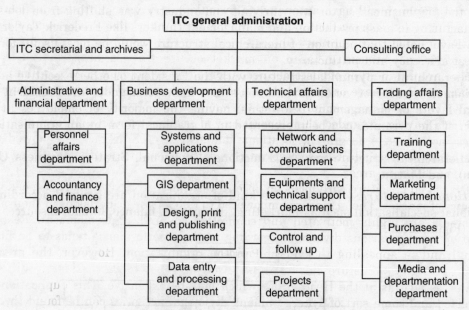

Figure 17.3 ITC functional structure.

Divisional structure: In divisional structure, business activities of an enterprise are organised as individual business units (also termed as divisions); each business unit is entrusted with the direct responsibility for its performance and fully empowered to discharge the same. As a firm grows in size and engages in several products lines in many related industries, the management finds it appropriate to adopt divisional structure as it allows divisional managers to respond effectively to the needs of their respective business units (Figure 17.4).

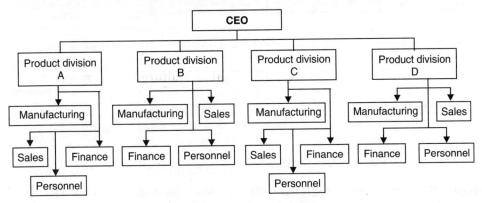

Figure 17.4 Divisional structure.

A divisional structure may be organised according to product, market or geographic areas. In product-based structure, the entire organisation is departmentalised according to product with a manager of the product division responsible for its performance. The divisional manager will have autonomy to formulate and execute strategy concerning his division. MNCs like Du Pont, General Motors and Procter and Gamble have adopted a divisional structure by product line.

A divisional structure based on market occurs when a firm's activities are organised around the type of customer needs served by an enterprise. MNCs like HSBC and Barclays Bank have organised their business according to the types of customers like, corporate customers, small business customers and retail customers.

Firms having expanded their operations in various regions may organise their business according to geographic locations; manager of each division is endowed with the authority of taking decisions, keeping in view the needs and attributes of consumers within the different areas.

Divisional structure with focus on decentralisation is relatively more responsive to dynamics of market. The managers empowered to take strategic decisions in their areas of business are highly motivated and committed to product development. Resource allocation among various divisions according to their performance tends to be highly rational and is appealing to everyone in the organisation. However, the greatest weakness of this structure lies in duplication of functions across many different divisions as well as at the Head Office which may be expensive. This duplication can be averted and some sort of synergy among divisional activities can be found through the use of committees and horizontal linkages.

Bharti Airtel has adopted a divisional organisational structure, as shown in Figure 17.5.

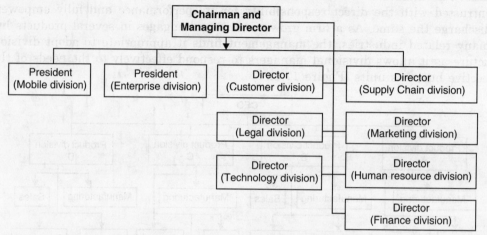

Figure 17.5 Organisational structure of Bharti Airtel.

Strategic Business Units (SBUs): SBUs are an extended form of the divisional structure. According to this structure, the entire firm is organised according to critical businesses working within the ambit of corporate office having its own product-market strategy to direct and run the business. Each SBU may have its divisions and functional departments, depending on the requirements, as depicted in Figure 17.6.

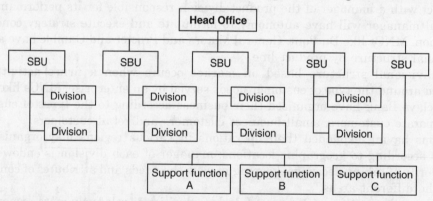

Figure 17.6 SBU structure.

The SBU structure provides ample scope of decentralisation and freedom to achieve market developments and customise strategies. Accountability for each business is the greatest strength of this structure.

However, this structure suffers from the problems of coordination and control. There is a lack of authority over financial affairs of the business. At times, objectives and strategies of the SBUs may not be coterminous with those of the firm which may have telling effect upon the overall success of an organisation.

Many leading organisations like Asian Paints, Godrej, Lupin, Dabur India and Piramal Industries have adopted SBU structure.

Tata Consultancy Services (TCS) had created in 2008 a verticalised organisation structure under which the company had carved out 24 business units, and each unit head reported to the CEO directly. In May 2011, TCS tweaked its structure in bringing in greater vertical focus within the company. TCS has now created 8 stacks of related operating units, and the stack heads will report directly to the CEO, thus reducing the instances of reporting from 24 to 8.

Matrix structure: Since the above-mentioned structures failed to cope with rapidly changing environmental developments and to increase the organisational flexibility, matrix structure was evolved. This structure is the combination of product and geographical patterns of departmentation in the same organisation structure or functional and customer structures operating in random. Functional departmentalisation is typically combined with product groups on a project basis. For example, a product group intends to develop a new addition to its line; for this project it obtains personnel from functional departments such as research, engineering, production and marketing. These personnel then work under the manager of the product group for the duration of the project. These personnel are responsible to two managers.

Although, matrix structure is necessarily complex, it has certain advantages.[11] Often, matrix structure proves to be an efficacious means for bringing together the diverse specialised skills required to handle projects. Problem of coordination, which is conspicuously absent in most functional designs, is minimised in this structure, because the most important personnel for a project work together as a group.

However, matrix structure has certain weaknesses. First, a state of conflict exists between functional and project managers, as both compete for limited resources. Secondly, role conflict, role ambiguity and role overload may result in stress for the functional and project managers as well as for the team members. Further, the morale of the people is dampened when they are rearranged once projects are completed and new ones begin.[12]

In order to overcome these problems and render matrix structure more effective one, it would be necessary to define the objectives of the project, clarify the roles, authority and responsibilities of the managers and team members. Special training in new job skills or inter-personal relationships may be necessary when a matrix overlay is first introduced or when a temporary overlay becomes permanent.

Tata Motors Ltd. has adopted matrix structure to organise its activities. As is evident from Figure 17.7, Tata Motors' structure is composite of functional and product structures. The Board of Directors, along with its committees, provides leadership and guidance to the company's management and directly supervises and controls the performance of the company. To focus effectively on the issues and ensure expedient resolution of the diverse matters, the Board has a set of committees which operate as empowered agents of the Board as per charter/terms of reference. The company has constituted independent SBU/centres for different product segments, viz., Commercial Vehicle Business Unit (CVBU), Passenger Car Business Unit (PCBU), and Engineering Research Centres (ERCs).

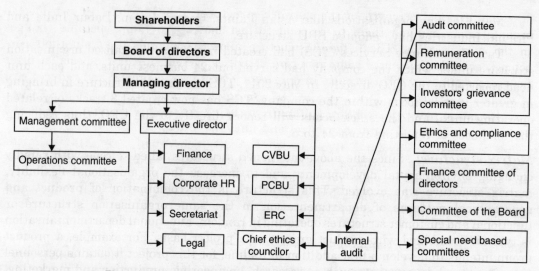

Figure 17.7 Organisational structure of Tata Motors Limited.

Network Structure

In recent years, Indian corporates have realised that hierarchical structure cannot ensure organisational success in highly complex, competitive and volatile milieu, for the fact that with too many layers it has contributed to delays, duplication of work, more proneness to mistakes, more interpersonal problems, more cost and has also ignored the multidimensionality of the environmental forces. As a result, hierarchies are being decimated to build more flexible, responsive and cost-effective flat and delayered structure, and unnecessary processes and procedures are being removed. Organisations have started thinking of developing multidimensional and flexible strategic capabilities. Hence, the evolution of networks shown here as Figure 17.8.

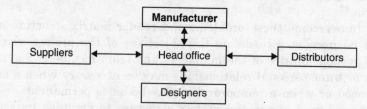

Figure 17.8 A network structure.

The salient features of the network structure are:

(i) Separate unit for each business bound to parent company through equity holdings.

(ii) Corporate affairs department monitors and coordinates the strategic issues including outsourced activities.

(iii) It seeks to build a set of negotiated and cooperative relationships involving several other partner firms, all doing what they do best.[13]

The greatest strength of the network structure is the flexibility it provides to organisations enabling them to respond to fast moving and unpredictable changes in the market place. The network structure allows companies to retain their core competencies at the centre while non-core activities are outsourced to specialist firms for greater efficiency. This results in spread of risk for the company and reduces cost of control overheads.

However, network structure suffers from the weaknesses of dilution of focus and synergies, difficulty of strategic control and unavailability of skill at group level.

According to Miles and Snow, network structure may fail because after having shed many non-core activities a firm may find that its expertise has become too narrow and that its role in the value chain has become more valuable.[14]

Multinational Companies like Apple Computer, Google, AT&T, Dell Corporation and Nike have this kind of structure.

Emerging Trends in Organisational Structure

All the aforestated structures, except network structure, focus on a vertical organisation. Such a vertical organisation is sometimes necessary, but may be a hindrance in rapidly changing environments. In hierarchy based structure, different people and functions do not operate completely independently. However, in the wake of rapid liberalisation and globalisation around the globe during the last three decades leading to increased competitiveness and business complexities, corporate leaders have felt the need to comprehend deeply the nature of interdependence and improve the functioning of organisations in respect to this factor so as to cope with fast-changing product-market development effectively. Thus, the trend towards flattening the organisation, developing the horizontal connections and de-emphasising vertical reporting relationships is emerging. At times, this involves simply eliminating the layers of middle management. For example, some Japanese companies including very large manufacturing firms have only four levels of management, viz., top management, plant management, department management and section management. Some US companies also have drastically reduced the number of managers as part of a downsizing strategy, not just to reduce salary expense, but also to streamline the organisation in order to improve communication and decision-making.[15]

Indeed, information technology has facilitated in flattening the organisation. The use of networks and software designed to facilitate group work within an organisation has certainly improved speed of communications and decision-making. Even more effective is the use of intranets to make company information readily accessible throughout the organisation. The rapid growth of such technology has made virtual organisations and boundaryless organisations possible, where managers, technicians, suppliers, distributors and customers connect digitally and physically.

In view of the above, organic model is replacing the traditional, mechanistic structure, because it is relatively simple and de-emphasises on job specialisation, relatively informal and decentralises authority. In organic structure, decision-making and goal-setting processes are shared at all levels, and communication ideally flows more freely throughout the organisation.

Another emerging trend that has buttressed the evolution of organic structure is conviction of the corporate leaders that any organisation structure capable of coping with tectonic developments in product-market milieu has to depend on the people for its success. Accordingly, corporations have tended to dismantle vertically functional departments and replace them with horizontal, cross-functional and process-centric teams. The objective is to assign ownership of each process to a group of people, making them responsible for its success or failure to ensure that it meets its target. As a result, the onus of performance is no longer on rigid systems, but on the resourcefulness, initiative and responsibility of the process owners.

Delegation of Decision-making Power

Another critical issue concerning an organisation seeking to execute strategy effectively is to decide about the delegation of the formal decision-making authority at different levels of the organisational hierarchy. The degree to which formal authority is delegated by the top management across the organisation runs along a continuum from decentralisation to centralisation. In a relatively decentralised organisation, considerable authority and accountability are passed down the organisational hierarchy. As opposed to this, in a relatively centralised organisation, considerable authority and accountability remain at the top of the hierarchy.

In a decentralised set up, decision-making is comparatively better because decisions are made closer to the scene of action, better training, higher morale and greater initiative at lower levels and more flexibility and faster decision-making in rapidly changing complex environment. But absolute decentralisation devoid of coordination and leadership from the top would defeat the very purpose of the organisation— efficient integration of sub-units for the pursuit of organisational goals through the strategy plan.

On the other hand, centralisation offers a variety of strengths such as specialised skills, talent and technology that are sometimes neither affordable nor practicable in multiple locations. Besides, it provides cohesiveness in the overall operations.

In real world, organisations can neither be totally centralised nor absolutely decentralised. The moot issue is to what extent authority should be delegated to lower level managers and how much autonomy they should enjoy in making decisions.

Deciding about Degree of Autonomy

While deciding about how much latitude and autonomy should be given to the divisional and local managers, a host of factors should be considered.

One such vital factor is environment force. High degree of autonomy has to be granted to the managers of those regions where environment is volatile, uncertain and rapidly changing. The unpredictability of such environment demands that the managers acquire and process considerable amounts of information promptly. Further, they must respond quickly and appropriately to that information. Autonomy allows the divisional managers to avoid the delays in responding to the environmental changes.

Level of autonomy is also the function of the local political environment and the sensitivity of an industry. Public utilities such as telecommunication, electricity-generating companies are prone to local political pressure because they are deemed essential to the welfare of the country. State governments may force the firm to grant more autonomy to its local unit.

The type of strategy pursued by the firm should also influence the type of authority system that it creates. A firm following strategy of product diversification has to provide greater latitude to the divisional managers so as to enable them to make suitable product decisions in the light of local requirements.

Mode of operations should also be considered while deciding about the degree of autonomy to divisional managers because mode of operations reflects the degree of involvement of the firm in offshore markets. International activities such as licensing and export functions are usually carried out from corporate headquarters but affiliates or subsidiaries require some degree of localised decision-making to keep operations efficient.

Another critical consideration is nature of the industry and its technology. Companies competing on the basis of product technology are more highly centralised than those competing on process technology. Where the process technologies need segmentation to cater to local requirements, high degree of centralisation is required. But firms, whose competitiveness is based on unique product technology, are more amenable to more centralisation because of the imperativeness of close monitoring of technologies involved.

The size and complexity of a firm also decide the degree of autonomy to divisional units. The larger an organisation, the more it needs autonomy. Likewise, the more complex an organisation is, the more it needs decentralisation to cope with its wide variety of organisational operations and types of decisions. Large and complex organisations such as Procter and Gamble or IBM need especially high levels of decentralisation.

Degree of autonomy to divisional and department heads depends essentially on the characteristics of its managers. If divisional personnel are of high quality with good experience and business judgement, they should be given more authority. High degree of autonomy will, however, not be appropriate if those managers do not have the requisite abilities or motivation to make the required decisions.

Nature and significance of decisions also influences the degree of autonomy. Generally, strategic decisions relating to turnaround business expansion through diversification and/or acquisition routes and entry in overseas markets, which have far reaching impact on the organisation's future, have to be made at the top level. However, the divisional and local managers should be actively engaged in deciding about specific programmes of action that need to be taken to achieve the above strategic decisions. This is what leading corporate houses in India, viz., Tatas, Birlas, Mahindra & Mahindra, Godrej and Bharti are practising.

STAFFING

Efficacious execution of corporate and business strategies demands that the organisation should be staffed with people endowed with required skills and behaviour best suited to achieving corporate objectives. This enjoins upon human resource (HR) managers the responsibility of tailoring manpower planning to corporate objectives and strategies and drawing a long-term hiring programme.

The recruitment process has to focus on acquisition of the right people who could act as missionaries at management level and mercenaries at activity level. HR manager should attempt to develop a competency matrix with the aid of internal resources keeping in view the firm's future demands. It should be followed by the personal interview to assess the behavioural competencies and the cultural aspects of a candidate.

National Thermal Power Corporation (NTPC) hires engineers/postgraduates through nation-wide open competitive examination and campus recruitments. Hiring is followed by 52 weeks induction training (fully-paid) consisting of theoretical input, on the job training, personality development and management modules.

In view of metamorphic changes in task requirements following wrenching changes in the business environment and the consequential changes in corporate objectives and strategies and serious talent shortage, organisations need to accord high priority to training and developing employees in order to update their knowledge and competence, and develop special skills of self-directed leadership, self-motivated team work and self-generated creativity and thus to realise their potentials. The training programme should be so designed as to link it to the corporate strategy and act as a catalyst between the people and strategy, between the customers and organisations. Focus of any training programme should be on honing the talents of the employees they possess. Once their potential skills are whetted and polished, they would love to stay and work for the organisation.

Further, the overall thrust of the training and development programmes of an organisation in today's scenario has to be on developing an overall global business perspective as well as understanding of business strategy formulation and relationships between cross and functional strategies and multi-skilling in cross-functional areas. This will go a long way in improving their marketability which may, in fact, serve as powerful instrument of motivation.

NTPC believes that efficiency, effectiveness and success of the organisation depend largely on the skills, abilities and commitment of the employees. Accordingly, a lot of emphasis is laid on the training and development of employees. Training in NTPC is carried out with short-term and long-term objectives to impart skills required to carry out various jobs and provide developmental input for the individual's and organisation's future growth. NTPC's training policy envisages 7 Mondays of training per employees per year. It has developed its own training infrastructure comprising Power Management Institute, Employees Development Centres and Simulator Centres. For the management development, NTPC has a set of planned interventions designed for each stage in a person's career. Each of these is a custom-made, medium-term training programme, specifically designed to give developmental input at a particular stage in the person's career.

The training philosophy at Infosys has been to equip the participants with the know-how to find the best solution, rather than to teach 'one way to do it' and also to relate to real life situations. The training plan provides a sequence of inputs as individuals grew through their professional career, commencing with a structured induction at the beginning to leadership training with assuming senior responsibilities. Training and development-initiatives are available at each milestone and cover-technical training by Education and Research Department, Quality Process Training, Personal Effectiveness and Managerial programmes and The Infosys Leadership System.

Tata Motors conducts various programmes to train their staff in the latest and the best technology and management practices. Through its in-house vocational training and apprenticeship programme the company trains its staff in the latest and the best technology and management practices. Structured training programmes, rotational assignments and cross-functional mobility allow employees to grow. Movement across functions is encouraged to help the employees develop a wider perspective and gain expertise in manifold functions.

Summary

Enduring success and competitive edge of an organisation depends essentially on designing of a structure that is tethered to its corporate and business strategies. The management must, therefore, ensure that the structure matches with the corporate objectives and strategies, otherwise the organisation may land in serious trouble.

Another critical consideration in designing structure for the organisation is identifying the business activities which are to be performed internally and those to be outsourced to highly specialised agencies.

Choosing the right kind of structure is another critical issue which should be decided after taking into consideration a host of variables, such as external environment, corporate objectives and strategy, size of the firm and its resources, the geographical dispersion of the firm's operations and the range of its businesses.

There has been in existence multiple structural variations, ranging from simple structure to hierarchical and network structure. In the initial stage, a company adopts simple and centralised structure to handle one-product business. With growing size of organisation and diversification of business, a company moves towards functional, divisional, SBU and matrix structures to cope with increased business complexities and increased organisational flexibility.

In recent years, Indian corporates have realised that hierarchical structure can no longer ensure organisational success in highly complex, competitive and volatile environment. Hence, network structure has come into vogue, where separate unit for each business is tied to a parent company through equity holdings.

There is now emerging a trend of flattening the organisation, developing the horizontal connections, de-emphasising vertical reporting relationships and eliminating layers of the middle management to effectuate the strategy effectively and promptly.

Another key factor in organisational strategy is location of the decision-making authority between headquarters and divisional offices. This issue is often referred to as centralisation versus decentralisation of control. There is no ironclad rule to handle this issue. In real world, companies are neither totally centralised nor totally decentralised. They generally adopt a structure that provides for decentralisation to encourage inputs, flexibility and responsiveness to local conditions with an overlay of centralisation to provide structure and cohesiveness in the overall operations.

Last but not the least is the critical question pertaining to structuring a firm's operations to decide how much autonomy should be given to the divisional and local managers. A host of factors including environmental force, corporate strategy, mode of operations, product technology, size of the organisation, and the like have to be factored in while addressing this issue.

Efficacious execution of corporate and business strategies is contingent upon staffing of the organisation with people endowed with right skills and behaviour. This enjoins upon human resource managers the responsibility of tailoring manpower planning to corporate objectives and strategies and drawing a long-term hiring and training programme.

Key Terms

Centralisation of authority

Decentralisation of authority

Divisional structure

Formal structure

Functional structure

Hierarchical structure

Horizontal structure

Matrix structure

Network structure

Outsourcing

Simple structure

Strategic alliances

SBU structure

Discussion Questions

1. "Structure follows strategy and strategy follows structure". Comment upon the statement.
2. "Without a vision, an organisation structure fails". Discuss.
3. What are the critical issues that need to be addressed while designing the organisational structure of a company?
4. Discuss the different forms of structure for organising a business.
5. How should a company attempt to achieve synergy among functions and business units?
6. What is network structure? Under what circumstances is this structure most suited to a company?
7. What important factors should the top management keep in view while deciding about the degree of autonomy to be granted to divisional and local managers?
8. How would a strategic manager determine locus of decision-making in the firm?
9. Trace out the emerging directions in organisational structure in India.

References

1. Weihrich, Heinz and Harold Koontz, *Management*, McGraw-Hill, New York, p. 244, 1994.
2. Chandler, Alfred, *Strategy and Structure*, MIT Press, Cambridge, 1962.
3. Ibid.
4. Miles, R.E., C.C. Snow, J.A. Mathews, G. Miles and H.J. Coleman Jr., "Organising in the Knowledge Age: Anticipating the Cellular Form", *Academy of Management Executive*, November, pp. 7–24, 1997.
5. Amburgey, T.L. and T. Dacin, "The Dynamics of Strategy and Structural Change", *Academy of Management Journal*, 37(6), pp. 1427–52, 1994.
6. "The Strategist", *Business Standard*, December, 2010.

7. Jennings, D.F. and S.L. Seaman, "High and Low Levels of Organisational Adaptation: An Empirical Analysis of Strategy, Structure and Performance", *Strategic Management Journal*, July, pp. 459–475, 1994.

8. *Business Standard*, December 3, 2010.

9. Chandler, A.D., *Strategy and Structure*, MIT Press, Cambridge, 1962.

10. Ibid.

11. Greiner, E., "Evolution and Revolution as Organisations Grow", *Harvard Business Review*, May–June, pp. 55–67, 1998.

12. Barlett, Christopher A. and Sumantra Ghoshal, "Matrix Management: Not a Structure, a Frame of Mind", *Harvard Business Review*, July–August, pp. 138–145, 1990.

13. Kirth, Christopher M., *International Business Environment and Management*, 2nd ed., Prentice-Hall Inc., Englewood Cliffs, New Jersey, 1985, p. 374.

14. Miles and Snow, op. cit.

15. French, Wendell L. and Cecil H. Bell, Jr., *Organisation Development*, Prentice Hall, Englewood Cliffs, New Jersey, p. 119, 1978.

Internet Resources

- *www.thehindubusinessline.com*
- *www.kingfisher.com*
- *www.itcportal.com*
- *www.airtel.in*
- *www.tatamotors.com*

18

Cultural Dynamics and Strategy Execution

LEARNING OBJECTIVES

The present Chapter aims at:

- Providing an incisive view of the dynamics of organisational culture and its tenets.
- Familiarising readers with the evolution of culture in an organisation and its perpetuation.
- Giving an understanding of influence of organisational culture on strategy execution.
- Presenting a vivid view of transformation of culture in changed environment.

INTRODUCTION

One of the most critical forces that influence performance of an organisation and its competence in gaining sustainable competitive advantage is its *culture*. In fact, effectiveness and efficacy of the organisation are dependent upon its culture which affects the way the managerial functions of planning, organising, staffing, leading and controlling are carried out.[1] Every company has an immanent culture, having its own business philosophy and principles, its own way of approaching problems and making decisions, its own embedded patterns of how it does things around here, its own moves, taboos and political don'ts—in other words its own ingrained beliefs, behaviour and through pattern, business practices and personality.[2] Every organisation has a culture that governs how organisational people behave. It helps us to predict their attitudes and behaviour.[3] It has significant impact on employees' turnover and possibly their job performance.[4] Organisational culture is, thus, the personality of an organisation. It is like the blood flow in the human system that connects and energises the various internal organs.

As such, it is important to comprehend concept and tenets of organisational culture, origin of culture in an organisation and power of culture in improving organisational effectiveness and creating a balance between strategy and culture.

CONCEPT OF ORGANISATIONAL CULTURE

Organisational culture is the collection of beliefs, expectations and values learned and shared by the corporation's members and transmitted from one generation to another.[5]

It exists despite one's desire to have it or not, whether noticed or ignored and whether articulated or not. It is reflected in how things are done and how problems are solved in an organisation.[6] Organisational culture embodies the values and standards that guide people's behaviour. It determines the organisation's overall direction. It governs what company stands for, how it allocates its resources, its organisational structure, the system it uses, the people it hires, the fit between the jobs and people, the results it recognises and rewards, what it defines as problems and opportunities and how it deals with them.[7]

It is evident from the above that the epicentre of an organisation's culture is its beliefs, shared norms, values and philosophy and about how its affairs ought to be conducted—the reasons why it does things the way it does.

Organisational culture has a host of unique attributes such as observed behavioural regularities (use of common language terminology, and rituals related to defence and demeanour), norms (standards of behaviour), dominant values (major values that the organisational espouses and expects the participants to share), philosophy (policies setting forth the organisation's beliefs about how the employees and/or customers are to be treated), rules of an organisational climate (overall feeling that is conveyed by the physical layout, the way the participants interact and the way members of an organisation conduct themselves with the customers or other outsiders.[8]

Corporate cultures vary widely, as can be noted from Illustrative Capsule 18.1, exhibiting organisational cultures of leading organisations in India.

ILLUSTRATIVE CAPSULE **18.1**

ORGANISATIONAL CULTURES OF MARUTI UDYOG LTD., ONGC, WIPRO, HINDALCO, RELIANCE INDUSTRIES

MARUTI UDYOG LTD (MUL)

Organisational culture of MUL has the following unique features:

- Participative management, teamwork, Kaizen (continuous improvement), communication and information sharing, open office culture for easy accessibility.
- Focus on quality and productivity.
- Empowerment to employees.
- Harmony, trust, respect, loyalty, benevolence, human feelings are key values of MUL culture.
- Customer orientation.
- Strict work discipline for individuals and organisation.

ONGC

ONGC has undertaken an organisation transformation exercise in which HR has taken a lead role as a change agent by evolving a communication strategy to ensure involvement and participation among employees in various work centres. Key elements of organisational culture of ONGC are participative and innovative. Policies and policymakers at ONGC have always had the interests of the large and multi-discipline workforce at heart, consultative, associative and administrative forum for interactive participation and for fostering an innovative culture. In fact, ONGC has been one of the few organisations where this method has been implemented. It has had a positive impact on the overall operations since it has led to enhanced efficiency and productivity and reduced wastages and costs.

WIPRO

WIPRO laid a strong emphasis on shared beliefs and leadership values. In 1993, much before it became fashionable to do so, Premji had articulated a set of beliefs that would shape Wipro's strong and distinctive organisational values.

The WIPRO's creative work environment practices a non-hierarchical structure and promotes free flow of information and expertise. The organisation believes in bringing together different interest groups to keep its employees' creative momentum on the upswing. WIPRO cares is an initiative that provides the opportunity to the employees to involve themselves in a social service set up. WIPRO takes its corporate responsibility seriously and expects its members to contribute their time and effort here.

HINDALCO

At the heart of HINDALCO's process and product, behind its growth and success, lies the story of the HINDALCO team. A multi-lingual, multi-cultural cross-section of people bound by the same values and pursuing a common mission—to create superior value, realise their full potential and steer the company towards a pre-eminent position amongst global metal majors. An achievement-focused and development-oriented, embedded with high standards of business ethics and supported by sound management practices is the defining characteristic of the HINDALCO work culture. The company is a learning organisation where motivation runs through the talent pool and skills set from the shop floor to the office desk.

RELIANCE INDUSTRIES

Reliance believes that good governance practices stem from the culture and mindset of the organisation. According to its policy, the company is unequivocally committed to all its stakeholders—employees, customers, shareholders, investors, vendors and policy planners. At Reliance, every team member is encouraged to ensure that the stakeholders' interests are uppermost. Reliance has a well-defined policy framework in this regard consisting of values and commitment, code of ethics, business policies, prohibition of insider trading, programme of ethics and management.

TENETS OF AN ORGANISATION'S CULTURE

According to a recent research study, organisation's culture is composed of the following:

(i) Innovation and risk taking: The degree to which the employees are encouraged to be innovative and take risks.

(ii) Attention to detail: The degree to which the employees are expected to exhibit precision, analysis, and attention to detail.

(iii) Outcome orientation: The degree to which the management focuses on the results or outcomes rather than on the techniques and processes used to achieve those outcomes.

(iv) People orientation: The degree to which the management decisions take into consideration the effect of outcomes on people within the organisation.

(v) Team orientation: The degree to which work activities are organised around teams rather than individuals.

(vi) Aggressiveness: The degree to which people are aggressive and competitive rather than easy going.

(vii) Stability: The degree to which the organisational activities emphasise maintaining the status quo in contrast to growth.

Each of these tenets exists on a continuum from low to high.

Depending on the degree to which the members of an organisation accept the norms, values or other cultural contents, organisational culture may be highly or lowly intensive.[10] Organisations with strong norms, promoting a particular value, such as Quality and Kaizen at MUL, have high degree of **intensive cultures**. The members in an organisation having intensive culture tend to exhibit consistent behaviour. Intensive culture shows the culture's depth.

Another attribute of organisational culture is **cultural integration** which refers to the extent to which units across the organisation share a common culture. This is the culture's depth. Organisations with a pervasive dominant culture may hierarchically be controlled and power-oriented and has integrated cultures. All or a majority of employees tend to hold the same cultural values and norms. This is known as **strong culture** which is characterised by the organisation's core values being both intensely and widely shared.[11] Strong culture companies typically have creed or value statements, and regularly focus on the importance of using these values and principles as the basis for decisions and actions taken throughout the organisation. A strong and dominant culture gives an organisation its distinct personality.

In contrast, an organisation will be weak and fragmented when many subcultures exist, few values and behavioural norms are widely shared and there are few traditions. Generally, large organisations structured into different units along functional and geographical lines have sub-cultures and a less integrated culture, reflecting common problems, situations or experience that the members face. For example, the purchase department can have a sub-culture that is uniquely shared by the members of that department. It will include the core values of the dominant culture plus additional values unique to the members of the department. Likewise, an office or unit of an organisation which is physically separated from its main operations may take on a different personality. Again, the core values are essentially retained but modified to reflect the separated unit's distinct situation.

It is important to note that the stronger an organisation's culture, the less the management need be concerned with developing formal rules and regulations to guide the employees' behaviour. These guidelines will be internalised in the employees when they accept the organisation's culture.[12]

CREATING AND NURTURING ORGANISATIONAL CULTURE

Creating and nurturing corporate culture, that not only fits into the design and rationale of the work practices of the company, but also meets the character and needs of a large and diverse workforce is the real challenge the chief executives encounter today. It is a matter of integrating and synthesizing the personal agendas of their employees with the collective agenda of the company.

An organisation's culture does not pop out of thin air. Beliefs and philosophy, norms, values and practices that become embedded in the culture of an organisation originate from a single person having idea for the new enterprise, division, department or from the bottom of the organisational hierarchy or the top.[13] The founders of an organisation traditionally have a major impact in establishing the early culture. They have a vision of what the organisation should be. They are not constrained by previous customs of doing things or ideologies. The small size that typically characterises any new organisation further facilitates the founders imposing their vision on all organisational members. Because the founders have the original idea, they also typically have biases on how to get the idea fulfilled. The organisation's culture results from the interaction between the founders' biases and assumptions and what the original members learn subsequently from their own experiences. There are slew of examples including Henry Ford at the Ford Motor Company, Thomas Watson at IBM, Sam Walton at Wal-Mart, David Packard at Hewlett-Packard, J.N. Tata at Tata Group and G.D. Birla at Birla Group where individuals had immeasurable impact in shaping their organisation's culture.

Once established, practices within the organisation act to maintain it by exposing the employees to a set of similar experiences.[14] A company's culture can be perpetuated by continuity of leadership, by screening and selecting new group members according to how well their values and behaviour fit in, by systematic socialisation of the new members in the fundamentals of cultures, by the efforts of senior group members to reiterate core values in daily conversations and pronouncements, by the narration of the company legends, by regular ceremonies honouring the members who display cultural norms and penalising those who do not.[15]

While screening the new members, companies are concerned with hiring those who will fit in and who embrace their prevailing culture. This attempt to ensure a proper match results in the hiring of people who have common values. Such members feel pleasure in serving the organisation for a long time. They play a major role in indoctorinating the new employees into the culture. Members whose values conflict with the organisation's values tend to leave quickly.

Applicants for entry-level positions at Procter and Gamble, Wipro, Infosys, HINDALCO and Maruti adopt an exhaustive application and screening process. Their interviewers are a part of a cadre who have been selected and trained extensively. Applicants are interviewed in depth for such qualities as their ability to "turn out high volumes of excellent work, identity and understanding problems and reach thoroughly substantiated and well-reasoned conclusions leading to action".

The actions of the current top management set the general climate of what is acceptable behaviour and what is not. How the employees are to be socialised will depend on the degree of success achieved in matching the new employees' values to those of the organisation in the selection process and the top management's preference for socialisation methods.

However, an organisation's culture is not static. It changes in consequence to environmental developments. Crisis and new challenges evolve into new ways of doing things. Arrival of new leaders and occurrence of tectonic changes in socio-economic milieu across the globe leading to change in corporate vision, objectives and strategy can cause a culture to evolve.

CULTURE AS ADJUNCT TO STRATEGY EXECUTION

Organisational culture plays significant role in successful implementation of the company's strategy, for the fact that it influences beliefs and core values of the members, increases their commitment to the corporate objectives and strategies and shapes their attitudes and behaviour.

It provides a climate and an umbrella of mutual trust, so that all the employees grow and develop under its aegis to their optimum potential and promise and contribute their best to translate into action.

A company's culture oriented towards strategy supporting values, practices and behavioural norms lends incredible support to strategy effectuation efforts. For example, Airtel's culture of frugality and thrift inspires its members to embark on cost-saving initiatives which will be immensely useful in the successful execution of a low-cost leadership strategy. Maruti's engendered values of quality, productivity and empowerment have facilitated the management in executing differential leadership strategy. Organisation culture, which focuses on taking initiatives, challenging the status quo, exhibiting creativity, embracing change, and promotes creative collaboration and drive to lead market change, yields to outcomes that are conducive to successful the execution of product innovation and technological leadership.[16]

It must, however, be noted that an organisation's culture can be helpful in improving organisational effectiveness through successful strategy execution only when it is excellent and performance-oriented and produces a work climate and *spirit de corps*.

In this type of culture, the corporate management is expected to pursue policies and practices that encourage people to do their best. They concentrate on product innovation and development initiatives, welcome new ideas and take calculated risks to create new business positions. They sincerely care about the well being of all the stakeholders and try to satisfy all the legitimate demands. Equity and fairness to all are a decision-making principle—a commitment often described as "doing the right thing".

Companies having performance-oriented culture are usually people-oriented and reinforce their concern for individual employees in every conceivable way. They treat their employees with dignity and respect, train them thoroughly, encourage them to use their own drive, initiative and creativity in performing this, set reasonable and clear performance standards, hold managers at every level responsible for developing the people who report to them, and grant employees enough autonomy to stand out, excel and contribute. To create a result-oriented organisational culture, a company must make champion of the people who turn in winning performance.[17]

Furthermore, performance and result-oriented culture should coalesce with the organisational strategy so that the employees are energised to perform their jobs in a strategy supportive manner, adding significantly to the power and effectiveness of strategy execution. Such cultures can promote sustainable excellent performance only when there is complete compatibility between strategy and culture. A strong strategy-supporting culture nurtures and motivates people to do their best; it provides structure and standards and a value system in which to operate; it promotes strong company identification among employees. All these make the employees feel genuinely better about their jobs and work environment and stimulate them to perform closer to the best of their abilities. Godrej consumer products has performance-oriented culture, detailed as Illustrative Capsule 18.2.

ILLUSTRATIVE CAPSULE 18.2

PERFORMANCE-ORIENTED CULTURE OF GODREJ CONSUMER PRODUCTS

Godrej consumer has a performance-oriented culture, created and maintained by its Chairman Adi Godrej. The company has valuable professionals on its Board. It has instituted a lot of business processes and other initiatives, which, the management believe, has created a performance-oriented and people-oriented organisation. There is a 360-degree evaluation for all senior people, including the CEO. The company has constituted a young executive Board. They do a lot of research, discussion and studies on issues of HR development, corporate governance, strategic planning and, once a quarter, report to the group management committee with a presentation. The company pursues policy of empowerment, providing opportunity to young executives to take decisions. Learning opportunities and development are other elements of Godrej culture. Focus on communication is a key to the company's culture. The Chairman regularly meets up with the managers and the President with the managers and officers. The Chairman communicates with all employees every quarter.[18]

Where there is a mismatch between culture and strategy and ingrained values and operating philosophies do not cultivate strategy-supporting habits and the very kinds of behaviour needed to execute strategy successfully, the culture becomes a stumbling block, hurting the organisational performance.[19]

The key to big Japanese success in the US auto market does not owe to strategy alone. It is also a culture that inspired the workers to excel at fits and finishes to produce mouldings that match and doors that don't sag.[20]

TRANSFORMING CULTURE IN CHANGING ENVIRONMENT

Strong compatibility between culture and strategy, as noted above, is precondition to culture serving as a powerful source of competitive advantage and sustained growth of an organisation. Non-compatibility between the two leads to disastrous results.

Organisational culture is not static. Like an organisation that changes and grows through its life cycle, the culture of a company must be changed in consonance with the environmental developments if it has to support its strategy making and execution efforts in the rapidly changing environment. According to John Kotter, companies with adaptive cultures, outperform other companies with 4 times more revenue growth, 8 times more employee growth, 12 times more stock price growth and 756 times more net income growth. It must, however, be noted that culture need not be changed every time on the occurrence of small or incremental environmental changes. It is only in the event of breakthrough changes or transformational changes, as witnessed in India since pursuance of the policy of liberalisation and globalisation, changing the business milieu of the country or occurrence of sub-prime crisis resulting in global economic chaos, that the management has to transform its existing culture that does not fit in the changing milieu, failing which the company may face problem of survival. If the existing beliefs, and core values and norms embedded in the company's culture do not measure up to current and future competitive demands, prevent it from adopting to changing economic contingencies and do not agree with those which influence the organisation's effectiveness, allowing such cultures to continue is very likely to result in stagnation and even extinction of the organisation.

Pepsi India transformed, for example, its culture of passivity to that of aggressiveness when the top management found that the existing culture will in no way help the company to become number one in the field of soft drinks. With change in the culture, the company could take on Coke directly; consumers have been advised explicitly to compare the tastes of the two colas. Thrust of the new culture is on winning at all levels and the employees' experience of their culture.

Top management of Ashok Leyland Ltd. (ALL) changed the organisational culture in 2009 to cope with emerging competitive challenge to the companys (Illustrative Capsule 18.3).

ILLUSTRATIVE CAPSULE 18.3

TRANSFORMING CULTURE BY ASHOK LEYLAND

By the turn of the century, it became apparent to the top management of Ashok Leyland Ltd. (ALL)— India's second largest manufacturer of commercial vehicles—that the company needed to undergo a complete transformation if it has to remain a significant player in the rapidly evolving market place. From just two players then the industry was all set to get crowded with the proposed entry of foreign truck majors such as *Volvo* and *MAN AG*. Most importantly, the mindset of customers had begun to change. They were no longer willing to wait for the delivery of vehicles, and customer loyalty could not be taken for granted anymore. Thus, the commercial vehicle industry was moving from being a sellers' market to a buyers' market.

It did not take the ALL brass too long to figure out what the company needed to do. It decided to become aggressive and more agile with a strong focus on innovation instead of remaining content with the number two position in the industry and a reasonable profit year after year. They also understood that in order to bring about this change ALL needed to turn younger. This transformation, the top management surmised, would not be possible with an executive team whose average age was around 50. By combining the exuberance of youth who are typically experimental, tech savvy, vibrant, and energetic with the experience of seniors who have depth, maturity and validated knowledge, ALL wanted to turn itself into a modern outfit and offer a serious challenge not only to Tata Motors, the market leader, but also to the other global majors who were planning an entry into the Indian Commercial Vehicle market. The Hinduja Group's flagship company soon began to be on youth like never before and by 2003–04, young executives (below 35 years of age) accounted for 37% of the management rising up to 40% by 2005–06.

However, to its dismay, the Human Resource (HR) department noticed increasing attrition levels among the newly recruited young executives from 4.8% in 2003–04 to 21.3% in 2006–07. The reason, according to various employee-feedback measures, was culture shock. The youngsters, to their rude surprise, found ALL to be a very different creature—a compliant organisation—where juniors seldom questioned the seniors, who for their part, demanded a culture of reverence from their subordinates. It was a company where freedom was not a given thing, and transparency in decision-making and knowledge sharing not often practiced. But youngsters had no qualm in questioning what they thought was incorrect. They gave more importance to knowledge than hierarchy and sought immediate results. They also wanted clear key result areas and goals and were unwilling to leave their career in the hands of their bosses. On the other hand, the seniors, who were used to a different environment, resented and resisted the approach of the youngsters and this, in effect, led to a generation gap. The young executives felt left out and unwanted.

R. Seshasayee, MD, ALL was perturbed to note the reasons that caused the young executives to leave. He felt strong that it was important to challenge the young executives at work and through that reinforce the reasons for them to stay on. It was then he decided "if the organisation had to change to suit the youth, so be it" and launched "MISSION YES" in 2006.

"MISSION YES", says Shekhar Arora, Executive Director, HR, "was conceived to engage, enable and empower youngsters who were feeling isolated and ignored". Under MISSION YES, banner projects, which were important to the company, were given to cross functional teams of young executives.

"Through these projects we engaged the youngsters. By offering them management time and lots of data (even confidential information) we enabled them to come up with a solution. Finally, when their recommendations were considered seriously and accepted, they felt empowered", says Arora. The youngsters grabbed the opportunity and, in their typical style, began to engage the top management. The Management Plan Budget (MPB) team consisting of 23 young executives, while drawing up the annual plan for the 2007–08, questioned the production capacity of one lakh units drawn up by the managing committee. They claimed that the capacity could be stretched by 10% to 1.10 lakh units. The team explained to the senior management how capacity could be raised through debottlenecking production at various units. The management committee accepted the recommendation and implemented it. Similarly, another team designed a modern bus (called *i-Bus*) for city transportation in nine months flat—from concept to prototype. ALL also formed "MISSION YES Organisation", which is run entirely by YES with an allocated budget. It conducts events, and knowledge-sharing sessions, and comes up with innovative ideas which then became a banner project.

As these efforts began to capture the imagination of the young executives, ALL rolled out a development linked career plan, seeking out high performing youngsters, identifying their aspirations and committing to help them get there in the organisation.

The importance given to the young executives triggered another round of culture shock within the company—this time among the seniors, who felt left out. It was then the company decided to rope them in as mentors. Having learnt things the hard way when they joined the company, seniors took to mentoring passionately. Today, many of them have come to be rated as ace mentors (an honour given based on the feedback by young executives).

These measures have broken the ice between the youngsters and the seniors, and both have come to respect each other. The results are beginning to show "Attrition rate came down from 21%, when MISSION YES was launched to 11.2% in 2008–09. Young executives have begun to take up leadership positions in the company. Not only that; the employees on the shop floor are now seeking a similar process for themselves, and most interestingly, many senior executives want the age criterion of 35 years removed so that they too could participate in MISSION YES", says Arora.

In early 2011, Mahindra and Mahindra changed its core values and purpose and adopted a new brand positioning—Rise—to cope with changed business environment[21] (Illustrative Capsule 18.4).

ILLUSTRATIVE CAPSULE 18.4

TRANSFORMATION OF CULTURE BY MAHINDRA & MAHINDRA THROUGH NEW BRAND POSITIONING

Thirteen years ago Mahindra & Mahindra (M&M)—$7.1 billion automobiles-to-IT conglomerate—outlined the group's core values where the celebration of being Indian was at the core. But with business expanding new geographies, the top management felt that the core value has to stand for something new, which is the new rainbow for the company, which is expected to lift its fortunes and take it to the next level.

On January 16, 2011 Anand Mahindra—Vice-Chairman & Managing Director—unveiled its new brand positioning, called 'Rise'. "Rise", according to Mahindra, "is going to be new rainbow—something everyone always tries to get close". "The idea is to communicate with one brand voice, one face and one Mahindra core purpose …. Rise … means achieving world class standards in everything we do and conquering tough global markets".

For non-Indian employees, who now comprise 10% of M&M's workforce, the earlier tag line "Indians are second to none", did not mean much. The Spirit of Rise, the group executives said, is based on three brand pillars—accepting no limits, alternative thinking and driving positive changes, involving organisational soul-searching and seeking to unite the Mahindra workforce as a group of unconventional thinkers who create world-class offerings.

To ensure that the 1,00,000 plus staffers are on the same page, M&M has started detailed human resource exercises which include incorporating Rise in performance management systems. It has, for example, launched a new metric called 'Employee Promotes Score'. Under this, people will be judged "how enthusiastic an employee is to recommend Mahindra products".

With employees as the core audience of the rebranding exercise, the human resource team has gone into an overdrive. Mahindra Group HR head, Rajeev Dubey, is spearheading efforts to ensure the new attitude filters down in the actions and decision-making of the company. "Rise culture will have to permeate our communication, performance and talent management, rewards and recognition and work designs", says Dubey.

Mahindra said he expects Rise to allow the employees to outperform and give them a reason why they should come back to work the next day.

The company has decided to spend ₹120 crore over the next three years to communicate the essence of the new positioning both within the company as well as its trade partners.

In view of the above, the top management needs to assess from time to time, the suitability of the existing organisational culture in the changed environment, and a consequent change in the organisational strategy. It has been recognised by the organisations around the globe that a strong culture cohered to strategy making and execution brings about material difference between successful and unsuccessful organisations. Hence, transforming the culture in consonance with change in corporate objectives and strategies can improve capability of a company to implement new strategies and perform better.

However, transforming the culture of an organisation is difficult and time taking process because it demands changing core values, norms symbols, myth and behaviour. As a matter of fact, it is tougher to reshape a deeply entrenched culture than it is to instill strategy supportive culture from the scratch in an upcoming enterprise.

Change in the organisational culture demands perspicacious understanding of the existing culture, identifying a sub-culture in the organisation and thereby deciding which aspects of the present culture are strategy friendly and which are hindrances. This should be followed by threadbare discussions of the top management with the concerned employees about those facets of culture that need to be changed and the actions being taken to establish new strategy-supporting culture. Symbolic actions in terms of the role models by the top management such as leading cost minimisation exercises, emphasising the importance of responding to customers, initiating measures to alter such policies and practices as hinder the execution of new strategy, according recognition to performing employees, and to those who displayed performance in the establishment of new culture, would convince the employees about seriousness of the management about transformation of culture.

The top management may further reaffirm the employees' belief in its commitment to create a new culture of taking strong measures such as replacing managers imbued with old cultures by new "breed" managers, changing long-standing policies and practices that are outmoded and dysfunctional or those that block new initiatives, linking incentives to the new measures of strategic performance and making major budgetary reallocation of resources from existing strategy-based projects to upcoming strategy projects.

For successful transformation of corporate culture, it is imperative to weave shared values, beliefs, and guiding principles into the fabric of day-to-day business. It is also essential to create an environment that fosters innovation, risk taking and generally encourages breakthrough results. Everyone should have shared responsibility to be involved in 'driving' and causing change. There is an emphasis on accountability and feedback where everyone either serves a customer directly or serves someone who does.

It is noteworthy that building an adaptive culture is a journey that demands ongoing commitment from all over long periods where everyone speaks a common language.

Summary

Sustained growth and success of an enterprise, depends, inter alia, upon its culture which affects the way the managerial functions are performed.

Organisational culture is the collection of beliefs, expectations and values learned and shared by the members of the enterprise and transmitted from one generation to another. It is reflected in how things are done and problems solved in the organisation.

Organisational cultures may vary widely. Depending on the degree to which members of the organisation accept the norms, values and other cultural contents, organisational culture may be highly or lowly insensitive. Organisations with strong norms, promoting a particular value have high degree of intensive cultures. In contrast, organisations with weak and fragmented culture, only few values and behavioural norms are widely shared.

An organisation's culture originates from a single person (generally from the founder) having idea for the upcoming enterprise. Because the founders have the original idea, they also typically have biases on how to get the idea fulfilled. Once established, practices within the organisation act to maintain it by exposing the employees to a set of similar experiences.

A company's culture can be perpetuated by continuity of leadership, by screening and selecting new group members according to how well their values and behaviour fit in, by systematic socialisation of the new members in the fundamentals of cultures, by the efforts of senior group members to reiterate core values in daily conversations and pronouncement, by the narration of company legends, etc.

Organisational culture plays a significant role in successful execution of the company's strategy because it influences beliefs and core values of the members, increases their commitment to the corporate objectives and strategies, and shapes their attitudes and behaviour.

However, a culture to be effective, must be performance-oriented that produces a work climate and spirit de corps. Furthermore, there should be strong linkage between culture and strategy, otherwise the organisation may face disastrous consequences. Accordingly, the culture will have to be changed to cope with dynamically changing environment and the concomitant change in the organisation's strategy.

Key Terms

Corporate culture
Cultural integration
Intensive culture
Performance-oriented culture

Strong culture
Weak culture
Transforming culture

Discussion Questions

1. What is organisational culture? Discuss its fundamental tenets.
2. How does culture originate in an organisation? Discuss ways with which culture can be perpetuated in an organisation.
3. Discuss how culture influences execution of strategy and organisational effectiveness.
4. What is intensive culture? Bring out its implications with reference to an organisation.
5. Bring out the redeeming features of performance culture.
6. "Organisational culture to be effective must be compatible with corporate strategy". Comment.
7. How can organisational culture be transformed in response to changes in environment and corporate strategy?

References

1. Weihrich, Hairiz and Harold Koontz, *Management—A Global Perspective*, McGraw Hill International Editions, p. 333, 1994.
2. Thompson, Arthur A. Jr. and A.J. Strickland III, *Strategic Management*, Irwin McGraw Hill, pp. 291–293, 1996.
3. Robbins, Stephen P., *Essentials of Organisational Behaviour*, Prentice Hall of India, New Delhi, pp. 236–237, 1997.
4. Cox, Charles J. and Cary L. Cooper, "The Irrelevance of American Organisation Sciences to the UK and Europe", *Journal of General Management*, Winter, pp. 29–30, 1985.

5. Schein, E.H., *The Corporate Culture Survival Guide*, Jossey-Bass, San Francisco, p. 12, 1990.

6. Flanagan, P., *The ABC of Changing Corporate Culture*, M.A. Cambridge, Ballinger, 1984.

7. Petrock, Frank, "Corporate Culture Enhances Profits", *HR Magazine* 35, November, pp. 64–66, 1990.

8. Luthans, Fred, *Organisational Behaviour*, McGraw Hill, 7 Singapore, pp. 497–498, 1995.

9. O'Reilly, C.A. III, J. Chatman and D.F. Caldwell, "People and Organisational Culture: A Profile Comparison Approach to Assessing Person-Organisation Fit", *Academy of Management Journal*, September, pp. 487–516, 1991.

10. Rousseau, D.M., "Assessing Organisational Culture: The Case for Multiple Methods" in *Organisational Climate and Culture*, B. Schneider (Ed.), Jossey Bass, San Francisco, pp. 153–192, 1990.

11. Wiener, Y., "Forms of Value Systems: A Focus on Organisational Effectiveness and Cultural Change and Management", *Academy of Management Review*, October, p. 536, 1988.

12. Robbins, Stephen P., op. cit., p. 240.

13. Kotter, John P. and James L. Heskett, *Corporate Culture and Performance*, Free Press, New York, p. 7, 1992.

14. Harrison, J.R. and G.R. Carroll, "Keeping the Faith: A Model of Cultural Transmission in Formal Organisations", *Administrative Science Quarterly*, December, pp. 552–82, 1991.

15. Schain, Edgar, *Organisational Culture and Leadership*, Jossey-Bass, San Francisco, p. 210, 1985.

16. Sashittal, "Cultures that Support Product-Innovation Processes", *Academy of Management Executive* 16, N3, August, pp. 42–54, 2002.

17. Waterman, Robert H. Jr., "The Seven Elements of Strategic Fit", *Journal of Business Strategy* 2(3), p. 70, Winter, 1982.

18. *Business Today*, November 18, 2007.

19. "A Business and Its Beliefs", *Mc Kinsey Foundation Lecture*, McGraw Hill, 1963, as quoted in Kotter and Heskett, op. cit., p. 17.

20. *Business Today*, December 13, 2009.

21. *Business Standard*, February 21, 2011.

Internet Resources

- *www.marutisuzuki.com*
- *www.ongcindia.com*
- *www.wipro.in*
- *www.hindalco.com*
- *www.ril.com*

19

Strategy Execution through Leadership

LEARNING OBJECTIVES

The present Chapter aims at:
- Providing conceptual exposition of leader and leadership.
- Distinguishing between a leader and a manager.
- Presenting a vivid view of how leadership influences strategy execution.
- Giving a lucid account of attributes of effective leadership.

INTRODUCTION

Outlining the importance of a leader in success and effectiveness of a business undertaking, it has been aptly observed that "no organisation is good or bad; it is the leader who makes or mars". This is for the fact that an individual by dint of formally designated managerial authority or by virtue of unique attributes drives the people towards accomplishment of the enterprise objectives. But not all leaders are managers, nor for that matter, are all managers, leaders. Just because an organisation provides its managers with certain rights is no assurance that they will be able to lead effectively. Non-sanctioned leadership, i.e., the ability to influence that arises outside of the formal structure of the organisation, is as important or more important than formal influence.[1] It is the quality of a leader that decides the quality of the environment which, in turn, determines the quality of talents on which depends the success of an organisation.

LEADER AND LEADERSHIP—CONCEPTUAL UNDERPINNING

The fundamental task of leaders is to prime good feelings in those they lead. That occurs when a leader creates the resonance—a reservoir of positivity that frees the best in the people. At its root, then the primal job of leadership is emotional. Primal leadership is, thus, about leading the people with values, and managing their own emotions effectively. Such leaders have the ability to empathise and see things from other people's perspective.

Leadership is generally about the style and behaviour of leaders for providing direction, influencing people, rousing their commitment and mobilising their talent and energies to achieve organisational objectives (Illustrative Capsule 19.1). An organisation's ability to mobilise its employees, trade partners, and suppliers to execute it relentlessly and vigorously for all the time to come everywhere in the world, is the most challenging task that a leader has to perform.

ILLUSTRATIVE CAPSULE 19.1

LEADERSHIP STYLE OF WIPRO TECHNOLOGIES[2]

In 1966, when Azim Premji took over the leadership of the company on the demise of his father, some of the shareholders even demanded that the company be sold to the highest bidder as they were unwilling to trust a 21-year old to run it. But Premji was determined to prove himself and with confidence asked them to come and see (the company) after five years.

Wipro, which was a small company then with a turnover of just ₹4 crore, started its business with the production of Sunflower brand of 'Vanaspati'. Today, the Group's turnover is more than ₹3,000 crore and it diversified along the way from manufacturing and marketing 'Vanaspati' to becoming a major in the global software services segment.

Premji believes in creating leadership at all levels in the company and his driving business philosophy is 'value for money by applying thought'. He admires the leadership qualities of Mahatma Gandhi and Jac Welch. He admires Welch for his ability to get things done and the way in which he moved the 2,40,000 strong organisation (General Electric) to go in a particular direction. He says he understands where and why these leaders succeeded and why they failed. They are inspirational role models for his own leadership styles and values.

A good leadership, according to Former Chairman, Eicher Motors, Subodh Bhargava, is always holistic and comprehensive. It does not just look at product development or IT or accounts or manpower efficiency. It has to take a systems approach to the entire thing so as to derive synergistic benefits inherent therein.

As such, leadership should not be considered merely as a matter of style and behaviour of individuals, but also inner motivation, values, beliefs, attitudes, insights, knowledge, skills and perceptions of the key functionaries in the organisation whose vision and aspirations provide the driving force and direction to the organisation. Alongside this, leadership also encompasses the development of processes, systems and cultural norms developed by the leaders of the organisation that support certain kinds of attitudes and behaviours which ensure setting challenging objectives and accomplishing high levels of performance.

The modern concept of leadership focuses on distributed leadership, where leadership does not only talk about corporate level leadership but also leadership at SBUs and their constituents and even include the people whose title does not imply leadership but who actually step forward in certain context at the functional and departmental levels. Traditionally, leadership was used to refer the top management who were expected to have all the answers to the problems the organisation was faced with. In today's complex business world, the senior executives do not have answer for all the problems because of demand for a broad range of critical skills which they do not possess. Individual executives just don't have the personal capacity to sense and make sense of all the changes swirling around them. The paradox is that the answers exist in the organisational people who do possess required skills. Hence, the thrust is now on people leading at every level of the organisation because of their unique leadership qualities. The corporate leaders need to distribute leadership responsibility, replacing hierarchy and formal authority with organisation bandwidth, which draws on collective intelligence. Executives need to relax their sense of obligation to be all and do all and instead become comfortable sharing their burden with the people operating in diverse functions and locations throughout the organisation. Distributed leadership energises transformation by enhancing adaptive capability and sharpening responsiveness to change.

Distributed leadership is becoming more popular in Indian corporate world in recent years to cope with recent cataclysmic changes in business environment. The corporate leaders in India have realised that success in today's unpredictable and uncertain environment is possible, only if they get leaders at multiple levels involved to drive that growth. Accordingly, they are focusing on the development of leadership at all levels. Infosys has embarked on institutionalisation of sound, robust and sustained leadership for all times to come. Infosys has three tiers of leadership besides the corporate leadership. Tier I leaders, about 50 in number, are just below the Board and are from the top management cadre. The next level has 150 leaders who are selected by Tier I leaders and a couple of internal members of the Board. Tier III of the leadership has about 450 leaders chosen from the middle management. Once the leaders are chosen, they come under the care of the Director of the Infosys Leadership Institute and are nurtured very carefully through training programmes and mentoring sessions designed by it.[3]

It is also notable that leadership is not by title; leadership has to do with whether an individual steps forward and takes a lead. In fact, there are people who have leadership titles, but do not lead. Leadership is about a set of behaviours. A fancy title is not only an opportunity; it is also an obligation to engage in certain behaviours. Indian business leadership has shown some distinctive tenets. Some of these are from India's spiritual tradition. Great corporate leaders have seen leadership not as power, privilege and enjoyment, but as a sacred trust and responsibility. There is stress on public good, on all the stakeholders, and not just the shareholders' value maximisation.

LEADERSHIP AND MANAGEMENT

Organisations to survive and thrive in turbulent times need both effective leadership and efficacious management. In fact, leadership and management are the two sides of a coin having two distinct but complementary systems of action. Strong leadership with weak management is no better, and is sometimes actually worse, than the reverse. Hence, the need to combine strong leadership and strong management and use each to balance the other.[4]

Not everyone can be good at both leading and managing. Some may have the capacity to become excellent managers but not strong leaders. Others have great leadership potential but, for a variety of reasons, have great difficulty becoming strong managers. Smart companies value both kinds of people and work hard to make them a part of the team. However, these companies forget that people cannot manage and lead unless planned endeavours are made to grow the top people to provide both. For this purpose, organisations must understand the basic difference between leadership and management.

Leadership is about coping with change so as to survive and grow effectively in a rapidly changing economic, technological, competitive and socio-cultural and political environment. Hence, setting the direction of the change is fundamental to leadership. For setting a direction, leaders gather a broad range of data and look for patterns, relationships and linkages that help explain things. This enables the leader to create vision and strategies in terms of what the organisation should become over the long-term, and articulate a feasible way of achieving this vision.

The management, on the other hand, is about coping with business complexity. In the absence of good management, complex enterprises tend to become chaotic in ways that may lead to their extinction. Good management brings a degree of order and consistency to crucial dimensions like the quality and profitability of products. The management handles business complexity by planning and budgeting and develops the capacity to achieve its plan by organising and staffing—creating an organisational structure and set of jobs for accomplishing plan requirements, staffing the jobs with competent people, communicating the plan to these people, assigning responsibility for carrying out the plan and devising systems to monitor implementation.

The equivalent leadership activity, however, is aligning people by communicating the new direction to those who can create coalitions that understand the vision, and are passionately committed to its achievement. Aligning invariably involves taking many more individuals than organising does. The target population can involve not only a manager's subordinates but also bosses, peers, staff in other parts of the organisation, as well as suppliers, government officials, customers and anyone who can help translating vision into action. Further, aligning leads to empowerment in a way that organising rarely does.

The management ensures achievement of planned targets by controlling and problem-solving: monitoring actual results against the plan by means of reports, meetings and other techniques; identifying deviations, and then planning and organising to solve the problems. In striking contrast, leadership to achieve a vision requires motivating and inspiring—keeping people moving in the right direction, despite major resistance to change, by appealing to basic but often untapped.

Nevertheless, the concept of leader and manager is different: the modern multiprong strategy has encouraged the fusion of both to overcome problems arising out of bewildering developments, giving rise to the modern leader-manager concept, and is ideal for an organisation. An organisation to be conceived, to be designed and to function effectively requires a leader who conceives vision and provides direction. At the same time, translation of the vision into practice is the responsibility of the manager. Because of these two types of jobs, it is not always possible that a leader can be a good manager and vice-versa. However, it may not be difficult for a manager to acquire leadership through various structured interventions.

An individual with a fusion of leadership and managerial qualities is relatively more capable of looking at various aspects inside and outside an organisation. Being a leader-manager he will be able to study the pattern from a variety of information, and he can interpret with them, can have a futuristic look and also set a direction so that the organisation can function effectively in a continuously changing environment. Being a leader-manager, he will be capable of forcefully convincing others about his vision with his suitable management of communication. Then as a capable manager he can sit down to plan details of the strategy developed by him. The designing of an organisation structure is not an easy task even if the direction has been set. It has to be a mixture of various pressures such as socio-economic and political environment, technology, and the like. The managerial aspect of leader-manager is tested here. He has to look at the needs and risks of designing the structure. He has to procure the necessary human resources for achieving the objective. Since it is not possible to do all these jobs effectively, he delegates many of these functions but he establishes mechanism to monitor the work delegated to others. This arrangement would give him time to give proper shape to his own vision or translate this to action through proper planning and to review it time and again. Being a manager also, his planning aspect acts as a complement to his goals setting.

A leader-manager will be able to communicate with the authority about his vision and decisions. He will know that the implementation of a strategy into action requires a proper cohesion between many internal and external forces. To bring the cohesion he will select a target group consisting of both people from inside and outside the organisation. With his communication and managerial skills, he will be able to convince them about the alternative future.

Then he can take up the task of aligning the people to organisational objectives and external forces. This is in fact a very delicate job. This is a major thrust area as far as the future of an organisation is concerned.

Apart from the above, the new leader-manager has to be highly reliable and consistent as far as his vision and subsequent planning are concerned. Besides, he has to understand the basics of inspiring and guiding human resources. He should focus on improving the quality of human resources which is key to excellent performance.

In view of the above advantages of leader-manager fusion, corporate enterprises in India like Tata Group, Infosys, Wipro, Mahindra & Mahindra (M&M), Hindustan Unilever, and the like have designed and developed leadership development programmes to select, train and mentor talented managers of their organisations. The leadership development programme has gained momentum in corporate world during the last two years of economic slowdown. The managers are being trained on how to succeed in a turbulent environment, how to rethink their product positioning and to innovate things closer to the customer. Potential leaders are imparted lessons to develop social leadership with the ability to understand diversity and integrators who can put teams together.[5]

ROLE OF LEADERSHIP IN THE EXECUTION OF STRATEGY

The role of leadership in the execution of corporate strategy is paramount inasmuch as its presence is strongly felt and its personality is reflected in each and every activity associated with effectuation of corporate strategy including articulation of functional and departmental objectives and goals, putting in place right infrastructure, people and resources, alignment of the entire organisation activities to the corporate objectives and strategies, ensuring continuous free flow of information across the organisation boundaries, preparation of action plans and allocation of resources and establishing the monitoring system to assess progress of execution of plans.

While strategy-making task falls within the province of the top leadership, responsibility of executing strategy is assigned to the functional and departmental leaders. However, the top leaders have a game plan that takes care of the overall picture. HDFC Chairman, Deepak Parekh leaves operations to his seniormost managers, but leads from the front when it comes to intuiting new opportunities and strategising ways to capitalise on them before rivals are off the starting blocks. The Founder Chairman of HCL Technologies is practically invisible and keeps himself away from day-to-day management.

Corporate leaders play the role of a guide in developing functional and operating policies within the framework of corporate strategy and coach the middle level and lower ring managers in drawing up action plans and in allocation of resources.

It is also the major responsibility of the corporate leaders to balance and integrate conflicting and competing goals and plans, diverse preferences and values of line managers and to accord due attention to the social expectations. Thus, they play the role of coordinator and act as "ring master" in keeping all the diverse efforts and operations of the company headed in the same direction. The corporate leaders have to present the plan in such a manner that appeal to the organisational people.

They have to design an appropriate structure, keeping in view the needs of the corporate strategy. The task of identifying key organisational activities, grouping them into departments, delineating authority and responsibility, and establishing working relationships among groups that will enable both the company and the individuals, and to realise mutual objectives rest primarily with the top leadership. The structure should be such as to secure wholehearted cooperation of the individuals to the satisfaction of all. Integration of differences can easily be achieved if the members are committed to a common cause.

Another major responsibility of the corporate leadership is to create convivial and congenial climate in the organisation where there is dignity and respect for the individuals, and people are pushed to be as good as they can be. They have freedom to put forth new ideas and take initiative to translate them into action and feel enamoured and enthralled to give their mind and heart to accomplish organisational objectives. It has to create learning ambience where organisational people strive relentlessly to coordinate and cooperate with wide technologies and production skills into competencies that enable the organisation to bring out innovative products of world class standards at competitive price to cater to the ever-changing needs of the customers.

Good leaders create a culture of meritocracy where talents bloom and blossom and people are performance-oriented. They also bring about transformational changes in the organisational culture when it is found that the existing guiding beliefs, values and norms embedded in the organisation's culture are not adequate enough to cope with the impending challenges.

Developing viable communication system in the organisation to facilitate constant interactions among the employees at different levels is the prime responsibility of the top leadership. The system should be such as to transmit information, ideas and instructions to the subordinates on the matters pertaining to corporate goals, plans, operating policies, procedures, job roles and responsibility of the subordinates in their day-to-day functioning and to get things done through them. The communication system should be so designed as to facilitate the top leadership to keep in touch with events and activities, to achieve a measure of control over them and to get feedback on the effectiveness of their decisions, actions and behaviour.

Once the plans are put into action and the structure is in place, it is also the responsibility of the corporate leaders and functional leaders to review and rejig the actual results against the targeted ones so as to ensure if the actual performance is in conformity with the planned performance. Where a company's strategy execution effort is not delivering desired results, the top leaders have to step forward and nudge corrective measures.

If the situation allows the managers to proceed more deliberately in deciding when to make changes and what changes to make, most managers seem to prefer a process of incrementally solidifying commitment to a particular course of action. The process followed in deciding on corrective adjustments is essentially the same for both proactive and reactive changes. They sense needs, gather information, broaden and deepen their understanding of the situation, develop options and explore their pros and cons, put forth action proposals, generate partial (comfort-level) solutions, strive for consensus, and finally adopt an agreed course of action. Thus, leaders play the role of evaluator and controller.

Although the task of executing strategy successfully and achieving the desired results is daunting in today's complex and uncertain business environment, the same can be dexterously performed if the corporate managers play the role of a leader than as a manager. Even as a leader, the role of the managers should be transformational instead of a transactional. Transformational leadership inspires organisational success by profoundly affecting the followers' values. Transformational leader creates a sense of duty within an organisation, encourages new ways of handling problems and promotes learning for organisational people. As a transformational leader, a manager must move from exercising gross power of authority, which only produces compliance to the subtle power of influence, which secures commitment and passes ownership down the risk. In contrast, transactional leaders guide and motivate their followers in the direction of established objectives by classifying the role and task requirements and watch and search and intervene only if standards are not met with. Transformational leaders inspire their people by way of vision creation and articulation, empowerment, trust, knowledge share and by performance. A manager has to be an effective leader endowed with unique attributes to ensure sustained success at an exponential pace.

ATTRIBUTES OF EFFECTIVE LEADERSHIP

Effective leadership is about envisioning with passion, positivity, inspiration, loyalty, expertise, extraordinary courage, empathy, adaptability and institution ability.

Leading by Vision with Passion

Leadership is about envisioning for the organisation. It is about creating a grand vision—a purpose, which is noble, lofty and aspirational. An excellent leader conceptualises the future and sees what others cannot see. He is not only the dreamer; he has a knack to translate the dreams into reality. He passionately owns the vision and drives it to completion. He shares the vision with the employees, customers, suppliers, collaborators, investors and other enlightened groups of the society to solicit their opinions that will enable him to crystallise it in terms of corporate purpose. Sharing of the vision generates excitement, brings order out of chaos and builds confidence and trust among the employees who will work harder to make it succeed. Sharing of the vision enables the corporate leadership to interpret, refine and make it operational.

Ratan Tata's conceptualisation and development of the *Nano* car in the face of great adversity is a case in point. The project was derided as impossible and as a pipedream by the so-called experts. He faced tremendous resistance from all quarters. However, with his obsession and determination, Tata brought together Tata Motors' employees, external suppliers and stakeholders and galvanised them into action, to produce the lowest cost car despite constraints of time and resources. The *Nano* is a tribute to Tata's exemplary leadership qualities.

The successors to Dhirubhai Ambani—Mukesh Ambani and Anil Ambani—are equally known for their ambition, dynamism and passion. They are passionate in each one of their businesses. A.M. Naik, the Chairman of L&T, leads the organisation by incorrigible passion which is so robust and so sustainable that at any point of the day he will gush about a strategic plan concerning L&T, or about vision concerning L&T, or something about the business or something about building the talent. He is very upbeat in terms of enthusiasm levels, and that is perhaps the engine and the fuel which really leads many people even through very difficult circumstances.

Leading by Inspiration

Good leaders are those who have the urge for supremacy in the industry and markets and who inspire their people to achieve this ambition by fostering trust and removing paranoia, generating a sense of pride and ownership in the organisation and providing life satisfaction to them. To truly inspire trust, leaders must be extremely fair and predictable in how they deal with the people. Trusted leaders generally enjoy a reputation of being 'apolitical' 'beyond favouritism' and 'above the fray'. Being fair is a more useful leadership trait than being nice. On inspiring leadership falls the mantle of embedding and embodying the specific values that will glue the diverse activities and initiatives of the people into a cohesive whole, directed at the organisational vision and mission. Such leaders recognise that people are not just resources, not just economic, social and psychological beings, they are also spiritual beings who want meaning.

A leader can demonstrate his faith and trust on his followers by empowering them in decision-making process. Successful leaders influence people by working and playing with them, showing concern for the people. Azim Premji inspires his people by spreading the message of people orientation, which involves showing concern for the followers' well being, status and satisfaction, thus enabling them to perform their self-appointed tasks and meet the organisational objectives. Godrej Group's Adi Godrej has been boosting and channelising powers of his people towards executing their self-determined strategies by fostering trust, generating a sense of pride in the organisation and tapping the individual synergies to enable a collective push towards the common objectives. Sapient provides a unique environment of freedom, flexibility and trust that allows an individual's potential to flower.

Leading by Positive Mindset

Leaders of Reliance, Wipro, Infosys, Tata Sons, Dr. Reddy's Labs, NTPC, Larsen & Tarbo (L&T), Hero Honda and several others have positive mindsets, never complain about the constraints in the external environment, and endeavour to convert threats into opportunities. Business leaders like L.N. Jhunjhunwala and B.M. Munjal and Dhirubhai Ambani were not deterred by the highly restrictive and hostile government policies towards private sector when they were establishing their companies and they faced atrocious tax loss, unwillingness of MNCs to give technology and similar other constraints. They had enormous self-confidence and found imaginative ways of overcoming the constraints to build highly competitive and successful organisations. The attitude of the leadership in these companies is similar to the 'Mirror and Window' approach described by Jim Collins.[6] They set challenging and ambitious objectives for themselves. When they failed, they looked into the mirror to examine the reasons within themselves for their failure and to learn from it. And when they succeeded, they looked out of the window at the blue sky to thank their stars.

Leading by Loyalty

Organisational success is contingent, inter alia, upon loyalty and commitment of the leadership for the fact that greater degree of loyalty of corporate leadership engenders high degree of loyalty and commitment among its customers, employees, suppliers and shareholders, leading to increase in the profits the company reaps.[7] Outstanding loyalty is the direct result of the words and deeds—the decisions and practices—of the committed top executives who have personal integrity.

According to Reichold, there are six principles of loyalty: preach what you practice, play to win-win, be picky, keep it simple, reward the right results, listen hard, and talk straight.[8]

The committed and loyal leaders believe the action speaks louder than words and walk the talk.

In building loyalty, it is not enough that the company's competitors lose. Its partners must win. The leader can achieve extremely high customer loyalty by fostering similarly high loyalty among the employees. Dedicated employees who put customers' needs ahead of their own short-term interests reinforce the organisation's capacity to generate superior results.

A practical leader knows that his organisation cannot satisfy all the customers at a time. Accordingly, he prefers to be very much selective about his customers and designs his value propositions to appeal to such customers.

An effective leader makes his organisation as flexible and speedy as he needs to be in an increasingly complex world. Great leaders understand that they must simplify the rules for decision-making. They keep their organisation focused on one simple rule: "Do whatever is in the customers' best interest". Simplicity has structural applications and the organisational complexity impedes the quick decisive action that a fast-changing business environment demands.

A great leader designs incentive structure in such a way as to reward the loyal and committed employees. He also values the customers' satisfaction. By incorporating the customer loyalty and employee development in the manager development process, a leader can improve the alignment of interests across several partner groups.

A successful leader is a good listener and talks straight. Long-term relationship requires honest, two-way communication and learning. True communication promotes trust, which in turn, engenders loyalty. Communication also enables business leaders to clarify their priorities and coordinate responses to problems and opportunities as they develop. The principle of straight talk with the customers, vendors and employees builds trust. Most of the successful leaders do not hesitate in telling the employees where they stand. The managers are required to submit annually to 360-degree feedback: performance reviews from bosses, peers and subordinates.

Leaders of great organisations take cognisance of the above principle. They break through the cynicism of the times by showing that they believe that business is into a zero-sum game, that an organisation thrives when its partners and customers thrive. The centre of gravity for business loyalty—whether of customers, employees, investors, suppliers, or dealers—is the personal integrity of the senior leadership team. Through loyalty to ideals, the leaders become worthy of loyalty from their partners.

Leading by Courage

Great leaders have courage to take risky pursuits, courage to view changes in opportunities than as threats, courage to take higher risks, courage to think differently, courage to give freedom to the people and encourage them to take risks, courage to actively disturb the status quo even when the going is good, courage to encourage criticism, courage to benchmark against the best, and courage to take decisions.

Leaders like Dhirubhai Ambani, Ratan Tata and Munjal have been bold enough to dream high, have courage to expect the impossible from fellow persons. They saw their business exponentially while Rahul Bajaj, the Chairman, Bajaj Group, saw the changes as threats to domestic companies and what followed was clearly an indication of his lack of courage to look at those economic changes as opportunities. This led to displacement of Bajaj Auto from its numero uno position by Hero Honda. Laggards in hugging reforms without inhibitions have continued to be laggards in the market place too, while others like Reliance, Tata Motors, TCS, Infosys and Wipro have zipped past them.

The leaders, who have demonstrated courage to think differently from others, have been able to show significant impact in their areas. Robert Goizuete, the CEO of Coca-Cola Inc., thought differently from others to recover the dwindling sales of Coke. Muhammad Yunus established the Grameen Bank for the upliftment of rural folks. ITC invented new ways of helping farmers to get the right price for their products by establishing e-choupals.

Courageous leaders focus on the company's well-being and future and give a lot of freedom to their potential leaders. Tata Group boasts of its excellent leaders like Darbari Seth, Russi Mody, Sumant Moolgaoker and Xerxes Desai who worked without any interference from the leadership. This was the sterling courage demonstrated by JRD Tata.

Effective leaders have to be audacious and venturesome to breakthrough old habits of thinking, to unleash fresh solutions to perennial problems, breakthrough the existing interpersonal barriers, breakthrough the cynicism that many people feel about their job and help them find meaning and intent in what they do. They need to breakthrough the limits imposed by the people's doubts and fears to achieve more than they believe possible. Courageous leaders like Welch do not wait for any crisis to occur to make change. They actively search for opportunities to change, grow, innovate and seek to disturb the status quo in times of stability.

Bold leaders try to benchmark everything they do with the best in their areas and at times even cross the boundaries to compare with the best from other industries. GE benchmarked itself against well-known companies in specific areas like inventory management (with Wal-Mart) or profitability (with P&G) in its quest to achieve the stretch targets.

The leaders very often do not hesitate to take decisions in the long-term interest of their organisation and pursue these decisions vigorously. Such leaders have an edge over others. Corporate giants like Ratan Tata and Kumar Mangalam Birla demonstrated exemplary courage when they decided to take over Corus and Novelis respectively who were bigger in size than theirs.

Leading by Expertise

In knowledge economy, the corporate leaders can influence their people and command respect in and outside the organisation not by virtue of traits and behaviour alone— but also on account of their mastery over a process that is crucial to the organisation. In an age where competitive advantages must be polished till they shine, the CEO-as-leader must champion this specific proprietary expertise, not only making it the pivot of the organisation's strategy, but also ensuring that it is passed up, down and across the organisation instead of being hoarded in the corner room. Late Dhirubhai Ambani was the hero of Reliance Group's employees because of his demonstrated and disseminated competence of financing and finishing mega projects on global scales.

Leading by Empathy

Real leaders empathise fiercely with the people they lead. It is the quality of feeling empathy towards the people that actually makes one a successful leader and eventually leads to the success of any organisation. They follow a unique approach—tough empathy—to give the people what they need, not what they want. Tough empathy strives respect for the individuals and for the task at hand.[9] Empathy is built from three major behaviours: (i) recognising your own shortcomings of past and present, (ii) listening to others and learning more about their lives and their private challenges, and (iii) explicitly aspiring for a noble ideal of the leadership. A leader cannot be a successful even if he has all the qualities of good leadership, if he misses the basic quality of feeling empathy towards the organisational members.

Leading by Adaptability

Excellent leadership is about resilience—the ability to constantly check how the environment is changing and proactively take initiatives to adjust and adapt to the changes before the latter take place. People who practice adaptive leadership use the turbulence of the current environment to build on and bring closure of the past. In the process, they change the key rules of the game, reshape parts of the organisation and redefine the work the people do.

In today's fast changing uncertain business environment, a successful leader requires not only problem-solving, crisp decision-making, the articulation of clear direction skills but also adaptability skills so that he adapts what and how things get done in order to thrive in tomorrow's world. He must develop "next practices" while excelling at today's best practices.

Corporate adaptability usually comes mainly from the accumulation of micro adaptations originating throughout the company in response to its many micro-environments. Even the successful big play is typically a product of many experiments, one of which finally proves pathbreaking.[10] To foster such experiments, corporate leaders have to acknowledge the interdependence of the people throughout the organisation. They should use leadership to generate more leadership deep in the organisation.

In the last two years Indian corporate enterprises have focused on adaptability skill of leaders at every level. The corporate management now feel that it lacks leaders who could handle a downturn. Leaders in a growing company have very different skills from those needed in a crisis. A company that has understood this lesson well is Bangalore's Mind Tree Consulting, an IT services firm. The Vice-Chairman, Subroto Bagchi, quaintly asserts that the slowdown never had any impact on his company. This was largely due to the company's model of leadership: it believes in looking at the next crisis and dealing with it.[11]

Leading by Institution Building Ability

Institution building ability is the essence of far-sighted visionary leadership that is deeply concerned with the sustained growth and success far beyond the terms of the leaders. GE has survived the exit of legendary Jack Welch and has, indeed, gone on to greater heights under the current CEO, Jeff Immelt. Goldman Sach has become stronger under Lloyd Blankfein than it was under Hank Paulson. In India, Reliance has expanded several times under the leadership of Mukesh Ambani after the demise of his legendary father. Ratan Tata has transformed the group of Tatas in a way not imagined. Kumar Mangalam Birla has gone to extraordinary achievements after the death of another corporate giant—Aditya Birla. Hindustan Lever has made rapid progress even after rare business leaders like Prakash Tandon, Ashok Ganguly and Vindi Banga have left that great institution.

These leaders firmly believed in developing leaders across the organisation. They have had the conviction that there is leadership capability in every human being and leaders exist at all levels. These leaders realised pretty early that their success depended on how well they could create a cadre of future leaders to handle higher revenues and profits, more customers and employees, challenges of innovation and competition, and ever increasing expectations of the society. They created systems for recruiting the best talent from universities and for training these people to aim high, take tough decisions, handle dilemmas, pursue values steadfastly, get their people to reach for the stars, reach out to the society and handle the ups and downs of business with equanimity. They then chose the most promising ones amongst these employees to climb the corporate ladder fast, and gave them opportunity to exercise these skills while providing a safety net for them. They evaluated their wards constantly and applauded them for their strengths in public, gave constructive feedback on their weakness in private and pushed them constantly towards 'stretch targets'. They mentored their wards and built confidence in them to handle tough situations.[12]

Summary

Organisational success depends, in the main, upon the quality of the leadership of the company because it decides the quality of the environment and strategic decisions and so also quality of their execution.

Leadership is about the style and behaviour of the leaders that influence the people and rouse their commitment and mobilise their talent for achieving the objectives of the organisation. The modern concept of leadership focuses on distributed leadership, which signifies existence of leadership at all levels.

It is also important to note that leadership is not by title; it is about set of behaviours. A fancy title is not only an opportunity; it is also an obligation to engage in certain behaviours.

In today's complex and fast changing business landscape, organisations to ensure sustained growth, need both leaders and managers. While leadership is about coping with changes by revisiting the existing visions, mission, objectives and strategies and communicating the same to the people and engaging them in translating the vision into action, the management is about coping with business complexities by planning and budgeting and developing capacity to achieve its plan, creating suitable structure and devising system to monitor implementation. Although the concept of leadership and management is different, the demand of the modern business world is a fusion of both, to overcome myriads of problems arising out of bewildering developments. This has given rise to the emergence of leader-manager concept.

Leadership has a paramount role not only in strategic thinking but also in its effectuation. A corporate leader influences each and every activity relating to strategy execution. Although the responsibility of implementing strategy falls within the jurisdiction of the functional and departmental managers, the corporate leaders have a game plan that takes care of the overall picture. In the process of strategy execution, they act as a guide in developing operating policies and coach the middle and lower-level managers in preparation of action plans and allocation of resources among different functions, divisions and departments. They play the role of coordinators to achieve conflicting and competing goals and programmes of line managers.

They also monitor the progress of implementation of the strategy and thus act as controllers.

Although the task of strategy execution in the current scenario is cumbersome, the same can be performed dexterously and efficaciously, if the managers play the role of an effective leader. An effective leader leads the organisation by passionately envisioning, positive attitude, inspiration and loyalty, expertise, extraordinary courage, adaptability and institution building ability.

Key Terms

Corporate adaptability	Empathy	Primal leadership
Corporate leadership	Envision with passion	Resilience
Culture of meritocracy	Leader-manager	Transactional leadership
Distributed leadership	Mirror and window	Transformational leadership

Discussion Questions

1. "No organisation is good or bad. It is the leader who makes or mars". Explain with illustrations.
2. Discuss the concept of leadership. What is distributed leadership? How is it different from corporate leadership?
3. "Leadership is not by title; it is about set of behaviours". Comment.
4. Distinguish between a leader and a manager. Why is the concept of leader-manager gaining prominence in modern business world?
5. Discuss how leadership influences execution of corporate strategy.
6. What are the different roles a corporate leader plays in implementing corporate strategy?
7. What is transformational style of leadership? How is it different from transactional leadership style?
8. Discuss, in brief, the attributes of an effective business leader.
9. How can a leader influence the behaviour of his people through vision?
10. How can people in the organisation be inspired by leadership?
11. "Great leaders must have extraordinary courage to lead the organisation to success". Discuss.
12. How can a leader influence his people by empathy?
13. "Effective leaders develop leadership at every level in the organisation in order to ensure sustained success in hyper competitive scenario". Comment.

References

1. Robbins, Stephen P., *Essentials of Organisational Behaviour*, op. cit., p. 139.
2. *Indian Management*, March, p. 78, 2006.
3. *Business Today*, January 9, 2011.
4. Kotter, John P., "What Leaders Really Do", *Harvard Business Review*, December 2001.
5. *Business Today*, December 12, 2010.
6. Collins, Jim, *Good to Great*, Random House, 2001.
7. Reichheld, Frederic F., "Lead For Loyalty"; *Harvard Business Review*, July–August, p. 76, 2001.
8. op. cit., pp. 77–84.
9. Goffee, Robert and Gareth Jones, Why Should Anyone Be Led by You?, *Harvard Business Review*, September–October, p. 68, 2000.
10. Heifetz, Ronald, Gran Shaw, Alexander and Marty Linsky, "Leadership in Crisis", *Harvard Business Review*, South Asia, July–August, p. 56, 2009.
11. *Business Today*, December 12, 2010.
12. Murthy, Narayan N.R., "A Lead on Growth", *Business Today*, January 9, 2011.

20

Strategic Audit and Recycling

The present Chapter aims at:

- Discussing the nature and scope of strategic audit.
- Describing the utilities of a strategic audit.
- Presenting a discussion on various methods of conducting strategic audit.
- Outlining the circumstances leading to recycling of strategy and the process of the strategy recycling.

INTRODUCTION

The responsibility of the corporate management does not end with strategy making and its effectuation, but transcends beyond it to encompass the task of auditing corporate other strategies. This is for the fact that an organisation to survive and thrive in a competitive scenario must ensure that the current strategy is based on resources and competencies to exploit opportunities or respond to impending threats and assess the suitability of the strategy in a changing environment and achieving the desired outcome. For this, the top management must conduct strategic audit periodically.

NATURE AND SCOPE OF STRATEGIC AUDIT

Strategic audit is an integral part of the corporate strategic management which is concerned with monitoring and assessing efficacy of various activities associated with strategic planning and strategy execution and taking suitable measures to improve business operations of the organisation. In addition, a strategic audit can be quite formal adhering strictly to established organisational rules and procedures or quite informal, allowing managers wide discretion in deciding what organisational steps to be taken and when the focus of strategic audit has to be an integration of related functions.

It is a systematic, structured and comprehensive review of the strategy and the strategic processes and operations to identify weaknesses, blind spots, reasons why profits are failing to reach predicted levels and new areas where potentially more value can be added.

Strategic audit consists of making something happen the way it was planned. It is a special type of audit that scrutinises the strategic management process to make sure that it functions properly. More specifically, strategic audit is exclusively concerned with determining the suitability of the company's overall strategy and its sub-strategies in the dynamically changing environmental conditions, and assessing how far the company's overall performance as well as the performance of the business unit, the divisional and department units are in conformance with the planned performance. In case the strategies are not found adequate to cope with the changed landscape or the actual result is not in accordance with the strategies, then the intent of strategic audit ensures that all outcomes planned during the strategic management process do, indeed, materialise.

A strategic audit can take many forms, but could focus on, for example, three areas of competitive positioning:

    (i) Competitors

   (ii) Customers

  (iii) Cost base

Strategic audit is supposed to be conducted by the Board of Directors which is primarily an oversight Board. But in professionally managed companies it is the CEO who conducts this job in consultation with independent Directors of the company who have reservoir of diverse knowledge and expertise. The CEO also constitutes cross-functional teams of the managers to assist him not only in monitoring operations but also in integrating the related functions. In this process, the senior management accountants should also be involved. But more junior financial managers need to be engaged to think about how they can add value to the business and may find that planning, coordinating or merely participating in a strategic audit process gives them the chance to take on a more strategic role.

UTILITY OF STRATEGIC AUDIT

Strategic audit of an enterprise is as important as strategy making because it provides an insight into the efficacy and effectiveness of the overall plan as well as subplans in attaining the desired results. It also enables the management to judge the suitability of the ongoing strategy in changing socio-economic, political and technological developments and corporate conditions and points out the need for modifications in strategy in order to seize emerging opportunities and minimise new threats.

On the basis of periodic strategic audit, the central management can determine precisely whether programmes are being carried out in such a way that the corporate objectives will be attained satisfactorily.

Very often companies run into trouble because quality of their strategy has deteriorated. The top management in that event has to struggle hard, no matter how much effort they put into improving short-term financial performance. A strategic audit can help the management to spot weaknesses before they become critical.

Strategic audit also influences the behaviour of events and ensures that they conform to the plans. It serves the 'steering function', to steer the organisation and the various sub-systems within it on the right track and to negotiate their way through a turbulent environment. It aims at promoting integration between short-range and long-range plans between the enterprise and the environment.

Strategic audit serves as a valuable instrument for the purpose of achieving stability and continuity, on the one hand, and adaptation and adjustment, on the other. Organisational stability is sought through appraisal of operational policies and procedures. This ensures the steady state of the organisation to establish itself, to derive and consolidate the gains from resources already committed, to preserve the system's vitality and viability. Periodic appraisal of the strategy provides an opportunity to the management to make requisite adjustments in the objectives, strategies and policies, in tune with the dynamics of the external environment.

Strategic audit can also help the management in making effective use of scarce and valuable resources of the enterprise. It strives for minimising the variability in the development of resources so that the intended goals are achieved with the least cost and few untoward consequences.

Strategic audit plays a significant role in addressing governance problems by forcing the managers to consider whether they are running the business to generate long-term shareholders' value, trying to maximise its short-term performance in order to increase their business payments.

In effect, a strategic audit is a business health check.

METHODS OF CONDUCTING STRATEGIC AUDIT

There are various methods of undertaking strategic audit to measure the organisational performance. Two commonly accepted methods of making strategy audit are qualitative organisational measurement and quantitative organisational measurement.

Qualitative Organisational Measurement

In this method the managers seek answer to critical questions relating to important facets of the organisational operations. Seymur Tillers in his article on the qualitative aspect of the organisational performance suggests several important questions to ask for measuring qualitatively the performance of an organisation.[1] These questions are:

Is Strategy Consistent with Corporate Objectives?

The basic idea underlying the formulation of a corporate strategy is to achieve the corporate objectives. Hence, the major criterion to evaluate the efficiency of the strategy is to determine how far it will be helpful to attain the desired results. For instance, if a firm aims at increasing its profits by 40% during the next five years through augmenting sales, the central management must verify whether the corporate strategy provides emphasis on market penetration, market development, product development and other measures that will help the enterprise to achieve the anticipated objectives.

Similarly, if a firm in its endeavour to fulfill social obligations sets the objectives of promoting social welfare, the management should verify how far the current strategy provides for social actions. Social responsibility concept must be embedded in the strategy, action plans and programmes of the company. Strategy, not providing explicitly for social welfare actions, cannot be considered effective and useful to the enterprise. The central management will also have to ensure that the organisational plan of the enterprise constituted at the corporate level staff department is endowed with social responsibility activities.

Is Organisational Strategy Consistent with Its Environment?

Another important yardstick to measure the effectiveness of the current strategy is to check its adequacy in exploiting present as well as future opportunities and/or counteracting impending threats. Instances are not rare when an enterprise formulates strategy to capitalise on opportunities in foreign countries while ignoring abundant opportunities existing inside the country. The management has to ensure that such sort of policy and strategy are not allowed to see the light of the day.

Further, it is also necessary to verify if the current strategy has been adapted and modified in accordance with dynamic developments in socio-economic, competitive, technological and political spheres of the country. An enterprise not bothering to interact with various environmental forces and adjust its objectives, strategies and programmes may experience disaster because external conditions may change to a hindrance rather than help. Such a check will help the management to verify the validity of the ongoing strategy.

To What Extent has Competitiveness of the Enterprise been Scrutinised?

This could involve asking generic questions, tailored to suit the context of the enterprise's competitors:

(i) Who are the company's rivals? How big are they? What resources do they have?

(ii) Does the management understand how customers perceive the company's competitors' value-added potential and how does this compare with their perception of what the company's value-added services mean to them?

(iii) Does the management know the rival's cost advantages/disadvantages in relation to the company?

  (iv) Which competitors pose the serious threats to the company and why?

  (v) Does the management know how customers perceive the value the company adds and the characteristics of the company's products and services that distract from this? Can the management break this information down by segment?

Is Organisational Strategy Consistent with Its Strengths?

A successful strategy is one which is supported by adequate resources of the enterprise. At times, the management swayed by high ambitions and initial successes may be tempted to choose a path of expansion without perceptive and penetrating enquiry into the company's past performance and present strengths. Such an overambitious growth plan can bring untold sufferings. To check the occurrence of such a possibility, it will be pertinent for the central management to ensure that the strategy is consistent with the resources of the enterprise. Further, it has also to ensure that the strategy is making maximum use of synergistic benefits.

Is Organisational Strategy Consistent with Management Values?

Effectiveness of strategy is dependent upon the personal involvement of those at the helm of affairs. Hence, in the formulation of the strategic and action plans, personal values, preferences and motives of the business executives must be given due consideration. Conflict between the personal values of the key members of the enterprise and the strategy is a sign of danger and a harbinger of mediocre performance or failure. It is, therefore, necessary for the evaluator to determine as to what extent the personal values of the key executives and other executives are reflected in strategy and other plans.

Is Organisational Strategy Appropriate to Its Plans and Programmes?

A strategy can achieve the desired results if the functional plans, action plans and programmes are consistent with it. This is why feasibility testing of the sub-strategies has to be made constantly. It ensures that they conform to the corporate strategic plan. If this is not done and inconsistency exists, it will be very difficult for the enterprise to achieve budgeted results within a specified period of time.

Is Organisational Strategy Consistent with Its Performance?

The central management should assess actual performance for a period of time and compare it against what was planned. If the comparison indicates that the performance is satisfactory, the ongoing strategy may be considered to be sound. However, the management, before giving testimony to the soundness of the strategy, should determine whether positive deviation was the outcome of mere change or due to current plans. Where the comparison indicates a large negative variations, the manager has to find out if the deviations have occurred because the plans were wrongly formulated.

Does Strategy Foster Organisational Motivation?

An enterprise aiming at achieving leadership in the product line and embarking on a massive diversification programme will have to formulate a strategy which can create a stimulating climate in the organisation and encourage the people to do their best and to adapt to change of events. This calls for clear-cut objectives, goals and a strategy that remove uncertainty and ambiguity and have a strong action focus. Involvement of lower-level executives in decision-making, provision of freedom of job, and provision of financial and non-financial incentives to those showing exceptional performance also motivate the employees to contribute their best to the organisation. It is, therefore, necessary to verify if the existing strategy constitutes stimulus to the organisational effort and commitment.

Is Organisational Strategy Too Risky?

Strategy and organisational resources together determine the degree of risk an organisation takes. The corporate management must determine the amount of risk (or potential for losing resources) it wishes to incur. In this regard, the management has to assess such issues as the total amount of resources a strategy requires, the proportion of the organisation's resources that the strategy will consume, and the time commitment the strategy demands.

Is the Time Horizon of the Strategy Appropriate?

The basic purpose of designing a strategy is to accomplish some organisational objectives within a certain time spectrum. The strategic auditors must determine if the time allotted for implementing the strategy and for reaching the related organisational objectives is realistic and acceptable, given the organisational circumstances. They have to ensure that the time allotted to achieve the objectives and the time necessary to implement the strategy are consistent. In case of any inconsistency between the two, it may be difficult to accomplish the objectives satisfactorily.

Besides these, there are other questions for qualitative organisational measurements. Some of these are:

(i) Are financial policies with respect to investment, dividends and financing, consistent with the expected opportunities?

(ii) Has the company defined the market segments in which it intends to operate, specially with regard to both product line and market segments?

(iii) Has the company defined the core capabilities it needs to succeed?

(iv) Will the business segments in which the company operates provide adequate opportunities for achieving the corporate objectives? Do they appear attractive enough to draw an excessive amount of investment to the market from the potential competitors?

(v) Does the company have a viable plan for developing a significant and defensible superiority over the competitors based on these capabilities?

(vi) Are the existing resources of the company really adequate to justify an expectation of maintaining superiority over the competitors in key capabilities?

(vii) Does the company have operations in which it cannot reasonably expect to outperform its competitors? If so, can the managers expect these operations to generate adequate return on invested capital?

(viii) Has the company selected the business segments that can reinforce each other by contributing jointly to the development of key capabilities?

(ix) Can the company's scope of business be revised to improve its chance against the competitors?

(x) Do the competitors combine their operation in ways that give them superiority in the key resource areas?

Qualitative measurement methods can be very meaningful if conclusions based thereon are drawn very carefully because of greater scope of subjective judgement. Strategic control actions based on invalid audit results can certainly limit the effectiveness of the strategy management process and may even spell disaster for an organisation.

Quantitative Organisational Measurement

This method of assessment of the organisational performance is based on numerical data. Quantitative measurements can evaluate the number of units produced per time period, production cost, production efficiency levels, levels of employee turnover and absenteeism, sales and sale growth, net profits earned, dividends paid, return on equity, market share and earnings per share. Three widely used quantitative techniques are: Return on Investment (ROI), Weighted Performance (Z) score and Stakeholder's audit[2].

Return on Investment (ROI)

This method seeks to evaluate the organisational performance by relating net income to total assets of the company. Comparing ROI values for connective years, and with those of similar organisations usually generates a more complete picture of the organisational performance in this area. The managers should employ this method keeping in view its limitations.

Weighted Performance (Z) Score

In this method, weights are assigned to five performance measures and summed up to arrive at an overall score.[3] The score forms a basis for categorising focus as healthy and unlikely to become bankrupt. The formula used for the purpose is:

$$Z = 1.2X_1 + 1.4X_2 + 3.3X_3 + 0.6X_4 + 1.0X_5$$

where

Z = Index of overall financial health

X_1 = Working capital to total assets

X_2 = Return of earnings to total assets

X_3 = Earnings before interest and taxes to total assets

X_4 = Market value of equity to book value of total liabilities

X_5 = Sales to total assets

Firms having score below 1.8 have relatively high probability of going bankrupt. Those with score of above 3.0 have low probabilities of becoming bankrupt. Firms having score between 1.8 and 3.0 are in a grey area. Thus, this method gives the top management enough idea about the financial health of a firm and insights into how to improve it.

Stakeholder's Audit

In this method, the organisational performance is monitored on the basis of the feedback generated by the stakeholders' groups which include the customers, suppliers, employees, shareholders, creditors, trade unions, social interest groups and so on. The tone and content of such a feedback can be an extremely valuable indicator of organisational progress toward financial and non-financial goals.

Table 20.1 exhibits several stakeholders' groups and measures to evaluate the short-term and long-term impact they may have on the organisational performance.

Table 20.1 Measurement of Organisational Performance by Stakeholders

Stakeholders	Near-term performance measures	Long-term performance measures
Customers	Sales (value and volume), new customers; number of new customers' needs met	Growth in sales turnover in customer base; ability to control price.
Suppliers	Cost of raw materials; delivery time; inventory; availability of raw materials	Growth rates of raw materials costs; delivery time; inventory; new ideas from suppliers
Creditors	Earnings per share, stock price, return on equity	Growth rate in return on equity, Debt-Equity Ratio
Employees	Number of suggestions; productivity; number of grievances	Number of internal promotions turnover
Government	Number of new pieces of legislations that affect the firm	Number of new regulations that affect the industry; return of cooperative to competitive encounters
Environmentalists	Number of environmental protection agency complaints, number of legal actions	Number of changes in policy due to environmentalists, number of calls for help initiated by environmentalists

Source: *Strategic Management: A Stakeholder Approach*, Boston, Pitman Publishing, 1984

PROBLEMS IN THE CONDUCT OF STRATEGIC AUDIT

Task of strategic audit suffers from the problems arising out of misinterpretation of the environmental forces and corporate resources. The evaluator may not always be correct when he questions the validity of the organisational strategy. This is because of the fact that determination of opportunities and threats is often as much as function of the perception and the attitude of the person making such exercise as it is of the factor itself. For instance, a dynamic and enterprising planner may perceive abundant opportunities emerging due to economic and technological developments and formulate expansion strategy. This approach may not be appreciated by an evaluator with a conservative attitude and closed cognitive style who holds the view that the enterprise should continue to maintain its present product-market posture owing to disquieting political developments.

Inaccurate assessment of financial, marketing, managerial and other resources of the enterprise and existence of synergistic benefits pose another obstacle to the strategic audit. Thus, for instance, a corporate planner chooses a diversification strategy because in his view the firm has adequate financial and managerial resources to support this plan. But the evaluator questions the utility of such a strategy because he doubts the skill and competence of the senior executives of the firm.

Another obstacle that is inherent in strategy appraisal is identification, evaluation and choice of the strategic alternatives. In the real world, it has been noted that some organisations without making independent appraisal of opportunities, choose a course of action because others in the same line of business have done so. This type of approach renders the product-market strategy weak.

Another source of difficulty involved in the appraisal of strategy is misinterpretation of current results. Generally, the CEO, without digging deep into the problem, regards the current strategy as unsound if the performance has not been satisfactory and directs the corporate planner to re-examine it. In the same vein, he labels the strategy as sound because of the excellent operating results. But such a hurried judgement may, at times, be erroneous. Poor results may have been due to improper execution of the strategy or outstanding profits were due to certain other factors such as war and product rationing. The management swayed by good results may not take serious note of implications of impending environmental changes and accordingly remain indifferent to any modification in the current plan for the future.

RECYCLING OF STRATEGY

Where the basic position of a company is changed and/or the fundamental premises on which the present strategy is founded are challenged, it becomes imperative to recycle strategy. Recycling of the strategy refers to reformulation or remaking of the strategy. Recycling may take place when the company's strategic position has undergone significant changes. Thus, for instance, the management's thrust of stability or survival of the organisation due to a sudden and impending decline in sales and earnings or due to emerging financial crisis, forces the organisation to take drastic actions and reformulate the corporate strategy to solve the immediate and future problems.

At times, phenomenal and unexpected changes in environment conditions occur in and outside the country. For instance, the energy crisis of the 70s and subsequent changes in the customers' preferences forced many automobile companies to reformulate their strategies. Global financial crisis of 2008 compelled MNCs—both Indian and foreign—to rejig their strategy to ensure their survival. In addition to external events, changes in the internal position of the company such as change in the top management of the company or formation of strategic alliance may bring about significant changes in the current strategy.

The general process of recycling of the strategy is the same as that entailed in the strategy making. However, recycling is less formal and is quickly formulated and executed because it is carried out in urgency and only those elements which are affected by the new strategy need the attention of the management.

Reformulation of strategy is managed by all those engaged in the formulation and execution of the corporate strategy. The management adopts a sensing-adjusting response mechanism for the reformulation of the strategy.

One of the major problems involved in reformulating the strategy is the success syndrome. Generally, the management of a successful organisation is not interested in change and often acts in too slovenly a manner to be effective. Another problem that may arise in the course of reformulation of the strategy relates to changes in the overall corporate policy. It has been found in real life that policy changes may not be appreciated by all the senior managers and may result in resentment and resignation of some sensitive managers. This, in turn, is likely to jeopardise the existing organisational structure which further complicates the situation.

Implementation of a reformulated strategy poses still greater problems because it requires a transitional period during which existing concepts and methods are discarded, new ones are tried and accepted, and the newly structured organisation is put into operation.

Summary

Strategic audit is an integral component of corporate strategic management concerned with comprehensive review of the strategy and the strategic processes and assessing strategic operations in a systematic and structured manner with a view to spotting weaknesses and finding reasons for not achieving the desired results and taking corrective measures to improve the performance of the company.

A strategic audit can take many forms but could focus on, for example, three areas of competitive positioning, viz., competitors, customers and cost base.

Strategic audit plays useful role in improving the performance of an organisation on sustained basis since it provides meaningful insights into effectiveness of the overall plan as well as the plans at the business unit and divisional and departmental levels in the context of the current and future business environment.

Strategic audit can be conducted by both qualitatively and quantitatively. While conducting strategic audit, the top management should ask searching questions especially with regard to the company's competitive positioning, compatibility of the strategy to the company's strengths and weaknesses, relevance of the current strategy in the changed environment, adequacy of the structure to execute the plans, and so on. Certain quantitative techniques may be useful to judge the performance of the company.

In case the fundamental position of the company is changed and/or the basic premises, on which the current strategy is founded, are challenged, the top management need to reformulate the strategy keeping in view the changing environmental forces.

Key Terms

Competitive positioning

Core capability

Financial policies

Organisation strategy

Return on investments

Strategic auditors

Stakeholders' audit

Weighted performance score

Discussion Questions

1. What is strategic audit? Discuss its utility in organisational success.
2. What are the various ways of conducting strategic audit in an organisation?
3. What are the major problems faced by the management in conducting strategic audit?
4. Under what circumstances should a strategy be recycled? How is recycling done?
5. How can competitive positioning of a company be audited?

References

1. Tilles, Saymour, "How to Evaluate Corporate Strategy", *Harvard Business Review*, July–August, pp. 111–121, 1963.
2. Lauenatin, Milton, "Keeping Your Corporate Strategy on Track", *Journal of Business Strategy*, 2(**1**), p. 64, Summer 1981.
3. Altman, Edward I. and James K. La Flour, "Managing a Return to Financial Health", *The Journal of Business Strategy* 2(**1**), pp. 31–38, Summer 1981.

SECTION V

Real Life Indian Cases in Strategic Management

CHAPTER 21. A Guide to Using the Case Studies in Strategic Management

21

A Guide to Using the Case Studies in Strategic Management

LEARNING OBJECTIVES

The present Chapter aims at:
- Providing a broad understanding of analysing real life business cases.

REAL LIFE CASES

List of Cases Studies

1. Maruti Suzuki India Ltd.
2. TTK Prestige
3. Dr. Reddy's Laboratories
4. Tata Tea's NEW Gambit
5. Amrutanjan: Pain for Suitors
6. *Nano's* Topsy-Turvy RIDE
7. Nokia India
8. Nano Filters
9. Vishal Retail
10. Harrison Malayalam
11. Go Air
12. Rohit Surfactants
13. Nerolac

CASE ANALYSIS AS A PEDAGOGICAL TOOL

There are three main routes to learning, viz., learning by rote, learning by doing and by discovery. Among these, learning by doing through case discussions has become most popular method of learning across the world especially in the management programmes where the participants are expected to develop problem solving skills. Learning through rote has not found favour in the management programmes because teaching through lectures becomes a didactic and mechanical one-way process. In fact, mere act of listening to lectures and sound advice about managing does little to develop communication, emotional and decisional skills among the participants. Students learning the management concepts, skills, paradigms, tools and techniques through textbooks, statement of fact and definitive lecture notes fail and falter in making decisions to resolve real life problems. Professor Charles Gragg rightly observed that managerial skills and expertise cannot be acquired through mere listening to lectures and reading books. This is because of the fact that each managerial situation is different from others with unique aspects, requiring its own diagnosis and judgement.[1]

In case method of learning, the participants of the programme are taught through discussion of real life cases. A case is a narration of the actual events and situations existing in an organisation. It sets a situation with all the ancillary facts, figures, opinions, emotions, views, grapevine, and the like. Through discussion of cases, the participants get to know the scene of the action and all the relevant facts about the industry as a whole, a single organisation and its competitors. Since cases contain detailed information about conditions and problems of different organisations belonging to different industries, discussion of these cases develops the analytical and problem solving skills. The participants are at the same time exposed to how organisations and their managers handle the problems.

It is important to note that in case method of teaching, there is no final one solution to the problem plaguing the organisation. Usually, case discussions may produce good arguments for more than one solution. There is always scope for differences of opinion and there may be myriad of feasible courses of action and approaches, each of which may work out satisfactorily. As such, if one does not find one strong unambiguous answer to the issue, it should not be frustrating. In the real business world, answers do not come in conclusive black-and-white terms. When one elects a particular course of action, there is no peeking at the back of a book to see if one has chosen the best thing to do and no one to turn to for a correct answer. The only valid test of the management action is the 'results'. If the results of an action turn out to be good, the decision to take it may be presumed right. If not, the action chosen was wrong in the sense that it did not work.[2]

UTILITY OF CASE ANALYSIS IN MANAGEMENT LEARNING

The case method provides to the learners an invaluable opportunity to apply the managerial concepts, skills, tools and techniques, which they had learnt from textbooks and lectures, to real life problem prone cases leading to sharpening of their problem-solving skills. Cases present actual business situations and as such enable the learners to analyse situations in both successful and unsuccessful organisations. This increases their understanding of what the managers should and should not do in guiding a business to success.

The primary objective of case method of teaching is to build skills of the learners in sizing up company resources, strengths and weaknesses and in conducting strategic analysis in a variety of industries and competitive situations, developing management judgement about what needs to be done and how to do it and gaining in-depth exposure to different industries and companies, thereby acquiring something close to actual business experience.[3]

Discussion of a wide variety of real life cases makes the learners actively engaged in identifying the central problem in the case, diagnosing the same, and then undertaking in-depth analysis of strengths, weaknesses, opportunities and threats to find out workable solutions. This, obviously, helps the learners in strengthening decision-making skills.

METHODOLOGY TO BE USED FOR CASE ANALYSIS

(i) Identify the Central Problem
(ii) Diagnose the Problem
(iii) Undertake the SWOT Analysis
(iv) Formulate overall objectives and strategies
(v) Develop the functional plans to implement strategies
(vi) Recommend measures to evaluate and control

Identify Central Problem

There will be no real life case if it does not entail problem for the organisation. It is, therefore, pertinent for the participants to identify the main problem which the enterprise faces and needs solution.

Diagnose the Problem

The next step is to find out why this problem has arisen. This problem could be change in external environmental forces, or ineffective execution of strategies, or both and lack of effective monitoring machinery. The participant is expected to dive into the case to find out the factors that contributed to the current problem.

Undertake SWOT Analysis

After identifying the main problem and diagnosing the same, it is now time to make perspicacious analysis of current and forthcoming changes in external environment so as to discuss business opportunities and threats and assess their likely impact on existing product market strategy of the company. The SWOT analysis should be made in the context of economic, technological, political and socio-cultural environmental forces. An analysis of the industry environment in which the company is operating should be conducted along the Porter's analysis of competitive forces, viz., threat of new entrants, rivalry among existing firms, threat of substitute products, bargaining power of the buyers, bargaining power of the suppliers and relative power of other stakeholders.

Simultaneously, a critical appraisal of the company's current strengths and weaknesses should be undertaken in order to underscore its core competencies and competitive superiority vis-a-vis its rivals, especially in terms of cost differentiation, infrastructure, and the like. The company's strengths and weaknesses need to be scanned with reference to marketing, production, research and development, human resource development, finance and general management.

Formulate Overall Objectives and Strategy

In context of the SWOT analysis, the participant should first of all assess the adequacy of the company's existing objectives and strategies to squeeze the emerging opportunities and counteract the impending threats. In case of the ineffectiveness of the current objectives and strategy, the next exercise should be to visualise new vision and mission and reset the new objectives. This should be followed by formulation of an overall strategy for the company. For this purpose, it would be pertinent to identify a few potential strategic alternatives and evaluate each of them in terms of pros and cons as also their potentiality to achieve the objectives. The next step would be to specify which one of the alternative strategies is recommended and why.

Developing Functional Plans to Implement Strategies

Within the framework of overall corporate objectives and strategy, the participant should then try to develop the objectives in each critical function and a suitable strategy to achieve these objectives. While doing so, care should be taken that all the sub-problems and causes responsible for these problems are adequately addressed. It would also be useful to investigate if the organisational and management restructuring are required. It would also be useful to specify who will be responsible for preparing each functional plan and how long each programme will take to complete.

Evaluate and Control

A participant's job of case analysis and case writing will be complete only after he/she specifies the type of evaluation and control machinery that is required to carry out the recommendation successfully. Also he/she should specify who should be charged with the responsibility for monitoring the operations. It has also to be ensured that if the present information system is adequate to conduct monitoring effectively and if not, required change in the information system should be recommended.

APPROACH FOR PREPARING A CASE FOR CLASS DISCUSSION

Meaningful discussions of real life cases are contingent upon thorough preparation of the case by all the participants. For this purpose, everyone is supposed to read the case and get deep insight into the situation presented and develop some reasoned thoughts and make recommendations based on a logical analysis of the facts contained in the case.

For preparing a case, a participant should proceed along the following lines:

(i) The learner should read the case quickly to get acquaintance with the situation including the types of issues and problems involved in the case.

(ii) He/she should again go through the case but this time thoroughly to grasp the facts and circumstances embodied in the case.

(iii) He/she should peep into all the data presented in the exhibits and try to analyse them.

(iv) On the basis of the above, the learner should attempt to analyse the case and the main problems facing the company and prepare a list of the issues involved.

(v) He should then delve into the case to identify precisely various causes responsible for this problem. These causes could be due to failure of the company to cope with changes in economic, technological, competitive, socio-cultural and political environment. Lack of operational efficiency, ineffective execution machinery and management incapability could also be the reasons for the present problem.

(vi) Penetrating analysis of the case requires some sort of number crunching—computing financial ratios on the basis of the data given in the case—to determine financial and operational performance, calculate growth rates of sales or profits or unit volume, check out profit margins and composition of the cost structure and gain insights into revenue-cost-profit relationships existing in the company.

(vii) Once the problem has been identified and the same has been diagnosed, the learner should proceed to scan the environment—both external and internal. The main source of such scanning will be the opinions and the data embodied in the case. At times, the case may contain contradictory views. In that case, the learner should make judgements about the validity of the data and information supplied in the case.

(viii) It is advisable to the learner not to restrict himself/herself only to the information presented in the case. He/she should undertake outside research into the environmental setting. To check the validity of the data, the business periodicals for that period may be screened. Access to computerised company and industry information services such as India Info line, India stats and other databases, available on CD-Rom or online at a library will be considerably helpful. Database capita online also provides access to corporate annual reports and other processed information. This will enable the participant to capture the real picture of the company.

(xi) On the basis of the above information, the participant should now prepare a list containing emerging opportunities for and impending threats to the company. Also, he/she stand draw a separate list containing those strengths of the company which are comparatively superior to its rivals. The existing weaknesses of the company may also be listed.

(xii) The next step would be to spell out the primary objective that can address the main problem. The primary objective should be supplemented by the functional objectives to cope with the various causal factors the problem.

(xiii) On the basis of the penetrating analysis of the situation in the case and conceptual understanding of the management and its various streams, the learner should identify strategic alternatives, evaluate each of them and recommend the one that will help the company to resolve its problem and achieve the objectives.

(xiv) The strategy recommended should unambiguously specify the course of action to be taken over a period of time. It should be noted that proposing realistic, workable solutions is far preferable to casually tossing out top-of-the head suggestions. Recommended action should be based on logical reasoning.

In case analysis, it may be reiterated that there is hardly just one right course of action because managing a company is not such an exact science that produces a single foolproof solution to a problem. There is always scope for more than one good way to analyse the situation and find better course of action. Of course, some analysis and action plan may be better than others. Hence, the learner should not lose confidence in the correctness of his/her analysis and judgement, if he/she has prepared the case along the lines suggested above.

PARTICIPATING IN CLASSROOM CASE DISCUSSION

Unlike learning by rote, in the case method of teaching, the learners have to play a very active role and do most of the talking. The role of the instructor is to facilitate discussions, encourage the participation of the learners and stimulate them to share insights, observations and thoughts about the case. He has to play the role of extensive questioner and listener, keep the discussion on track and offer, where necessary, alternative views. Class discussion of a case begins with presentation by a participant of the situation given in the case; his analysis, and the actions he recommends for the company to take, and explain the reasons therefor. The instructor then opens the case for discussions and encourages other participants to offer their opinions.

Active and objective engagement of the participants in case discussions leads to emergence of many insightful things, challenging the analysis, assumptions and conclusions by the presenter and thus enriching his thinking about the case. Group discussions, obviously, pave way for deeper analysis, better applications of concepts and techniques and more sound conclusions. As such, meaningful case discussions are inevitable for developing emotional understanding, analytical and problem-solving skills. For this, the following things should be factored in:

(i) In the case method, as noted earlier, it is the learners and not the instructor who play active role.

(ii) At the instance of the instructor, a participant presents the case in the class. While presenting the case, he/she is expected to provide a brief profile of the situation in the case, highlighting the main problem, and causes for the problem. He/she has also to present the SWOT analysis and course of action he/she suggests for the company alongwith logical explanations and evidence.

(iii) There is no harm if the learner discusses the case with few of his/her friends before presenting his/her findings in the class because this helps him in refining his own thinking.

(iv) Every participant is expected to prepare the case thoroughly, make his/her own SWOT analysis and draw his/her conclusions. Each of them speaks without fear, or favours his/her thinking about the case, challenging someone's position or defending one's own. However, this should be based on facts, logics and the prevailing scenario.

(v) Being a potential manager, the learner should be a good listener and patiently hear all the comments sportingly and react wherever necessary with solid arguments.

(vi) Participants should never hold a rigid attitude, but try to learn new ideas and thoughts emerging out of the discussions. This will broaden their horizon of thinking and sharpen analytical and decisional skills.

FINANCIAL ANALYSIS AS AN AID TO CASE ANALYSIS

An analysis of strengths and weaknesses of a company requires analysis of financial statements of the company to check out its financial health and recent performance in terms of sales, profits, profit margins, make-up of the cost structure and understand cost-volume profit relationships. As such, financial analysis of the company is very essential while analysing the case.

Financial analysis is the process of determining financial strengths and weaknesses of the company by establishing strategic relationship between the components of balance sheet and profit and loss statement and other operating data. There are two types of financial analysis, viz., vertical analysis and horizontal analysis. **Vertical analysis** studies relationship as between different individual components of the financial statements and as also between these components and their totals for a given period of time. In **Horizontal analysis**, changes in different components of the financial statements over different periods of time with the help of series of the statements are analysed to get insights into the changing profitability and financial conditions of the company.

One of the most powerful financial tools employed very frequently for assessing financial strengths and weaknesses of an enterprise is **Ratio analysis**. It is the process of determining and presenting in arithmetical terms the relationship between figures and group of figures drawn from financial statements.

Financial ratios used for case analysis can be categorised into five basic groups, viz., liquidity, ratios, leverage ratios, coverage ratios and profitability ratios. A bird's eye view of these ratios may be had from Table 21.1.

Where the company's financial health is found highly unsatisfactory, the analyst may use **Altman's Bankruptcy Formula** to calculate its z-value.[4] The z-value can be computed by combining five ratios by assigning weights to them according to their importance to a company's financial strength. The formula is:

$$Z = 1.2X_1 + 1.4X_2 + 3.3X_3 + 0.6X_4 + 1.0X_5$$

where,

X_1 = Working capital/Total assets (%)

X_2 = Retained earnings/Total assets (%)

X_3 = Earnings before interest & taxes/Total assets (%)

X_4 = Market value of equity/Total liabilities (%)

X_5 = Sales/Total assets (number of times)

Scores below 1.81 indicate significant credit problems, whereas a score above 3.0 suggests a healthy organisation. Scores between 1.81 and 3.0 raise question marks.[5]

Table 21.1 Summary View of Important Financial Ratios

Particulars of Ratios	Purpose of Ratios	Formula to Compute Ratios
• **Liquidity ratios**	To measure the short-term solvency of the firm	—
1. Current ratio		$\dfrac{\text{Current assets}}{\text{Current liabilities}}$
2. Acid test ratio		$\dfrac{\text{Quick assets (Current assets – inventories)}}{\text{Current liabilities}}$
• **Leverage ratios**	To measure the long-term solvency of the firm	—
3. Debt to total assets ratio		$\dfrac{\text{Total assets}}{\text{Total debt}}$
4. Debt-equity ratio		$\dfrac{\text{Total debt}}{\text{Total equity}}$
• **Coverage ratios**	To measure the firm's ability to repay its obligations	—
5. Interest coverage ratio		$\dfrac{\text{Profit before interest and tax}}{\text{Interest cost}}$
6. Dividend coverage ratio		$\dfrac{\text{Net profit after tex}}{\text{Dividend amount}}$

(Contd.)

Table 21.1 Summary View of Important Financial Ratios (*Contd.*)

Particulars of Ratios	Purpose of Ratios	Formula to Compute Ratios
• **Profitability ratios**	To measure profitability performance of the firm	
7. Gross profit to sales	To measure the operating efficiency of the firm	$\dfrac{\text{Cost of goods sold}}{\text{Gross profit}}$
8. Operational profit to sales	To judge managerial efficiency of the firm	$\dfrac{\text{Operating profit}}{\text{Sales}}$
9. Net profit to sales	To judge managerial efficiency of the firm	$\dfrac{\text{Net profit}}{\text{Sales}}$
10. Return on capital employed	To assess utilisation of funds	$\dfrac{\text{Net profit}}{\text{Total capital employed}}$
11. Return on investments (ROI)	To measure earning power and overall operating efficiency of the firm.	$\dfrac{\text{Net operating profit}}{\text{Investment}}$

So as to determine if the company can sustain its growth through its internally generated funds, it would be useful to calculate Index of Sustainable Growth. The formula to compute this index is:

$$g = \frac{[P(1 - D)\,(1 + L)]}{[T - P(1 - D)\,(1 + L)]}$$

where

P = (Net profit before tax/Net sales) $\times$ 100

D = Target dividends/profit after tax

L = Total liabilities/Net worth

T = (Total assets/Net sales) $\times$ 100

If the planned growth rate calls for a growth rate higher than its g, external capital will be needed to fund the growth unless the management is able to improve operating efficiencies, decrease dividends, increase the debt-equity ratio or reduce assets by renting or leasing arrangements.[6]

Another useful financial tool employed in the case analysis is Break-Even Analysis (BEA). This technique is used to study cost-volume-profit relationship at varying levels of output and to determine the point at which revenues and costs agree exactly. If the firm is operating at a level above the Break-Even Point (BEP), it indicates that the firm is making profit. Cost-revenue relationship at the BEP can be expressed as:

Total Fixed Costs + Total Variable Costs = Total Sales Revenue

Break-even point (BEP) of a firm can be determined by using the following formula:

$$\text{BEP} = \frac{F}{(I - V)/P}$$

where

F = Fixed costs

I = whole number

V = variable cost per unit

P = selling price per unit

Units needed to break-even = $F/(P - V)$

This technique can enable the management to know at what level of activity the operations of the firm will break-even and to estimate the level of operations that will yield optimum profits. The management can also use cost-output relationship in establishing or reviewing pricing policies. If the management is contemplating to reduce the price of the product, it may use the relationship to determine what changes in volume of sales would be necessary to compensate the price rise being considered.

References

1. Gragg, Charles I., "Because Wisdom Can't be Told" in M.P. Mc Nair (Ed.), *Case Method at the Harvard Business School*, New York, p. 11, 194.

2. Thompson, Arthur A. Jr. and A.J. Strickland III, *Strategic Management— Concepts and Cases*, Tata McGraw-Hill, New Delhi, 2001.

3. Schoen, D.R. and Philip A. Sprague, "What is the Case Method?", in M.P. Mc Nari (Ed.), *Case Method at the Harvard Business School*, pp. 78–79.

4. Wheelen, Thomas L., Hunger, J. David and Krish Rangarajan, *Strategic Management and Business Policy*, Pearson, New Delhi, p. 318, 2010.

5. Fridson, M.S., *Financial Statement Analysis*, John Wiley & Sons, New York, pp. 192–194, 1991.

6. Bangs, D.H., *Management by the Numbers*, Upstart Publications, Dover NH, pp. 106–107, 1992.

CASE STUDY 1

Maruti Suzuki India Ltd.

Despite impressive volume growth Maruti Suzuki India Ltd. (MSIL)—India's largest passenger vehicle maker—is feeling headwinds in the form of new competition, higher input costs and capacity constraints.

MSIL—a partial subsidiary of Suzuki Motor Corporation of Japan—accounts for over 45% of the domestic car market. Maruti Udyog Ltd. (MUL) was established in February 1981. It commenced production in 1983 with the *Maruti* 800 which at the time was the only car available in India. Its only competitors—The Hindustan Ambassador and Premier Padmini—were both around 25 years out of date at that point. Now, Maruti Udyog Ltd. offers a complete range of cars from entry level *Maruti* 800 and *Alto* to hatchback *Ritz, A Star, Swift, Wagon-R, Sedan's Dzire, Sx4* and Sports Utility Vehicle *Grand Vitara*.

The company annually exports more than 50,000 cars and has an extremely large domestic market in India selling over 7,30,000 cars annually. On September 17, 2007, Maruti Udyog Ltd. was renamed Maruti Suzuki India Ltd. The company crossed the one million mark in passenger vehicle sales for 2009–10, a 29% growth high over the previous years.

However, during the last two years the company is facing problems on many fronts. While exports doubled in 2009–10 over 1,47,000 units in the previous financial year, and rural sales accounted for 16.5% of total 2009–10, against 9.5% in 2008–09, the company has been losing market share on the back of new launches in March quarter, 2010.

In the March quarter, Maruti saw its market share decline by over 400 basis points year-on-year sequentially to 41.5% due to intense competition in the AZ segment (over 70% of its sales) due to recent launches of new models such as Volkswagen *Polo*, Chevrolet *Beat* and Ford *Figo*. While Maruti has been able to regain quite a bit of its market share from 41.5% to about 48% now, analysts believe the new launches from Toyota and Honda, later in current year 2011 could make it tougher to maintain the share and increase prices. Given the pricing of the *Etios* (just under ₹5 lakh), a citi report says that Maruti's *Dzire* and the *Sx4* which fetch MSIL (Maruti) about 15% of revenues will be impacted. Further, it believes the *Etios Sedan* hatchback, which was launched by Toyota in April 2011, at an attraction price point (₹4.3 lakh), could impact the Swift, which contributes to about 14% of the company's revenues. Toyota's pricing is part of its strategy to more than triple its market share to 10% over the next five to seven years. Honda's *Brio*, too, when it is launched towards the end of 2011, could cut into Maruti's share.

However, analysts believe the new launches are expanding the market rather than leading to market share erosion for the existing players. They believe that car makers are attracting buyers by creating a niche for themselves with unique features and aggressive pricing, thus helping expand the market. Despite intense competition for the April–October 2010 period, Maruti's domestic car market share fell only 150–200 basis points year-on-year to 48.2%.

According to Vivek Mahajan, head of research at Aditya-Birla Money, "Given the fact that the passenger vehicle segment is expected to grow 15% every year, Maruti should benefit from a volume upsurge with a marginal market share loss. Maruti has been taking steps to keep its product stable fresh with the launch of new and updated models. Since the start of 2010, the company with the launch of *Eeco* has been able to boost its C segment sales. In the A$_2$ segment, the company launched BS-IV compliant *Wagon-R*, *Alto K-10* and five CNG models across segments.

Another issue plaguing Maruti management is capacity constraints. The company's plants at Gurgaon and Manesar have been running at full capacity of a million units for some time now. The management believes, it will be able to increase the capacity by 70,000 units by reducing bottlenecks and improving productivity. The company plans to add a capacity of 2,50,000 units at the Manesar plant by 2011–12.

The key concern area for Maruti is its Ebdita margins, which contracted about 200-basis print year-on-year to 10.7 in September quarter, 2010 on the back of higher input costs and royalty. Since the March 2010 quarter, royalty has jumped from 3.4% to 5.3% of sales. On the raw material front, both steel and copper prices have gone up 15%, while rubber prices have doubled over the last year. Higher raw material costs coupled with rising labour cost could increase pressure on margins going ahead, unless Maruti can improve efficiencies by an equal proportion. Shinzo Nakanishi, MD said, "We will keep up our efforts in localisation and cost reduction to protect and enhance our profit margins".

Analysts believe, what will stand in good stead for the market leaders are its unparalleled distribution network, cost competitiveness and product strength. The company can bank on these advantages to get a bigger pie of the automobile sector, expected to grow 10%–15% in 2010–11. The script is trading at 12.2 times its 2010–11 earnings per share estimate of ₹104 and should deliver about 20% returns over the next one year.

Maruti's ability to sustain market share and improve profitability will determine whether its stock will shine or continue to underperform the broader markets, as has been the case in the recent months.

CASE STUDY 2

TTK Prestige

On June, 2010, while addressing shareholders at TTK Prestige's 54th annual general meeting in Hosur, Chairman T.T. Jagannathan made an interesting detour. Not so long, he told the shareholders, the company was in the grips of a crisis. The combination of high excise and sales taxes had punched a hole in its pocket, and exports had taken a hit after the 9/11 terrorist attacks on the United States. The low point was reached in 2002–03. Sales had slumped to ₹113 crore, there was an operating loss of ₹17 crore, on the company's books, and the debt burden had mounted to ₹80 crore. With quiet pride, Jagannathan then read out the numbers for 2009–10: Turnover of ₹516 crore, operating income of ₹76 crore and free cash balance of ₹30 crore, inspite of capital expenditure of ₹40 crore.

The dip in the fortunes had actually prompted a significant course correction for the company. TTK Prestige at that time had a single product in its portfolio: pressure cooker. Ten percent excise duty meant that the unorganised sector had a field day, indeed, local price-warrior brands that functioned under the radar screen of the excise collections enjoyed a share in excess of 50% in the 900 crore market. And TTK Prestige was heavily dependent on the southern markets for sales. Though it had some presence in the west, its visibility was nominal in the north and the east. There was an urgent need to guard itself against these risks.

The question was in which direction should it expand? Its flagship brand *Prestige*, had, over the years built a strong equity amongst women in the kitchen (the group was launched in the mid-1920s) by T.T. Krishnamchari who went on to serve as India's finance minister. This was a strength TTK *Prestige* could leverage. Accordingly, the management decided to grow in kitchen appliances and other items that go into a kitchen. Some bit of the diversification plan was driven by market research, some by gut feel, and some by simple observation. Jagannathan had observed a small village with a population of 5,000 and found that nobody had a pressure cooker. This was not odd; what caught his attention was that every household had a mixer. That was an indication of where the business potentiality lay. Over the years, the company has launched stoves, mixers, grinders, grills, coffee makers, toasters and even chimneys and modular kitchens. All told, it has over 500 stock-keeping units in its portfolio.

TTK *Prestige* operates 224 *Prestige Smart Kitchen* outlets in 136 towns to show case its range of products. Kitchenware in India has always been sold through multi-brand outlets. As a result, brands often offer higher profit margin to the retailers to gain a prime slot on the display window. Aware that this game can bleed the company, TTK *Prestige* has gone for its own flagship stores. In addition to *Prestige Smart Kitchen*, the company also runs the *Prestige* kitchen boutiques for modular kitchen. It had even set up *Prestige* lifestyle stores for top-end products, but the initiative has been mothballed. Ever since the exclusive *Prestige Smart Kitchen* stores came up, claims TTK *Prestige* executives, sales have picked up in the multi-brand outlets as well.

The expansion in the product portfolio and retail network was accompanied by outsourcing. Production capacity, it was felt, ought not to derail the company's plans. The other reason is that many kitchenware items are reserved for production in the small-scale sector; and outsourcing is a convenient way to overcome this hurdle for a large company like TTK *Prestige*. "I blame my grandfather for the present condition of Indian industry. The policy of reservation did not allow any body to scale up. Meanwhile, look where China's industrial sector has reached today", says Jagannathan.

So, what has been the result on the ground? Pressure cooker, which contributed the bulk of TTK *Prestige's* sales, now accounts for 46%. Kitchen appliances contribute 20% to the overall sales, non-stick cookware 17%, gas stoves 12%, and others including modular kitchens 5%. Its share in the kitchen appliances market is small, less than 10%.

This is not to suggest that TTK *Prestige* has put the pressure cooker business on the backburner. In 2005, the government reduced the excise duty on pressure cooker from 10% to nil. This resulted in the decline of market share of the local unorganised brands to about a third. Of the two-thirds, TTK *Prestige* lords it over half. Jagannathan is perhaps aware that it will not be easy for him to raise his market share from here; that is why the foray into kitchen appliances makes sense. TTK *Prestige* has tried to create some differentiation through innovation in design.

Some rivals and observers feel that TTK *Prestige* has not created enough technological barriers in the new areas it has entered. "Many others, who entered the business, had to exit as they could not meet consumer demands and were unable to provide high-quality products", says Maharaja Appliances Chairman and Managing Director Harish Kumar. "Appliances make a technology- and design-driven business. It requires a lot of work and constant innovation to improve your products". He also cautions against the use of imported products, especially from low-cost producers in China, because of the quality problems.

Still others feel *Prestige*, being a hardcore pressure cooker brand, doesn't lend itself to extension to appliances. *"Prestige's* association with the pressure cookers makes it a little difficult to have an impact in kitchen appliances," says Milagrow Business & Knowledge Solutions founder and former Philips Chief Executive Rajeev Karwal. "People will be a little skeptical of its appliances as it is better known for its pressure cookers and non-stick cookware. It will have to ensure quality and features to attract the consumers.

Jagannathan, on his part, is convinced that the company is on the right track, though he knows there are issues that need to be sorted out. One issue is how to tackle the rural markets. With increased income, the demand for pressure cookers and even kitchen appliances is on the rise. These markets, it so happens, have always been serviced by local players and national brands do not have much of a presence.

TTK *Prestige* has formed a new business model involving Non-Government Organisations or NGOs and self-help groups to sell pressure cookers in rural India. The initial investment will come from the company, while the management will be provided by the Non-Govermental Organisations (NGOs). The company hopes to boost its revenues from the rural market with this model in place.

The other issue was expansion in the North. TTK *Prestige* had in 1997 set up a factory in Uttarakhand for inner-lid pressure cookers. The company decided to expand this factory to make kitchen appliances like mixers and grinders, gas stoves and induction cooktops, and so on. But it will need to look at its products strategy for the North carefully. Unlike the South, meal preparations in the North do not require heavy grinding and blending; as a result, the food processor market there is different from the Southern states. What TTK *Prestige* seems to be banking on is its high expenditure on sales and promotion. "Without tagline, *Are you ready for a smarter kitchen?*, we have always aimed at making the loudest noise in the kitchen appliances market", says TTK *Prestige* Executive Vice-President (marketing) Chandra Kalro.

The company essentially focuses on the domestic market, since it has after all got singled badly in markets overseas. Exports were a huge focus for TTK *Prestige* in the 1990s and the early years of the current decade. It had started a new brand called Manttra for the US market and even set up a subsidiary there, called Manttra Inc., to develop the market. A team of 25 salesmen was taken on board and soon several retailers were setting Manttra pressure cookers. Then the bankruptcies began to happen and TTK *Prestige* was in a soup. "They killed US with charges and bankruptcies.

I decided to withdraw from the market", says Jagannathan. At the moment, only sears and K-Mart sell its wares. One retailer has not paid the company for 3,00,000 pieces, while another one rejected a consignment of 4,00,000 pieces. Wal-Mart, the biggest retailer on earth, is out of bounds because it wants deliveries within 24 hours. Wiser now, Jagannathan says: "When the Indian market is doing so well, we are not very keen on exports".

CASE STUDY 3

Dr. Reddy's Laboratories

Little did Dr. Wolfgang Niedermaier, Former CEO of betapharm, who has since left the company, realise that what was to unfold was the puzzle itself. Just a year after the acquisition, the German healthcare market changed almost overnight. Drug prices came crashing down as the German government took to healthcare sector reforms, turning the once attractive branded generics market into a predominantly commoditised, tender-riven business. As a result, the carrying value of betapharm declined to $90 million in March 21, 2010 from the acquisition cost of $480 million after four rounds of impairments in its books. The Indian company, for its part, has been feeling the pain of the buyout—gone bad. It went into the red in 2008–09, thanks to huge write-downs because of betapharm.

To ensure it is viable, Dr. Reddy's brass has been working on betapharm's cost structure—four years after the acquisition; 35% of betapharm's products (by value) have been transferred to India, and the workforce downsized from 400 at the peak to around 80 today. At the same time, the German major's business model has been modified to make it more attuned to winning tenders.

But making betapharm—and therefore, Dr. Reddy's work is going to be a long haul. "I do not think we have dealt with betapharm. What we have dealt with is writing down the value of betapharm, and we have cut costs". Says G.V. Prasad, Vice-Chairman & CEO, Dr. Reddy's Labs, adding: "We have not grown but shrunk the business". Prasad is clear what needs to be done. Turnaround betapharm, "Convert it into a growth engine and create value out of it. It is still an unfinished task and will take another 2–3 years", he adds. It is, perhaps, because of uncertainties like these that there are reports that big MNCs like Glaxo and Pfizer could be eyeing a stake in Dr. Reddy's.

Dr. Reddy's Laboratories, founded by Dr. Anji Reddy, is another innovation-focused drug major that knows a thing or two about treating ulcers. It has made a small fortune by knocking off the generic version of the best-selling anti-ulcer drug *Zintac*. But it is not just betapharm that is a source of heartburn for the company. US operations of the company have been plagued with product recalls and audits by the US Food & Drug Administration have impacted production schedules. That explains why revenues for the third quarter of 2009–10, at $373 million were 6% lower than a year ago, and the consolidated bottom-line was in the red to the tune of ₹522 crore.

To be sure, Dr. Reddy's future hangs not just on betapharm's fate but going beyond it to build a solid base for operations in key global markets. And it is here that learnings from the betapharm experience will stand the company in good stead. For instance, like Germany, a number of overseas markets are getting price-regulated, and Prasad's shift in strategy—to go after government tenders—will come in such countries, too.

Consider Russia, for instance where the Government has been talking of imposing some form of price control. For Dr. Reddy's, clearly, the worry is whether its Russian operations—which along with the CIS Region account for some 13% of sales—will also go the betapharm way, "Given our experience in Germany, we think we are better prepared to catch early signs and act quickly", says Umang Vohra, Senior V.P. and CEO of Dr. Reddy's, although he does not think Russia imports a lot of medicines and 40% of the total Russian market is 'Over-the Counter' (OTC). Another big opportunity is existence of biosimilars (newer versions of generic equivalents of biopharmaceutical products whose patents have expired). Both OTC and biosimilars would not come under the purview of price control.

That is why Prasad has shortlisted Russia and the CIS amongst the company's five key markets. The other markets it will focus sharply on are the US, Europe (mainly Germany and the UK) and India till 2008. Dr. Reddy's Red spread itself thin across as many as over 30 markets including such countries as Trinidad & Tobago and Haiti. Today, that number is down by half, and will go down further.

For each of its key markets, Dr. Reddy's has worked out a different strategy. For instance, in the markets of the US and Europe, the company will focus on generics that are either difficult to make or in which competition is limited. For Russia, it will be OTC and biosimilars. And in India, it will be to move into rural markets and aggressively launch products.

Dr. Reddy's is not the only Indian Pharma firm following such a strategy of tapping niche opportunities. Lupin, for instance, is targeting the less competitive oral contraceptive market in the US which is worth close to $4 billion. What is more, Lupin has built a significant presence in Japan, the world's second-largest Pharma market, where the government has reforms to increase consumption of cheaper generics.

Yet, there is little doubt that margins are going to be under pressure for Indian Pharma as more and more countries follow the European model of price control. Says Prasad: "We need to have globally-competitive costs, for which the whole company must be oriented towards competing in commodity markets with a low-cost structure and a frugal work culture.

Indeed, Dr. Reddy's is one of the pioneers in drug discovery in India. However, the results are still not proportionate to the effort. The fear is that those efforts will now be compromised at the altar of cost-rationalisation. Prasad dismisses such speculation. "We have only restructured our research to spend more money on programmes and projects and less on overheads".

However, the pipeline of NCES has withered from 6–7 molecules a few years ago to just three now. The company's defence is that rigorous measures were applied to evaluate the molecules. And Prasad loves to point out that Dr. Reddy's is still the only company in India with a Phase III asset (Balaglita zone, Dr. Reddy's anti-diabetic NCE candidate). Dr. Reddy's is also widening its scope beyond NCES to "differentiate formulations", where improvements are made in existing products. The probability of success here is higher although returns in absolute terms would not be as huge as if an NCE gets to market. As margins come under pressure with increasing competition and governments attempting to restrain prices, Dr. Reddy's is currently seized with the main issue as to how to improve business performance of the company.

CASE STUDY 4

Tata Tea's NEW Gambit

Tion, the cold beverage from Tata Tea, which has extracts of tea, ginseng and fruit, was launched with much fanfare in 2009. But a year on, the product exists only in two states—Tamil Nadu and Kerala.

According to Sangeeta Talwar, executive director, marketing and regional President, South Asia, Tata Tea, the product is doing well and will see the phased roll-out across the country in time. The response from the market place has been good. She says, "We recently launched an orange flavour, which complements our portfolio of apple, peach and mango".

But according to experts, in a competitive segment such as fruit drinks, estimated to be ₹2,000 crore in size, growing at a steady clip is not enough. "You need to have the wherewithal, the muscle power and the strength to carry on in a competitive segment such as this", they say.

Even if one were to take into account the practice of launching a product selectively in a few regions before going in for a full-blown national launch, Tata Tea's *Tion* appears to be tad slow on that count, not to mention that it is hardly visible in the market place.

This piecemeal approach to the brand, say experts, lies in the company's inability to compete with the likes of Pepsi Co and Coca-Cola in a segment that they clearly dominate.

Tion, a year on, is now doing sales of about 2 million per month in the 250-ml segment while the larger 400-ml variant is small with sales of about 2,00,000 bottles per month. Against this, *Nimbooz*, a lemon flavoured drink launched by Pepsi Co in 2010 is said to be clocking sales of over 2,00,000 bottles per day or 7 million bottles per month. Coca-Cola's *Minute Maid Nimbu Fresh*, launched a few months earlier, is also doing sales of about 2.5 million bottles per month.

Under the circumstances, Tata Tea tied up recently with its competitor Pepsi Co, announcing it had signed a memorandum of understanding with the latter for a new non-carbonated beverage entity. Tying up with Pepsi Co will allow Tata Tea to leverage the latter's skills in the non-carbonated beverage business—something it needs so badly if it has to emerge as a well-rounded beverage major.

Tata Tea has articulated off and on its keenness to go beyond tea and coffee. Its acquisitions in the last few years have echoed this sentiment. Whether it be the buoyant of Mount Everest Mineral Water, which owns the Himalayan brand of packaged water, or energy brands in the US, the 30% stake of which was subsequently sold to Coca-Cola in 2007. Tata Tea has been looking to diversify its product portfolio for long.

Health and wellness is a market too hard to resist given that overall beverage consumption is moving these, whether in India or abroad. According to a recent report prepared by the Tata Strategic Management Group, health and wellness beverages in India are likely to grow at 22% year-on-year to touch ₹17,350 crore by 2014–15. The market at the moment is about ₹6,200 crore in size including fruit juices, fruit drinks, energy and sports drinks, etc. Worldwide, the health and wellness market is already over $460 billion in size.

Pepsi Co knows well the implications of playing in this market. It already has a $10 billion health-drink business worldwide.

Pepsi Co's global Chairperson and CEO Indra Nooyi, in fact, has said recently that she is looking to triple Pepsi Co's health-drink business over the next ten years as she sees huge growth areas for its "good for you" drinks. Tie-ups in the area are likely to help further the cause as Pepsi Co looks to shed its image as a maker of cold drinks. Nooyi has also laid out a roadmap to reduce salt, saturated fats and added sugar in the company's products in the next five years, while sugar and saturated fat will be brought down in ten years. The MoU with Tata then in the Indian market is yet another step in this direction.

What would be the future of *Tion* and other products like it is a million dollar question which Tata Tea management is seized with.

CASE STUDY 5

Amrutanjan: Pain for Suitors

The Chennai-based Amrutanjan has been in the news as a takeover target over the past couple of years. And the buzz just refuses to die down even though the promoters have denied times without number.

Because of the takeover reports, the scrip has gone up over 150% in the last one year. What added fuel to the fire was Emami Chairman R.S. Agrawal's reported statement in April 2010 that he was interested in buying Amrutanjan. His company, however, was quick to clarify that the Chairman had only expressed his desire to acquire any fast moving consumer goods or Pharma business or company, including Amrutanjan, within its financial and operational resources. Meanwhile, names of various other suitors including Dabur have been doing the rounds.

Despite the takeover rumours, 115-year old Amrutanjan sits firm in the market place with a share of 29%—second only to rival Zandu, which has a share of 45%, and was acquired by Emami in 2008.

For Amrutanjan, retaining its number two slot over all these years has been far from easy in a market that has seen competition growing at the same time. As an FMCG analyst points out, "When competition increases, the first to be attacked are the number two and three brands. They are the ones challengers go after typically. The number one is secure in that sense because challengers are not buying for its blood at the first instance. The number two always has a greater threat of seeing market share eroding as challengers increase".

So as to stay relevant and meet competitive pressure, Amrutanjan has transformed itself into a youthful product with new packaging and variants. There are three key variants as of now—a pain balm, a strong balm and a maha strong balm. Plus, the brand has extended into segments such as roll-on liquids, cold gel packs, reusable gels, joint ache creams and sprays in quest for new users.

Amrutanjan's pricing of its balm is also on a par with leader Zandu—₹20 for the standard 8-gm.pack. Tiger is slightly expensive at ₹22, says observer. "So that gives consumers a choice of two products at the same price point", says a source.

That's not all. To increase brand recall, Amrutanjan has also changed its advertising strategy moving away from regional-level campaigns to a national-level exercise replete with a new tagline—*Be ready with Amrutanjan.*

As the brand makes the transformation from regional to national, it has retained one attribute through its grip over rural and semi-urban markets. That has been the heart of Amrutanjan's distribution strategy-keeping its key consumer profile intact even as it seeks new users.

Amrutanjan, as rivals point out, is strong in non-metro markets. "By and large, pain balms are strong in tier two and three cities. It's not an urban phenomenon because consumers in small towns and cities are comfortable using pain balms as opposed to pain rubs or creams", says an executive from Elder Healthcare.

In small towns and cities, the fight is a square one between Amrutanjan and Zandu, say analysts. Both have their strong holders—Zandu in the north, and Amrutanjan, in the south. Both over the years have moved to allied areas—taking the battle to each other's doorsteps in the process. So Amrutanjan has been fighting hard for share in the north, while Zandu has been seeking consumers in the South. Have they succeeded? For now, Zandu seems to be having an upper hand with greater market share, say analysts, though Amrutanjan is not giving up yet in its quest for market share beyond the south.

What it is banking on is its trademark properties, say sources, its distinctive yellow balm with a strong aroma. It is these medicinal properties that have ensured that consumers in the south have remained loyal to it despite the onslaught of Zandu. As an executive with a rival healthcare firm says, "People love applying a balm before retiring for the night in the south. And if that is an Amrutanjan nothing like it".

CASE STUDY 6

Nano's Topsy-Turvy RIDE

With a price tag of just ₹1 lakh, the *Nano* was meant for all those Indians who wanted to drive a car but could not afford to buy one. Once it's out on the road, Pundits had said, the market will explode. Every nook and cranny of the country will be crammed with the small wonder, Ratan Tata, the Chairman of the Tata group had told the *Mc Kinsey Quarterly* when the *Nano* was being conceived that such a car could sell up to a million pieces in a year. It was a jolt of sorts for all when Tata Motors reported the same numbers for November, 2010: but actually it had sold only 509 *Nanos*. The slide had actually started earlier. *Nano* sales had peaked at 9,000 in July 2010 and then fell to 8,103 in August, 5,520 in September and 3,065 in October. November, 2010 was, of course, the lowest point for the car that was launched amid much fanfare in March 2009.

These numbers, to be fair, show what Tata Motors has sold to its dealers and not what the customers bought from the dealers. So it doesn't capture fully what is going on at the market place, though it somewhat mirrors the trend. Automobile experts insist that dealers do not like to hold large inventories because of the cost attached to it. But the Tata Motors may have picked up large stocks of the *Nano* in view of the launch-time euphoria, and that perhaps could be the reason for the low November numbers. Whatever the reason, the dip in the sale graph is worrisome. The car market has grown at a fast clip percent in the last several months. The two-wheeler market, which the *Nano* was supposed to feed on, too has shown no signs of a slowdown in months together.

The *Nano* experienced hiccups even before it was born. Work at the *Nano* factory at Singur in West Bengal had to stop midway in October 2008, thanks to the agitation over compensation to the landowners. The company, a week later, announced that it had got land at Sanand in Gujarat for the factory.

Meanwhile, as a makeshift arrangement Tata Motors began to roll out the *Nano* from its plant at Pantnagar in Uttarakhand. This plant is dedicated to the Ace mini-truck; the engineers said they could put together up to 50,000 *Nanos* in a year—not enough for open sales where customers walk into a showroom and drive out in a car. So, the company decided to gauge the demand and streamline production. The bookings were opened on March 23, 2009 and closed on April 25, 2009—as many as 2,06,000 people applied, 1,00,000 were shortlisted by June, and the first delivery was made in July by Ratan Tata in Mumbai.

The Sanand Factory went on stream in June 2010; the company started to do open sales in several states like Kerala, Karnataka, Maharashtra, Uttar Pradesh, West Bengal, Chattisgarh, Madhya Pradesh, Andhra Pradesh, Bihar, Gujarat and Punjab. It hoped to cover the whole country by March 2011. This may be a good indication that the supply constraints on the *Nano* have begun to lift, though some observers say production is yet to peak because all component suppliers have not been able to set up shop near the Sanand Factory. But the booking delays, most experts insist, worked against the *Nano*. People who missed out in the lottery were unhappy. The deliveries were to be completed over the next year-and-a-half; some lost interest midway and cancelled their bookings. Though Tata Motors had said the 1,00,000 bookings will be delivered by December, 2010. There were just 71,000 *Nanos* on the road as of November, 2010. As this includes sizeable off-the-shelf numbers as well, cancellations clearly have been huge. There was also some bit of confusion in the market—advance booking for an automobile, after all, is not something the current generation of Indian car buyers has heard of.

Moreover, it is no longer a ₹1 lakh car. The cheapest a customer can buy a *Nano* in the country is around ₹1.24 lakh (ex-showroom); the top variant can cost up to ₹2.05 lakh. Spread over 60 or even more installments, the difference does not add up too much. But the catchy ₹1 lakh tag is gone, though the *Nano* remains the cheapest car in the world.

There were also a few incidents of the car catching fire. Tata Motors, on its part, claims the fires were caused by the addition of foreign electrical equipment like music system and air-conditioners which were not supported by the car. The company adds that internal and international experts have twice analysed the *Nano* in 2010 and arrived at the conclusion that the reasons for the incidents in a few *Nanos* are specific to the cars, and there are no generic defects. It also claims that over 80% of the current *Nano* owners are either satisfied or very satisfied with the car. But don't these incidents still play on the consumers' mind? Has this caused the demand for the *Nano* to taper off in recent times? What would be the future of *Nano* in the wake of emergence of small cars by the rivals? These questions are currently engaging the serious attention of the Tata Motors management.

CASE STUDY 7

Nokia India

At the launch of Nokia's latest communication device E7 in 2011 D. Shiva Kumar, Managing Director and Vice-President for Nokia India, was inundated with questions from the media on Nokia's steady decline in market share and gradual increase of Android's—Google's open source mobile operating systems—share in India. But Shiva Kumar displayed no signs of irritation while he patiently addressed journalists' questions. He got the company's brand ambassador Shah Rukh Khan to address the media about the newest device and his experiences with the E7.

But behind a facade of calm, Nokia is preparing for a bitter battle for market shares. While at the lower end of the market, smaller local manufacturers are giving the world's top cell phone maker a run for its money, at the upper end—in the critical smartphone segment—Nokia is struggling against stiff competition from innovative software makers Apple and Google.

Finland-based Nokia—once mighty mobile phone maker—has been facing the heat of economic downturn in 2009 and bruising competitive environment since 2010 and onwards, raising doubts among the shareholders and executives about the company's ability to sustain its 4% dividend.

Although Nokia still commands 37% of the world's handset market, it is facing tough competition in the lucrative high end of the industry where Apple's *i-phone* and Research in Motion's *BlackBerry* have grabbed the cool factor in smartphones that can surf the web and handle e-mail.

Olli-Pekka Kallasvmo, the company's taciturn Former Chief Executive, admits the mood out there is gloomy, especially on the Wall Street. "We are not getting the benefit of the doubt", he said in an interview the day after the analysts' meeting. "We need to change that".

Nokia's problems have grossly been acute in North America, where its hold on smartphones equals a barely visible 3.9%, compared with 51% for Research in Motions and 29.5% for Apple, according to an analyst, Gartner. As if to underscore its problems in the US, Nokia announced in December 2009 that it would shutter its flagship stores in New York and Chicago.

"We made wrong decisions in the American market", says Kai Oistamo, Executive Vice-President for devices. For example, Nokia was slow to make the change to so-called clamshell phones, sticking with "monobloc" models even as consumers abandoned them.

While Nokia first offered touchscreen technology in 2004—three years before the debut of the i-phone—Apple's models quickly made Nokia's competing products look stodgy. Most of Nokia's touchscreen phones can't quickly transform their screen with the jab of a finger, which is among the factors that make the i-phone seem so much more slick.

Until recently, according to both Nokia executives and industry experts, the company did not want to produce phone specifically tailored for American consumer tastes and it resisted demands from the major carriers to come up with phones based around their brands and individual specifications.

Nokia has also been hobbled by its traditional weakness in phones employing CDMA, the wireless technology offered by Sprint and Verizon wireless that is used by about 50% of American consumers. (Sprint's current line up does not include any Nokia models). Nokia focuses instead on GSM phones for AT&T and T-Mobile. However, AT&T's exclusive deal with Apple has hurt Nokia in the high-end smartphone market.

Though Nokia sells a lot of smartphones elsewhere in the world, its share of the global smartphone market has fallen to 39.3% in 2010, down from 42.3% in 2009. Even in Nokia's home base of Europe, the i-phone is rapidly gaining in popularity.

Sensing erosion of its market share in smartphone in Europe and the US, Nokia is now focusing on emerging markets of Asia to exploit burgeoning opportunities. According to Stephen Elop, who took over at the helm at Nokia in September 2010, "the reality is 90% of the world does not have or cannot afford a smartphone or a high-end device. This gap creates an opportunity". Elop has decided to increase investment in low-end phones that have sold well in Asia, as well as in emerging market countries elsewhere.

Even in emerging markets Nokia is facing fierce competition. Three years ago Nokia's position in emerging markets looked impenetrable, occupying leadership position in China and India. "But low chip sets and growing scale have helped a number of Asian manufacturers to price aggressively and seize market share", said Geof Blabber, an analyst at the mobile communications research firm CCS insight in London.

The battle for cheap phone market could get even together. Nokia has relied on its brand and distribution chain across emerging markets, home to 1.7 billion mobile phone subscribers. But ZTE and its larger Chinese rival, Huawel Technologies, which have traditionally been in the network equipment business, are aggressively muscling in on mobile devices. ZTE expects to ship more than 80 million mobile phones this year (2011), up by a third from 60 million units last year, He Shiyou, Executive Vice-President for the company's mobile device unit, said in April 2011.

While demand for low-end cell phones has surged across emerging markets since the economic crisis began to ease, Nokia's sales of basic cell phones have fallen for three consecutive quarters. In the January-to-March quarter of 2011, Nokia sold 84.3 million handsets other than smartphones, 2% less than a year earlier.

For Nokia, India is the second biggest market after China having contributed $2,809 million to the company's worldwide sales in 2009. However, in recent times, Nokia has been struggling against stiff competition from the global as well as local players. The company's market share dropped to 30.2% in 2010–11 from 49% a year ago.

Nokia India has noted tremendous opportunity existing in India for business expansion. As per Analysys Mason data, the Indian mobile handset market has grown by 30.17% from 116 million handsets as on December 31, 2008 to 151 million handsets as on December end, 2009. The growth has been driven by the growth in mid-priced devices—in the range of ₹2,000 to ₹5,000. According to Cyber Media Research Survey (CMR), the Indian mobile handset market would tend to grow by 25% in terms of volume in 2011 to 210 million units, with small phones contributing sales of nearly 12 million.

But competition is breathing down Nokia's neck. It is not only competing with established brands like Research in Motion—the maker of *BlackBerry*—Apple and Samsung but also from smaller local players, who have unleashed tsunami of copycat models with almost similar features that match those of high-end branded models, but at much lower prices. Result: brands like Micromax, Gfive, Spice, among others, have already grabbed a sizeable chunk of the domestic handset market.

Nokia India has been hit the handset because of the availability and success of Google's free open source Android platform that made entry and expansion in the small phone market easier for a number of hardware manufacturers in India which have chosen to join Android eco system, especially at the mid-to-low range of the smartphone market.

According to CMR, Indian buyers are increasingly more feature conscious, rather than being plain 'brand loyal' in the traditional sense of the term. He adds, "Emerging mobile handset players with their highly innovative features have been able to influence the first time buyers, especially, the youth and blue collar executives".

Korean electronic giants like LG and Samsung have already upped their R&D focus to make value additions for Indian mobile users. Samsung says it has made significant investments in its software R&D centre in Noida. Samsung India Software Operations Vice-President Dipesh Shah says, "We are sure to capture a market share of at least 40% in 2011". Shah is hopeful that the company's Android-based smartphones as well as those running on Bada, its own mobile operating system, will provide enough differentiation to give it a big market push in 2011. LG, too, is betting big on smartphones. Since the demand for smartphones is accelerating with 3G in India, "LG expects to generate 20%–25% revenue from new smartphones", says Vishal Chopra, business head, mobile communications, LG India.

Having seen a market share erosion of more than 40% during the last three years in India, Nokia is keen to uphold itself as a brand that can be trusted—a direct answer to naysayers who believe the local handset brands have eaten into Nokia's share at the entry level. This is why Nokia is wooing popular Bollywood Stars like Shah Rukh Khan and Priyanka Chopra as the brand ambassadors for its devices who can communicate the 'trust' factor to the consumers. But smart marketing will not alone save Nokia and the company knows that. That is why Shiva Kumar says, "Nokia excels at providing low-cost handsets in high volumes—affordable, simple user interfaces and handsets with software that one can consume and not just fancy". Nokia claims that it has five-tuned its approach for the entry level. "We will launch several low-cost dual SIM handsets with features like camera and radio that are much in demand", says Shiva Kumar.

Until very recently, Nokia believed its competitive position in smartphones could be improved with Symbian—that's when it launched the Nokia8 device that supported Symbian 3OS. This older operating system did not stand a chance against new mobile OSes like Android and Apple iOS, Shiva Kumar admits. He feels that for the long-term, the Symbian platform will not be sufficient in pocketing the small phone users.

On February 11, 2011 Nokia India announced its new strategy, leadership team and operational structure for devices and services business, designed to focus on speed, results and accountability. Effective from April 1, 2011, there will be two business units. Smart Devices, focused on smartphones, and mobile phones, focused on mass-market mobile phones. "The new strategy also involves changing our mode of working and culture to facilitate speed and agility in our innovation, product development and execution and accountability for results", lists Shiva Kumar.

In March 2011, a broad strategic partnership was announced between Microsoft and Nokia. Microsoft's Windows Phone would serve as Nokia's primary smartphone platform, announced Nokia's CEO, Stephen Elop. "A renowned approach to capture volume and value growth to connect the next billion to the internet in developing growth markets", underlined Elop.

Nokia outlined the risks of its decision to partner with Microsoft, in a regulatory filing highlighting many of the issues raised by critics, primarily the hiatus period before it can launch devices running Windows Phone 7 (WP7)—a period that condemns the company to another year in the smartphone wilderness. Nokia says it is aiming to expand the Microsoft operating system into mass markets. Other risk factors highlighted by Nokia include the relative immaturity of the Windows Phone 7, a mobile operating system developed by Microsoft as the successor to its Windows Mobile Platform.

Recently, Nokia unveiled new mobile phones at both ends of its range to fend off competition from cheap unbranded handsets and smartphones powered by Google Inc's Android. The C2-03 model would target consumers in emerging markets by making it easier to switch between different phone numbers, said the Executive Vice-President. Nokia also showed the N9, a touchscreen smartphone, based on its Mec Go Software.

"Nokia now recognises it needs to move more quickly to make up for lost ground in emerging markets, particularly India, where agile opportunist competitors have taken market share", said Ben Wood, a London-based analyst with CCS Insight.

However, market analysts believe that Nokia woke up late to fight its smart rivals. "Nokia should really have begun this fight back two years ago, and leaving it so late in a very tough competitive position", said Neil Mawston, an analyst at the research firm strategy Analytics.

Market analysts are wondering if Nokia India would be able to recapture its past glory.

CASE STUDY 8

Nano Filters

According to a 2007 United Nations report, half of the world's hospital beds are occupied by patients suffering from water-borne diseases. In India, such diseases affecting nearly 4 million people cause more than 1.5 times the deaths caused by AIDS and double the deaths caused by road accidents.

Water purifiers thus far have been used in middle and upper class homes, though water-borne diseases affect all income classes. The cost of water purifiers—acquisition as well as maintenance—has been too steep for poor household. The existing state of affairs suggests a need gap-purifiers.

Sensing this need gap, the Tata Group has launched—Swatch, the world's cheapest water purifier at price points of ₹749 and ₹999. The genesis of Swatch (clean) began nearly a decade ago as a corporate social responsibility initiative of Tata Consultancy Services. Between 2000 and 2003, the company launched a water filter called 'Sujal' and distributed it among several NGOs. When the tsunami ravaged parts of Coastal South India in 2004, these water filters were distributed in the affected regions.

The offtake was brisk because the product worked well. That is when the company sat up and took notice of a tremendous commercial opportunity in water purifiers. That was also the time when Tata Motors was working on its ultra low cost car, the *Nano*. Could it do a *Nano* in water purifiers?, Tata thought.

Soon thereafter, Tata Chemicals, Tata Consultancy Services and Titan Industries got together to take things to the next level. The result is *Swach*. Scientists working on the project have used rice husk ash and silver nano particles to filter out the bacteria and other germs. The filter was made by Tata Consultancy Services. Tata Chemicals did the silver nanotechnology and Titan created the precision machine tools to make the filter. "We see this as an opportunity to provide solutions to the have-nots", says the head of the Water Purifier business of Tata Chemicals.

Swach—the water purifier—does not require electricity; instead it runs on a replaceable cartridge with a shelf life of 3,000 litres. This would last a family of five for about 200 days.

At the launch, Chairman Ratan Tata said, "safe drinking water is the most basic of human needs. The social cost of water contamination is already enormous and increases every year".

On the pricing front, Swach costs far less than rivals Hindustan Unilever's *Pureit* and Eureka Forbes' *Aquasure*, which cost ₹2,000 and ₹1,950 respectively. Still, *Swach* is not being sold at a loss. There is, to be sure, keen sense of business as well. At present, the total water purifier market is about ₹1,500 crore. Water purifiers can be found in 10% of urban homes, while rural penetration is less than 1%. Thus, Tata is placing his bet on the 200 million households that do not have access to safe drinking water.

While the price of *Swach* is the lowest in the market, Tata would have an assured flow of income from the sale of cartridges. At the same time, it significantly eliminates the need for after sales services, unlike its peers in the business.

As for brand building, Tata is following a two-pronged approach. The first comprises conventional marketing of the product, while the second will concentrate on the causes related to unsafe drinking water.

For distribution, Tata will bank on other Tata firms, including Rallis, the company's farm retail business, Tata Salt, which caters to 53 million households, as well as some non-profit outfits.

With all this, will Nano Filters be able to sell one million units a year in the next five years?

CASE STUDY 9

Vishal Retail

Three years before Kishore Biyani set up his first Pantaloon store on Kolkata's high street, Garahat, in 1997, Ram Chandra Agrawal had set up a large garment store, Vishal Garments, at Kolkata's Tiger Cinema, which was converted into a sprawling store.

But Agrawal's first-mover advantage did not last long. While Biyani's store is still there, Agrawal's has long closed, after he moved to Delhi in 2001 and founded Vishal Retail. Both grew at a frantic pace after that, but while Biyani prospered, growth became a liability for Agrawal.

Today, the Chairman of Vishal Retail is eagerly waiting his date with the Corporate Debt Restructuring Cell of lenders in the third week of November, 2009. With unpaid debt of ₹730 crore, Agrawal is hoping his lenders would give him a new lease of life.

The lenders, led by State Bank of India, have to take a call on restructuring Vishal's ₹730-crore debt: reduce interest rates, prolong its repayment of the principal and offer some sort of moratorium on repayment of interest and principal.

The lenders are even seeking a change in management, though executives and people close to the company feel there is no need for it. "Agrawal is open to change, but what will the lenders do by taking over a company? They cannot run a retail company", says a former Vishal executive.

Vishal's Group President, Ambeek Khemka says, a Bankers have validated its business model, which is value-retailing and catering to markets in tier-II and tier-III cities. The only mistake we made was to grow our business through short-term debt". The 'only mistake', however, proved too costly. In June 2007, Vishal raised ₹110 crore through an IPO but this was not enough to meet its scorching growth. It had 50 stores by then and was looking to add 130 more in a year. It tapped the short-term debt market, as it could not bring in a follow-on offer before a year after the IPO.

"The thinking was that once we expand, have the top line, we could hit capital market again to fund expansion and retire short-term debt or convert into long-term debt", says Khemka. Before it could do, (industry sources say Vishal was talking to private equity investors, who withdrew at the last moment), the Lehman Brother collapse happened.

Anticipating its expansion, Vishal had placed order with suppliers (in apparels Vishal had to place orders six months in advance). When the stores did not happen, deliveries piled up and consumption slowed. "The supply chain got choked, not just for Vishal but many retailers globally", says Manmohan Agarwal, a former CEO at Vishal.

Vishal is saddled with huge stocks, valued at ₹550 crore that it is trying to liquidate. This is the second big problem and responsible for back-to-back quarterly losses in the last two quarters of 2009. According to Khemka, losses are likely to continue till June end 2010.

Vishal made many other mistakes. When it was ramping up, it spread itself too thin, opening stores across the country. Given that it was selling over 20,000 items in its stores, this made its supply chain complex.

According to suppliers, distribution centre-led model failed as it could not build on IT network which meant that buying at the warehouses was not aligned to customer needs, and it ended with dead inventory. "It seems the sourcing managers had a brief to buy at the best cost. But there was a mismatch", says the sales head with an FMCG major. Also, Vishal tried to develop private labels in every single category, but did not have the competence (had limited scale) to support these.

Though the impact has still been minimal so far, Vishal has been trying to get back on track. Khemka is working on a turnaround to reduce its debt burden, get rid of inventory, and fuse liquidity. Vishal has brought down monthly expenses from ₹46 crore to ₹36 crore, which includes an interest burden of ₹8.5 crore. It has reduced interest costs by ₹2.5 crore a month, which will come down further if the CDR agrees to a moratorium on interest payment for two years. It could use this for replenishing stocks, upgrading stores.

Vishal's capital structure remains a problem. One good thing working for it is that it has brought rentals on its properties down to ₹23.25 per sq.ft. from ₹50–60 per sq.ft.

It has also closed two dozen stores and warehouses. At one point, Vishal had a warehouse space of 1.1 million of sq.ft (26 warehouses) to service a retail space of 2.6 million sq.ft. Today, it is servicing 2.5 million sq.ft. of retail space through one central warehouse of 3,50,000 sq.ft. It plans to close another 12 stores in the next three months, which will bring the number from 150 to about 135. Vishal's stores used to sell over 40,000 SKUs (Stock Keeping Units); Khemka has brought it down to 15,000 SKUs.

Vishal does not like to be compared with Subhiksha, unable to pay and being suspended operations, as it is meeting its obligations. Unlike Subhiksha, lenders are willing to consider its debt recast. "It is a running company. There is no reason to stop supporting it …. Lenders made money on Vishal for seven years. They can now support it for two-three years", says Manmohan Agarwal.

On March 14, 2011 Vishal Retail announced the completion of the sales of its retail and wholesale business to the Chennai-based Shriram Group and to TPG wholesale— the Indian arm of US-based TPG, respectively.

CASE STUDY 10

Harrisons Malayalam

When Pankaj Kapoor took over as the Managing Director of Harrisons Malayalam (HM) in April 2008, his brief was clear—unlock the potential for growth in the company whose revenues, in the previous six years between 2002–03 and 2007–08, grew by less than 10% on year from ₹124 crore to ₹209 crore.

Kochi—headquartered HM, an RPG Group Company, is the largest grower of tea in South India with an annual production of 17 million kg from its plantations across Kerala and Tamil Nadu spanning 15,000 acres. It is also the single largest producer of rubber in the country with 18,300 acres under cultivation in Kerala and an annual output of 12,200 tonnes. It has a project division too that does engineering projects.

It did not take Kapoor and his top team too long to understand that the business in its current form offered very little headroom for growth. "We could not grow by expanding the plantations as it is very difficult to acquire land. Also there were limitations to improving the productivity of our existing land", says Kapoor. HM's productivity at 5,750 kg/acre for tea was already higher than the industry average of 4,500 kg/acre. In the case of rubber, HM's productivity at 666 kg/acre is marginally lower than the India average of 740 kg/acre. "We realised that HM should move away from cultivating and selling the produce as commodities in auctions if it has to achieve higher growth", he adds.

The situation, Kapoor and his top managers surmised, called for significant transformation in the way the company was hitherto doing its business. A two-stage plan to propel HM's growth was arrived at.

As a first step, HM decided to mine more value from existing operations, by upping land productivity (through re-planting old tea bushes and rubber trees with new high-yielding varieties and inter-cropping pineapples, bananas and other crops with rubber), labour productivity (through mechanisation) and factory output (through modernisation). It also improved the capacity utilisation of its factories by buying produce, both rubber and tea, from other growers. These efforts have begun to show results and taken revenues from ₹209 crore in 2007–08 to ₹293 crore in 2008–09 and the company hopes to close 2009–10 at ₹350 crore. "These measures were aimed at not only bringing in a burst of immediate growth but also improve further the overall productivity and quality of output—an important pre-requisite for the company's second category", says N. Dharmaraj, Vice-President, Tea Division.

Their second strategy, clearly more challenging but with the potential to take the organisation to a high trajectory growth path, was to convert HM into a fast moving consumer goods (FMCG) company. "HM have always had its tea brands. In fact, we launched our first brands (Surya and Mountain Mist) along with Tata Tea way back in 1970s", points out Kapoor. But HM's branded tea business never really took off on a large scale for a variety of reasons. Those tracking the tea industry say that the company tried to act like an FMCG background to run its branded tea business as the company's wage structure more suited the plantation sector. So the responsibility invariably landed on the executives from the plantation sector who were not trained to listen to consumers. That explains HM's decision to package and sell only those teas it cultivates resulting in the company being absent in popular segments such as Darjeeling tea and Assam tea. HM's brands thus remained regional with presence only in a few pockets.

Unlike in the past, the branded tea strategy that the top management drew up now was thought through, sincere and long-term in approach. To start with, the company began by convincing its employees that it was possible for HM to become an FMCG company. "Our knowledge of tea is unquestionable. We are among the best," says Kapoor. "This fact needs to be coupled with a mindset change where the customer is seen as the king. The earlier inward-looking approach (controlling cost and selling at auction) had to go", he adds.

The company started a consumer marketing division and began recruiting FMCG professionals offering them a competitive pay structure. A detailed market research followed and the brands were revisited. It was decided that HM will have its brand across the price spectrum and tea will be purchased from other plantations for processing and packaging in the case of Assam or Darjeeling Tea. Today, HM's tea brands are available in packs priced from ₹150 (economy segment) to over ₹300 (super premium segment).

Once the people and the brands were ready, the company began to set up its distribution network. Unlike most other FMCG launches, which are big bang affairs, HM began to roll out its distribution network and products in a calibrated fashion. It first started with Kerala and Karnataka and followed it up with Tamil Nadu. It recently forayed into parts of Maharashtra. The roll out was followed by localised brand promotion. "This is a conscious strategy. We will first get the back-end ready and then go for mass branding, which is too costly. There are no shortcuts in this", explains Kapoor. HM will enter Orissa and Andhra Pradesh in 2010–11 and hopes to cover most parts of the country in four years time.

Also, the company is very clear that it does not want to take on Tata Tea or Hindustan Unilever—at least for now. "We can't compare ourselves with them. They are global brands. We are not even a national brand yet. There is a third brand in every market and our hope is to grab that slot in three to four years", says Kapoor. HUL and Tata Tea between them, account for 52% of the 500 million kg branded-tea market in the country.

In 2008–09, HM's branded-tea business earned revenue of ₹8 crore. It was expected to be ₹20 crore in 2009–10. In four years, income from branded tea business is expected to touch ₹100 crore. The results have already begun to reflect on the bottom line—realisations, the company says, have already improved by 20%. The stock market too has taken note of this. HM's share price at the Bombay Stock Exchange has doubled from ₹60 levels in April 2008 to the current level of ₹121.

HM is readying its next move, "Once we gain enough scale, we will look at buying an international tea brand. That will then lay the foundation for our next big leap", reveals Kapoor. Plans are also afoot to acquire tea gardens abroad, especially in Africa. HM is also planning to leverage its distribution chain by launching brand extensions. For instance, it will soon add value to the fruits it grows such as pineapple and banana by offering packaged table-top fruits. It is also planning to enter packaged-juices segment.

In rubber too, the company is looking at products. "As a forward integration strategy we are looking at developing new products such as thermo-plastic natural rubber. We are also considering acquisition of companies that are in the business of manufacturing rubber products such as threads or gloves", says C. Vinayaragharan, Vice-President, Rubber Division.

The company has also financially readied itself for this growth. "Our debt-equity ratio at 0.54 and free reserves at ₹153 crore offer us enough flexibility to fund over growth plans including acquisitions", says K.N. Mathew, Vice-President, Finance.

HM, with all these measures, hopes to double its current revenues to become a ₹600-crore company in three years. Will the company be able to accomplish the desired results?

CASE STUDY 11

Go Air

Go Air, which touched a new low in March, 2009 when its planes were flying half-empty, is trying to stage a comeback.

The Wadia Group's budget carrier, which had 2.6% market share in the first quarter of 2009, has increased it to 5.8%. It carried 52% more passengers, last quarter compared to the same period last year and 153% more in 2009–10 compared to year before, albeit on a low base.

The numbers are still very small compared to what relatively new comers such as SpiceJet and Indigo have achieved. It is also a fact that despite its focus on driving efficiencies, the airline is at best catching up with its rivals. In May, Go Air had a lead factor of 85.7% but its peers did better than that—Indigo clocked 92.3% and SpiceJet 90.4%. Even on on-time performance, most airlines scored higher than Go Air.

But everyone agrees that the numbers are a sharp improvement for an airline which everyone had written off. No one had thought that the airline will be in a position to talk about building scale and will finally exercise the option of buying 10 more planes from Airbus. It is, in fact, trying to prepone deliveries, which are slated to start in January 2012. What is more, the airline is making the pre-delivery payments for these planes from its accruals, and is no more looking to induct a financial or strategic partner.

Go Air managed to almost double market share by adding just two aircraft. "You do not gain market share only by dumping more capacity in the market. Without passengers, the added capacity will only dilute the load factor. So Go Air must be doing something right. "Once you get a bad reputation (for service and reliability) it takes a long time to re-achieve a good one", says Steve Forte, a former CEO of Jet Airways.

While Go Air has been riding the recovery in demand, it has come a long way from the lows it hit in the second half of 2008–09. At one point, the airline was cancelling 20–22% of its flights, which began to erode the confidence of fliers and travel agents. That's when Chairman Nusli Wadia stepped in, and in April, 2009 replaced CEO Edgardo Badiali with a management led by Kaushik Khona, who was then working as Vice-President, Finance, in the Chairman's office.

Khona's brief was to make the airline profitable in a way that it could sustain its growth. The immediate challenge was to restore confidence of fliers and trade and return the old planes, the root cause for cancellations.

Three old planes were returned in May–July 2009. "We told ourselves that we will never cancel a flight and always fly on time. This helped us gain stability and instil confidence in consumers and trade", says Khona. This started showing results: in April, 2010, Go Air carried 1,40,000 passengers against 70,000 the previous month.

The airline went for a rebranding exercise: it changed the colour of the logo and uniform of its crew to solid blue. "We wanted to be seen as a serious player and a corporate airline", says Khona. So, it tried to shed its youth-oriented image. Ground staff, who used to dress in Jeans and T-Shirt, switched over to blazers and suits. "It helps in the overall look and feel of the airline", says Rakesh Tiwary, Go Air's Vice-President, commercial.

Go Air used customers' feedback to ramp up its customers' service, benchmarking them with the best in the business. For instance, if it took Indigo or Jet Airways a minute to check in a passenger, it tried to achieve the same. "With a 360 degree approach, we aligned all departments, trained them for better customer delivery", says Tiwary. With new planes, Go Air was also the first to harp on-time performance leading to least cancellations.

The airline also altered its distribution strategy to reduce its dependence on consolidators and now it directly reaches over 600 travel agents who generate 22%–28% of its sales. As a result, distribution costs fell to 5% from 13% before April 2009.

Go Air's network strategy focused on how it could flog its assets and connect tier-II towns not serviced by other low-cost carriers (LCCs). It operates 16 flights a day on the Delhi-Mumbai-Delhi Sector, which caters to its corporate customers and sustains the airline. It was the first LCC to launch a business class (in the first two rows, minus the middle seats with meals and more leg space), which comes at a third of the price charged by full service carriers. It offers a flexi fare—for ₹150 more and allows people to reschedule flights without a fee.

LCCs like to dominate city-pairs with higher frequencies than spread themselves too thin. But Go Air believes in connecting more cities with fewer planes. Khona believes it helps him widen his reach and carry more people.

Not everyone is impressed. A senior executive with a rival LCC says, "Go Air changes its routes strategy every six months and cannot decide what to do. The best flights in the networks are always the ones which have been there for a long time in the network. How many times they started flying Ahmedabad-Bangalore, stopped flying, and resumed flying? They are an airline without a thought", he says.

However, many experts say it's smart thinking to build a network of cities that tries to avoid direct confrontation with larger and more established airline. "Once their strength increases, they can start nipping at the major flanks", says Forte. This strategy helps it flog its planes' move—at 7.6 flights a day per aircraft, it has the highest aircraft utilisation per day, followed by 6.5 flights a day per aircraft by Indigo and Kingfisher. Khona says this allows him do one extra flight per day.

The management's next target is to improve the airline's market share to 7.5% by December 2011 and improve efficiency. How far the company will be able to achieve the target in the competitive market place, is a question that, according to analysts, future developments will answer.

CASE STUDY 12

Rohit Surfactants

Rohit Surfactants—the maker of *Ghari* detergent power and bar and a bigger challenger to Hindustan Unilever's dominance of the detergent market—resides in a non-descript three-storey building situated in the city of Kanpur. Men here can be found working on newer ways to take on Hindustan Unilever and others in the fiercely competitive Indian fast-moving consumer goods market. In 2009, the company has come out with a premium detergent called *MRZ*, *Ghari Gold* for modern trade, *Xpert* dish cleaner and *Venus* soap. Next in the works is *Ghari Urn* for woollens and *Venus* shampoo. At the moment, these businesses, are small: out of Rohit Surfactants's ₹1,940-crore turnover in 2009–10, *Ghari* contributed as much as ₹1,825 crore or 94%. But the intent is clear.

Much of the confidence, of course, stems from the success of *Ghari*. The detergent market in the country is estimated at ₹11,000 crore per annum. About two-thirds of that is powder and the rest is bars. Hindustan Unilever (*Surf, Rin* and *Wheel*) leads the pack with around 17%—ahead of Procter and Gamble (16%) and *Nirma* (8%). Of all its rivals, only *Wheel* sells more than *Ghari*. While the market is growing at a lower rate of 5% to 7% per annum perhaps because the market is more or less saturated; *Ghari* is growing faster at 10% to 15%.

The detergent market has three well-defined segments. Premium which is about 15% of the market and includes brands like Hindustan Unilever's Surf and Procter & Gamble's Ariel, midscale (40% of the market; main players are Hindustan Unilever's Rin and Procter and Gamble's Tide) and popular (45% of the market where *Ghari*, *Nirma*, Hindustan Unilever's *Wheel* and Fena's *Fena* operate). *Ghari* is positioned at the bottom of the market where the real volumes lie. Rohit Surfactants Chairman & Managing Director, Murlidhar is very clear where his flagship brand is slotted. "*Ghari* is everybody's brand. It is the best solution available in the market and gives you value for your money".

According to FMCG experts, detergent is bought largely by the housewife once a week or month, and she happens to be an extremely value conscious consumer. Consumers, they also say, especially those in villages and small towns, have begun to look for cheaper options in staples like soap, detergent and toothpaste so that they can spend more on discretionary items like mobile phones, televisions and automobiles. Their choice of detergents is inevitably one that gives the maximum results at the lowest price.

There are indications that the popular segment is growing faster than the other two. KPMG Manager (Advisory Services) Anand Ramanathan says that regional detergent brands have grown much faster than the national brands in the last one year. He puts their growth in the year till July 2010 at 40.7%. And all regional brands are price warriors—they have nothing to offer by way of quality or brand. *Ghari* power is priced at ₹5 for 145 grams. This is way below brands like *Surf, Ariel, Henko* and *Tide*, though it is more or less the same as *Wheel, Nirma* and *Fena*. So far, the aggressive price tags seem to have worked. "One of the factors that have contributed to *Ghari's* success is the price-quality ratio", says Sansika Marketing Consultancy Chairman & Managing Director, Jagdeep Kapoor, who had in the past worked with *Nirma*.

Murlidhar and family believe in low margin of 9%—the industry average is 12% to 13% for the premium players. In other words, they are ready to sacrifice some profit for market share. Companies the world has used this strategy to get a foothold in the market; profit margins can be raised subsequently. "We have kept our profit margins low, which is not an easy thing to do for large companies", says Murlidhar. What helps is one—Rohit Surfactants is a closely-held company and Murlidhar need not justify this strategy to a large body of shareholders and analysts. Two, the company works on a shoestring advertising and marketing budget. In 2009–10, while *Ghari* did a turnover of ₹1,825 crore, its marketing team was handed out only ₹35 crore, or less than 2%, to promote the brand through above- and below-the line activities. Most national brands have a marketing budget that adds upto 13% to 15% of their turnover.

Three, Rohit Surfactants keeps its wage bill on a tight leash by not hiring high-profile marketers on sky-high salaries. "We hire smart people from local institutes, and train them in house", says Shushil Kumar Bajpai, President (Corporate affairs) Rohit Surfactants.

Rohit Surfactants's trick in marketing because of the small budget is innovation. Bajpai set the ball rolling by taking the brand to trains. The first campaign was the Ghari Detergent Express (a summer special) in 2008 that ran between Lucknow and Guwahati for two months. Taking the cue from there, *Ghari* has now advertised in Pushpak Express that runs between Lucknow and Mumbai. The brand can also be seen on railway crossings in West Bengal and Uttar Pradesh. "The train is the medium that the masses interact with", says Bajpai. "We started putting up advertisements inside the bogies of Swarna Jayanti Express (from Trivandrum to Hazarat Nizamuddin in Delhi) in 2010 that cuts across three or four states in South India". This is a clear indication that the company wants to take *Ghari* down South.

In addition, Rohit Surfactants promotes *Ghari* at roadside shows, magic shows and exhibitions in smaller towns and cities. Customers are unlikely to see other brand at these places—an innovative idea to break the clutter. The magic shows, says Bajpai, have given *Ghari* good visibility in cities like Jaipur, Indore, Kota, Alwar and Kanpur. Of late, the company has taken some tentative steps towards the popular media. It has sponsored a show, 'Rakt Sambandh', on NDTV Imagine. Three television commercials are also in the pipeline.

Before going national, which would have spread its resources very thin, Rohit Surfactants focused on Uttar Pradesh to begin with. Uttar Pradesh, with a population of 167 million, accounts for over 12% of the country's FMCG sales. Nine of the company's 18 manufacturing units are in Uttar Pradesh with 900 out of 300 *Ghari* dealers. Once the home base was secured, it spread out to other states. According to Bajpai, 60% to 70% of Ghari's sales now come from Uttar Pradesh, Madhya Pradesh and Maharashtra.

And now it wants to sell in the South. There could be problems, warn experts. "The company needs to have its supply chain close to three markets. This will help it control the transportation costs", says former Dabur India Chief Operating Officer, Kannan Sitaram. Indeed, outside the "cow belt", Rohit Surfactants' only unit is at Aurangabad in Maharashtra. Bajpai says that plans are afoot to set up one in Karnataka. Also it will have to bind brand awareness from scratch. What may work in Ghari's favour is the higher profit margin of 9% the company offers its dealers; rivals seldom offer better than 6% or 7%.

Also, as it grows in size and adds more products to its portfolio, Rohit Surfactants will have to compete in the market for top talent. Can the low-profits company do that? Bajpai says it plans to go to the Indian Institutes of Management to recruit from the campus.

In the final analysis, are all these good enough to snatch market share from heavy weight rivals like Hindustan Unilever, Procter & Gamble and *Nirma*? Sitaram says that *Nirma* has the advantage of backward integration because it makes soda ash, the key raw material for detergent. Hindustan Unilever, on its part, straddles all price points. Its *Wheel* sells more than *Ghari*. KPMG's Ramnathan says that "the company will protect its market share with great energy because detergents account for almost 40% of its turnover. Some years back when *Nirma* posed a threat to it, Hindustan Unilever responded with its rural marketing strategy and restored its market position. This indicates that for Hindustan Unilever the detergent category is important, and it is unlikely to let go off its market leadership".

Is the journey ahead going to be cakewalk for Murlidhar, Bajpai and their team?

CASE STUDY 13

Nerolac

Nerolac—the number three player in the decorative paints market in India—has a share of 13% to leader *Asian Paints'* 47%, and number two player, *Berger Paints'* 18%. *Nerolac* has its sights at the top, putting in place a three-prolonged strategy that includes focusing on differentiated products, greater brand building and more retail initiatives on the ground. "If you have to improve share you have to go that extra mile", says Anuj Jain, Vice-President, Sales and Marketing, *Nerolac*.

Nerolac's enthusiasm to wrest market share from rivals, especially *Asian Paints* does not appear to be completely misplaced, since the company leads the pack in the ₹4,000-crore industrial paints market. It has a share of 62% in the automotive segment

—a key one under industrial paints. Overall, it has over 40% share in industrial paints to Asian Paints' 13%. "It is the undisputed leader in industrial paints", says an executive with a rival firm.

This leadership in industrial paints then is clearly goading it to take on its archrival on the decorative side. But it certainly would not be easy. This is because Asian Paints has ensured there are not chinks in its armour on the decorative side at least. The decorative segment accounts for almost 70% of the ₹13,000 crore overall paints market. Following is a comparative study:

Market Share

Players	Decorative	Industrial
Asian Paints	47%	13%
Berger	18%	18%
Kansai Nerolac	13%	40%

Rivals such as *Nerolac, Berger, Dulux* and *Nippon,* have been trying hard to wrest market share from *Asian Paints* for some time now. But the latter's formidable grip over the paints distribution network in the country, its ability to churn out new products as well as its high decibel ad campaigns have ensured that it stays ahead of the curve.

Asian Paints has over 25,000 dealers to *Berger's* 9,500 and *Nerolac's* 6,500. Asian's overall marketing strategy for 2010–11 was ₹244 crore as against *Berger's* over ₹70 crore and *Nerolac's* ₹68 crore.

"So no matter how much you shout, *Asian Paints* simply outshouts you", admits *Berger Paints'* Senior Vice-President, Sales and Marketing, Abhijit Roy. "Tell me one gap in their marketing strategy and I would be ready to attack them", he says.

In contrast, Jain of *Nerolac* strikes a positive note, "There is no denying of *Asian Paints'* domination in the decorative market. But how do you stand out? You have to do something different. We rather benchmark ourselves to international standards".

In the last one year, *Nerolac* has launched products such as lead-free paints and paints with a heat guard, keeping the objective differentiation in mind. It is now in the process of rolling a low VOC or Volatile Organic Compound Paint. Low VOC paints are designed to perform like conventional paints without the harmful ingredients", Jain says.

According to market analysts, these initiatives are really not different. Asian paints has a low VOC portfolio for about five to six years now, says the company's Vice-President, Sales and Marketing, Amit Syngle. "Our lead-free portfolio has been around for the last two and a half years", he says. Berger, meanwhile, is the process of introducing its low VOC range in near future. Lead-free is also something that it already has in its portfolio, says Roy.

According to Syngle, "Lead-free is a standard that the industry moved to sometime ago. It is a moral obligation to take it up because these products are not harmful to the human body. But Jain of *Nerolac* insists these trends were actually introduced by it in the industry. "We were the first ones to introduce lead-free paints last year. The others have followed us", he insists.

The one-upmanship does not end here. Jain says that as far as retail initiatives go, each company has a different model. "Asian Paints has a dealer-centric network of stores, while we are doing shop-in-shops". *Nerolac* is in the process of rolling about 100 mini-stores in 35 cities. *Asian Paints*, in contrast, already has some 3,000 critical stores that act as colour select outlets. It is also rolling out high-end concept stores called **colour ideas** in different cities. It is here that prospective buyers/customers will get a glimpse of what the company has to offer in terms of colour and share. *Berger*, meanwhile, is experimenting with franchisee stores. It has 45 such franchisee outlets at the moment.

"There is nothing unusual with a retail footprint. It is an industry norm", says Syngle.

So, can *Nerolac* really beat *Asian Paints* at its game?

Index